AMERICAN IMPORTS

COMMITTEE ON AMERICAN IMPORTS

THE POLICY statement which appears as Chapter 25 of this book was formulated by the Committee on International Policy of the National Planning Association, co-sponsor of the study with the Twentieth Century Fund. The following are the members of this committee who signed the policy statement.

FRANK ALTSCHUL, *Chairman*
Chairman of the Board,
General American Investors Company

LOUIS BROWNLOW, *Vice Chairman*
Washington, D.C.

STANLEY ANDREWS
Executive Director, National Project
in Agricultural Communications,
Michigan State College

SOLOMON BARKIN
Director of Research, Textile
Workers Union of America

RICHARD M. BISSELL, JR.
Economic Consultant,
Washington, D.C.

JOHN F. CHAPMAN
Associate Editor,
Harvard Business Review

CARTER GOODRICH
Professor of Economics,
Columbia University

LUTHER H. GULICK
City Administrator of the
City of New York

KENNETH HOLLAND
President, Institute of
International Education

ISADOR LUBIN
New York State Industrial Commissioner

T. G. MACGOWAN
Manager,
Marketing Research Department,
Firestone Tire and Rubber Company

JOHN C. MCCLINTOCK
Assistant Vice President,
United Fruit Company

HELEN HILL MILLER
Journalist, Washington, D.C.

PHILIP E. MOSELY
Council on Foreign Relations

GEORGE NEBOLSINE
Coudert Brothers

PAUL NITZE
Washington, D.C.

CHARLTON OGBURN
New York City

LITHGOW OSBORNE
President, The American-
Scandinavian Foundation

CLARENCE E. PICKETT
Honorary Secretary, American
Friends Service Committee

VICTOR G. REUTHER
Assistant to the President,
Congress of Industrial Organizations

MORRIS S. ROSENTHAL
New York City

WAYNE CHATFIELD TAYLOR
Heathsville, Va.

ROBERT WEST
Warner, New Hampshire

WALTER H. WHEELER, JR.
President, Pitney-Bowes, Inc.

DAVID J. WINTON
Chairman of the Board,
Winton Lumber Company

AMERICAN IMPORTS

By

Don D. Humphrey

---

*A study jointly sponsored
by the Twentieth Century Fund
and the National Planning Association
with a policy statement by the
Association's Committee on International Policy*

NEW YORK · The Twentieth Century Fund · 1955

COPYRIGHT, © 1955 BY THE TWENTIETH CENTURY FUND, INC.

Library of Congress Catalog Card Number: 55-8798

PRINTED IN THE UNITED STATES OF AMERICA BY

WM. F. FELL COMPANY, PHILADELPHIA, PENNSYLVANIA

FOREWORD

THE PROTECTIVE tariff as a means of fostering domestic industry by limiting competitive imports has been a political issue since the days of Alexander Hamilton. Until after the United States emerged as a creditor nation following World War I, however, import policy and the tariff were regarded solely as domestic issues. Since the end of World War II, which greatly strengthened our creditor position, the "import problem" has appeared under a new guise in the form of the "dollar gap." This is said to measure the "inability" of the people of the rest of the world to sell enough goods and services to Americans to pay for their purchases from us, or, alternatively, our "unwillingness" to buy enough from foreign countries to enable them to meet their obligations to us.

To what extent is American tariff policy responsible for the dollar gap? What American industries depend upon existing tariffs for their competitive existence? To what extent would further tariff reductions—for the Reciprocal Trade Agreements program over the past two decades has already brought drastic cuts—bring larger imports? What is America's "capacity" to consume larger amounts of foreign goods and services, even if no tariffs existed?

These are some of the questions which led the trustees of the Twentieth Century Fund in 1950 to authorize this study of American imports. The project has been carried out jointly with the National Planning Association. The Committee on International Policy of the NPA has served as the advisory and policy committee for the study, while the Twentieth Century Fund has been in charge of the research and responsible for the publication and dissemination of the findings.

The NPA Committee is therefore solely responsible for the views and recommendations set forth in the final chapter of the report. Don D. Humphrey, Professor of Economics at Duke University, served as research director of the project and, except for Chapter 11, is solely responsible for the research report. Calvin B. Hoover, of Duke University, prepared Chapter 11 and served as consultant on the project.

The Fund is deeply indebted to Mr. Humphrey for the energy and competence he brought to the difficult task of analysis, and is grateful to the National Planning Association and its International Committee for their cooperation in carrying this project through to its successful conclusion.

J. FREDERIC DEWHURST, *Executive Director*
The Twentieth Century Fund

330 WEST 42ND STREET
NEW YORK 36, N. Y.
AUGUST 1955

vii

PREFACE

IMPORTS PRESENT the kind of problem that is not solved once and for all. Conflicts of interest between those who gain and those who lose by freer trade must be resolved again and again.

Although the decline of protectionism has lagged behind the rise of America's competitive strength in world markets, support for freer trade is stronger, after twenty years of experience with lower tariffs, than it was at the beginning of the program. At the same time, important segments of the community are more fearful of foreign competition than at any time in recent years.

Our tariff law reflects both sides of the shield of public opinion—a desire to expand trade and a growing fear of foreign competition.

The consumer's voice is too small to be heard in the tariff debates, and the Congress is left to reconcile, as best it can, the growing demand for export markets with the conflicting claim that competition from cheap foreign labor destroys American industry. Still another influence concerns whether or not to sacrifice local business to the broad requirements of foreign policy, which call for expansion of world trade in the national interest.

The present study attempts to make some small contribution to a better understanding of American attitudes toward the tariff and a wider understanding of the economic analysis of imports. It ventures to predict who would be hurt by freer trade and gives considerable attention to the question of injury from foreign competition.

One wonders if either liberals or protectionists would have predicted that American tariffs could be reduced as drastically as they have been, with so little increase in imports and so little injury to import-competing industries. It may be that both sides of the debate have claimed too much for the tariff. Certainly protectionists predicted more immediate injury than has occurred, and my impression is that liberals sometimes implied greater material benefits than have, in fact, been realized. After twenty years of tariff reduction, the over-all picture is that home industry has displaced imports instead of imports displacing home industry.

To interpret this development in a dynamic setting, the present study attempts to bring into account the effects of business cycles, historical growth, technological advance and institutional factors which hamper international specialization and trade.

I have received a great deal of help at various stages of the study. Herbert W. Hargreaves and Herbert K. Zassenhaus served as staff associates for about a year. I appreciate their contribution and regret that they were called to other duties before the project was completed. It was my good fortune to have the assistance of Harry Eastman for a time, and I am grateful for his help in drafting several chapters. I also want to thank Sheila Eastman for research assistance and for the careful checking of tables and other data.

For assistance in obtaining data, acknowledgment is due Ben Dorfman of the Tariff Commission, Sam Schurr of the Bureau of Mines, W. T. M. Beale of the State Department, and James P. Cavin of the Bureau of the Budget, who was helpful in obtaining data pertaining to agriculture.

George Soule's contribution to the organization and readability of the manuscript went far beyond the duty of an editor, particularly on Chapters 2, 3 and 4, and I am grateful for his assistance.

Walter S. Salant gave the manuscript a careful reading and I have profited from his criticism.

My greatest debt, and one that cannot be adequately expressed, is to Calvin B. Hoover. As originally planned, he was to have been a co-author, and I am confident that the final product would be a better one if he had not been pressed, by a sense of duty, into other services. He has continued as adviser and critic at every stage of the study and his generous support has been invaluable.

The author is responsible for the views expressed and for the flaws that have crept in.

DON D. HUMPHREY

A NOTE ON IMPORT STATISTICS

In order to obtain a calendar year series of imports for comparison with output, it is necessary to use the "general imports" published in *Monthly Summary of Commerce and Finance*. These have not been edited as were the fiscal year series published in *Historical Statistics of the United States, 1789–1945*.

In Chapter 4, which deals with the tariff, it is necessary to use a fiscal year series of "imports for consumption" because tariff statistics are related to this series.

In addition to the difference between "imports for consumption" and "general imports," the fiscal year and calendar year series are not entirely identical owing to the fact that the fiscal year data have been edited. The series published in *Historical Statistics* is for fiscal years up to 1915. This series includes imports by economic classes.

"General imports" include the total arrivals of merchandise, whether they enter consumption channels immediately or are entered into warehouses under customs custody to be subsequently withdrawn for consumption or exportation. "Imports for consumption" include entries for immediate consumption and withdrawals from warehouses for consumption.

In *Historical Statistics*, Series M 62–67 are identified as "general imports" through 1932 and "imports for consumption" thereafter. *Statistical Abstract of the United States, 1939*, Table 545, identifies the series as "general imports through 1933."

On the measurement of import prices in various periods, see T. J. Kreps, "Import and Export Prices in the United States and the Terms of International Trade, 1880–1914," *Quarterly Journal of Economics*, August 1926; T. J. Kreps, "Export, Import, and Domestic Prices in the United States, 1926–1930," *Quarterly Journal of Economics*, February 1932; P. T. Ellsworth, "Export, Import and Domestic Prices, in the United States, 1931–1936," *Review of Economic Statistics*, November 1937. These sources leave serious gaps in the period covered by the present study, and for this and other reasons have been used only as a general source of reference. Indexes of the unit value and quantity of imports by the Departments of Commerce and Agriculture have been used where available.

D. D. H.

CONTENTS

TABLES

APPENDICES

FIGURES

PART I

THE TROUBLESOME IMPORT DEFICIT

Chapter 1

The Export Surplus

THE UNITED STATES imports too little and has for a long time. As a result it has been virtually impossible for other nations to repay their debts and to buy as much as they would like to buy here.

Our export markets suffer because we import so little. We could unquestionably sell more to the rest of the world if we bought more from abroad. Greater international specialization and trade offer the possibility of higher living standards for all.

The classical gains from trade are more vital to the rest of the world than to this country because we occupy a vast subcontinent, rich in natural resources, and because we already have so much specialization and free trade within our own borders. But political considerations, as well as the prospect of economic benefits, dictate the expansion of our foreign trade. America has a vital interest in the well-being and security of the free world, and American leadership would be strengthened if the level of trade with Europe, Japan and the undeveloped nations could be raised.

Large-scale foreign aid provided by the Marshall Plan, the Mutual Security Program, the Point Four Program and other measures has served to dramatize the problem. The rest of the world needs American food, machinery, military equipment and investment capital. If the United States stood ready to buy more of the goods and services offered by other countries, it would be more nearly possible for them to service their debts and to pay for the goods they need.

The "Favorable" Balance Becomes Embarrassing

Ever since the early 1870s at least, the United States has sold abroad goods and services of a total higher value than the goods and services bought there. Until after World War I, this situation was regarded with satisfaction by most American citizens and their elected officials. The excess of exports over imports was called a "favorable balance of trade," because it meant that in foreign commerce Americans were taking in more money than they spent—a goal which every businessman and every individual consumer normally chooses in his own affairs. The excess earnings could be employed to pay the interest on foreign debt, to reduce the principal of the debt itself, or to enlarge investment abroad. A "favorable balance of trade" seemed just one of the ways in which a nation could become richer.

3

After World War I the advantages of the export surplus began to be doubted, and little by little informed opinion came to regard it as an unfortunate anomaly. Even before 1914, the foreign debt of Americans had been greatly reduced, and by the end of hostilities the United States had become a net creditor nation instead of a debtor nation. This would have remained true even if the intergovernmental war debts had immediately been cancelled. How was Europe to pay past debts unless Europeans sold Americans more than Europeans bought? It was argued that the historic and proper role of a creditor nation was to accept service of the debt by importing goods and services.

Farmers, who suffered in 1920–1921 from a drastic fall of prices, were told that unless Americans bought more European goods, Europeans could not buy enough wheat, cotton and tobacco, or at least could not pay remunerative prices for them. Most manufacturers had in the past been concerned chiefly with the domestic market, but now large industries were reaching out for export markets, and saw that their prospects were at least in some degree dependent on the ability of foreigners to buy their products. Yet high tariff barriers were restored in 1922 by the Fordney-McCumber Act, and were not modified during the decade.

America maintained an export surplus chiefly because Americans after 1923 invested substantial sums abroad. Net earnings from foreign trade were thus in effect left outside the country, except insofar as the dollars lent to foreigners came back in payment of interest and amortization of the war debt. But towards the end of the boom, which culminated in 1929, foreign investing by Americans began to fall away, and the decline played a role in the ensuing world-wide economic collapse.

A flow of investment abroad could not suddenly be discontinued without peril. In the early years of the great depression, American purchases of foreign goods and services fell drastically too. Many foreign debts were perforce defaulted, nations went off the gold standard, moratoria became necessary. In the ensuing international scramble to increase exports without increasing imports, and to conserve scarce supplies of foreign exchange, the nations erected a network of new barriers against the free flow of commerce. The United States had already invited retaliation by enacting extremely high duties in the Hawley-Smoot tariff of 1930.

The Attempt to Expand Trade

American farmers and some American industries in the early 1930s again suffered from the greatly restricted ability of foreigners to buy their products. Though the collapse of domestic markets was to a far greater degree responsible for the general distress than the collapse of demand from abroad, the federal government after 1932 included among its measures designed to speed recovery a program to enlarge American exports by removing trade barriers.

The Reciprocal Trade Agreements Act, which became law in 1934, permitted a reduction of import duties, yet its aim was far wider than that of measures for tariff reduction passed under former Democratic administrations. Through reciprocal agreements, it was designed to bring about international recovery by world-wide removal of trade barriers. Secretary of State Hull expressed the view that the United States must assume leadership in freeing the world of obstacles to trade—a role which it was under obligation to fulfill because of its previous traditional position as an outstanding exemplar of protection. Ever since that reversal, it has been the official policy of the United States to further the growth of an expanding international economy through removal of obstacles to world-wide free competition.

Nevertheless, the excess of exports from the United States persisted. Foreign governmental war debts could not be paid and were allowed to lapse. Americans no longer had the confidence, even if they had had the means, to make private investments in foreign lands. Now the export excess was mainly paid for, not as in the 1920s by an outflow of loans, but by large and continual shipments of gold from abroad—gold for which the United States apparently had no use except to swell excess bank reserves. Just as previously the nation had provided an excess of goods and services to foreigners in exchange for promises to pay which in many cases turned out to be worthless, now it was providing an export excess in exchange for a precious metal for which it had no need. If, instead of gold, the United States had obtained food, clothing or other manufactured articles in exchange for all its exports, the import-competing industries in the United States would have suffered. And since unemployment was widespread in the 1930s owing to low levels of investment, the workers displaced by increased imports might not have found re-employment in other industries. The export surplus would have disappeared, to be sure, but at the risk of creating a decline in national income. An export surplus of goods and services is favorable to domestic employment in the same way that domestic investment provides income and employment to workers without creating immediately a corresponding increase in the supply of consumption goods. It is safest to eliminate an export surplus when domestic resources are fully employed and domestic investment is expanding.[1]

1. See Calvin B. Hoover, *International Trade and Domestic Employment*, McGraw-Hill, New York, 1945. This work contains in embryonic form some of the findings developed in the present study.

War and Postwar Crisis

When new war broke out in 1939, the need of Hitler's enemies for American goods was greatly increased, while their ability to manufacture goods for export was reduced. The new neutrality legislation of the United States forbade loans to finance war purchases, the Johnson Act forbade loans to nations whose World War I debts were in default, and indeed the European belligerents would probably have been unable to borrow if no law had stood in the way. By the device of lend-lease the American government was enabled to finance the necessary export surplus to those who eventually became its Allies, without creating uncollectible war debts. But with the end of lend-lease in the summer of 1945, the old problem of how the European nations were to pay for the goods and services they needed from the western continent reappeared in exaggerated form. The export surplus of the United States soon became widely known by a new name emphasizing the difficulties it involved for other nations, and especially for Europe—"the dollar gap."

It was important for the United States that the dollar shortage be ended, not just for the old reasons, but for new ones as well.

1. Without enough dollars to buy goods that must be imported, war-disrupted nations could not feed their populations adequately or buy materials essential for their industries. Economic and social calamity might ensue unless prompt and generous aid was forthcoming.

2. Until this peril was allayed, no nation in danger could take the risk of relaxing restrictions on imports or control of foreign exchange; thus the program of removing trade barriers as an aid to an expanding world economy was blocked.

3. The challenge of Soviet Communism to the free world made it imperative that nations which had not succumbed be bulwarked against hunger, unemployment and the political disturbances that would be sure to follow economic collapse.

4. American agriculture was greatly expanded by the war and needed foreign markets.

The export surplus of the United States had now become much more than troublesome or embarrassing; it was a problem of the first magnitude to the whole free world. No longer could it be regarded by any intelligent person as a "favorable" balance of trade. It was now financed by the American taxpayer.

Exports Exceed Imports by $49 Billion, 1946–1953

In order to understand the implications of the export surplus, and the choice of possible remedies, it is well at this point to turn to the accounts which show, in rough figures, the economic transactions of the United States with the rest of the world in recent years. This type of account is often called the "international balance of payments" of the United States.

It shows (1) the volume of exports and imports of goods and services, (2) the surplus or deficit of exports over imports, and (3) the means by which the balance of trade was financed.

American imports of goods and services increased rather consistently from $7 billion in 1946 to $16.6 billion in 1953. This was chiefly due to the rapid expansion of the American economy and to the high levels of production and employment that prevailed. At the same time, the increase of exports from $14.7 billion in 1946 to $21.3 billion in 1953 was only somewhat less great, so that we consistently exported more than we imported of both goods and services.

America's export surplus reached a postwar peak of $11.5 billion in 1947. In 1950, because of speculative buying touched off by the sudden outbreak of war in Korea, America outbid the rest of the world for raw materials. Because of an increase of imports and a decline of exports, the export surplus fell to $2.3 billion. But the following year exports rose more than imports, and the annual surplus of exports approximated $5 billion, in round numbers, in 1951, 1952 and 1953.

Continued growth of exports was sustained after 1951 by foreign military aid, which increased as economic aid declined. Also, the great bulk of the rise in total imports from 1951 to 1953 did not consist of commercial imports, but represented services purchased by American military establishments overseas. The export surplus of goods and services of all kinds was reduced by only $500 million from 1951 to 1953. (See Figure 1.)

Although exports of services exceeded imports of services each year, the export surplus of services alone was reduced to minor proportions in 1953 when imports reached $4.7 billion compared with exports of $4.9 billion.

Commodity imports rose from $5.2 billion in 1946 to $11.9 billion in 1953, but because of the rise of exports, the surplus of commodity exports was reduced only from $6.5 billion to $4.5 billion. The export surplus of commodities increased each year from 1950 to 1953. (See Table 1.)

Total exports of goods and services exceeded imports by approximately $49 billion in the seven-year period 1946–1953. This means that the dollars which the rest of the world earned by the sale of goods and services to the United States fell short, by $49 billion, of paying for the goods and services bought from the United States.

About $4 billion of this $49 billion gap was financed by private gifts and remittances to relatives and friends outside the United States. Another $3 billion was financed by private investments, that is, by a net outflow of capital from the United States.

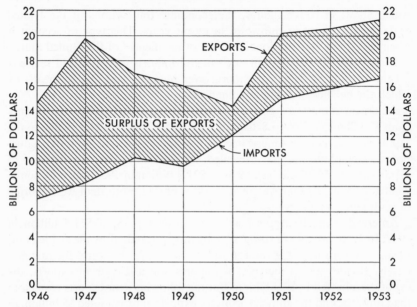

FIGURE 1. UNITED STATES EXPORTS AND IMPORTS OF GOODS AND SERVICES,
1946–1953

Sources: Economic Report of the President, January 1954, p. 219; *Survey of Current
Business*, March 1954.

This leaves a gap of $42 billion between exports and imports in the
period 1946–1953 that was financed by loans and grants of the United
States government. Without this extraordinary financial assistance, the
rest of the world could not have bought so much more here than it sold.
Thus, *the size of the dollar gap shown by statistics was determined chiefly by
the public loans and foreign aid that were made available to finance it.*

Statistics do not measure the dollar shortage, which is best defined as the
excess of demand for dollars over the supply of dollars at current exchange
rates. Foreign nations arbitrarily suppressed their demand for American
goods and services because they had insufficient means of paying for them.
They also maintained arbitrary exchange rates which tended to enlarge
their demand for dollar goods. These factors all have to be taken into
account in evaluating the problem of the dollar shortage.

An export surplus of goods and services is the only way that the United
States can provide a net addition to the resources of foreign nations and,
hence, the dollar gap shown by the balance of payments reflects mainly the
assistance which we were willing to provide for the security and well-being
of friendly peoples. Under the circumstances, it was believed necessary in

TABLE 1

UNITED STATES EXPORTS AND IMPORTS OF COMMODITIES AND SERVICES, 1946–1953

(Billions)

Year	Exports		Imports		Export Surplus	
	Commodities	*Services*	*Commodities*	*Services*	*Commodities*	*Services*
1946	$11.7	$3.0	$ 5.2	$1.8	$6.5	$1.2
1947	16.0	3.8	6.1	2.2	9.9	1.6
1948	13.3	3.7	7.8	2.4	5.5	1.3
1949	12.3	3.7	7.1	2.5	5.2	1.2
1950	10.7	3.7	9.3	2.8	1.4	0.9
1951	15.5	4.7	11.7	3.4	3.8	1.3
1952	15.8	4.8	11.5	4.3	4.3	0.5
1953	16.4	4.9	11.9	4.7	4.5	0.2

Sources: Economic Report of the President, January 1954; *Survey of Current Business,* March 1954.

our own interest to finance such an export surplus, and in this sense a dollar gap was desirable. *Reference to elimination of the dollar gap means that we wish to eliminate the conditions that made it necessary:* (1) by improving the capacity of other nations to pay their own way, and (2) by making it possible for them to do so through mutually beneficial trade, which, on our part, requires opening the American market to competitive imports.

Both Imports and Exports Enlarged by Military Expenditures

In interpreting the dollar gap as shown by the excess of American exports over imports, some writers are inclined to overemphasize the distinction between economic and military aid and to exclude the export surplus financed by military aid from the balance-of-payments problem.

There is, however, no sharp distinction between economic and military aid, for a nation receiving military aid is enabled to direct more of its own resources to the production of civilian goods while a nation receiving economic aid is enabled to devote more of its own resources to defense requirements. In a purely technical sense, moreover, the distinction between economic and military assistance is by no means as sharp as the figures might suggest. Although roughly $10 billion of total foreign aid is termed military grants, these cover not only American exports of military end-items, but also commodity exports intended to encourage the shift of foreign production from civilian to military goods. Military aid has been used to finance not only raw materials and machinery but also consumption goods, including foodstuffs, which were treated as "defense support." In requesting appropriations for foreign assistance from the Congress, responsible officials asserted that military aid to cover these "defense-support" items is inseparable from assistance to provide military end-items.

The practice of excluding all foreign military aid from the problem of the dollar gap is also misleading because the level of American imports as well as exports has been raised substantially by military programs. Largely as a result of expenditures for American military establishments overseas, direct military imports amounted to $1.3 billion in 1951, $1.9 billion in 1952 and $2.5 billion in 1953. This has provided an easy source of dollar earnings to the outside world because most military imports do not have to compete directly in the American market; they represent services provided by foreign nations which could not be converted to production of commercial exports except at a heavy cost. In the period 1947–1953, military imports totaled approximately $8 billion compared with foreign military aid of $10 billion including "defense support."

American imports have also been enlarged, temporarily, by expenditures of several billions of dollars in the building of a stockpile of strategic and critical materials. This represents, of course, an increase in inventory over and above the requirements of current production.

Finally, it is entirely possible that the huge expenditures for national defense at home have raised the level of American imports by providing a higher over-all level of employment and income at home than would otherwise have prevailed. It is also possible that domestic production for the military requires a larger component of imports (wool, natural rubber, petroleum, uranium, copper and other minerals) than would be required for production of civilian goods.

In sum, the volume of American imports and, hence, the ability of other nations to earn enough dollars to pay their own way have been greatly enlarged by the same threat to the security of the free world which created the need for American military aid to other nations.

How the Export Surplus Was Financed

Loans by the United States government and its agencies provided $7 billion toward financing our peak export surplus of $11.5 billion in 1947. Thereafter, public loans fell rapidly to $200 million in 1953.

Foreign economic aid reached a peak of $5 billion in 1949 under the Marshall Plan, and then declined each year to $1.8 billion in 1953. As economic aid declined, military aid rose from $200 million in 1949 to a peak of $4.7 billion in 1953. (See Table 2.)

Initially, public loans were the most important means of financing the export surplus. As the inability of other nations to pay became clear, loans were largely replaced by economic aid, which, in turn, has been substantially replaced by military aid. In a limited technical sense, the means of

TABLE 2

How the Export Surplus of Goods and Services Was Financed, 1947–1953

(Billions)

Year	Export Surplus to Be Financed	Private Remittances	Public Loans	U.S. Government Economic Aid	U.S. Government Military Aid	Gold Reserves and Dollar Assets[a]	Private Investments	Errors and Omissions[a]
				Means of Financing				
1947	$11.5	$.7	$7.0	$1.8	$ .1	$ -1.9	$1.0	$ -1.0
1948	6.7	.7	.9	3.7	.4	-1.2	.9	-1.0
1949	6.4	.6	.6	5.0	.2	-.1	.6	-.8
1950	2.3	.6	.2	3.5	.6	3.6	1.3	-.2
1951	5.2	.5	.2	3.0	1.5	.4	1.1	-.5
1952	4.8	.6	.6	1.9	2.6	1.2	1.1	-.6
1953	4.7	.7	.2	1.8	4.7	2.5	.1	-.3

Sources: *Economic Report of the President*, January 1953, January 1954; *Survey of Current Business*, March 1954.
a. Minus signs indicate net inflow of gold and capital to United States.

financing the export surplus has changed, but the American taxpayer has continued to pay the bill in each instance.

A nation that imports more than it exports on short-term swings in the balance of trade may finance its deficit with the world by drawing down its gold and dollar reserves. It may also borrow from private foreign sources to cover that part of its imports which is not paid for by exports. These items, however, have played only a minor role in financing the total surplus of American exports since the second world war.

In 1947, the total of public loans, private investments and foreign aid was insufficient to cover America's export surplus of $11.5 billion, and in order to pay for their imports from the United States other nations had to draw down their already depleted reserves of gold and dollars by $1.9 billion. Foreign reserves fell well below the critical point. This situation was reversed by the increase in foreign aid, by the devaluation of foreign currencies in 1949, and by the unexpected increase in the value of American imports the following year when war broke out in Korea. In 1950 other nations increased their reserves by $3.6 billion through transactions with the United States because they sold us more goods at higher prices and because they bought less from us than in previous years. Foreign assistance and investments of all kinds continued to exceed the surplus of American exports to be financed, and other nations succeeded in adding to their reserves, though by smaller amounts, each year through 1953. (See Table 2.) This strengthening of their impaired financial position was indispensable to the restoration of orderly world trade.

In most years, Americans invested abroad $1 billion net, in round numbers. Although this is shown as a net item in the balance of payments, it must be adjusted downward owing to "errors and omissions," which consist largely of unrecorded capital movements flowing into the United States. Thus, the true net movement of private capital was even smaller than it appears from Table 2.

Foreign Investment Plays a Minor Role

As the richest nation in the world, the United States has the largest reservoir of capital available for investment. This has led to exaggerated notions of the contribution which private investment is likely to make to the elimination of the dollar shortage. The first point to consider is the character of private foreign investment.

Sale in the United States of foreign bonds and other securities may provide dollars which other nations can use to buy American exports of goods and services. Portfolio investments, as this type is called, were popular in the 1920s, but have been of minor importance since that time.

Although private long-term investments abroad rose by $10 billion in the seven-year period 1946–1953, less than $1 billion of the increase was of the portfolio type, and most of this was for Canada.[2]

Direct investments which involve active participation in management of foreign enterprise account for more than 90 per cent of our long-term private investment abroad since the second world war. Investments by American steel companies in the production of iron ore in Labrador, Venezuela and Liberia are examples. Such investments typically involve the export of American machinery and equipment. They do not provide other nations with dollar exchange with which to buy goods of other kinds except to the extent that the investment dollars are spent locally for labor and materials, and so reach the exchange market through conversion into local currencies.[3] A large proportion of these direct investments are for the purpose of obtaining raw materials, which eventually provide the means of repayment. American oil companies have been the largest private foreign investors.

Because of exchange restrictions dictated by the shortage of dollars, there has been little opportunity for private foreign capital to flow into the United States. Most of the increase in foreign holdings in this country represents reinvestment of earnings of affiliates of foreign corporations and rising market prices of corporate securities.

Total American investments abroad, both private and public, roughly doubled from $18.7 billion in 1946 to $39.5 billion in 1953. At the same time, total foreign investments here rose from $15.9 billion to $23.6 billion. As a result the net creditor position of America rose from $2.8 billion in 1946 to $15.8 billion in 1953.

Earnings from our investments abroad are far greater than foreign earnings from investments here. In 1953 American investments abroad earned $2.6 billion while foreign earnings here were only $500 million. This is because our investments are largely in productive enterprise, while foreign investments are largely in short-term assets. Because of this excess of earnings due Americans from foreign investments, the effect of our net creditor position on the balance of payments is even more important than appears from the figures on investments.

2. "International Investment Position of the United States," *Survey of Current Business*, May 1954.

3. The conclusion of one writer is that: "In sum, United States private investment cannot be considered as making any appreciable contribution either directly or indirectly to alleviation of the dollar shortage. Whatever the cause—whether it stems from the direct investment technique used, or from the breakdown of the prewar pattern of trade, itself a casualty of the dollar shortage—this state of affairs seems irreversible as long as American investors react to the dollar shortage problems as they have in the postwar period." Ernest Block, "United States Foreign Investment and the Dollar Shortage," *Review of Economics and Statistics*, May 1953, pp. 159–160.

The Creditor Nation Argument

Ever since the first world war, when America became a creditor nation, it has been argued that this position implies an obligation to accept an import surplus of goods and services. This widely held belief may involve possible confusion between a net creditor position and a stage of maturity when the people of a creditor nation wish to consume the fruits of their past investments. The two things are not at all the same. Nothing happens to raise the propensity to consume simply because a nation shifts from a debtor to a net creditor position.[4]

At some date in the distant future Americans may decide to live off their past investments. At that time it should be easy to accommodate an import surplus of goods and services because consumption will rise faster than income produced. But this is certainly not the situation today, and there is no indication that it will become so in the foreseeable future.

Net repayment of past investment would create a dilemma for a nation like the United States where people generally try to "get ahead," that is, to consume less than their income. Actually, in the United States, the total of investment has almost invariably become larger year by year; the people of the nation as a whole have seldom consumed as much as they have produced. Similarly, a nation which does not wish to consume the fruits of its foreign investments may reinvest them abroad and thus continue to maintain an export surplus.[5] This is what we should expect when a nation first acquires a net creditor position, and it is precisely what happened during the 1920s when America's net foreign investments rose from $3 billion in 1919 to $8.8 billion in 1930.

The real difficulty arises when a creditor nation not only seeks to stop investing abroad, but also does not wish to consume the fruits of its investments. This calls for a net import surplus of goods and services without a corresponding increase in consumption. Earnings from foreign investments must then either be sacrificed or be accepted in the form of goods and services which, in effect, are reinvested at home. This presents a two-edged threat: a painful readjustment and the danger of over-all deflation.

A shift from an export surplus to an import surplus is bound to exert a deflationary influence, and unemployment would result unless domestic investment were expanded by an equivalent amount. How deflationary it

4. An increase in demand for dollar exchange to service our net investments as a creditor nation may tend to lower the price of imports, but there is no reason to suppose that the proportions of total American income consumed and saved will be significantly affected as a result.

5. "If the rate growth on all foreign investment could exceed its yield the problem would be solved . . ." Evsey D. Domar, "The Effect of Foreign Investment on the Balance of Payments," *American Economic Review*, December 1950, p. 809. Cf. Walter S. Salant, "The Domestic Effects of Capital Export under the Point Four Program," *American Economic Review*, Papers and Proceedings, May 1950.

would be would depend to a large extent on the relation between the required import surplus and the gross national product. In the United States, to accept $5 billion more in imports than at present would be to accept something like 1.3 per cent of the gross product. At the same time that some home industries were embarrassed by an increase of competitive imports or by a loss of export markets, some industries would be called on to increase their rate of investment for the purpose of producing more consumer goods in the future.[6]

The alternative is to continue investing more and more abroad each year, always postponing the time when imports would need to exceed exports. While this offers a theoretically possible escape from the dilemma, compound interest produces astonishing sums over the long run. Even after allowing for ordinary business losses, there would seem to be little prospect of expanding foreign investment over the decades on a scale which would take care of the ever-growing sums available for reinvestment. In this respect the analogy between foreign and domestic investment is at a highly abstract level which ignores the risks of war and the forces of modern nationalism.

The modern nation no longer limits the role of the state primarily to protection of private property and enforcement of contract. Other nations resist the growth of foreign ownership and influence in the pattern typical of the nineteenth century. Private portfolio investments abroad have been largely replaced by public loans, and direct investments are increasingly limited to a minority interest. The age of colonialism is past.

By private management contracts and licensing agreements as well as by public programs, American know-how is made available to the outside world with a minimum of international capital movement and foreign control. Technical knowledge, which required decades to develop and cost millions of dollars, is spreading throughout the world and is recorded in the balance of payments only through the receipt of management fees and royalties.

Foreign investment can and should play a role in the economic development of other countries, but the past affords little guidance as to the character of the debtor-creditor relationship which will eventually emerge.[7]

6. Such an adjustment would be only somewhat less formidable if the rest of the world could supply investment goods more cheaply than they are produced at home. But as will be indicated in later chapters, most of America's potential imports appear to consist of agricultural products and nondurable goods.

7. In the Victorian Age, Britain poured 40 per cent of her total investments into foreign countries and, by 1914, about one tenth of her national income was derived from foreign investments. If today the United States were to devote the same share of her resources to foreign investment, "the entire Marshall Plan would have to be carried out twice a year." A. K. Cairncross, *Home and Foreign Investment, 1870–1913*, Cambridge University Press, 1953, p. 3.

Elimination of the Export Surplus

Now, suppose the American taxpayer were to stop financing a surplus of exports, or, in other words, our foreign trade were to be balanced except for the minor effect of private capital movements. What are the possible means of achieving this result and what would be the economic consequences?

The first way would be for foreign nations to cut their purchases of American goods. United States exports of military end-items regarded as essential for mutual security might be stopped or exports of cotton, wheat, machine tools and other industrial equipment might be reduced. In 1953, American commodity exports would have had to be cut by 27 per cent to bring them into balance with commodity imports. If we should reduce imports for American military establishments overseas or complete our stockpiling program, the cut in our exports would have to be even more drastic. The loss of $4 or $5 billion worth of exports might not seriously affect the economy as a whole, but specific producers in the export industries would suffer.

A second way to eliminate the export surplus would be for America to buy more from abroad, and continue to sell as much as at present. In 1953 this would have meant an increase in imports of goods and services by 28 per cent. This seems a large undertaking, and indeed it would be difficult to accomplish. But the magnitude of the adjustment seems small in view of the fact that gross national product was $367 billion. The requisite increase of imports is but 1.3 per cent of that.

The least disturbing adjustment would be to raise gradually the level of both imports and exports, and to close the gap by a more rapid growth of imports than of exports.

The dollar gap can be eliminated either at high or at low levels of foreign trade, but with an important difference. It would be cheaper for America to import many products which are now produced at home, and to pay for them with exports. What is perhaps more important, the expansion of mutually beneficial trade would be a symbol of the responsible conduct of foreign policy and of the leadership which history has placed in American hands.

Such arguments seem so strong that the question arises why they have not long since prevailed. Are there causes of the export surplus which do not yield to argument? What are the difficulties in the way of enlarging imports? If all tariff barriers were removed, who would be hurt? These questions must be considered if effective action is to follow persuasion in eliminating the export surplus.

Chapter 2

Imports and Economic Growth

IF AN EFFORT is to be made to remedy the imbalance in the foreign trade of the United States by an expansion of imports, it is well to know something of their history. Have total imports, whether measured by value or by physical quantity, shown a tendency to increase? In particular, have they increased in proportion to the growth of the American economy? What kinds of goods have been imported, and in what order of volume? Has the composition of imports changed? What are now the chief imports?

Our examination of these questions will support the following conclusions.

1. Domestic production supplanted the long-term growth of imports in the last decade of the nineteenth century and, again, after 1937. Imports appear to have kept pace with the growth of domestic commodity output from the Civil War to the 1890s and from the end of the century to the 1930s.

2. The composition of imports since the Civil War has greatly changed. Most significant is the trend of crude materials, which increased much more rapidly than other imports until the first world war, but have since declined in relative importance. By 1948, crude materials represented a smaller piece of the import pie than in 1900. Semimanufactures, on the other hand, have increased in relative importance.

3. Imports are highly concentrated in a few commodities and the degree of concentration is growing. Our largest imports more than doubled in value from 1929 to 1949 while all other imports failed to rise in value despite the inflation of prices. Eight items alone accounted for almost all the growth in the value of imports between 1929 and 1949.

These developments signal an element of danger. The strongest industrial economy in the world seems to have become relatively less dependent on imports of crude materials as well as other imports. Growth has been limited increasingly to a small group of imports, and the rich variety of products which characterize domestic trade have been of diminishing importance in foreign trade. Postwar shortages have probably accentuated these developments, but at least some of the trends were evident before the war.

THE RELATION OF IMPORTS TO DOMESTIC PRODUCTION

Imports by Value

Imports of goods, measured by value, can most logically be compared with the value of total United States output of finished commodities, at prices charged by producers. In both cases only goods are included. A more frequent basis of comparison—imports of goods with the gross national product of the United States—greatly distorts the actual situation chiefly because the gross national product includes services as well as goods, and services have occupied a growing share of the national output. The comparison of imports with finished commodities at prices charged by producers in the United States avoids this serious defect.

Data on United States commodity output before 1890 exist only for the single years 1869, 1879 and 1889. In this period the ratio of imports to domestic commodity output changed little, though a dip occurred in 1879. Beginning in 1890, annual data are available. The year-to-year record is irregular because of the business cycle; imports rise more than domestic production in booms and fall more in depressions. Wars also limit imports, though not domestic output.

Three trends, however, are clearly visible. There was a sharp drop in the ratio of imports to domestic output between 1890 and 1900. After 1900 the ratio remained about the same until 1929, except for variations due to depressions and World War I. During the depression of the 1930s another sharp drop occurred. Some recovery took place between 1935 and 1937, but the ratio ends in 1939 at the lowest point reached in the whole series. (See Figure 2.)

It is difficult to account for the fall of the ratio between 1890 and 1900. Depression characterized the early years of the decade and the Spanish-American War occurred in 1898. But if these were the main influences in bringing about the downward trend, why did not the ratio of imports to domestic output return to the pre-1890 level during prosperity and rapid industrial expansion between 1900 and 1914? Domestic prices turned up in 1896 after a decline of one third from the Civil War to 1896. There was a shift in the domestic terms of trade favorable to agriculture as prices started up. Unfortunately we know very little about the foreign terms of trade. Moreover, the whole structure of world trade shifted at this time. The growth in domestic industry displaced imports of finished goods and it may be that changes in the tariff contributed to the displacement. This question will be examined later.

In any case, it is remarkable that there was no downward tendency of the ratio in the long period from 1900 to 1929, except in depression and

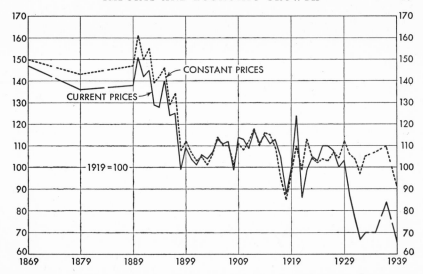

FIGURE 2. INDEX OF GENERAL IMPORTS AS PER CENT OF FINISHED COMMODITY OUTPUT AT CURRENT AND CONSTANT PRICES,[a] CALENDAR YEARS 1869, 1879 AND 1889–1939

Source: Appendix 1.

a. Imports deflated by wholesale prices before 1919; quantity index thereafter.

war. As the United States industrial economy and population expanded, so did the value of imports.

A sharp drop in the ratio between 1929 and 1933 would be expected because of the great severity of the slump. But what accounts for the failure of the value of imports to recover as did the value of domestic output between 1933 and the end of the decade? Usually this break in the historic trend is associated with the many obstructions to trade that originated during the depression, including the high American tariff and the devaluation of the dollar, which hampered imports much like an abrupt rise in import duties.

Imports by Physical Volume

If, however, the quantity of imports is compared with domestic commodity output in constant prices, the ratio between them does recover after 1933. The constant trend which was in evidence since 1900 continues until 1938, interrupted only by a decline which would normally be associated with the fall of American production and employment between 1929 and 1933. Indeed, the parallelism between imports and domestic production is far closer than would be expected in the deepest depression of recent times.[1]

1. Repeal of prohibition increased imports of alcoholic beverages.

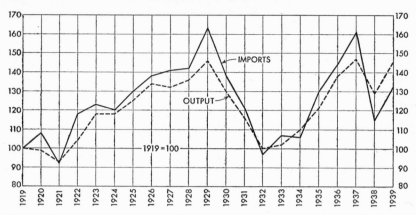

FIGURE 3. INDEXES OF QUANTUM IMPORTS AND FINISHED OUTPUT AT CONSTANT PRICES, 1919–1939

Source: Table 11. The output series in constant prices has been adjusted for net exports.

The effect of deflating a value index by an index of prices is of course to give an indication of the change of physical quantity.[2] What apparently happened after 1933 was that the United States continued to buy a quantity of foreign goods which made up about the same percentage of its domestic physical output as in the thirty-five previous years. The ratio stated in terms of current prices without this correction fell only because of a greater relative fall in the prices of the kinds of goods imported than in the prices of domestic output as a whole. This conclusion is not surprising, because imports consisted to an important extent of mineral and agricultural products, the prices of which fell further and recovered more slowly than the prices of industrial products. The domestic output of the United States, however, consisted to a greater degree of industrial products than did imports.

2. In this period, we are comparing an index of the quantity of imports with output in constant prices. The official quantity series of the U.S. Department of Commerce is available for 1913 and annually beginning in 1919. For an explanation of method, see *Foreign Trade of the United States, 1936–1949*, International Trade Series No. 7, U.S. Department of Commerce, 1951, p. 6. Imports before 1919 were deflated by wholesale prices. "Output in constant prices" is the series by the National Bureau of Economic Research.

The constant prices series before 1919 shows only changes in the relative importance of imports on the assumption that import prices behaved like wholesale prices. Although the broad trend of import and wholesale prices was similar, the deflation is inadequate. Prices of leading imports after 1898 rose less rapidly than domestic prices and it may be that the displacement which persisted after this time was chiefly in the value rather than in the quantity of imports relative to output.

The student who wishes to pursue the subject of prices may begin with T. J. Kreps, "Import and Export Prices in the United States and the Terms of International Trade, 1880–1914," *Quarterly Journal of Economics*, August 1926.

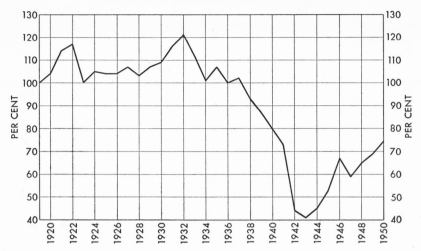

FIGURE 4. QUANTUM IMPORTS AS PER CENT OF INDUSTRIAL PRODUCTION,
1919–1950

Source: Appendix 2.

Prices of farm products in the United States rose more than prices of foreign agricultural products in the 1930s, because of the drought and the recovery measures of the United States government. What has to be accounted for is not any decline in the relative quantity of imports, but the unexpectedly large amounts that the United States bought from abroad in these years of unemployment. (See Figure 3.)

It should, of course, be remembered that though the figures indicate a surprising capacity of domestic consumers during the depression to use imports (measured by quantity), the dollar earnings from imports are the main consideration of the foreign sellers. These did fall drastically in spite of the increased quantity sold, because of low prices. The ability of foreigners to buy from the United States without exchange shortages and other embarrassments was correspondingly reduced.

A frequently used comparison—that of imports with industrial production in the United States—may easily be misleading because about half of imports consist of agricultural products. Nevertheless the comparison is of some interest since at times when industrial production is high, purchasing power for all varieties of imports is high. Also, industries use as raw materials many imports, including such agricultural products as rubber. An index of imports, measured by quantity, as a percentage of industrial production in the United States showed no sharply declining tendency in the 1930s until after 1937; indeed in 1932 it reached its peak for the series beginning in 1919 and ending in 1950. Apparently the steep fall after 1939

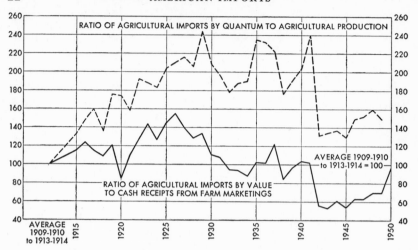

FIGURE 5. INDEXES OF RATIO OF AGRICULTURAL IMPORTS TO AGRICULTURAL
OUTPUT, BY VALUE AND QUANTUM, 1910–1914 TO 1950

Source: Appendix 3.

was due in part to the competition of new synthetics with silk, and in part
to war in the Far East, which disrupted production and trade not only in
silk but also in such products as rubber and tin. Though a rising trend
began in 1943, the index in 1950 was still far below the prewar level. (See
Figure 4.) The displacement of imports in the depression of 1938 was
unusually severe and subsequent recovery has been incomplete.

Agricultural Imports

It may be enlightening to compare agricultural imports with agricultural
output[3] in the United States. The demand for food and clothing, whether of
domestic or foreign origin, is strongly affected by population growth, and
to a smaller extent by domestic purchasing power. The ratio, in terms of
quantity, rose sharply between 1910–1914 and 1929. (The more rapid
growth of agricultural imports than of domestic farm production had begun
in the nineteenth century.) The ratio shows sharp drops during the depression of the early 1930s and again in the 1938 slump, but by 1941 was back
near the 1929 peak. The war brought a precipitate fall in 1942, but after
that a moderate rise began, and since World War II the ratio has been about
half again as high as before World War I. (See Figure 5.)

The ratio of the value of agricultural imports to cash receipts from
domestic farm marketings indicates the disadvantage suffered by foreign

3. Production for sale and home consumption.

producers of United States agricultural imports because of the greater fall in prices of their products than of farm products in the United States. It begins to fall in 1926, three years before the onset of depression; before that it had never risen so far above the 1910–1914 base as the ratio in terms of quantity. By 1932 it was below the level of 1910–1914, and since then exceeded that level only in 1935–1937 and 1940–1941. The last figure, that for 1950, shows a marked rise from the previous year, but is still some 2 per cent below the pre-World War I level.

CHANGES IN THE COMPOSITION OF IMPORTS

Changes between the Civil War and World War I

In 1866 by far the largest class of imports, measured by value, consisted of finished manufactures. Next in rank, though far below it in value, was manufactured foodstuffs. Crude foodstuffs and semimanufactures (partly manufactured goods principally used as industrial materials) came next, and were about equal in value. At the bottom of the list stood crude materials.

By 1914, the year of the outbreak of World War I, a striking change in this order had taken place. No class of imports had shrunk, but some had grown much faster than others. Now far in the lead was crude materials, which had occupied the last place just after the Civil War. Finished manufactures was in second place. Third came semimanufactures. Some distance below stood crude foodstuffs, and lowest of all, manufactured foodstuffs, which in 1866 had occupied second place. (See Figure 6.)

The situation in the mid-nineteenth century was that of a nation which, though its manufactures were growing, still needed to buy abroad more manufactured products than industrial materials. Both fabricated consumer goods and capital goods were imported in major volume. At the end of the long period of industrial expansion from the Civil War to World War I, industrial materials in crude and semimanufactured form had risen markedly in the scale, though foreign finished manufactures were still in large demand. There was no sign, however, that the United States was approaching the situation of a highly industrialized nation like Britain, which specialized in manufacture at the expense of production of farm products. Foodstuffs, both crude and manufactured, were at the bottom of the list even in 1914.

Crude materials showed an upward trend throughout the entire period. It was not until 1898, however, that they definitely took first place from finished manufactures. Semimanufactures (of which wood pulp is a good example) did not show any marked rise until after the beginning of the twentieth century.

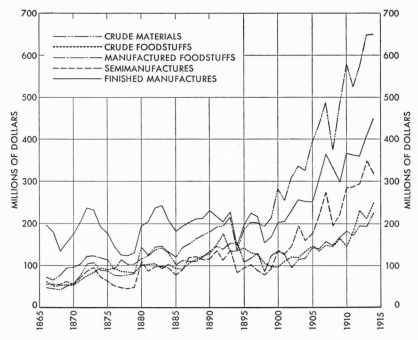

FIGURE 6. VALUE OF IMPORTS, BY ECONOMIC CLASSES, 1866–1914

Source: Historical Statistics of the United States, 1789–1945, pp. 246–247.

No important inference can be drawn from the more or less level trend of the absolute value of imports before 1898, contrasted with its rapid rise thereafter, except that the shift reflects the difference in long-term price movements. In general, prices were falling between 1866 and 1896; increases in physical volume of imports were not reflected in their total value during this period. Thereafter, because of generally rising prices, values rose more rapidly than volume.

The fact that crude materials occupied a so much larger place in the total value of imports after 1900 than before doubtless helps to account, in a technical sense, for the previously noted fact that the ratio of total imports to domestic production never was as high after this date as previously. A nation which imports mainly manufactured articles is likely to import more in relation to its domestic production than one which imports mainly raw materials and does most of its own fabricating. This will be the case, whether the measure is by value or by quantity. Change in composition of imports, however, is a result rather than a cause of more fundamental factors which determine the growth of imports and output.

382.50973 H884a

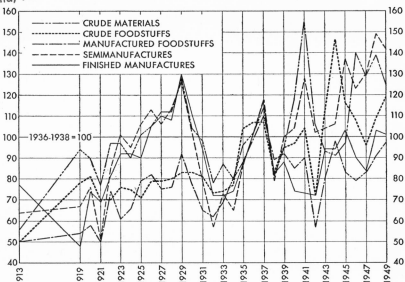

FIGURE 7. INDEXES OF CHANGES IN QUANTITY OF IMPORTS, BY ECONOMIC CLASSES,
1913 AND 1919–1949

Source: *Foreign Trade of the United States, 1936–1949*, International Trade Series
No. 7, U.S. Department of Commerce, 1951, Table 13.

Change in the War Years, 1913–1919

The war years, of course, brought a tremendous increase in the value of imports: 170 per cent in the two food groups, 130 per cent in crude and semimanufactured materials, but only 20 per cent in finished manufactures. The rise in value of the three categories of fabricated imports was due largely to price inflation. It was only crude materials and crude foods imports which rose sharply in physical quantity. (See Figure 7.)

By quantity, total imports rose about one fourth; finished manufactures dropped sharply, while semimanufactures and manufactured foods increased only slightly. Apparently, crude goods were available in world markets though fabricated goods were not available until the postwar year 1920. This was a natural consequence of the fact that the chief manufacturing nations were at war. The most rapid increase in the value of imports of manufactured foods and finished manufactures was in 1920, after the end of the war, and when the inflation of nonfarm prices reached a climax.

Change in the 1920s

The 1920s witnessed an entirely new development. Only crude foodstuffs lagged behind the rise in the other categories. This is the only period in which the three groups of fabricated imports rose more rapidly than the two groups of crude imports. But the postwar rise must be interpreted against the background of the war period when the crude materials had increased rapidly. Generally, the imports which had suffered during the war increased most rapidly in the postwar period, while those that had increased rapidly during the war lagged during the 1920s. The broad differentiation among the classes of imports with respect to the rise from 1913 to 1929 is between foods and nonfoods. The war had expanded domestic production of foodstuffs, and imports suffered. (Figure 7.)

Change in 1929–1949

The Great Depression is discussed in a later chapter. We are here concerned with the period only as it affected long-term growth. All categories of imports fell sharply in the depression, but both crude and manufactured foods declined less, by quantity, than nonfoods. In the latter 1930s, the nonfoods also failed decisively to regain the 1929 high, while the foods established highs in 1937 well above all previous peaks.

The differences which characterized the behavior of the several categories of imports during the second world war are only, in part, similar to the disparities during the first world war. The relatively low groups in both wars were manufactured foods and finished manufactures. But imports of crude materials failed to rise consistently during the second world war, as they did in the first. This doubtless reflects the effects of war in the Pacific.

The failure of imports to rise absolutely during the twenty years 1929–1949 seems strange. Despite the increase of two thirds in real gross national output, the quantity of imports increased only 3 per cent. The only increase of importance in the quantity of imports over the two decades was in semi-manufactures and in crude foods, which was relatively low in the 1920s. The fall in finished manufactures is, perhaps, not unexpected; but *the failure of crude materials to rise far above the 1929 peak in 1948–1949 is an astonishing development.* Retardation in the growth of crude materials extends back to 1919. All other imports increased twice as much as crude materials from 1919 to 1949.

Finished manufactures fell 10 per cent from the 1929 peak to the 1937 peak and 22 per cent from 1929 to 1949, as compared with a rise of 171 per cent from 1919 to 1929 and 69 per cent from 1913 to 1929. The absolute fall in finished imports, however, is but the continuation of a long-term pattern. Relatively, finished imports have been falling since very early times, but there are some indications that this decline may be leveling off.

Manufactured foods increased only 5 per cent by quantum in the twenty years 1929–1949, in sharp contrast to a rise of 80 per cent in the preceding sixteen years 1913–1929. This group has also been declining relatively since

TABLE 3

PERCENTAGE INCREASE IN OUTPUT AND IMPORTS, BY ECONOMIC CLASSES, SELECTED
PERIODS, 1919–1949

	1919–1929		1929–1937		1937–1949		1929–1949	
	Value	Quantum	Value	Quantum	Value	Quantum	Value	Quantum
Gross national product	28	30	−13	2	183	62	146	66
Finished commodity output	10	46	−17	a	a	a	a	a
Total imports	13	63	−32	−2	120	5	50	3
Crude materials	−9	36	−38	−11	91	10	19	−2
Crude foods	−1	6	−23	29	223	11	147	43
Manufactured foods	−24	70	4	20	69	−12	75	5
Semimanufactures	45	90	−28	−7	125	20	61	12
Finished manufactures	102	171	−45	−10	127	−14	26	−22

Sources: Gross national product, U.S. Department of Commerce; output, Simon Kuznets, *Commodity Flow and Capital Formation*, National Bureau of Economic Research, New York, 1938, Vol. I, Tables II-5 and II-7; imports, *Foreign Trade of the United States, 1936–1949*, International Trade Series No. 7, U.S. Department of Commerce, 1951.

a. Not available.

the end of the nineteenth century, but the downward trend has leveled off since 1926–1930.

The apparently anomalous failure in crude materials imports remains to be accounted for. Why should they have been in less demand at the end of two decades which, as a whole, were characterized by gigantic growth of industrial production? (See Table 3.)

LAG IN IMPORTS OF CRUDE MATERIALS AFTER 1929

Typical of the broad historical trend of crude materials imports until recently are hides, furs, crude rubber, tobacco and raw silk. Imports of these materials rose rapidly and almost without faltering for a century until the years 1926–1929. Thereafter, the volume of imports either declined or failed to reach new peaks despite the further expansion of trade and of domestic production. (See Figure 8.) During the early years of the twentieth century, crude materials imports were increasing vigorously; the five under examination were expanding more rapidly than the average for all raw materials. But after 1925, raw materials imports either expanded more slowly or declined more rapidly than most of the other economic classes. These five raw materials fell from two thirds to two sevenths of all crude materials imports.

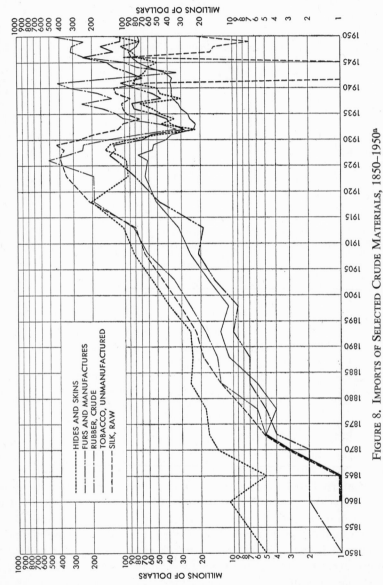

FIGURE 8. IMPORTS OF SELECTED CRUDE MATERIALS, 1850–1950[a]

Source: Appendix 4.

a. 1950 reflects speculative buying of hides and stockpiling of rubber.

28

Hides and Skins

The United States has imported hides and skins from the earliest days of its existence.

Cattle hide imports are only a supplement to domestic production. Imports are marginal in the sense that they are made to fill the gap in any year between the variable domestic production and domestic requirements. Thus, the volume of imports varies from year to year with changes in demand, which are much greater than changes in domestic consumption. Sheep and goat skins, on which we depend more heavily for imports, do not show the sharp variations shown by cattle hide imports.

Hides are used primarily for the manufacture of boots and shoes, which is no longer a rapidly expanding industry. Once a population has reached a level of consumption of two pairs of shoes per capita annually, there appears to be little prospect of further growth in the consumption of shoes with leather uppers. Increases in consumption, apart from cyclical variation, take place with increases in population.

Since cattle hides supplement domestic production, we might expect that imports would rise faster than shoe production in a period of sustained prosperity. This, in fact, is the case. Hide imports reached short-period peaks in World War I, in 1929 and in 1948. Each of these peaks, however, was lower than the preceding one, and while hide imports rose 200-fold in the hundred years preceding 1920, they have since fallen by more than half. This long-term decline is attributable primarily to the increased cattle raising in the United States because of the high price of meat, to the development of substitutes for leather and to the depletion of European herds during the war.[4] (See Figure 8.)

Furs

The young, pioneering United States was an importer of furs at least as early as 1821. Fur imports increased from $1 million a century ago to over $125 million in the late 1920s. The increase was tenfold from 1850 to the turn of the century, and more than tenfold in the first quarter of the twentieth century. However, despite the enormous increase in both prices and real income since 1929, imports of fur in 1949 were well below the 1925–1929 average in current values. (See Figure 8.)

The failure of fur imports to maintain their earlier levels was not due to a shift from raw to manufactured furs. Most fur imports are unmanufactured skins—95 per cent of the total in 1949. Domestic breeding of fur-bearing animals accounts for part of the decline in imports, but both the domestic industry and imports have suffered from other factors including, apparently, changes in taste and style. Other possible factors affecting

4. See Chapter 13.

consumption are a long-term trend to warmer winters, shift of population to warmer regions and less outdoor life in formal dress. Imports of certain furs were embargoed in 1952, but this could not account for the failure of imports to keep pace with consumer expenditures in earlier years.

Rubber

Rubber consumption is continuing to grow year by year. But world natural rubber production has been entirely inadequate to meet the demand for new rubber in recent years. Much of the present acreage is superannuated and new production will be offset in part by a destruction of old plantings.

The rest of the world outside the United States, Russia and Canada has no adequate synthetic rubber facilities and has used natural rubber almost exclusively. Immediately after the war, United States rubber users were required by law to use about a quarter of a million tons of certain types of synthetic rubber annually. This is roughly one fourth of the capacity for the production of chemical rubber which was developed during the war. A certain amount of natural rubber is needed, but the relative proportion of chemical and natural rubber is still affected by prejudice in favor of the natural product. If this prejudice should wane, we could get along with smaller rubber imports than we have had.

The use of reclaimed rubber declined following the war. The use of chemical rubber in the United States greatly exceeded the minimum legal requirement because of the imbalance between world demand and current world production of new natural rubber.

Imports for stockpiling contributed substantially to the rise in imports after 1950.

Tobacco

Tobacco is indigenous to this continent and the United States is the world's leading exporter of tobacco, accounting for more than one third of world exports.[5] Nonetheless, owing to the many types of tobacco, we have imported tobacco for more than a century.

Cigarette production expanded 133-fold, from 3 billion in 1901–1905 to 400 billion in 1948. The tobacco used in cigarette manufacture in this period increased from 12 million to 1 billion pounds.

Imported tobacco leaf is indispensable to the well-established cigarette blends. Imported leaf declined from 11 per cent of the tobacco leaf used in all manufacture in 1927 and 1928 to 6 per cent in 1943–1945 and 6 per cent

5. Henry C. Taylor and Anne Dewees Taylor, *World Trade in Agricultural Products*, Macmillan, New York, 1943.

in 1948. Imported leaf is indispensable to the blend, but the proportion apparently is variable.

The consumption of tobacco in making cigarettes increased fivefold between 1921–1925 and 1948, while imports of tobacco leaf increased only 20 per cent.

Raw Silk

Raw silk imports constitute one of the dramatic and familiar technological casualties. In the decade of the 1920s imports of silk rose at an exceptional rate—more than doubling from 1920–1921 to 1929. Even in the depressed 1930s raw silk fared relatively well. In 1931–1935 imports averaged 75 million pounds, a decline of 14 per cent from 1926–1930. The recovery of the later 1930s did not bring with it a renewed expansion of silk imports. The average silk importation of 1936–1940 was 33 per cent below 1926–1930. Artificial silk fibers were gaining ground at the expense of real silk.

Continued improvement in artificial fibers and the development of new ones such as nylon would, no doubt, have reduced the consumption of silk much further even in peacetime. The war, by cutting off raw silk imports, delivered a decisive blow to silk consumption by giving the synthetic fabrics an opportunity to establish themselves in the consumer's taste. In 1949 imports were 5 per cent of the 1926–1930 level and no substitute imports in the fiber field had appeared.

DECLINE IN PROCESSED RAW MATERIALS

A second group of five items that also failed to increase as rapidly as might have been expected are not classified by the census as crude materials. But, in an economic sense, they are raw materials, for they are purchased by industry.

In order of importance these raw materials are copper ore and manufactures, tin including ore, burlaps, vegetable oils and fats, and fertilizer. With the progressive industrialization of the United States and the displacement of manufactured imports by domestic products, it could be expected that the proportion of raw materials in total imports would increase. This was not the case with this group of commodities, which formed a constant 10 per cent of total imports in the three periods 1906–1910, 1926–1930 and 1949.

Copper Ore and Manufactures

Imports of copper have not increased much more rapidly than total imports in the periods under examination because of the depressing effects on imports of the technological progress in mining methods which has taken place in the United States, the increasing accumulation and therefore importance of secondary copper, and the decline in American exports.[6]

Tin, Including Ore

The most important factor causing an absolute decline in the value of tin imports from 1929 to 1949 has been the development of the electrolytic process for applying tin to iron plate in a much more sparing manner than had hitherto been possible. In addition, substitutes have appeared for tin in its two main functions of food preservation and solder.[7]

Burlap

Imports of jute sacking continued to increase from 1926–1930 to 1949, but not so rapidly as imports in general. Demand for burlap has suffered from the expanding use of other materials for packing, such as paper bagging, and also from development in methods of handling materials which avoid the necessity of packing at all.

Vegetable Oils and Fats

Imports of vegetable fats and oils increased more rapidly than all imports during the first quarter of this century, but suffered an absolute decline between 1926–1930 and 1949. In physical volume, 1949 imports were approximately one half of the prewar level. This decline is attributable to the appearance of competing domestic vegetable oils in large quantities. The most important of these is soybean oil. In addition, supplies of animal fats and oils increased in this period, and they are substitutes for vegetable fats and oils in some of their uses. Furthermore, technical research has developed detergents which are not made with fats and oils. In 1940 two fifths of the fats used in soap were of vegetable origin.[8]

Fertilizers and Materials

The history of fertilizer imports is accounted for by the development of domestic sources of supply, both natural and synthetic. Fertilizer imports rose from $27 million in 1906–1910 to $68 million in 1926–1930, but fell to $63 million by 1949.

Before World War I, Germany had practically a monopoly of potash, and Chile was virtually the single source of nitrogen. After the war new potash deposits were discovered in other countries, the United States producing 9 per cent of the world's output. New methods developed in Ger-

6. See Chapter 15.
7. See Chapter 15.
8. See Chapter 13.

many for fixing the nitrogen in the air were introduced in the United States, and capacity for nitrogen fixation was expanded to 600,000 tons in 1939. World War II caused a vast expansion in the United States production of both these chemicals as well as in the production of phosphorus, of which this country had always been a major source. The increase in American supplies combined with severe shortages elsewhere to retard the growth of American imports.

HIGH CONCENTRATION OF IMPORTS

Coffee has been in recent years by far the largest import of the United States; it increased from $150 million in 1937 to $800 million in 1949, and accounted for one eighth of total imports. The nonferrous metals as a group make up another eighth. If to these two kinds of imports are added petroleum, sugar and rubber, half the imports are accounted for.

Coffee is not grown in the United States. Of the nonferrous metals, tin and nickel are not found in the United States; others are imported to add to domestic supplies, rather than to replace them. Petroleum is in this category. Sugar is competitive with the domestic product, but no natural rubber is grown in the United States. Though all these products may be subject to competition from domestic substitutes, most of them do not directly compete with domestic products. They are imported chiefly because of international differences in the distribution of natural resources. Noncompetitive imports are rarely subject to protective tariffs.

Agricultural imports alone make up about one half of total imports. Half of these, such as bananas, cocoa, silk and natural rubber, are not produced in the United States and are not subject to import duties. It is significant that so large a proportion of imports is concentrated in products of this type.

The Growth of Concentration

Nine imports for each of which $100 million or more was spent in 1929 made up 40 per cent of total imports in that year. The same products twenty years later accounted for 54 per cent of total imports. Of these nine, six were a larger percentage of total imports in 1949 than in 1929—nonferrous metals, coffee, sugar, newsprint and paper manufactures, petroleum and its products, and wood pulp and paper base stocks. Three shrank as a proportion of the total—rubber, hides and skins, and undressed furs. (See Table 4.)

Imports in 1949 for which $150 million or more was spent are twelve in number. In 1929 these imports constituted 43 per cent of the total value

TABLE 4

LARGEST IMPORTS^a IN 1929 AS PER CENT OF TOTAL IMPORTS, 1929–1949

	1929	1933	1937	1949
Nonferrous metals	7.5	6.7	7.9	12.7
Coffee	7.0	8.6	5.0	12.1
Rubber, crude	5.5	3.2	8.2	3.6
Sugar	4.8	7.2	5.5	5.6
Newsprint and paper manufactures	3.7	5.4	4.6	6.9
Petroleum and products	3.3	1.8	1.5	7.2
Hides and skins, raw	3.1	3.1	2.4	1.1
Wood pulp and paper base stocks	2.7	4.5	3.9	3.2
Furs, undressed	2.5	2.3	2.6	1.6
$100 million imports	40	43	42	54
	(Millions)			
$100 million imports	$1,753	$ 618	$1,251	$3,564
All other imports	2,646	832	1,759	3,034
Total imports	$4,399	$1,450	$3,010	$6,598

Source: Office of International Trade, U.S. Department of Commerce tabulations of census data (July 1950).

a. $100 million and over in 1929. Note: Percentages computed before rounding.

of imports; in 1949 they were no less than 61 per cent.[9] This list includes four products not found among those for which $100 million each was spent in 1929—wool, cocoa or cacao beans, sawmill products and oilseeds. One in the former list is not included—hides and skins. (See Table 5.)

Though some of these items are groups rather than individual commodities, substitution of the individual items would not change the picture. A complete list of imports includes many thousands of items, but more than half of the total by value consists of a very few commodities, and the proportion of the total represented by these few has been rapidly increasing.

The Imports Which Grew

Eight items alone accounted for almost all the growth in value of imports between 1929 and 1949. Taken together they increased about $2 billion, while the value of all imports grew about $2.2 billion. These imports are (1) coffee, (2) nonferrous metals, (3) newsprint, wood pulp and the like, (4) petroleum and its products, (5) raw wool, (6) machinery and vehicles, (7) watches and clocks, (8) diamonds. (See Table 6.)

The physical quantity of these eight imports grew as well, since their value increase (at current prices) was 169 per cent, as against a rise in

9. In 1952 these twelve items accounted for 64 per cent of total imports. The increase in concentration from 1949 to 1952 was due chiefly to a great increase in coffee prices.

The increase in unit value of crude material imports from 1929 to 1949 was less than that of other categories of imports.

TABLE 5

LARGEST IMPORTS[a] IN 1949 AS PER CENT OF TOTAL IMPORTS, 1929–1949

	1929	1933	1937	1949
Nonferrous metals	7.5	6.7	7.9	12.7
Coffee	7.0	8.6	5.0	12.1
Petroleum and products	3.3	1.8	1.5	7.2
Newsprint and paper manufactures	3.7	5.4	4.6	6.9
Sugar	4.8	7.2	5.5	5.6
Rubber, crude	5.5	3.2	8.2	3.6
Wool, unmanufactured	2.0	1.3	3.2	3.4
Wood pulp and paper base stocks	2.7	4.5	3.9	3.2
Cocoa or cacao beans	1.1	1.3	1.7	1.9
Sawmill products	1.0	0.6	0.7	1.7
Furs, undressed ·	2.5	2.3	2.6	1.6
Oilseeds	1.8	1.8	2.1	1.4
$150 million imports[b]	43	45	47	61
		(*Millions*)		
$150 million imports	$1,876	$ 646	$1,412	$4,046
Other imports	2,523	804	1,598	2,552
Total imports	$4,399	$1,450	$3,010	$6,598

Source: Office of International Trade, U.S. Department of Commerce tabulations of census data (July 1950).

a. $150 million and over in either 1948 or 1949 (because of the variation of individual items in these years). The computations, however, are for the year 1949 only.

b. Owing chiefly to the great increase in the price of coffee from 1949 to 1952, these twelve items accounted for 64 per cent of total imports in 1952.

Note: Percentages computed before rounding.

import prices (unit values) of 47 per cent. All other imports, taken together, *decreased* greatly in quantity. The decrease would amount to about 40 per cent if it could be assumed that the unit value of all imports was representative of this group.

The eight items did not increase faster than other imports until after 1937. The increase was from 27 per cent of total imports in 1929 and 1937 to 48 per cent in 1949.

Coffee and diamonds must be imported if the United States is to have them at all. Nonferrous metals, newsprint and wood pulp are used increasingly to supplement domestic industrial materials, because of the complete lack or gradual exhaustion of domestic sources. For light on the increased demand for wool and petroleum, see Chapters 13 and 15. Only two classes —machinery and vehicles, and watches and clocks—directly supplanted American manufactured products, and only these two consist mainly of products from industrialized nations of Europe. In neither case was domestic production absolutely displaced by the growth of imports.

TABLE 6
GROWTH IMPORTS, 1929, 1937 AND 1949[a]

	1929	1937	1949	Percentage Increase, 1929 to 1949
	(Millions)			
Nonferrous metals	$331	$236	$836	152
Coffee	302	150	796	164
Newsprint, printing paper, wood pulp and pulpwood	252	235	635	152
Petroleum and products	144	45	478	232
Wool	87	96	222	155
Machinery and vehicles	42	25	135	221
Watches and clocks	17	11	51	200
Diamonds, uncut and industrial	14	15	44	214
Total, growth imports	$1,189	$ 813	$3,197	169
All other imports	3,210	2,197	3,401	6
Total imports	$4,399	$3,010	$6,598	50
Ratio of growth imports to total imports (per cent)	27	27	48	

Source: Office of International Trade, U.S. Department of Commerce tabulations of census data (July 1950).

a. General imports in 1929, imports for consumption thereafter.

It is remarkable that in a twenty-year period when there occurred a tremendous expansion of the population and income of the United States, and a great diversification of products, the citizens and industries bought only eight major imports in increasing amounts.

ECONOMIC GROWTH AND IMPORTS

Two interrelated aspects of the relation between imports and economic growth are of main significance for the question whether imports can be sufficiently increased. One is the trend of total imports as compared with the growth of production in the United States. The other is the change in the composition of imports that has occurred because of changes in the domestic economy.

If the import deficit is to disappear and the international trade of the United States is to grow at the same time, both imports and exports must increase, but imports must increase at a faster rate than exports. This would be unlikely to occur unless imports grew at least as rapidly as domestic production of commodities.

By and large, imports increased as rapidly as domestic production from 1900 to 1937, if measured by physical quantity. Wars and depressions have interrupted the parallelism, but it has continued over the long term. By *value*, however, the slump in imports which occurred in the 1930s had not been fully erased by 1949. And it is the value of imports which is decisive in the purchasing power of foreigners for United States products, and in the elimination of the import deficit of the United States.

The decline in value of imports as a percentage of domestic production is due mainly to shifts in the kinds of products imported. Crude materials and agricultural products have in the past fifty years formed the major part of our imports, and these in general have suffered more from declines in prices (at least before World War II) than have manufactured products, which bulk larger in domestic production than in imports.

Many believe that this disadvantage of exporters to the United States will be remedied by relative rises of world raw material prices, as well as by the possibility that the extraordinary growth of American industry, accompanied by the depletion of domestic mineral resources, will greatly expand the importation of industrial materials. If so, the trend of the second quarter of the twentieth century will have to be reversed. The pronounced increase in import of crude materials taken as a whole was ended a quarter century ago. In 1948 crude materials formed a smaller proportion of imports than in 1900.

The decline of manufactured imports as a percentage of total imports has been less sharp in the past twenty-five years than in the first quarter of the century. In the generation ending in 1925, the percentage of finished manufactures to total imports fell by one third; in the generation since 1925, it fell by only 10 per cent. Semimanufactured goods—which are industrial materials—have shown some increase in relative importance. If the United States could markedly increase its imports of finished manufactures and semimanufactures, not so much reliance would have to be placed on increased import of raw materials as a means of eliminating the import deficit.

The prospects for increased importation of food products, whether crude or manufactured, are mixed. The United States supplies the bulk of its own food staples, and doubtless will continue to do so in the indefinite future. The demand for food in general does not expand with the growth of consumer purchasing power but rather with the growth of population. As levels of living rise, the percentage of family income spent for food declines. Nevertheless these broad observations conceal the fact that with rising incomes people buy larger quantities of "luxury" foods and beverages which sell at relatively high prices—such commodities as coffee, cocoa and chocolate, or tropical fruits and vegetables. The main food imports have been of this nature.

The high and increasing concentration of imports among a few commodities represents a distinct element of danger for the prospect of increase in imports. It implies that a growing proportion of domestic wants has been supplied by domestic production. This might not be surprising if wants were becoming less varied and simpler, but the opposite has been the case.

Technological advance, which may at any time decrease the need for one of the few categories of imports—as it has in the case of silk, rubber, fertilizers and tin—or a change in popular taste for consumer goods, could cause a downturn in the total United States purchase of foreign products. To make possible a reliable and important increase in imports it would be desirable if possible to increase demand for a wide array of items, even if at the beginning the demand for any one of them seemed small or the increase in its import were minor.

So far in this study the effects on imports of the business cycle or of the tariff and other trade obstacles have not been examined. To these subjects we must now pass on. From the evidence already summarized, however, it seems clear that economic growth has been one of the most important influences on the value and volume of imports.[10]

10. A number of studies have attempted to sort out the influence of income and relative price changes on imports by multiple correlation analysis. See, for example, John H. Adler, Eugene R. Schlesinger and Evelyn Van Westerborg, *The Pattern of United States Import Trade since 1923*, Federal Reserve Bank, New York, May 1952.

A detailed criticism of these technical studies is beyond the scope of the present work, which is intended for the general reader. It seems extremely doubtful if the statistical techniques that have been employed can provide a precise measurement of price elasticity. The efforts to measure income elasticity fail to deal with the important distinction between short and long run. See the convenient summary of results and a brief criticism by J. M. Letiche, "A Note on the Statistical Results of Studies on Demand Elasticities, Income Elasticities, and Foreign Trade Multipliers," Saertryk af *Nordisk Tidsskrift For Teknisk Okonomi*, 1953, pp. 39–54. For bibliography and criticism, see also G. H. Orcutt, "Measurement of Price Elasticities in International Trade," *Review of Economics and Statistics*, May 1950.

Chapter 3

Imports and the Business Cycle

IN EACH MAJOR BUSINESS CYCLE since the Civil War, American imports have fluctuated more widely both by value and by quantity than has domestic output.

1. Following the two peaks in 1872 and 1882, the fall in imports was at least twice as great as in manufacturing output.

2. In the depression from 1892 to 1894 the fall in import values was twice as great as in finished commodity output at producers' prices. A second decline in the 1890s resulted in a fall in import values in 1896 five times as great as the decline in output.

3. In the depression of 1908, the fall in import values was twice as great as in commodity output.

4. In the sharp slump of 1921, the fall in import values was two-thirds greater than in commodity output.

5. In the great depression from 1929 to 1932, the fall in import values was one-third greater than in commodity output.

6. From 1937 to 1939 the fall in import values was five times as great as in commodity output.

Insofar as can be determined from statistical evidence, each recovery from the relative displacement of imports in depression appears to have been approximately complete except for an extraordinary displacement near the end of the nineteenth century,[1] and again following the peak of 1937.

Depressions Hamper Maximum Specialization

The classical theory of foreign trade bases its main opposition to trade barriers on the benefits of specialization; in this respect it makes no distinction between domestic and international markets. Both consumers and producers will gain from wide and free markets supplied by producers each of whom concentrates on what he can do best and at the least cost.

The maximum possible specialization, however, depends on conditions seldom found in the actual world. Competition must prevail both in the selling of goods and in the hiring of labor and other resources. Both labor

1. This displacement may have been due to the Dingley tariff and the normal forces of economic development.

and capital must be mobile within each nation. Prices must be flexible. These premises of the classical theory are often explicitly stated. Another premise is high-level employment so that bidding for resources will equalize marginal returns between competing home industries.

In a dynamic economy this means continuous expansion of national output. The shift of resources (and especially of labor) from less efficient to more efficient uses will be seriously hampered unless business is active and expanding and a high level of employment prevails. Otherwise competition from imports may lead, not to the transfer of less efficiently utilized labor and capital to other occupations where they can be more productively employed, but only to reduction of prices and wages in the import-competing industries and areas which suffer from an excess of resources.

The theory abstracted from short-term changes and the interaction of the business cycle with foreign trade has been slighted in theoretical discussion, except for the effect of changes in national income and purchasing power. There are important short-term structural distinctions between foreign and domestic trade as well which also require examination.

Historical data indicate clearly that in the case of the United States, imports have suffered more severely from depression than has domestic production, and in prosperous periods imports have risen more rapidly than domestic output. The data and the probable reasons for the disparities they show need scrutiny.

REASONS FOR CYCLICAL INSTABILITY OF IMPORTS

Why do cyclical fluctuations affect imports more than domestic production? Imports apparently represent a marginal source of supply; many are used to supplement rather than to replace domestic output at high-level employment. In addition, the kinds of goods imported differ in composition from those produced at home. A larger proportion consists of agricultural products or raw materials, the prices of which characteristically have wider cyclical swings than the prices of manufactured goods. This would affect the total value of imports even if the quantity were relatively stable. A larger proportion, too, consists of luxuries or semiluxuries, the consumption of which is probably reduced first when income falls. In combination with these influences is the well-attested fact that business inventories show wide swings during the cycle; and imports are, of course, additions to domestic inventories from the production flow of foreign producers.

Relative Deflation of Import-Competing Industries

While differences in composition account for part of the relative instability of *total* imports as compared with *total* output, it is clear from the empirical evidence which will be reviewed that a major part of the difference cannot be explained by this factor. Imports of wool, for example, fluctuate more widely than domestic mill consumption. Petroleum imports fluctuate more widely than domestic production. The same is generally true of specific finished goods like jewelry, silverware, clocks and watches. In fact, all agricultural imports fluctuate more widely than domestic agricultural production, and imports of all finished goods fluctuate more widely than output of all finished goods.

The evidence also seems to show that the comparative instability of imports is not explained by the elasticity of demand with respect to income. Imports which compete directly with domestic production fluctuate more widely than imports of the same class which are not produced at home. *This suggests that the key to the relative instability of competitive imports lies in relative changes between the costs of domestic and foreign goods which take place in the expansion and contraction of the business cycle.*

The hypothesis is that deflation and inflation in the domestic import-competing industries are relatively larger than in the same industries abroad. These short-term changes in comparative costs may be due to two factors: (1) Fluctuations in income may be more severe at home than abroad. (2) Deflation and inflation of America's import-competing industries may be greater than in the rest of the economy. If this hypothesis is correct, foreign producers will meet more severe competition from domestic import-competing industries in depression than in prosperity and will find it advantageous to divert exports from the relatively deflated American market in periods of depression.

For reasons which will become apparent in later chapters, the bulk of American imports consists of the products of agriculture and the older non-durable-goods industries. Prices in American import-competing industries appear to be more flexible than in the rest of the economy. With some notable exceptions, the import-competing industries suffer from a relative inelasticity of demand and the capacity to produce surpluses as the result of technological advance. Continuous expansion of the more dynamic home industries is, therefore, needed in order to draw labor out of agriculture and to avoid relative deflation of the import-competing industries.

In order to avoid a decline in the importance of imports relative to output, it does not suffice to avoid serious depression. The comparative instability of imports appears to be relatively greater in a slight recession than in serious depression and even a leveling off of the growth of domestic production will usually result in an absolute fall in the relative importance of imports.

The hypothesis is that continuous expansion of total domestic output is required in order to avoid idle or underemployed resources accompanied by relative deflation in the import-competing industries. Thus the cyclical behavior of imports is a corollary of the dynamics of internal growth and of the concentration of imports in relatively stagnant industries. Only when total output is expanding vigorously will competition among home industries be strong enough to raise wages and incomes in the import-competing home industries equally with those in the more progressive industries. Let employment be less than full and the effect will be felt first in agriculture and the older nondurable-goods industries, which are the principal import-competing industries.

The absolute fall in imports which usually accompanies a leveling off in expansion of output may be due in part at least to the inventory factor. This relationship, or acceleration effect, is quite familiar in business cycle analysis. However, the inventory factor can help to explain the relative instability of imports only on the assumption that inventories of imports fluctuate more widely than those of domestically produced goods.

Tariffs also play a role in the cyclical changes in comparative costs. Specific duties represent a rigid cost element in the delivered price of imports with the result that such tariffs may provide greater protection in depression than in prosperity.[2]

It is also possible, though by no means clear, that transport, handling and selling costs are relatively more rigid than producers' prices of some products and represent a more serious barrier to trade in depression than in prosperity. Long-distance trade, whether domestic or foreign, may fluctuate more widely than trade within the smaller community. Because of the relatively small volume of imports compared with sales of domestic goods, and the rigidity of wages and rents, selling costs may discourage imports in periods of depression.

The control of foreign production by American companies may provide still another explanation in the case of imports like petroleum. Foreign reserves may be used as a marginal source of supply regardless of comparative costs.

The effect of these various factors cannot be isolated in considering the empirical evidence. It seems doubtful, however, whether factors other than the relative deflation of import-competing industries will account for the systematic differences between fluctuations in domestic and foreign trade.

Price Fluctuation of Imports

The instability of producers' prices of imports compared with domestic producers' prices is explained largely by the different composition of imports and national output. Roughly one half of imports are agricultural products, for which prices are characteristically more volatile than manu-

2. On the importance of specific duties see Chapter 6.

facturers' prices. For this reason import values fluctuate more violently than national output in prosperity and depression.

Import prices of manufactured goods too are probably more flexible, in some respects, than domestic prices. Import prices are not so subject to the many monopolistic controls and institutional rigidities that characterize the domestic market. International cartels did not usually try to fix prices of manufactured goods to the American market. They rather agreed to stay out of the American market in return for reciprocal treatment by American producers. Product differentiation, resale price maintenance and related "controls" have resulted in comparatively rigid prices for finished goods.[3] In the main, however, these monopolistic influences are weakest in the import-competing home industries.

Comparison of import with domestic prices presents conceptual difficulties. Domestically we attempt to measure changes in the price of the same product in the same market. The statistics used for import "prices" are unit values which reflect changes in commodity composition and geographical source as well as price measured in the more usual sense of the same product in the same market.[4] Unit import values and domestic producers' prices, for this reason, do not compare like and like. The difference, moreover, is not entirely statistical, for the possibility of radical shifts in international sources of supply means also the possibility of price changes greater than within a single national market.

In addition to differences in composition and source of supply, import and domestic prices are not subject to the same forces of inflation and deflation. While imports underwent a radical change in composition during World War I, import prices (unit values) emerged from the war well behind the rise in wholesale and gross product prices. At the 1920 peak, however, the rise in import prices from a 1913 base was about the same as in wholesale prices and one-fifth greater than in gross product prices. (See Table 7.)

Import prices fell almost one half from 1920 to 1922, or three times more than the deflation in gross product prices, a half greater than finished commodity prices and appreciably more than wholesale prices.[5]

3. On inflexible prices of finished goods compared with raw material prices, see the diagrams in D. D. Humphrey, "Nature and Meaning of Rigid Prices, 1890–1933," *Journal of Political Economy*, October 1937.

4. See *Foreign Trade of the United States, 1936–1949*, International Trade Series No. 7, U.S. Department of Commerce, 1951, Table 13. For a comparison of domestic and international prices, see T. J. Kreps, "Export, Import, and Domestic Prices in the United States, 1926–1930," *Quarterly Journal of Economics*, February 1932. The Kreps-Ellsworth index of import prices declined 48 per cent from 1926 to 1933, which is less than the change in unit values but greater than the change in domestic prices. P. T. Ellsworth, "Export, Import, and Domestic Prices in the United States, 1931–1936," *Review of Economic Statistics*, November 1937.

5. Most of the industrial countries of the world suffered in the depression of 1921 with the exception of Austria and Germany. See Willard Thorp and W. C. Mitchell, *Business Annals*, National Bureau of Economic Research, New York, 1926, pp. 94–95.

TABLE 7

PERCENTAGE PRICE CHANGES FOR SELECTED PERIODS, 1913–1950, GROSS NATIONAL PRODUCT, FINISHED COMMODITIES, WHOLESALE PRICES, AND IMPORT UNIT VALUES BY ECONOMIC CLASSES

	1913–1920	1920–1922	1922–1929	1929–1933	1933–1937	1937–1938	1938–1948	1948–1949	1949–1950
GNP prices	+103	−16	+2	−25	+13	−2	+79	−0.7	+2
Finished commodity prices	+107	−31	−0.4	−31	a	a	a	a	a
Wholesale prices	+121	−37	−1	−31	+31	−9	+110	−6	+4
Import unit values	+122	−46	+3	−44	+40	−11	+145	−5	+8
Crude materials	+80	−39	0	−61	+78	−16	+116	−4	+9
Crude foods	+60	−34	+37	−56	+33	−19	+273	−4	+38
Manufactured foods	+436	−76	−13	−36	+36	−12	+130	−5	+0.5
Semimanufactures	+199	−38	+7	−43	+35	−9	+124	−8	−3
Finished manufactures	+19	−32	−5	−42	+7	+7	+151	−3	−2

Sources: GNP prices are the implicit price index; finished commodity prices are the implicit price index from Simon Kuznets, *Commodity Flow and Capital Formation*, National Bureau of Economic Research, New York, 1938, Vol. I, Tables II-5 and II-7, and William Howard Shaw, *Value of Commodity Output since 1869*, National Bureau of Economic Research, New York, 1947, Tables I-1 and I-3; wholesale prices, Bureau of Labor Statistics; import unit values, see *Foreign Trade of the United States, 1936–1949*, International Trade Series No. 7, U.S. Department of Commerce, 1951, Table 13.

a. Not available.

The rise in import prices from 1922 to 1925 and the decline from 1925 to 1929 were substantially greater than in domestic prices. In the depression from 1929 to 1933, import prices fell about one-half more than wholesale and finished commodity prices, and increased about one-third more in the rise from 1933 to 1937.

The decline in import prices and wholesale prices was of the same order of magnitude from 1937 to 1938 and was far greater than the decline in gross product prices.

In the decade from 1938 to 1948, import prices rose about one-third more than wholesale prices and almost twice as much as gross product prices. Import and wholesale prices declined roughly the same in the slight deflation of 1949, but the rise in import prices was twice as great in 1950.

In a perfectly competitive market, prices of imported and domestically produced goods would, of course, be identical for the same product. But the real world is so far from a perfectly competitive market that this observation by no means disposes of the issue.

The importance of the price factor should not be dismissed as superficial. The relative instability of import prices has serious repercussions on the income of foreign producers and the ability of other countries to buy American exports.

The Inventory Cycle

Changes in inventories undoubtedly contribute to the cyclical instability of imports. Stocks of raw materials must be increased in order to supply an orderly expansion of production. Similarly, retailers and distributors must maintain larger stocks of finished goods as sales are expanded if their shelves are to be continuously filled with an ample range of choice as to size, color, quality, etc. The inventory cycle arises from the fact that an additional increase in current imports beyond the requirements of rising consumption is needed to build up stocks as the economy expands from a lower level to a higher level of production and sales. But once the rise in consumption levels off, the rate of imports will decline by the amount which has been going into stocks even though consumption were now stabilized.

The opposite occurs in a downswing. Since a lower inventory is needed to supply a lower level of consumption, current imports can be reduced by more than the fall in consumption while stocks are consumed. But as soon as the decline in consumption is abated, imports will rebound toward the normal relationship of imports to consumption. The inventory cycle is a special case of the acceleration principle familiar in business cycle analysis, which applies to domestically produced inventories and imports alike.

The inventory cycle is augmented by speculation, which is encouraged by the great instability in import prices. Some evidence of the speculative character of the inventory cycle has been noted in imports of raw cotton in the Netherlands. Since the Dutch raise no cotton at home, net imports in the long run must equal consumption, but annual net imports sometimes exceed and sometimes fall short of consumption. The difference between consumption and imports in the period 1922–1938 was an inventory cycle of roughly two years' duration, which Tinbergen attributes to the speculative character of raw material markets.[6]

The inventory cycle of imports is further augmented by the time lag between the placing of orders and the receipt of goods that is inherent in the production period and shipping time from the foreign source to the importers' warehouse and display counter.[7] Rostow believes that "there was, undoubtedly, a tendency for British foreign trade to fluctuate cyclically, in what we might call an inventory cycle."[8]

The greater instability of import prices, the greater uncertainty and the longer planning period for imports than for home-produced goods create a presumption that the inventory cycle may be more pronounced for imports than for home-produced goods.

The empirical evidence on year-to-year behavior of United States imports in relation to changes in home production and consumption strongly suggests an inventory cycle. Thus, the expansion from 1928 to 1929 produced what certainly appears to be an excessive increase in imports in relation to the rise in consumption. Again and again one observes a rise in imports one year and a lag the following year that seems excessive in relation to changes in production and consumption. Thus, finished commodity output in constant prices increased 3 per cent and quantum imports 10 per cent from 1932 to 1933; but the following year, output rose 11 per cent and imports declined 1 per cent. Similarly, from 1921 to 1922 finished output rose 12 per cent and imports 29 per cent; but the following year

6. Jan Tinbergen and J. J. Polak, *The Dynamics of Business Cycles*, University of Chicago Press, Chicago, 1950, p. 96.

7. For a general theoretical treatment of time lags and inventory cycles, though not with reference to imports, see Lloyd Metzler, "The Nature and Stability of Inventory Cycles," and "Factors Governing the Length of Inventory Cycles," *Review of Economic Statistics*, August 1941 and February 1947, respectively. See also the exhaustive empirical study by Moses Abromovitz, *Inventories and Business Cycles*, National Bureau of Economic Research, New York, 1950.

8. W. W. Rostow, *British Economy of the Nineteenth Century*, Oxford University Press, New York, 1948, p. 40. "Thomas Tooke's *History of Prices* is the best source of data on the course and the mechanics of short cycles in foreign trade, his account deriving vitality and authority from a merchant's long experience. The institutional arrangements, with their time lags, credit arrangements, and dependence on expectations, are described by N. S. Buck, *Anglo-American Trade, 1800–1850;* for the system of credit advances on consignments, and the 'interlacing of credits' and speculation with foreign trade operations see especially pp. 12–14, 23, and 39; for reference to the inventory nature of the foreign trade crises of 1816 and 1831 see pp. 138–9." *Ibid.,* note 1.

output increased 14 per cent and imports only 4 per cent. The buying of imports for inventory was probably encouraged in 1922 by anticipation of higher duties under the Fordney-McCumber tariff.

Luxuries

When incomes fall in a business slump, expenditures are not reduced in the same proportion on all kinds of goods, but are reduced first on luxuries while the consumption of necessities is more nearly maintained. About 30 per cent of total imports in 1929 were luxury and semiluxury goods.[9] These imports fell about 65 per cent from 1929 to 1933, or more than half again as much as the decline in consumer expenditures of 40 per cent.

Luxury imports other than foods, which totaled $800 million in 1929, fell more than 70 per cent from 1929 to 1933—three-fourths more than the fall in consumer expenditures. Fur imports dropped 70 per cent, diamonds 80 per cent, clocks and watches 90 per cent, china and porcelain 75 per cent, photographic goods 65 per cent, jewelry 95 per cent, automobiles, parts and motorcycles 85 per cent, cotton-embroidered and lace handkerchiefs 95 per cent.

Imports of semiluxury foods, which amounted to $500 million in 1929, fell 57 per cent from 1929 to 1933. While considerably greater than the 40 per cent fall in consumer expenditures, this decline in semiluxury foods was considerably less than the decline in other luxury imports. Indeed, it was much less than the decline in total imports. Apparently consumers regard semiluxury foods as more essential than other luxury imports. Otherwise the characteristically greater instability of agricultural prices might be expected to produce a greater decline in the value of luxury foods than in nonfood luxury imports.

Most luxury foods are not produced domestically and do not compete directly with home production as do most other luxury imports. This suggests that the comparative instability of the nonfood group is due to their competitive character as well as to their luxury character. The fact that competitive imports are more unstable than noncompetitive imports of the same general category suggests that the former are, broadly speaking, marginal to domestic production. The issue raised is important because the instability of total imports has usually been explained exclusively in terms of their elasticity with respect to changes in domestic income.

9. A common-sense notion of luxuries has been used. No scientific pretensions are attached to the use of the term. Luxury imports are less important in the trade of many countries than in the United States, and world imports therefore are not subject to the same degree of instability for this reason. However, the countries which sell us luxury goods suffer from the instability in income which attends the unstable markets for these products, and their own capacity to buy imports is affected by the instability in their earnings from luxury exports to the United States. For data and discussion of individual items, see Chapter 17.

TABLE 8

PERCENTAGE CHANGES IN CONSUMPTION, PRODUCTION AND IMPORTS OF JEWELRY,
SILVERWARE, CLOCKS AND WATCHES, BUSINESS CYCLE PERIODS, 1892–1914

Cycle Period	Consumption	Production	Imports
Contraction, 1892 to 1894	−35	−30	−56
Expansion, 1894 to 1895	+19	+15	+49
Contraction, 1895 to 1896	−16	−12	−29
Expansion, 1896 to 1906	+197	+160	+410
Contraction, 1906 to 1908	−26	−16	−59
Expansion, 1908 to 1910	+45	+27	+156
Contraction, 1910 to 1914	−17	−9	−43

Source: William Howard Shaw, *Value of Commodity Output since 1869*, National
Bureau of Economic Research, New York, 1947.

The belief that the comparative instability of competitive luxury imports
is attributable to their marginal character can be tested by comparing the
cyclical behavior of a luxury import with domestic production and consumption of the same product. The best available statistics which meet this
requirement are those of the National Bureau of Economic Research for
jewelry, silverware, clocks and watches. Imports were a significant proportion of consumption, ranging from roughly 25 per cent of domestic production in prosperous years to 15 per cent in depressions.

In each of the major business cycles covered by the data, which extend
from the 1890s to the first world war, the rise and fall in imports was about
twice as great as the fluctuations in domestic consumption.[10] Moreover,
fluctuations in consumption were in each instance greater than in domestic
production. From 1906 to 1908, for example, production declined 16 per
cent, consumption 26 per cent and imports 59 per cent. (See Table 8.) This
seems to demonstrate that the instability of competitive luxury imports is
not explained solely by their luxury character.

Imports absorbed some of the shock of cyclical changes to domestic
production and employment by bearing a disproportionate share of the fall
of consumption in depression and of the rise of consumption in prosperity.
Thus, competitive imports which are marginal to home production serve as
a stabilizing influence on cyclical fluctuations in home production and
employment.[11] This, however, only transfers the instability of employment
to the exporting nation.

10. Consumption represents production adjusted for net exports.

11. This is a dubious benefit, for, clearly, the burden of domestic instability is only
shifted to our neighbors. The contrary is emphasized by Folke Hilgerdt: "Conversely,
one of the greatest—but largely overlooked—benefits of international trade in goods
(particularly manufactured goods) is that it moderates business fluctuations." "Foreign
Trade and the Short Business Cycle," *Economic Essays in Honour of Gustav Cassel*,
Allen & Unwin, London, 1933, p. 288. This statement seems to overlook the effect of
exports.

The notable instability of imports is not, as has been assumed, entirely due to the elasticity of demand with respect to changes in income. It is a striking fact that the 65 per cent decline in total luxury and semiluxury imports from 1929 to 1933 was slightly less than the decline in all other imports. The instability of noncompetitive semiluxury imports also appears to have been less than that of the competitive nonluxury imports.[12] Both facts appear as anomalies in terms of the income explanation of the instability of imports.

IMPORTS FLUCTUATE MORE WIDELY THAN DOMESTIC PRODUCTION

Major business cycle peaks were reached in 1872, 1882, 1892, 1895 and 1907, with troughs in 1875, 1885, 1894, 1897 and 1908 respectively.[13]

There was a greater cyclical variation in imports than in domestic output at both current and constant prices. Virtually every rise and fall in output was accompanied by a still greater change in imports. Although the deflation of imports is inadequate, the disparity between changes in imports and output is so great that there can be no doubt as to relative instability of imports in real terms.

Cycles in the 1870s and 1880s

The fall in total imports following the two major business cycle peaks in 1872 and 1882 was at least twice as great as in manufacturing output. Since annual data on commodity output are not available for this period, imports have been compared with manufacturing output.[14] The increase in imports relative to manufacturing output deteriorated in the three periods of business expansion.

In the expansion from 1869 to 1872, the increase in imports was 2.7 times as great as that in output. In the expansion from 1876 to 1882, the increase was 1.2 times as great, but in the expansion from 1885 to 1892, the rise in imports was only 0.8 times as great. (See Table 9.) The reduced rate of rise may have resulted from the tariff of 1883 or the faltering of production in the expansion phase of this cycle, which was interrupted by two minor recessions in 1888 and 1891 and increased less than in the previous cycle.

12. See below the comparison of competitive and noncompetitive agricultural imports, pp. 63–66.

13. See Edwin Frickey, *Economic Fluctuations in the United States*, Harvard University Press, Cambridge, 1942; *Production in the United States, 1860–1914*, Harvard University Press, Cambridge, 1947. Frickey's standard pattern is reproduced in Arthur Burns and Wesley Mitchell, *Measuring Business Cycles*, National Bureau of Economic Research, New York, 1946, p. 112.

14. To obtain figures of physical quantity, this comparison requires the deflation of imports by a price index, for which adequate data are not available. For want of anything better, import values have been deflated by wholesale prices, which may perhaps be used to indicate the order of magnitude of change.

TABLE 9

INSTABILITY OF IMPORTS AT CONSTANT WHOLESALE PRICES COMPARED WITH
MANUFACTURING ACTIVITY, BUSINESS CYCLE PERIODS, 1869–1892

| | Percentage Change | |
Cycle Period	Manufacturing	Imports
Expansion, 1869 to 1872	+24	+66
Contraction, 1872 to 1876	−10	−24
Expansion, 1876 to 1882	+75	+92
Contraction, 1882 to 1885	−4	−9
Expansion, 1885 to 1892	+68	+55[a]

Sources: Imports, Monthly Summary of Commerce and Finance, November 1911,
p. 1051; manufacturing, Edwin Frickey, Production in the United States, 1860–1914,
Harvard University Press, Cambridge, 1947, Table 6.
a. There is a divergent movement in this period between wholesale prices and Kreps'
index of import prices. His deflated index of imports increased 27 per cent from 1885 to
1892; however, his median index of the quantity of imports increased 55 per cent. T. J.
Kreps, "Import and Export Prices in the United States and the Terms of International
Trade, 1880–1914," Quarterly Journal of Economics, August 1926.

However, despite the cyclical instability and the deterioration in the expansion of imports relative to output, the growth of imports over the
twenty years 1869–1889 was greater than the growth of manufacturing.[15]

Depressions of 1894, 1896 and 1908

The most significant global measure of changes in the importance of
imports is their relationship to finished commodity output at producers'
prices. This ratio compares like and like in the sense that both imports
and output represent commodities before distribution costs have been
added. Broadly speaking, we may think of finished imports as competing
with finished output and all other imports as supplying materials for
domestic production of finished commodities. Annual data on finished
commodity output begin in 1889.

In the depressions of 1894, 1896 and 1908, the fall of imports in each
instance was at least twice as great as the fall of commodity output at
current prices. From 1892 to 1894, imports fell 20 per cent and output 10
per cent. In the second depression of the 1890s, from 1895 to 1896, imports
fell 15 per cent and output 3 per cent. In the depression of 1908, imports
fell 22 per cent in a single year while output fell 11 per cent. (See Table 10.)

The relative instability of imports is also evident in minor business cycles.
Fluctuations in imports conformed to these cycles more closely than fluctuations in total commodity output. The reference troughs of five minor
cycles are 1891, 1901, 1904, 1911 and 1914. The ratio of total imports to

15. See the use of Frickey's data to illustrate cycles in this period in Alvin H. Hansen,
Business Cycles and National Income, Norton, New York, 1951, pp. 25–29.

TABLE 10

PERCENTAGE DECLINE IN COMMODITY OUTPUT[a] AND TOTAL IMPORTS AT CURRENT
AND CONSTANT PRICES IN THE BUSINESS SLUMPS OF 1894, 1896 AND 1908

Year	Current Prices		Constant Prices	
	Output	Imports	Output	Imports[b]
1892–1894	10	20	5	12
1895–1896	3	15	0.2	11
1907–1908	11	22	12	19

Sources: Output, William Howard Shaw, *Value of Commodity Output since 1869*,
National Bureau of Economic Research, New York, 1947, Tables I-2 and I-3; imports,
Monthly Summary of Commerce and Finance, November 1911, p. 1051.
   a. Finished commodity output excluding construction materials.
   b. Imports at constant wholesale prices.

commodity output fell in 1891 and 1901, rose in 1904,[16] fell in 1911 and
rose in 1914.[17]

Instability of Imports and Finished Commodity Output

The slump of 1921 following the first world war produced a decline of
about one third in the value of commodity output and a decline in imports
about two-thirds greater. (See Table 11.) This disparity is small compared
with earlier depressions, presumably because of the unusually severe decline in domestic prices. If we must have slumps in business, and if deflation
is desirable, the slump of 1921 was an economist's dream of what a deflation should be. It was, above all, a drastic but quick scaling down of the
cost and price inflation cumulated during and immediately after the first
world war. In a single year the deflation was completed: real commodity
output[18] had declined 6 per cent while the fall in quantity of imports was
two and a half times as great. After deflation of prices, recovery was immediate and complete:[19] real output rose 12 per cent in the following year
and the increase in imports was two and a half times as great. The ratio of
imports to output at constant prices reached a peak in 1922. This unusually
high level of imports was probably due to inventory buying in anticipation
of the higher duties of the Fordney-McCumber tariff.

Imports generally increased more than output after 1921 as long as
output was rising. But the leveling off in real output in 1924 produced an
absolute decline in both the value and quantity of imports. A similar de-

16. However, imports for consumption declined in fiscal 1904.
17. The increase in 1914 may represent speculative buying of imports as a result of
the war in Europe.
18. Kuznets' constant price series has been adjusted also for changes in net exports
and thus represents "output destined for consumption." The unadjusted series has been
used in current prices in order to have comparable data beyond 1933.
19. The effect of deflation on employment and production, which depends upon
expectations and other factors, is not usually so beneficial.

TABLE 11

RATIO OF IMPORTS TO FINISHED COMMODITY OUTPUT,[a] 1919–1939

(*Index: 1919 = 100*)

	Current Prices			Constant Prices		
Year	Imports[b]	Output	Ratio of Imports to Output	Imports[b]	Output[c]	Ratio of Imports to Output
1919	100	100	100	100	100	100
1920	135	109	124	108	99	110
1921	64	74	86	92	93	99
1922	79	78	99	118	104	113
1923	97	92	105	123	118	104
1924	92	89	103	120	118	102
1925	108	98	110	130	125	104
1926	113	103	110	138	134	103
1927	107	99	108	141	132	107
1928	104	104	100	142	136	104
1929	113	110	103	163	146	112
1930	78	90	87	138	130	106
1931	53	69	77	121	116	104
1932	34	51	67	97	100	97
1933	37	53	70	107	102	105
1934	—	—	—	106	110[e]	96
1935	52	74[d]	70	130	121[e]	107
1936	—	—	—	144	138[e]	104
1937	77	92[d]	84	161	147[e]	110
1938	—	—	—	115	129[e]	89
1939	58	88[d]	66	132	145[e]	91

Sources: Simon Kuznets, *Commodity Flow and Capital Formation*, National Bureau of Economic Research, New York, 1938, Vol. I, pp. 138 and 159; *Foreign Trade of the United States, 1936–1949*, International Trade Series No. 7, U.S. Department of Commerce, 1951.

a. Excluding construction materials.

b. General imports through 1933, imports for consumption thereafter. The import series on the right is a quantity index rather than imports at constant prices.

c. Same output series (in constant prices) with Kuznets' adjustments for net exports (i.e., "output destined for consumption").

d. Unofficial data from Department of Commerce tied to Kuznets' series.

e. William Howard Shaw, *Value of Commodity Output since 1869*, National Bureau of Economic Research, New York, 1947. Shaw's output series tied to Kuznets' series in 1929. If the two series are tied together in 1932, the result is a slightly higher level in the years 1933–1939.

cline in domestic output in 1927 was accompanied by a sufficient decline in import prices to produce a decline in the ratio of imports to output at current prices, but the ratio of imports to output by quantity increased slightly. The rapid rise of 8 per cent in output in the single year 1928 to 1929 produced a striking acceleration in imports, which increased almost twice as much. A large part of the sharp relative increase in imports in 1929 is probably explained by changes in inventories.

Each year of the great depression following 1929 witnessed a greater decline in imports than in output, at both current and constant prices. In 1931 the decline in imports by quantity was about the same as the decline in output—12 per cent compared with 11 per cent. This anomalous behavior followed immediately the higher duties of the Hawley-Smoot tariff, effective June 1930. This suggests that the effect of raising the tariff was to force import prices down; they fell 60 per cent more than domestic commodity prices[20] from 1930 to 1931. Thus, at current values imports fell a half more than output in the single year 1931, but at constant prices the decline was about the same.

The collapse of imports from 1929 to 1932 has been greatly overemphasized because of the failure to recognize that imports characteristically fall more than domestic production. The 70 per cent fall in import values is spectacular, but viewed as a decline only one-third greater than the fall in domestic production, the relative decline of imports in the great depression appears moderate. Every cycle of record shows a greater relative decline than this. In the depression of 1894, the fall in import values was twice as great as in domestic production. In the depression of 1896, the fall in imports was four to five times as great, in 1908 twice as great and in 1938–1939 five times as great as in home output. (Of course, the relative decline of imports cannot be so great when the fall of domestic production is large.)

The decline in imports by quantity from 1929 to 1932 was only one-fourth greater than the decline in domestic production, compared with a decline two and a half times as great as that in production in 1921 and two and a half times as great from 1937 to 1938.

In 1932 quantum imports reached only about the same proportion of commodity output as in 1919 and 1921.

The slight recovery in 1933 which brought an increase of 3 per cent in real commodity output[21] produced a rise in imports three times as great. A large part of this relative rise in imports probably represents inventories that were worked off in 1934.

While imports at current prices failed to regain the 1929 ratio to commodity output, the quantity of imports in 1937 virtually reached the 1929 level.[22]

The much-discussed collapse of foreign trade in the early 1930s was no more than normal cyclical displacement from the drastic collapse of domestic production, plus the severe deflation of import prices (unit

20. Kuznets' finished output series, *Commodity Flow and Capital Formation*, National Bureau of Economic Research, New York, 1938.

21. Gross national product continued to decline in 1933.

22. The ratio of quantum imports to gross national product in 1937 recovered almost to the 1929 level. Since the distribution and service component of gross national product is relatively stable over the cycle, the decline of imports in relation to GNP in the early 1930s was greater than in relation to commodity output and the recovery slightly less.

values), which fell 60 per cent more than domestic producers' prices between 1929 and 1932. Once the price factor is eliminated, there appears to have been no decisive change in the trend of total imports relative to commodity output from 1913 to 1937 although there were great changes in their composition.

The surprisingly high level of real imports during the great depression has been generally overlooked because of the relative deflation of import prices. Incomplete economic recovery would be expected to result in a lower level of imports relative to output. But in the later 1930s there were special conditions: imports of grain and foodstuffs were exceptionally high owing to the drought of 1934–1936. The repeal of prohibition provided an extra fillip, though its importance to imports is usually exaggerated. Increases of domestic prices under the New Deal were a stimulant to imports.

The more serious displacement of imports took place in 1938, when the ratio of quantity of imports to output declined by one fifth to reach the lowest level since the Civil War. Moreover, imports in 1939 failed to recover substantially as did output. (See Figure 2.) Data on commodity output are not available for later years. Insofar as can be judged by comparison with gross national product, the ratio of imports to output has never recovered the level of 1899–1937.

As will be shown later, imports of all *finished* commodities in 1937 had failed to recover as fully as all other imports; and it seems likely that the virtually complete recovery of total imports in 1937 was due to special conditions. There is some justification, therefore, in regarding the incomplete recovery of the 1930s as having resulted in a displacement in imports relative to output.

It is notable that the permanent displacement of imports in both 1898 and 1938 followed a second depression within each decade from a submerged cyclical peak.

In the fourteen business cycles—both major and minor—during the half century from 1889 to 1939, total imports increased faster than commodity output in prosperity and fell faster than output in depression with but few exceptions.

The single important divergence in the relative rise and fall in imports from the reference cycles as measured by the National Bureau was in 1897–1898.[23] In view of the multiplicity of forces that affect foreign trade, the correspondence between reference cycles and the relative rise and fall in imports seems surprisingly good.[24]

23. This may be explained by the Dingley tariff, which became effective July 24, 1897. The role of tariffs will be considered in the next chapter.
24. Wesley C. Mitchell measured the "conformity" of fluctuations in total imports, by value, over sixteen business cycles from 1867 to 1938. *What Happens During Business Cycles*, National Bureau of Economic Research, New York, 1951, Table 31, p. 256. For his explanation of indices of conformity, see *ibid.*, p. 15.

Competitive Imports More Unstable Than Noncompetitive Imports

There was a relatively greater decline in competitive than in noncompetitive imports from 1929 to 1933; it appears to be illustrated in almost every commodity group.

All mineral imports fell from 9.2 per cent of domestic mineral production in 1929 to 5.2 per cent in 1933. Petroleum imports, which are competitive, fell from 4.4 per cent to 1.5 per cent of domestic output. All nonmetallic minerals, however, some of which are not competitive, fell from 5.6 per cent to 3.3 per cent of domestic output. (See Table 48.) While all metal imports remained unchanged at about 21 per cent of domestic production in both 1929 and 1933, imports of noncompetitive nickle, tin and manganese ore fell 25 per cent, 50 per cent and 55 per cent respectively, while competitive zinc ore, lead, aluminum and copper fell 90 per cent, 70 per cent, 70 per cent and 75 per cent respectively.

Domestic shoe production fell 7 per cent from 1929 to 1933. But hide imports fell two thirds in value, and cattle hides, which are produced in relatively greater quantities at home than sheep and goat skins, fell three fourths in value. By quantity, imports of cattle hides fell about one half, while the less competitive sheep and lamb and goat and kid skins fell only one fifth.

Vegetable products are produced at home and supplies are easily expanded. Imports of vegetables and preparations fell 70 per cent, while noncompetitive fruits, although in the luxury category, fell only 50 per cent.

In the inedible vegetable commodity classification, imports of naval stores, which are competitive with home production, fell 80 per cent, while largely noncompetitive drug imports fell only 50 per cent.

In the textile group, imports of cotton and woolen manufactures, which are competitive, fell 55 and 85 per cent respectively by value, while imports of flax and ramie, which are less competitive, fell about 50 per cent. By quantity, imports of cotton cloth declined about one third and woolen and worsteds more than one half, while imports of linen fabric did not decline. Imports of silk manufactures, which are competitive, fell by quantity more than one half. Silk is significant as a case where the raw material import was more stable than the manufactured product, presumably because of the fact that the raw material was complementary to[25] and the manufactured product competitive with home production.

Noncompetitive imports of cork and cork bark increased slightly in quantity and cork waste declined less than one half. But competitive hardwood logs fell nine tenths and saw mill products three fourths.[26]

25. Before nylon was introduced.

26. The comparisons above were selected from the commodity group classification and are rather general. A more definitive examination of competitive and complementary imports is provided by agricultural imports. See p. 65.

TABLE 12

GROSS AGRICULTURAL INCOME AND AGRICULTURAL IMPORTS, 1869–1914

Crop or Fiscal Year[a]	Gross Agricultural Income	Agricultural Imports	Imports as Per Cent of Income
	(*Millions*)		
1869	$2,554	$188	7.4
1870	2,514	195	7.8
1871	2,309	227	9.8
1872	2,373	279	11.8
1873	2,408	285	11.8
1874	2,471	274	11.1
1875	2,550	266	10.4
1876	2,391	239	10.0
1877	2,440	255	10.5
1878	2,109	241	11.4
1879	2,405	240	10.0
1880	2,959	324	10.9
1881	2,995	309	10.3
1882	3,358	345	10.3
1883	3,044	341	11.2
1884	3,011	333	11.1
1885	2,717	286	10.5
1886	2,679	318	11.9
1887	2,817	339	12.0
1888	3,071	355	11.6
1889	2,862	378	13.2
1890	3,054	399	13.1
1891	3,339	438	13.1
1892	3,043	457	15.0
1893	3,138	444	14.1
1894	2,768	380	13.7
1895	2,810	392	14.0
1896	2,780	408	14.7
1897	3,218	419	13.0
1898	3,285	340	10.4
1899	3,432	388	11.3
1900	3,867	453	11.7
1901	4,126	422	10.2
1902	4,371	441	10.1
1903	4,445	489	11.0
1904	4,582	504	11.0
1905	4,792	606	12.6
1906	5,106	602	11.8
1907	5,284	690	13.1
1908	5,551	579	10.4
1909	6,175	703	11.4
1910	6,546	794	12.1
1911	6,149	767	12.5
1912	6,590	882	13.4
1913	6,815	909	13.3
1914	6,875	993	14.4

(*Notes opposite*)

56

AGRICULTURAL IMPORTS

Since agriculture all over the world has tended to maintain production in depression despite drastic deflation of crop prices, the behavior of agricultural imports in depression and prosperity is of special interest. In agriculture, too, competitive production and flexible prices have approximated the conditions postulated by classical economics.

Between the Civil War and the first world war, agricultural imports can be compared with gross farm income.[27] The pattern of fluctuations in agricultural imports conforms tolerably well to these major reference cycles when allowance is made for the recording of imports by fiscal years. In four of the five minor cycles from 1889 to 1919, agricultural imports either declined or leveled off with the decline in (fiscal year) minor reference cycles of the National Bureau of Economic Research.[28]

Fluctuations in domestic gross agricultural income followed the business cycle pattern less closely than did imports. The peak and trough in income occurred three years later than in industrial production in the depression of the 1870s, and the agricultural income data show no decline in the depressions of 1897 and 1908.

Agricultural imports rose from about 7 per cent of agricultural income in 1869 to 12 per cent in the business cycle peak of 1872, then fell to 10 per cent in the depression of 1875.

In the next cycle imports increased to 11 per cent of farm income in 1883 and declined to 10.5 per cent in 1885.

Imports expanded more vigorously, to 15 per cent of farm income in the peak of 1892 and declined to 14 per cent in 1894. During the prosperity of domestic agriculture in the "golden era of agriculture" beginning about 1895, imports reached a peak of 15 per cent of farm income in 1896 but again fell to 10 per cent in 1898. Imports again rose to 13 per cent of farm income in 1907 and fell to 10 per cent the following year. (See Table 12.)

27. Frederick Strauss and Louis H. Bean, *Gross Farm Income and Indices of Farm Production and Prices in the United States, 1869–1937*, U.S. Department of Agriculture, Technical Bulletin No. 703, December 1940.

28. The reference troughs of the five minor recessions were 1891, 1901, 1904, 1911 and 1915; agricultural imports rose in 1890 and 1891, declined in 1901, leveled off in 1904, declined in 1911 and leveled off in 1915.

Notes to Table 12

Sources: Income, F. Strauss and L. H. Bean, *Gross Farm Income and Indices of Farm Production and Prices in the United States 1869–1937*, U.S. Department of Agriculture, Technical Bulletin No. 703, December 1940; imports, 1869–1908, U.S. Department of Commerce from census data, 1909–1910 from Bureau of Agricultural Economics, thereafter from *Agricultural Statistics, 1940*.

a. Income by crop years, imports by fiscal years.

The fluctuations in agricultural imports were consistently somewhat greater than in domestic farm income both in the "hard times" of the nineteenth century and the "golden era" of the twentieth century.

Wool

The instability of imports relative to domestic mill consumption was most striking in the case of wool. However, the cycles in the case of wool do not follow closely the standard reference business cycles, particularly before 1890. In the nine cycles from 1866 to 1911, wool imports invariably rose or fell far more than domestic mill consumption. Since the first world war, imports have fluctuated even more violently.

The 15 per cent decline in mill consumption[29] from 1866 to 1868 produced a decline in imports four times as great. The rapid expansion of 44 per cent in consumption to a cyclical peak in 1872 produced a rise in imports ten times as great, so that imports rose to 45 per cent of consumption in 1872.

In the depression following the peak in 1872, a decline of one quarter in mill consumption produced a fall in imports almost three times as great. The first year of general recovery from the trough in 1874 produced a more rapid increase in imports than in consumption; but the leveling off of consumption in the next four years produced an absolute decline in imports. (See Table 13 and Figure 9.)

Here we see a significant and characteristic acceleration effect: the decline in the rate of growth of consumption, which increased only 10 per cent in four years from 1875 to 1879, was sufficient to produce an absolute decline of 29 per cent in wool imports so that imports fell one third in relative importance, from 22 per cent of consumption in 1875 to 14 per cent in 1879. The total effect of the severe depression in the 1870s was to reduce imports from 45 per cent of consumption in 1872 to 14 per cent in 1879.

The rapid rise of consumption in 1880 produced a magnified increase in imports to 35 per cent of consumption and a corresponding accelerated decline the following year. When consumption rose from a trough in 1881 to a peak in 1886, imports rose from 17 per cent to 29 per cent of consumption. In the following years, slight changes in consumption always produced magnified changes in imports.

It is possible that the increase in duty in 1890 and the shift of wool to the free trade list in 1894 contributed to the instability of imports by causing the mills and importers to postpone purchases in 1894 until wool could be

29. The data on raw wool consumed adjusted by Frickey for changes in stocks show exactly the same pattern except for the period 1894 to 1900. See *Production in the United States, 1860–1914.*

TABLE 13

COMPARATIVE INSTABILITY OF WOOL IMPORTS IN RELATION TO DOMESTIC MILL
CONSUMPTION, 1866–1946

Fiscal Year	Cycle	Mill Consumption[a]	Net Imports[a]	Mill Consumption[b]	Net Imports[b]	Imports as Per Cent of Consumption
		(Millions of Pounds)		(Percentage Change)		
1866	Peak	224	70			31
1868	Trough	190	23	−15	−67	12
1872	Peak	274	124	+44	+439	45
1874	Trough	206	36	−25	−71	18
1880	Peak	357	124	+73	+244	35
1881	Trough	290	50	−19	−60	17
1886	Peak	424	123	+46	+146	29
1890	Trough	378	102	−12	−17	27
1893	Peak	471	168	+25	+65	36
1894	Trough	347	49	−26	−71	14
1897	Peak	601	347	+73	+608	58
1899	Trough	335	64	−44	−82	19
1900	Peak	437	150	+30	+134	34
1901	Trough	402	100	−8	−33	25
1905	Peak	542	247	+35	+147	46
1908	Trough	431	120	−20	−51	28
1909	Peak	591	263	+37	+119	45
1911	Trough	448	129	−24	−51	29
1923[c]	Peak	603	274	+35	+112	45
1932	Trough	440	21	−27	−92	5
1937	Peak	580	158	+32	+652	27
1938	Trough	514	39	−11	−75	8
1946	Peak	1099	842	+114	+2059	77

Sources: Statistical Abstract of the United States, 1909, 1913; U.S. Department of Agriculture, Wool Statistics, 1949.

a. Total U.S. consumption and net imports of all types of wool, greasy shorn basis, 1866–1911; U.S. mill consumption of apparel wool, greasy shorn basis, 1923–1946.

b. Percentage change from previous peak or trough.

c. Calendar years beginning 1923.

imported duty-free. However, there was a depression in 1894 and the relative decline in imports seems only slightly greater than in similar cyclical declines. The reimposition of a duty on wool in 1897 was accompanied by a sharp decline in imports, which, however, soon regained former levels.

The acceleration effect of small changes in consumption is striking. Thus, the rise in consumption in 1902 produced a greater increase in imports, which rose from 25 per cent of consumption in 1901 to 34 per cent in 1902.

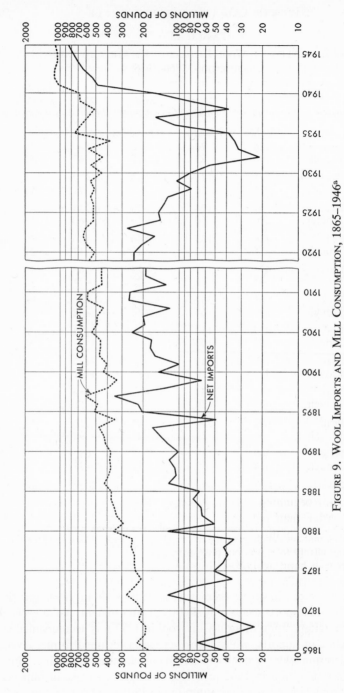

FIGURE 9. WOOL IMPORTS AND MILL CONSUMPTION, 1865–1946[a]

Sources: Statistical Abstract of the United States, 1909, 1913; U.S. Department of Agriculture, Wool Statistics, 1949.

a. Apparel wool after 1919.

A further rise in 1905 increased imports to 46 per cent of consumption. But with the 10 per cent decline in 1906, imports fell to 40 per cent of consumption, and, with the sharper fall in 1908, imports were reduced to 28 per cent of consumption.

While it seems likely that the import lows in 1894 and 1899 and the high in 1897 reflect, in part, speculative timing of imports because of the shift of wool to the free trade list in 1894 and back again to the dutiable list in 1897, it is clear that the sharp short-term changes in the relative importance of imports are connected almost invariably with changes in mill consumption, which produced a magnified change in imports. The numerous changes in duty from the Civil War to the first world war failed to reduce the secular trend in the proportion of raw wool imports to domestic mill consumption. (See Figure 9.)

Following the first world war, imports in 1923 reached a peak equal to 45 per cent of consumption, proportionately as large as in the earlier peaks of 1872 and 1909. From the early 1920s consumption declined gradually while imports declined faster until the collapse following 1929, when imports reached a low in 1932 equal to 5 per cent of mill consumption. Recovery brought an increase in the relative importance of imports, but only to 27 per cent of consumption at the peak in 1937. In the slump of 1938, the fall in imports was almost seven times as great as in consumption, despite the fact that their relative importance at the peak in 1937 was only a little more than half as great as at earlier peaks.

In recent years imports have accounted for a larger proportion of consumption than ever before.[30]

Sugar

The percentage of domestic sugar consumption supplied by imports has declined slightly with each cyclical fall in consumption[31] since the Civil War; after the beginning of the twentieth century, imports increased and decreased faster than consumption in each major and minor business cycle.[32] The degree of instability is less pronounced than in the case of wool. American sugar prices appear to be more stable than wool prices. Since Cuba is close at hand, transport costs are less important for sugar imports than for wool, which must be carried from Australia, New Zealand and Argentina.

30. See Chapter 4 on the tariff, for an explanation of how imports have displaced about half of this highly protected home industry.

31. "Retained for consumption," that is, continental production plus territorial shipments plus foreign imports minus exports. Imports exclude shipments from the territories of Puerto Rico, Hawaii and the Philippines.

32. Including those where, as in the depression of 1921, sugar consumption actually increased.

TABLE 14

COMPARATIVE INSTABILITY OF SUGAR IMPORTS IN RELATION TO DOMESTIC
CONSUMPTION, BUSINESS CYCLE PERIODS, 1874–1938

Fiscal Year	Cycle[a]	U.S. Consumption[b]	Imports from Foreign Countries	Imports as Per Cent of Consumption
		(Millions of Pounds)		
1874	Peak	1,782	1,512	83
1878	Trough	1,646	1,292	76
1884	Peak	2,975	2,198	71
1886	Trough	2,818	2,113	69
1894	Peak	4,936	3,819	76
1895	Trough	4,322	3,175	73
1897	Peak	5,598	4,329	77
1898	Trough	3,469	2,062	59
1901	Peak	5,585	3,970	71
1902	Trough	5,019	3,020	60
1903	Peak	6,380	4,197	66
1904	Trough	5,662	3,639	64
1907	Peak	7,090	4,367	61
1908	Trough	6,591	3,334	50
1920	Peak	9,735	7,550	63
1921	Trough	10,546	6,673	56
Yearly Average, or Year Beginning July 1				
1923	Peak	11,291	6,874	58
1924	Trough	13,073	7,863	56
1926	Peak	13,031	7,938	59
1927	Trough	13,128	6,832	50
1928	Peak	14,381	8,231	55
1933	Trough	13,028	2,713	20
1937	Peak	12,390	3,485	27
1938	Trough	13,309	3,333	24

Source: Statistical Abstract of the United States, 1909, 1923, 1939.

a. Approximate business cycle peak and trough (fiscal years 1874–1921), which was peak for imports though not always for apparent sugar consumption.

b. "Retained for consumption," that is, continental production plus territorial shipments plus imports from foreign countries minus exports.

The fact that the instability of sugar imports relative to consumption is moderate and characterizes minor and major cycles alike suggests that these fluctuations may be partly explained by inventory speculation. The decline of imports in 1898 must be interpreted against the background of the Dingley tariff of 1897 and the Spanish-American War in 1898. Similarly the fall of imports in 1933 reflects both the decline in consumption and the

Hawley-Smoot tariff of 1930. Sugar imports maintained roughly the same importance in the cyclical fluctuations from 1923 to 1928 as in 1907–1908 despite the increase in duty in the Fordney-McCumber tariff of 1922, which was greater than the increase in either the Dingley or the Hawley-Smoot tariffs. (See Table 14.)

Hides

Hides, like wool, illustrate strikingly the magnified effect of changes in consumption on changes in imports. Shoe production, which consumes most hides, fell only one eighth from 1929 to 1932. Consumption[33] of cattle hides declined about one fifth, but the relative fall in imports was four times as great. Expansion of shoe production to a new high in 1937 brought a 50 per cent increase in consumption of cattle hides and a relative increase in imports four times as great. Similarly, the relative decline in imports in the slump of 1938 was five times as great as the decline in the consumption of hides. The greater recovery of imports the following year restored the 1937 relationship to consumption.

Goat and sheep skins follow the same pattern as cattle hides, but though imports fluctuate more widely than consumption of domestic skins, the relative instability is less pronounced than in cattle hides.

Hides, like wool, exemplify the marginal character of competitive imports with respect to both business cycles and secular growth. While domestic cattle hides established a new high in 1937, imports recovered to only half of the 1929 level. But the relative instability of imports continued. Imports fell from 12 per cent of consumption in 1937 to 7 per cent in 1938 and then rose to 15 per cent in 1939. (See Table 15.)

In the years after the second world war, hide imports amounted to only 4 per cent of consumption. The inflationary development in 1950 produced an increase in imports of cattle hides to 14 per cent of consumption.

Competitive and Noncompetitive Agricultural Imports

Beginning with the 1920s the quantity of total agricultural imports, which account for roughly half of the total, can be compared with domestic farm production and the value of imports with cash receipts from marketings. Moreover, the careful classification of agricultural imports into competitive and noncompetitive groups since 1924 shows that the imports which compete directly with home production fluctuate more widely than those which are not produced at home.

The fall in quantum agricultural imports in the depression of 1921 was almost twice as great as the 10 per cent decline in home production. The

33. These data of the National Tanners' Council represent leather production, that is, consumption of hides.

TABLE 15

INSTABILITY OF HIDE IMPORTS IN RELATION TO DOMESTIC CONSUMPTION, 1929–1939

(Millions of Hides and Skins)

Year	Cattle Hides			Goat and Kid Skins			Sheep and Lamb Skins		
	Consumption	Imports	Imports as Per Cent of Consumption	Consumption	Imports	Imports as Per Cent of Consumption	Consumption	Imports	Imports as Per Cent of Consumption
1929	19	6	29	56	60	108	39	26	66
1932	15	1	8	37	35	93	29	15	52
1937	22	3	12	47	52	111	34	23	66
1938	19	1	7	32	30	94	29	15	50
1939	22	3	15	40	39	97	39	29	73

Sources: Imports, *Foreign Commerce and Navigation;* consumption, *Survey of Current Business,* compiled by Tanners' Council of America.

Note: Percentages calculated before rounding figures in millions.

TABLE 16

PERCENTAGE CHANGES IN COMPETITIVE AND NONCOMPETITIVE QUANTUM AGRICULTURAL IMPORTS AND AGRICULTURAL PRODUCTION IN BUSINESS CYCLE MOVEMENTS, 1920–1939

| | | Agricultural Imports | | |
Cycle Period	Agricultural Production	Total	Competitive[a] (Supplementary)	Non-competitive[a] (Complementary)
Slump, 1920 to 1921	−10	−18	b	b
Recovery, 1921 to 1929	+19	+84	b	b
Depression, 1929 to 1932	−3	−29	−48	−16
Recovery, 1932 to 1937	+10	+38	+93	+12
Slump, 1937 to 1939	−3	−23	−37	−12
Recovery, 1938 to 1939	+3	+11	+15	+10

Sources: Quantum imports by calendar years, courtesy of the Office of Foreign Agricultural Relations, U.S. Department of Agriculture; production, *Historical Statistics of the United States, 1789–1945* and *Statistical Abstract of the United States*.

a. These are official series which the U.S. Department of Agriculture calls "supplementary" because the imports compete directly with home production and "complementary" because the products are not produced at home. For further detail see Chapter 13.

b. Quantum data not available.

increase in imports during the following year was three times as great as the 10 per cent rise in production. In the longer expansion from 1921 to 1929 the rise in imports was 4.4 times as great as the rise in production.

While cash marketings of farmers fell from $11.3 billion in 1929 to $4.7 billion in 1932, physical production declined only 3 per cent. Competitive agricultural imports, however, fell almost one half by quantity. Despite the great importance of semiluxury products in noncompetitive agricultural imports (which probably accounts for their instability), this group fell only about one sixth.

The relative instability of competitive imports is likewise shown in the expansion from 1932 to 1937. Agricultural production increased 10 per cent while competitive agricultural imports increased 93 per cent and noncompetitive imports only 12 per cent. The rise of competitive agricultural imports was accentuated by drought conditions in the mid-1930s.

In the slump of 1938, agricultural production declined only 3 per cent, while competitive imports fell 37 per cent and noncompetitive imports 12 per cent. In the limited recovery from 1938 to 1939, agricultural production increased 3 per cent while competitive imports increased 15 per cent and noncompetitive 10 per cent. (See Table 16.)

The instability of agricultural imports relative to home production is even greater at current values. Thus the value of agricultural imports fell two thirds in the depression of 1921, while domestic marketings fell one third. The relative instability of imports appears even in the minor cycles: agricultural import values declined in both 1924 and 1927 although the value of domestic marketings increased. Despite the dramatic fall in cash marketings from 1929 to 1932, agricultural imports fell from 20 per cent of domestic marketings in 1929 to 14 per cent in 1932.

In the slump of 1938, domestic marketings fell one eighth in value while competitive imports fell almost one half and noncompetitive imports one third.

IMPORTS OF FINISHED COMMODITIES

The comparison of imports of finished commodities with finished output is of particular interest since, broadly speaking, finished imports are competitive with home production. Annual data begin in 1889.

Depressions of 1894, 1896 and 1908

The depression from 1892 to 1894, which was accompanied by a decline of 10 per cent in finished output, produced a decline in finished imports three times as great.[34] Output of producers' durables fell 25 per cent while imports of producers' durables fell 60 per cent. Output of consumers' durables fell 24 per cent while imports of durables fell 37 per cent; production of semidurables fell 21 per cent and imports 38 per cent. Output of perishable commodities increased slightly in this depression while perishable imports declined 15 per cent. (See Table 17.)

Although not every individual item exhibits the relative instability characteristic of imports as a whole, the more important products do. The decline which reduced output of industrial machinery 18 per cent produced a 60 per cent decline in imports of the same goods. A 5 per cent decline in output of toys, games, etc., resulted in a 37 per cent decline in similar imports. Output of dry goods and notions fell about 25 per cent while dry goods imports fell 42 per cent.

Recovery from the depression of 1894 was interrupted before output regained the previous peak of 1892, a development which would be expected to have a severe effect on imports. Finished output fell 3 per cent from 1895 to 1896 while finished imports fell 12 per cent. Output of industrial machinery declined 10 per cent and machinery imports fell almost 40 per cent.

In 1898 output increased, but imports fell absolutely, and there has been no subsequent recovery in the ratio of imports to output.

34. Shaw's series, *Value of Commodity Output since 1869*, National Bureau of Economic Research, New York, 1947. These imports of finished goods include duties, as do the data in Table 8.

TABLE 17

PERCENTAGE CHANGES IN FINISHED COMMODITY OUTPUT AND FINISHED IMPORTS
IN BUSINESS SLUMPS OF 1894 AND 1896

	1892 to 1894		1895 to 1896	
	Output	Imports	Output	Imports
Total, finished commodities[a]	−11	−30	−3	−12
Perishables	+1	−15	−5	−6
Semidurables	−21	−38	−3	−5
Consumers' durables	−24	−37	−2	−14
Producers' durables	−25	−60	+6	+8

Source: William Howard Shaw, Value of Commodity Output since 1869, National Bureau of Economic Research, New York, 1947, Table I-1.
a. Excluding construction materials.

The depression of 1908 brought in one year an 11 per cent decline in domestic output of finished goods and a 20 per cent decline in imports of finished goods.

The decline in imports of clothing and personal furnishings was almost one-fourth greater than the decline in home production. Dry goods and notions, toys and sporting goods also showed the characteristically greater decline in imports than in home production. In the case of house furnishings, however, the decline in imports and in home production was of the same order of magnitude. In sum, domestic output of semidurables fell 10 per cent while finished imports fell about 30 per cent.

Furniture imports also declined more than domestic output. But imports of books and other printed matter moved parallel with domestic production, while domestic production of musical instruments and floor covering declined more than imports. In sum, home production of consumers' durables fell about 15 per cent while finished imports of consumers' durables fell about 30 per cent.

The ratio of finished imports to output declined in each minor cycle from 1889 to 1919 except in 1901 when the ratio leveled off after a decline the preceding year.

Cyclical Fluctuations, 1929–1939

In the severe depression from 1929 to 1933, finished commodity output fell by almost one half at current values while imports fell by almost two thirds.[35] The fall in imports was greater than in output for each major class.

In the expansion from 1933 to 1937, the rise in finished imports was about one-half greater than the 73 per cent rise in output. Imports of perishables, semidurables and consumers' durables each rose faster than

35. Data are not available on all finished imports for the early 1920s.

TABLE 18

PERCENTAGE CHANGES IN FINISHED COMMODITY OUTPUT AND FINISHED IMPORTS,
BY VALUE, 1929–1933, 1933–1937 AND 1937–1939

	Contraction, 1929–1933		Expansion, 1933–1937		Contraction, 1937–1939	
	Pro- duction	Imports	Pro- duction	Imports	Pro- duction	Imports
Total, finished commodity output	−49	−65	+73	+106	−4	−21
Consumers' perishables	−40	−52	+57	+122	−5	−17
Consumers' semidurables	−48	−67	+42	+51	+4	−35
Consumers' durables	−54	−76	+94	+116	−7	−20
Producers' durables	−73	−79	+233	+127	−10	−36

Source: U.S. Department of Commerce, unpublished data.

output of the same class. Production of producers' durables, however, increased more than imports. (See Table 18.)

Although output in 1937 had recovered the 1929 level, resources remained unemployed. At the 1937 peak, the ratio of finished imports to output had failed to recover the 1929 level. The hypothesis advanced with respect to the effect of unemployment on the relative deflation of import-competing industries would lead us to expect this result. We cannot be sure, however, that the empirical results do not reflect the effect of changes in the tariff and normal growth.

From the submerged peak of 1937, the decline in finished imports to 1939 was five times greater than the 4 per cent decline in output. Moreover, each major class of imports fell more than output. (See Table 18.)

SPECIALIZATION AND MARGINAL IMPORTS

Probably half or more of American imports cannot practicably be produced at home and are not directly competitive with domestic production. We do not have the climate to produce coffee or the natural resources to produce tin. The instability of this group of imports depends entirely on changes in demand.

It is clear that noncompetitive agricultural imports fluctuate more widely than domestic production. This may be due to the fact that these imports are semiluxury in character compared with domestic agricultural production.

The chief marginal imports compete directly with home production and, consequently, suffer not only from instability in demand but also from the advantage that domestic producers derive from the deflationary effects of unemployment in the domestic economy. Where domestic production can be substituted for imports and vice versa, most American imports are in a sense marginal, and the expansion and contraction of consumption in prosperity and depression will produce a disproportionate change in imports. Home production is supplemented by imports in prosperity; imports will suffer first in depression.[36]

Short-term changes in demand produce magnified changes in competitive imports. In the early stages of a depression originating in the home market domestic producers may derive a competitive advantage from the relative deflation of prices and costs, but, as the deflation spreads from the home market to the rest of the world, this initial advantage is reduced, with the result that the "acceleration effect" on imports is moderated. Thus we might expect the decline in imports relative to home production to be greater in the early stages of a domestic slump than in the later stages of a long world-wide depression. On the other hand, the "acceleration effect" may be due in part at least to changes in inventories.

But quite apart from the relative deflation at home and abroad, domestic producers will always have an advantage over foreign competitors to the extent that transportation and selling costs favor local sources of supply. Distance is a real barrier to trade. In a depression, when goods sell below the cost of production, transportation and selling costs, which are comparatively rigid, become more important in determining the source of supply. The decline in specialization is a familiar depression experience. The disintegration of trade in a business slump may be caused first by the differences in deflation in the various national markets and second by the substitution of local supplies for more distant sources of supply.

On the other hand, railroad rates are more rigid than ocean freight rates and for some products deflation may favor foreign over domestic trade. It

36. Haberler's emphasis seems to be that there is no reason to expect any systematic relationship, such as is described in this chapter, between cyclical changes in imports and home production though at one point he does indicate that imports may rise faster than home production, a development which he explains in terms of the classical mechanism.

"It must not be assumed that the proportion of expenditure in any country which finds its way abroad in payment of imports will remain the same in all phases of a cyclical movement. As a local expansion or contraction develops, there will be changes in the distribution of income and expenditure which may involve a greater or smaller proportion of purchases from abroad; but there is no reason to expect any systematic movement . . .

"We can say, however, that the further a local expansion goes the more it is likely to 'spill over' into other regions—and that for a different, a third, reason. Imports will increase, not merely *pari passu* with incomes, but faster. As the expansion goes on, stocks are taken up, unemployed workers reabsorbed, and plant is used to fuller capacity. Hence wages and other prices will rise and, by the operation of the mechanism described in the classical expositions of international trade theory, both home and foreign demand will be switched away from local products to foreign substitutes." Of course, Haberler was concerned with foreign trade in general rather than the particular character of the American market. Gottfried Haberler, *Prosperity and Depression*, United Nations, New York, 1946, p. 411.

is not an invariable rule in every industry that imports fall more than domestic production.

Specific duties impose a rigid cost factor and require more drastic deflation of f.o.b. prices of foreign goods than of competing domestic goods if foreign exporters are to maintain their share of the domestic market in depression.

Will a depression that begins abroad produce a corresponding expansion in American imports relative to home production, owing to the relative deflation in the depressed country? In this situation the tariff may have played a significant role—at least, in the past.

Until recent years, the American tariff structure included a mass of surplus duties which were ineffective because, under normal business conditions, these home industries did not need tariff protection.[37] The advantage of relative deflation accompanying a business slump originating in his own country would enable the foreign producer to sell more in the American market. But duties which were ineffective under prosperous conditions may become effective when foreign costs are deflated relative to domestic costs. The effects of relative deflation at home and abroad are not symmetrical where the tariff structure is filled with obsolete and normally ineffective duties which become effective with a greater fall of f.o.b. import prices than of domestic prices.

Cyclical Expansion

Just as a decline in consumption will produce a greater decline in imports, the expansion of consumption will tend to produce a greater expansion in imports. But the cards appear to be stacked against imports, for the effect of expansion and contraction is not entirely symmetrical. While the slightest recession will immediately produce a displacement of imports, recovery of the previous peak after a long depression may fail to restore the relative importance of imports.

The effect on imports of domestic expansion depends on the margin of underemployed resources as well as on the income effect. Normal growth is required merely to maintain the relative importance of imports; recovery to a submerged peak below the long-term growth line would be expected to leave underemployed resources in the import-competing industries and to result in relative displacement of competitive imports. Once domestic production has been substituted for imports, the resources become more difficult to dislodge. High levels of employment must be sustained to equalize costs between competing home industries and in order to permit the full operation of the principle of comparative costs.

37. The Trade Agreements Program has cut out much of the surplus protection. See Chapters 5 and 6.

Wages are not equally flexible for all types of employment and in all areas. Among the major economic groups, farm wages probably fall most during depression. In general it is the wages of the marginal workers that are most volatile. The degree of unionization varies widely among industries and geographic areas. Whereas union wage scales hold in the metropolitan centers, smaller employers in suburban areas are able to hire workers for less. Although it may not appear in the statistics, the wage and income structure is knocked out of shape by a depression.

This phenomenon is particularly important in the United States, with its great geographical distances and sharply differentiated rates of industrial growth. The normal increase in labor supply, for example, is twice as high in the South as in the industrial Northeast.[38] As a consequence, the pressure to deflate wages in a depression is greater in some areas than in others. Local producers in the areas where wages are "out of line" on the low side will be able to compete with imports more effectively than under a more rational wage structure which would entail competitive and, therefore, higher wage costs in the relatively stagnant industries.

In a progressive economy, labor must be continually shifted from the relatively stagnant to the more dynamic industries. Unless the growing industries expand each year, labor will be unemployed or underemployed in agriculture and the relatively stagnant industries. As will be shown in later chapters the incidence of competitive imports is concentrated in the relatively stagnant home industries. There is little occasion to expand imports which compete with home industries that suffer from an excess of labor and are capable of producing surpluses. Thus, continuous internal growth is essential to avoid relative deterioration of foreign trade.

For these reasons an incomplete or halting recovery will not usually permit a recovery of the relative market for competitive imports which existed before the preceding depression.

---

38. *State and Regional Variations in Prospective Labor Supply*, Bulletin No. 893, U.S. Department of Labor, Table 1.

Chapter 4

Imports and the Tariff

CHANGES IN THE amount of goods a nation buys abroad are conditioned partly by its economic growth and partly by the cyclical fluctuations of its economy—subjects discussed in Chapters 2 and 3. These forces operate whether or not the nation strives to protect domestic industries. What role has the protective tariff played in the hampering of imports by the United States? Because the protective policy was adopted with the express purpose of keeping out goods competitive with home products, the natural assumption is that it has been effective. Yet tariffs may not always have accomplished their ostensible purpose. Considering the deliberate efforts to destroy foreign trade, it is remarkable how well it has survived. The opposite of this proposition is that reduction of tariffs may not increase trade as much as the great debates would lead one to suppose.

Five sources of possible misunderstanding of the role of tariffs may be noted.

1. The existence of a tariff on the statute books is not proof that it is effective. In a dynamic economy, tariffs would have to be continually adjusted in order to maintain the same degree of protection. Infant industries grow up. In the course of historical growth a constant tariff structure may become less effective as time goes on. Owing to changes in relative costs, fixed duties do not provide constant protection.

2. The import-competing industries compete with each other as well as with export and other industries for resources. Consequently, restriction of certain imports may increase imports of other products. The over-all restrictive effect of a broad tariff structure may be less than appears from the individual items taken separately.

3. The character of world demand for a nation's exports has an important bearing on the effect of its tariffs. Tariffs may improve a nation's terms of trade and, if demand for its exports is inelastic, the favorable effect on its terms of trade will more than offset the effect on domestic prices of imports. In this event, tariffs encourage expansion of export industries at the expense of the import-competing industries for which protection was intended.

4. The income effect of tariffs may raise the level of certain classes of imports. If protection is successful in stimulating home production, certain

72

imports will be displaced. But, under some conditions, the entire level of national income and employment will be raised, and the effect of higher income on total imports may go a long way toward offsetting the restrictive effect on the price of certain dutiable imports.

5. It is a mistake to assume that the explanation of changes in the relative importance of imports necessarily lies in tariffs and other deliberate obstacles to trade. Imports may naturally rise faster than national output at one period of development and decline in relative importance at a later stage.

The United States Has Followed a Protective Policy

The United States has, at least until 1934, rather consistently followed a policy of protection ever since the Civil War. In 1865 the average duty on dutiable imports (equivalent ad valorem rate) was 48 per cent. Between that date and 1935 the average rate never fell below 39 per cent except in the period when the Underwood Law was in effect (1914–1921), the average rate of which was 27 per cent. During the years of World War I, however, foreign producers of many dutiable products were unable to supply or in some cases even to deliver them, and American industry needed little protection since at least from 1916 to 1920 it found difficulty in producing enough to satisfy domestic demand.

These data indicate only the broad contours of changes in tariffs. They are realized average duties and, owing to changes in the composition of imports, do not necessarily measure the precise change in duties. The average duty collected reflects changes in the composition of imports caused by many factors including the effects of duties themselves. Almost any measurement of the height of tariffs is ambiguous. Nonetheless, a review of tariff history indicates that the average rate collected on dutiable imports shows fairly well the direction of the change under individual tariff laws. But we cannot be sure whether the amount of change was greater or less than is indicated by the average duty. The increase under the Dingley Law, for example, may have been greater than is indicated by the realized average duty.

Before the Underwood Law, tariff reductions were moderate and transitory. The act of 1870 lowered the average rate on dutiable imports to 43 per cent. The act of 1872 reduced it again, to 39 per cent, but this law was repealed three years later, and duties rose by steps to 48 per cent under the McKinley Law, 1891–1894. For two years under the Wilson Law, 1895–1897, the rate came down to 41 per cent, but the Dingley Law, 1898–1909, restored it to 47. The Payne-Aldrich Law, effective 1910–1913, resulted in a rate of 41 per cent. After the ineffectual reduction of the Underwood Law, protection was again established by the Fordney-McCumber Law in 1923

TABLE 19

AVERAGE RATE ON DUTIABLE AND TOTAL IMPORTS BY TARIFF LAWS, 1865–1952

Period or Year[a]	Tariff Law	Equivalent Ad Valorem Rate[b]	
		Dutiable Imports	Total Imports
		(Per Cent)	
1865–1870	Act of 1864	48	44
1871–1872	Act of 1870	43	38
1873–1875	Act of 1872	39	27
1876–1883	Act of 1872 repealed in 1875	43	29
1884–1890	Act of 1883	45	30
1891–1894	McKinley Law	48	23
1895–1897	Wilson Law	41	21
1898–1909	Dingley Law	47	26
1910–1913	Payne-Aldrich Law	41	19
1914–1922	Underwood Law	27	9
1923–June 17, 1930	Fordney-McCumber Law	39	14
June 18, 1930–1933	Hawley-Smoot Law	53	18
1934	Trade Agreements Act	47	18
1935		43	18
1937		38	16
1939		37	14
1941		37	14
1943		33	12
1945		28	9
1947		19.3	7.6
1949		13.5	5.5
1950		13.1	6.0
1951		12.3	5.5
1952		12.7	5.3

Sources: 1865–1945, U.S. Tariff Commission, Statistical Division, February 1951; 1947–1952, Statistical Abstract of the United States, 1953, Table 1077.

a. Fiscal years through 1918; calendar years thereafter.

b. Annual average for years tariff laws were in force.

Note: Average ad valorem equivalent rates of duty are arrived at by arithmetical computation and do not necessarily show the extent to which the degree of protection has actually been modified. They give an indication only of the general level of protection.

with a rate of 39 per cent. On June 30, 1930, this was superseded by the Hawley-Smoot Law, with a rate of 53 per cent on dutiable imports—the highest on record since the Civil War.

In 1934 the Hawley-Smoot Law was amended by the Reciprocal Trade Agreements Act, which inaugurated a gradual reduction of duties. Even under this policy, however, the rate on dutiable imports did not fall below 39 per cent until 1937, when it touched 38, and did not reach the Underwood rate until after 1945—the last year of World War II. Thereafter the rate fell rapidly to 13.1 per cent in 1950 and 12.7 in 1952. (See Table 19.)

It is the effect of changes in duties rather than the level of duties themselves which is our chief concern.

Effect of High Duties Which Totally Exclude Imports

A tariff which is raised so high as to exclude imports altogether might result in a decline in the average rate that is actually collected. On the other hand, if the relative volume of high-duty imports were increased as a result of the reduction of such duties, the average duty collected might rise. While it is important to recognize this logical possibility, there is considerable evidence to indicate that, historically, the average realized rate has generally reflected the direction of real changes in the height of the tariff.

We know, for example, that the unusually high tariff of the 1920s was again raised very substantially by the Hawley-Smoot tariff of 1930. In addition, the ad valorem equivalent of specific duties, which applied to the bulk of dutiable imports, was raised still higher by the precipitate drop in prices after 1929. Here is a period in which a decline in the average realized duty might be expected as a result of a tariff structure so high as to totally exclude or drastically restrict imports bearing the highest duties. The fact, however, is that the average realized duty rose under the Hawley-Smoot tariff and continued to rise as a result of the fall in prices.

The average rate on all dutiable imports was as follows:

	Per Cent
1929	40
1930	45
1931	53
1932	59

Moreover, the average realized duty declined from 1933 to 1937 as the ad valorem equivalent of specific duties was reduced by rising prices and as some duties were reduced by trade agreements. (See Table 20.)

Examination of individual tariff schedules in the highest brackets generally shows similar results, namely, that the direction of changes in

TABLE 20

FREE AND DUTIABLE IMPORTS FOR CONSUMPTION AS PER CENT OF GROSS NATIONAL
PRODUCT AT CURRENT VALUES, AVERAGE DUTIES AND PER CENT OF FREE IMPORTS,
BY TARIFF LAW PERIODS, 1910–1950

Fiscal Year (1910–1918)[a] or Calendar Year	As Per Cent of GNP			Average Rate on Dutiable Imports	Free Imports as Per Cent of Total Imports
	Free Imports	Dutiable Imports	Total Imports		
Payne-Aldrich Law August 6, 1909					
1910	2.0	2.1	4.0	42	49
1911	2.0	1.9	4.0	41	51
1912	2.2	1.9	4.1	40	54
1913	2.4	1.9	4.2	40	56
Underwood Law October 4, 1913					
1914	2.9	1.9	4.7	38	60
1915	2.3	1.4	3.7	33	63
1916	3.1	1.4	4.4	31	69
1917	3.0	1.3	4.3	27	70
1918	3.1	1.1	4.2	24	74
1919	3.3	1.4	4.7	21	71
1920	3.4	2.2	5.6	16	61
1921[b]	2.1	1.3	3.5	29	61
1922[b]	2.5	1.6	4.1	38	61
Fordney-McCumber Law September 22, 1922					
1923	2.5	1.8	4.2	36	58
1924	2.4	1.7	4.1	37	59
1925	2.9	1.6	4.4	38	65
1926	2.9	1.5	4.4	39	66
1927	2.7	1.5	4.2	39	64
1928	2.7	1.4	4.1	39	66
1929	2.8	1.4	4.2	40	66
1930	2.3	1.1	3.4	45	67
Hawley-Smoot Law June 18, 1930					
1931	1.8	.9	2.8	53	67
1932[c]	1.5	.8	2.3	59	67
1933	1.6	.9	2.6	54	63
1934[d]	1.5	1.0	2.5	47	61

(Continued on facing page)

average realized duty reflects real changes in the height of the tariff. The
duty on chinaware, for example, was already so high (68 per cent) in 1929
that it would be easy to assume that a further increase in duties by almost
one half would reduce the average realized rate on all china tableware and

TABLE 20 (*Continued*)

Fiscal Year (1910–1918)[a] or Calendar Year	As Per Cent of GNP			Average Rate on Dutiable Imports	Free Imports as Per Cent of Total Imports
	Free Imports	Dutiable Imports	Total Imports		
Reciprocal Trade Agreements Act June 12, 1934					
1935	1.7	1.2	2.8	43	59
1936	1.7	1.3	2.9	39	57
1937	2.0	1.4	3.3	38	59
1938	1.4	.9	2.3	39	61
1939	1.5	1.0	2.5	37	61
1940	1.6	.9	2.5	36	65
1941	1.6	.9	2.5	37	63
1942	1.1	.6	1.7	32	64
1943	1.1	.6	1.7	33	65
1944	1.3	.5	1.8	30	70
1945	1.3	.6	1.9	28	67
1946	1.4	.9	2.3	26	61
1947	1.5	.9	2.4	20	61
1948	1.6	1.1	2.7	14	59
1949	1.5	1.1	2.6	14	59
1950	1.7	1.4	3.1	13	55

Sources: Imports for consumption and tariff data, U.S. Tariff Commission; GNP, U.S. Department of Commerce.

a. Imports for consumption and related tariff data are available only by fiscal years before 1919. Consequently, it has been necessary to compare fiscal year imports with calendar year GNP for the earlier period.

b. The Emergency Tariff Act became effective on certain agricultural products on May 28, 1921, and continued in effect until September 22, 1922.

c. Subsequent to June 21, 1932, certain commodities which had previously been on the free list were made taxable, and since that date have been reported as dutiable commodities. The principal commodities affected were petroleum, copper, lumber and coal.

d. Trade Agreements Act passed as amendment to Hawley-Smoot Law June 12, 1934. Under it many rates of duty have been decreased from time to time. First agreement effective September 12, 1934, with Cuba.

kitchenware by virtually excluding those items bearing the highest rates. Yet we find that the ad valorem of compound duties rose from 68 per cent in 1929 to 94 per cent in 1933, and thereafter fell as prices rose.

The ad valorem equivalent rates of compound duties on household china tableware and kitchenware from 1928 to 1937 were as follows:[1]

Year	Per Cent	Year	Per Cent
1928	68	1933	94
1929	68	1934	88
1930	73	1935	87
1931	84	1936	86
1932	93	1937	84

1. Compiled by U.S. Tariff Commission from data by U.S. Department of Commerce.

Importance of Duty-Free Imports

The rate on dutiable imports does not, of course, tell the whole story. The rate on all imports was at its highest point in 1865–1870—44 per cent— and after that showed a generally declining tendency, reaching 14 per cent under the Fordney-McCumber Law in the 1920s, and rising to only 18 per cent even under the Hawley-Smoot Law. The Reciprocal Trade Agreements Act reduced it gradually to 6.1 per cent in 1950.

The figures of the average rate on all imports, including those which came in free, are quite ambiguous as a test of the degree of protection, however. The over-all rate would be reduced by the transfer of formerly dutiable articles to the free list; such a shift would imply a narrowing of protection. The rate would also be reduced merely by a rise in the relative volume of nondutiable commodities, entirely aside from any change in the commodity composition of the two groups.

Nondutiable imports *have* become a larger percentage of total imports, at least since the passage of the Payne-Aldrich Law in 1909, when they comprised 49 per cent. Their rise, however, has not been large or steady and has frequently been reversed. Nor does their course reflect closely the changes in tariff law. The highest points of nondutiable imports have been 74 per cent in 1918 and 70 per cent in 1944. Both of these years occurred in periods of low tariffs; yet probably both reflected the effect of war conditions rather than that of import duties. In peacetime, relatively high percentages between 60 and 70 were reached under the regime of protection which prevailed in the late 1920s. Since World War II, the percentage of nondutiable imports, under a low-tariff regime, fell as low as 55 in 1950, but this figure is no lower than was that of the last year of the protective Payne-Aldrich Law—1913. (See Table 20.)

TARIFF THEORY

The classical economic theory opposes protective duties on the ground that absence of interference with freedom of trade, whether within a nation or among nations, will promote specialization in production and favor the more efficient competitors. Under such a regime, consumers everywhere would benefit, and each nation would make the best possible use of its resources.

A logical inference from this doctrine is that an effectual tariff must be either a bonus to an industry which does not need it or a subsidy to an industry which otherwise would suffer from its relative inefficiency. Whether the tariff is subsidy or bonus, those who are not protected pay the bill. And to the extent that wages and profits are equalized by competition between industries, in the long run all will suffer.

Effective tariffs of course compel consumers to pay higher prices for the protected article, even if it is not imported. If the demand for the article is elastic, consumers will in consequence spend less for it, and resources will be diverted to less important uses than if no tariff existed. If the demand is inelastic, they may buy as much as they might have bought at a lower price, but in consequence will have less to spend for other things, and unprotected industries and occupations will suffer accordingly. No import duty can directly protect industries which by their nature meet no foreign competition, such as transportation, the distributive trades and services of all kinds.

Attempts have been made to broaden protection by subsidizing the merchant marine and exports of surplus agricultural commodities (dumping). Nevertheless, a major part of our imports are duty-free and no such subsidies have been extended to the large fraction of the population engaged in the production of goods or services not competitive with foreign producers.[2]

A necessary conclusion is that even if it were feasible to extend equal protection to all producers in a nation, none would be able to benefit from it. "Equal protection for all" would mean that no one was enabled to bid resources away from others as a result of tariffs and subsidies. Thus the structure of home industry would remain unchanged.

If protection is to provide a subsidy or a bonus to the protected, the subsidy or bonus must be paid by somebody.

The protection given to some necessarily injures others. If resources are drawn into import-competing industries, other home industries are constricted as a result. Furthermore, even those engaged in the protected industries may not prosper as much as if no protective duties existed. For, insofar as the tariff is effective, it serves only to bring about a less efficient allocation of resources than would have occurred without it, and since the world as a whole is less productive than it might be, all, including the protected industries themselves, may suffer lower real incomes in the long run.

In this respect the logic of the classical theory is unassailable, provided its assumptions are granted—such as the existence of relatively free competition, internal mobility of capital and labor, and high-level employment. The qualifications concern chiefly the effect of tariffs on (1) the terms of trade and (2) the distribution of income. A particular nation may gain more from tariff restrictions which improve its terms of trade than it loses from the misuse of resources. A particular factor of production may also gain at the expense of the other factors. But the gains to one nation or to one factor

2. Resale price maintenance and other market restrictions introduce elements of protection chiefly against domestic competition. In the case of petroleum and other extractive industries, resources are attracted by favorable treatment with respect to taxes.

are less than the losses to others because tariff restrictions reduce total world income.

The classical case for free trade was based on a cosmopolitan outlook which abstracted from the effect of tariffs on the terms of trade. From the national standpoint, however, it would be possible to gain from tariffs at the expense of the outside world, provided that other nations do not retaliate. An unusually high degree of technical knowledge and administrative discretion would be required in order to exploit monopoly gains via the ratio of export prices to import prices.[3]

Tariffs affect not only the level of income but also the distribution of income. International trade is a substitute for immigration and foreign investment and, under certain conditions, would have the same effect on the distribution of income. Restrictions on imports which encourage domestic production of labor-intensive products like sugar beets, and discourage exports of capital-intensive products like automobiles, tend to raise the relative return to labor.[4]

Income Effect of Tariffs

Let us assume that tariffs are raised and that certain classes of imports are restricted as a result of the effect on prices. What will be the effect on total imports? Domestic employment and income will be stimulated by the shift of demand from imports to products of home industry, and some part of the increase in national income will be spent on imports. Thus, even though the relative importance of certain categories of imports is reduced, the income effect will raise the level of duty-free and, possibly, other classes of dutiable imports which were not restricted.

Will Tariffs Necessarily Protect Import-Competing Industries?

Under some conditions, the favorable effect of tariffs on the terms of trade will produce altogether different results from those which were intended. The intention is to protect domestic import-competing industries against foreign competition by an import duty which raises the domestic price of imports and enables the protected industries to expand. It is misleading, however, to consider only the effect on domestic prices.

The secondary effect of tariffs on world prices must also be brought into account. Although tariffs may raise the domestic price of imports, they

3. Cf. Jacob Viner, *International Economics*, Glencoe, Illinois, 1951, pp. 10–11; Tibor de Scitovsky, "A Reconsideration of the Theory of Tariffs," reprinted in *Readings in the Theory of International Trade*, Irwin, Illinois, 1949.

4. It is unlikely, moreover, that the particular factor of production which enjoys a higher relative return will suffer a lower real return. If tariffs raise labor's share of national income, real wages will be raised, and conversely. Wolfgang F. Stolper and Paul A. Samuelson, "Protection and Real Wages," in *Readings in the Theory of International Trade*.

lower the price in world markets by restricting the demand for world goods. If world demand for the nation's exports is elastic, the effect on domestic prices will be greater than the effect on its terms of trade. In this case, tariffs enable domestic import-competing industries to expand at the expense of its export industries.

But if world demand for the nation's exports is inelastic, the favorable effect on its terms of trade is greater than the effect on domestic import prices. In this case, tariffs enable domestic export industries to expand by bidding resources away from the import-competing industries for which protection was intended.[5]

The favorable effect of tariffs on the terms of trade has probably played a role in the history of America's foreign trade. Demand for primary products has usually been regarded as relatively inelastic and demand for manufactured products as elastic. In the earlier part of American history, the great bulk of our exports consisted of primary products. Exports of manufactures expanded only gradually with the development of industry. In 1900, for example, crude materials and foodstuffs of all classes still accounted for as much as two thirds of total exports. These classes of exports accounted for half of the total as late as 1913 and, even today, America remains an important exporter of agricultural products although finished manufactures account for the bulk of our exports.

A nation which is an important exporter of primary products and which faces an inelastic demand for its exports is in a position to benefit from the favorable effect of tariffs on the terms of trade. From this factor alone we should expect that tariffs were often ineffective in keeping out imports in the earlier period of American history, and that they became more effective as the character of our exports gradually shifted from primary products to finished manufactures. But in any event, the effect of tariffs on the shift of resources from export industries to import-competing industries would be less than it appears from the effect on domestic prices of imports.

Will an Effective Duty Necessarily Remain Effective?

Of course a specific duty—that is, one specified in dollars and cents—will become less effective in an era of rising prices and more effective when prices fall. But even more important considerations than this are involved.

Let us introduce a highly important realistic factor of change which characterizes modern industrial society in general, and characterizes the United States in particular—technological advance.

Technological change is uneven in its incidence. New industries grow; old industries may stagnate or decline. Some industries experience a more

5. Lloyd A. Metzler, "Tariffs, the Terms of Trade, and the Distribution of National Income," *Journal of Political Economy*, February 1949.

rapid increase in output per man-hour than others. In a period of relatively full employment, expanding and highly efficient industries tend to draw labor and other resources from contracting industries which in many cases, though not always, employ labor less efficiently. It is the less efficient industries which need, and mainly demand, protection.

If the domestic competition of the more efficient bids up wages and the prices of other resources, the less efficient may in the end have to incur higher costs in order to remain in production. In that event, a protective tariff which once was high enough to subsidize the less efficient will become inadequate. Under these circumstances, protective duties will have to be periodically revised upward in order to remain effective.

If, on the other hand, a protected industry becomes more efficient than before, and is able to pay higher wages and expand its market, a historically necessary duty may become higher than the industry needs. This industry may reach a point where it could not lose its market to foreign competitors even if the duty were removed.

Such an unnecessary duty is ineffective in the sense that it does not in fact keep out foreign goods, because the foreign goods in question would not be imported even if the duty did not exist. If the industry in question is competitive, its prices may already have fallen low enough to meet foreign competition. If it is subject to more or less monopolistic control, it may profit from protection at the expense of consumers, but still would be capable of survival if it had to meet foreign competition on even terms. To lower or remove the tariff in this case might not appreciably increase imports, although it would benefit consumers by reducing prices to competitive levels.

Will Even an Effective Duty Necessarily Keep Out Imports?

Let us suppose that a duty is effective in the sense that the domestic price is raised above the world price by the full amount of the duty. Will this fact necessarily prevent the growth of imports which compete with the protected industry? The answer is "No." The protected industry may be unable to expand enough to satisfy the full domestic demand for its products. It may even be forced to contract because more efficient home industries are bidding away its labor force and expanding at its expense. Tariffs may be more or less restrictive depending on the rate of growth of competing home industries and on prosperity and depression.

The adjustments called for by the basic principle of trade depend on competition for resources between home industries. The principle called by economists the theory of "comparative advantage" states that a nation may import articles that could be produced more cheaply at home than abroad, for the reason that the nation has other industries still more efficient, in which its resources can be more productively employed. Thus, it will be cheaper to import an article that costs 20 per cent less to produce at home than abroad, if that article can be paid for with exports that cost, say, 50 per cent less to produce at home than abroad. Complete operation of the principle requires that the efficient industries draw labor and other resources from the less efficient until the wages of comparable labor are equal between the two industries. If wages in the import industries remain lower than wages in the more efficient home industries, they may be able to maintain production and compete against imports.

If an effective tariff is cut in time of depression, the result may be, not to increase imports, but to force a reduction in wages and prices in the protected industries—an adjustment that is facilitated by the existence of unemployment. Whether the consequence of a tariff cut is lower wages or unemployment, it may not during the period of depression facilitate a more efficient allocation of domestic resources.

On the other hand, an increase in tariff during a world-wide depression may not reduce imports. Instead, it may force a reduction of the prices (before duty) of imported products. It is possible that this was one effect of the Hawley-Smoot tariff of 1930, for while the value of imports fell drastically, the volume fell no more than we should expect (relative to domestic production) if there had been no increase in duties.

Does Protection of Some Industries Necessarily Restrict the Rate of Growth of Total Imports?

In the beginning, an undeveloped country may not be able to shift resources from primary production to manufacturing by means of a protective system on imports of manufactured goods. This is because world demand for its raw material exports is likely to be inelastic, and the effect of tariffs on its terms of trade will more than offset the effect on domestic prices of manufactured products.

At some later stage, when the nation is able to export goods for which the demand is elastic, a protective system may attract resources to "infant industries" by restricting imports of their products. But as time goes on, it will not result in a progressive restriction of total imports unless the protected industries continue to grow disproportionately to the unprotected, or the more highly protected continue to grow at the expense of the less highly protected. To jump from the premise that the United States has followed a protective policy to the conclusion that imports as a whole have grown less rapidly because of protection of infant industries is unwarranted. The *level* of imports is lower because of tariffs, but this does not mean that the *rate of growth* of total imports has been lower.

It is a reasonable presumption that duties require a considerable period of time in order to become fully effective. In a dynamic economy, however, many other factors are also at work which may offset the expected effect of import duties. Some industries will increase in efficiency until they no longer need protection or profit from it. On the other hand, resources may be drawn away from the "protected" industries unless duties are progressively increased. If duties are extended to more and more industries, these industries will compete with each other as well as with the free sector of the economy for resources. Higher restrictions for some industries may lead to increased imports in others. The over-all effect of a protective system cannot be judged by examining the effect of duties on individual items taken separately.

In a nation with the vast resources of the United States, it is difficult to believe that the course of industrial growth has been greatly distorted, at least in the twentieth century, by tariffs. However important protective duties may have been in one detail or another, there is little basis for believing that the broad sweep of historical growth has been seriously affected and there is some ground for believing that the protective system became less rather than more effective as time went on.

For the same reason, an attempt to increase imports by reducing the tariff may be disappointing.

To suggest this possibility is not to defend the tariff, but merely to say that it may not have done so much harm to the national economy—or to the world economy—as it would have done if it had been effectual.

TWO ENLIGHTENING INSTANCES

Let us now turn from theory to a few illustrations of the actual operation of a tariff.

The Illuminating Case of Wool

Wool is a fascinating case study of how protection can cease to exclude imports. Although the gross returns to sheep raisers are about the highest in history, wool imports in recent years have displaced almost half of the domestic industry. Product differentiation and other institutional rigidities are often more important barriers to trade in manufactured goods than the tariff.[6] But wool is a highly protected, standardized product traded on a basis of price, and therefore particularly suitable for study with respect to the effect of the tariff.

The tariff on wool is a method of maintaining prices of domestic wool above the world market level, and the sheep industry in the United States has become

6. See Chapter 10.

established with this protection provided, and on the assumption that it would be continued. Although a price-support program for wool is in effect, growers continue to look to the tariff as a more basic factor influencing the economic stability of their industry.[7]

In the face of a protective tariff, apparel wool imports increased from 30 per cent as much as home production in 1935–1939 to 217 per cent in 1945–1949. In spite of mandatory price supports in the domestic market in addition to tariff protection, and in spite of about the highest returns in history to sheep growers, sheep numbers declined by almost one half between 1940 and 1949.[8]

Wool production is, of course, a joint product with mutton. About half of the income from sheep raising in the past forty years has been from wool and half from lamb and mutton. The price of all grades of lamb[9] increased almost threefold, from $15 to $44 per hundred pounds, between 1940 and 1949. Gross values from the slaughter of sheep and lamb doubled from the decade of the 1930s to the 1940s. That the decline in sheep numbers did not result from low lamb and mutton prices is made crystal clear by a study of the U.S. Tariff Commission.[10] Between 1940 and 1948 income from sale of sheep and lambs increased two and a half times and cost increased almost as much while income from wool had increased only one and a half times.

How is it, then, that imports have displaced almost half of this protected industry? The answer cannot be found in sheep raising alone but lies in the dynamics of technology, full employment and competition for resources. Tariff protection has been overshadowed by the relative rise in efficiency of *competing home industries*.

Sheep compete directly with cattle for pasture on the western ranges. With a nearly fixed pasture area, sheep and cattle numbers tend, under prosperous conditions, to move in opposite directions according to the relative value of cattle and sheep. When the ratio of cattle prices to sheep prices in the years 1910–1915 rose sharply above the long-term average, cattle numbers increased and sheep numbers declined. On the other hand, when the ratio of cattle prices to sheep prices fell between 1923 and 1930, sheep numbers increased and cattle numbers declined. Since 1942, the ratio of cattle to sheep prices has been slightly above the long-term average. This

7. *Domestic Wool Requirements and Sources of Supply*, U.S. Department of Agriculture, June 1950, p. 23.

8. The Agricultural Act of 1949 makes the support of wool prices mandatory under the conditions that have prevailed.

9. *Domestic Wool Requirements and Sources of Supply*, Table 15, p. 80.

10. *Estimated Costs of Production of Wool, Sheep, and Lambs, in 1948*. In 1948, estimated costs per head (excluding interest) in the western region were $9.83; total income was $10.83.

would account for a modest decline in sheep numbers but is not sufficient to account for the greatest decline on record.

About half the total decline in sheep numbers has occurred in the eleven western states and Texas, where sheep compete with cattle for pasture. In the rest of the United States the alternating movement between sheep and cattle numbers that has characterized the west does not occur. None the less, sheep numbers in the states[11] where sheep raising is incidental to general farming have declined to the lowest level in more than one hundred years.

A reason for the decline in sheep raising in these farm-flock states,[12] and the greater than "expected" decline on the basis of cattle numbers in the western range states, is contained in the replies from questionnaires mailed to 16,000 sheep raisers in twenty-nine states. Losses from dogs and wild animals[13] were listed as the most important reason. But this reply must be subject to further explanation since it seems unlikely that dogs and coyotes have increased in numbers or ferocity in the past eight years.

The reply reflects the fact that farmers were too busy with more profitable work to provide the customary care and protection given sheep. The real reason for the decline was well expressed, *"Too much farm work and had to cut down on something."* The most important reason given for reducing sheep numbers in most states east of the Mississippi, particularly where dairying is important, was competition with other livestock. In addition, the largest percentage decline in sheep occurred in areas where the production of cash crops, particularly soybeans and wheat, has been greatly increased.

In the western range states, where large-scale sheep raising requires specialized labor, many replies noted that the labor available consisted of "old" men. Even relatively high wages, apparently, are not sufficient to attract young men from the neon lights to the sheep herder's home on a chuck wagon. An earlier survey, made in 1948, shows that more than half of those who had sold out their sheep were not going back into the business.[14] By far the most important cause was the competition from other crops and livestock. The next most important was that the operator was too old and the sons were not interested in sheep raising.

Wool Imports Are Substituted for Imports of Hides, Oil and Cheese

Here we see the abstract theory of foreign trade richly studded with the events of current history. On the western ranges, sheep gave way to cattle;

11. Excludes eleven western states and Texas.

12. The sheep ranch of over 1,000 head accounts for less than one half of the total wool clip. The reduction in sheep numbers is common to all sizes of operations in all areas.

13. *Domestic Wool Requirements and Sources of Supply*, p. 52.

14. *Ibid.*, p. 55.

in the east, wheat, soybeans and dairying have claimed more of the farmer's labor. The displacement of imported hides, vegetable oils and cheese by the expansion of domestic cattle, soybeans and dairying has as a corollary the displacement of domestic sheep raising and the expansion of wool imports.

This demonstrates that technological progress does not necessarily destroy foreign trade. Research has fostered the dramatic expansion in soybean production. Improved technique in quick drying for the preservation of proteins in hay has increased efficiency in cattle raising and in dairying. *The same technological changes, however, which contributed to the decline of dairy and oil imports, by shifting the relative efficiency of competing home industries, have contributed to the rise in wool imports.*

Here we see comparative costs at work. As one import is substituted for another in a technological revolution, the tariff becomes ineffective. The "old" men who are too specialized will continue to keep sheep on the pastures that are too poor for anything else. The tariff will provide them a higher return than a free market price, so that income will continue to be diverted to them, but neither tariff nor price supports, though a hindrance, have prevented the expansion of the more efficient types of farming.

There is nothing inevitable about such compensating adjustments in foreign trade. This substitution in imports probably would not have taken place under depressed economic conditions. Full and sustained prosperity to the point of inflation was necessary to shift resources. It is only when domestic producers are so fully employed that they "have to cut down on something" that imports have a chance to increase. Without the tariff and other rigidities, less inflation would be necessary to shift resources. But, if left alone, a tariff may not destroy more and more trade; instead it is likely to become less and less effective owing to the more rapid increase in the efficiency of certain industries than of others.

A Duty Becomes Vestigial in Rice

The case of wool showed how imports have displaced home production despite the protective tariff. The case of rice shows how a high tariff was rendered more or less innocuous by revolutionary changes in the technique of production.

The United States raised about half of the rice it consumed in the latter part of the nineteenth century and imported an equal amount, over a tariff wall as high as 77 per cent. A substantial reduction in duty in 1890 failed to increase imports significantly. But with the development of machine methods about the turn of the century and the opening up of the prairie country in Louisiana, Texas and Arkansas, the costs of home production were dramatically reduced while much of the rest of the world continued to rely on the water buffalo, the sickle and the flail.

As a consequence, home production increased eightfold in about twenty years and the United States became an exporter of rice. Exports of 15 million pounds in 1910 were increased rapidly to 500 million pounds in 1921 and in the more recent years, 1948 and 1949, over 900 million pounds of rice were exported from annual crops of about 2,700 million pounds.[15]

The fact that the United States can profitably export rice in competition with the lowest-paid labor in the world should lay at rest once and for all the old notion that all American producers need protection against cheap foreign labor. Rice farmers have been able to pay somewhat higher wages than neighboring cotton and sugar growers and sell rice in competition with India, Thailand and Indo-China, where rice is produced at the lowest of subsistence wages. The answer, of course, is that "For each day's work the American farmer may produce from twenty to fifty times as much rice as the oriental farmer."[16]

Rice illustrates how the dynamics of comparative costs may produce a decline in the relative importance of certain imports and, *at the same time, reduce the importance of a tariff wall.* But the repercussions are more interesting still. Since cotton and sugar did not experience comparable revolutionary changes in costs of production, rice producers were enabled to pay higher wages and expand at the expense of these competing enterprises.

To the extent that resources were scarce and substitutable, the expansion of rice could have been directly or indirectly at the expense of sugar production and would have as a corollary a rise in the imports of sugar. If resources were withdrawn from cotton the result would be a reduction of cotton exports. On the other hand, if the labor and land employed in the expansion of rice represented merely the reduction of disguised unemployment, the opening up of new land and the more efficient use of both land and labor, then the revolution in rice need not have produced compensating repercussions on foreign trade in sugar and cotton.

An increase in the tariff on sugar would have made it more difficult for rice growers to bid resources away from sugar producers. But no additional tariff protection would be needed to keep those resources in sugar which were specialized and could not be shifted to rice.

In fact, Louisiana sugar cane acreage was reduced substantially at the time that rice acreage was rapidly expanded. In 1902–1906 sugar cane sup-

15. *Gross Farm Income and Indices of Farm Production and Prices in the United States, 1869–1937*, Technical Bulletin No. 703, U.S. Department of Agriculture, December 1940, p. 71; *Agricultural Statistics*, 1936 and 1950, pp. 297 and 500, respectively.

16. Theodore W. Schultz, *Agriculture in an Unstable Economy*, Committee for Economic Development Research Study, McGraw-Hill, New York, 1945, p. 152, note.

plied 11 per cent of domestic consumption, but declined to 6 per cent in 1912–1916 and to 2 per cent in 1927–1931.[17]

A Sketch of Tariff History

It is impossible to give, within brief compass, an account of the manifold complexities of changes in the American tariff since the Civil War. Nor is it necessary for the present purpose, which is to evaluate its over-all effectiveness. Were the changes in duties frequent enough and systematic enough to match the changes in cost? Our chief concern is whether the successive tariff laws increased the over-all protection of the American economy. Most of the history that has been written cites the impressive increase in duties and creates the strong impression that this was responsible for a progressive hampering of imports relative to the growth of home industry.

We know from the way tariffs were made that the whole process was most unsystematic. Important items were shuttled back and forth between the free and dutiable list. The House passed one bill, the Senate another; each revision represented a compromise of compromises. But the dominance of the protectionist's view, abetted by the logrolling process, insured what appeared to be a broad and high tariff wall.

From the Civil War to 1900

The American tariff structure after the Civil War was a legacy of the scramble to raise revenue during the war. As internal taxes were levied on domestic producers, protectionists seized the opportunity to raise the duty on imports sharply and indiscriminately. With the coming of peace, the internal taxes, except on liquor and tobacco, were soon repealed, but the bulk of Civil War duties on imports remained largely unchanged for twenty years and more. The resulting tariff structure, while high, was in no sense carefully considered or systematic.

Soon after the end of the war the duty on wool and woolens was raised substantially. A flat cut of 10 per cent in 1872 was repealed three years later. The first general revision, in 1883, sought to give the appearance of reducing the tariff while retaining protection. Individual duties were jock-

17. Beginning in 1921 the mosaic disease caused a reduction in sugar cane yield and acreage harvested. Harold Barger and Hans H. Landsberg, *American Agriculture, 1899–1939*, National Bureau of Economic Research, New York, 1942, p. 91. The decline in cane production, however, was offset by the expansion of beets in other areas. The Tariff Act of 1890 provided a cash bounty payable directly to growers from 1891 to 1894. The sums involved in the bounty, however, were far less than those from the duty which were remitted. F. W. Taussig, *The Tariff History of the United States*, 8th edition, Putnam, New York, 1931, p. 277.

eyed up and down, cottons were raised slightly, chinaware sharply, but the reductions were generally nominal and the changes unsystematic.

Looking at the tariff system as a whole, it retained substantially unchanged, the high level of duties reached during and after the Civil War. No new line of policy was entered on, in one direction or the other . . .[18]

The McKinley tariff of 1890 raised average duties. Woolens were given a duty of 100 per cent or more. The order of magnitude of the increase on cottons is indicated in the dragnet clause, covering cotton goods not elsewhere provided for, which raised the duty from 35 per cent to the 50 per cent level.[19] The revenue duty on raw sugar was repealed, and raw sugar placed on the free list. The high duty on rice was moderated.

The 50 per cent level of duties under the McKinley tariff was short-lived. In 1894, the Wilson tariff made reductions of 10 and 20 per cent in the items of greater practical importance. On the finer cotton goods, for example, the 50 per cent duty of 1890 became 40 per cent in 1894; the reduction on knit goods was greater though the duty remained high—50 per cent. Duties on various silks were cut from 60 per cent to 50 per cent and from 50 per cent to 45 per cent. Similar reductions were made on quality linens, and the duty on dressed flax was reduced by one half, while bagging of jute, flax and hemp was made duty-free. Raw sugar was again made dutiable, but raw wool was shifted to the free list.

The Dingley tariff of 1897 represented a return to 1890 and, on some items, pushed duties higher than ever before. The rates on china and glassware were restored to the 1890 level. Higher duties were imposed on silks and linens. Raw wool was restored to the dutiable list with the old system of high compensating duties on woolens. The Dingley tariff, which was about the highest since 1865, was also the longest-lived and for this reason provides a suitable period for testing our view that even a high tariff, if it remains fixed, does not progressively restrict total imports.

Payne-Aldrich Law, 1909

Some of the most important tariff schedules remained virtually unchanged under the Tariff Act of 1909. The duty on sugar, which had been chiefly a revenue duty until 1897, remained at the protective rates fixed in 1897.[20] The extra duty on refined sugar, which protected the refineries, was reduced sharply from 12½ cents to 7½ cents per hundred pounds. The

---

18. Taussig, *op. cit.*, p. 250. The present sketch relies heavily on Taussig.
19. *Ibid.*, p. 267.
20. With the exception that 300,000 tons were admitted duty-free from the Philippines.

wool schedule was left intact, except for a reduction of about 10 per cent on yarns and dress goods.

Hides were shifted to the free list and the duty on leather, shoes and harness reduced to nominal rates. Zinc was added to the dutiable list.

Duties on mercerized cottons and fashioned hosiery were advanced, but the most important increase was in the silk schedule—chiefly the finer grades. There is some evidence that, in the revision of 1909, duties like those on silks, mercerized cotton hosiery and cutlery were shoved up a notch on those qualities which continued to be imported notwithstanding the high duties in the earlier Dingley tariff.

Over-all, the Payne-Aldrich Law shaded average duties slightly.

The Underwood Tariff—Effective October 4, 1913

The Democratic Congress under President Wilson's leadership in 1913 gave the American tariff the only large downward revision made by the Congress since the Civil War.[21] Most important was the shift of sugar and wool to the free list, effective immediately on wool, and with a delay of two and a half years in the case of sugar. The compensating specific duties on woolen goods likewise went by the board; ad valorem woolen duties of 50 per cent and 55 per cent were cut to 35 per cent.

Duties on cotton goods were, likewise, cut drastically, though the practical effect was less significant, since the cheaper grade cottons were produced as efficiently in the United States as abroad.

The reduction in rates on silk fabrics was less than on cottons and woolens and duties remained high—about 45 per cent.

Chinaware and crockery were left with duties of 35 per cent and 40 per cent, which, though high, represented a reduction from 55 per cent and 60 per cent.

Agricultural machinery was put on the free list. Leather and shoes also were made duty-free.

Fordney-McCumber Tariff of 1922

The Underwood tariff was in effect chiefly during the first world war and, consequently, there is no opportunity to observe its effect. In 1921 an emergency tariff bill imposed high duties on agricultural products including the important items, wool and sugar, as well as a list of "bogus" duties devoid of economic significance.

In the main, these were incorporated and even raised in the Fordney-McCumber tariff of 1922. Raw wool was protected with a duty of 31 cents

21. Under the Trade Agreements Act, the Congress delegated authority to the President.

per pound, with compensating rates on woolens, which were also protected by a duty of 50 per cent.[22]

Silk manufacture was protected by a 55 per cent duty as it had been most of the time since the Civil War. The more important classes of cotton manufactures were made dutiable at 40 per cent, which was about 10 per cent below the high rates of 1897 and 1909.

Chinaware was raised to unprecedented rates of 60 and 70 per cent, imitation jewelry to 80 per cent and laces to 90 per cent. Extremely high duties, from 75 per cent to several hundred per cent, were also levied on cutlery, razors and guns. Duties on dyestuffs and other chemicals were also extremely high.[23]

The Fordney-McCumber Law extended the list of dutiable items and appeared to have increased protection beyond all earlier tariffs.

Hawley-Smoot Tariff Bill

The climax of raising duties by logrolling was reached in the futile and absurd Hawley-Smoot tariff of 1930. Duties in all schedules were increased substantially.

Cuba had become our chief source of sugar imports. Under the 1913 tariff, the Cuban duty had been fixed at one cent a pound. Under the reciprocity agreement, Cuba received a 20 per cent reduction, which, under the Tariff Act of 1922, made the Cuban duty 1.76 cents. This high duty was increased still further to 2 cents in 1930. The difference in cost of production between Cuban sugar and American beet was no more than 1.5 cents. The principle of setting duties to equalize cost went out the window.

The sugar producers, especially the beet-sugar people, asked all they thought it possible to get; the Republicans in House and Senate gave them, more or less grudgingly, what seemed necessary to fulfill campaign pledges and to hold their party associates in line. The final rate was merely the result of give and take, maneuvering and compromise.[24]

Duties were raised on cotton cloth, the finer grades of woolens and silk. China and glassware also received the dubious benefits of higher rates—dubious because the increase amounted chiefly to surplus protection. Rates on scientific instruments and watches were increased. Aluminum utensils now shared in the effort to protect everyone. Import prices had started down in the mid-1920s and the ratio of import values to national output was already declining in the late 1920s. The Hawley-Smoot tariff was

22. Carpet wool, which is not produced domestically, was taxed, but the tax was remitted when the wool was used in making carpets. Taussig, *op. cit.*, p. 462.

23. *Ibid.*, p. 453.

24. *Ibid.*, p. 502.

enacted after the depression had already begun and imports were falling rapidly in relation to output.

Did Higher Duties Increase Protection?

Have higher duties under the successive laws made the tariff a more effective over-all barrier to trade, or were the dynamic changes in comparative costs more potent than the tariff makers?

In the textile industries and chinaware protectionism ran rampant. These specific industries may be used as tests to bring out the effect on imports of extraordinarily high duties.

When the average rate of duty on cotton manufactures was increased from 46 per cent under the Wilson tariff (1895–1897) to 55 per cent under the Dingley Law (1898–1909), imports dropped from $36 million in 1897 to $27 million in 1898.[25] However, imports of cotton manufactures increased almost two and one half times from 1899 to a peak of $73 million in 1907. (See Table 21.)

The pattern for earthenware and chinaware is similar. The increase in duties from a level of 34 per cent to 55 per cent in 1898 was accompanied by a reduction in imports from $10.5 million to $6.5 million; but, by 1907, earthenware and chinaware imports had reached almost $14 million.

When the tariff on woolen manufactures was increased from 46 per cent to more than 90 per cent, imports of woolen manufactures were greatly restricted. The greater part of the enormous increase in woolen duties in 1897, however, as in 1890, consisted of compensating duties for the tariff on raw wool. When home manufacturers paid more for raw wool because of the duty, the tariff on manufactured woolens included both protection to woolen manufactures and additional compensating duties to cover the higher domestic price of raw wool. The increase in the rate under the Dingley tariff was accompanied by an immediate decline in woolen imports from almost $50 million to about $15 million in the normal business year of 1900. By 1907, imports had risen, but only to $22 million.

A similar pattern is shown under the earlier tariff laws. The increase on cotton manufactures and chinaware in the tariff of 1883 was accompanied by a sharp decline in imports (allowance should be made for the fact that 1884 and 1885 were recession years). But by 1890, chinaware imports had risen by one half under duties averaging 57 per cent; cotton manufactures, however, remained at about the same level as in 1884.

Duties were reduced with the advent of the Wilson tariff, effective August 28, 1894. We may compare fiscal 1894,[26] the last year under the McKinley tariff, with 1897 since both were depression years. The cut in

25. 1897 and early 1898 were recession years.
26. Imports are on a fiscal year basis.

TABLE 21

IMPORTS AND DUTIES ON COTTON MANUFACTURES, WOOLEN MANUFACTURES,
EARTHENWARE AND CHINAWARE, 1882–1913

(Value in Millions, Duty in Per Cent)

Year	Cotton Manufactures		Woolen Manufactures		Earthenware, Stoneware and Chinaware	
	Value	Duty	Value	Duty	Value	Duty
1882	$31.3	39	$37.3	68	$ 7.0	43
1883	32.4	38	42.6	68	8.9	43
Law of 1883						
1884	28.6	40	41.5	66	4.6	56
1885	27.2	40	36.2	67	4.8	56
1886	29.2	40	40.5	67	5.0	57
1887	29.2	40	44.2	67	5.7	57
1888	28.7	40	47.2	68	6.3	57
1889	27.1	40	52.7	67	6.5	57
1890	29.3	40	54.2	69	7.0	57
McKinley Law October 6, 1890						
1891	29.1	51	43.2	81	8.1	57
1892	28.7	57	35.8	96	8.7	58
1893	33.3	57	37.0	99	9.4	58
1894	21.6	56	19.6	97	6.7	58
Wilson Law August 28, 1894						
1895	33.6	47	36.5	57	9.3	35
1896	32.3	46	48.3	48	10.5	34
1897	35.5	46	48.9	46	10.5	34
Dingley Law July 24, 1897						
1898	26.7	55	13.2	77	6.5	55
1899	31.7	56	14.0	95	7.6	59
1900	39.8	55	15.6	92	8.7	58
1901	39.8	55	14.7	91	9.4	58
1902	44.6	55	17.0	92	9.7	59
1903	51.7	54	19.3	91	10.5	58
1904	48.9	54	17.6	93	11.9	58
1905	49.0	54	18.0	92	11.7	58
1906	61.8	54	22.4	90	12.8	59
1907	73.1	53	22.4	89	13.7	59
1908	66.1	52	19.1	91	13.1	59
1909	61.9	53	18.1	90	10.1	59
Payne-Aldrich Law August 6, 1909						
1910	68.3	56	23.1	90	11.2	59
1911	64.3	56	18.8	88	11.4	58
1912	63.4	56	15.2	83	10.1	58
1913	62.1	55	15.0	82	10.0	58

Source: Statistical Abstract of the United States, 1899 and 1914.

duty on cotton manufactures from 56 to 46 per cent was accompanied by an increase in imports from $22 million in 1894 to $36 million in 1897. The cut in woolen duties from 97 per cent (including compensating rates) to 46 per cent was accompanied by a rise in imports of woolen manufactures from $20 million to almost $50 million. Similarly, in chinaware, the cut in duty from 58 per cent to 34 per cent was accompanied by a rise in imports from $6.7 million to $10.5 million. It is impossible to estimate, however, the extent to which the increase in imports was a result of price elasticity, of the difference in severity of the depressions, or of secular growth.

Relative Decline in Imports of Semidurables

The specific commodity groups which account for the fall in total imports values in the last five years of the nineteenth century were dry goods, clothing and personal furnishings. As a result, imports of semidurable finished goods fell decisively at this time, although certain groups like toys, games and sporting goods held up until the first world war.

Imports of the other major classes of finished goods did not fall decisively relative to output until the first world war. These included the perishables, consumers' durables, producers' durables and construction goods.[27]

Chiefly as a result of the behavior of textile and clothing items, each succeeding peak representing imports of finished goods as a percentage of the total national output of finished goods is lower than the one before it. "Finished imports" fell from almost 6 per cent of "finished output" in 1869 to 5.5 per cent in 1890, to 4.6 per cent in 1895, to 3.5 per cent in 1909, to 2.5 per cent in 1929, to 2 per cent in 1937. The decline in the relative importance of these imports, however, has not been gradual and continuous but was concentrated in three periods. The first decline occurred just before the turn of the century, the second was during the first world war, and the third was during the depression of the 1930s.[28] (See Figure 10.)

The National Bureau import series include duties, and the ratio of the relative importance of imports is correspondingly affected by a change in duties. Thus the decline in the relative importance of finished imports from

27. These data on finished imports, published by the National Bureau of Economic Research, should not be confused with the so-called "economic class" of finished manufactured imports as published by the census. The finished goods series of the National Bureau accounted for from 27 to 29 per cent of total imports. William Howard Shaw, *Value of Commodity Output since 1869*, National Bureau of Economic Research, New York, 1947. The National Bureau has told the present writer that there is some doubt as to whether or not all of the items in Shaw's series are finished goods but that on the whole the possible discrepancy is not very important.

28. The Shaw data extend only to 1919. It has been possible to supplement these published series with unpublished biennial data from 1929 to 1939, furnished by the U.S. Department of Commerce. Unfortunately, this leaves a gap between 1919 and 1929 and nothing later than 1939.

FIGURE 10. IMPORTS[a] OF FINISHED GOODS AS PER CENT OF TOTAL OUTPUT OF FINISHED GOODS,[b] 1869–1939

(*Current Values*)

Source: 1869–1919, Table 22; 1929–1939, unpublished data by U.S. Department of Commerce.
a. Including duties.
b. Excluding construction materials.

1909 to 1913 may be in part due to reduction of duties under the Payne-Aldrich tariff of 1909, as well as to rising prices. It was the durable-goods component which was chiefly responsible for the decline in this period.

The fall in relative importance of finished imports during the first world war also was accentuated both by the lower duties of the Underwood tariff of 1913 and by the inflation of prices.

Though the decline in imports of finished goods relative to output was arrested in the first decade of the twentieth century, some components continued to decline. Thus, imports of dry goods and notions, which amounted to as much as one fourth of domestic production in the 1890s, fell slowly from 20 per cent in 1899 to 16 per cent in 1909. Similarly, imports of clothing and personal furnishings, which amounted to 7 per cent of domestic output in the 1890s, fell to 4 per cent in 1899 and to almost 3 per cent in 1909.

The relative displacement of these specific imports by home production in this period was presumably abetted by the relatively high tariffs on dry goods and clothing. But a single case of this kind is not equivalent to an

TABLE 22

IMPORTS[a] OF FINISHED GOODS BY MAJOR CLASSES AS PER CENT OF OUTPUT OF
FINISHED GOODS OF THE SAME CLASS, 1869, 1879 AND 1889–1919

(*Current Values*)

Year	Total[b]	Perishables	Semi-durables	Consumers' Durables	Producers' Durables	Construction Materials
1869	5.9	4.0	12.4	8.4	.73	3.7
1879	4.0	2.9	7.4	7.2	.36	1.8
1889	4.5	2.7	9.9	9.3	.73	2.4
1890	5.5	3.6	11.6	9.0	.67	1.8
1891	4.5	2.9	9.0	8.7	.79	2.1
1892	4.7	3.0	9.1	9.0	.74	2.0
1893	4.1	2.5	9.3	9.1	.64	2.3
1894	3.6	2.5	7.3	7.5	.39	1.9
1895	4.6	2.4	11.5	9.7	.57	2.4
1896	4.2	2.4	9.9	8.5	.59	2.7
1897	3.9	2.3	9.0	7.4	.38	2.1
1898	3.0	1.8	6.3	7.1	.43	1.9
1899	3.2	2.2	5.7	8.2	.36	2.1
1900	3.1	2.2	5.5	7.8	.57	1.9
1901	3.1	2.1	5.6	9.2	.42	1.9
1902	3.4	2.4	5.9	9.0	.51	2.3
1903	3.4	2.5	5.4	9.4	.47	2.5
1904	3.3	2.6	4.9	8.6	.38	1.9
1905	3.4	2.5	5.1	9.2	.36	1.9
1906	3.5	2.6	5.2	9.7	.40	2.1
1907	3.5	2.7	5.5	8.5	.38	2.0
1908	3.1	2.6	4.2	6.7	.40	1.7
1909	3.5	2.9	4.6	8.7	.73	1.9
1910	3.3	2.7	4.8	7.5	.65	1.8
1911	3.1	2.6	4.0	7.1	.66	1.7
1912	3.1	2.8	4.2	5.8	.63	1.8
1913	2.9	2.8	3.8	5.5	.42	1.7
1914	3.0	3.1	3.7	4.5	.51	1.9
1915	2.2	2.4	2.6	3.2	.26	1.8
1916	2.0	2.1	2.0	3.2	.17	1.5
1917	1.6	2.0	1.6	2.3	.09	1.4
1918	1.3	1.8	1.2	1.6	.10	1.6
1919	1.5	1.6	1.3	3.6	.14	1.5

Source: William Howard Shaw, *Value of Commodity Output since 1869*, National
Bureau of Economic Research, New York, 1947, Table I-1.

a. Including duties.   b. Excluding construction materials.

increase in the over-all effectiveness of the tariff structure. Imports of other
finished manufactures increased relative to home production. Thus, imports of consumers' durable goods rose from roughly 8 per cent of home
production in 1900 to 10 per cent in 1906, while imports of finished
perishable goods increased substantially faster than home production in the
decade ending 1909. (See Table 22.)

How Generally Effective Was the Tariff?

When a historical effect may be traceable to several independent variables, it is difficult to distinguish the influence of any one of them. If, however, a correlation of the over-all result with any one of the possible causal factors turns out to be negative (that is, uncorrelated) in a number of crucial instances, it is at least reasonable to assume that other causes were more influential. Let us compare the behavior of imports since the Civil War with the general changes in tariff which occurred, bearing in mind that the average duty collected reflects changes in the composition of imports as well as legislative changes in duties. The ratio of imports to commodity output provides the best over-all measure of changes in the importance of imports. (See Table 23.)

From the Civil War to Dingley

Despite an increase in duty on a few items, the rise in dutiable imports from 1869 to 1872 was more than half again as great as the rise in domestic manufacturing activity.[29] Duties were cut 10 per cent across the board in 1872. Dutiable imports fell 26 per cent from 1872 to 1875, while manufacturing activity fell 7 per cent. The tariff reduction proved abortive. Duties were restored in 1875 and imports fell a further 10 per cent in the following year while manufacturing activity remained stable.[30]

The higher duties of the McKinley tariff of 1890, contrary to the assumption of most authors, do not appear to have been more restrictive of total imports than earlier tariffs. The ratio of imports values to output under the McKinley tariff compares favorably with that in 1869 and 1889.

An important study of *Industrialization and Foreign Trade* has attributed a decline in manufacturing imports relative to manufacturing output to the McKinley tariff: "In the United States industrial protection after two decades of relatively liberal trade policy was sharply increased by the McKinley Tariff of 1890."[31]

In point of fact, the McKinley tariff raised the average duty on dutiable imports less than 10 per cent and, *by shifting important items to the free list,*

29. In relating imports to the tariff, we use "imports for consumption," which are available only by fiscal years for the period 1869–1918.

30. At constant wholesale prices, the fall in total imports was about two and a half times as great as the fall in manufacturing from 1872 to 1876. We compare imports with manufacturing only because there are no annual estimates of commodity production before 1889. Deflation of imports by wholesale prices is inadequate. Import prices are probably more unstable than wholesale prices.

31. League of Nations, Columbia University Press, 1945, p. 87. The data in this study are five-year averages, which, because of the importance of the cyclical changes, may give a misleading impression of the timing. The National Bureau of Economic Research series of finished commodity imports shows no secular fall in imports relative to commodity output under the McKinley tariff, nor under the Wilson tariff which followed. The decisive fall came with the later Dingley tariff. These data are in current values.

lowered the average duty on all imports by 25 per cent. There was no fall in total imports relative to output (current values) to be explained, except in 1894 when a sharp depression occurred. Dutiable imports declined as a percentage of output from 1890 to 1893, but this does not compare like with like, owing to the removal of revenue duties and the shift of important items like sugar from the dutiable to the free list.[32] (See Table 23.)

The tariff reduction of almost 20 per cent under the Wilson tariff was not accompanied by an increase in the import-output ratio.

The Dingley Tariff

The Dingley tariff of 1897 stands out as the most restrictive (at current prices) of the protective tariffs and possibly the only revision which effectively increased over-all protection. The ratio of imports to output by value fell decisively and has never since regained the levels of 1869 to 1897. There is some evidence, however, to indicate that this represents a displacement in the value rather than the quantity of imports relative to output. Domestic prices rose faster than import prices and more favorable terms of trade prevailed. From 1895–1899 to 1910–1914, the rise in the level of domestic prices was more than one-half greater than the rise in Kreps' index of import prices.[33] It is possible that the higher duties of the Dingley tariff contributed to the relative deflation of import prices.

But even here account must be taken of the fact that 1897 and part of 1898 were depression years which followed quickly on the heels of the depression of 1894.[34] The blowing up of the battleship *Maine* in the Havana harbor and the brief war affected sugar and certain other imports substantially. Wool was shifted to the dutiable list, yet the import-output ratio fell sharply from previous levels for free goods as well as for dutiable imports.

Three quarters of the fall in import values in 1898 can be accounted for by sugar, raw wool and woolen manufactures. However, imports of both

32. Unfortunately we have no statistical series on commodity output at producers' prices after 1939. This is much the best base against which to measure changes in the over-all importance of imports. Estimates of national income for the earlier period were based on sales by producers to which distribution costs were added. Income estimates for later years, however, represent projections of such a benchmark based primarily on retail trade and sales tax data. Cf. 1951 National Income Supplement to the *Survey of Current Business*, Part III.

33. T. J. Kreps, "Import and Export Prices in the United States and the Terms of International Trade, 1880–1914," *Quarterly Journal of Economics*, August 1926. This index of import prices is based on 29 commodities, which represent from 30 to 40 per cent of imports. But the behavior of the index is dominated by the price of coffee, sugar and wool.

34. Although output did not decline for the entire year 1898, the standard pattern of business cycles fell briefly in 1898 to the level of the trough at the end of 1897. The standard pattern remained well below the secular trend line. Edwin Frickey, *Economic Fluctuations in the United States*, Harvard University Press, Cambridge, 1942, chart 34, following p. 338. See also W. M. Persons, *Forecasting Business Cycles*, Wiley, New York, 1931, p. 198.

TABLE 23

FREE AND DUTIABLE IMPORTS FOR CONSUMPTION AS PER CENT OF FINISHED
COMMODITY OUTPUT[a] IN CURRENT VALUES, BY TARIFF LAW PERIODS, 1869, 1879
AND 1889–1939

Fiscal Year (1869–1918) or Calendar Year	As Per Cent of Output[b]			Average Rate on Dutiable Imports	Free Imports as Per Cent of Total Imports
	Free Imports	Dutiable Imports[c]	Total Imports		
1869	0.8	13.7	14.5	47	6
1879	4.1	8.5	12.6	45	32
Law of 1883					
1889	5.0	9.5	14.5	45	35
1890	5.3	10.1	15.4	44	34
McKinley Law October 6, 1890					
1891	7.1	8.7	15.8	46	45
1892	8.4	6.6	15.0	49	56
1893	7.8	7.3	15.1	50	52
1894	7.7	5.3	13.0	50	59
Wilson Law August 28, 1894					
1895	7.2	6.8	14.0	42	52
1896	7.3	7.7	15.0	40	49
1897	7.0	7.5	14.5	42	48
Dingley Law July 24, 1897					
1898	5.0	5.0	10.0	49	50
1899	4.4	5.7	10.1	52	44
1900	5.0	6.4	11.4	49	44
1901	4.3	5.9	10.2	50	42
1902	4.7	6.0	10.7	50	44
1903	5.0	6.5	11.5	49	43
1904	5.1	6.0	11.1	49	46
1905	5.4	6.0	11.4	45	48
1906	5.0	6.1	11.1	44	45
1907	5.5	6.6	12.1	43	45
1908	5.1	6.4	11.5	43	44
1909	5.1	5.8	10.9	43	47
Payne-Aldrich Law August 6, 1909					
1910	6.0	6.2	12.2	42	49
1911	6.0	5.8	11.8	41	51
1912	6.2	5.3	11.5	40	54
1913	6.6	5.2	11.8	40	56

(*Continued on facing page*)

TABLE 23 (*Continued*)

Fiscal Year (1869–1918) or Calendar Year	As Per Cent of Output[b]			Average Rate on Dutiable Imports	Free Imports as Per Cent of Total Imports
	Free Imports	Dutiable Imports[c]	Total Imports		
Underwood Law October 4, 1913					
1914	8.1	5.3	13.4	38	60
1915	7.0	4.2	11.2	33	63
1916	7.7	3.5	11.2	31	69
1917	7.2	3.1	10.3	27	70
1918	6.7	2.3	9.0	24	74
1919	7.6	3.1	10.7	21	71
1919[d]	7.8	3.2	11.0	21	71
1920	8.3	5.3	13.6	16	61
1921	6.1	3.9	10.0	29	61
1922	7.0	4.4	11.4	38	61
Fordney-McCumber Law September 22, 1922					
1923	6.8	4.9	11.7	36	58
1924	6.9	4.7	11.6	37	59
1925	8.0	4.3	12.3	38	65
1926	8.2	4.2	12.4	39	66
1927	7.8	4.3	12.1	39	64
1928	7.5	3.9	11.4	39	66
1929	7.6	3.8	11.4	40	66
1930	6.7	3.3	10.0	45	67
Hawley-Smoot Law June 18, 1930					
1931	5.8	2.9	8.7	53	67
1932	5.1	2.5	7.6	59	67
1933	5.0	2.9	7.9	54	63
1935	4.7	3.3	8.0	43	59
1937	5.6	3.9	9.5	38	59
1939	4.6	2.9	7.5	37	61

Sources: Imports and duties, U.S. Tariff Commission; finished output, 1869–1919, William H. Shaw, *Value of Commodity Output since 1869*, National Bureau of Economic Research, New York, 1947, Table I-1; 1919–1933, Simon Kuznets, *Commodity Flow and Capital Formation*, National Bureau of Economic Research, New York, 1938, Vol. I, Table II-7; unpublished output data, 1935–1939, U.S. Department of Commerce.

a. Output excluding construction materials.

b. Imports and duties are for fiscal years 1869–1918, calendar years thereafter; output is for calendar years.

c. Excluding duties.

d. Kuznets' output data.

sugar and raw wool were spectacularly high in 1897, presumably in anticipation of the higher duties of the Dingley tariff. Moreover, despite the duty, raw wool imports, once the inventory had been consumed, rose to higher levels in relation to domestic mill consumption than in previous decades.

Imports of hides and lead continued to increase under the Dingley tariff although the duty on both had been increased.

Coffee imports, which were duty-free, declined substantially in 1898 because of a sharp fall in price. But imports of raw silk and rubber increased.

If anything, Dingley duties became less, rather than more, restrictive in the course of time.

A Doubtful Interpretation

The fall in average duties within the life of the Dingley tariff, from 52 per cent in 1899 to 43 per cent in 1907, returned average duties to the level of the previous Wilson tariff. At the conclusion of *The Tariff History of the United States*, Taussig attempts to explain this substantial decline, which continued under the Payne-Aldrich Law of 1909:

> From 1897 to 1912 there is a slow decline in the average rate of duty, due to the circumstance that the free imports form a larger proportion of the total, which again is due to a tariff so high as often to prohibit the importation of dutiable articles.[35]

While high duties unquestionably exclude some imports, there is no evidence that the entire tariff structure became progressively restrictive, which is the point of question.

In the first place, dutiable imports increased faster than free goods under the Dingley tariff.[36] It is only the decline in the average rate on dutiable imports that requires comment. The explanation probably lies in the rising price level, which necessarily reduced the ad valorem equivalent of specific duties. Import prices increased one third between the years 1898 and 1907. The decline in average rates of duty was gradual during the decade, precisely as would be expected from the gradual rise in prices. The blind forces of inflation and deflation produced changes in effective duties as great as those made by Congress.

Taussig apparently mistook the effect of rising prices on average duties for an increase in the effectiveness of high duties. Actually duties were lowered. The point is an important one because Taussig's explanation has been used by various writers in an effort to reconcile a fall in duties with a fall in imports.

It is difficult to equate the 50 per cent average duty on dutiable imports in 1893–1894 with the 50 per cent average duty in 1901–1902 because of the

35. *Op. cit.*, p. 530.

36. The data in Table 23 are not identical with Taussig's. As he observed, the figures in successive editions of the *Statistical Abstract of the United States* were not always consistent. The more rapid rise of dutiable imports was probably a depression-to-prosperity phenomenon.

shift of items from the free list to the dutiable column under the Dingley tariff of 1897. There was a substantial increase in the average rate in relation to total imports. But the reduction from 50 per cent on dutiable imports in 1901–1902 to 40 per cent in 1912–1913 unquestionably represented a real reduction, not a bogus one as Taussig assumed. The ratio of imports to output, however, never recovered to earlier levels. Changes in composition of imports and the necromancy of the averages may have played a role here, but it seems more likely that this failure reflects chiefly the fact that the effect of raising and lowering the tariff is not symmetrical in a world of changing costs.

The Golden 1920s

The experience under the Fordney-McCumber tariff of 1922 is one of the most interesting in American tariff history. Protection is commonly re-garded as having reached a new high at that time. It was with reference to this tariff bill that Taussig wrote:

> The outcome was a tariff with rates higher than any in the long series of pro-tective measures of the whole period. It went beyond the acts of 1890, 1897, 1909. The special conditions of 1921–1922 led to an extreme of protection which few had thought possible.[37]

This evaluation creates the impression that over-all protection was in-creased. It is quite clear, however, that no decline in the relative importance of total imports took place. On the contrary, the ratio of imports to output under the Fordney-McCumber Law compares favorably with that under the earlier Dingley and Payne-Aldrich laws.

Dutiable imports were definitely lower in relation to output, but this was offset by higher imports of free goods. If there was any period in American tariff history in which lower average duties resulted from duties so high as to totally exclude certain imports, it was probably the early period covered by the Fordney-McCumber tariff. But this is not at all clear.

The efficiency of American industry, which had been given a special boost by the experience of the first world war, increased rapidly in the 1920s. According to some writers, this would be expected to have retarded the growth of imports. The facts, however, indicate the contrary.

It is the present custom to look back with regret on the relatively high level of imports in the 1920s—and not without reason. The same percentage of imports to domestic output now would solve most of our problems—or so it appears. It is curious that those who attribute the failures of trade to the tariff are apparently untroubled by the fact that imports were high in the era of the 1920s, which represented "an extreme of protection which

37. Taussig, *op. cit.*, p. 453.

few had thought possible." This is not to imply that prosperity was chiefly due to the tariff. The favorable level of imports was due to prosperity, and the effect of high incomes more than offset the increase in the tariff.

In view of the favorable experience under the higher duties of the Fordney-McCumber tariff, definitive conclusions with respect to the displacement of imports under the earlier Dingley tariff would seem unwarranted. A more adequate measure of import prices is needed to determine if the quantity as well as the value of imports declined relative to output. We would also like to know a good deal more than we do about the shifts in terms of trade when prices turned up in 1897 following the long decline which had begun at the close of the Civil War.

It seems most extraordinary that the Dingley tariff, which has not been regarded as a particular high-water mark in the rising tide of restrictionism, should have appeared so much more restrictive than the McKinley or the Fordney-McCumber tariffs.

The Tariff and History

Short-term changes in the value of imports appear to correlate more closely with prosperity and depression than with changes in the tariff. With the possible exception of the Dingley tariff, the changes in duties which began in 1872 did not decisively reduce the over-all importance of imports in relation to domestic output. In this respect, the McKinley tariff of 1890 seemed to have had no important effect. Similarly, there is little evidence of a decisive change in the relative importance of total imports due to changes in the tariff during the first three decades of the twentieth century.[38] *Tariff levels were not the controlling factor in determining the over-all importance of imports.*

Broadly speaking, to be sure, the American economy since the Civil War has become less and less dependent on the outside world for imports of finished goods. This general trend probably was accelerated by tariff protection, but might have taken place in any event. Until 1938, the relative decline in importance of finished commodity imports was offset (except for the break in 1897–1898) by rising imports of agricultural products and industrial crude materials.

We proceed now to examine the Trade Agreements Program, which inaugurated a policy of lower tariffs.

38. The relative decline in dutiable imports under the lower Underwood duties during the first world war is explained by the fact that manufactured imports were not available.

PART II

OBSTACLES TO IMPORTS

Chapter 5

The Trade Agreements Program

THE RECIPROCAL TRADE AGREEMENTS ACT of 1934 represents an innovation in traditional American tariff making. Sumner Welles hailed it as "one spot of sanity in a world outlook that seemed wholly and hopelessly dark."[1]

By this new departure the United States took the lead in seeking tariff reduction through bargaining with other countries. Reduction of American duties depends on the reciprocal reduction of foreign restrictions on our exports. As a corollary, the tariff-making process is shifted from the Congress to the executive branch of government. The American Trade Agreements Program does not seek to provide for the exchange of specified quantities of specified commodities. Trade is left in the hands of private traders. The agreements provide for reciprocal reduction of tariffs and bind certain commodities against tariff increases, though they often permit the substitution of other restrictions on trade.

However, the policy underlying tariff concessions is not nearly so liberal as many supporters of the program have supposed and would have liked. It is important to recognize at the outset that the Trade Agreements Program does not represent a clear and unconditional victory of freer trade over protectionism. There has always been a dualism in the new policy. Tariffs are to be reduced—but home industry is to be protected against serious injury from foreign competition.

Background of the Program

The basic historical fact is that innovations, mechanization and development of mass production techniques have given America's largest industries a competitive advantage in world markets. The weight of our vastly greater wealth means high productivity and low unit costs compared with other nations, which cannot afford so much capital equipment and such frequent modernization. America's dynamic industries no longer need the protection of a high tariff wall to the same extent as in the nineteenth century. The other side of this coin is that our relatively stagnant industries are often less able to compete in a free world market because their costs have not been reduced as rapidly as costs in the more progressive home

1. Sumner Welles, "Postwar Trade Policies of the United States," *International Conciliation*, May 1943, p. 394.

industries. It seems reasonable to believe that the Trade Agreements Program was made possible by the historical change which gave leading American industries higher productivity and a superior competitive position. However, the growing export interests of leading home industries have rarely asserted their new position as effectively as do the lesser industries which continue to benefit from protection. The American market is more important than the potential export market and fear of impairing the price structure in the home market has outweighed the interest in exports.

Beyond a doubt, the new competitive position of American industry after the first world war would have justified a continued downward revision of protective tariffs that was well begun with the Underwood tariff of 1913. Instead, with the Fordney-McCumber duties of 1922, there came an attempt to establish a new high tariff peak. This was followed by the futile effort to raise the wall of protectionism still higher under the Hawley-Smoot tariff of 1930.

One of the most common arguments for lower tariffs since the first world war is the change of the United States from a debtor nation to the world's largest creditor. With the collapse of foreign investment in the 1930s, many were convinced that our high tariff policy must be reversed if we were ever to collect the more than $1 billion annual debt service due this country. Although the service on debt owed by foreigners does create a serious problem in a severe business depression, the general argument that a creditor nation must lower its tariffs is a dubious one. It neglects the possibility that continued expansion of new foreign investment may offset the return flow of repayment on past debt. There is no economic law requiring creditors to consume the service and amortization payments on past debts; they may be reinvested instead. Fundamentally, creditor-debtor relationship is no different in foreign trade than in domestic trade, provided exchange difficulties do not arise. It is desirable for both economic and political reasons that America should have a net outflow of capital, which means also a net outflow of goods. In a peaceful and orderly world, this might continue for generations after we had become a creditor nation. To become a creditor nation does not create economic forces which dictate that service and amortization payments will exceed new foreign investment; and the failure of foreign investment is not associated with either creditor nation status or high tariffs, but with nationalism and world disorder.

The historical change calling for lower American tariffs was not the change by which the United States became a creditor nation; it was the revolutionary improvement in the productivity and cost position of home industry. The infant industries of Hamilton, Clay and McKinley were grown up, and by 1934 the time for a change was overripe. American commodity exports had long exceeded imports, and this export surplus increased with the growth of foreign investment in the 1920s. Thus, American business had become increasingly export-minded. The anomaly is that apparently a great depression was required before this new interest in exports could be brought to bear on the tariff question.

From the indefensible position the United States had assumed with the Hawley-Smoot duties, any time was a good time to reduce tariffs. Nonetheless, it is a relatively poor time to cut duties when industry already suffers from long and severe unemployment. The objective of tariff reduction is to shift workers and other resources which are relatively unproductive in the protected industries to more productive employment. But inefficient production is better than no employment at all, and the case for suffering painful adjustments in the name of "the best use of resources" has a rather hollow sound when millions of workers are producing nothing at all. Although the policy of tariff reduction has been executed mainly in a period of recovery and prosperity, the destiny of the Reciprocal Trade Agreements Program has been affected by its origin as an emergency measure in the midst of a long and severe depression. The plain fact is that the new policy was sold to the Congress mainly as a means of increasing American exports by reduction of foreign duties rather than by the acceptance of more competitive imports. Competitive imports were not wanted and were to be regulated in accordance with the needs of home industry. Thus, the circumstance of its origin is vital to understanding the future of the program.

Tariffs versus American Exports

Between 1929 and 1933 the volume of world trade had dropped two thirds by value and about one third by quantity. For the United States the decline was even greater—the United States share of world trade had dropped from 16 to 11 per cent in the five years following 1929. The export industries and agriculture suffered acutely from this loss of export markets.

In the light of subsequent efforts to restore world trade, there is a nightmarish quality about the fact that the duties actually collected under the Hawley-Smoot tariff[2] during the years 1930–1933 amounted to an average rate of 53 per cent on all dutiable items. Duties under the Hawley-Smoot

2. Hearings on tariff revision were begun in the spring of 1929 before the collapse of the stock market. The intention was to seek additional protection for agriculture, which had not shared equally in the prosperity of the 1920s, owing in part to the decline of world agricultural prices. But the Congressional tariff-making process of logrolling got out of hand and the ill-fated act of 1930 turned out to be a wholesale effort to increase protection. The act was not well received at home and the world depression brought increased restrictions against American exports. How much of this was retaliation is open to question. (For the retaliation argument, cf. J. M. Jones, Jr., *Tariff Retaliation*, University of Pennsylvania Press, Philadelphia, 1934.) The Hawley-Smoot tariff was old-fashioned protectionism and not primarily an antidepression measure. On the other hand, the widespread increase in restrictions by other countries which followed seems to have been primarily an effort to support home employment in the depression.

tariff, many of which were unnecessary at the time even from the viewpoint of a protectionist, were substantially increased in effect by the subsequent fall in prices. Average duties collected on dutiable imports had increased from 27 per cent under the Underwood tariff, 1913–1922, to 39 per cent under the Fordney-McCumber Law, 1922–1930. It was estimated that the Hawley-Smoot Act would raise the average duty to about 45 per cent (with stable prices).

The United States tariff schedule carries many specific duties[3] of so much per unit or per pound. Thus, the result of the great fall in prices was to raise duties as a percentage of import values: by 1932 they amounted to 59 per cent.

Leading Reasons for the Trade Agreements Act

The father of the Trade Agreements Program was Cordell Hull, then the new Secretary of State from Tennessee. His persuasive powers managed to combine the appeal of export markets with the broad civilizing function of world trade in which destiny had cast the United States for the leading role. There is a revealing passage in Hull's *Memoirs:*

The year 1916 is a milestone in my political thinking. Then for the first time openly I enlarged my views on trade and tariffs from the national to the international theater. Hitherto, I had fought hard for lower tariffs, largely because of their immediate domestic effect. I believed that high tariffs meant a higher cost of living for American citizens. They assisted in building up monopolies and trusts. By cutting down the sales by other countries to us, they also cut down the purchases by other countries from us.

But toward 1916 I embraced the philosophy I carried throughout my twelve years as Secretary of State, into the Trade Agreements . . . to me, unhampered trade dovetailed with peace; high tariffs, trade barriers and unfair economic competition with war . . . I reasoned that, if we could get a freer flow of trade— freer in the sense of fewer discriminations and obstructions—so that one country would not be deadly jealous of another and the living standards of all countries might rise, thereby eliminating dissatisfaction that breeds war, we might have a reasonable chance for lasting peace.[4]

This was not, however, the argument that carried the day in Congress. At the time of debate by Congress, the leading reasons given by the Secretary of State for asking enactment of the Trade Agreements bill were: (1) the failure of trade to maintain the prewar rate of growth, (2) world unemployment, (3) the need to expand exports. Secretary Hull argued that if world trade had continued to expand at the same rate as before World War I it would have amounted to $50 billion instead of $12 billion. He said that 30 million workers were unemployed in the world and that "nearly 80

3. Specific duties are in contrast to ad valorem duties, which are expressed as a *percentage* of the value of the import.
4. *The Memoirs of Cordell Hull,* Macmillan, New York, 1948, Vol. I, p. 81.

per cent of the world's population of 2 billion persons are living below the poverty line. Some enterprising nation or nations will and must produce and export the many different commodities necessary to supply these people thus in need."[5] This great opportunity belonged to the United States but something had to be done to reverse the trend of restrictionism throughout the world. This was to be achieved by the process of tariff bargaining.[6] "The primary object of this new proposal," Hull later told the Ways and Means Committee, "is both to reopen the old and seek new outlets for our surplus products."[7]

With Hull, this emphasis was not merely an *ad hoc* argument to meet the exigencies of the day. A survey of his earlier career in the Congress shows that he emphasized primarily, though not exclusively, the exchange of (1) noncompetitive goods, and (2) those goods which supplement but do not displace home production.

The new trade policy of 1934 owes much to the influence and persuasive powers of Cordell Hull. His view of the nature of foreign trade was a far cry from classical liberalism. He emphasized that international trade "does not mean the displacement of established home production and trade of one country by another," but "is really the mutually profitable exchange by nations of their surpluses."[8] Hull declared:

International trade is simply a system of barter or exchange of goods and products between nations. Each nation must sell its surpluses to other nations needing or desiring them, while in turn it purchases from others such goods and commodities as it may specially desire, chiefly those it does not itself produce at all, or in sufficient quantities, or the production of which is not economically justifiable.[9]

The Trade Agreements Act

The policy of reciprocal trade agreements is that trade will be expanded "without injury to American producers." In asking for passage of the bill, President Roosevelt termed it necessary for the "successful building up of trade"; the aim was "to modify existing duties and import restrictions in such a way as will benefit American agriculture and industry"; the measure was "part of an emergency program necessitated by the economic crisis,

5. *New York Times*, March 9, 1934, Report of House Hearings.

6. France doubled the duties on certain United States exports in March 1934. This can be interpreted either as delayed retaliation against the Hawley-Smoot duties or anticipation of the bargaining under the Hull Program. See *Congressional Record*, March 24, 1934.

7. Hearings on H.J.Res. 407, 76th Cong., 3d sess., 1940, pp. 7–8.

8. *Congressional Record*, December 19, 1925, p. 1182 and April 14, 1926, p. 7472. Cf. W. R. Allen, "The International Trade Philosophy of Cordell Hull, 1907–1933," *American Economic Review*, March 1953, pp. 101–116.

9. *Congressional Record*, May 10, 1926, p. 9103, quoted in Allen, *op. cit.* The final phrase allows Hull some leeway for traditional liberalism.

. . . an essential step in the program of national economic recovery." The classical principles of trade were submerged by the stress on exports and national recovery. Exercise of the authority to reduce duties "must be weighed in the light of the latest information so as to give assurance that no sound and important American interest will be injuriously disturbed . . . the adjustment of our foreign trade relations must rest on the premise of undertaking to benefit and not to injure such interests."[10]

This commitment to maintain the protection of home industry under executive paternalism has dogged the program from the outset. Even in the triumphant early days of the New Deal majorities, hostages were given in order to get the legislation through Congress. Otherwise, perhaps, there could have been no "new" policy.

The search for export markets for agricultural surpluses was one of the principal supports for the program. On the industrial side the program was presented as a means to reduce unemployment.

The opposition placed its emphasis on the argument that a depression is a poor time to seek lower tariffs. Senator Barbour said:

I am opposed to international bargaining with our tariff because I am convinced that, no matter how we may proceed or for what purpose, it means only in the end no real bargaining at all but simply the undermining of our protective policy, *actually more necessary than ever before.*[11]

While the argument for national self-sufficiency was mentioned by the opposition, the admissibility of noncompetitive imports was never seriously questioned.

The persistent dollar shortage since the second world war has been interpreted as showing an urgent need to increase American imports. Consequently, the Trade Agreements Program has come to be regarded in many quarters as an instrument for substituting "trade for aid" by increasing American imports.

This view, however, is derived from events. It was never the purpose of the act to increase imports more than exports. On the contrary, the bill was enacted expressly "for the purpose of expanding foreign markets for products of the United States"[12] and in the interests of combating "the present economic depression."

The policy was that tariff reduction would be *reciprocal* and, therefore, that exports would be increased. The act recognized, however, that in

10. Text of President Roosevelt's Message to Congress, *Operation of the Trade Agreements Program, June 1934 to April 1948*, 1949, Part II, U.S. Tariff Commission.

11. *Congressional Record*, March 5, 1934, p. 2680. (Italics supplied.)

12. ". . . as a means of assisting in the present emergency in restoring the American standard of living, in overcoming domestic unemployment . . ." Public Law 316, Section 350(a), June 12, 1934.

order to gain foreign markets, the United States would need to afford "corresponding market opportunities for foreign products in the United States." But the provision for the admission of imports was, in turn, modified by euphonious language foreshadowing the "escape clause." A cardinal principle of the program provides for suspension of tariff concessions which "cause or threaten serious injury" to domestic producers.[13] In the declaration of the act, imports were to be admitted "in accordance with the characteristics and needs of various branches of American production." This ambiguous language seriously compromised the program, for "by regulating the admission of foreign goods" in accordance with the needs of individual industries, it was intended, apparently, to limit competitive imports to levels which would not displace home production.

Executive Powers

The act authorized the President, when he found tariffs and other restrictions "unduly burdening and restricting," to negotiate trade agreements which reduce duties and other barriers to trade. Thus certain tariff-making powers were delegated to the President, who was given wide discretion to reduce import duties.[14] Reciprocal reduction of restrictions by other countries is not formally required by the act, but is firmly established by legislative history and usage.

A maximum reduction of 50 per cent from the 1930 tariff schedule was provided by the 1934 law. No item may be shifted from the dutiable to the free list. When the act was extended in 1945, an amendment provided a *further* 50 per cent limit on reductions from the January 1, 1945 duties, "however established." Thus, the maximum possible reduction of those duties already reduced by 50 per cent became 75 per cent from the 1930 level. But since the actual reduction from 1930 levels in effect on January 1, 1945, averaged 32 per cent, the maximum permissible average reduction was 66 per cent of the 1930 level and varied from 50 to 75 per cent on individual items.

The power to reduce tariffs by a maximum of 50 per cent of the 1945 level has not been fully utilized and no further power was delegated by the

13. See "Escape Clause," p. 116.

14. As a departure from tariff making by the Congress, the trade agreements differ fundamentally from the earlier "flexible tariff" provision of the act of 1922, which authorized the President to raise or lower duties by not more than 50 per cent on the "equalization of cost" principle. The earlier delegation of power was not discretionary. See F. W. Taussig, *Free Trade, The Tariff and Reciprocity*, Macmillan, New York, 1920, p. 135. For a somewhat more charitable view see Mark A. Smith, "The United States Flexible Tariff," in *Explorations in Economics*, McGraw-Hill, New York, 1936, pp. 169–178.

Congress until 1955. Tariff concessions from 1945 to 1953 reduced average rates by 32 per cent.

The act of 1955 extends the power to reduce rates by up to 15 per cent, spread over three years, and further provides that ad valorem rates above 50 per cent may be reduced to 50 per cent. In all, the Congress has made three grants of power to reduce rates, in 1934, 1945 and 1955.

The act of 1934 lays down no criteria for the modification of duties beyond the general provisions (1) that duties "unduly burdening and restrictive" can be modified and (2) that imports are to be admitted "in accordance with the characteristics and needs of various branches of American production." Within the 50 per cent limit, executive discretion appears to be limited only by the broad objective of expanding exports.

The virtual absence of criteria has not given the American tariff negotiators a free hand, but rather the contrary. They have been free to reduce duties only where it would have little immediate effect on competitive imports. Whatever the law may provide, the real power of the President in important matters has been narrowly circumscribed. First, the Congress has held close rein by enacting the law for short periods so that it has been necessary for the President to come back to Congress ten times in twenty-one years for extension of the act. Second, the President has had to use his delegated power in a manner that would not injure even individual branches of home industry.

Congress renewed this authority to negotiate trade agreements at three-year intervals until 1943, and thereafter renewed it in 1945, 1948, 1949, 1951, 1953, 1954 and 1955—ten times in all. The form of the act remained intact until 1948, when the so-called "peril point" limitation was imposed. Under this provision, the Tariff Commission must determine in advance the maximum concession that can be offered without danger to home industry. Although this limitation was eliminated in the extension of 1949, even more restrictive provisions were added in the renewal of 1951. These were again renewed in 1953. Crippling amendments to the escape clause in 1955 are the most serious of all. These restrictive amendments reflect a shift in the balance of power from the President to the Congress.

Flexible Tariffs a Danger

Little has been heard in recent years of the flexible tariff provision of the act of 1930,[15] which provides for tariff adjustment to equalize the difference between foreign and domestic costs. It is still in effect, however, on those items not covered by trade agreements. Under this provision, the Tariff Commission investigated the foreign cost of producing almonds in 1949 to determine if higher duties were needed.

15. Section 336, Title III.

United States production of almonds tripled from 1935–1939 to 1949, while world production increased less than 10 per cent. United States production increased from 9 per cent of world production in 1935–1939 to 24 per cent in 1949. Imports fell from a major to a minor share of domestic consumption.

A majority of the Commission, with Brossard and Gregg dissenting, was unable to make a finding "owing to the fact that the available evidence on costs of production in the principal competing country (Italy) does not disclose adequate information on which to base a finding of costs of production of almonds in that country."[16] The dissenting Commissioners believed that the cost data showed that United States costs exceeded Italian costs by "at least as much or more than the existing duty."

The flexible tariff could do much harm. Rising prices and tariff concessions have already taken care of most of the tariff reduction that would be possible under the flexible tariff principle. In any event, this is unimportant since it only permits the scaling down of excess protection. The principal hope for expanding trade lies in the expectation that American costs in some industries will rise faster than foreign costs. Through domestic competition for resources, rising productivity in the more progressive industries should raise costs in the less progressive industries, thus creating higher costs which are not matched by higher productivity. The flexible tariff is expressly designed to provide higher tariffs in this situation. It has fallen into disuse in recent years because it was not needed, but we may hear more about it in the future. The flexible tariff is more restrictive than the escape clause. Many industries, although not seriously injured, might be entitled to protection on a showing of costs.

The flexible tariff was first enacted in the law of 1922. In the twenty-seven years 1922–1949, the Tariff Commission made 112 cost investigations. In 71 cases the President changed the duty in accordance with the findings of the Commission: rates were increased in 44 cases, decreased in 20 cases, and both increased and decreased in 7 cases. The Commission recommended no change in 36 cases and in 5 cases the President did not make the changes recommended by the Commission. The administrative difficulty of cost studies is one thing which operates against extensive use of the principle.

Protection of Home Industry

It is difficult for responsible officials to claim that tariffs were reduced in order to shift domestic resources to more productive employment. On the contrary, the administration has always vigorously defended its stewardship in maintaining essential protection.

16. *Almonds*, U.S. Tariff Commission, Report No. 167, 1950, p. 5.

In 1940 Secretary Hull told the Congress:

We have reduced duties only in those cases in which, after a most careful examination of all relevant factors, it was found that existing duties were unnecessarily and unduly burdensome, and we have done so only in those cases in which other countries have agreed to accord better treatment to our exports in return for tariff adjustments on our part. We have reduced duties only to the extent to which, after an equally careful examination, it was found that such adjustments would not be prejudicial to any established branch of production in agriculture, in mining, or in manufacturing industry. Where necessary, as an additional safeguard, we have limited the amount of imports which would be permitted to come in at the reduced rate of duty.[17]

In hearings on the Extension Act of 1945, which provided permissible reductions in duty of 50 per cent from the level of January 1, 1945, Will Clayton, one of the stalwart supporters of the program, testified:

A rumor has freely circulated that certain American industries have been singled out as inefficient industries and that if the additional authority provided for in the bill is granted the State Department will use such authority to trade off these inefficient industries for other industries which can compete in the world market. Nothing could be further from the truth than this. The State Department has never construed the Trade Agreements Act as a license to remake the industrial or agricultural pattern of America.[18]

When Harry Truman became President he reaffirmed the commitment against injury to home industry in a letter to the Speaker of the House, Sam Rayburn.

I have had drawn to my attention statements to the effect that this increased authority might be used in such a way as to endanger or "trade out" segments of American industry, American agriculture, or American labor. No such action was taken under President Roosevelt and Cordell Hull, and no such action will take place under my Presidency.[19]

Escape Clause

The "escape clause," which provides for suspension of concessions that "cause or threaten serious injury" to any home industry, is a cardinal principle of American policy. Without the commitment that no branch of home industry will be endangered by tariff concessions, the trade agreements legislation probably could not have been renewed and extended. The

17. Hearings on H.J.Res. 407, Secretary Hull, before the House Committee on Ways and Means, 76th Cong., 3d sess., 1940, p. 9, quoted by William Diebold in *New Directions in Our Trade Policy*, Council on Foreign Relations, New York, 1941, pp. 16–17.

18. Before the Senate Finance Committee, quoted by Senator Millikin, *Congressional Record*, September 8, 1949, p. 12647.

19. Quoted by H. Wickliffe Rose, *Improving Our Tariff Program*, American Tariff League Publication No. 127, p. 7; cf. Senator Millikin's statement, *Congressional Record*, September 8, 1949, p. 12651 f.

"escape clause," as such, was first formally expressed by Executive Order No. 9832, February 25, 1947, requiring that all new trade agreements reserve for the United States the right to withdraw a concession, if unforeseen results of the concession threaten or cause serious injury to any branch of home industry. It was subsequently included in prewar agreements. Substantially the same protection was included in the General Agreement on Tariffs and Trade at Geneva in 1947. No concession is ever made which is expected to injure home industry. The escape procedure is a final protection against "unforeseen" developments.

An appreciation of the commitment not to injure home industry is indispensable to understanding the program. It helps to explain why the substantial reduction of American tariffs has had so little effect on imports. As will be shown in more detail, our negotiators were under the heavy obligation to reduce precisely those duties which would have no serious effect on competitive imports.[20] This leaves open the possibility of permitting increased competition from imports sufficient to retard the growth of less efficient home industries. This is a long-term process. Moreover, it will require that "serious injury" be interpreted to mean only the *absolute* displacement of home industry. In other words, the United States would accept the *relative* displacement of home industry by imports, and tariff concessions would not be withdrawn because imports absorbed a larger share of a growing market.

How Trade Agreements Are Made

The statistical accomplishments in tariff reduction are quite impressive.[21] However, it is procedure rather than statistics that must be examined to understand why the impressive reduction in tariffs has had so little effect on imports. In brief, all tariff concessions are thoroughly screened and American negotiators are authorized to make only those concessions which do not threaten home industry. The results tend to produce a maximum of tariff reduction with a minimum of imports.

The entire trade agreements plan has never been an exclusive State Department responsibility. The President is required by law to consult the Departments of State, Treasury, Commerce, Agriculture and Defense, and the Tariff Commission. In practice the Department of Labor and, in later years, the ECA have been consulted, as have other agencies when problems of particular interest to them arose. The Department of Interior, for example, is consulted when minerals are involved and became a regular

20. The question of injury and the specific industries which claim to have been injured are considered in Chapter 19. See also Chapter 21 on handmade glass and Chapter 22 on watches.
21. These are considered in the next chapter.

member in 1952. Thus, the decisions which emerge from the executive departments represent the consensus of specialists representing the diverse interests of the Cabinet and other executive agencies. This form of working organization is not only required by law but is dictated by the sensitivity of Congress to protection of American industry.

The Interdepartmental Committee, known as the Trade Agreements Committee, explores the advisability of a trade agreement. After a study of the pertinent facts, if the conclusion of the Trade Agreements Committee is favorable, and if an exchange between governments indicates a reasonable prospect of a successful negotiation, and if the President concurs, a public announcement is made of this government's intention to negotiate. The announcement is accompanied by a "public list" of import items on which concessions will be considered. Careful preliminary screening by all interested governmental departments goes into the preparation of this list.

The lists of items for possible concession and notices of hearings are widely disseminated; copies are sent to every member of Congress, to district offices of governmental departments and to other distribution points where they are available to interested parties. Publication of the list is an open invitation to interested parties to express their views and, judging from the voluminous records of the hearings, at least one and frequently several witnesses appear personally to make representations about each product.[22]

Members of Congress may make representations for constituents. Up to January 1940, more than 160 members of Congress had appeared before the Committee Panels.[23] The adequacy of the opportunity for being heard has seldom been questioned. Complaints on the hearing procedure have usually centered upon the time limitation imposed by the volume of work to be done and upon the ineffectiveness of the hearings from the public viewpoint. Business representatives have sometimes complained to the Congress that the hearings were courteous but futile.

The decision to offer concessions is made with solicitous care for domestic interests. After information and views are obtained from written memoranda and from hearings, the Trade Agreements Committee reviews the data item by item and makes recommendations as to what concessions should be offered to the negotiating countries. No concession is made except from the published lists.

22. The records of these hearings, except the briefs and other testimony given in confidence, are available for examination in the Office of the Secretary, Committee for Reciprocity Information, U.S. Tariff Commission, Washington.

23. There may be some duplication in this figure. See *Extension of Reciprocal Trade Agreements Act*, Hearings, House Ways and Means Committee, 76th Cong., 3d sess., 1940, pp. 1097–1103.

In making its decisions, the Committee considers such factors as (1) the importance of imports in relation to domestic production, (2) the trend of imports, (3) the extent to which they are competitive with domestic output, and (4) the competitive strength of domestic industry in third markets as indicated by the trend of exports. The Committee also considers the relative importance of hand labor and machinery in production, the extent to which an industry is diversified or concentrated geographically, and the national security significance of skills and equipment peculiar to the industry. These and many other factors relating to the competitive strength and national importance of an industry are weighed against the possibility of import injury to the import industries.

Safeguards

Decisions of the Trade Agreements Committee have generally been unanimous because of its reluctance to recommend concessions where any member feels strongly that a domestic producer will be injured.[24] Because of the diversity of opinion embodied in the recommendations, the practice of unanimous consent produces extremely cautious results.

Ways have been found to reduce duties and, at the same time, avoid increased competition from imports. The evidence is palpable in the wide use of such restrictive devices as (1) narrow product descriptions and classifications, and (2) quotas which set an absolute limit on the volume of imports or limit the amount which can be imported at reduced duties. In a memorandum prepared for the information of members of Congress, the State Department described the use of these safeguards:

> . . . the Committee considers whether it would be desirable or possible to make a concession on only part of the tariff category that may be involved. For example, it might well be that a substantial reduction in the tariff on imports of a product above a certain value would not have any appreciable effect on the domestic industry, whereas a comparable reduction on lower value products might have a considerable impact.
>
> The Committee may also take into consideration the advisability of making a limited reduction through the use of a tariff quota or other devices. For example, the Committee may decide that a reduced duty should apply to only a specified percentage of average U. S. consumption of the product. Or to take another example, the Committee may decide to reduce the duties but to reserve the right to increase the rates if imports exceed a certain percentage of U. S. production of similar products.

This procedure represents a faithful and conscientious carrying out of the law. The objective is not to shift resources out of protected industries, but

---

24. Executive Order No. 10082 provides that if any member of the Trade Agreements Committee dissents "from any recommendation to the President with respect to the inclusion of any proposed concession in the trade agreement, the President shall be furnished a full report by the dissenting member . . . giving the reasons . . ."

to reduce duties in such a careful and discriminating way as to retain essential protection. The best that can be hoped for is that it may be possible to limit the future growth of protected industries. The trade agreements have greatly complicated the already unduly complex United States tariff schedule. Tariff classifications have been subdivided, rates have been differentiated seasonally, and tariff quotas have been imposed to limit the quantity of imports at reduced rates.

The Negotiation

In negotiating, the American team is bound by the statutory list of negotiable items prepared beforehand by the Trade Agreements Committee and by its instructions as to concessions. (The law itself does not permit the transfer of dutiable items to the free list; the maximum possible concession is a 50 per cent cut in the duty in effect on January 1, 1945.) The bargaining position of the American team is weakened by the fact that it is not free to change its position in return for reciprocal concessions of greater value by the other country.[25]

These rules of procedure are so restrictive that the negotiating teams cannot press their demands upon the other country first and then consider what can be offered in return, as is the customary technique of bargaining. The maximum concession permitted by law is known to all in advance, as is the escape clause policy. Regardless of possible gains, no branch of domestic industry may be exposed to serious injury. And if a mistake is made the concession is to be withdrawn.[26] When the inducements that the United States can offer are limited and known to others, as they are under these circumstances, all the United States can do is ask the other side to concede as much as possible. Typically, the United States has offered more extensive concessions than other countries and has been unable to justify, on the reciprocal principle, the full use of negotiating authority.

Prior to 1947 trade agreements negotiations were conducted with individual countries. While the negotiations were bilateral, the concessions made by the United States were multilateral. The same concessions extended to the negotiating country were also extended to other countries under the unconditional most-favored-nation principle.[27]

25. See the statement by H. R. Kemp, Senate of Canada, *Proceedings of the Standing Committee on Canadian Trade Relations*, 1947–1948, No. 2, pp. 48–49.

26. Since 1951 the Tariff Commission determines in advance the "peril point" beyond which tariff concessions will seriously injure or threaten domestic producers. Concessions to Venezuela on residual fuel oil went beyond the Commission's recommended peril point. This is the President's legal prerogative, which he may lose if he makes much use of it.

27. Except for Cuba and the Philippines, to which the United States has long extended preferred treatment, trade agreement concessions made by the United States apply equally to imports from all countries except those with policies contrary to the purpose of the act. Only prewar Germany and Austria were denied the benefits of lower trade agreement rates.

In 1922 the United States abandoned the conditional form of most-favored-nation treatment, which is based on reciprocity and extends the concessions of trade agreements to third parties only on condition that they reciprocate with some equivalent concession.[28] The unconditional form does not require reciprocation from third parties.

In carrying out the unconditional most-favored-nation principle, the extension of the substance of concessions to third countries has been limited by use of the "principal supplier" approach in the negotiation of agreements.[29] According to this principle, concessions are granted to the nation which is the chief source of supply for any commodity. It follows that other countries which receive the most-favored-nation treatment can only be lesser suppliers, except as sources may shift subsequently. Certain prewar agreements contained the so-called third-country clause wherein the United States retained the right to withdraw concessions if the major benefit shifted to any third country. In defense, it is argued that this approach is necessary in order to avoid being deprived of bargaining power before an agreement is made with each country.

The benefits of the agreement also tend to favor the country that is party to the agreement as a result of the practice of subdividing the tariff schedule into minute classes and granting concessions only on the particular class of goods supplied by the contracting party.

The classic example of reclassification is the concession on cattle imports granted by Germany to Switzerland in the agreement of 1902 extended by the most-favored-nation clause to all other exporters of cows to Germany. The reduction of the tariff was limited to "large dapple mountain cattle or brown cattle reared at a spot at least 300 meters above sea level and having at least one month's grazing each year at a spot at least 800 meters above sea level."[30]

As it has worked out in practice, the devices which are justified in the name of bargaining serve primarily to restrict the effect of concessions.

General Agreement on Tariffs and Trade (GATT)

Foreign trade was inevitably impaired by the dislocations of the second world war and United States exports were especially affected by the acute

28. The practice of trade discriminations may have been inherent in the earliest trade, which took the form of personal grants to traders who carried on their business in a suspicious and often hostile environment; frequently, in fact, as a right of a conqueror in a defeated enemy state. See R. C. Snyder, *The Most-Favored-Nation Clause*, King's Crown Press, New York, 1948. The most-favored-nation principle is thought to have had its origin in the successful efforts of the European states to obtain terms from the middle eastern states as favorable as those extended to neighboring countries.

29. Only rarely have critics argued that the principal supplier approach has not been strictly followed. The concession on zinc in the Canadian agreement is sometimes said to be a case in point. The most important instance was the 1943 agreement with Mexico, which provided lower duties on petroleum than had been provided by the 1939 agreement with Venezuela in 1952.

30. Charles P. Kindleberger, *International Economics*, Irwin, Homewood, Illinois, 1953, p. 199, note.

shortage of dollars (lend-lease was abruptly stopped in 1945). Of course, the dollar shortage merely reflected the fact that the rest of the world desperately wanted to buy more American goods than it could pay for. This reflected the need for trade as well as aid. As early as 1945 the United States government published its *Proposal for Expansion of World Trade and Employment*. After discussion at the United Nations, this led to the Geneva conference in 1947 where the United States for the first time negotiated multilaterally with twenty-three countries while, at the same time, they negotiated with each other. The Geneva negotiations, together with preliminary conferences on the establishment of an International Trade Organization, have been described as "the most prolonged, sustained, and complex series of interrelated negotiations ever undertaken in the field of international economic relations."[31]

The General Agreement required seven months to negotiate, covered more than 45,000 items and represented two thirds of the imports of the signatory countries. American participation was undertaken under the authority of the Trade Agreements Act. Never before in history have so many nations come together to negotiate among themselves about trade.

In order to support the tariff provisions, it was necessary to reach agreement also on a number of general provisions.[32] The principles underlying these are:

1. Nations should give each other unconditional most-favored-nation treatment.

2. Restrictions on trade should be in the form of tariffs and only at the customs frontier.

3. Customs administration should be simplified and improved in order to lower the "invisible tariff."[33]

4. Nations should consult before taking action which might be harmful to another nation's interest.

The General Agreement provides numerous exceptions to its rules. Among the more important are:

1. The preferential system between Britain and the Commonwealth nations, between France and her Overseas territories, and between the United States and Cuba are maintained, although preferential treatment may not be increased.

2. If imports cause or threaten serious injury to domestic industry, concessions may be withdrawn. (This is the American "escape clause.")

31. William Adams Brown, Jr., *The United States and the Restoration of World Trade*, The Brookings Institution, Washington, 1950, p. 1; cf. U.S. Department of State, *Analysis of General Agreement on Tariffs and Trade*, 1949, p. 3.
32. See "Treatment of American Exports," pp. 142 ff.
33. See Chapter 9.

3. Quotas which are prohibited for normally protective purposes are permitted in order to maintain or increase essential monetary reserves and to support domestic farm programs.

4. Under certain conditions, undeveloped countries may use restrictions on trade in order to encourage infant industries.

5. Nations may dictate their own policy in buying for their armed forces and for strategic stockpiles.

The contracting parties have no power of enforcement but rely on the sanction of their collective judgment. The underlying principle is that a nation contemplating action which might injure another should give advance notice, if possible, and that nations should consult in order to resolve conflicts of interest. Escape clause action, for example, requires consultation except under conditions of extreme emergency.

In 1947 United States imports amounted to $3.5 billion on the free list and $2.0 billion of dutiable goods—a total of $5.5 billion. After GATT, the duty was reduced on 94 per cent of the dutiable items, and 86 per cent of the goods on the free list were bound against increases in duty. The reductions in duties ranged from 45 to 65 per cent on $1.3 billion of imports. While the scale of the Geneva negotiations may have been revolutionary, the form and results were not.

The General Agreement is not basically different in principle and intent from an ordinary tariff agreement between two countries. It follows the precedents set by the bilateral agreements previously negotiated by the United States, all of which contained general clauses designed to protect the tariff concessions contained in them, and all of which had to be "administered" by the two contracting parties. . . . The fact that on certain matters the contracting parties are authorized or required to take joint action does not alter the nature of the Agreement. It does not make the GATT an international organization in the usual sense of the term . . .[34]

The future may alter this judgment. Since the decision of the administration in 1950 not to press Congress for approval of the charter of the proposed International Trade Organization, the State Department has indicated that it would advocate an expansion of the consultative functions of GATT.

In 1949, ten additional countries, raising the total to thirty-three, participated in further trade negotiations at Annecy. In the fall of 1950 further negotiations were begun at Torquay. Seven new countries participated, including Korea, Austria and Germany. It proved impossible to obtain the inclusion of Japan in the Torquay meeting.

The constitutionality of GATT has been challenged, chiefly by protectionists, both in and out of Congress. Section 10 of the Trade Agreements

34. Brown, *op. cit.*, pp. 238–239.

Extension Act of 1951 expressly provided that the Congress was neither approving nor disapproving GATT by extending the Trade Agreements Law. The question of GATT's legal status arises in an acute form when the Congress passes laws which violate GATT, as in Section 104 of the Defense Production Act of 1951 (the cheese amendment).[35]

That the President has the power to enter into the General Agreement seems clear enough. At the same time, it is recognized that the contracting parties cannot overrule acts of the Congress or the Chief Executive. The obligation is to consult and review concerning the discharge of the undertaking.

The administrative customs law of the United States requires modification, particularly with respect to valuation, marking and countervailing duties, in order to conform to the General Agreement.

The present status of GATT is that the Executive has entered into a binding agreement, but the terms are applied only provisionally and to the extent that they are consistent with the relevant law in effect on October 30, 1947.

A thoroughly sympathetic writer has made the following evaluation of GATT:

One might say that the rules it lays down are riddled with exceptions; that the principles accepted are too vague to be meaningful; that a mere promise to consult is not much guarantee of good behavior; that there has been no sacrifice of national sovereignty; that the tariff concessions made will not really hurt any domestic industry no matter how uneconomic; that to agree on principles of multilateral trade under present world conditions is to ignore realities and live in an ivory tower; that it was foolish to go to all this trouble under the appalling uncertainties of present conditions; that the wiser course would have been to wait until conditions were stabilized; until the shape of things to come could be more clearly discerned. All of these things could be and are being said, and each of them contains a modicum of truth.

But it can also be said that the deepest need of the world today is agreement and a sense of direction. Nations can no longer solve their problems alone. National boundaries have long since ceased to confine either depression or prosperity. When things are uncertain and confused, when there is a likelihood of nations working at cross purposes, when there is a common need and wide difference of opinion as to how to meet it, then is the time to reach agreement on the direction in which nations are to go. And the General Agreement set the direction of over three-quarters of the world's trade and took the first steps along the course thus charted.[36]

As a result of experience to date, those with intimate knowledge of the operation of GATT have come to regard the consultative function as per-

35. Nine nations protested this law as a violation of GATT, a view supported by the State Department.

36. Winthrop G. Brown in *Foreign Economic Policy for the United States*, edited by Seymour Harris, Harvard University Press, Cambridge, 1948, pp. 269–270.

haps its most valuable contribution. This has served, for example, to mitigate somewhat the harmful effects of the ill-advised "cheese amendment" and apparently aided in ending discrimination by Belgium.[37]

Politics of Tariff Making

The unfortunate experience with tariff making which resulted in the Hawley-Smoot Act convinced some responsible leaders in Congress that the legislative body should never again undertake to fix the schedule of duties.[38]

Most writers have been extravagant in praise of the new procedures established in 1934.

Never in the past has the United States followed such a careful and expert method of dealing with problems of foreign trade. Never before has consideration of tariff matters been so free from logrolling, politics, and narrow sectional influences. Formerly professional lobbyists frequently crowded others off the stage. Now there exists an effective means, available to all without cost, whereby everyone is assured of a careful and impartial hearing by trained officials who have no party interest to serve.[39]

There has been astonishingly little criticism of political influence in the negotiation and administration of the program.[40]

There is no doubt whatever that the established trade agreement method represents a signal improvement over the logrolling process of earlier days. However, the eulogy of improvement should not neglect the defects. The President was always obligated to use his powers with great restraint and the "history of trade agreements since 1934 has been a story of the gradual weakening of the executive's freedom of action . . ."[41]

This prewar evaluation has been doubly true since the end of World War II. During the war there was less concern about the danger of imports.

37. See p. 252 on the cheese amendment and p. 145 on discrimination. For details, see reports of the GATT secretariat, for example, *The Attack on Trade Barriers*, Interim Commission for ITO, 1949; *Liberalizing World Trade*, 1950; *GATT in Action*, 1952. See also *Reports on the Discriminatory Application of Import Restrictions*, Geneva, 1950, 1951, 1952.

38. See E. E. Schattschneider's study under the revealing title, *Politics, Pressures and the Tariff: A Study of Free Private Enterprise in Pressure Politics, as Shown in the 1929– 1930 Revision of the Tariff*, Prentice-Hall, New York, 1935.

39. Francis B. Sayre, *The Way Forward: The American Trade Agreements Program*, Macmillan, New York, 1939, p. 96. See also John D. Larkin, *Trade Agreements: A Study in Democratic Methods*, Columbia University Press, New York, 1940, Chapters 3 and 4.

40. In numerous interviews conducted in connection with this study there was only one charge of political influence—and that a careless one—in connection with relief granted under the escape clause from import of women's fur felt hats. The implication was that other cases were equally deserving of relief but that hats had been selected in order to aid the Democrats in the Connecticut state election of 1950. It was not explained why Republican members of the Tariff Commission voted for injury, if this were the case.

41. Carl Kreider, "Democratic Processes in the Trade Agreement Program," *American Political Science Review*, April 1940, pp. 322–332.

The anticipation of increased imports prompted a formidable attack on the program in 1948. Despite the fact that the "escape clause" had been formalized by an Executive Order, the Congress added the so-called "peril point" amendment. This requires the Tariff Commission to determine in advance of any negotiation the limit of "safe bargaining" beyond which tariff reduction may imperil any branch of home industry. A similar procedure has always been followed by the Interdepartment Committee; the amendment gave the Tariff Commission alone additional responsibility for protection of home industry.

In 1948, Will Clayton argued that American tariff policy should not provide "absolute protection to all American producers under any and all circumstances," but should be based on "broad national consideration" in which he included:

(1) Markets for surplus agricultural and industrial products; (2) payment of interest and amortization on governmental and private debts; (3) the ability of the United States to satisfy the economic requirements of the growing and prosperous population.

Clayton indicated that the criteria of injury should include the loss of export markets as well as loss of the home market to competitive imports.[42] However, his argument did not persuade the Congress, and the "peril point" amendment was passed.

The debate was renewed the following year when Willard Thorp, Assistant Secretary of State, asked that the "peril point" provision be deleted:

The third major objection to the 1948 Act is that the peril-point reports are necessarily unduly restrictive. In them the Tariff Commission is required to report what it finds to be the minimum tariff and other import restrictions necessary to avoid the threat of serious injury to domestic industry producing any article under consideration for trade agreement concessions by the United States. The determinations by the Commission are to be made without regard to any national or international considerations such as benefits to be obtained from other countries, long-term needs of our economy for expanding markets, the necessity of obtaining the best possible use of domestic resources, including considerations of conservation, possible strategic considerations, and the possible repercussions of our actions upon policies of other countries toward us.[43]

Thus the criterion "best possible use of domestic resources" finally appeared, though still pretty well submerged. Thorp had argued that in the give and take of negotiation, it was necessary to use some criteria in choosing the items on which concessions were to be made, and that one

42. *Extension of Reciprocal Trade Agreements Act*, Hearings, Senate Finance Committee, 80th Cong., 1st sess., 1948, pp. 23 and 29.

43. *Extension of Reciprocal Trade Agreements Act*, Hearings, Senate Finance Committee, 81st Cong., 1st sess., 1949, p. 304.

criterion among others is the efficient use of resources. Senator Millikin answered this on the floor of the Senate:

Nijinsky never executed a *grand jette* rivalling this leap into undelegated power. There is nothing in the Reciprocal Trade Agreements Act of 1934, and there is nothing in any extension of it that makes the reciprocal trade system a vehicle for obtaining "the best possible use of domestic resources."
I believe the general opinion around here is that reciprocal trade should deal with commodities after they are produced . . . that those administering the system have not been charged with responsibility . . . of judging whether to grant or deny concessions on the ground that the particular commodity represents the "best," "good," "indifferent" or "bad," use of our domestic resources.[44]

In Senator Millikin's view the criteria for the selection of concessions based upon conservation and strategic considerations were equally objectionable, because these responsibilities were lodged elsewhere in the executive departments of the government. Moreover, the Senator objected strenuously to any qualification whatever of the assurance that domestic producers would not be injured, on the ground that home industry should not be subordinated to "the opportunism, the shifting demands, and the logrolling of our diplomacy." Senator Millikin was quite clear that the program should not be used to shift domestic resources:

It does not require qualification of the safeguarding rule unless it is in mind to swap injury to one domestic industry for the benefit of another. And there are no odds in that so far as the welfare of the over-all economy is concerned.[45]

The administration sought to retain the nominal power to negotiate by promising not to use the power in a way that would imperil domestic industry. To this the opposition replied that if the administration conceded that the power would not be used, it could also concede the principle of "prevention" by leaving the determination of "peril points" in the hands of the Tariff Commission. The administration won on this point in 1949, but lost again in 1951. Protectionists have consistently fought to increase the power of the Tariff Commission, which is regarded as a safer guardian than the President or his Cabinet.

The House amendments to the Trade Agreements Extension bill of 1951 showed how far sentiment in the House had moved toward statutory safeguards. As passed by the House, the bill included both "peril points" and "escape" provisions.

Upon application of any interested party, the Tariff Commission would be required to hold hearings for the purpose of producing evidence, and to report its findings and recommendations to the President. Moreover, the

44. *Congressional Record*, September 8, 1949, p. 12651.
45. *Ibid.*

Commission would be required to consider "a downward trend of production, employment and wages in the domestic industry concerned, or a decline in sales and a higher or growing inventory attributable in part to import competition, to be evidence of serious injury or a threat thereof."[46] The Commission is also required in every appropriate instance to report the reasons why it did not find evidence of injury. This paragraph appears to have been designed to insure a finding of "injury" when a domestic industry is not fully employed and domestic sales decline more than imports.

The administration bowed to the inevitable by offering to accept, in modified form, both the peril point and escape clause procedures. The Secretary of State conceded that amendments could be worked out on both issues which would permit the program to continue in workable form. Such amendments permitted the Tariff Commission to continue to participate in the work of the Trade Agreements Committee and in actual negotiations, but required that it heed certain danger signals in its analyses of injury. In thus accepting still further safeguards, the administration saved the form of the program by an even more abject sacrifice of substance. The act of 1955 provides additional avenues for protection under the escape clause.[47]

Reciprocity

The overriding factor limiting American exports in recent years has not been the tariffs of other nations but the shortage of dollars. Most trade agreement countries have found it necessary because of their internal policies to impose direct controls on purchases of American goods. Under the circumstances, tariff concessions to the United States have not freed trade.

There is little evidence to show that world protectionism of existing industry has been seriously undermined. Other nations have apparently pursued the same objective as the United States; the trade agreement system has been used as a politically expedient approach to the modification of tariffs without seriously breaching the protection of home industry. Thus, a successful trade agreement was negotiated with Great Britain in 1939 although neither country seriously modified the principle of protection. At the Torquay negotiations in 1950–1951, Britain and the Commonwealth nations continued to maintain the system of preferential treatment within the Commonwealth. The salutary prospect is that *expansion* of protected industries may be restricted.

Before attempting to sum up the effect of tariff concessions on American imports, it seems desirable to indicate the scope of the negotiations and the magnitude of the concessions. This is the subject of the next chapter.

46. H.R. 1612, 82d Cong., 1st sess., Section 7 (c).
47. See Chapter 19. For complaints of injury, see Appendix 6.

Chapter 6

Tariff Reduction under Trade Agreements

THE REALIZED AVERAGE DUTY on dutiable imports was 47 per cent in 1934 and 14 per cent in 1949—a decline of 70 per cent. This decline reflects (1) tariff concessions, (2) higher prices, and (3) changes in the composition of imports.

The over-all effect of changes in the composition of imports on average duties has been minor. As a result of further tariff concessions and the renewed increase in import prices after 1949, the average duty on dutiable imports declined to 12 per cent in 1952—a decline of almost 75 per cent from the 1934 level.

The effect of rising prices on specific duties is illustrated by the 1930 tariff of 1.5 cents a pound on garlic. The ad valorem equivalent at that time was 40 per cent. In 1950, owing to the rise in price, the ad valorem of the 1930 rate was 22 per cent. But in the meantime, the rate had been reduced by trade agreement to .75 cents a pound so that the ad valorem equivalent rate in 1951 was 11 per cent. A major part of American imports bear specific duties and, as a result, rising import prices have been about as important as have trade agreements in the reduction of tariff rates. Inflation has probably had a greater effect on imports than have trade agreements because inflation is not selective.

Interpretation of tariff statistics is a formidable task. The average rate may reflect changes in the composition of total imports as well as changes in the duty on individual items. These difficulties can be overcome by comparing the duties in different years on imports of one year, which leaves the composition and price of imports unchanged.

Thus, the average rate of duty based on and weighted by imports in the years indicated was as follows:

	Before Any Agreements	After Agreements
1934 imports	46.7	a
1947 imports	28.3	15.0 (to Jan. 1, 1949)
1949 imports	25.8	13.9 (to Jan. 1, 1951)
1952 imports	24.4	12.2 (to Jan. 1, 1953)

a. No agreements had been made.

129

Trade agreements accounted for a 50 per cent reduction in duty on 1952 imports. The change before any tariff concession from 46.7 per cent in 1934 to 24.4 in 1952 was due to rising import prices and changes in the composition of imports.

Thus, the average rate on the dutiable imports of 1947, if calculated at the duties in force in 1934, before any tariff concessions under reciprocal trade agreements, was 28.3 per cent. By January 1, 1949, the calculated rate at the duties currently in force had been reduced to 15 per cent on the same imports (those of 1947), a reduction of 47 per cent, solely as a result of tariff concessions. (See Table 24.) The realized average duty in 1949 was 13.8 per cent, and differs from the 15 per cent calculated rate because of changes in the composition and price of imports between 1947 and 1949.

The actual realized average duty in 1934 before trade agreement concessions first were made was 46.7 per cent. The calculated duty at 1934 rates on 1947 imports was 28.3 per cent. (See Table 24.) Thus, average duties were reduced from 46.7 per cent to 28.3 per cent by changes in price and composition of imports between 1934 and 1947. (See Table 25.)

In order to separate the effect of changes in (1) price and (2) composition, the average duty on 1947 imports was calculated using the realized 1934 rates (by 15 tariff schedules). This was compared with the actual realized duty in 1934 to indicate the broad effect of changes in composition between 1934 and 1947, when the composition would presumably be distorted by postwar dislocations in supply. The actual realized average duty in 1934 was 46.7 per cent. The calculated duty on 1947 imports using 1934 duties (by 15 tariff schedules) was 49.2 per cent (not shown in table). Thus changes in composition among schedules raised the average duty by 2.5 points, or about 5 per cent.

Since the combined effect of changes in composition and price between 1934 and 1947 was to reduce the average duty by 39 per cent (Table 25), and the effect of changes in composition alone raised the average duty by about 5 per cent, it follows that the effect of rising prices from 1934 to 1947 was to reduce the ad valorem equivalent of duties by 41.5 per cent. This figure compares average 1934 duties with average 1947 duties, eliminating the effect of tariff concessions.

Import prices, which rose 44 per cent between 1947 and 1951, have continued to reduce the ad valorem equivalent of specific duties. Additional tariff concessions since January 1, 1949 were made at Annecy and Torquay.

On January 1, 1953, after all concessions including Torquay, the calculated rate (based on and weighted by 1952 imports) was 12.2 per cent—an average reduction of 50 per cent from preagreement rates. (See Table 26.) Rising prices since 1934 reduced the ad valorem equivalent of average

TABLE 24

REDUCTION IN DUTY UNDER TRADE AGREEMENTS TO JANUARY 1, 1949, BY TARIFF SCHEDULES

(Based on Imports in 1947)

Tariff Schedule	Dutiable Imports		Ad Valorem Equivalent Rates		
	Total Value	Per Cent Subject to Reduced Rates	Before Any Agreements	On January 1, 1949	Average Reduction
	(Millions)			(Per Cent)	
1. Chemicals, oils and paints	$ 119	67.2[a]	17.9	11.9	34
2. Earths, earthenware and glassware	44	87.2	35.7	21.2	41
3. Metals and manufactures of	246	91.8	32.0	17.1	46
4. Wood and manufactures of	42	99.0	11.8	4.7	60
5. Sugar, molasses and manufactures of	437	98.2	30.0	10.6	65
6. Tobacco and manufactures of	92	100.0	37.2	25.9	31
7. Agricultural products and provisions	312	84.6	17.6	10.0	43
8. Spirits, wines and other beverages	67	95.9	92.5	28.9	69
9. Cotton manufactures	16	91.5	37.6	25.8	31
10. Flax, hemp, jute and manufactures of	150	95.6	12.0	5.5	54
11. Wool and manufactures of	199	99.7	54.0	36.8	32
12. Silk manufactures	11	19.0[b]	50.4	44.4	12
13. Manufactures of rayon or other synthetic textile	16	99.8	31.6	21.2	33
14. Papers and books	23	86.5	19.8	11.9	40
15. Sundries	208	50.6[c]	23.1	15.5	33
Free list taxable	229	95.8	12.3	6.3	49
Total	$2,212	88.7	28.3	15.0	47

Source: U.S. Tariff Commission, *Effect of Trade Agreement Concessions on United States Tariff Levels Based on Imports in 1947*, May 1949, Tables 2 and 3, pp. 9 and 10.

a. 32.5 per cent of the dutiable imports of Schedule 1 were subject to "no concession."
b. 81.0 per cent of Schedule 12 were subject to "no concession."
c. 40.4 per cent of Schedule 15 were subject to "bound rates."

TABLE 25

REDUCTION IN DUTY FROM 1934 TO 1947 BEFORE TRADE AGREEMENT CONCESSIONS

Tariff Schedule	Ad Valorem Equivalent Duty		Percentage Reduction 1934 to 1947 from Changes in Price and Composition of Imports
	1934 Imports	Before Any Agreements 1947 Imports	
	(Per Cent)		
1. Chemicals, oils and paints	38.2	17.9	53
2. Earths, earthenware and glassware	55.6	35.7	36
3. Metals and manufactures of	35.1	32.0	9
4. Wood and manufactures of	22.9	11.8	48
5. Sugar, molasses and manufactures of	67.3	30.0	55
6. Tobacco and manufactures of	89.1	37.2	58
7. Agricultural products and provisions	38.4	17.6	54
8. Spirits, wines, and other beverages	84.6	92.5	+9[a]
9. Cotton manufactures	45.3	37.6	17
10. Flax, hemp, jute, and manufactures of	24.8	12.0	51
11. Wool and manufactures of	79.4	54.0	32
12. Silk manufactures	55.9	50.4	10
13. Manufactures of rayon or other synthetic textile	72.5	31.6	56
14. Papers and books	24.7	19.8	19
15. Sundries	37.2	23.1	38
Free list taxable	29.3	12.3	58
Total	46.7	28.3	39

Sources: Col. 1 from *Statistical Abstract of the United States, 1949*, Table 981; Col. 2 from Table 24.
a. The increase in this schedule reflects the change in composition owing to repeal of prohibition.

TABLE 26

REDUCTION IN DUTY UNDER TRADE AGREEMENTS TO JANUARY 1, 1953, BY TARIFF SCHEDULES
(Based on Imports in 1952)

Tariff Schedule	United States Dutiable Imports, 1952	Average Ad Valorem Equivalent Based on Rates in Effect:			Percentage Reduction in Rates from:	
		Before Any Agreements	On January 1, 1945	On January 1, 1953	Preagreement to January 1, 1953	January 1, 1945 to January 1, 1953
	(Millions)	(Per Cent)				
1. Chemicals, oils and paints	$ 164	25.1	20.0	12.4	51	38
2. Earths, earthenware and glassware	118	40.6	36.7	24.7	39	33
3. Metals and manufactures of	901	23.7	18.9	12.1	49	36
4. Wood and manufactures of	215	10.9	7.5	4.7	57	37
5. Sugar, molasses and manufactures of	385[a]	25.8	13.5	9.4	64	31
6. Tobacco and manufactures of	83	45.6	34.7	20.3	56	41
7. Agricultural products and provisions	774	16.2	12.5	9.4	42	24
Fishery products	119	13.3	11.0	8.4	37	24
Other	655	16.8	12.8	9.7	42	24
8. Spirits, wines and other beverages	127	81.4	41.6	23.1	72	45
9. Cotton manufactures	42	36.8	30.0	21.8	41	27
10. Flax, hemp, jute and manufactures of	162	12.2	9.0	5.2	58	43
11. Wool and manufactures of	462	36.7	30.2	22.4	39	26
12. Silk manufactures	29	58.8	52.7	31.0	47	41
13. Manufactures of rayon or other synthetic textile	35	32.8	31.0	17.7	46	43
14. Papers and books	39	20.4	15.2	9.4	54	38
15. Sundries	294	31.8	26.5	19.1	40	28
Free list taxable	660	10.2	5.3	4.1	60	23
Total	$4,490	24.4	17.9	12.2	50[b]	32[b]

Source: U.S. Tariff Commission, *Effect of Trade Agreement Concessions on United States Tariff Levels Based on Imports in 1952.*

a. Chiefly cane sugar ($324 million), imports of which are regulated by quota.

b. If imports of cane sugar, which are regulated by quota, were excluded, the percentages would be 49 and 32, instead of 50 and 32.

duties by roughly the same amount.[1] The actual course of realized average duties, which declined by almost 75 per cent in this period, does not seem to give too distorted an over-all picture of the combined effect of tariff concessions and rising prices.

Trade Agreement Countries

The number of trade agreement countries has grown in four steps: (1) the bilateral agreements before the Geneva conference; (2) the General Agreement (GATT) at Geneva in 1947; (3) the Annecy Conference in 1949; (4) the Torquay Conference in 1950–1951. After Torquay, over 80 per cent of world trade was accounted for by trade agreement countries.

Before 1940 agreements were negotiated with Canada, France, Switzerland, Sweden, Finland, Czechoslovakia, Turkey, the United Kingdom, the Benelux group and eleven Latin American countries. Of these, the preferential agreement with Cuba and the agreements with Canada and the United Kingdom were most important, although the United Kingdom agreement negotiated in 1939 became unimportant almost immediately because of the war. Our trade with some of the Latin American countries is not a substantial part of our total trade, and our imports from them, consisting largely of tropical products, are not substantially affected by tariff manipulation, either because they are on the free list or because of limited industrial demand.

Postwar multilateral negotiations at Geneva resulted in new agreements with eight of the pre-Geneva countries and fourteen other countries with which agreements had not previously been made or were not in force. The additions at Geneva included eight members of the British Commonwealth of Nations, Chile, China, Czechoslovakia,[2] Lebanon, Norway and Syria. The accessions at Annecy included ten countries and five more were added at Torquay.

Three bilateral agreements were terminated by joint agreement: that with Colombia on December 1, 1949; that with Mexico on December 31, 1950; that with Costa Rica on June 1, 1951.

In 1951, the United States suspended all obligations with Czechoslovakia under the General Agreement and all obligations under bilateral agreements with satellite countries. Three countries—China, Lebanon and Syria—have withdrawn from the General Agreement.

Two of the countries—Brazil and Korea—with which the United States concluded negotiations at Torquay had not signed the agreements by June 30, 1952.

1. See U.S. Tariff Commission, *Operation of the Trade Agreements Program, June 1934 to April 1948*, 1949, Part III, pp. 3–5.

2. Czechoslovakia is included in both the prewar and Geneva groups. Its agreement had been suspended during the war.

TABLE 27
STATUS OF TRADE AGREEMENTS, JUNE 30, 1952

19 Countries—Geneva		9 Countries—Annecy	
Australia	Jan. 1, 1948	Denmark	May 28, 1950
Belgium[a]	Jan. 1, 1948	Dominican Republic	May 19, 1950
Brazil[a]	July 30, 1948	Finland[a]	May 25, 1950
Burma	July 29, 1948	Greece	Mar. 9, 1950
Canada[a]	Jan. 1, 1948	Haiti[a]	Jan. 1, 1950
Ceylon	July 29, 1948	Italy	May 30, 1950
Chile	Mar. 16, 1949	Liberia	May 20, 1950
Cuba[a]	Jan. 1, 1948	Nicaragua	May 28, 1950
France[a]	Jan. 1, 1948	Sweden[a]	Apr. 30, 1950
India	July 8, 1948		
Indonesia[b]	Mar. 11, 1948		
Luxembourg[a]	Jan. 1, 1948	4 Countries—Torquay	
Netherlands[a]	Jan. 1, 1948	Austria	Oct. 19, 1951
New Zealand	July 30, 1948	Western Germany	Oct. 1, 1951
Norway	July 10, 1948	Peru[a]	Oct. 7, 1951
Pakistan	July 30, 1948	Turkey[a]	Oct. 17, 1951
Southern Rhodesia	July 11, 1948		
Union of South Africa	June 13, 1948		
United Kingdom[a]	Jan. 1, 1948		

Bilateral Agreements—11 Countries			
Argentina	Nov. 15, 1951	Iran	Jan. 28, 1944
Ecuador	Oct. 23, 1938	Paraguay	Apr. 9, 1947
El Salvador	May 31, 1947	Switzerland	Feb. 15, 1936
Guatemala	June 15, 1936	Uruguay[c]	Jan. 1, 1943
Honduras	Mar. 2, 1936	Venezuela	Dec. 16, 1939
Iceland	Nov. 19, 1943		

Source: U.S. Tariff Commission, *Operation of the Trade Agreements Program,* Fifth Report, July 1951–June 1952, pp. 171–173, mimeographed.

a. Had previously concluded a bilateral trade agreement with the United States.

b. The Netherlands negotiated concessions on behalf of the Netherlands Indies at Geneva in 1947. On February 24, 1950, the United States of Indonesia (now the Republic of Indonesia) was recognized as a contracting party to the General Agreement in its own right.

c. Uruguay negotiated for accession to the General Agreement at Annecy, and also negotiated at Torquay, but had not, by June 30, 1952, signed either the Annecy or the Torquay Protocols. She has signed since that date.

Thus, the United States was a party to trade agreements with 43 countries on June 30, 1952. (See Table 27.)

Importance of Specific Duties

The relative importance of specific duties has increased by almost one half since 1931.[3] The duty was specific on 76 per cent of dutiable imports

3. Specific duties have played an important role in American tariff history. They produce perverse results but are regarded as more enforceable than ad valorem rates, which require valuation of imports. The Tariff Act of 1789 carried predominantly specific rates. Under the Walker tariff of 1846, all rates were on an ad valorem basis. Subsequently specific and compound rates were introduced wherever possible.

TABLE 28

IMPORTANCE OF SPECIFIC AND OTHER DUTIES, 1931 AND 1952

	Per Cent of Dutiable Imports	
Type of Duty	1931[a]	1952[b]
Ad valorem	35	20
Specific	54	76
Compound	8	4
Unsegregated	4	0

Sources: R. Elberton Smith, *Customs Valuation in the United States*, University of Chicago Press, Chicago, 1948, pp. 10 and 11; U.S. Tariff Commission, *Operation of the Trade Agreements Program*, Fifth Report, July 1951–June 1952, Table 9.

a. Year ending September 30.

b. Rates in effect January 1952, weighted by 1949 imports.

in 1952, compared with 54 per cent in 1931. (See Table 28.) A small part of this shift may be due to the effect of tariff reduction produced by higher import prices.

The highest duties at present are compound rates, which averaged 30 per cent in 1952. Ad valorem duties averaged 18 per cent, and specific duties 11 per cent.

There is a strong presumption that the fortuitous reduction in the tariff resulting from inflation is more significant for trade than the concessions made by trade agreement, although the magnitudes of the decline are roughly the same. Our negotiators were under obligation to cut duties which would not result in injury to home industry. The forces of inflation are blind. This makes it all the more remarkable that such a comprehensive cut of almost 75 per cent reaching into every tariff schedule and bracket should produce such meagre results in enlarging imports.

Tariff Concessions

In order to show that American tariffs have been greatly reduced for several years, most of the following data are based on duties in effect on January 1, 1949 and January 1, 1950. Time is so important for the adjustments in supply that data for the earlier years are probably more significant than the concessions made after Annecy. The further concessions made at Torquay do not substantially change the broad picture.[4]

Slightly less than 90 per cent of both agricultural and nonagricultural imports (1947 composition) were subject to reduced rates on January 1, 1949. Of these imports, the over-all rate had been reduced from 29.9 per cent to 14.8 per cent since the beginning of the Trade Agreements Program, a reduction of 50 per cent. The average agricultural rate was slightly higher than the nonagricultural rate before any agreement, and its reduction was

4. See Table 26 for 1952 data; also Table 31.

TABLE 29

REDUCTION IN DUTY UNDER TRADE AGREEMENTS TO JANUARY 1, 1949, BY ECONOMIC CATEGORIES

| Economic Class | Total Value | Dutiable Imports Subject to: | | | Ad Valorem Equivalent Rates in Effect: | | Percentage Reduction[a] |
| | | Reduced Rates | Bound Rates | No Concession | Before Any Agreements | On January 1, 1949 | |
	(Millions)	(Per Cent)			(Per Cent)		
All classes	$2,212	88.4	5.7	5.9	29.9	14.8	50
Agricultural	1,056	89.4	4.0	6.6	31.6	16.3	48
Nonagricultural	1,156	87.4	7.2	5.4	28.3	13.4	53
Crude materials	585	98.8	.4	.8	30.9	19.7	36
0—Agricultural	358	99.7	.1	.2	37.7	26.2	31
1—Nonagricultural	227	97.3	.8	1.9	19.9	9.2	54
Crude foodstuffs	138	85.0	2.4	12.6	17.2	8.2	52
2—Agricultural	117	82.7	2.8	14.5	19.5	9.4	52
3—Nonagricultural	21	97.9	—	2.1	6.5	2.4	64
Manufactured foodstuffs and beverages	617	92.0	3.7	4.3	36.4	12.6	65
4—Agricultural	524	91.2	3.8	5.0	29.8	10.6	64
5—Nonagricultural	92	96.7	2.9	.4	71.4	23.0	68
Semimanufactures	420	71.9	18.9	9.2	16.3	8.4	48
6—Agricultural	54	18.0	35.2	46.8	16.7	8.6	49
7—Nonagricultural	365	79.9	16.5	3.6	16.3	8.4	48
Finished manufactures	452	86.3	4.1	9.6	33.3	17.8	47
8—Agricultural	3	94.5	—	5.5	23.3	8.6	63
9—Nonagricultural	450	86.2	4.2	9.6	33.4	17.8	47

Source: U.S. Tariff Commission, *Effect of Trade Agreement Concessions on United States Tariff Levels Based on Imports in 1947,* May 1949, Tables 5 and 6, pp. 13 and 14.

a. Excluding imports on which duties were not bound or reduced.

137

slightly less by 1949. The largest rate reductions on agricultural products were made on manufactured foodstuffs and finished manufactures; the lowest on crude materials and semimanufactures. The smallest reductions in the nonagricultural group were on semifinished and finished manufactures. (See Table 29.)

The sixteen principal commodities on which duties were reduced account for over 57 per cent of total imports with reduced duties and for 53 per cent of the total reductions. Cuban cane sugar was by far the largest item, and the rate on it was reduced 65 per cent. (See Table 30.) The duty on wool was reduced by 25 per cent and on burlap by 50 per cent. The tax on crude petroleum was also reduced by 50 per cent.

Only 6.6 per cent of dutiable imports (1952 composition) remained untouched by tariff concessions.[5] The average rate on these was 18 per cent on January 1, 1953. A further 4 per cent were bound against increases from preagreement rates. The average rate on these was 14 per cent.

The duties which had not been reduced or bound by concessions on January 1, 1953 averaged 53 per cent on earthenware, 56 per cent on silk manufactures, 31 per cent on beverages, 33 per cent on cotton manufactures, 32 per cent on flax, hemp and manufactures, 48 per cent on wood and manufactures, 26 per cent on fishery products and 29 per cent on sundries. (See Table 31.) There is a strong presumption that most of these imports would increase substantially if duties were cut by 50 per cent. The total value of 1953 imports on which duties had not been cut in these eight categories was only $75 million.

The reductions in duty extend through all size classes of rates, that is, the 20–30 per cent class of preagreement rates was reduced by 50 per cent, the 70–80 per cent class by 46 per cent, etc. (See Table 32.)

In sum, while there have been no across-the-board cuts, tariff reduction has been comprehensive by industrial classes and by height-of-duty brackets.

The average reduction by trade agreement to January 1, 1949 on all dutiable imports was 47 per cent. (See Table 25.) Excluding those imports on which duties were not bound or reduced, the corresponding figure was 50 per cent (Table 29); including the concessions at Annecy, the average reduction to January 1, 1950 was 52 per cent (Table 32); including the Torquay concessions, the average reduction to January 1, 1952 was 55 per cent based on 1949 imports and 54 per cent based on 1952 imports.

The calculated average rate (weighted by 1947 imports) on January 1, 1950 was 14.3 per cent. The maximum permissible reduction under the law would have reduced the average rate to 9.8 per cent. On January 1, 1953 after Torquay, the calculated average rate (weighted by 1952 imports) was 12.2 per cent. (See Table 26.)

5. Weighted by 1949 imports, the corresponding figure was 5.5 per cent.

TABLE 30

Commodity	Value of Imports, 1947	Rate of Duty or Ad Valorem Equivalent in Effect:		Percentage Reduction
		Before Any Agreements	On January 1, 1949	
	(Millions)	*(Per Cent)*		
Schedule 3				
Watches, 16 or 17 jewels, 0.6–0.8 inches wide	$ 17	62.8	37.7	40
Nickel in pigs, etc.	34	9.9	4.1	59
Lead pigs and bars	34	17.5	8.8	50
Schedule 5				
Cane sugar, from Cuba	405	31.6	11.1	65
Schedule 6				
Cigarette leaf tobacco, unstemmed, except Latakia	51	38.1	32.6	14
Cigar filler tobacco, stemmed, from Cuba	24	27.0	13.5	50
Schedule 7				
Castor beans	25	5.6	2.8	50
Tomatoes in their natural state, except from Cuba	20	36.4	18.2	50
Cotton, staple 1¼ inch or over	33	17.3	8.6	50
Schedule 8				
Whisky, aged in wood 4 years, in containers of 1 gallon or less	49	106.8	32.0	70
Schedule 10				
Jute burlaps, not bleached, etc.	109	4.9	2.4	50
Schedule 11				
Combing wool, finer than 56s, in the grease	120	47.9	36.0	25
Schedule 15				
Bristles, sorted, bunched, or prepared	19	1.0	1.0	Bound
Diamonds, cut but not set, suitable for jewelry, except from Cuba	53	10.0	10.0	Bound
Free list, taxable				
Crude petroleum	162	13.0	6.5	50
Residual fuel oil	35	15.4	7.7	50

Source: U.S. Tariff Commission, *Effect of Trade Agreement Concessions on United States Tariff Levels Based on Imports in 1947*, May 1949, Table 11, pp. 20–23.

TABLE 31

IMPORTS BOUND TO PREAGREEMENT AND IMPORTS ON WHICH NO CONCESSIONS WERE MADE UNDER TRADE AGREEMENTS IN EFFECT JANUARY 1, 1953[a]

(Based on 1952 Imports)

Tariff Schedule	Imports Subject to Preagreement Rates Bound against Increase		Imports Subject to Rates on Which No Concessions Have Been Made	
	Total Value	Ad Valorem Equivalent of Rates of Duty	Total Value	Ad Valorem Equivalent of Rates of Duty
	(Millions)	(Per Cent)	(Millions)	(Per Cent)
1. Chemicals, oils and paints	$ .2	20.1	$ 6.4	15.0
2. Earths, earthenware and glassware	1.3	52.2	15.2	53.4
3. Metals and manufactures of	12.0	16.0	91.3	13.2
4. Wood and manufactures of	—	—	4.8	48.5
5. Sugar, molasses and manufactures of	—	b	—	b
6. Tobacco and manufactures of	—	—	—	—
7. Agricultural products and provisions, total or average	82.8	18.7	128.6	12.3
Fishery products	17.3	12.4	8.2	25.8
Other	65.5	20.4	120.4	11.4
8. Spirits, wines and other beverages	b	—	2.8	30.9
9. Cotton manufactures	—	b	3.3	33.2
10. Flax, hemp, jute and manufactures of	6.5	3.3	1.6	32.0
11. Wool and manufactures of	.7	8.2	2.7	11.6
12. Silk manufactures	—	—	3.2	56.2
13. Manufactures of rayon or other synthetic textile	—	—	—	b
14. Papers and books	—	—	.6	20.2
15. Sundries	76.3	9.2	35.3	29.2
Free list taxable	b	b	1.0	9.1
Total or average	$180.0	14.2	$296.8	18.3

Source: U.S. Tariff Commission; see Table 26.
a. Including U.S. tariff concessions at Torquay.
b. Imports too small to make computation of ad valorem equivalent significant.

TABLE 32

AVERAGE RATES BY HEIGHT-OF-DUTY BRACKETS BEFORE AND AFTER CONCESSIONS[a]

(*Per Cent*)

Rate of Duty before Any Agreements (Per Cent Ad Valorem)	Ad Valorem Equivalent Based on Rates in Effect:			Reduction in Rate Preagreement to:	
	Before Any Agreements	January 1, 1945	January 1, 1950[a]	January 1, 1945	January 1, 1950[a]
10.0 or less	5.8	4.4	2.6	25	55
10.1 to 20.0	15.0	9.1	7.5	39	50
20.1 to 30.0	26.6	19.0	13.4	28	50
30.1 to 40.0	33.0	19.3	13.2	42	60
40.1 to 50.0	47.0	40.0	30.9	15	34
50.1 to 60.0	55.3	39.6	30.8	28	44
60.1 to 70.0	65.6	46.8	35.8	29	45
70.1 to 80.0	75.2	55.1	40.9	27	46
80.1 to 90.0	87.8	64.2	48.7	27	44
90.1 or over	107.3	55.1	35.9	49	66
Total, all rates	29.6	19.6	14.3	34	52

Source: U.S. Tariff Commission, *Operation of the Trade Agreements Program*, Third Report, July 1949–June 1950, p. 107.

a. Based on 1947 imports and including tariff concessions made by the United States at Annecy.

Terms of Trade

Tariff reduction may affect the terms of trade as well as the volume of trade. Particularly if the supply of imports is inelastic or imports are regulated by quota, as in sugar, a nation exporting to the United States may gain dollars by increasing its export prices without paying any more for its imports, as a result of reductions in the American tariff.

The most important single gain from tariff reduction has been to increase returns to Cuban sugar producers. As a result of the 65 per cent reduction in duty, the substantial revenue formerly collected by the U.S. Treasury on sugar imports now goes to foreign sugar growers in the form of higher export prices, because the quantity of imports is regulated and the American price is held up by highly restrictive quotas.

Other countries in general may have gained more from American tariff reduction through the resulting increase in their export prices than by the increased quantity of their exports to us. But it cannot be established who gained through the terms of trade as a result of reciprocal tariff reduction. If the rest of the world gained on balance, as a general rule, the result would be salutary (although not what the Congress intended).

There is little reason why the rich United States should tax the poor world as a source of revenue. However, in addition to support of agricultural prices by government programs, the demand for American exports has been so distended by foreign aid that the cost of our exports to the recipients may have offset the price benefits to other countries of tax (import duty) reductions on their exports to us. In any event these factors were but waves on the rising tide of inflation abroad and at home.

"Between 1936–1938 and 1946 United States import prices rose 13 per cent more than export prices, and by the end of 1948 they were 24 per cent higher." During the postwar years "the cost of imports in terms of exports has risen with very little interruption."[6]

We should, however, generally expect import prices to rise (and fall) more rapidly than export prices because raw materials and foodstuffs are about twice as large a share of total imports as of total exports and these prices are more flexible than other prices. The cost of imports in terms of exports in 1948–1949 was roughly the same as in 1923–1925. Following the Korean War, import prices increased more rapidly than export prices.

Treatment of American Exports

The original objective of the Trade Agreements Act was to eliminate restrictions and discrimination against American exports. The concessions received do not appear to have been so great as those granted. But this is quite impossible to measure. In any event, the concessions received are largely on paper, except for the effect on the terms of trade.

Owing to the acute postwar dollar shortage fostered by the internal monetary policies of foreign governments, the restrictions and discrimination against American exports since World War II have been greater than before. The lowering of foreign tariffs could not substantially increase our exports except as the world's dollar earnings from American imports were increased. Under the circumstances quantitative controls which discriminate against American exports have been widely used. The need for quantitative controls is dictated primarily by the internal policies of other governments with respect to money, taxes, exchange rates, wages and employment.

The concessions for which the United States has bargained under trade agreements are of two kinds: (1) general provisions concerning commercial policy, and (2) reductions in the barriers against imports of specific commodities.

Some of the general provisions are designed to protect scheduled concessions while others prevent discriminatory and other unfavorable treatment of United States exports. The United States itself has employed quotas on agricultural imports but, as a rule, has not imposed other restrictions, such as exchange controls and quantitative discriminatory treatment of imports from different sources.

6. H. K. Zassenhaus and F. C. Dirks, "Recent Developments in the U.S. Balance of Payments," *Staff Papers*, International Monetary Fund, April 1952, p. 231.

Halting and reversal of the trend toward extension of these practices, therefore, have been prime objectives of the United States in its trade agreements program, and for these objectives the general provisions of the agreements are of major importance.[7]

American exporters are said to have benefited from most-favored-nation treatment,[8] which assures the United States the benefit of concessions granted by trade agreement countries to third countries. The 1936 Canadian agreement is, perhaps, the most significant instance where tariff discrimination against our exports was eliminated. By the most-favored-nation provision, duties were reduced on about 43 per cent of Canada's total dutiable imports from the United States. The French agreement of 1936 provided a similar benefit, although it covered a smaller volume of trade.

The preferential tariff systems of the United Kingdom and the Commonwealth nations, and to a lesser degree that of France Overseas, have been a major target in the general provisions sought by the United States. Although the preference features of the United Kingdom and Canadian tariffs were somewhat modified by specific concessions in pre-Geneva trade agreements, the most-favored-nation provisions of these agreements did not directly affect the preferential system. Moreover, up to a certain date new and increased preferences could have been introduced, either by raising rates on imports from the United States or, in the case of commodities covered by scheduled concessions, by reducing duties on imports from Commonwealth sources.

The General Agreement on Tariffs and Trade contains a most-favored-nation clause which, while not banning the imperial preference system, greatly limits its scope and magnitude. A general provision of the Geneva agreement pledges the contracting countries (1) not to introduce new preferences for imports from countries with which preferential trade relations have existed in the past, and (2) not to increase existing preference margins.

Not only does the Geneva provision protect many concessions against the serious impairment which might result from subsequent increase in the margins of British Preference, but also, for many commodities not covered by the schedules of concessions, its effect is equivalent in importance to the binding in previous tariff treatment.[9]

7. U.S. Tariff Commission, *Operation of the Trade Agreements Program*, Part I, p. 28. ". . . the importance of the trade agreements to the export trade of the United States may well lie as much in the general provisions of these agreements as in the scheduled commitments made by the other contracting countries regarding their treatment of imports of specific commodities . . . especially in the long run." *Ibid.*, p. 33.

8. "The obligation to extend most-favored-nation treatment in customs and related matters to other contracting parties is a cornerstone of the (General) agreement. . . ." William Adams Brown, Jr., *The United States and the Restoration of World Trade*, The Brookings Institution, Washington, 1950, p. 251.

9. U.S. Tariff Commission, *Operation of the Trade Agreements Program*, Part IV, p. 7; see also Brown, *op. cit.*, pp. 250–253.

In general, the terms of pre-Geneva agreements committed foreign nations, except in time of war, not to apply quantitative restrictions against the United States imports listed in the scheduled concessions unless quotas were set forth in the schedules, and not to apply quantitative restrictions in a manner discriminating against imports from the United States.

The Geneva agreement limited the use of quantitative restrictions on both scheduled and unscheduled items and continued the earlier prohibitions against discriminatory treatment. However, the Geneva agreement added the important qualification that countries in balance-of-payments difficulties may apply quantitative restrictions in a discriminatory manner.

Whereas earlier trade agreements prohibited use of exchange controls to discriminate against United States exports, the general articles of the Geneva agreement do not deal directly with the use of exchange controls. These matters are now handled by the International Monetary Fund. Although the Fund agreement aims in general to limit the use of exchange control devices, the "scarce currency" provision permits discriminatory quantitative restrictions on imports under certain conditions. The Fund agreement also recognizes exchange controls during the "transition," which is not defined. Not only may discrimination be practiced against United States exports under postwar agreements, but provisions against quantitative import and exchange restrictions in the earlier agreements may be temporarily suspended to meet balance-of-payments difficulties.

For some time to come, therefore, the provision against discriminatory use of quotas will remain largely inoperative, and in consequence the value to United States exporters of many of the scheduled concessions will remain problematical. Moreover, quantitative restrictions imposed for balance-of-payments reasons may often afford additional protection to the industries of the countries imposing them and encourage the development of new industries.[10]

Twenty-three of the contracting parties to the General Agreement indicated in November 1951 that they were then resorting to quantitative restrictions for balance-of-payments reasons. These included twelve continental countries, all the British Commonwealth countries except Canada, and Brazil, Chile and Indonesia. For the same reason, quantitative restrictions on imports are employed by the following countries with which the United States has bilateral agreements: Argentina, Ecuador, Paraguay, Uruguay, Iceland and Iran.

Only a few countries employed few or no quantitative restrictions on trade in 1951–1952. These included Canada, the Dominican Republic, El Salvador, Guatemala, Haiti, Honduras and Liberia.[11]

10. U.S. Tariff Commission, *Operation of the Trade Agreements Program*, Part I, p. 32.

11. *Ibid.*, Fifth Report, July 1951–June 1952, pp. 28–33. For the progress made in many countries toward greater freedom in trade and payments, see the annual reports of the International Monetary Fund on exchange restrictions.

There is some doubt as to the wisdom of the great emphasis the United States has placed on nondiscriminatory multilateral trade in the postwar years. The doctrine was "sold" to the world on paper but not in practice. The value of this and other concessions to the United States depends on the elimination of the dollar shortage, that is, on the restoration of balance and order in world trade. Many countries were unwilling to cut their standard of living and investment plans. The result was inflation, open or controlled. Under these conditions, convertibility of currencies was impossible and discrimination against dollar purchases became the general practice. By 1953, however, continental thinking was turning toward more orthodox economic policies. Some liberalization of policy toward dollar imports was adopted by Belgium, Germany and Britain. America has made important contributions toward this objective by large-scale foreign aid, which represents a net addition to the resources of receiving countries. We have also made it possible for the outside world to increase its dollar earnings by maintaining a high level of national income and by a domestic stockpiling program, both of which have increased American imports. These factors have doubtless played a more important role than tariff reduction in enabling other countries to pursue more liberal trade policies.

Multilateralism

The refusal of the United States substantially to increase competitive imports together with its insistence on equal treatment of American exports has exacerbated the balance-of-payments difficulties of other countries. Under trade agreements other countries can discriminate against United States exports only after they get into serious balance-of-payment difficulties.

A foreign country suffering from shortage of dollars often might buy more of what it needs from nations in the nondollar area, and thus economize dollars without restricting the total of its imports. But if, as is often the case, the prices of goods from the nondollar area are higher than those of the same goods from the United States, this practice requires quota restrictions on dollar imports and, thus, discriminates against American exporters—a practice forbidden by trade agreements. The policy of insisting on equal treatment of American exports is defended on the ground that it will force other supplying countries to bring their prices and costs down in order to balance their receipts and payments. The issue, therefore, depends on whether other countries are able and willing to pursue internal policies which will keep their costs competitive with American goods.

This problem is illustrated by the restrictions imposed by Belgium in 1951 on dollar imports. These were designed by Belgium to shift her imports to European sources and, thus, to reduce the surplus that Belgium had with the European Payments Union. The United States and Canada complained that this discrimination against dollar imports was a violation of GATT. When Belgium subsequently announced at the seventh session of GATT that she planned to relax the quotas on dollar imports, France, Italy and the Netherlands expressed apprehension lest this step should prove harmful to the balance-of-payments position of other European countries whose exports had benefited from Belgium's discrimination against dollar imports. The United States and Canada refused to condone this argument for intra-European trade based on discrimination against dollar goods and insisted that Belgium should conform to its obligation under GATT.[12]

As long as there are hard and soft currencies, the volume of world trade could be increased by permitting systematic discrimination against hard currency goods. The danger of maintaining discrimination, of course, is that the soft currency countries may be relieved of the pressure to make the fundamental internal adjustments required to get their costs and prices in line with hard currency countries. But if they are unable or unwilling to make these adjustments, the volume of trade may be restricted by the nondiscrimination rule.

The effect of trade agreements on trade has been completely overshadowed by historical developments which culminated in the second world war and by the disorder following the war.

The statement that expansion of international trade "is vital to peace and prosperity" is a half-truth at best. It is more nearly true that peace and prosperity beget trade.

Balanced trade as we knew it before the first world war was conditioned by certain accepted internal policies of government. The institutional framework of foreign trade has changed with the rise of the welfare state. Trade agreements policies were not conceived against this background and are not designed to meet the problems of disequilibrium and the dollar shortage. The best that can be hoped for is that if order can be restored in the balance-of-payments problems, the salutary effect of lower tariffs may have an opportunity to work. But this is as much a question of national monetary and fiscal policies as of international commercial policies.

Evaluation

In face of the vagaries of statistics, most investigators, after citing the data, turn to a priori reasoning to defend the Trade Agreements Program. Only modest claims are made on the general ground that at last the United States is headed in the right direction.

. . . the primary importance of the Hull policy lay in the fact that in 1934, for the first time since the Underwood Act of 1913, United States tariff rates started

12. Press Release, GATT/101, European Office of the United Nations, Geneva, November 11, 1952.

moving downwards, and the apparently irresistible drive toward increased protection was checked.[13]

A prewar monograph found that because the program had helped to reduce discrimination

It is reasonable to conclude that the United States has enjoyed a gain in trade, as compared with the volume of trade that would have been transacted if there had been no trade agreements program.[14]

Even supporters of reciprocal trade who believe that the tangible benefits of larger trade have been substantial have viewed the program as vastly more important to us "in terms of international good will and future economic relations."[15]

The State Department has stressed the significance of the program as an instrument of agreement among the free nations of the world and as a "shield" in the struggle against the expansion of Soviet power.

The implication that trade agreements have been an important instrument promoting the common cause of the West against the Soviet Union and her satellites seems strained. The United States has been able to negotiate agreements with free nations because of a common interest, to say nothing of loans and aid. Reduction of American tariffs was overdue. Because of the acute dollar shortage it has been particularly important to avoid the appearance of keeping out imports even though lower duties have not, in fact, contributed appreciably to the restoration of balance in world trade.

Thus far, the policy of free multilateral trade has failed, and it may be doubted if the trade agreements approach has appreciably improved the economic integration and political solidarity of the free world. Certainly the program deserves full credit for a successful break with the Hawley-Smoot tradition. But it should not be assumed that a return to Hawley-Smoot tariffs is the only alternative to the present trade agreements policy.

The objective of trade agreements has now swung full circle. Originally hailed as a program to expand export markets in the midst of a depression, it is now regarded in many quarters as a means of substituting "trade for aid," which requires increased imports without increased exports.

Since the inauguration of the Reciprocal Trade Agreements program, the relative and absolute increase of our exports has exceeded that of our imports. This is the most important criticism that can be legitimately directed against the

13. William Diebold, *New Directions in Our Trade Policy*, Council on Foreign Relations, New York, 1941, pp. 23 and 24.

14. Grace Beckett, *Reciprocal Trade Agreements Program*, Columbia University Press, New York, 1941, pp. 112 and 113.

15. Mary J. Bowman and George L. Bach, *Economic Analysis and Public Policy*, 2d edition, Prentice-Hall, New York, 1949, p. 888.

program. Its failure to achieve a more adequate reduction in United States tariffs has seriously limited its contribution to the solution of the "dollar-shortage" problem.[16]

There is no legal authority whatever to reduce tariffs for the purpose of balancing trade, especially when exports are distended by foreign aid. Tariff reduction can make it a little easier to balance imports and exports at *high* levels rather than *low* levels. But tariff reduction, especially reciprocal tariff reduction, affects imports and exports alike. Tariffs affect the *level* of trade and not the *balance* of trade.

The protectionists score a point when they complain of the disingenuous shift in the arguments supporting tariff reduction.

The Trade Agreements Act was introduced in 1934 for the purpose, as stated in the preamble, of restoring employment and correcting the effects of the depression. When it was extended in 1937 war had started in Asia, and proponents of the Act said a major purpose was to prevent war. When the Act was extended in 1940, war had started in Europe; preparations for war had ended the depression; and the Trade Agreements would help keep us out of the war. In 1943 the Act was extended again, and then the Act was said to be necessary to win the war it could not prevent. In 1945, the extension was advocated to reconstruct and restore normal trade with Europe. In 1948, there was an extension of one year, as mentioned before, with the intention of studying and improving the tariff system; but in 1949 the Act was extended again for the avowed purpose of closing the dollar gap in our foreign trade, of restoring multilateral trade, and of preventing the spread of communism. In 1950 a special study for closing the foreign trade gap was in progress when the communists attacked in Korea, and the subsequent rearmament moves helped to close the gap. Nevertheless, the President's special assistant, Gordon Gray, went ahead and made a voluminous report recommending, among other things, approval of the Havana Charter for ITO (now dead), and more Trade Agreements and reductions of tariff. Then the Secretary of State stated that the planned Torquay conference must go forward as tariff reductions would help curb inflation, under these new war conditions.[17]

The Trade Agreements Program is Janus-faced. It looks, in one direction, toward the liberal tradition of free multilateral trade, and in the other, toward the protection of home industry.

The program is two-faced because it was never strongly supported for the right reason and was sometimes supported for the wrong reason. *Trade is good—not because it will create additional jobs, but because it will make some jobs more productive. Trade is good—not primarily as a substitute for foreign aid, but because trade is mutually profitable.*

16. J. M. Letich, *Reciprocal Trade Agreements in the World Economy*, King's Crown Press, New York, 1948, pp. 30 and 32.

17. *Improving Our Tariff Program*, American Tariff League Publication No. 127, pp. 8 and 9.

But the explanation of why trade is good exposes the real problem. *The gains from trade are derived from the shift of domestic resources to more productive employment and depend, therefore, on the injury and liquidation of industries that need protection, or on the restriction of their growth in comparison with the growth of consumption.* Some gains to the total economy may also be realized from the abolition of tariff subsidies to industries that could survive and grow, though at lower prices, without protection.

The escape clause does not guarantee domestic producers against increased competition from imports, but against serious injury. To what extent can trade increase under this policy?

(1) Imports may rise, but less rapidly than home production. This represents the relative disintegration of foreign trade. (2) Imports may increase more rapidly than home production where the domestic market is growing. This represents relative, though not absolute, displacement of home production. (3) Where a business produces many products, imports may displace one product without *seriously* injuring the industry. (4) Imports which do not directly compete with the specific products of home industry may increase without injury.

Noncompetitive imports create no difficulty except in borderline cases where it is difficult to determine whether the specific import is directly competitive with domestic products or creates a new market of its own. The growing market offers the most promising prospect for increased imports under present policies. The rub is that, apparently, foreign countries enjoy a comparative advantage chiefly in those domestic markets which are relatively stagnant.[18]

Tariff concessions have been circumscribed with solicitous care for maintaining essential protection of home industry. The procedure established for screening tariff concessions is expressly designed to reduce the tariff without seriously increasing competitive imports as a result. The heart of the matter is the principle that no domestic industries shall be seriously injured. Much ingenuity has been employed to reduce the tariff without injury. Concessions have been circumscribed in four ways:

First, the tariff classification has been subdivided in order to limit the effect of tariff reduction. In effect, this amounts to discrimination by multiplication of tariff classes; it serves to exclude third parties from the benefits of concessions.

Second, the advantage of the multilateral extension of concessions to third parties is limited by the policy of tariff bargaining which makes concessions only to the principal supplier. Tariff bargaining with individual countries on the principal supplier approach is inimicable to the multi-

18. Cf. Chapters 19–22.

lateral expansion of trade. This point has become less important since GATT.

Third, tariff reduction has been offset by quantitative controls. Quotas were imposed on 15 of the 38 imports with a value of $1 million or more on which duties were reduced 50 per cent or more between 1934 and 1948.

Finally, the general escape clause requires that concessions be suspended in case the resulting imports threaten serious injury to any branch of home industry. The principle of protection has not been seriously breeched by tariff concessions, which have been so conscientiously screened that it was rarely necessary to suspend any concession that was granted.

The program initiated by Cordell Hull has been commonly referred to as "our liberal Trade Agreements Program." This is something of a euphemism; the policy does not represent classical liberalism. In order to avoid serious injury, tariffs have been systematically reduced where the cuts would do the least harm and provide the least benefit. This criticism is essential to understanding the limitations of the Trade Agreements Program. In the spring of 1951, Secretary Acheson told a Congressional Committee that where low wages in foreign countries created competitive problems "the record of action under the Reciprocal Trade Agreement Act demonstrates clearly that we have been fully aware . . . have carefully acted . . . in a manner that would avoid serious injury to the industry and workers involved."[19] Acheson's statement is supported by the facts.

There can be no possible doubt as to the careful and conscientious work of the Trade Agreements Committee. It is remarkable that tariffs could be reduced so much and imports increased so little. Imports have increased but less than income, compared with the high-tariff 1920s.

Because so many other factors were at work, it cannot be demonstrated conclusively how much or how little imports have increased *as a result of tariff concessions*. The evidence must be weighed.

First, all experience shows that American imports increase more rapidly than home production in periods of rapid expansion. Yet the quantity of imports rose less than 4 per cent in the twenty years[20] 1929–1949, a period in which real gross national product increased by two thirds. In part as a result of the war in Korea, the quantity of imports increased 20 per cent from 1949 to 1951 while real gross national product increased 16 per cent. The increase in imports after 1946 includes substantial inventories for the stockpiling of strategic materials.

Second, efforts to check the specific items which might be expected to increase most as a result of tariff reductions have turned up relatively few

19. Prepared statement before House Ways and Means Committee, January 22, 1951, mimeographed.
20. Quantity data for dutiable imports alone are not available.

instances where imports have increased faster than domestic production. More important, domestic producers themselves are alert to competition from imports. Requests for relief under the escape clause provide a good indication of the relative unimportance of the industries where imports have increased faster than domestic production as a result of tariff concessions. Escape clause proceedings show only three "industries" which had been seriously injured as of June 30, 1952: (1) women's fur felt hats, (2) hatters' fur, and (3) dried figs. Imports of filberts and almonds were also found injurious to domestic marketing programs. Up to January 1955, the escape clause was also invoked on alsike clover seed and watch movements.

The President has declined to invoke the escape clause, as recommended by the Tariff Commission, on garlic, tobacco pipes, scissors and shears, groundfish fillets, lead and zinc, handblown glassware, spring clothespins, screen-printed silk scarves and screws.

Imports of certain agricultural products on which tariffs were reduced are restricted by quota;[21] otherwise, some of these imports would have increased substantially, in part as a result of tariff concession, but also as a result of growth of population and incomes.

Compared with prosperous prewar years, the quantity of imports has fallen drastically in relation to national product. It may be, of course, that without tariff concessions the relative decline would have been still greater. But the overwhelming weight of evidence is that the increase in America's trade as a result of tariff reduction has been in no way commensurate with the magnitude of the undertaking.

Nonetheless, the comprehensive reduction of duties (1) by about 50 per cent as a result of tariff concessions, and (2) by a like amount as a result of rising prices, may produce more substantial results in the future, particularly if a high rate of internal growth is maintained and business fluctuations are moderated. *In time, it is probable that the dynamic changes in relative costs will produce an increase in imports if the present level of duties is held and if unemployment can be avoided.*[22] This may not be possible, however, under the escape clause. We shall return in Chapter 19 to the question of "Injury and the Escape Clause," which is of decisive importance.

21. Cf. pp. 406 ff.
22. This statement makes no allowance for possible technological displacement of raw material imports such as has taken place since the 1920s. See Chapters 14 and 15.

Chapter 7

Attitudes toward the Tariff

ATTITUDES TOWARD the tariff have changed since the 1920s and again since the 1930s. The evidence which will be reviewed indicates that support for freer trade is stronger in the business community than ever before. At the same time, attempts to reduce trade barriers seem to have arrived at a virtual impasse, and evidence can be cited which seems to point to a resurgence of protectionist strength. These apparently contradictory developments require interpretation.

In 1934 when the Congress first authorized reduction of tariffs, the overriding considerations were expansion of *domestic* production and employment in the midst of depression. It was hoped that by reciprocal tariff reduction on a selective basis, exports could be expanded without increasing those imports which would damage home industry. As the United States became deeply involved in the problems of the outside world, the focus changed. Considerations of *foreign* rather than domestic policy have come to play a decisive role. The second authorization (in 1945) to reduce duties was part of a larger program to restore world order, which had been completely shattered by depression and war.

Support for the Trade Agreements Program has been derived from three different sources: (1) There is a growing awareness on the part of exporters that the export market is limited by the volume of imports. (2) Prosperity and full employment at home have provided a favorable climate. (3) As the threat of Soviet expansion became apparent, the need for strengthening the free world by expansion of trade became more compelling. On the other hand, as surplus tariff protection was eliminated, the import-competing industries became increasingly apprehensive and, except for the cold war, it is doubtful that the Trade Agreements Act could have been extended repeatedly since 1945. In sum, there seems to be a consensus that more trade would be a "good thing," but American industry and agriculture are not prepared to accept the consequences.

The key to the dilemma is that after almost twenty years of experimenting with lower tariffs, the program still lacks that firm foundation which can be provided only by acceptance of the *principle* that the direct economic gains from trade outweigh the damage to home industry. Many of those who have been converted to the "liberal" side were influenced more by international developments than by the doctrine of Adam Smith.

This conversion was graphically described by Clarence B. Randall, President of Inland Steel, member of Harvard's governing board and Chairman of President Eisenhower's Commission on Foreign Economic Policy:

> Until 1948—until Paul Hoffman tagged me to go to Europe for him, I was the most isolationist guy you ever saw. Then I got a first-class scrubbing of my ideas. . . . We ought at least to make it clear that the tariff level won't be raised for, say, five years.[1]

The Impasse in Tariff Policy

The doctrine of foreign trade which asserts that high-cost domestic producers in the import-competing industries should be liquidated in favor of the expansion of exports has never been widely accepted.

> In the universities, a succession of brilliant economists such as William Graham Sumner, Frank Taussig and Jacob Viner exposed the fallacies of protection and put the case for freer trade forcefully and with great clarity. Hundreds more of teachers of economics made tens of thousands of undergraduate students familiar with the theory of international trade. But this teaching had little impact on public opinion. The American business community, until recently, maintained a fairly solid protectionist front. It either ignored the professors or dismissed their arguments as "theoretical."[2]

So long as the case for lower trade barriers is based primarily on the needs of the outside world, the advocate is caught in the embarrassing position of seeming to sanction immediate damage to home industry for the remote objective of providing a basis for world order. This position is so uncomfortable that it is scarcely tenable without the reinforcements which can be provided only by the theory of foreign trade. The theory shows that *the nation itself can gain directly as a result* of the liquidation of its high-cost industries and the shift of resources to more productive employment. It is rare, however, that those who have asked the Congress to reduce trade barriers are prepared to stand up and be counted in favor of the liquidation of any home industry.

We have now had four high-level reports to the President in almost as many years which called for lower trade barriers and increased imports.[3]

1. *Fortune*, March 1953. For a considered statement of Randall's views, see his Charles R. Walgreen Foundation lectures, *A Foreign Economic Policy of the United States*, University of Chicago Press, Chicago, 1954.

2. Percy W. Bidwell in the Foreword to *Foreign Trade and U.S. Tariff Policy*, edited by Joseph Barber, Council on Foreign Relations, New York, 1953.

3. In addition see the report of the Sawyer Mission, *Foreign Commerce Weekly*, December 22, 1952, and *Report of the ECA Commerce Mission* (Taylor Mission), October 1949.

1. The Gray Report called for lower trade barriers and concluded that "This nation has nothing to fear from liberal import policies."[4]

2. The President's Materials Policy Commission showed the need for increased imports of materials for growth and security.[5]

3. The Public Advisory Board for Mutual Security advocated tariff reform in the national interest.[6]

4. The Randall Commission asked for extension of the Trade Agreements Act for three years with new authority to reduce duties by only 15 per cent.[7]

The Randall Commission included five senators, five representatives and five public members. Apparently, the Commission sought to win the support of its most strongly protectionist members for continuation of the Trade Agreements Program by recommending only a symbolic cut in duties. Even so, the effort failed. The *Minority Report* asserts that the majority was *"primarily concerned* with the steps that this country can take toward *solving the world's dollar problem . . ."* and that this misconstrues the congressional directive to "deal with the enlargement of international trade in a manner consistent with a sound domestic economy."[8]

President Eisenhower's 1954 Message to Congress on foreign economic policy was based largely on the majority recommendations of the Randall Commission. It asked for very little and in the view of most observers "promised to get even less."

Emasculation of the program by commodity amendments was avoided by a compromise measure in 1955. This extension of the act reflects accurately the attitudes responsible for the impasse in policy. Tariffs may be further reduced by up to 15 per cent and duties higher than 50 per cent may be reduced to a maximum of 50 per cent, as recommended by the Randall Commission. On the other hand, crippling amendments make it much easier for domestic producers to obtain tariff relief from damaging foreign competition. Increased protection under the escape clause and national security amendments may more than offset the effect of further cuts in the tariff. Thus, the Congress has authorized the President to move forward and backward at the same time.

4. *Report to the President on Foreign Economic Policies*, November 1950.

5. *Resources for Freedom*, Vol. I, *Foundations for Growth and Security* (Paley Report), June 1952.

6. *A Trade and Tariff Policy in the National Interest* (Bell Report), 1953.

7. *Report of the Commission on Foreign Economic Policy*, January 1954. This report has been widely criticized at both the popular and academic level. See, for example, the editorial in *Life*, February 15, 1954, and *A Critique of the Randall Commission Report*, prepared by Klaus Knorr and Gardner Patterson on the basis of a conference held at Princeton University in 1954.

8. *Minority Report*, Commission on Foreign Economic Policy, January 1954.

Support and Opposition

The consumer interest does not appear from the record to have played a significant role in the determination of tariff policy. Support for the program has been based almost wholly on the export argument and foreign policy considerations. Churches, women's clubs and cultural groups have generally supported trade agreements on the broad ground of improving international relations.

A close contest occurred in 1940, when mounting grievances of "exposed" industries threatened to defeat extension of the Trade Agreements Act. The Senate vote in 1940 was 42 to 37 in favor of the act, with 17 members not voting.[9]

A substantial part of the mass production and heavy engineering industries presented favorable statements either directly or through the Department of Commerce. The hard core of support for the program has centered among the cotton and tobacco growers, the shipping industries and import merchants.

Representative groups supporting the program in 1940 or 1948 included:

Agricultural

American Farm Bureau Federation
Texas Federation of Women's Clubs
Tobacco growers (not an association)
Dried Fruit Association of California

Manufacturing

Business Advisory Council for the Department of Commerce
Automobile Manufacturers Association
Remington Rand
United States Cuban Sugar Council
American Trade Association for British Woolens
American Watch Assemblers Association
Baldwin Locomotive Works
Atlantic Refining Company

Merchant

National Council of American Importers
Foreign Trade Committee, Detroit Board of Commerce
Merchants Association of New York City
National Foreign Trade Council

9. H.J.Res. 407, 76th Cong., 3d sess., 1940.

Straw Goods Importers Association
Foreign Trade Section of the Proprietary Association (pharmaceuticals)
Cuban Committee of the National Foreign Trade Council

Transportation

Merchant Marine Institute
W. R. Grace and Company (also trading)
Brotherhoods of Railway Trainmen and Clerks

The support of some of the groups was predicated on proper safeguards. The Texas Women's Club was interested chiefly in cotton exports. Tobacco growers wanted both foreign markets and a protective tariff. The Dried Fruit Association was interested in disposing of export surpluses.

The opposition was based almost entirely on the threat to import-competing home industries. Those interested in protection who favored serious modification of the program are here identified with the opposition. Representative groups opposing or wishing to seriously modify the program in 1940 or 1948 were:

Mainly Producers of Primary Products

National Wool Growers Association
National Grange
National Cooperative Milk Producers Federation
American National Livestock Association
National Council of Farm Cooperatives
American Mining Congress
American National Fox and Fur Breeders Association
National Board of Fur Farm Organizations
Massachusetts Fisheries Association
Independent Petroleum Association
National Coal Association
American Zinc Institute and Tri-State Zinc and Lead Ore Producers
    Association

Manufacturing Industries

Tariff Committee, National Association of Manufacturers
United States Potters Association
Vitrified China Association
American Glassware Association
National Association of Wool Manufacturers
National Association of Cotton Manufacturers
American Lace Manufacturers Association

Domestic Manufacturers of Watches
Wine Institute
National Lumber Manufacturing Association
Synthetic Organic Chemical Manufacturers

Allied Groups

Governors' Conference of New England
Workers Protective Conference
American Tariff League

In addition, there has always been a sprinkling of opposition from local agricultural interests subject to import competition. Typical are the California and Florida fruit growers, the California calavo growers, the Southwestern pecan growers and mushroom growers. Vegetable and dairy interests near the Canadian and Cuban border have been aggravated by the agreements with Canada and Cuba.

The active opposition of representatives from a score of very small industries, such as bicycles, motorcycles, pins, gloves and candied fruit, seems to have increased since 1948.[10]

Support for Freer Trade

The shift of sentiment in favor of freer trade is indicated by business leaders and organizations with a wide range of views.

The extreme position is taken by the Detroit Board of Commerce, which has declared for completely free trade. The senior officials of automobile companies, big oil companies, banks and other large concerns are now prominent among the active supporters of lower trade barriers. Henry Ford II makes this discerning comment:

A serious flaw in the present trade legislation is that it fails to provide any means for weighing the factor of national interest in the determination of tariff rates; by the same token, it fails to provide for indemnifying, financially or otherwise, a producer who suffers injuries in the national interest.[11]

Organization of the Committee for a National Trade Policy adds a long list of distinguished names to the roster of those who actively support freer trade. One of the directors, Charles H. Percy, president of Bell and Howell, believes that the United States will be better off in the long run

10. See *Trade Agreements Extension Act of 1953*, Hearings, House Ways and Means Committee, 83d Cong., 1st sess., pp. 8–9.

11. *Expanded Trade and World Peace*, reprint of an address sponsored by the Committee for a National Trade Policy, October 26, 1953. See also the statement in favor of freer trade by Eugene Holman, Chairman of the Board of Directors, Standard Oil of New Jersey, before the annual meeting of the National Foreign Trade Council in November 1953. (Reprinted as a public interest advertisement in the February 1954 issues of *Harper's Magazine* and the *Atlantic Monthly*.)

with freer trade. His company produces cameras, which are protected, but is also very interested in foreign markets for advanced sound-producing equipment.[12]

Percy was a star witness before the Ways and Means Committee in January 1955 when opposition threatened to wreck the Trade Agreements Program. The Committee for a National Trade Policy is doing an extremely useful job in mustering support for liberal policies. Its president, Charles P. Taft, provided the best informed and most forceful attack on misguided protectionists in the long history of congressional hearings on trade agreements. This is all the more important because surveys of opinion show that the tariff is rather far down on the list of issues which are of pressing concern to business executives.

The National Association of Manufacturers has substantially changed its position. In 1934 the Association advocated protection of home industry because of unemployment. The NAM held that the main handicap to trade was the low level of domestic production, and that prosperity at home must precede the revival of foreign trade.[13] Later, trade agreements were criticized as inconsistent with the cost-raising policies of the New Deal. The NAM held that trade agreements before the war had produced no significant benefits to our export industries. With the outbreak of war, it asked that further negotiations be stopped. In 1952, by contrast, the NAM was calling for better access to American markets for foreign producers.[14]

A 1953 survey of 825 influential citizens by the Council on Foreign Relations showed that 98 per cent believed that the United States should continue to reduce tariffs in return for reciprocal concessions. A majority of two thirds recognized that in some cases increased imports would damage home industry.[15]

A poll of 500 business and labor leaders by the Research Institute of America showed that 92 per cent believe the United States "should actively work for greater freedom in international trade" and 60 per cent "favor further lowering of our tariffs."[16] Other polls show roughly similar results.

The marked shift of business opinion toward freer trade is shown by a poll of 903 executives in 1954 by the National Opinion Research Center at the University of Chicago. The results, analyzed by the Center for International Studies at the Massachusetts Institute of Technology, show that one third of the executives interviewed had changed their attitude since 1939,

12. *Fortune*, March 1953.
13. See hearings on *Reciprocal Trade Agreements, 1934*, House Ways and Means Committee, pp. 127 and 395; *ibid.*, Senate Finance Committee, p. 299.
14. See the report on National Association of Manufacturers, *New York Times*, November 7 and December 4, 1952, and the Association's October declaration.
15. Joseph Barber (editor), *Foreign Trade and U.S. Tariff Policy*, Council on Foreign Relations, New York, 1953.
16. *Saturday Review*, January 23, 1954, p. 33.

and more than three fourths of these had shifted toward a more liberal policy. In 1939 a poll of executives by *Fortune* showed that 31.5 per cent were in favor of higher tariffs, 19.4 per cent (about half of whom had reservations) favored lower tariffs and 34.5 per cent wanted no change. Fifteen years later the M.I.T. analysis, published in *Fortune* (April 1955), showed the following attitudes:

Higher tariffs	5 per cent
Lower tariffs	38 per cent
Leave unchanged	31 per cent
Don't know	22 per cent
Refused to generalize	4 per cent

The effort to mobilize support for freer trade is assisted by such national publications as *Life* and *Fortune*. At the popular level, *Life* Magazine with its large circulation has devoted editorials to the need for lower trade barriers. Under the sanguine title, "Free Trade Is Inevitable," *Fortune* compared the shift in American attitudes today to the British drive for free trade a century ago, led by Manchester businessmen Richard Cobden and John Bright.[17]

It is apparent, however, that the American drive is stalled far short of free trade. The typical attitude is believed to be approximately the position taken by the United States Chamber of Commerce, which has supported the Trade Agreements Program from the outset.

The United States should pursue a realistic and constructive policy which will encourage the maximum flow of international trade and at the same time afford reasonable protection for American industry and agriculture against destructive and unfair competition from abroad. . . .

Imports required by our economy and industry help the United States maintain its export trade by providing foreign nations with the means of paying for our exports, and help to supply them with goods vital to their economies and improved standards of living. Therefore, for the benefit of the American economy as a whole, business and government should encourage increased United States imports, without, however, subjecting our own domestic producers or manufacturers to unfair or unreasonable disadvantage in competition.[18]

Three things are notable about this 1952 declaration: (1) The direct dependence of exports on imports is expressly recognized. Compared with the days of high tariffs, this represents a significant advance. (2) The importance of trade to other countries is recognized and the isolationist position is rejected. (3) The emphasis, however, is on the imports which

17. March 1953. See *Life's* editorial February 15, 1954. *Time* Magazine also carries special features in the Business section designed to fill an editorial function outside the area of spot news. See "The Case for Free Trade," May 25, 1953.

18. *What the National Chamber Stands For in World Affairs*, Washington, 1952, pp. 4 and 5.

are needed and it is not made clear that we "need" the kind of imports which compete directly with high-cost domestic production. In 1952, "constructive and realistic policy" to the Chamber meant maximum trade with reasonable protection—a highly elastic formula.

The following year the Chamber reviewed its position and, while still holding to the escape clause, adopted a somewhat more liberal attitude toward competitive imports.[19] The 1953 policy is that "Unreasonable or unethical competition must not be the cause of serious injury to domestic producers, but the determination of injury due to imports should be judged in the light of the national interest."[20]

Although the policy is still ambiguous, introduction of "the national interest" is a step forward which goes beyond the express provisions of existing legislation. The National Chamber has an underlying membership of 1,600,000 businessmen. It now appears to have joined the vanguard of public opinion in support of slightly more liberal criteria than have been sanctioned by the Congress.

Committee for Economic Development

Unlike many supporters of trade agreements, the Committee for Economic Development advocates the *principle* of freer trade, and its spokesman has gone farther than most of those who testify before congressional committees in accepting the consequences. CED has made a contribution by its sustained support of liberal policy based on traditional economics as well as on political considerations. Its recent testimony may help to explain why even an able pleading of the case for liberalism has not been sufficiently persuasive to win popular support and carry the day.

A liberal trade policy contributes to our objective of strengthening our domestic economy by increasing productivity and living standards. It does this by enabling us to use our resources in the most effective manner, specializing on what we can produce best and exchanging these products for goods which other countries produce more cheaply than we can make them. For the same reason, a liberal trade policy contributes to our objectives of strengthening our allies. Enabling them to produce and sell more of the products which they can make most efficiently increases their productivity and helps them to become self-supporting and strong. . . .

The C.E.D. believes that the logical course is a gradual and consistent policy of tariff reduction. . . .

The rate of technological progress of our economy outstrips that of the rest of the world. . . .

Aimed particularly at those classes of goods which our major allies are best able to produce and export, our present tariff policies reduce the ability of other

19. See the address by the president of the National Chamber, Richard Bowditch, *Our Stake in Foreign Trade*, June 12, 1953.

20. Quoted in *Trade Agreements Extension Act of 1953*, Hearings, p. 1712.

countries to sell their products in the American markets. We then tax ourselves, or go into debt to give our allies the dollars they need to buy the exports we will not let them earn for themselves. Our restrictive trade policies thus add substantially to our tax burden and lower our living standards. . . .

Last year United States imports totalled $11 billion. . . .

Most of these imports consisted of raw materials essential for our own production, which we would continue to buy even if their prices were increased. . . .

Our imports of finished goods totalled $2 billion, and of this $2 billion only about $1 billion, or three-tenths of one per cent of total national output, were subject to duties. It is around the question of a moderate increase or decrease in this $1 billion of imports that the tariff question revolves.

The extent of hardship which might result from gradual reduction of the tariff, however, is another question which needs to be put in proper prospective. The area of possible hardship is small. . . . Moreover, the extent of dislocation resulting from gradual tariff reduction will ordinarily be considerably less than that which our industries frequently experience from domestic causes, such as new technological progress or new products introduced by competitors, geographic shifts in industry, or changes in consumers' tastes. . . .

Furthermore, we believe that the Trade Agreements Act should be renewed without the peril-point and escape-clause provisions that have been added to it in recent years. . . .

The lowering of American trade barriers is not a panacea; it will not overcome all the world's economic troubles. Tariff reduction by the United States will not cause imports to rise sufficiently to end the dollar shortage. . . .[21]

Here we have a more liberal and a more able statement of the case than is usually made by supporters of the Trade Agreements Program. It boils down to this: (1) The direct economic gain is relatively small because the potential increase in imports is small. (2) Foreign trade is vital to many countries and is important to the United States because we have a stake in a strong free world. (3) Potential damage to domestic industry is small because the potential increase in competitive imports is small.

These problems will be examined in later chapters. The point here is that it is extraordinarily difficult to arouse the public about the tariff because the issues are intricate and the effect of further tariff reduction on the American standard of living is relatively unimportant compared with the potential gains from internal growth.

Congress of Industrial Organizations

A major part of organized labor has generally supported the Trade Agreements Program but opposed increased imports which would undermine domestic wage standards or create unemployment. While recognizing the need for expansion of foreign trade, organized labor has joined with management in seeking to restore higher duties in those specific industries which claim serious injury as a result of tariff concessions.

21. *Trade Agreements Extension Act of 1953*, Hearings, pp. 1699–1702. The CED spokesman was Meyer Kestnbaum.

The rise of mass industrial unions has helped to create a somewhat more liberal attitude toward foreign trade than had previously characterized unions organized along craft lines. In labor circles, it is chiefly the CIO unions which have emphasized that "American industry has nothing to fear from foreign competition."[22]

Even in the traditionally import-sensitive cotton textile industry, labor spokesmen have stressed that improvements in productivity provide a substantial measure of protection. Emil Rieve of the Textile Workers Union held that "with the exception of such countries as Japan" for a wide range of products the United States can "meet and beat the manufacturing costs of countries which pay lower wages."[23]

At the same time, the Textile Workers Union in no sense advocates a policy of free trade. Solomon Barkin has expressly stated that the adjustment of domestic production to foreign competition requires a domestic policy for maintenance of full employment.[24] Labor's sympathetic attitude toward expansion of trade is premised on four conditions:

1. The deflationary effect of imports should not be permitted to create unemployment.

2. Labor standards abroad should be raised.

3. American labor should be protected by a continued rise in the efficiency of American industry.

4. The pattern of trade should be based largely on the expansion of manufactured exports in return for imports of raw materials and noncompetitive goods.

Given these conditions, tariff reduction is regarded as compatible with the aspirations of labor unions. But as soon as unemployment appeared, labor representatives appeared before the proper committees "to attest the impropriety of reducing tariff rates on textile items."[25]

22. See testimony of Stanley Ruttenberg in the various hearings on extension of trade agreements. The auto workers are among the strongest supporters of trade agreements. CIO steelworkers have also supported the program. David McDonald's proposal of governmental assistance in cases of injury caused by increased imports is of special interest. See *Report of the Commission on Foreign Economic Policy* (Randall Report), January 1954, pp. 54–58.

23. *1945 Extension of Reciprocal Trade Agreements Act*, Hearings, Senate Finance Committee, 79th Cong., 1st sess., p. 514.

24. *1945 Extension of Reciprocal Trade Agreements Act*, Hearings, House Ways and Means Committee, 79th Cong., 1st sess., Vol. 2, pp. 2379 and 2382. Compare testimony of Amalgamated Clothing Workers, CIO, and International Ladies Garment Workers, *ibid.*, p. 2372; *Extension of Reciprocal Trade Agreements Act*, Hearings, House Ways and Means Committee, 76th Cong., 3d sess., Vol. 3, pp. 2884 and 2885.

25. Statement of Emil Rieve before the Committee for Reciprocity Information, June 1, 1950, mimeographed.

American Federation of Labor

As a loose confederation of largely autonomous unions, the AF of L promotes the position of its affiliated unions. In a formal sense, this means that the Federation may ask the Congress to raise some duties and lower others. The practical effect, however, seems to favor protection. Organization of labor by crafts seems to result in stronger emphasis on tariff protection than organization on an industry basis. The AF of L has a long history of support for protectionism and, although it has come to recognize expressly the importance of expanding trade in recent years, its position with respect to protection of American labor standards is an extreme one.

In 1921 a convention of the Federation urged Congress to "immediately enact an adequate tariff on crude oil and its by-products" to protect the domestic oil and coal industry against imports from Mexico.[26] In 1925 the Federation protested repeal of the duty on ship repairs in foreign ports. Three years later it proposed to stop imports of Chinese-made shingles from British Columbia.

In 1937 the Federation sought to extend to foreign commerce the principle of the Connery Wage and Hour Bill, which was designed to stop the movement in interstate commerce of products produced by sweatshop labor. Similarly, it has criticized the Trade Agreements Program on the ground that it is inconsistent with laws protecting American labor, such as the Fair Labor Standards Act, the Walsh-Healy Act, the Bacon-Davis Act and the Oriental Exclusion Act.[27]

The 1938 resolutions of the Executive Council called on the Federation to exercise all possible efforts to prevent imports under trade agreements where such imports were based on lower wages and living standards than prevail in competitive American industries.[28] The unions said to be "seriously affected" by competitive imports represent a rather surprising list including the Painters, Decorators and Paper Hangers; the United Brotherhood of Carpenters and Joiners; the Bricklayers, Masons and Plasterers.[29] It is the railroad and maritime unions of the AF of L which have supported the Trade Agreements Program most consistently.

After safeguarding amendments were added to the Trade Agreements Act in 1951 (Public Law 50), the AF of L gave the program qualified endorsement. In supporting extension of the act in 1953, president George Meany wrote that the Federation "favors a maximum of trade, subject,

---

26. *Extension of Reciprocal Trade Agreements Act*, Hearings, House Ways and Means Committee, 76th Cong., 3d sess., 1940, p. 1367.

27. Statement of Matthew Woll, vice president of the American Federation of Labor, *ibid.*, p. 1394.

28. *Ibid.*, p. 1369.

29. For the complete list, see *Extension of Reciprocal Trade Agreements Act*, Hearings, Senate Finance Committee, 78th Cong., 1st sess., 1943, p. 82.

however, to the conditions that imports from low-wage countries do not undermine our wage standards." Although this might seem to indicate a change in attitude, it is not clear that the Federation has altered the substance of its policy. The Executive Council declared that "The American Federation of Labor cannot condone wage competition from abroad when we have made elimination of wage competition in this country a cardinal principle of our legislation."[30]

Protection of American Wage Standards

Labor's position with respect to protection of American wage standards imposes serious obstacles to any liberal trade policy. The extreme protectionist wing of the AF of L, led by Matthew Woll, appears to deny that trade between nations with different wage levels can be mutually advantageous. Any such belief is, of course, mistaken. Nonetheless, it is true that freer trade would affect labor and capital differently, to the relative disadvantage of American labor. Under fully competitive conditions, free trade would tend to have an effect on wages similar to the effect of immigration.

This question cannot be adequately explored here. It must suffice to say that there is a grain of truth hidden in the wage argument, which lends support to labor's position, although the argument, as it is stated, is unsound. Total income may be increased by expansion of foreign trade in competitive products, but the effect on the *distribution* of income will be unfavorable to American labor and favorable to capital. This is because the import-competing home industries generally employ relatively more labor and less capital than the export industries.[31] Consequently, liquidation of the import-competing industries and the corresponding expansion of exports will raise income, but will tend to shift the larger real income from labor to capital.

The relevance of these considerations here is to indicate that the shift of resources from the labor-intensive, import-competing industries to more productive employment in the capital-intensive, export industries does not serve the interest of owners and workers alike. And whether or not the arguments advanced by businessmen and labor are stated correctly, we should recognize that they do not have identical interests in free trade. The reason, to repeat, is that the export industries require relatively less labor and more capital than the import-competing industries, provided always that the internal economy is in balance.

30. *Trade Agreements Extension Act of 1953*, pp. 559–561. These hearings reprint the text of the Executive Council's Report to the 70th Convention of the American Federation of Labor, San Francisco, 1951. Meany's statement sounds more liberal than the Executive Council's Report.

31. Provided that wages are in balance between the import and export industries.

Outside of the immediate import-competing industries, we should expect that the business community will recognize increasingly that its interest lies in free trade. The same cannot be said of labor.

As a practical matter, however, the effect of foreign trade on the distribution of income is overshadowed by the effect of increasing productivity via internal developments. The volume of potential imports is too small relative to internal development to seriously affect the American wage standard, provided there is no decline in the rate of new investment and growth. The practical problem is that displaced workers in the import-competing industries may not be able to find more productive employment within a reasonable length of time. Labor unions correctly interpret their own interest when they emphasize a domestic policy of full employment as a condition for reduction of trade barriers. And if this demand were realized, labor could probably afford to forget about the effect of competition from low-wage countries on the American wage standard.

Sophisticated Arguments for Tariffs

Protection of infant industries during the period of their development was long regarded by economists as the only sound case for tariffs. It followed from this thesis that protection should be eliminated once the industries were well established. Solomon Barkin of the Textile Workers Union has developed a variant of this thesis which can be regarded as an extension of the infant industry argument to the highly developed country. It justifies protection in the interest of rapid technological progress.

It is sometimes argued that technological advance has reduced the importance of international trade and that tariff protection is, therefore, less harmful than it used to be. Barkin goes further and argues that tariff protection may foster rapid innovation and thus produce lower costs than could be realized from international specialization. The premise is that complete international specialization may result in a slower rate of technological advance in other countries than can be achieved by American industry.

Most cotton textiles, for example, are said to be cheaper today than they would have been if the industry had remained concentrated in Britain. In woolens, too, costs have been reduced by introduction of automatic looms and the American system of spinning worsted yarns. Cost reduction as a result of the dynamics of technological advance is said to offset the benefits of international specialization.

In sum, the argument states that protection may be justified in the capital-rich nation which will exploit new methods and can afford rapid innovation. In some respects this recalls the late Professor Schumpeter's position, although he stated the case differently:

In any case, however, protection increases the rate of profit. Whatever we may think about this from other standpoints, in a rapidly progressing country it will have the effect of accelerating the pace of that progress by propelling investment and making it easier to face risks.[32]

These arguments are mentioned chiefly to illustrate the fact that support for tariffs is not limited exclusively to the injury, unemployment and low-wage argument.[33]

National Labor-Management Council

The National Labor-Management Council is among the most vigorous protectionist groups in the United States today.[34]

The membership of most business and labor organizations includes elements on both sides of the tariff issue. Unlike these organizations, the National Labor-Management Council is composed exclusively of elements which favor higher tariffs and most of its members would be seriously affected by loss of protection.[35]

The National Labor-Management Council holds that all high-cost industries are entitled to protection and that "the degree of protection should be roughly equal to the advantage of foreign producers in this market as a result of their lower labor standards, modified by relative productivity."[36]

Spokesmen for the group attempt to win political support on the ground that tariff protection is a measure to help small business. It is asserted that the total production of many import-competing industries is smaller than the exports of large-scale industries such as automobiles, iron and steel, electrical machinery, agricultural machinery, meat products and office equipment. Testifying before a congressional investigation of small business and monopoly power, O. L. Strackbein declared that lower trade barriers benefit big business by expansion of exports and, at the same time, injure and in some cases destroy small industries by foreign competition.[37]

32. "Influence of Protective Tariffs on Industrial Development of the United States," *Proceedings of the Academy of Political Science,* May 1940; reprinted in *Essays of J. A. Schumpeter,* edited by Richard V. Clemence, Addison-Wesley, Cambridge, 1951, p. 168.

33. Considerations of the loss of revenue from tariff reduction and the effect on the terms of trade do not appear to have played an important role in determining American attitudes toward commercial policy.

34. Membership in the National Labor-Management Council is composed of both labor and management. The chairman, O. R. Strackbein, is also executive secretary of the American Wage Earners' Protective Conference. Matthew Woll is president of the Wage Earners' Protective Conference, which is composed of unions affiliated with the American Federation of Labor.

35. In the aluminum industry it was the Kaiser and Reynolds companies which asked for escape clause investigations. Presumably aluminum imports were mainly from the Canadian plants of the Aluminum Company.

36. Statement of Principles, adopted March 21, 1950, mimeographed.

37. Before the Subcommittee of the House Judiciary Committee on the Study of Monopoly Power, November 9, 1949, mimeographed.

The realignment of forces which made possible the reduction of trade barriers is described as follows:

Southern low-tariff perennials, speaking for cotton and tobacco, joined forces with the mass production industries that had outgrown the domestic market, and the international bankers who had a heavy stake in foreign countries. . . . The trusts, the monopolies, the big banks of the financial East were now sitting piously in the same pew with the Northern liberals, many of whom had won their political spurs by denouncing the sins and evils of the "bloated plutocrats," "oligarchies" and "robber barons."[38]

The National Labor-Management Council seeks to extend the use of quotas. In part, resistance to tariff reduction is due to the uncertainty as to the volume of imports which will result. It is stated, or implied, that the import-competing industries would often accept a larger volume of imports than we actually have in exchange for quotas which would eliminate the risk that imports might be still larger. There may well be something to this argument. Quotas can be used to liberalize as well as to restrict trade. Such a scheme would be dangerous, however, unless unusual precautions were taken to insure that responsibility for setting the quotas was lodged with administrators who were dedicated to the expansion of trade.

Farm Organizations

Farmers and farm organizations are in a favorable position to support the Trade Agreements Program because agriculture is to some extent protected by quantitative restrictions on imports in connection with domestic marketing programs.[39]

The American Farm Bureau Federation has supported the trade agreements policy, subject to proper safeguards. The Bureau is, of course, concerned with expansion of agricultural exports. But it also recognizes the balance-of-payments problem and, everything considered, its position can be described as a moderate one. The policy statements of the Bureau recognize the importance and complexity of the issues created by domestic support prices and the need to expand foreign trade. Apparently the Bureau is prepared to support some adjustments in domestic production in the interest of balancing imports and exports.[40]

38. O. R. Strackbein, *The Tariff Issue Reviewed and Restated,* Washington, 1950, pp. 10 and 11.

39. Section 22 of Public Law 320 as amended by the Agricultural Act of 1948.

40. *Trade Agreements Extension Act of 1953,* p. 797. For the earlier attitude of the Bureau, see *Operation of the Trade Agreements Act and the Proposed International Trade Organization,* Hearings, House Ways and Means Committee, 80th Cong., 1st sess., p. 683; *1949 Extension of Reciprocal Trade Agreements Act,* Hearings, House Ways and Means Committee, 81st Cong., 1st sess., p. 668.

In the early period, the National Grange took an unfavorable view of trade agreement policies.[41] In 1953, however, its spokesmen supported extension of trade agreements, opposed the Simpson bill and emphasized that lower tariffs can increase the American standard of living.[42] This position must be interpreted in the light of special protection for agriculture.

The attitude of the National Farmers Union has been, in a sense, quite liberal. For example, it was the only major farm organization which fully supported the now defunct Charter for an International Trade Organization and criticized restrictions on imports to hold up domestic farm prices.[43] In recent years, however, the Farmers Union has endorsed full parity prices for farmers, which greatly complicates the problem of reducing trade barriers. The Farmers Union still supports trade policies designed to shift resources in accordance with their best use, but it also wants programs designed to avoid impoverishing farmers in the process.[44]

Resurgence of Protectionism?

Some observers interpret developments, particularly in the Congress, as indicating resurgence of protectionist strength.

1. The Congress has sought to provide easier relief from foreign competition under the escape clause and, by the peril point amendment, has made tariff reduction more difficult.

2. The so-called "cheese amendment" in the War Powers Acts of 1950 and 1951 provided mandatory restrictions on certain imports in violation of GATT. As a result, five nations protested and declared themselves free to retaliate.

3. Passage of at least some features of the Simpson bill was narrowly averted in 1953.[45] The bill provided for quotas on petroleum and residual fuel oil, higher duties on lead and zinc, and would have opened the door to higher duties via the escape clause. The provision designed to strengthen protectionism by increasing the membership of the Tariff Commission was resolved only after a long struggle in conference between House and Senate.

Congressional concern with manning the protectionist ramparts may be taken less as an indication of resurgent protectionist strength and more as a reflection of increasing competition from imports. More serious competition from imports in a number of lines has resulted from (1) recovery of

41. See testimony of Albert Goss, *Operation of the Trade Agreements Act and the Proposed International Trade Organization*, pp. 668–669.

42. *Trade Agreements Extension Act of 1953*, pp. 778–792.

43. *Operation of the Trade Agreements Act and the Proposed International Trade Organization*, pp. 1725–1726.

44. See the statement of James G. Patton, *Trade Agreements Extension Act of 1953*, pp. 907–914.

45. H.R. 4294, 83d Cong., 1st sess.

European production since the Marshall Plan, (2) widespread devaluation of currencies in September 1949, (3) speculative bidding of American buyers for imports following outbreak of war in Korea, and (4) decline of American farm prices. The apparent resurgence of protectionism may be taken chiefly as reinforcement of the commitment against injury from tariff reduction.

There is, apparently, a disparity between the strength of protectionists in Congress and the growing support for freer trade among business leaders. The old saying that "free traders win the argument while protectionists win the votes" requires some explanation. Condemning congressmen for supporting the interest of their constituents is not only futile but beside the point. In the democratic process, the clamor for protection should be offset by pressures from the export industries which would leave the Congress as a whole free to pursue the public interest.

There is little reason to suppose that congressmen are less responsive to demands from their export-minded constituents than to demands from the import-competing industries. The voluminous testimony taken by congressional committees suggests, however, that the export industries have not exerted as much pressure as have those seeking protection. When a businessman is threatened by imports he sees his congressman. But how many potential exporters call on their congressman with the same urgency? After almost twenty years' experience with trade agreements, Congressman Sadlack had never heard of exports from Connecticut that were attributed to trade agreements, and denied that there were any.[46]

In the 1953 hearings the export side of the argument was developed in some detail. Until recently, however, the export argument seems to have served mainly as a background factor which has helped to change the climate of opinion. It has often failed to deliver the votes because exporters failed to pinpoint the specific areas that would benefit. Outside of the export branches of agriculture, the export industries in the past have been largely preoccupied with the very much larger domestic market. This has thrown a heavy burden on the executive branch of the government in its attempt to liberalize trade.

Return of the traditionally high-tariff Republican Party to power after twenty years brings to the fore the conflict within the party itself. President Eisenhower has taken a stand in favor of international trade but has attempted no innovations in trade policy. Chairmanships of important congressional committees were held by apparently intransigent protectionists in 1952–1953.

Secretary of State Dulles took a neutral position with respect to trade barriers in 1953 pending the report of the Randall Commission—a sub-

46. *Trade Agreements Extension Act of 1953*, p. 1379.

stantial departure from the role of Secretaries since Cordell Hull. Here are excerpts from his testimony:

I do not think that domestic industry and agriculture should be sacrificed in the interest of exporters, or that local business should alone pay the price of foreign policies designed to promote international unity and economic health. . . .

I want to say to you that, as Secretary of State, I have no preconceived ideas and no policies to which I feel committed. I have a completely open mind in this respect.[47]

Representative Jenkins inquired about "a half dozen big industries in this country that are ready to fold up if we do not do something about them. What would be your advice in cases like that?"

Dulles: . . . While I believe that there should be a considerable measure of protection against foreign competition, the mere fact that there are businesses in the United States which are having difficulty in the face of new types of competition is nothing new to American life. In fact, it is characteristic of American life.

Jenkins: That is not the point. . . .

Dulles: If the causes of the situation you speak of are due to foreign competition rather than domestic competition, that is certainly one of the things that should be studied and gone into, and it might very well be a basis for increased tariff protection.[48]

Representative Eberharter: In other words, Mr. Secretary, you are saying that we may change our policy to a higher tariff policy. . . .

Dulles: . . . I would not attempt at the present time to prejudge the question of whether it will be a change up or a change down.

. . . I recall that when I was in the Senate in 1949 I voted for introduction at that time of the peril-point clause. . . .

Eberharter: Do you think the adoption of the peril-point was generally considered satisfactory to our friends of the free world at the time of its adoption?

Dulles: . . . As long as our tariff restrictions are reasonable, we can explain them and can give them good reasons for what we do, I do not fear the consequences.

Eberharter: Mr. Secretary, my experience has been that when one wants to avoid meeting an issue head on, the escape is always to appoint a commission or board to reexamine or examine a problem so the issue can be decided at some later date.

Dulles: The fact that that has been the experience of the world for so many centuries indicates there must be a little merit in it or it would not have survived so long.[49]

The testimony of other Cabinet members differed in detail but indicated that they believed in the principle that home industry should not be displaced by foreign competition. Even allowing for the fact that the administration's tactics were to postpone the issue, it can scarcely be said that the

47. *Trade Agreements Extension Act of 1953*, pp. 590 and 591.
48. *Ibid.*, p. 593.
49. *Ibid.*, pp. 595 and 596.

first appearance of the new Cabinet inspired confidence in the future of a liberal trade policy. In the past it has been necessary for the executive branch to provide aggressive leadership in order to avoid crippling amendments. Here the Cabinet seemed to take a position of benevolent neutrality. Fortunately, the Committee for a National Trade Policy, led by Charles P. Taft, came to the rescue in 1955.

Recent Demands for Protection

Recent attempts to restrict imports of petroleum, lead and zinc provide some lessons about tariff debates. Although the Simpson bill was scotched in 1953, the forces of protectionism have not been decisively defeated and the same issues are likely to emerge again.

The slight recession of 1949 precipitated a demand for protection which was postponed only by the increased consumption and stockpiling of materials associated with the Korean War. Several congressional committees have investigated the effect of petroleum imports on domestic industry. The coal industry and certain railroads joined independent petroleum producers in seeking to restrict imports of crude and residual fuel oil. The Neely Committee concluded that

. . . the importation of foreign oil has had a substantial injurious effect on the coal, oil and railroad industries of the Nation . . . the evidence dispels every doubt and every shadow of a doubt that oil imports have played a major role in increasing unemployment among miners, petroleum workers, and railroad employees.[50]

A more accurate statement would be that the *evidence presented to the Committee* showed these results. Protectionists are able to obtain congressional hearings on the difficulties of specific industries adversely affected by imports. The findings of such investigations cannot purport to include the broader interests of import-consuming industries and export trades which would suffer from restrictions on imports.

There is no question about the serious problems faced by communities like Shallmar, Maryland, or the Panther Valley region of Pennsylvania. A number of mines were closed in 1949 and some communities with no other industries faced destitution. Concerning the cause of the difficulty, one witness said:

We do not contend that the importation of foreign oils is the only factor contributing to the plight of these miners and the coal industry in these areas of Pennsylvania and Maryland—but it appears by far the most damaging. Most of the coal in both areas has been sold in eastern markets which have borne the brunt of foreign oil dumping.[51]

50. *Causes of Unemployment in the Coal and Other Specified Industries*, S. Rept. No. 2042, 81st Cong., 2d sess., 1950, p. 17.
51. Statement of John Crichton, General Superintendent of Pennsylvania Mines, representing the Johnstown Coal and Coke Co., *ibid.*, pp. 381 and 382.

Labor and industry representatives estimated the displacement of labor in 1949–1950 at 50,000 workers, evenly divided between the mines and coal-carrying railroads.

Coal mining is the victim of substitute fuels for space heating, for transportation and for the generation of electric power. The coal industry and railroads have been hurt by the growth of the automotive and trucking industries. Although the competitive position of railroads has improved as a result of dieselization, this development has further reduced the consumption of coal. Still another angle to the import problem is that the interest of coal-hauling railroads in coal as a source of revenue apparently exceeds their interest in oil imports as a source of fuel. Finally, extensive lists of electric power plants converting from coal to oil were read into the record for the purpose of showing the damage from imports.

The political strength of protectionism is explained in part by the fact that the American economy is so dynamic. The coal industry can claim that it is seriously injured by petroleum imports, but actually it was already injured by substitution of domestic oil for coal. Proponents of freer trade are prone to neglect this point and to argue that the potential injury from imports is insignificant compared with the adjustments that are taking place as a result of technological change and development of new products. While it is true that imports alone would rarely result in serious injury, this is not the issue which the Congress has to face. The Congress is under pressure to consider the total dislocation and adjustment to which a community is subjected by the combined forces of internal growth and external trade.

It is apparent that restricting imports of petroleum would be a most awkward and expensive way to protect stranded coal miners and railroad workers. This important policy issue has never been threshed out. *In the meantime, the import-competing home industries which are injured primarily by domestic competition demand tariff protection on the ground that they are injured by the marginal foreign competition.*

In the case of lead and zinc, demands for protection arise from depletion of domestic ores and instability of market prices.

The Bureau of Mines has described the general problem facing the mining industry:

During the past several decades, the trend of mining has been toward exploitation of leaner ores and ores at greater depths. The present outlook is for an expansion of this trend because of the dwindling reserves of higher grade ore and the exhaustion of shallow deposits. . . . Underground mines at increasing depths are bringing burdensome problems in drainage, ventilation, and support of mine openings.[52]

52. Staff of the Bureau of Mines and Geological Survey, *Mineral Position of the United States*, published as Appendix to *Investigation of Natural Resources*, Hearings, Senate, Public Lands Committee, 80th Cong., 1st sess., 1947, pp. 207 and 208.

These factors place the extractive industries in a different position from the manufacturing industries.[53] An investigation by the House Small Business Committee warned that the output of mines suffering depletion of ores was threatened by "an inadequate tariff structure."[54] The acute problem, however, arises because of the instability of prices, which requires a sudden rather than a gradual adjustment to depletion of ores. A sharp break in prices in 1949 and again in 1953 led to unemployment and a strong demand for tariff protection.

During 1949–1950 the number of operating mines in the Tri-State mining area declined from twenty-five to fourteen and production of zinc concentrates fell from 17,500 tons to 10,000 tons monthly. In Utah, the Silver King Coalition and Park Utah Consolidated closed because the fall of metal prices did not warrant operation of such high-cost mines. The increase in lead imports was blamed for the break of about 50 per cent in prices.

These difficulties of the lead and zinc mines were relieved by the advent of the Korean War, but reappeared in 1953 when prices again dropped 30 to 50 per cent. While the basic background consideration is the depletion of high-grade ores, the case for protection derives its strength from the instability of prices. Pleas for protection of high-cost, marginal mines are also tied in with the argument for military security. Once mines are abandoned, flooding and caving in are said to make the cost of reopening shafts and tunnels prohibitive. If mines are not in continuous operation, it is claimed that they will deteriorate so badly that they cannot be reopened. This leads to the paradoxical argument that production from low-grade reserves should be subsidized by tariff protection in the interest of conserving national resources.

An industry which is victimized by a sudden collapse of prices will almost always be able to make a *prima facie* case showing injury. And when imports are increasing at the same time, it is not surprising that a Senate Committee should attribute the unemployment to imports. Protectionists derive a tactical advantage from the fact that raw material producers are damaged by short-term instability even though the instability is not primarily due to imports. The President declined to invoke the escape clause as recommended by the Tariff Commission in 1954.

Although tariffs are an expensive and inadequate means of protecting raw material producers from the injury resulting from unstable demand, the pressures for protection are likely to become formidable each time there is a sudden collapse in the market.

53. See Bureau of Labor Statistics, *Trends in Output per Man-hour: Mining 1935–1949*, August 1950, mimeographed.

54. *Small Independent Mines*, H. Rept. No. 1101, 80th Cong., 1st sess., 1947, p. 2.

Chapter 8

The American Tariff League

PROTECTIONIST SENTIMENT in the United States is not confined to a handful of small industries like handmade glass and pottery, which are at a competitive disadvantage because labor costs constitute a high proportion of total cost. The protective tariff has been a tradition in the American business community. Much of today's protectionist sentiment is largely a vestigial survival from the infant-industry argument of the nineteenth century. A major part of some industries associated in the protectionist camp no longer need protection or profit from it; in fact, a high tariff policy is contrary to their interests as potential exporters.

Organized protectionist sentiment has long centered in the American Tariff League, which was founded in 1885. Its membership includes about 80 different branches of industry and agriculture and some 300 companies and agricultural groups. The League's primary objective is to provide wholesale protection to a widely diversified American industry. It publishes a monthly information service which keeps its members well informed on proposed changes in tariffs and trade policies and which also needles its members by emphasizing any current increase in imports.

The case for the protective tariff, as stated by the leading organization which advocates protection, merits examination. The League attempts to be all things to all protectionists, and it is probably for this reason that the language of its spokesmen sometimes seems ambiguous and even contradictory. This chapter endeavors to interpret these ambiguous points fairly and not unsympathetically.

The League stresses the value of wide diversification in home industry. Protection affords an opportunity to utilize the entire range of domestic resources and talents, some of which would remain unexploited without it. A corollary of a diversified and balanced home industry, according to the League, is industrial progress and a dynamic economy. The effect of excessive specialization, on the other hand, is said to be stultifying.

The League stands for the "scientific" tariff, which would equalize domestic and foreign costs. But this by no means represents a wish to destroy all foreign trade, as a literal interpretation might suggest. International trade is desirable and even necessary but should be restricted largely to noncompetitive goods which supplement domestic resources and capacities. The Tariff League regards the "scientific" tariff as a formula which would limit competitive imports and provide changes in duties to match changes in costs. One primary objective is flexible rates which would maintain constant protection in a changing world.

The League is opposed to the present Trade Agreements Program because it has not raised as well as lowered duties, because it has increased uncertainties and because it has shifted the tariff-making process from the Congress to the executive branch of government. Members of the League charge that tariff reduction under trade agreements is partly responsible for the increase in other trade barriers and for the deterioration of trade. They point out, moreover, that the Trade Agreements Program was originally presented as an antidepression measure, but that its sponsors have, disingenuously, changed their supporting arguments with every passing season.

The Reason for Trade

In spite of its opposition to the Trade Agreements Program, the American Tariff League holds the view that an expansion of mutually profitable trade is both necessary and desirable. The League regards international trade as essential because: (1) natural resources and population are unevenly distributed; (2) climates vary; (3) cultural differences among the various nations are pronounced; (4) the state of the arts is in different stages of development among the various nations.[1] The growth of trade is a natural corollary of spreading industrialization and, in fact, depends on industrial development because poor countries have less goods to trade. The League's position is that internal growth is a prerequisite to the expansion of external trade, since "no people or nation can long have more or consume more than it produces." Small countries lack the "opportunity for mass production at low unit-costs." Backward countries lack the "skill and the arts and sciences."[2] This view is derived from the League's emphasis on such trade as does not compete with or at least does not injure home production.

The League maintains that two conditions are essential to the development of mutually profitable trade. One, trade must be "regulated" in the national interest. Second, international trade in competitive products should be limited. This is the object of regulation.

1. The interpretation of the League's position given in this chapter owes much to private interviews with its leading spokesmen. Published sources are quoted wherever possible. See *1945 Extension of Reciprocal Trade Agreements Act*, Hearings, House Ways and Means Committee, 79th Cong., 1st sess., 1945, p. 1335. For a detailed statement of the League's views and proposals, see the League's memoranda and testimony before the House Ways and Means Committee in 1945 and 1948. The League's proposals for a substitute for the Trade Agreements Act are contained in the *Declaration of Principles and Program for World Trade* reprinted in *Trade Agreements Program*, Hearings, House Ways and Means Committee, 80th Cong., 2d sess., 1948, pp. 29–41.

2. *1945 Extension of Reciprocal Trade Agreements Act*, p. 1328.

The League holds that free trade is impossible. "So long as there are nations and political boundaries preventing the free movement of people, there cannot be free movement of goods . . ."[3] Any national drive to put the world on a free trade basis will conflict with particular national interests. In their own national interest nations will inevitably impose barriers that dry up the flow of trade. "If the country wants to and can trade, it will not place a barrier in the way of trade. If there is a real need for goods, it would be dangerous for a government to bar trade. If there is not, it is practically impossible to trade under any conditions that do not create confusion and ill will."[4]

The best that can be hoped for is freer trade under a system of "regulation" as opposed to rigid "barriers," that is, under a system which provides the minimum interference with trade compatible with the national interest. Since the prosperity of its people is the primary responsibility of a government in economic affairs, and since "almost infinite diversification" is the key to a dynamic and prosperous economy, competitive imports should be controlled.

The League contends that it does not advocate the total exclusion of competitive imports, but a tariff to equalize differences in cost. It thus favors "regulation" and opposes "barriers."

The "regulation" of trade by a "scientific" tariff is not control in the League's eyes. The League does not believe in "planned, managed or state controlled economy" nor in "intergovernmental cartels." There is one exception: the League would use import quotas as a tool for controlling business cycles.

Under conditions of economic difficulty, the government could well institute a program for price stabilization, and the use of quantitative quotas under such circumstances could well serve to prevent chaos in our domestic economy, without preventing foreign imports.[5]

Industrial Diversification

The key to prosperity for the national economy, which, in the League's conception, must always be the first concern of governments, lies in a diverse and dynamic economy. Diversity is the key to effective utilization of national resources. "Almost infinite diversification of economic activity has given this country's economy its dynamic character. Specialization would tend to make it static."[6] The League denies that specialization is the prin-

3. *Declaration of Principles and Program for World Trade*, in Hearings, p. 29.
4. *Ibid.*, p. 36.
5. *Ibid.*, p. 41.
6. *Ibid.*, p. 29.

cipal key to national wealth. A nation can overspecialize and so lose the capacity for dynamic growth.

Instead, the League emphasizes the role of diversification in the development of wealth. Diversification permits development of a wider range of individual talents and natural resources, gives wider scope to individual initiative and inventiveness, and fosters growth. Complete specialization, on the other hand, tends to freeze patterns of production, hastens the exhaustion of the best natural resources, affords less employment for specialized skills, and permits the exploitation of the people by the producers of other countries.[7]

The League believes that the case for tariffs is supported by the experience of the United States.

Relatively high rates of duty were generally imposed in order to attract foreign capital and to stimulate immigration of persons with special talents, and in turn to provide employment as well as to provide local markets for home-grown products and the products of forests and mines.[8]

The duty on rayon, for example, in the Tariff Act of 1909 is credited with the establishment of the first successful rayon mill in the United States in 1910 with British capital and skill. Without the tariff the United States would have continued to import rayon from Europe.[9] Thus protection for "infant industries" attracted foreign capital and skill and eliminated American dependence upon foreign suppliers whose skills enabled them to exploit the American people. On the other hand, the cartel type of restrictions, which results in the allocation of markets and industries among nations, as in the case of the German dye industry, is an evil. The rapid growth and relative self-sufficiency of the American economy under the protective tariff should serve as an example to other countries.[10]

Tariffs Reduce Costs

Domestic requirements should dictate foreign economic policy rather than the other way around. Competitive imports are harmful. The League favors laissez-faire at home but a "scientific" tariff to regulate foreign commerce in order to subordinate international trade to domestic requirements. These views are supported by an amazing argument.

Exchange of competitive goods through foreign trade may provide a wider choice of goods—but usually at a somewhat higher cost because of charges for transportation, insurance handling, loss, spoilage, etc. This is a real handicap to small nations, or to those with meager natural resources or with poor climate, or

7. *1945 Extension of Reciprocal Trade Agreements Act*, p. 1322.
8. *Ibid.*, p. 1332.
9. *Ibid.*, pp. 1365–1366.
10. *Ibid.*, pp. 1329–1330.

to backward peoples. They are deprived of the advantages of mass production for a big market and must work longer hours or with other disadvantages to secure a good standard of living because they must bear the cost of getting things from foreign sources.[11]

The League apparently believes that other countries can seriously compete with America's leading mass production industries. Consequently, it is argued that imports will hamper the efficiency of mass production. In order to acquire and maintain the advantages of large-scale production, a country must preserve the home market for its own producers.

The home market is the main basis of American industrial efficiency. Without a market of such size, our assembly-line technique would not be nearly so efficient in terms of low unit costs. If tariffs are traded down to the point where imports impair productivity, our net prosperity is impaired.[12]

The League's president, H. Wickliffe Rose, even uses as an example the American automobile industry to argue the point that imports impair mass production. "Reduce that market and the same industry will become less efficient, for the labor per unit produced will become higher, as will its costs."[13] Just why more trade would reduce the market for American automobiles is not clear. To many observers both at home and abroad it appears that United States mass production industries could supply both home and foreign markets if we imported more of the other products. The League's concern over imports which compete with our mass production industries is exceeded by the apprehension of foreign producers regarding America's superior productivity.

Imports Are Deflationary

While the League sympathizes with the idea of high employment in the export industries in order to maintain domestic prosperity, it warns of two dangers. (1) An artificially high level of exports from war-expanded industries will degenerate into gifts because of America's limited ability to absorb imports. (2) If imports are increased to balance exports, the net result will be unemployment. At this point the supporting argument is not quite what we should expect. Spokesmen for the Tariff League vigorously deny and abhor the Keynesian explanation of unemployment. The case that imports are deflationary is made to rest on the contention that most exported products require less labor per unit of value than goods competing with imports. The issue is illustrated by the trade of automobiles against textiles. The League's memorandum argued that if one fourth of the domestic output of automobiles were exported and an equal value of foreign cotton

11. *Ibid.*, p. 1328.
12. *Declaration of Principles and Program for World Trade*, in Hearings, p. 35.
13. *1945 Extension of Reciprocal Trade Agreements Act*, p. 1321.

goods imported, exports would provide 100,000 jobs but imports would displace 400,000 jobs. The difference is attributed largely to the higher labor content of America's imports compared with her exports.[14] So far so good; but clearly this shows the *potential* gains from trade. The services of 300,000 workers would be made available to produce additional goods and services. Something more is needed to show the danger of unemployment.

The League holds that domestic prosperity is the overriding objective. In order to achieve this goal it is necessary to avoid overspecialization and underutilization of resources. Competitive imports produce overspecialization, underutilization of natural resources and stultification of many skills. Domestic prosperity, therefore, requires the regulation of foreign trade. But, while preventing excessive imports, the system of regulation should not interfere with the "free" movement of goods and with the freedom of people to determine the specific terms of regulation. The "scientific" tariff is such a system of regulation.

Scientific Tariff

The League proposes to substitute for the present Trade Agreements Program a "scientific" tariff and a system of "truly reciprocal agreements." Apparently, a desirable "agreement" means to the League quantitative agreement. "Truly reciprocal" seems to mean balanced trade. Presumably such agreements would involve chiefly the bilateral exchange of industrial goods for raw materials and foodstuffs. Trade would be regulated under a properly constituted international trade organization. Such a program, the League contends, would not injure domestic efficiency as does the present program. A "scientific" tariff would promote a more peaceful world by extending the same privilege to other nations. By providing the simplest regulatory mechanism, the system would preserve freedom. Finally, the League's program would increase trade through "natural channels" and contribute to the prosperity of all nations. Presumably, this means that national expansion, based on protection and diversification, would increase trade in noncompetitive goods with perhaps some competitive imports if they are needed to supplement national production.

The characteristics of such a "scientific" tariff are three: (1) it must equalize costs; (2) it must be flexible; and (3) it must be equitable. Since costs continually change, duties must be flexible in order to maintain the intended protection.

As most of the purposes of a customs duty are served when the duty on imports equalizes certain differences in cost of production in the United States and abroad, such as wages, taxes, and social security, a system which defines and provides for equalization is necessary to implement the doctrine of scientific tariff.[15]

14. *Ibid.*, pp. 1326–1327.
15. *Declaration of Principles and Program for World Trade*, in Hearings, p. 30.

An equitable tariff is one which is "just, fair, reasonable, balanced, impartial . . . A rate which is too high to admit goods or is too low to produce appreciable revenue is not equitable as a revenue tariff. If it is too low to equalize those elements of cost or too high to admit any foreign goods, the rate is not equitable."[16]

A tariff on competitive products should be used to prevent injury. The rate of duty should be adjusted to different costs. In the League's language, this will not exclude competitive products, but only provide domestic and foreign producers "equal access" to the American markets. The net result of an equitable tariff system, so the argument goes, is to give efficient domestic producers an equal opportunity to sell in the domestic market in competition with imported goods.

The League objects to ad valorem duties because "the country with the lowest foreign costs pays the lowest amount of duty . . . Thus the countries already at a competitive disadvantage with higher costs, must pay larger amounts of duties and suffer additional disadvantages."[17]

A flexible tariff, by imposing differential rates on the basis of differences in foreign costs, would not exclude imports but only place them on a competitive footing with domestic producers "in efficient industries and plants."[18] In view of the League's emphasis on diversification and utilization of a nation's own natural resources, this does not mean that high-cost industries would be liquidated. "Efficiency" probably means technical efficiency rather than low cost. Thus, a technically efficient mining or textile industry would be protected from low-cost imports. On the other hand, the League recognizes that national self-sufficiency is neither practicable nor desirable. It would protect such high-cost industries as are practicable and permit a smattering of imports in most industries.

The purposes of the tariff as itemized below sum up the League's position:[19]

(1) economic necessity
(2) military security
(3) government revenue
(4) to assist in providing parity for certain agricultural products
(5) to offset drastic changes in the value of foreign currency
(6) to promote diversification through a multiplicity and variety of jobs and products distributed widely over the United States
(7) to protect domestic private enterprise in competition with foreign concentrations of economic power and government enterprise

16. *Ibid.*, p. 32.
17. *Ibid.*, p. 39.
18. *1945 Extension of Reciprocal Trade Agreements Act*, p. 1322.
19. *Declaration of Principles and Program for World Trade*, in Hearings, pp. 40–41.

(8) by preventing foreign monopoly of the United States market, to maintain for domestic consumers,
   a. continuity of supply
   b. fair prices
   c. good quality
   d. needed volume
(9) to offset higher domestic taxes, representing social security and a higher standard of living than in foreign countries
(10) to offset lower foreign wages in a unit cost of production
(11) to make possible the importation of perishable seasonal products in the off-season, particularly agricultural products, while maintaining domestic production and sale in season
(12) to strengthen our economy and strategic position by stimulating the importation of foreign inventions, capital, and productivity, while providing sources of dollars for the foreign nations with which to buy our goods
(13) to encourage risk capital investment in the United States
(14) to discourage rather than to encourage the exploitation of the lowest paid wage earners in the world
(15) to discourage the dumping of foreign goods in our market
(16) for retaliation against nations which discriminate against the United States

Trade Agreements

The *Declaration* recognizes the need for expansion of imports. "The greatest economic problem of the United States is to increase imports in terms of dollars, to balance at least a larger part of our tremendous exports, without injuring our productivity."[20]

But this objective, according to the League, cannot be realized under the Trade Agreements Program, which has created international antagonisms and has led to the substitution of "barriers" for "regulation."

The way to achieve balanced trade is to remove the "threats, fears, and misgivings which are caused by the Trade Agreements Act" and to substitute truly reciprocal agreements which would encourage "mutually profitable trade." The Hull-type agreements are not "reciprocal" and are not "trade agreements" but merely tariff agreements.[21] More useful is the type of agreement negotiated by the United Kingdom with Argentina, Sweden and Russia while the United States wrangled at Geneva and Havana over theory and policy. That the present tariff agreements do not

20. *Ibid.*, p. 37.
21. Testimony of H. Wickliffe Rose, *Trade Agreements Program*, Hearings, House Ways and Means Committee, 80th Cong., 2d sess., 1948, p. 10.

lead to reciprocal trade is demonstrated by the present sad state of affairs where trade is unbalanced and American goods are more discriminated against than before the program was begun. Tariff agreements have only led to the substitution of more inflexible barriers. The League attributes the growth of new restrictions on trade to tariff concessions under the present program.

The present tariff system as embodied in the Trade Agreements Program, the League argues, contributes nothing either to domestic or to foreign welfare. On the contrary, it has been inimical to prosperity at home and abroad because it denies the legitimate aspirations of the participating peoples for increased industrialization. The world has sought to avoid the deterioration that would result from the present trade agreement system by replacing tariff barriers with barriers that are less satisfactory. This process of replacing tariffs with rigid barriers has resulted in a less healthy world situation. The trade agreements have jeopardized the prosperity of the several parties and, because of the "threats, fears and misgivings" associated with the program, world trade has been reduced. Thus, reciprocal tariff concessions have not led to reciprocal trade but to the increase of other barriers to trade.

The indictment of the Trade Agreements Program includes three principal charges.

First, the failure to distinguish between tariffs and barriers has led to the paradoxical situation in which a program which purported to promote peace by increasing trade has led instead to new restrictions to trade and to increasing international tensions. This was caused in large measure by the fact that the agreements system shifted the regulatory power from the area of conflicting domestic interests to that of conflicting international interests. "Regardless of the high ideals which may have motivated the Trade Agreements Act, the result has been international political trading" in which the United States tried to prevent other countries from protecting their new and rising industries, thereby impinging on national sovereignty.

Second, the program has worked against scientific regulation, which would have promoted trade in the interests of all, and has also threatened domestic freedom by shifting tariff making from the Congress to the executive branch of government.

Third, the League contends that the trade agreements system has distorted trade from its "natural channels":

Channels of international trade must be natural, that is, the flow of goods must be from sources of available supply to points of consumer demand. If the channels are not natural in this sense but are forced, artifically created, or diverted, the flow can be only intermittent and undependable.[22]

22. *Declaration of Principles and Program for World Trade*, in Hearings, p. 36.

In plain language this is an argument against efforts to increase imports of Europe's manufactured goods which compete with American industry. The League's "natural channels" of trade would provide imports from Latin America and Asia, which sell us raw materials and crude foodstuffs that do not compete with domestic production.

A paradox exists in our fundamental policy of restoring multilateral trade, and at the same time trying to stimulate more bilateral trade between the United States and Western European countries. While the traditional normal channel of trade between United States and Western Europe is trilateral—flowing from U.S.A. to Europe to South America to U.S.A.—nevertheless, last year Paul Hoffman, then head of ECA, conducted an extensive campaign toward closing the trade gap in merchandise directly between the United States and countries of Western Europe. The effort continues actively through our own government officials who are in Europe, at our public expense, urging and training European producers to ship more competitive goods here, regardless of multilateral and more normal channels of trade.

This pressure by ECA to balance the merchandise trade with the countries of Western Europe points up another paradox.[23]

The League's second paradox is the effort to use tariff reduction for the purpose of increasing imports in order to balance the exports provided by economic aid. This directly contradicts the express terms of the Trade Agreements Act, which provides for "regulating the admission of foreign goods" in accordance with the needs of American production.

The League opposed the Havana Charter for an International Trade Organization and proposed that it be renegotiated to encourage (1) adoption of the scientific tariff; (2) treaties to prevent unfair practices against foreign investors and traders; (3) elimination of barriers against mutually profitable trade; and (4) preparation of information useful in trade.

The League insists that Congress should write the policy standards into the law and should create a United States Commission for International Trade to determine appropriate changes in duties under those standards. Changes in duty, however, should be submitted to the House Ways and Means Committee so that the Congress, if it chose, could act on proposed changes. This procedure would safeguard the democratic process.

The results of such a general scheme of reform would, in the League's view, produce substantial benefits:

If these proposals are adopted, it should then be practical to resume our foreign trade where it has ceased, to increase it where it exists, and to develop new channels and new commodities in trade. . . . The system should improve our foreign relations . . . and encourage the adoption of similar systems in other countries to the mutual benefit of all.[24]

23. H. Wickliffe Rose, *Improving Our Tariff Program*, American Tariff League Publication No. 127, p. 6. (A statement before House Ways and Means Committee, January 25, 1951.)

24. *Declaration of Principles and Program for World Trade*, in Hearings, p. 30.

Such, in outline, is the American Tariff League's diagnosis of the Hull program and its prescription for a substitute.

The Tariff Commission

Protectionists find the Congress more responsive to their interests than the executive branch of government and seek to keep tariff making in the hands of elected representatives. Beyond this, an important part of the struggle over policy is the question of who is to administer the law. The League is partial to the Tariff Commission and would like to see the powers that must be delegated by the Congress lodged with the Commission. The League insists that all such matters as the "escape clause" and "peril points" be administered by the Commission. The League would doubtless favor an increase in the Commission's staff and if necessary in the number of Commissioners as a secondary defense against more liberal trade policies.

When Colonel Sidney Morgan resigned from the secretaryship of the Tariff Commission in the spring of 1950, an office he had held for twenty years, the Tariff League published his address as guest speaker at its sixty-fifth annual meeting. The theme of Colonel Morgan's address was a plea for strengthening *Our Vital Tariff Commission*.

The Tariff Commission needs friends . . . friends on the outside, intelligent friends, sympathetic friends, militant friends, if need be. I think the Commission would have a great many more friends than it has if people knew the whole story of its service during the trade-agreement years. The enormous amounts of factual information that have been prepared on so many countless occasions, I think, have served American industry wonderfully well.

If you want that kind of service, the agency that produces it deserves something better than quiet strangulation up a dark alley. That's what it's been getting for the past five years . . . [25]

A Reinterpretation of Demands for Scientific Tariffs

So peculiar is the use of words in the League's official memoranda and in the testimony of its spokesmen that its program requires considerable interpretation in order to grasp what its members really stand for. Thus, the League's most insistent demand is for a tariff policy to "regulate" imports. At the same time, it opposes "barriers" and does not advocate total exclusion of competitive imports. Indeed, it repeatedly calls for "equal access" of domestic and foreign producers as well as for expansion of trade in "natural channels" and for increased American imports to balance at least part of our export surplus. Much of the ambiguity and apparent inconsistency derives from the League's central position calling for a "scientific" tariff.

25. American Tariff League Publication No. 128, 1951, p. 8.

The principle of the so-called scientific tariff is that import duties should equalize the difference between domestic and foreign costs. An important part of the formula is the emphasis on flexibility. Duties would be continually adjusted to fit changes in relative costs.[26]

Economists who swear by the principle of comparative costs have usually scorned the "scientific" tariff because, taken literally, "it means simple prohibition and complete stoppage of foreign trade."[27] This, however, is not what the protectionists seek. Not even the Tariff League wishes to stop the great bulk of duty-free imports like coffee, tea, cocoa and tin. On the contrary, they wish to increase imports of this class, which have accounted for more than half of America's total imports since 1910. The League blatantly overstates the case, but the argument is that tariffs encourage national industrial development, and thus they lead to the expansion of international trade, chiefly in noncompetitive goods that are free from international rivalry.

The emphasis on flexibility is the vitally important part of the "scientific" tariff. Fixed duties, whether stated as specific or ad valorem rates, do not provide constant protection in a world of changing costs.

Thus, duties become less protective as a result of relative changes in productivity or, on the other hand, protection may become redundant and unnecessary. The "scientific" tariff represents, primarily, the search for a formula to maintain tariff protection in a dynamic world. By a too literal interpretation of the demand that tariffs be adjusted to costs, economists have overlooked this important insight. The neglect may be due to the fact that the doctrine of foreign trade has never been fully integrated with the problems of growth and cyclical fluctuations. Quite patently, protectionists would like to be fully protected; their demand for a flexible tariff is but an acknowledgment of the importance of changes in comparative costs.

The League says that it does not seek duties so high as to protect individual companies which are inefficient. It does seek to retain, despite relative changes in productivity among home industries, the degree of protection established by the Congress.

Evaluation

The Tariff League is a registered lobby and obviously a special pleader. Its arguments grossly overstate the case for protection and neglect the

26. The Tariff Commission rather than the Congress would adjust duties to equalize the cost of production at home and abroad. As early as 1908, the Republican Party embraced the principle of the "scientific" tariff and the idea was bandied about in the tariff debates of 1909. The general principle was formally enacted in the tariff law of 1922. Cf. Mark A. Smith, "The United States Flexible Tariff," in *Explorations in Economics*, McGraw-Hill, New York, 1936.

27. Frank W. Taussig, *Some Aspects of the Tariff Question*, 2d edition, Harvard University Press, Cambridge, 1915, p. 363.

interest of the nation as a whole including the producer interest of (1) export industries, and (2) other home industries which would enjoy a larger domestic market if the burden of foreign aid were reduced by increased imports.

Some of the League's arguments are more defensible than others. The "unemployment" example used by the League is the strongest possible argument for precisely the kind of international trade that the League seeks to prevent, namely, trade in competitive goods. The example shows that the exchange of automobile exports for textile imports would create only 100,000 new jobs making automobiles, but would displace 400,000 textile workers because relatively more labor is required to produce textiles of equal value. While these figures probably exaggerate the realistic possibility of automobile-textile trade, the example does show, and for the right reason, the potential annual savings of the labor of 300,000 workers as the result of international specialization and trade in competitive products. Unemployment will be a serious problem only if the American economy fails to expand enough to re-employ the displaced workers in producing additional goods and services with which to raise our level of living. Since any implication that expansion will cease is contrary to the conservative economic views of the League's members, the general unemployment argument is peculiarly inappropriate for this particular organization.

Imports without exports are deflationary because they absorb domestic purchasing power without providing domestic employment. But for those who are acutely concerned over inflation and labor shortages, this should be an argument for relatively more imports. By increasing imports (or reducing exports) we may reduce foreign aid and (1) avoid public borrowing, which increases the national debt, or (2) reduce taxes, which will enable the taxpayer to spend more and, thereby, increase employment and production for the home market.

The League's emphasis on tariffs to encourage development of diversified home industry is on safer ground. Specialization in a changing world can become overspecialization. Our knowledge of the dynamics of growth is still in the formative stage and it is not prudent to insist that the principle of comparative costs is always the overriding consideration. It is, however, an important consideration. Moreover, there remains the practical question how much protection and for how long. America has already achieved a richly diversified home industry.

The really disturbing thing is not the arguments of the Tariff League, but the wide range of industries which continue to support a wholesale tariff policy when their predominant interest as Americans, as taxpayers, and as producers lies in the expansion of trade, including competitive products. One of the largest companies in the chemical industry, for example, is among the most powerful influences in the Tariff League. Yet our chemical exports are three or four times greater than imports. Probably no other industry has made so many innovations and produced so many important new products. It would seem that the broad interest of the chemical industry lies in freer trade.

Leaving the consumer interest entirely aside, it seems questionable whether the American Tariff League represents the broad interest of the scores of industrial groups affiliated with it. The explanation seems to be in part a historical one. Protection is a tradition in American industry. Many business groups and trade associations have not taken careful stock of the improvement in their competitive position in world markets, a position which has not been fully exploited owing to the shortage of dollars.[28]

Increasingly since the first world war, foreign producers have come to fear, and rightly so, the superior productivity of American industry. But there is one fact which helps to explain the persistence of American protectionism in the face of historical changes which have improved America's over-all competitive position in world markets. There remain small segments of many an industry which would be partially liquidated by freer trade, although perhaps concerns representing nine tenths of the production in that industry would benefit. Because of inertia, the tradition of protection and, apparently, a belief that the potential foreign market is relatively unimportant, the energetic protectionist tail has been able to wag the apathetic foreign trade dog. If details of tariff making were restored to Congress, or tariff changing were delegated to a commission instructed to "equalize costs," the record of history indicates that the same outcome would be visible in tariff schedules.

28. The outstanding testimony of Charles P. Taft showed that some leading opponents of freer trade may be acting contrary to their own interest. Taft also attacked the misleading advertisements of the American Tariff League. See *Trade Agreements Extension*, Hearings, House Ways and Means Committee, 84th Cong., 1st sess., 1955, pp. 2454–2510.

Chapter 9

The Invisible Tariff

IT WAS A customs lawyer who remarked, "Let me write the Administrative Act and I care not who fixes the rates of duty."[1] Administrative regulation and procedure as well as substantive customs law represent a serious barrier to imports which may be as restrictive as tariffs.[2] Not to be found in the formal schedule of duties, this "invisible tariff"[3] presents a trap for the inexperienced and a test of stamina for the experienced importer.

American customs regulations are antiquated, cumbersome and ambiguous. They were devised to meet nineteenth century conditions which no longer exist. Customs law is excessively rigid and fails to allow reasonable discretion in its enforcement. Customs procedures are so uncertain and inequitable that they would not be tolerated in any other branch of national government. Modernization and simplification are long overdue. Customs laws, administrative regulations and procedures were slightly improved in 1938, but have never been thoroughly overhauled. The codification of 1922 failed to simplify and modernize regulations and the act of 1930 extended an outworn system. Only a few undesirable requirements were modified in 1953.

ADMINISTRATIVE HURDLES FOR IMPORTS

Three primary issues concern the classification, valuation and marking of imports. The customs classification is hopelessly complex. The valuation

1. Benjamin Arthur Levitt, *Through the Customs Maze*, Customs Maze Publishing Co., New York, 1923, p. 11, quoted in Percy W. Bidwell, *The Invisible Tariff*, Council on Foreign Relations, New York, 1939.

2. See *Report of the ECA Commerce Mission* (Taylor Mission), October 1949; "Customs Administration Procedures between Canada and the United States," *Report on Invisible Tariffs to the Joint Canadian and United States Chamber of Commerce Committee on Simplifying United States Customs* by the U.S. Associates of the International Chamber of Commerce. Since the present chapter was drafted, the subject was treated in *A Trade and Tariff Policy in the National Interest*, A Report to the President by the Public Advisory Board for Mutual Security, Washington, 1953, Chapter 7.

3. "Each successive tariff act was a major legislative event, attended by months of public discussion. Meanwhile, there was arising a second tariff structure, a comprehensive system of administrative controls over import trade. Attracting much less attention in the public press, rarely debated in Congress, and never the subject of discussion by women's clubs or business men's forums, the invisible tariff has spread its intricate network over an ever-increasing area of our foreign trade. Today, administrative measures are more comprehensive than the visible tariff, since they affect goods which are on the free list as well as those which are dutiable; they are more effective since they make use of quotas and embargoes as well as tariff duties; they can be put into operation more promptly, since they do not need to wait upon discussion in legislative assembly." Bidwell, *op. cit.* p. 2.

formulas are unnecessarily costly and almost impossible to apply equitably. The marking requirements are a booby trap for the unwary.

Classification

Classification difficulties delay imports.[4] United States customs rates differ greatly on the basis of highly technical and minute determinations under the several thousand different headings. Many countries have broad, simple tariff classifications and the rate does not differ much among the categories in which a product may be classified. Under the American classification, the rate may differ more than 100 per cent, depending on the weight, size and other characteristics of an article. Thus bottles and jars containing toilet preparations may be taxed at 12½, 20 or 25 per cent ad valorem, depending on the method of manufacture of the container. (Was the jar produced by automatic machinery and was molten glass automatically fed to the machinery?) A dinner or luncheon set, the pieces of which are obviously of the same materials, since they are bought and sold as sets, may have as many as three different rates applied to individual pieces because of differences in size, value and the like.

The complexity and ambiguity of the classification has been multiplied by trade agreements. Under the act of 1930, for example, Wilton rugs and "like material" were taxable at the same rate as velvet carpets and "like material," namely, at 40 per cent ad valorem if valued at not more than 40 cents per square foot. Under a trade agreement, the rate on velvet rugs and carpets of like description was reduced to 30 per cent, while the original 40 per cent duty was retained on Wilton rugs and carpets of like description. This has made it necessary to determine whether rugs of "like material and description" are like Wilton or like velvets, a question which, despite much time-consuming endeavor, remains a matter of opinion.

Where an imported article might fall under more than one tariff item, the classification adopted is often to the exporter's disadvantage. A frequently recurring example of this is the classification of articles with fringes on them as "fringes" at a rate of duty of 45 per cent. The fringes can be removed from the article before shipment in order to escape the levy of 45 per cent of the value of the whole article. In such a case the fringes pay 45 per cent duty and the rest of the article comes under a different classification—but only if the two parts enter the United States on different ships.

Still other difficulties arise from classifying new articles produced by technological change. The difference in duty is enormous, depending on the administrative decision with respect to classification. Radar sets, for ex-

4. Since this chapter was written the Congress has ordered the Tariff Commission to make a complete study of classification for tariff purposes and report within two years. Public Law 768, Chapter 1213, 83d Cong., 2d sess., approved September 1, 1954.

ample, were unknown when the 1930 tariff was enacted. A radar set would be dutiable at a rate of $4.50 plus 65 per cent ad valorem if classed as a measuring device but at 25 per cent ad valorem if classed as an electrical instrument. After four or five years of litigation, radar sets were placed in the latter classification by court decision.

The multiplication of classes for customs purposes, under trade agreements, has delimited tariff concessions to narrower classes of imports. Thus, the breaking down of tariff classifications into minute categories has been used as a restrictive device. At the same time that duties were reduced, the invisible customs barrier has been raised by the proliferation of already complex classes.

A characteristic of American customs classification which, until November 1950, was particularly irritating to American importers and foreign exporters was the impossibility of obtaining binding decisions on questions of tariff classification. Customs officials refused to give binding opinions in advance of importation though they did give advisory opinions as to the tariff item under which a particular commodity would fall. The complexity of the tariff is such that no one can be certain what will be the decision, and so the delivered cost of imported goods is uncertain.

Owing to occasional reclassification of imports, an importer could not be sure of the rate of duty even after some shipments had already gone through the customs. A commodity on which a certain rate of duty had been paid might suddenly be reclassified and the importer would have to pay a higher rate of duty on past shipments as well.[5] Such an arrangement caused losses for the importer, who frequently had already sold the imported commodities when notified of the additional levy and could therefore not even attempt to pass it on. An example of this is the case of a foreign supplier of table-top cookers, the sample shipment of which was classified under Paragraph 353 of the Tariff Act of 1930 as "cooking stoves and ranges having as an essential feature an electric heating element," at 17½ per cent. The importer foresaw substantial sales until the main shipment, which entered at a different port of entry, was reclassified under Paragraph 339 as "household utensils having an electric heating element," at 40 per cent ad valorem.

This source of uncertainty was modified in November 1950 by a Treasury ruling under which importers can submit samples and obtain from the Commissioner of Customs, in advance of importation, a formal declaration of tariff classification of merchandise.[6] The requirements, however, are so long and tedious that the practice has seldom been used.

5. The customs service explains some of these reclassifications thus: the initial shipment was small and did not justify serious study. Later shipments in volume justified the time and attention required for proper classification.

6. *Journal of Commerce*, November 2, 1950.

Before being classified under a particular heading, goods are examined with great care, the examination often being lengthy.[7] The delay connected with such inspection has at times been responsible for losses by causing failures to meet delivery dates and by causing such merchandise as holiday gifts and women's clothes to miss the season and fashion for which they were destined.[8] The Customs Court received about 13,500 classification cases in fiscal 1952 but disposed of only a fraction of that number.

Valuation

The determination of value for duty purposes has been a complicated procedure under existing law and produces a final result that often seems strikingly inequitable. Four general methods of determining value are provided and a fifth is required on certain goods. Under Section 402(a) of the act of 1930, value for duty purposes is based on (1) foreign value or (2) export value, whichever is higher. If these are not ascertainable, (3) "United States value" and (4) "cost of production" are used in this order. By the use of documents and contracts it is possible to take advantage of these multiple formulas and there is a certain amount of jockeying by experienced importers to find the value formula that is most favorable.

The determination of "foreign value" is costly and time-consuming, and the result represents neither the price paid for the goods nor the price for which they were sold in the American market. Neither importers nor customs officials know the "foreign value" without investigation, which places an onerous burden on both the customs service and the foreign producer. The 1930 statute defined "foreign value" as the price "at the time of exportation" to the United States "at which such or similar merchandise is freely offered for sale for home consumption to all purchasers . . . in the usual wholesale quantities and in the ordinary course of trade . . ."

The "export value" is the price at which merchandise is offered for sale to American importers. "United States value" is the price in the United States with allowances for profits, duty and other expenses, on which

---

7. The problem is most acute with new products. In general, the difficulties are greatest with manufactured products.

8. The United States is, of course, not the only country with restrictive and sometimes bizarre customs regulations. When snow was needed for ski jumping contests on Britain's Hampstead Heath, fifty-five crates of snow were imported from Norway. British customs service promptly announced a duty of twenty pounds sterling.

The newspapers enjoyed a field day. The *Evening News* printed a cartoon picturing ogre-like customs men waiting to pounce on returning travelers with the caption: "Ready, men? Watch out for French air in the bicycle tires, Swiss mud on the ski boots, Italian sunburn, Continental élan." The London *Times* wrote: "If the taxation is for revenue, the interest of the Exchequer demands the utmost effort to stimulate trade with the Polar region . . ."

Bureaucracy triumphed, however, when it was discovered that by filling out the proper forms and making sworn declaration that the snow was for fun and would not be resold as mineral water, it could be admitted duty-free. (From *Time*, April 9, 1951.)

arbitrary maxima are placed. The "cost of production" is composed of the sum of the cost of materials and fabrication plus additions for general expenses and profits on which arbitrary minima are placed.

Some hidden protection to domestic manufacturers is provided by the interpretations which have been placed on the wording of Section 402. The two most important phrases are "in the usual wholesale quantities" and "freely offered for sale," which occur in the definition of both "foreign value" and "export value."

"In the usual wholesale quantities" is interpreted to mean the value at which the largest number of transactions take place rather than the largest volume of sales. For instance, if a British exporter sent 80 per cent of his output to two American firms in two lots at a discount of 25 per cent and sold the remainder of his output to firms in the United Kingdom in small lots at a discount of 10 per cent, the value for duty purposes in the United States would be based on the 10 per cent discount. As a result, exports from countries with a small home market, such as Norway and the Netherlands, can have a higher value for customs purposes than the same merchandise selling at identical prices in larger national markets. The reason is that "usual wholesale quantities" are smaller in the smaller countries.[9]

The "freely offered for sale" proviso serves two functions. One of them is to facilitate the determination of dutiable value by the use of "offered" prices as the evidence of value even where no actual sales are made. The second and less constructive function is the use made of the proviso to gear dutiable value to the highest wholesale price in existence, and sometimes even to the retail price, on the ground that offers at lower prices are restricted as to purchaser or disposition.[10]

In addition to the above four methods of valuation there is also value based on "American selling price." In the case of coal-tar products and a few other commodities designated under Section 336 of the Tariff Act of 1930, duties are based on the American selling price of competitive goods produced in the United States. This method produces a higher value than the others and thus provides a higher duty. One result is that the rate of duty in relation to cost is far higher than would appear from the schedule.

The entire customs regulation is so complex and ambiguous that the same goods may be classified and valued differently by different appraisers and at different points of entry. Appraisers differ in thousands of cases each year.

Under existing laws and regulations, the customs service is unable to handle the growing volume of business. At any given moment in 1952, the number of cases held by appraisers for more than 90 days exceeded 100,000.

9. R. E. Smith, *Customs Valuation in the United States*, University of Chicago Press, Chicago, 1948, p. 172.

10. *Ibid.*, pp. 175–181.

Although value for customs purposes is not the price actually paid by the importer for the merchandise, if the importer enters a value lower than that finally decided upon by the customs officials, he may be penalized. Under Section 489 of the administrative provisions of the Tariff Act of 1930, penalties for undervaluation are 1 per cent of the appraised value for each 1 per cent excess of appraised over entered value. Remission is only made for clerical errors upon the order of the Secretary of the Treasury or upon the finding of the United States Customs Court. In the case of overvaluation where the entered value is higher than the appraised value, duty is levied on the entered value. In recent years the customs service has permitted an importer who cooperates by giving up all rights of appeal to amend his entry without penalty. These onerous requirements and penalties resulting from errors were modified by Public Law 243, Chapter 397, 83d Cong., 1st sess. Some experience under the amended law will be required before its effect can be evaluated.

As with difficulties arising from problems of classification, delays arise in the process of valuation. A delay of more than a year may take place between the provisional estimate of valuation made when customs clearance is given and the final estimate. The final estimate may result in the necessity to pay further duty even though the goods have already been sold. Roughly 15,000 cases involving valuations were received by the Customs Court in fiscal 1952. Less than one fourth of that number were disposed of, so that the backlog was increasing rapidly.

Customs procedure of the United States, as of other countries, places impediments in the path of importers by requiring extensive documentation. The information which must be given in consular invoices required for any consignment with a dutiable value exceeding $250 is not only detailed, but is often of a confidential nature. Foreign producers complain at the exposure of information that is required. When a shipment consists of more than one package, the invoice must indicate the value and content of each. Certain commodities must be accompanied by special certificates.

Marking Requirements

Section 304 of the Tariff Act of 1930 provided that, unless exempted by Treasury decision, "every article imported into the United States, and its container, and the package in which such article is imported, shall be marked, stamped, branded or labeled, in legible English words, in a conspicuous place, in such manner as to indicate the country of origin of such article."

While the Secretary of the Treasury has power to exempt articles from the marking requirements, exemptions are not so widely granted as to free the customs service from the charge of being excessively severe. The more important exemptions are given in cases where marking is impossible, where it would be injurious or unduly expensive and where the commodity is to be used by the importer.

Since 1938, imported articles which are improperly marked may be re-marked and imported without penalty in most cases. In certain instances, however, the law will not allow re-marking even in a foreign trade zone and the articles must be re-exported. In other cases improper marking is subject to a fine even where the improper marking was unintentional.

Marking requirements increase the cost of engaging in foreign trade. Indelible marking may involve expensive processes such as countersinking in the case of commodities such as sheet glass and iron and steel products. Marking may also detract from the value of the import in the case of fancy goods such as dolls' clothespins and may even prevent the entry of some products by rendering them virtually valueless as in the case of dice.

Uncertainty is introduced by the apparent inconsistency of court decisions like those which hold that diamonds mined in South Africa and cut in Holland should be marked "Holland" but that rabbit skins produced in one country and processed in another should be marked with the name of the producing country.

Certain commodities were subject to special marking requirements under the Tariff Act of 1930. Cutlery of all kinds, scientific instruments, dental and surgical instruments had to have the country of origin "die sunk conspicuously and indelibly" below the name of the maker or purchaser. In some cases, these requirements were physically impossible to execute.

Special marking requirements greatly increase the uncertainty involved in importing because of the complexity of the law and its rigid enforcement. For instance, a shipment of pocket knives bearing the manufacturer's name on one side of the blade and the country of origin on the other was refused entry because of a ruling that both markings must be on the same side and on the tang of the blade and one below the other. The knives were sent to Mexico to be re-marked, then shipped again to the United States. Marking requirements were modified by the Customs Simplification Act of 1953.

Special labelling requirements are also to be found in the Food, Drug and Cosmetic Act. Packages of imported foods must be plainly labelled so as to indicate quantity contained. The labelling requirements must follow rigid rules as to use of words.

Under the Federal Seed Act, Title 3, certain imported seed, mostly grass and legume, must be stained different colors depending on the country of origin. The purpose is to warn against seeds grown in southern countries which are likely to winter-kill in the United States.

The marking requirements insure that goods produced for other markets cannot be diverted to the United States.

The effect of the marking requirements is not only restrictive but is also discriminatory in that they operate in favor of established concerns which have the resources, stamina and experience needed to cope with the regulations.[11]

Dumping and Countervailing Duties

The Antidumping Act requires the Secretary of the Treasury to make public a finding whenever he discovers that the price paid for an imported commodity is below its "foreign-market value," or in its absence "cost of production."[12] A statement by the Secretary that an industry in the United States is being injured or is likely to be injured or prevented from being established by the importation of the goods being dumped is a prerequisite to antidumping action. After such a finding has been made, a dumping duty equal to the difference between "foreign market value" and "purchase price" is levied on all importations of the described class. However, "liquidation of entries" is suspended on mere suspicion of dumping. This has the effect of embargo.

American producers may hold up imports by filing a charge of dumping. There have been cases when the delay associated with investigations on the part of the Secretary of the Treasury was responsible for losses to the imports of perishable products.

Countervailing duties are for the purpose of offsetting foreign subsidies on exports and are equal in amount to the subsidy. No finding of injury to domestic producers is necessary in order to impose countervailing duties. They were imposed on Uruguayan wool tops in 1952. Many foreign governments have used numerous devices to stimulate dollar exports. The American Tariff League insists that our law on countervailing duties has not been enforced in recent years.

In two leading cases the Supreme Court of the United States[13] stated that the refund of excise taxes or drawbacks of import duties upon exportation, though not in excess of the amount actually collected from foreign producers by their governments, constituted bounties on exports. Secretaries of the Treasury have not been disposed to take advantage of these decisions, however.[14]

11. The Wool Products Labelling Act, which is administered by the Federal Trade Commission, provides that any product containing woolen fiber imported into the United States, with some exceptions, shall be labelled with the name of the manufacturer or merchant selling it and a statement of content. This same labelling is required of domestic wool products and thus cannot be considered as protective.

12. Since this was written the Antidumping Act of 1921 was amended so that the Treasury now determines if the import is to be sold at less than its "fair value." Public Law 768, Chapter 1213, 83d Cong., 2d sess.

13. *Downs* v. *United States*, 187 U.S. 502, 515.

14. See Bidwell, *op. cit.*, p. 88.

Under Section 307 of the Tariff Act of 1930 all goods produced by convict or forced labor are excluded from the United States. Under this section imports of phosphate rock mined in French Morocco by convict labor were excluded in 1928. Several crabmeat cases occurred more recently. In 1930 legislation excluding the products of indentured as well as forced labor was passed. This legislation was aimed primarily at tobacco from Sumatra and Java, but when it was discovered that a considerable part of the raw materials used by American factories might be cut off, a proviso was introduced exempting goods not produced "in such quantities in the United States as to meet consumptive demand." This proviso was invoked by American cigar manufacturers to prevent the prohibition of Sumatra leaf. In 1931, a general order was issued by the Treasury excluding lumber and pulpwood from the White Sea area of Russia on the grounds that it was produced by convict labor. The order was rescinded in 1933.

Appeal from Customs Decisions

Article X, Paragraph 3(b) of the General Agreement on Tariffs and Trade obligates contracting parties to maintain a tribunal, independent of the agencies entrusted with customs administration, to review administrative action relating to customs matters.

In the United States, the courts of law have always performed this function of an independent tribunal. The only appeal from the decisions of customs appraisers is to courts of law. In recent years about half of the cases received by the customs courts were appeals concerning valuation. Appeals are tried by a single judge of the United States Customs Court, from whose decision the importer or the collector of customs can again appeal to a decision of three judges who review the case. A further appeal on questions of law may be taken to the Court of Customs and Patent Appeals. The government has, in the past, won a majority of the cases.

Though the customs law affords liberal opportunity for appeal from administrative decision, the system suffers from the disadvantage that appeal to the courts involves both expense and delay. The delay sometimes extends to several years and not uncommonly to periods between six months and two years. Delay, uncertainty, and cost of litigation constitute a barrier to trade.

The Customs Bureau may decide to ignore a court ruling in order to have the case tried again. In one instance the court ruled that certain bottles were to be entered under Paragraph 218(e) as bottles produced by automatic machinery, at 25 per cent. (C.A.D. 408.) Collectors were instructed (T.D. 52439) to disregard this decision until the issue had been retried, and that similar bottles were to enter the United States as "bottles, otherwise produced than on automatic machine," at 75 per cent. In another instance collectors of customs were instructed (T.D. 51417) to overlook the decision of the courts (C.D. 949), which had ruled that dogfish liver oil was to enter under Paragraph 1669 as a crude drug, and to classify the oil under Paragraph 34 as a drug advanced in value.

Domestic interests are given the power to intervene in customs administration by Section 516(a) and (b) of the Tariff Act. Whenever an American manufacturer, producer, or wholesaler believes that the appraised value or classification is mistaken, he may file a complaint with the Secretary of the Treasury. The Secretary may bring action in the United States Customs Court if he thinks it warranted. If not, the American interest may bring action, though this is rare. The intervention of private citizens in the relations between the government and importers can be abused to harass the importer. This is especially the case as such court actions are between the domestic interest and the importer, not the government, and the importer is placed in the position of having to bear the expense of defending administrative acts.

Many importers believe that a great improvement would be made by allowing appeal from appraisers' decisions to be made to a tribunal, either within or outside the customs service, before appeals to the Customs Court. Such a tribunal would facilitate the solution of minor problems and save much time and expense. The present system is so rigid that in order to correct errors the appraiser himself must institute court proceedings (through the collector), for he has no authority to revise an appraisement and must therefore resort to appeal if additional evidence indicates that his original decision was incorrect. Rectification of simple clerical errors frequently requires an act of Congress in order to provide relief for the importer.

Discriminatory Excise Taxes

In some instances, revenue taxes discriminate against imports.

The processing taxes imposed on coconut, palm and palm-kernel oil under Section 2470 of the Internal Revenue Code are of this sort. If protection is the objective, the internal tax should be changed into an import duty.

Sections 2306, 2327 and 2356 of the Internal Revenue Code impose internal revenue taxes on imported oleomargarine, adulterated butter and filed cheese which are not applied to like domestic products.

A discriminatory tax is imposed on imported perfumes containing distilled spirits under Sections 2800 and 1650.

More important than the above examples is the provision under Section 2800 which levies internal revenue taxes on imported and domestic distilled spirits on the basis of the proof gallon, or wine gallon when below proof. In practice, this operates inequitably as between domestic and imported distilled spirits, since the domestic spirits are always or nearly always above proof at the time of tax payment while imported liquors are almost always below proof. The result is that imported liquor is taxed on the basis of wine gallons (i.e., as though it were 100 proof), whereas in the case of domestic spirits the tax is collected on the basis of proof gallons.

Customs Simplification

The urgent need for customs reform is clear. The question was brought up at the United Nations Preparatory Committee for the International Trade Conference in London in the spring of 1946 and was further discussed at Geneva in 1947. The ECA Commerce Mission[15] found Europeans loud in their complaints about our restrictive administrative procedures and substantive customs law.

In the customs appropriation for 1948 the Congress specifically authorized funds for study of the customs service by a private firm of management consultants. The objective was to improve the efficiency and reduce the cost of customs service. A report including recommendations was made by McKinsey and Company. The Bureau of Customs is acutely aware of the delays and inequities in its regulations and procedures; many of the recommendations reported by the private management consultants were suggestions offered by the Bureau or its employees.[16]

The recommendations were included in a bill[17] prepared by the Treasury —the Customs Simplification Act of 1950.

In 1951, the House passed a slightly amended bill. The Senate held hearings in the spring of 1952 but failed to act on the measure before Congress adjourned. Extremely minor changes on a score of administrative matters were made in the Customs Simplification Act of 1953. Requirements for marking and the handling of errors and mistakes were eased slightly.[18]

When a bill for simplification was first submitted in 1950, the ECA and State Department were currently emphasizing the need to increase imports. Partly as a consequence, the proposal was heralded in some quarters as a measure to increase trade. This probably did not win votes in the Congress. The fact is that the effect on trade was an incidental and minor aspect of the proposed legislation, which was conceived and designed by the Treasury primarily as a measure to modernize and improve the efficiency of the customs service. The Treasury proposal went scarcely half-way toward

15. *Report of the ECA Commerce Mission.*
16. Management Survey of the Bureau of Customs, Customs Administration and Procedure Enacted in the Smoot-Hawley Tariff Act of June 17, 1930, 46 Stat. 590. This act was slightly revised by the act of June 25, 1938, 52 Stat. 1077.
17. H.R. 8304.
18. Public Law 243, Chapter 397, 83d Cong., 1st sess.

what is needed to end the needless delays and injustice in customs administration. The quite different bill passed in 1953 scarcely touches major issues.

The proposed law would eliminate "foreign value" and substitute "export value" as the primary basis for valuation. Such a step would expedite customs administration and reduce its cost by reducing the necessity for determining facts and conditions in foreign countries. Valuation would be based upon transactions in the import trade of the United States. This would have the added advantage of decreasing the frictions with foreign manufacturers and governments which arise from the investigations of Treasury agents abroad. The proposal would also repeal "American selling price" as a basis of valuation. The version passed by the House eliminated this proposal.

The proposed formula is not as simple in demonstration nor as predictable in results as the British formula of realized price. The reason for retaining the more complex and uncertain formula is the Treasury view that the people of the United States would not want the larger importer to receive any advantage as the result of the lower price associated with large quantities.[19]

Another proposed change would make necessary the finding of material injury to a domestic industry in order to levy countervailing duties; under present law, it is only necessary to prove injury before dumping duties are levied.

The determination of both "foreign value" and "export value" requires that the valuation be made in the foreign currency with which the merchandise is purchased. The problem is that of determining what rate of exchange to use. The provision for quarterly findings by the Director of the Mint of rates of exchange based on the metallic content of coins has had no application since the departure of the United States from the gold standard. The proposed legislation provided for use of par values established by the International Monetary Fund. Where multiple rates exist, the Secretary of the Treasury is to issue regulations concerning their use for customs purposes or, in the absence of such regulations, the Federal Reserve Bank of New York is to certify one or more of such rates to the Secretary for such purposes.

Of the three major problems—classification, valuation and marking—marking requirements have been modified. The Treasury recommendations, which apparently the McKinsey Survey followed in many matters, were very conservative. The Treasury has been primarily concerned with measures to improve the efficiency of customs service rather than with reducing barriers to trade. Customs reform involves intricate issues and requires

19. In this matter the Treasury view appears to go beyond legislation affecting domestic markets. The Robinson Patman Act allows quantity discounts when based on cost.

expert knowledge. Adequate revision will require a major effort by liberal forces. Proposals for more extensive simplification have been pending in the Congress for several years.

At no time since the first tariff act of July 4, 1789 has so long a period elapsed without a comprehensive re-examination of classification and the rate structure. A complex structure of rates is the natural result of the bargaining process.

Those who seek protection have a better chance of getting it if the article is narrowly defined. Importers who seek lower duties have a better chance of success if the reduction is delimited to the article in which the importer is interested. When tariff concessions were made by bilateral agreement, the concessions were so defined as to exclude third nations, insofar as possible, from the benefits of the concessions. When the Tariff Commission recommends tariff relief under the escape clause, its proposal is limited to that class of imports which threatens serious injury. Thus, the increase of duties on women's fur felt hats was restricted to imports valued at $9 to $24 per dozen. This selective and discriminating process has resulted in enumeration of tariff classes which requires a book the size of a big-city telephone directory. Referring only to duties of 50 per cent and higher in 1953, there were 50 tariff classes of watches and clocks, 20 of handkerchiefs and 9 of pocket knives.

In 1954 the Congress asked the Tariff Commission to suggest simplification without significant changes in rates. The most that can be accomplished under this directive would seem to be rather limited. The Commission's interim report, *Tariff Simplification Study*, March 1955, does not portend the type of revision recommended by the Public Advisory Board for Mutual Security. The Commission's view is that "multiplicity of enumerations does not necessarily produce tariff complexity. The contrary is more often true."

"Buy American" and Other Restrictions

Though the War Department had been restricted as early as 1875 in the purchase of foreign materials for river and harbor improvement, it was not until 1933 that federal legislation required that preference be given American goods by all governmental purchases.

The basic policy is laid down in the "Buy American" Act of March 3, 1933. This provided that "unless the head of the department or independent establishment concerned shall determine it to be inconsistent with the public interest, or the cost to be unreasonable" only materials produced in the United States, and only goods manufactured in the United States of United States materials, shall be acquired for public use. The 1933 law does not apply to goods acquired for use outside the United States nor does it apply if the materials are not available in the United States in sufficient commercial quantities and of a satisfactory quality.

"Buy American" provisions of similar character are also to be found in the Rural Electrification Act, in the Appropriations Act for the National Military Establishment for 1949 and for 1950, in the Strategic and Critical Materials Stockpiling Act of 1946, in the Merchant Marine Act of 1936 and in federal housing legislation (Sec. 1946(c) of Title 42, United States Code).

The "Buy American" movement owes its initial success to depression and unemployment. Perpetuation of the policy under the opposite conditions when the government was acutely concerned with shortages and inflation does not make sense. Nonetheless the policy has been reaffirmed and even extended at a time when some people fear that the cost of national defense is a threat to our economic system.

A step backward was taken most recently when the defense appropriation for fiscal 1953 provided that preference be given domestic food, clothing, cotton and wool in all forms whether for use at home or abroad. Previous legislation had excluded goods for foreign use.

An administrative rule interpreted "unreasonable cost" of American goods as a 25 per cent differential above the delivered cost of foreign goods. This 25 per cent rule has been modified in different ways by various departments when the additional cost of American goods involved large sums.

The further requirement that goods must be made "substantially" from American materials and component parts has been interpreted to mean 75 per cent. This allows foreign manufacturers to supply, as subcontractors, up to 25 per cent of the materials or parts.

The "public interest" provision was not generally used, as it might have been, to help avoid inflation and unnecessary taxation. It would seem that the Treasury has been unduly timid in its failure to rescind the 25 per cent ruling at a time when the cost of national defense imposed such heavy burdens. According to a Washington news release in March 1955, the Defense Department was prepared to ease this ruling. Contracts would be given to foreign low bidders when the difference between the lowest foreign and domestic bids is 6 per cent or more of the foreign bid, except in cases where the American firm involved is vital to the public interest.

"Buy American" policies are most important in connection with expenditures for national defense, which account for about 80 per cent of the materials purchased by government.

It should be recognized that foreign supplies could be considered for only a small part of federal purchases, in any event. Very little military equipment for the American army would be purchased abroad. Many other factors operate against large purchases abroad, even if there were no legal impediments. Problems of quality and specification naturally lead government purchasing agents to favor traditional sources of supply. To the purchasing agent, there are substantial advantages in dealing with a few large firms that are known to be reliable. Nonetheless, these factors do not exclude some foreign buying and the Defense Department has occasionally let contracts to foreign firms that offered large savings. Despite these exceptions, however, the "Buy American" policies remain the main obstacle to cooperation with foreign countries in the sphere of military procurement.[20]

State and local governments spend billions of dollars yearly on materials and equipment. Twenty-two of the states have laws giving some degree of preference to local residents and materials produced within the states on all procurement contracts. This has the effect of discriminating against imports from outside the state, but none of the acts discriminate specifically against imports from outside the United States.

Local building codes also constitute a barrier to imported materials as many of them specify performance standards and specifications which bar foreign supplies.

The "Buy American" laws do not provide rigid requirements but establish preference as a general policy. Administrative interpretation could make more liberal use of the "national interest" clause in order to avoid inflation and reduce the cost of national defense. The public sentiment supporting such legislation, which was strong in 1931 and 1932, has long since disappeared. "Buy American" is contrary not only to the national interest, but also to the declared foreign economic policy of the government, which seeks to strengthen the free world by the expansion of trade. Repeal of the laws would be consistent with the declared objectives of the United States.

Food and Drug Restrictions

The Food and Drug Administration is responsible for the administration of the Federal Food, Drug and Cosmetic Act, among others. The purpose of this act is to protect consumers against adulterated or misbranded foods, drugs and cosmetics of both domestic and foreign origin. A food is held to be adulterated if it contains any potentially injurious substance, if it contains any filth or decomposed substance, if it has been prepared or packed under unsanitary conditions or if any substance has been added or subtracted to make it appear of greater value than it is. Misbranding exists where labelling is false, or fails to show the name and address of the producer and the weight of the product, and where the containers are judged to be misleading.

These definitions of adulteration or misbranding have at times given results which foreign exporters have considered unwarranted, as in the case

20. G. B. Howard, "United States Defense Procurement in Canada," *International Journal*, Autumn 1950, Toronto.

of a European chocolate manufacturer whose product was refused admission to the United States because the package was deemed too large relative to its contents despite the fact that the weight was clearly marked on the package and that the exporter considered such a package necessary to protect the product.

Samples of all imported food, drugs, devices and cosmetics are inspected and entry is refused to adulterated or misbranded commodities. Delay in sampling does not legalize importation. An importer may obtain the goods upon posting of bond to the invoice value of the imports pending decision, but he must be prepared to deliver them again should they be refused entry and must thus keep them intact. Should he fail to do so his bond must be forfeited. A shipment not tested at the time of importation may later be sampled or seized. Thus an importer's risks are increased by the fact that his goods are in danger of seizure upon importation and may remain in that state for some time.

The Food and Drug Administration also enforces the provision of the Federal Milk Import Act of 1927. This act requires that milk imported into the United States must be produced by shippers who hold a valid permit from the Secretary of Agriculture. To obtain the permit foreign farms must conform to sanitary standards equal to American milk-producing farms. The Secretary accepts, in lieu of inspection by United States inspectors, certified statements from Canadian inspectors. American inspectors visit the certified herds from time to time. Canada is the only important foreign source of fresh milk and cream.

Importation of fresh milk and cream from Canada fell drastically after the passage of the act. Imports of milk, which were over 7 million gallons in 1926, fell to 1,000 gallons in 1934. Cream fell from 5 million gallons in 1926 to virtually nothing in 1934. This entire contraction, however, cannot be attributed to the Federal Milk Importation Act. A major part of it was due to the large rise in duty in 1930, and, particularly, to state barriers to imports raised under the guise of sanitary regulations.

Today the rate of duty on milk of 2 cents a gallon is less than from 1922 to 1930, when it was 2½ cents a gallon. The rate of duty on cream is the same as then at 20 cents a gallon. There is a quota on imports of Canadian milk of 3 million gallons a year and on imports of cream of 1½ million gallons, but these are of no immediate importance as imports are less than 500 gallons a year.

Canadian authorities believe that the real barriers to Canadian exports are to be found in state sanitary regulations such as those of New York State.[21] These regulations provide that the only fluid milk that can be sold

21. Senate of Canada, *Proceedings of the Standing Committee on Canadian Trade Relations*, No. 5, 1948, p. 99.

in the State of New York is milk that has been inspected and approved by state authorities. These authorities have let it be known that they will not send their inspectors to Canada. Much the same methods are used to exclude milk from other states. The federal government evidently does not find itself in a position to prevail upon states to modify these practices, which nullify the undertakings of the government of the United States under its various trade agreements.

Restriction of Imports of Animals and Animal Products

The Bureau of Animal Industry of the Department of Agriculture was created in 1884 to combat animal diseases and their introduction from abroad. The original purpose was to raise American standards of animal health in order to maintain exports, which were threatened by foreign embargoes placed on American animals and meats on the grounds of health. Animal exports from the United States later declined in importance and the controls now serve to protect domestic industry. Despite regulations which seem severe, an outbreak of anthrax was recently traced to imported bone meal.

Importers of ruminants and swine are required to produce certificates signed by the chief veterinary authority in the country of export stating that that country has been free for sixty days from foot-and-mouth disease, rinderpest, contagious pleuropneumonia and surra. For cattle, certificates showing negative results on tuberculin and Bang's disease tests are required in addition. For swine, certificates must show the premises of origin and adjoining premises to have been free of hog cholera, swine plague and erysipelas for 60 days prior to exportation.

Upon importation in the United States cattle are tested for tuberculosis again and are quarantined for thirty days. Other ruminants and swine are held under observation for fifteen days. The owner must bear the cost of feed and care during quarantine, so that these measures afford economic protection to domestic consumers even though this was not the primary reason for the regulations.

Regulations covering imports of animals from Canada and Mexico are less severe than the measures described above. If certificates are presented showing negative tuberculin and Bang's disease tests, the tests are not repeated nor are the animals held in quarantine.

The principal feature of the present law is the provision for embargoes on imports of animals and fresh meat from any countries in any part of which foot-and-mouth disease or rinderpest is known to exist. This provision is to be found in Section 306(a) of the Tariff Act of 1930. Before 1930 the Bureau had full authority to impose embargoes against any country or part of a country found to be infected, but country-wide embargoes are now mandatory.

This measure seems unnecessarily severe and serves as an instrument for economic as well as sanitary protection. The legislation was pushed by livestock interests in the United States and opposed by the Department of Agriculture. The Secretary of Agriculture wrote to the Committee on Ways and Means when asked for an opinion in 1929: "It is the view of this department that this section is entirely unnecessary, since the department already has adequate laws to prevent the importation of cattle and cattle hides which will tend to the introduction or spread of contagious or infectious diseases among the cattle and other livestock of the United States."[22]

The countries affected most severely by the provision for nationwide embargoes are Argentina and Uruguay, though imports from all sources but a few European countries, the Caribbean and North America have been prohibited too. Argentina and Uruguay are the largest potential suppliers of fresh meat and yet can export only canned meat to the United States because parts of these countries are infected.

Many American states have even more severe regulations regarding animal diseases.

Restriction of Imports of Plants and Products

Despite the fact that approximately one half of the injurious insects in the United States were of foreign origin, it was not until 1912 that the United States sought to control imports of plants and their products by the Plant Quarantine Act of 1912.

The act, which is administered by the Bureau of Entomology and Plant Quarantines of the Department of Agriculture, provides that the Secretary may regulate, restrict or prohibit the importation and movements in interstate trade of nursery stock, fruits, vegetables and other plants which might result in the introduction of injurious plant diseases.

The official view is that the purpose of plant quarantine is to exclude pests and not to give tariff protection and that it should operate to permit the best possible movement of goods while employing reasonable safeguards against importing disease.[23]

Certain aspects of present regulations, which cannot be justified on biological grounds, do offer very substantial economic protection to domestic interests.

Steps in import procedure for plants are complex, involving obtaining of import permits and foreign certificates of inspection, elaborate marking of

22. Hearings of the House Ways and Means Committee, 70th Cong., XVI, 9952, quoted in Bidwell, *op. cit.*, p. 213.

23. P. N. Armand, "Today in Foreign Plant Quarantine," *Journal of Economic Entomology*, April 1950, pp. 139–145.

shipments, filing of notices of arrival and of shipment, inspection by American officials and, in certain cases, inspection by state officials.

Nursery Stock, Plant and Seed Quarantine No. 37 is based on a policy of decreasing the danger of introducing foreign pests and diseases by preventing the importation of all plants but those absolutely essential to the horticultural, floricultural and forestry needs of the United States. It was felt in authoritative quarters that, though decreasing imports would undoubtedly decrease the amount of infection, the law was defective as an instrument of biological protection.[24]

Furthermore, economic protection is given nursery men by allowing unlimited imports of rose stocks, the raw material for nurseries, whereas finished roses, bud sticks and cuttings, the finished products, are limited in quantity by the law. There is as much danger of disease from rose stocks as from other forms of rose imports.

The Fruit and Vegetable Quarantine No. 56 requires permits and inspection for all imports of fruits and vegetables except those originating in Canada. Certain exceptions were made allowing unlimited entry after inspection of certain fruits and vegetables believed free from infection. Embargoes were placed on Spanish grapes during the 1930s to prevent imports of the Mediterranean fruit-fly. Quarantine 28 was applied in 1917 to citrus fruits from sources infected with the citrus canker.

The question of how rigid biological protection should be is difficult of solution, since measures calculated to make absolutely certain that no infected plants are imported would be intolerably protective from the economic viewpoint. The problem is that of balancing risk of infection against the welfare of the consumer. Complete security from disease is unfeasible.

The Grain Branch of the Department of Agriculture administers the Federal Seed Act, which prohibits the importation of seed that is adulterated or unfit for seeding purposes, requires the staining of certain imported seeds, and prohibits the importation of screenings of seeds which do not have value for other than seeding purposes.

The act operates as a discriminatory barrier against foreign seeds in that domestic seed is only labelled and inspected whereas seed of foreign origin may be denied entry. Furthermore, the staining of certain seed does not serve a useful technical purpose, as in the case of the staining violet of alfalfa and red clover seed grown in Canada.

Copyrights

For many years, American copyright laws gave very substantial protection to American printers. The law not only prohibited the importation of

24. Lee A. Strong, *Plant Quarantine Act and Quarantine No. 37*, pp. 3 and 4, quoted in Bidwell, *op. cit.*, p. 239.

piratical copies of books, which is in accordance with the principle of copyright, but also prohibited the importation of English language books copyrighted in the United States and manufactured abroad, which is not in accordance with those principles.

Section 16 of Title XVII, United States Code, provided that in order to be accorded copyright protection in the United States a book in English must, with small exceptions, be printed in the United States from type set or plates manufactured in the United States. Section 107 prohibited importation of a book in English during existence of the American copyright.

This protection of the American printing industry, under copyright law, has recently been modified under the Universal Copyright Convention. With ratification by twelve members, the Convention becomes effective September 16, 1955. Public Law 743 (83d Cong., 2d sess.) carries out American ratification by amending the copyright law to permit imports manufactured in countries that give reciprocal treatment to American works.

Nongovernmental Action to Stop Imports

The restriction of imports is not limited to governmental agencies. Some interests in the United States which fear competition from imports have undertaken private action calculated to prevent the importation of certain commodities. These measures include both persuasion and threats of coercion.

Imports from countries behind the Iron Curtain are particularly vulnerable to attack by private agencies. Longshoremen refused to unload Russian crabmeat even though it was owned and shipped by British merchants.

The American Flint Glass Workers' Union of North America, AFL, has undertaken to put pressure on retail merchants to prevent them from selling foreign glassware which is cheaper than American handmade glass. The Union's campaign consists of a plea to merchants to sell only domestic handmade glassware in order to prevent the creation of unemployment in the glass industry, which would damage the maintenance of "a sound and healthy national economy for the economic chain cannot be stronger than its weakest link."[25] Similar pleas were made regarding plywood, shingles and doors.

25. Harry H. Cook, International President, American Flint Glass Workers' Union, Letter to the Retail Merchants of the United States, May 16, 1950; cf. Chapter 21.

Chapter 10

Domestic Handicaps

THE LITERATURE of international trade has created the impression that the tariff has been the most important barrier to trade, if not the only one, and from this, it was sometimes assumed that foreign trade would grow equally with domestic trade but for deliberate restrictions by government. More recently, customs regulations have been emphasized as obstacles also, and in many countries direct governmental controls have become the most serious barrier of all. Some writers mention the national differences in engineering specifications which impede the free flow of tools, machinery and other equipment in international trade. It is less well known that there are a host of other practical considerations which favor domestic trade.[1] Some of these institutional obstacles are related to customs procedures, but many are not.

Consider, for example, some of the "housekeeping" problems of the retailer. He must evaluate the reliability of his source of supply as to quality and delivery dates. The mere matter of returning goods not up to specifications is illustrative of the little things that mitigate against imports. To return goods purchased from a domestic producer may involve nothing more troublesome than picking up the telephone or dictating a letter. But in the case of imports, if there has been some delay in discovery of the defect, the prospect of arranging the return and going through customs in reverse is so discouraging that the buyer will usually decide not to attempt it. The difficulties are compounded by the fact that foreign suppliers do not operate commonly on the business practice familiar in domestic affairs. Communication is slower and misunderstanding is easy.

Less difficult, perhaps, than returning goods is the problem of prompt delivery on re-order of identical shipments. In the case of domestic products, a buyer can often try out a small order and quickly expand his inventory if sales go well. With foreign-produced goods this practice is uncertain or even impossible.

Few foreign producers can deliver the quantity of consumer goods required for national distribution in the United States.[2] It is not unusual for a

1. Except as otherwise credited, most of the information in this chapter is based on conversations with a score of importers and a few ECA officials. The author has profited especially from conversations with Mr. Gutter of the R. H. Macy Company, Mr. Morris Rosenthal of the Stein Hall Company and Robert Oshins of ECA.

2. Some of the issues presented in this chapter are considered from the point of view of European exporters by Professor Hoover in the following chapter.

British producer to face the alternative (1) of selling either a negligible volume in the American market or (2) of being called on for more than his total output. The expansion of facilities to satisfy the American buyer often seems a dubious and risky venture.

This explains the case of the Scottish textile manufacturer who, when approached by an American buyer after a profitable trial period of handling the producer's goods, agreed that he could supply a substantially larger volume in the future but stated that the price would have to be higher. His reason was that the modernization and expansion of plant needed to supply the larger volume would raise the costs. Perhaps, too, his uncertainty as to the duration of larger sales in the American market led the Scottish producer to the view that capital costs would need to be amortized in a shorter than normal period.

A producer of a famous china was reluctant to expand his production further for the American market, although the demand was unsatisfied, on the ground that it was not prudent business judgment to put more eggs in the risky American basket.

Communication itself is more highly developed in the United States than elsewhere in the world. No American businessman would tolerate the telephone service that characterizes most foreign countries. But the communication problem is more far-reaching. The catalogue displays of American concerns are, as a British Mission noted, "admirably produced" and "encyclopedic." It is rare that the foreign producer devotes as much energy and expenditure to sales as do Americans; in fact, his volume of sales will rarely warrant the expenditure on catalogues that American mass producers can afford.

Selling Imports

The economics of international trade has been written as if it were concerned only with standardized products like rubber and tin, which are sold on a basis of price. But consumer goods are not sold in an auction market and imports do not sell themselves; they have to be sold.

Experienced merchandizers have found that higher markups are required on imports in order to realize a profit margin equivalent to that on domestic goods. Some of the reasons advanced for this are: (1) higher inventory losses, (2) higher losses due to defects in quality, (3) greater breakage in shipping, (4) low volume and slow turnover, (5) product not advertised by manufacturer, (6) high cost of servicing durable goods. As a result of these factors the risks on imports are greater, the losses are larger and the selling costs are higher.

The importance of modern merchandising techniques was emphasized by Richard Bissell, Deputy Director of ECA, in writing of the effects of devaluation of European currencies in 1949:

But price was by no means the only obstacle; the European countries could not expand their exports to the United States virtually at will merely by the process of devaluation. This was soon recognized; and by the summer of 1950 the other aspects of selling, namely product design, packaging, credit terms and advertising, were receiving major attention in Manchester, Brussels, Turin, Lyons and elsewhere. Although it cannot be said that the sales problem was "solved" in the sense in which the production problem was, the devaluations, plus the growing adoption of modern merchandising techniques, plus the boom in the United States in early 1950 indicated that this knot too would be unraveled far ahead of schedule.[3]

Systematic market research is required in order to find the niche in the American market that Europe can supply. Sales promotion is necessary. There are wide differences between national markets in style, taste, color, size, packaging, and methods of marking sizes. Production has to be adapted to the American market. It is widely believed, moreover, that if a mass market were developed for an imported product, American producers could often take it over with a mass-produced product.

The American market for consumer goods presents the European exporter with a formidable selling problem. The European market is one in which production has never been so abundant as to put a heavy premium on the services of the salesman. In the past much consumption tended to be customary and in accordance with a "station" in life. The selling process, therefore, was largely a matter of putting goods into channels for distribution to an established clientele. In part this was because of the role of cartels in limiting production and dividing markets. In the United States "selling" is more highly developed, and the more highly developed the sales effort, the greater the emphasis on product differentiation, which reduces the importance of small differences in price.

Those who appraised the 1950 World Trade Fair in Chicago stressed that the exhibitors who did not do well "apparently did not put forth enough effort to attract buyers . . . the consensus seemed to be that the aggressive exhibitor was agreeably satisfied with sales, with prospects for future orders, and with information on marketing methods in the United States to be used as a guide to future business."[4]

A team of private American marketing experts visited Britain to explain American markets. The British view, they found, was that selling cost should bear a fixed relation to manufacturing cost. The implicit assumption was that higher selling costs either reduce profits or necessitate a price increase. As opposed to this view, the Americans extolled the "expansionist" theory of sales management, which asserts that higher selling costs

3. Richard M. Bissell, Jr., "The Impact of Rearmament on the Free World Economy," *Foreign Affairs*, April 1951, pp. 386 and 387.

4. "Chicago Success Invites New Trade Fairs," *Foreign Commerce Weekly*, October 16, 1950, p. 2.

when effectively used make possible volume production at lower unit cost. "In Britain, selling is something designed to fill the needs of the public."[5] The Americans emphasized that selling must create wants, if American imports are to be expanded.

The Time Factor

The most elementary economic considerations favor the domestic supplier. How long in advance must the retailer anticipate his market? Must he carry inventory or can he rely on the manufacturer to perform this costly function?

The delivery date is a goddess of the American market that must be propitiated. "American buying technique in many cases called for larger quantity of goods than were available or for earlier delivery than was possible, and some sales were naturally lost because of inability of the exhibitor to supply quantity shipments within specified delivery dates."[6]

The International Chamber of Commerce also commented on the uncertainties of the exhibitors themselves as to quantities available and delivery dates. Foreign suppliers are not usually accustomed to the close scheduling practiced by American retailers, who plan advertising and display dates months in advance. It is, of course, not merely the scheduling of production but shipping space, customs clearance and even such matters as drayage from dock to customs building that must meet a time schedule laid out months in advance.

When interviewed, one of the most experienced direct retail importers in the United States had a shipment of goods at the dockside. His advertising spread, planned months earlier, was then in the newspaper office for Sunday's papers; his problem was to insure that the goods cleared customs in time to be displayed for Monday's sale. There were only three bonded draying companies in New York City authorized to haul these goods between the dock and customs. Shipping was piled up at dockside in far greater volume than could be cleared through customs within the time schedule. The importer was faced, therefore, with the unpleasant task of trying to push his goods through customs ahead of shipments to others, some of whom were in the same position as he.

This experience must have been a common one because it had formerly been an established customs practice to permit clearance of urgent shipments on payment of a premium drayage fee by the importer. But this practice had to be abandoned because so many importers elected to pay the premium that priority lost its significance.[7] In this case the importer had to

5. "Yankee Salesmen in King George's Court," *Harper's*, January 1951.
6. "Chicago Success Invites New Trade Fairs."
7. The customs staff apparently was not expanded with the volume of imports through the port of New York.

fall back on the wiles of personal contacts, "friendship," etc.—a practice distasteful alike to both importer and customs officials.

In 1950 some goods imported specifically for Christmas piled up in customs and missed the Christmas trade. The principal responsibility apparently lay with the inadequate customs staff. At this period, twenty to twenty-five days were required to clear customs, compared with the four or five days regarded as normal.[8]

Style

Differences in style between national markets are sometimes enormous and always important. Following World War II, at least two years were required for German producers to get abreast of the style requirements of other outside markets. The same applies in a lesser degree to other products and other countries. Foreign producers, to sell in this country, must be able to create the style in silverware, glassware, china, prints and clothing, or they must be able to follow quickly the styles created in the United States. Women's clothing is a familiar and extreme case. One of the notable developments in the past generation has been the effect of the movie industry on styles. Though the Paris label is still treasured, the Parisian fashion makers have real competition from Hollywood.

The American mass market, while notable for uniformity at any one time, is characterized by rapid change. Unquestionably, there is more variety in the more uniform American market than elsewhere in the world; the variety is obtained by rapid change.

To keep abreast of the changes in taste, style and novelty interest, a high degree of organization and communication is required. The control of inventory is a more serious problem in a changing market. When a producer "hits the market" with a slightly new and different product, he must be able to turn out supplies for mass consumption quickly. Much of this is alien to foreign organization and capacities. Change is costly because of inventory losses. The European producer suffers especially from change because of high overhead in relation to comparatively small volume.

The use of color is another difference between the American and foreign markets. In France, for example, virtually nothing but white socks are manufactured for children. Linoleum is an excellent example of the importance of color and design. The British industry is outstanding and American imports are restricted by a tariff. But imports are also handicapped by the American preference for the colors and designs supplied by home industry.

The art director of the Homer Laughlin China Company observed that "the Japanese, English and European manufacturers have lagged in catching the contemporary feeling."

8. "Clearing customs" does not include the fixing of tariff liability. That comes later.

Differences in the size of women's hands create a difficulty in importing gloves. There are differences in the lasts of shoes, and differences in the system of marking sizes, which, for example, render the continental marking of children's clothing unintelligible to American buyers. While these are obviously not insuperable barriers, they are barriers.

Quality

The American market combines mass and quality as does no other market in the world. There is some disposition to think of imports as "quality" goods because of their traditional prestige and because the items that are imported represent the cream of Europe's production. But if European suppliers are to broaden their American market, the demand for quality looms as a large obstacle. To bring this realization to the foreign producer is one of the educational tasks of the importer. Many European producers of pure cashmere sweaters regard 98 per cent as commercially pure and are astonished that Macy's requires 100 per cent.

Assisted by the requirements of the Wool Labelling Act, the Pure Food and Drug Act and related legislation, the American buyer and hence the American retailer demand and get a quality that is, as a general rule, unknown in the run-of-the-mill markets of Europe.

Although the evidence is contradictory, the attitudes of merchants toward imported products reflect skepticism concerning the superiority of certain imported products which have enjoyed traditional prestige. A Canadian importer of both British and American woolens found the American product competitive in price and superior in quality. The British sales representative who happened to be in Canada at the time was called in and shown the difference in quality with the implied threat that the Canadian would shift to the American source unless the British quality were improved. The agent's reply was, "They won't like this."

The best quality British woolens are not produced for mass distribution. These woolens and worsteds have been regularly purchased in the United States by a few merchant tailors and manufacturers of expensive ready-to-wear suits, because British woolens have long stood for quality design and classic colors. A few buyers would have no other if the British product were available. But many merchants and consumers are not impressed. The heart of the matter was indicated by a store executive who said:

> British woolen manufacturing is geared to custom-made trade, i.e., five or six pieces, or short-suit lengths in exclusive or restricted colors. . . . To merchandise British woolen lines for the entire American market would require complete revamping and retooling of the entire industry.[9]

Some United States merchants contend that certain American woolen products offer better values than imports because of less shrinkage, better

9. *The Market for United Kingdom Consumer Goods in the United States,* a survey by Time, Inc., 1948.

colors and better sizes.[10] In the case of knit woolen clothing, British firms are well equipped to supply small orders in a wide range of colors and with careful attention to finishing detail.

American toys are highly protected, but merchants frequently found them to be more appealing because they were replicas of modern machinery, not antiques. In many other instances, the superiority of the domestic product is a matter of better adaption to local requirements. Some people object to pushing heavy British "prams" over hills and therefore prefer the lighter American models.

Bicycles

British bicycles have generally been held in esteem in countries where bicycle transportation is important, but United States merchants have expressed the view that dollar for dollar American mass production has provided a better bike.[11] Their opinion, however, may be based on considerations other than high quality.

Scores of American travelers, plus a large ECA Mission in Britain, have turned up frequent instances where it appeared that British organization was inadequate or that British industry was not straining every muscle to compete in the American market. The results might be surprising if a similar survey were made of the irrationalities in the American distribution of imported products. A newsletter, *Space and Time*, published the following account:[12]

British Bicycles: A Westchester subscriber has described to us the unbelievable obstacles placed in the path of a 16-year-old boy who wished to purchase a British-made bicycle: (a) Two shops tried to tout him to "British-type" (but American-made) wheels (b) Another store which confessed to having sold 12 British bikes seemed to resent their popularity, had not re-ordered, did not want to (c) There was a general resistance to the insistence of the boy and his chums that British product was superior (d) Youth had to demonstrate many of the features; the clerks didn't know about them (e) Finally the boy got a British bike at a mark-down from a dealer wanting to close out the line, apparently because they sold too well and upset him. Don't ask us to explain this weird report except to observe that contrary to our p. 1 story on "scientific merchandising" in groceries, it ain't no science. Boy's theory: dealers like bikes needing frequent repairs.

Monopolistic Patterns

In the case of the domestic market, product differentiation and a score of related monopolistic devices have modified the role of price.[13] But in

10. *Ibid.* This comparison presumably included the tariff.

11. Nonetheless bicycle imports increased sharply in 1951 and 1952.

12. May 1950, published by R. J. Landry, 18 West 70th Street, New York.

13. See D. D. Humphrey, "Nature and Meaning of Rigid Prices, 1890–1933," *Journal of Political Economy*, October 1937, pp. 651–661.

international trade, scant attention has been paid to the monopolistic factors in the retail markets, such as rigid prices, producer-distributor tie-ins, product differentiation, packaging, etc. Quite apart from the tariff, it seems clear that the obstacles to a free market in which price is the controlling force are greater in the case of imports than for domestically produced goods.

The procurement procedure for the great bulk of consumer goods imports is quite different from the purchase of standardized raw materials. The large department stores and retail organizations search for foreign producers whom they can develop as suppliers. The development of a supplier requires time and investment. His ability to produce goods may be adequate, but his designs may be unsatisfactory and his general knowledge of the American market sketchy. The American importer supplies designs, encourages and assists the producer in the development of his own designs and sometimes sends him shopping in a third country. At some stage the producer is likely to be brought to the United States to "shop" the American market. This usually proves an eye-opener, for apparently few foreign firms have an adequate conception of the quality and diversity of products with which their product must compete. One retailer commented that this education of the supplier was one of the most valuable investments his company made.

The mass distributors in the American market are mass buyers. The hard bargains that they are able to drive with domestic manufacturers in the form of discounts, premiums and advertising allowances are familiar. The Congress has from time to time investigated these problems. The Robinson-Patman Act and other legislation have been designed to encourage "fair competition." But the consumer goods market remains a highly differentiated one characterized by administered and relatively inflexible prices. Price is a consideration, but competition also takes the form of style, design and packaging. In this way the retailer seeks to obtain a modicum of exclusive control and price protection on products that he advertises and carries in stock. It is difficult and costly to find foreign suppliers who can provide volume, quality and product differentiation. In the case of some specialty items, however, the foreign producer who will handle small lots has an advantage over large-scale domestic producers.

Protection from Competition

Business seeks "protection" from all competition—domestic as well as foreign. The long complex history of trade associations, resale price maintenance, and a host of related practices directed against "unfair" competition testifies to the insistence of the businessman on protection from a free market.

From the business point of view the injury from competitive imports cannot possibly be measured by their volume in relation to domestic output. Imports are harmful because of the threat of spoiling the market, because of the uncertainty created by potential imports, because of the effect on price maintenance and informal price stabilization. Even the suggestion of "uncontrolled" imports represents a threat to a delicately balanced internal price structure.

Price protection is another "service" extended distributors by American producers that cannot be easily duplicated by foreign suppliers. By resale price maintenance, by refusal to sell to price cutters, by trademarks and nationally advertised brands, the domestic manufacturer provides the distributor with "protection." These considerations do not affect small "fill in" lines as much as the volume items.

Import Distribution

The rise of large retail stores has tended to displace the import wholesaler and jobber. Some information on the organization of importing is provided in the comments of merchants in the Time survey, which indicated that, for a variety of reasons, merchants prefer not to do business through import jobbers. Direct contact with the supplier is preferred. They feel that the jobber system is too slow and cumbersome to keep pace with the rapid adjustments required in modern merchandising. The American merchant prefers to begin at the production stage to gear the product to his promotional activity. He wants to advertise a product which is or can be made to appear unique. He needs to know how quickly goods can be supplied on re-order before determining his initial advertising spread. He wants, as far as possible, to gain the advantage of "confined distribution" on the product he advertises.

The jobber system, it is said, does not provide adequate interchange of information on changing consumer tastes in styles, color and pattern. In addition, the experienced representative of the larger American retail organization feels better equipped to cope with the idiosyncrasies of the tariff schedule. Thus, goods with braided elastic may be dutiable at 45 per cent, but by the substitution of equally satisfactory woven elastic, the duty can be reduced. Tassels on children's clothing raise the duty. Embroidery on cotton shirts raises the duty by 100 per cent from a rate of 25 per cent to 50 per cent. Foreign producers often appear strangely oblivious to the large differences in the duty associated with the trim.

The import duty is 110 per cent ad valorem on pocket lighters but only 30 per cent on table lighters. By putting a detachable base on lighters, they can be imported as "table" lighters and sold as pocket lighters.

Indirect importing of a wide range of consumer goods through import merchants worked well enough for small-scale business. But the development of mass distribution in the domestic economy has tended to displace the old manufacturer-wholesaler-retailer relation by combining the functions in larger units without the wholesaler. The parallel development in Canada has been described as follows:

> The system in 1900, whereby commodities moved from producer to consumer via the wholesaler and a retail network of thousands of small merchants, has given way to the complex system of the present day, in which the wholesaler plays a relatively minor part and the independent retailer is dwarfed by those huge corporate enterprises, department and chain stores, which in 1930 transacted 31.1 per cent of the total retail trade of the country.[14]

While this trend can be conducive to increased distribution of certain imported consumer goods, the elimination of regular wholesale importing operates against wide and regular distribution of a wide range of products. British shoes have been selling in chain shoe stores and mail order houses; fancy jams, preserves and confectioneries have found their way into the supermarkets. In one instance, a supermarket sold British automobiles by the pound. But the interest of distributors in foreign merchandise in many instances is to "fill out" lines in order to appeal to a wider range of customers interested in special styles and quantities.[15] The imported items are carried chiefly to attract customers by offering a larger choice.

The packaging and merchandising of food products are affected by the almost universal use of home refrigeration in the United States. How different the American from the European kitchen! The heavier British beers, for example, will not stand American refrigeration without deterioration. Prepared foods, ready for cooking or partly cooked, have found a ready market in the United States. The high price of domestic help is a critical factor affecting the differences between the American and European market.

Electrical equipment has to be adapted to American-type outlets, differences in current and safety requirements. Foreign producers must face the test of the American Standards Association and the Underwriters Laboratory. These and similar differences must be included in the cost calculation, including the cost of knowing in advance that the Pure Food and Drug Administration looks with a jaundiced eye on "custard creams" containing neither custard nor creams.

The New and Novel

While a cost advantage is requisite, far more is needed to establish a product successfully in the American market. Merchandising firms operat-

14. *Report of the Royal Commission on Price Spreads*, Ottawa, 1935, pp. 200 and 201.
15. See *Organization for Importing*, Studies in Business Policy, No. 29, National Industrial Conference Board, New York, 1948.

ing in both foreign and domestic markets emphasize the "new and novel" items which must compete in an economy rich in the "new and novel." It is said that the American consumer likes to buy something that is new.

Mere mention of the new products that have achieved wide consumer acceptance since the end of the war indicates something of the character of the successful new product. Television is the outstanding example. Nylon shirts achieved sudden popularity. Ammoniated tooth paste, antihistamines and new prescription drugs have reached the popular market. Foam rubber mattresses and cushions have found consumer acceptance. Aluminum foil has become a common kitchen product; quick frozen orange juice and precooked foods have suddenly found an accepted place. The breading of shrimp before freezing and the preparation of packaged frozen chicken for the frying pan have increased sales substantially.[16] Other new items include such products as magnesium ladders and glass fishing rods. Many of these products are the result of extensive and expensive research or, in the case of foods, depend on the electric refrigeration which characterizes the American kitchen.

There are numerous items produced in Europe that are almost unknown in the United States market, but substantial risks and development costs must be borne in order to introduce them successfully here.[17] Any European product, says the J. Walter Thompson Company (advertising), which fills an existing or potential need can be sold in the American market provided it has "some distinctive feature or unusual character to set it apart from competing products."[18] "The distinctiveness or superiority of a product may be in design, finish, quality, appearance, ease of use, style, size, economy, packaging, reliability, simplicity, cleanliness, lower price, novelty or any number of other characteristics." It is notable that price is among the qualifications but only one of many, as the practical problem is seen by the successful marketing expert.

Class vs. Mass Markets

Emphasis on the "new and novel" reflects the rapidity of change in the American market. This, in turn, is related to the whole problem of class versus mass markets.[19] The American market has the peculiar characteristic that American luxury consumption is expressed more by a rapid turnover than by the purchase of fine wares for lifetime use. The striking increase in

16. *Newsweek* carries as a weekly feature a list of new items on the market.

17. Experienced observers in the Chicago Fair stated that "undoubtedly the most important single accomplishment of the Fair, businesswise, was the introduction of many hundreds of new products to United States businessmen." "Chicago Success Invites New Trade Fairs," *Foreign Commerce Weekly*, October 16, 1950, p. 1.

18. *The American Market for European Goods*, Samuel W. Meek and Virgil D. Reed of the J. Walter Thompson Company, February 1950, p. 15, mimeographed.

19. Cf. Chapter 17 on imports of luxury goods.

income, together with the rise in income taxes, has affected the pattern of living, but by transforming the class market into a mass market rather than the opposite. Any departure from standardization is enormously expensive.

The prestige value of foreign wares is falling under the shadow of American eminence. American products are now coveted by much of the world. Mrs. Eleanor Roosevelt has recalled some of the late President's personal spending habits: "Franklin could see no sense in spending money in a restaurant when he had a home to eat in, and he had a lot of little economies. For example, he never paid more than two dollars for a shirt, and boasted when he found he could get one for $1.50, and he never would buy more than two pairs of shoes, though *he bought those and other things in England, as his father had.*"[20] One wonders how many Americans continue to buy these things in England as their fathers did.

It is even possible that the eating mode itself, with its emphasis upon the wholesome, mitigates against the consumption of imported foodstuffs, which are thought of in the champagne and caviar class. The mass society, which to some brings the vulgarization of taste, certainly does not emphasize the differentiation and refinement characteristic of luxury food and drink.[21] The fact that pasteurized, processed and packaged American cheeses can compete with, even displace, the rich full flavors of Europe's goats' cheese, well-seasoned in caves, testifies to the vulgarization of the refinements. A French proverb states that even the best wine is improved by a change after the second glass. Such refinements are not recognized by the American palate. Even if America were to become a wine-drinking nation, merchandisers would probably standardize the product except for trade names and different bottles.

Experienced distributors report that current methods of mass distribution militate against imports. In the days of class, the well-to-do buyer was seated and served by sales personnel who called her by name. This personal relationship made it possible to refer to a recent shipment of anchovies from Norway and Roquefort from France. The present method of self-service and displaying goods under a price tag has completely depersonalized the sales relationship and with it much of the opportunity to push import specialties.

The Changing Market

"Overseas manufacturers," says the advertising expert, "will be successful in proportion to their ability to foresee and adapt their forms and plans to changes in potentialities, needs and preferences in the market. No manu-

20. *This I Remember*, Harper, New York, 1949, pp. 49 and 50. Italics added.
21. The problem does not exist abroad because those who can afford the refinements are few in number. Our problem is how to sell differentiated luxuries to a class so big that it tends to become a mass market again.

facturer or industry can ignore basic trends and changes in this market and attain real success."[22] The adaptation of production and marketing to a rapidly changing market entails a cost not included in the usual explanation of comparative costs. It also involves a system of communication and a form of business alertness and organization which are a distinctive feature of the American market. In the textile field, vertical integration of the American textile industry, combining mills, converters, and their sales organizations, has brought the production operation closer to the consumers' market and quickened the response of the industry to changing tastes and market conditions.

The pressure for novel products in quantity is resisted by European producers of quality goods who are accustomed to "pat" production patterns. The Japanese, who are more willing to pattern their production to suit American fancy, have trouble on the side of quality. In the past both British and German fabricators have produced a great variety of fabrics in small amounts to satisfy the requirements of old customers in many parts of the world. A mass distribution of a particular fabric in the United States and the accompanying pressure for quantity price adjustments would interfere with their accustomed trade connections the world over. The importing nation which emphasizes volume forces foreign producers to compete with American producers in unaccustomed ways. One of the ways involves the tailoring of production and sales to suit the whims of buyers whose ideas are different, in an institutional framework where the domestic producer concentrates on making the market different.

The Ad and the Cashmere Sweaters

The effect of "irregular" marketing is illustrated by the case of *the ad and the cashmere sweaters.*

A small operator had made a favorable purchase of about 1,000 cashmere sweaters. Lacking experience with the American market, he consulted with a leading advertising agency and received the advice that a one-page ad in the *New York Times Magazine* could be expected to sell perhaps 600 to 700 sweaters. This seemed sufficiently attractive to the small entrepreneur and the advertisement appeared. He received 3,900 replies enclosing payment. Unable to replenish or augment his original stock of 1,000 sweaters, the dealer was in the embarrassing position of having to return the cash on almost 3,000 orders. But the effect on his source of supply was appalling.

The department stores who regularly merchandise cashmere sweaters, and who have established a reputation on the principle of underselling, denounced the foreign producers for supplying this "fly-by-night" dealer at favorable prices and threatened to discontinue handling the producers'

22. *The American Market for European Goods,* p. 9.

goods. The entrepreneur sold his sweaters, but the disturbance to the market greatly prejudiced the prospect of duplicating the experience. All this from one ad, and 1,000 sweaters. Expressed as a percentage of American expenditure on clothing, the sale of 1,000 sweaters is nothing, but its impact on price, competitive marketing relations and source of supply appeared for a time as a minor earthquake.

Differences in National Markets

The comparison of producers' prices between national markets may be misleading. Not only are the selling costs on imports often higher than on domestic goods; the materials specification and design of foreign production itself must frequently be adapted to the American market, and this adaptation involves higher costs.

Much that has been written creates the impression that goods are first produced and then sold in those markets of the world which offer the highest prices. This proposition, which is substantially true for primary products, misses the mark in the case of finished products. It was the view of the importers interviewed by this writer that the great bulk of finished goods imports are produced specifically for the American market and usually to the order of a specific class of buyers.

The importance of differences between national markets can be illustrated by reference to the British market, which, for historical reasons, is probably closer to the American market than are the styles, designs and specifications of other national markets.[23]

In order to produce furniture for the American market British firms would face the problem of finding materials which will stand up under central heating and American climatic changes. As a result, American interest in British furniture is limited to antiques and a few reproductions.

American shirt and pajama manufacturers require a minimum width of 36 inches in the manufacture of cloth, which limits access to the market for some British mills with equipment producing 31–32 inch fabrics acceptable to the British and European markets. American preference in colors and patterns also differs from the British and European.

American women refuse to accept "anything of a scratchy nature" in fabrics other than travel coats. In addition, the light-weight fabrics required by converters who sell in the American market is foreign to general usage among British weavers. Fashion is an additional obstacle.

In the case of men's wear, too, it was found that British manufacturers must conform to American standards, for example, lasts in the case of shoes

23. The information that follows is condensed from *What American Stores Are Buying in British Markets*, Economic Paper No. 10, American Chamber of Commerce, London, September 1950. Replies in this survey, which covered sixteen categories of consumer goods, stressed the tariff as the chief obstacle in only one category, namely, toys.

and sizes and styling in the case of clothing, except in a few instances where such firms as Burberry and Mackintosh have established American consumer acceptance of trade name products. Thus, the problem of adaptation exists even in the case of men's wear, where styles are comparatively stable and for which London was long the arbiter of fashion.

The British manufacturer now finds it advisable to "cater well to the requirements of the (American) market for special weights, designs, etc.," even in the case of the established fabrics for men's wear, such as Huttersfield and other Yorkshire worsteds, west-of-England flannels, Scottish tweeds and cashmeres. British manufacturers find it increasingly necessary to "first, study the demand and adapt their merchandise" to the special requirements of the American market.

Among the factors which British producers must study are geographical differences in the American market. It was found, for example, that British fine cotton raincoats enjoyed a ready sale in the eastern United States but encountered resistance elsewhere.

British luggage was too heavy to suit American tastes; American demand was limited to the lighter types and to matching sets.

The development of new fabrics in the United States has seriously affected the market for women's leather gloves formerly supplied by the British. Demand is now "largely confined to fine quality gift items for holiday selling." British tannage and workmanship in leather bags and wallets found ready acceptance provided the styles followed those developed by American manufacturers.

In the case of cutlery too it was found that "styling must be brought up to American standards."

British "narrow carpeting is not of much interest to the American public," although, in some other floor coverings, it was felt that British manufacturers should be able to "develop much wider acceptance."

The importance of sales outlets is illustrated by upholstery and drapery. British fabrics are now sold in the United States chiefly by interior decorators, whose markup is much higher than that of department stores. Britain has produced fine, hand-blocked chintzes and some manufacturers are seeking department store outlets with their larger volume and lower markup.

An earlier survey of *The Market for United Kingdom Consumer Goods in the United States*, by Time, Inc., in 1948 reported complaints about high British prices but reflected also other objections to British suppliers. Deliveries were poor; facilities for replacement and repair were inadequate; open stock pieces for replacement of china sets were not available; there was a lack of trade representation and promotion. Some American buyers thought that British producers rely too much on "old standbys"—clothing, cutlery and silverware.

The Time survey appears to support the British view that many of their products sell on a prestige basis. An English tray at $200 was competing with an American model of equal quality at one half the price, and an English tea set selling for $100 could be duplicated for much less. Prestige made up the difference with some buyers; with others it did not.

Towel Racks and Maple Syrup

Despite the fact that invidious comment on British plumbing is a commonplace, the British produce a warm towel rack which would probably interest American comfort lovers—but for the importing obstacles. The tariff is definitely the least part of this barrier. A man building a home in the Washington, D.C., area purchased the towel racks in Britain and had them shipped into the port of Baltimore. The cost of getting the articles through customs, as distinguished from the duty itself, seemed monstrous. The forwarding agent's handling charge was several times the customs duty and the total cost of getting the goods *after* they were landed in Baltimore exceeded the purchase price and transportation costs to Baltimore. Obstacles of this sort will not be eliminated by tariff reduction or even by customs reform.

A vacationer in Canada discovered a delectable maple syrup which was favorably priced. Later, he placed orders by mail for small quantities for personal use and Christmas gifts to friends. Each recipient had a different experience and was charged a different handling cost, although the duty was so small that in some instances it was not collected. In one case the shipment was delivered by parcel post without difficulty or extra service charge; in another a personal trip to the customs office was necessary; in still another, a personal trip plus the payment of a substantial handling charge for customs clearance and forwarding was required.

As far as quality, price and tariff are concerned, the purchaser would like to continue importing for his personal use and occasional gifts to friends. But he will do so only if he feels like taking risks because he cannot be certain that his gifts will not involve the recipient in excessive personal inconvenience and forwarding costs. The diversity of experiences in the shipment of identical packages to different receivers seems baffling.

Airplane Screws[24]

In the spring of 1951 screws were one of the small but critical items of supply that worried airplane makers. The making of aircraft requires many types of screws but a relatively small number of each type. Because the screw must be made to close specifications and because a plane maker will order perhaps 500 different types, but only 50,000 of each type, these orders

24. The information on airplane screws was obtained through ECA.

are not the most attractive kind of business to American screw makers. In fact, aircraft manufacturers feel that the screw makers dislike their orders.

It is not too difficult to understand the reason. At this time manufacturers faced large backlogs and steel was allocated. The setting and adjusting of screw-producing machines for close specifications requires the services of an extremely skilled and highly paid workman. After the machine is finally set, it is operated only an hour perhaps before it is necessary to stop and reset for another type. The result is that, when engaged in the production of screws for aircraft, the machine may be more out of use than in use. The screw manufacturer naturally prefers the standardized order that he is geared to produce, an order that will keep his expensive equipment in continuous use for a long stretch.

The organization of European producers is on a different basis. They have the skilled workers and, since the Marshall Plan, have acquired modern equipment. They are not, however, organized on the mass production basis which characterizes American industry. It would appear, therefore, that European screw producers, because they are set up to serve smaller specialized markets, are well suited to supplying the makers of aircraft.

The aircraft manufacturers were amazed at the suggestion that they import screws. Here are companies, with large and experienced purchasing staffs, facing a critical situation and apprehensive about supplies. Nonetheless, the idea of imports appalls them. How reliable is the foreign manufacturer? Will the screws be made to exact specifications and of dependable quality? The prospect of sending purchasing agents abroad, of learning customs routine, of coping with all the known and unknowns in getting goods across national lines seems too much. Their job is making planes, at which they are magnificent.

The duty itself has nothing to do with this problem.[25] What is needed and is lacking, it was said, is an import wholesaler to assume responsibility for matching the capacities of European producers with the needs of American users. But this entrepreneurial problem is not inconsiderable. The problems of timing, inventory, dependability as to quality, specifications and delivery dates involve far greater risks, at least for a time, than dealing with home suppliers. It may well be that these services cannot be supplied by an ordinary import wholesaler operating on a narrow margin. Domestic producers themselves are in a favorable position to carry inventories of imported screws.

The import agents who would handle this kind of transaction are regarded as "fly-by-night" operators looking for a 200 per cent markup. Domestic screw producers are not so hard to please in more normal times,

25. Imports of wood screws made of iron and steel increased greatly in 1950–1951 and domestic producers have sought escape clause investigations.

and the duration of this type of import business is highly uncertain. The overhead costs in establishing an import service organization to supply periods of abnormal demand may be comparable to the capital costs of supplying war material and, in the view of the importing agent, would probably need to be amortized in one year—an attitude not unlike that of the plane producers themselves. The risks are considerable and must be paid for; therefore the importer's margin will appear exorbitant in comparison with the margin on standard products like rubber and tea.

Capital Goods

Except for specialized items, the British government was prepared in 1950 to write off the potential American market for machinery because of the vast engineering resources of this country. "No large increase in machinery exports to the United States is expected because of its vast engineering resources but it is believed that progress can be made in the field of highly specialized equipment."[26] On a number of occasions British firms have offered the low bid on industrial power installations. Their bids were rejected because of the lack of standardization and the problem of servicing. In other cases where the Army was concerned, the Buy American Act has been an obstacle.[27]

Some insight into the problem can be gained from a British survey of United States and British competition in a third market.[28] Britain has the advantage in Canada of long political association and commonwealth tariff preference. The report of the Gilpin Mission, however, reflects the diffidence of the British export industry with respect to the Canadian market. Interchange of technical education and information between the United States and Canada and the common ownership of industry have led to similarities of industrial design and specifications that require special adaptation of many British products. The use of some American equipment in one branch of an industry has led to master contracts under which American exporters supply most of the principal ancillary plants, as in the case of coke ovens. Tied contracts in the rental of can-making machinery, the supply of cans and the integration of American parts with Canadian products in Canadian assembly plants have favored American suppliers, as has rapid innovation in wrapping machines and meat-packing equipment.

26. *European Cooperation*, Memorandum submitted to the Organization for European Economic Cooperation . . . H.M.S.O., January 1950.

27. Cf. pp. 200–202.

28. This discussion is based on *Exports to Canada*, Report of the United Kingdom Engineering Mission to Canada, 1948, H.M.S.O., London, 1949, known as the "Gilpin Mission Report."

The absence of Britain from the market during the war stimulated these and similar developments and left the British position doubly difficult. The uncertainties and dislocations of war are not immediately forgotten. Canadian buyers order American parts and service by telephone and express the fear that another war would make it impossible to service British equipment.

The Gilpin Mission investigated many complaints that United Kingdom prices on engineering products were higher but found few specific instances in which the complaints seemed justified. Orders had been lost to American producers for road-building equipment, biscuit-making equipment, evaporaters and roller dryers for the production of dried milk products because of lower prices and better delivery dates. But the high cost of maintaining service facilities discouraged British exporters of road-building equipment and similar lines. Prices of brewery equipment were comparable. In general, while prices were not a negligible factor they were, in the Mission's view, a subordinate one.

. . . The Mission is satisfied that over a wide range of engineering products the prices now being quoted to Canada are competitive. . . . It is unwise to be dogmatic on such a question, but the general impression remained with the Mission that, for all but mass produced equipment, the United Kingdom manufacturer has little to fear from foreign competition in the Canadian market so far as prices are concerned."[29]

Representatives of the American Tariff League assert that if foreign producers can compete with the United States in third markets, they can compete in the domestic market and use third-market competition as a yardstick of the need for tariff protection. This contention neglects many factors which favor domestic producers in their home market. Foreign suppliers are better adapted to produce comparatively small lots to meet a buyer's specifications, but, by the same token, are less well adapted to produce the volume demanded in American mass markets. The importance of provisions for service and parts scarcely needs to be spelled out. Servicing is a most serious obstacle to imports of durable goods, for replacement parts and servicing costs strongly favor the mass producer.

Failure to Exploit Import Opportunities

A very small staff in ECA scoured the field in search of neglected opportunities for imports, and turned up a number of apparently attractive opportunities. The question is why such opportunities remain neglected. The tariff appears less important and the other obstacles more important to

29. *Ibid.*, p. 35. Elsewhere, this general conclusion is modified somewhat by the admission that the British advantages in the Canadian market are offset to some extent by the high cost of packing and freight as compared with American exports.

those who have worked with the details of encouraging imports for a couple of years.

A survey of the European paper industry revealed a large number of items that can be obtained in Europe at lower costs, including transport and customs duty. Another case concerns a paper cone with plastic cap used in the production of all rayon in the United States. Only one United States manufacturer produces this item, which, it appears, can be turned out better and cheaper in Europe. Yet no enterprising distributor has undertaken to supply the American users. The speculative importer seeking the several hundred per cent markup apparently does not find the return sufficiently attractive, although to the outsider it seems generous.

Having discovered these neglected opportunities, the ECA was at a loss to know where to turn to find an entrepreneur. *Foreign Commerce Weekly* sometimes publishes a list of similar opportunities, which appears to offer the prospect of matching identified foreign supplies with known demands at home. The batting score in bringing the two together appears to have been very low.

As this is written a cement shortage impends in the American market. Like steel, United States cement capacity is permanently low in relation to capacity output for the entire economy. Before the war appreciable imports were customary. The specific trade relations, however, were destroyed by the war and have not been restored. Other countries can supply cement at a price which will permit absorption of transportation costs, but, at the present time, no one appears to be exploiting this opportunity on an organized and large-scale basis. Periodic flurries of cement imports have sold at exorbitant gray market prices. Why is not regular importing of cement established?

Importing risks are associated with cyclical uncertainty. In order to avoid carrying a large inventory with storage costs, the timing of import arrivals to match current demand requires both skill and accurate judgment of the market. The dependability of the foreign producer, shipping space and forwarding dates all impose risks and uncertainties that are inherent in importing. Apparently, importers view the market for imported cement in terms comparable to a new capital investment. Since the demand seems temporary and uncertain, the overhead costs must be covered in a short time.

Distribution Tie-ins

Expert opinion holds that foreign distribution facilities can be tied to American manufacturing more easily than foreign manufacturing can be tied to American distribution facilities. Only rarely has the latter been attempted. British interests bought control of the Indian Motorcycle Company and its distribution outlets in order to obtain distribution of British motorcycles and bicycles. The tendency, however, has been the other way. Factory assembly and sale of automobiles abroad is a familiar illustration. More recently, sixteen large American industries established factory and assembly facilities in Scotland.[30] *American investment in directly competing foreign enterprise is one of the most important developments that can help to overcome the handicaps that imports face in the American market.*

Integration of American production with foreign production and distribution for the purpose of export is, of course, dependent upon the development of sufficient volume to make it pay. Occasionally, the problem of returning foreign balances to this country, or of maintaining a volume of exports in the face of the dollar shortage, results in the development of a "compensatory" import business. Westinghouse International Company, for example, has imported a wide range of consumer goods, including printed silk fabrics, leather products, alabaster, silverware, canned lobster and Cuban canned pineapple, mainly for wholesaling to department, chain and specialty stores. Such importing is a side line undertaken on the theory that the company's export business would profit.[31] The American moving picture industry has engaged in many different enterprises in its efforts to repatriate foreign earnings.

Exporting and Importing

There is little question that the primary interest and drive, until recently, has been far greater in the field of exporting than of importing. American import-export organization favors exporting. One standard textbook, which emphasizes the more practical problems of international trade, contains an extensive bibliography on exports but is hard pressed to find a single up-to-date work on the technique of importing. In fact, only two books are listed in the bibliography, both published more than a score of years ago.

While data on the number of firms operating in foreign trade are volatile and perhaps misleading, the differences between the Department of Commerce lists of importers and exporters are striking. American firms registered as exporters numbered 19,284 against 2,690 importers, as of March 24, 1947.[32] It is presumed that the small number of importers reflects, in part at least, the many institutional handicaps which favor domestic production over imports. A number of monographic studies are needed on these institutional barriers to trade both at home and abroad.

30. *Report of the Thirty-sixth National Foreign Trade Convention,* 1949, p. 225.
31. *Organization for Importing,* pp. 37 and 38.
32. Cf. *Congressional Record,* March 3, 1948, p. 2076.

Chapter 11

The European Exporter's Point of View[*]

THE FOREIGN TRADE of the United States is traditionally thought of as consisting of exports of raw materials to Europe and imports of manufactured goods from Europe in payment for these exports. This has long since ceased to be true. Europe has not for a long time been able by the sale of manufactured goods or, indeed, by the export of commodities of whatever category to the United States to pay for more than a part of what was imported from the United States. Indeed, payment by any means, whether by "invisible exports," by indirect trade, by means of borrowing or by a combination of all these, has not been large enough to permit European governments to allow their people to buy goods freely in the United States market. This has been true since the great economic depression of the 1930s.

The smallness of United States imports of goods from Europe is unquestionable, measured by any standard. Our imports of goods from Marshall Plan Europe amounted to only about one half of one per cent of our national income in 1950. They were sufficient in that year to pay for only about 43 per cent of European imports from the United States.[1]

Why are our imports from Europe so small? What are the barriers or inhibiting forces which prevent the flow from being larger? The orthodox answer has been that if it were not for our barriers against European imports these goods would move into the United States in the quantities which one would expect according to the principles of comparative advantage. Our trade barriers were held to be almost the sole reason for the failure of the volume of imports to be as high as it apparently would be if the principles of comparative advantage had been allowed to operate without hindrance.[2]

* This chapter was written by Calvin B. Hoover.

1. In this chapter only our trade relations with "Marshall Plan Europe" are considered. In 1929 our imports from Marshall Plan Europe amounted to about one and four tenths per cent, in 1937 to nine tenths of one per cent and in 1948 to four tenths of one per cent of our national income. See *Report of the ECA Commerce Mission*, October 1949, Table 6, p. 36.

2. With much less logic it was often assumed that our trade barriers were likewise responsible for the failure of our imports from Europe to be as large as our exports to that continent. Conceivably our trade barriers might have been responsible for greater "triangularity" in intercontinental trade and in this sense might have had some causal effect in the imports-exports disparity. It is, however, a part of an orthodox doctrine that barriers to trade must inevitably operate to limit trade not only in one direction but equally in both directions. Thus our trade barriers could, according to orthodox doctrine, reduce the volume of both imports and exports. They could create conditions which foster disequilibrium between two areas.

Preceding chapters have demonstrated that this explanation certainly is an oversimplification of a very complex matter, which does not permit so easy an answer. Since international trade must be reciprocal if it is to be truly trade and not merely the donation of goods and services without recompense, it seems appropriate to inquire whether the causes for the diminutive level of United States imports from Europe might not also be found in part in Europe's attitudes toward the American market as well as in America's attitude toward imports. Many of the issues discussed in Chapter 10 will now be considered from the point of view of European exporters.

Looked at in the simplest possible way, the question becomes: Suppose there were no United States tariffs or other like barriers to imports from Europe, are there either forces or barriers in Europe itself which would nevertheless limit the flow of goods to the United States? If these inhibiting forces or barriers exist can their effects be mitigated in any way?

Inquiry in Europe

It seemed worthwhile not to rely solely either on the answers which could be deduced from the theory of international trade or even upon what could be deduced from an examination of the purely statistical evidence. The writer of this chapter decided that it might be profitable to make some on-the-spot case studies, even if only of the sort which could be made by an individual investigator in a very limited time.[3]

Accordingly, during 1950 most of the Marshall Plan countries of Western Europe were revisited. In the various countries, not only our own diplomatic representatives and ECA officials, but European economists, bankers, industrialists, merchants, exporters, importers, editors, estate owners and managers, peasants, labor leaders, governmental officials and others were interviewed.[4]

The task of getting the Europeans' point of view with regard to exports to the United States was greatly facilitated by the "Dollar Export Committees," which had been set up with ECA encouragement in most Marshall Plan countries to stimulate the export of goods and services that could earn dollars.[5] These committees were quasi-official in character. It had been

---

3. The writer had had the opportunity of looking at this problem from a number of different angles on previous assignments, as a member of the research staff of the Committee on Economic Development in 1944, as Economic Advisor to the U.S. Group of the Control Council for Germany in 1945, as a member of the President's Committee on Foreign Aid in 1947 and as Economic Advisor to the Economic Cooperation Administration in Paris in 1948.

4. The United Kingdom, France, Germany, Italy, Switzerland, Sweden, Denmark, the Netherlands and Belgium were visited. It was not possible, of course, to see in each of these countries representatives of every category to which reference is made.

5. These committees were called by various names in the different countries.

hoped by ECA that they would be primarily nongovernmental in character and made up largely of industrialists and businessmen. In actual practice, the character and composition of the committees varied from country to country. In some cases the committees seemed to have been set up largely "to keep the Americans happy" and as the result of governmental prodding. In other countries, particularly in the United Kingdom and in France, there was evidence of considerable national initiative, and private business and industry did assume the greater share of the responsibility.

These committees functioned with varying degrees of activity from one country to another. There was evidence that their members were aware of the desirability of increasing dollar earnings through exports to the United States. Plans were made to develop definite policies and programs for enlarging these exports. A number of specific steps were taken in the different countries to stimulate dollar exports. A good deal of "economic gadgetry" was invented and developed to further this end. *Nevertheless, European industrialists and other businessmen were almost unanimously skeptical about the potentialities for expanding exports to the United States on a scale which would bridge the "dollar gap." They indicated that they intended to make every effort in all good faith, but they were not very sanguine about the probable results.*[6]

Although, as is explained below, this lack of confidence is by no means without reason, Europeans did not adequately realize the factors in the United States which were favorable to an increase in European dollar exports. There was no widespread knowledge of the reductions in our tariff which had taken place under the Reciprocal Trade Agreements Act.[7] There was little realization of the basic shift in public opinion in the United States towards European imports which had taken place in recent years.

This shift in public opinion meant that while the producers of particular commodities which have to meet European competition would still fight as hard as ever to keep out competing products, "imports" in their generic sense had come to be treated in our press and radio and in public discussion as a "good" instead of a "bad" word. When this was called to their attention, Europeans were inclined to discount the practical significance of this general change in public opinion in its effect upon their ability to compete on the United States market. Reference to the special sales promo-

6. This does not mean that they were hopeless about the possibilities of closing the dollar gap, for most countries of Western Europe. They did not believe, however, that their efforts to "push" their products on the United States market would be a major factor in closing the gap. They were much more hopeful of being able to sell their exports in "third markets" outside the United States. The statistical evidence indicates that just prior to the Korean War this hope was in process of realization. Concurrently, these "third markets" were in some degree supplanting the United States as a source of European supply.

7. Granted that the reductions in duties under the act were apparently not a major factor in increasing United States imports of European goods.

tion campaigns for European imports which had been and were continuing to be staged on a grand scale by United States major department stores from New York and Philadelphia to Houston and Denver did not overcome European skepticism.[8]

What explains this lack of confidence of Europeans in their ability to sell goods on the American market? The answers may be set down as follows.

Tariff and Customs Barriers

Europeans fear our visible and invisible tariff barriers.

The European producer, of course, calls attention to the tariff as the first hurdle which he must surmount to get into the United States market. He points out that it is not merely a question of the existing rates of duties. He may be aware that these rates have been lowered as a result of reciprocal trade agreements. He points out, however, that just as soon as his exports to the United States show signs of cutting substantially into the market, the American producer will be certain to claim injury and the tariff rate is likely to be raised once more.[9] He will likewise point out the barrier which our administration of customs raises in the form of the "invisible tariff." Almost any European exporter can relate tales of woe in this connection. A Stockholm manufacturer of Swedish hard bread claimed, for example, that when he exported his product to the United States his American competitor succeeded in getting the imported product held up by raising the question whether the product was free of "foreign matter," that is, whether it consisted solely of the substances stated. But since no product is actually "100 per cent pure," what are the accepted limits of tolerance? He claimed that he could never get a "solid" ruling and that this caused endless trouble.

A shipbuilder of Gothenburg pointed out that his field of manufacturing was one in which the Swedes could claim a real comparative advantage, resulting in construction costs as low as any in the world. But when the question of constructing some small ships for United States coastal trade was raised, it was found that there was a prohibition in United States law against their construction abroad.

Mass Market Difficulties

Europeans do not believe that they can compete successfully in the American mass market for consumer goods. European producers are fond

8. The marked upsurge in European dollar exports which took place during the year following these discussions in 1950 seems to have demonstrated that at least during a period when inflationary forces were operating more strongly in the United States than in Europe, the European producers with whom the writer talked were unduly pessimistic.

9. The fact that this has actually happened in relatively few cases indicates the extreme care exercised with respect to United States tariff reductions. Every effort has been made to administer these so as to be sure that not enough imports will come into the United States to give grounds for domestic industry to claim injury successfully. Cf. Chapter 19.

of repeating the story of the European exporter who had succeeded in interesting an American importer in an item. The price was low enough and the American importer was convinced of its sales appeal. Indeed, the American was enthusiastic and ordered 50,000 units monthly to be delivered, starting within three months. The European producer gasped: "I can deliver 5,000 per month, starting in nine months." The American promptly lost interest. This story in various forms is told all over Europe.

A further illustration is the case of an American official of the U.S. Chamber of Commerce in London. Shortly after the close of World War II, he succeeded in getting a large manufacturer of a nationally advertised line of men's suits interested in importing a large quantity of British woolen cloth. The American manufacturer could afford to import the cloth at all, however, only if he could obtain a large enough quantity to justify an advertising campaign on a large scale. Upon inquiry, it was found impossible to obtain commitments for anything like the requisite quantity. Individual British manufacturers who were approached pointed out that to fill such a commitment they would have to withdraw from the domestic market and shut off completely exports to traditional markets.

European industrialists believed that in order to produce goods on a scale large enough to interest United States importers, they would find it necessary to expand their capital facilities or to concentrate on supplying one American buyer to the exclusion of their own domestic or the intra-European market. If they did either, they did not know how long they could depend upon continuance of United States demand for the product. Further, they were likely to say, "If we do succeed in building up a demand for some product which we manage to get into the United States market, you will copy it and by your mass production methods, very soon undersell us."[10]

European producers firmly believe that the superior productivity of American industry renders their own competition in the United States market for most commodities of mass consumption out of the question. Economists have traditionally scorned this type of argument. As John H. Williams puts it, "The classical economists would dispose of differences in comparative productivity by having them reflected in comparative money wages and prices. Once this process is worked out no trade problem

10. Undoubtedly the inability alleged by European manufacturers to compete successfully in the American market against "low cost, mass production methods of American manufacturers" is matched by the belief of some of these American manufacturers in their inability without tariff protection to compete in this same market against "imported low-cost goods, manufactured by low-wage–European labor." These American manufacturers, however, would consist mainly of those from small-scale and relatively unimportant industries. The shift from an almost morbid insistence upon tariff protection for domestic industry to an attitude of confidence in their ability to compete anywhere in the world is one of the most significant developments in the state of mind of American industrialists.

remains."[11] But Williams points out that this is primarily a static concept and that changes in relative productivity of different countries through time may produce unfavorable changes in terms of trade for the country in which productivity lags.

In addition, European manufacturers complained that in order to obtain sales outlets for their commodities in the United States they were required to pay a higher percentage of the price of their goods to distributing agents than did their American competitors. These American agents explained that this was necessary because of the greater uncertainty and smaller volume.

Taste and Style Changes

European manufacturers fear the fickleness of the United States consumer goods markets. European manufacturers are appalled at the difficulties of attempting to forecast United States tastes and styles. They understand that these tastes and styles can be guided and manipulated to a large degree by advertising. They well realize, however, that the scale of their own production is not ordinarily such as to justify advertising expenditures of a size sufficient to affect a mass market. They feel that their relative geographical and psychological isolation from the United States market puts them at an almost hopeless disadvantage in competing with the American producer in serving rapidly changing consumer tastes. They are appalled by the fact that suppliers of the American mass market may be required to make quick shifts in design and style upon the demand of the wholesaler or retailer.

By contrast, goods sold on their own domestic market or elsewhere in Europe, or indeed almost anywhere other than in the United States, require little change in style and design. Indeed, customers are likely to require almost the same product year after year. Europeans realize, furthermore, that effective advertising has to be timed and carefully geared to the delivery of the goods. The difficulties of providing deliveries at precise times are often almost insurmountable.

They are further discouraged by the realization that the mass character of United States consumer markets does not depend on a limited choice of items and styles. It has been pointed out, for example, that the average American has a wider range of fabrics to choose from when he buys a

11. *American Economic Review*, Papers and Proceedings, May 1951. See also John H. Williams, "Europe after 1952: The Long-Range Recovery Problem," *Foreign Affairs*, April 1949. A serious block to trade can develop if the country for which the terms of trade are worsening is not willing to have these more unfavorable terms of trade reflected in exchange rates and in domestic wage rates. Indeed, the block to trade may arise even if the terms of trade do not worsen, if the government of the country in which productivity lags is unwilling or unable to prevent a rise in wage rates which outstrips the smaller increase in productivity.

ready-made suit than does a Britisher who orders a custom-made suit. The Britisher may order a suit from his tailor to be made from a piece which has been especially woven to his tailor's order. American retailers, by contrast, can afford to carry in their inventories more different "weaves" in ready-made suits than are woven in Britain to special order plus those used in ready-made suits. The Britisher thus does indeed have an advantage in exclusiveness but not in variety.

Prospects for Luxury Exports

Europeans have small confidence in the future export possibilities of luxury products. According to the doctrine of comparative advantage, one would expect Europeans to concentrate upon the production of goods with a relatively high labor content, paid at comparatively low wage rates, in order to exchange them for United States goods produced with more capital equipment and with labor compensated at high wage rates. In actual fact, Europeans neither place reliance upon the expansion of this type of export nor wish to. Indeed, they greatly overdiscount their potentialities in this direction, particularly the possibility of selling such goods to American tourists. They argue that it is impossible to pay the wages which labor demands by continuing to rely upon hand methods of production. Some members of the French Dollar Export Committee emphasized their belief that France's traditional luxury goods industries could no longer be relied upon to carry the burden of providing exports to pay for French imports. They were hopeful that the production of small precision-type machines could be developed as one substitute.[12]

This trend in the handicraft industries is illustrated by the experience of the wicker-weaving industry in the little French village of Bussières-les-Belmont. The production from osiers of extremely well-made wicker articles such as trout creels and wine bottle holders, and of rather crudely made articles such as wastepaper baskets, is carried on in barns, largely as part-time employment, in this peasant village of some five hundred inhabitants. In years gone by, there had been considerable production for export, some of which was sold in New York department stores. These export sales had long since ceased. The proprietor of one establishment employing some thirty persons displayed with pride a plush-lined jewel case woven of extremely tiny osiers. "We have not made one of these for thirty years," he said sadly. "I doubt whether anyone could do it now. Labor is far too expensive and besides who would buy such things now-a-days? Now the demand is mostly for those waste baskets such as you see for sale in the cheap shops in Paris."

12. When the competition which would probably have to be met is considered, this alternative does not seem a very hopeful one.

It is useless to tell most Europeans that employment in handicraft industries and the exchange of these products for United States goods would often afford the best realizable means for paying wages as high as the national economy can afford. They argue that it is difficult to induce young people to undergo the careful training necessary to become the kind of craftsmen essential for this type of production. They then return to the wage argument and say that only by machine can a level of productivity be attained which will permit the payment of "tolerable wages." But can the European economy afford to purchase the machinery? "Ah, that is what the Marshall Plan is intended to do for us!" they answer.

The development of a more egalitarian type of society throughout the world, accompanied by a great increase in productivity in machine industry and a rise in the average standard of living, seems largely to account for the shift in demand away from handmade lace, vintage wines, custom-made clothes, shoes and the like. It is pointed out in Chapter 17 that a great increase in the average standard of living is almost inevitably associated with a decline in the production of the "exclusive" type of luxury goods and services. An increased equalization of income through taxation or socialization accentuates this trend.[13]

It is a notable feature of the postwar economic policy of all governments, except that of the United States, that old-style luxury products are scorned and well-nigh rejected as imports. This return to mercantilist sentiments and practices reflects, in some degree, the residuum of the national "siege economies" which characterized the war and postwar period. It reflects as well a shift in social and political power to the masses, so that no government in Europe or in Asia any longer holds to the dictum of the international trade theorist that a dollar's worth of perfume is exactly as important as a dollar's worth of flour or coal or capital equipment. European governments are still anxious to sell luxury products to other countries. However, they simply do not want to try to expand productive facilities in these industries and to rely upon a market which they think is becoming largely obsolete.

Some Concrete Examples

Everyone who has worked with the data of trade agreements in Europe during the immediate postwar period is acquainted with the case of country A whose government had to accept some fine cheese from country B in order to sell its products in that country. Country A did succeed in requiring a third country, C, to accept some of its own fine cheese. Country C

13. Since this was written, essentially the same point was made by Ingvar Svennilson in *Growth and Stagnation in the European Economy*, United Nations Economic Commission for Europe, Geneva, 1954, pp. 39–40.

repeated the process with still another country and forced this country to take some cheese. This country turned out to be country B, which had originally disposed of its fine cheese by economic *force majeure*!

The assiduity with which the negotiators of bilateral trade agreements attempted to require importing countries to accept hot-house grapes, azaleas, tulip bulbs, wines and liquors, as a condition of the importing countries selling their own exports and obtaining "solid" commodities such as iron ore, coal, grain and the like, became a standing joke. The reduction in import quotas and the development of the European Payments Union have greatly reduced, but have by no means removed, the aversion to allowing foreign exchange to be used for the purchase of nonessential imports.

Looked at from the standpoint of selling specialized luxury products in the United States, the case may be illustrated by that of vintage wines. Quite a good Burgundy, a Gevry-Chambertin, 1945, for instance, could be purchased at retail in Washington, D. C., at the time of writing for about $1.50 a bottle. This price is surprisingly little more than the price at which a reasonably good domestic wine can be bought. It is only in the large cities of the Eastern seaboard, however, that imported wines can be bought at such a low figure, if indeed they are to be bought at all. In Durham, N. C., for example, in a chain grocery a domestic "Burgundy" also sells for $1.50. The grocery does not stock imported wines.

Why, one might ask, could not substantial amounts of imported wines be sold throughout the United States in chain stores when the price would apparently be competitive with domestic wines? Those who discount such a possibility argue that too few people know much about varieties, vintages, "estates" and "domains." It is said that the very variety which the connoisseur finds so delightful, in being able to choose between hundreds of different wines, is a distinct disadvantage in the American market. It is claimed that the typical American who buys a wine and likes it cares only about being able to get one that tastes about the same the next time. He does not have to remember scores of tongue-twisting names if this is all that he cares about. It would be impossible, it is further argued, to stock from the limited supply of particular varieties of wines a large enough inventory to satisfy customers even if consumer demand for particular varieties could be developed by advertising.

It is necessary to consider the effect upon price of an attempt at mass distribution. Good vintages and varieties of wines can be obtained so cheaply in a few cities in the United States precisely because the national demand is limited. Chain grocery stores would be interested in stocking imported wines throughout the United States only if they could continue to be obtained at prices reasonably competitive with domestic growths. The price rise which would accompany a considerable increase in United States demand for European wines would be likely to limit the market automatically before volume sales on the national market could be attained.

Some of these difficulties could be overcome, however. A small booklet describing the characteristics of the different types of imported wines could accomplish much, if it were made readily available in retail outlets where wine is handled. It might be feasible to "sell" Americans on the advantages of sampling a number of different varieties of Burgundies, clarets, Rhine wines, Moselles and the like, so that it would not be necessary to keep continuously in stock exactly the same special types within the main classifications of wines. The growth in variety of delicatessen-type foods of somewhat exotic character stocked by chain groceries gives some hope that imported wines might well serve to satisfy this craving for variety among a substantial number of American consumers.

Much could thus be done to increase dollar income from sales of wines. Nevertheless, limitations of supply and the limiting effect of rising prices of the finer types of imported wines which would be the inevitable accompaniment of a greatly increased demand are likely to restrict this import opportunity to a relatively minor role as a dollar earner.

Everywhere the story was the same. In Italy it was pointed out that there was little expectation for continuing even existing levels of exports of special food products such as cheeses, wines, olive oil, *pasta* and the like, as the Italian-born population of the United States ages out. It was pointed out also that a new regulation had been put into effect by the United States against the importation of Italian cheese made from goat's milk which did not conform to certain minimum sanitary standards. No one denied the reasonableness of the regulation—neither the goats nor their owners could be called sanitarily fastidious—but it limited still further the potentialities of Italian cheese as a dollar earner, while at the same time protecting the market for domestic processed cheeses in the United States.

General Problems of International Trade in Consumer Goods

The head of the Federation of British Industries, Sir Norman Kipping, has pointed out that the trend was away from dependence upon the export of traditional consumer goods such as textiles, not only to the United States, but generally to all countries. The very impressive increase in British exports which nevertheless has taken place has been accounted for to a notable degree by the products of the engineering industries, that is, machinery, while the production and export of textiles, the traditional field of British excellence, has lagged.[14] It was argued that the undeveloped and

14. Postwar international trade in textiles has recovered to no more than 70 per cent of its prewar level. See the statement by Dr. Claudius Murchison, Director of the Cotton Textile Institute, in the *New York Times* of September 7, 1951.

developing countries of the world wish to raise the income of their people by employing them in manufacturing. Consumer goods, such as textiles, are naturally those first produced.[15] It was further argued that the British would have to count primarily on selling these countries the machinery to produce consumer goods rather than the goods themselves.

European exports of raw materials and semimanufactured goods do not face the same difficulties in getting on the United States market as exports of finished consumer goods. However, even these commodities are likely to go to soft-currency areas rather than to the United States where they could be sold for dollars.[16] In the case of newsprint, high-grade iron ore, scrap metal, rayon yarn and staple, and similar commodities, an outright price comparison will tell whether the goods will move to the United States or to a soft-currency area, so long as the producer is free to ship where he wishes.

These types of commodities are especially likely to move to the United States during periods when price controls are in effect on the domestic market. If the United States has a price ceiling on steel, for example, accompanied by a stringent scarcity, European steel may move into the United States to be sold on the black or gray market for as long as the situation exists. When the price differential disappears the shipments stop. There is no question here of changing tastes, styles, stocking of inventories or such complicating features. These types of goods pursue the "fast buck" whenever and wherever it can be found. Established trade channels are of less importance in this field when large profits can be made on a single transaction.

Not so, for example, with the market for a line of British-made raincoats to be sold in the United States. A British exporter explained how carefully he must plan his sales campaign, develop his contacts and provide for warehouse stocks before he expects to sell in any volume. There could be no question of sending over half a shipload of raincoats because a British manufacturer suddenly noted that there had been a sharp increase in the price of raincoats on the United States market.[17]

15. The argument, of course, does not immediately follow in the case of durable consumer goods such as automobiles, refrigerators and the like.

The insistence of underdeveloped countries on developing the manufacture of all types of consumer goods through the protection of these industries by trade barriers is in itself a substantial cause for the diminution of world trade and of international geographic specialization.

16. Economic developments which have brought world currencies closer to full convertibility since this was written have mitigated the importance of soft currencies in this connection.

17. Of course the assumption of a sudden increase in the price of raincoats in relation to the price of other commodities is itself an absurdity. This reflects a fundamental and important difference in the pricing process of nonstaple consumer goods and the pricing of bulk commodities which is of great significance in international as in domestic trade.

Scarcity of Goods and Profitability of Other Markets

A fundamental limitation upon the export of European goods to the United States was the scarcity of goods available for export at the current price in dollars—this in spite of the recovery of industrial production in Western Europe to much above the prewar level and the recovery of agricultural production to prewar levels. There was in some instances, indeed, an actual physical shortage of goods.[18] It was frequently difficult, if not impossible, to obtain for any export market some patterns and types of highest quality products, such as a particular pattern of china, in the quantities which could be sold at existing prices.

The scarcity of goods for the dollar market which exists because the total output could be sold more advantageously in the domestic or other soft-currency markets was also important. Almost any European government does, indeed, prefer that its nationals sell in the dollar market rather than elsewhere,[19] but to the particular producer the soft-currency market is likely to be more attractive since he is largely sheltered against competition from American industry.

A British manufacturer who produces, let us say, cutlery, and sells it in the United States, is not allowed to keep the dollars which he receives in payment or to dispose of those dollars at the highest price in pounds which he can obtain. He must turn the dollars in to a government agency. He receives pounds in exchange for them at an officially determined rate.

A somewhat similar process takes place in every country in Europe. So long as the manufacturer can sell his goods at a price on the domestic market or on a soft-currency market which will net him as large a return in pounds as if he had sold his product for dollars, he has no special economic motive for selling his goods for dollars in preference to selling his goods for other currencies, however soft they may be.[20] Indeed, if it is a question of the trouble and expense of developing a *new* market in the United States, he would have to receive a substantially *higher* price in the United States market to make it worth his while.

This is true with respect to sales of a British manufacturer in the French market, for example, as compared with sales in the United States market. Restrictions upon the import of goods from Britain or from any other

18. This scarcity in any absolute sense has now been largely eliminated. The normal operation of the price system which "rations" supplies has largely superseded absolute scarcity as a controlling factor in limiting the supply of goods available for export to the United States.

19. This was not strictly true during the early days of the Marshall Plan when the level of ECA aid depended largely upon the dollar deficit in the particular nation's balance of payments. The smaller the dollar sales the greater the deficit. The larger the deficit the greater the economic aid. This is no longer a major influence in the economic policy of most European countries, however.

20. See footnote 16 with reference to the diminished significance of soft currencies.

European country will be much less stringent than upon the import of United States-made goods requiring dollars for payment. The French or importer of other European nationality can offer his currency for British or other European-produced goods with much greater freedom than he can offer dollars. Consequently sales by nationals of soft-currency countries in soft-currency areas are likely to be relatively easy and profitable.

The existence of huge amounts of "blocked sterling," as in the case of India, likewise greatly increases the ease of selling goods in such areas rather than in dollar markets, since when "blocked sterling" is released it usually can be used for purchases only in the sterling area. The British exporter to India is thus selling in a market sheltered from competition with imports from American industry.

Effects of Full Employment and Currency Devaluation

The stronger "pull" of the domestic and intra-European market as compared with the dollar market is vastly accentuated so long as full employment continues. Full employment is both cause and effect of a very high level of consumer purchasing power. So long as a domestic market is "hungry" for all goods which can be produced and markets of neighboring countries are both "hungry" and short of dollars, it can be seen that special inducements or noneconomic motives would have to be depended upon in considerable degree to direct European-produced goods into United States markets.

This superior attractiveness of the European over the United States market, as well as the "dollar scarcity" itself, reflects in considerable degree both inflationary national economic policies and the overvaluation of European currencies in terms of the dollar. Indeed, both restrictions upon dollar imports, including exchange controls, and United States economic aid itself may be regarded as means of maintaining an "artificially" high value on European currencies. If the exchange values of the pound, franc, krona and other European currencies were allowed to fall drastically enough in relation to the dollar, dollar imports would automatically be curtailed and dollar exports expanded, provided that stability in the new exchange rates could maintain itself. Under such circumstances the superior "pull" of the soft-currency markets would disappear.

The Case of Swedish Newsprint

That the matter is not simple, however, is illustrated by the case of Swedish newsprint. Before the devaluation of British sterling, the European market was taking the greater portion of the exports of Swedish newsprint and wood pulp while only a small proportion went to the United States market. When Sweden devalued the krona concurrently with British sterling the government hoped that sales of Swedish newsprint and wood pulp to the United States would increase sharply, since Swedish producers would receive a greater number of krona per dollar of sales than before devaluation. It was assumed that the United States market would thus become relatively more attractive than either the domestic or the European market, since the krona had not been devalued in relation to other European currencies in the same degree. In this way it was hoped that the Swedish dollar balance of payments would be greatly strengthened.

However, the expected result did not happen. The price of newsprint and wood pulp simply rose enough on the European market to offset the added attractiveness of the United States market which had been brought about by the devaluation of the krona in relation to the dollar. It may be that only ECA economic aid gave the other European countries an exchange position such that their nationals could be allowed to use francs, lira and other relatively soft currencies to buy newsprint at these higher prices. Nevertheless, a large-scale reorganization of the European domestic and external economic and monetary mechanisms would be required to overcome the situation which keeps goods from being available for the United States market through the "unnatural" attractiveness of the European markets themselves.

It might appear a relatively simple matter for the governments of Western Europe to institute a deflationary domestic economic policy and at the same time allow their currencies to sink to an exchange ratio with the dollar which would balance their imports from the dollar area with their dollar earnings from export. Aside from other difficulties, however, two fundamental obstacles have so far proved insurmountable in following this policy. It is feared that as soon as inflationary forces are stopped from operating industrial production will be curtailed as demand drops off, with consequent unemployment. To allow the exchange value of currencies to fall in relation to the dollar is likely to start demands for wage increases and to cause capital to attempt to flee into goods or into gold or dollars.

In some of the countries of Western Europe which have in the recent past experienced hyperinflation, the psychological vulnerability to inflationary forces is now so great that they do not dare to carry out policies of credit expansion adequate for full employment and maximum capital investment. This has been particularly true in the case of Italy. On the other hand, in France inflationary fiscal and monetary policy has largely lost its potency as a stimulus to investment even though the French economy remains vulnerable to the evil effects of inflation. Conservative economic policies help to keep the costs of production of exported goods at a competitive level on the international market. This choice between alternative economic policies is a hard one to make. Governments are torn between demands of those who suffer from or fear unemployment and the demands of those who have suffered from and fear the evils of inflation.

Stimulation of Exports by Controls and Inducements

Since Europeans have not considered it feasible to decrease dollar imports and increase dollar exports by the more comprehensive means of devaluing currencies in relation to the dollar, most of the Western European countries have attempted to obtain the desired results by means of direct prohibition of dollar imports and stimulation of dollar exports by special inducements of one kind or another.

In the United Kingdom it was possible to stimulate exports directly by means of the numerous controls over industry available to a government which has a high degree of control over industry. Thus, automobiles were withheld from the domestic market and directed into export markets through direct government intervention and control. Governmental guarantees against loss in advertising campaigns and against credit losses in dollar markets are available to exporters.

British manufacturers and governmental officials agreed that noneconomic motives had to be depended upon to an important degree in order to induce increased dollar exports. It was apparently the rare case where a British manufacturer could not have sold for at least as high a price on the domestic or on some soft-currency market the goods which he was being urged to send to the United States.

After one British manufacturer had explained how much time, planning and expense were necessary in order to build up a market for his goods in the United States, he was asked why he went to all the trouble. His answer was, "I just wanted to prove to myself and to our own sales people that we still could sell in a truly competitive market. I wanted to prove, too, that we could sell in the toughest market of all, the United States. I think we can sell our goods on the American market for about twenty per cent more than American manufactured goods of comparable quality would sell for. By capitalizing on this snob appeal I think we can thus do our bit in the drive for dollars without loss. We do not expect to add to our profits by selling the goods in the United States rather than in our customary markets."

In addition to outright governmental intervention and control, there has been in the United Kingdom the system of "remission of purchase tax" by various devices familiar to all tourists. This system has the net effect of an export subsidy, since foreign purchasers for dollars can obtain goods substantially cheaply than can Britishers themselves. There is likewise a special exchange rate for dollar travelers' checks used in the purchase of goods by tourists in France. There are in other Western European countries a wide variety of somewhat similar schemes intended to stimulate dollar exports.

The Free Dollars Plan

A scheme which seemed to offer great advantages was often proposed, and was eventually put into practice in some countries, notably in the Netherlands. For many years in all countries of Europe, exporters have not been allowed to retain the foreign exchange which they received in payment for their exports. They have been required to turn over to the government this foreign exchange for local currency at the official rate. This official rate, in the case of dollars, was always less than the "free" rate or the black market rate.

It was widely argued that exports would be stimulated if the exporter were allowed to retain at least a part of the dollars which he received for export sales instead of having to turn them into the central bank or other governmental agency. This argument seems plausible at first glance. But, if an exporter is to be allowed to retain part of the dollars which he receives, why not simply devalue the local currency by a percentage which would give the exporter the same advantage?

Other difficult questions must be answered. Who should receive the "free dollars"? Should it be the producer of the goods for export? But who is "the producer"? The laborers in the plant? The Chairman of the Board of Directors? The corporation as legal entity? In practice it can only be the corporation or other legal proprietor of the business which is exporting the commodity. But a corporation cannot use dollars for its own personal consumption. It might, indeed, find a use for dollars to pay for imported raw materials or to buy machinery from abroad. However, this would be of advantage only if the particular corporation needed the raw material or machinery and could not otherwise obtain permission to import them.

Consequently, if "free dollars" are to be an incentive they must in most cases be transferable. That is, the exporting corporation must be free to "sell" the dollars to some other company or individual which needs dollars. Unless the purchasing company or individual can use the dollars for some purpose other than to exchange them for local currency at the official rate, however, there would be no reason to pay a premium for them, and hence no incentive effect for the exporting company.[21]

For what, then, are the "free dollars" to be used so that they will retain some incentive value? In the Netherlands the 10 per cent of "free dollars"

21. The corporation or individual purchasing the dollars might prefer to hoard them and often would pay a premium if allowed to do so. Countries trying out this particular economic gadget, however, quite logically have refused to permit this "use" of scarce dollars.

made available to the exporter could be used to purchase commodities for which import licenses would not otherwise be granted. It turned out that when this scheme was first put into operation it paid to use the free dollars to buy raisins for import. By selling the raisins thus obtained on the domestic market a return per dollar could be obtained roughly double the official dollar-guilder rate. Officially only the exporter of goods for dollars could use the dollars to buy raisins. However, since there was no sense in compelling a producer of, say, electric light bulbs to become a raisin importer, a market for free or "raisin dollars" quickly developed and was at least winked at by the Netherlands government. The net result was a dual exchange rate for dollars—the official dollar rate and the "raisin dollar rate."[22]

Not only was the scheme difficult to administer, but Dutch importers and exporters, bankers and others with whom the writer talked were exceedingly skeptical of whether it had stimulated exports to an important degree. Exporters who would have exported for dollars even though the scheme had not been in effect shared in its advantages. It seems probable that the experience of the Netherlands followed a rather general pattern. As soon as the balance-of-payments situation improved the scheme was abandoned with few regrets.

22. Exactly this result had been forecast by Hjalmar C. Hammarskjöld, the economist who was at that time Secretary of the Swedish cabinet and who opposed the introduction of this scheme into Sweden. He argued quite correctly that it would simply produce a dual rate in foreign exchange.

Chapter 12

Agricultural Policies and Trade

BECAUSE THE United States is the world's leading exporter of food, cotton and tobacco, more American farmers are concerned with export markets than with competition from imports. A major part of agriculture in the South[1] opposed protection of industry until after the first world war, and northern farmers, though normally Republican, often favored tariff reform. After the war protectionism gained strength.

Beginning in 1919 under the impact of agricultural depression, our farm policy has been characterized increasingly by the intervention of the federal government in domestic markets for the purpose of raising farmers' incomes. This intervention has tended to isolate domestic prices of agricultural staples from world markets. Hence, our farm policy has become increasingly nationalistic. Our foreign trade policy, on the other hand, after a century of high protection, has recently been moving toward freer trade. Since 1934, when the Reciprocal Trade Agreements program was inaugurated, this country has abandoned the strictly nationalistic, unilateral approach to commercial policy and has made a large number of international commitments for the expansion of multilateral trade. Thus farm policy and trade policy, moving in opposite directions, have come into conflict.[2]

In the past American agriculture has suffered from a chronic excess of workers and the capacity to produce more than could be sold at prices regarded by farmers as fair. Most of the time, free market prices would have resulted in farm incomes well below the return on comparable resources employed in other parts of the economy. This fact presents an unusually difficult foreign trade problem. In the absence of price supports, the prices of crops of which the United States has an exportable surplus will be determined by world markets.

The doctrine of foreign trade assumes that the workers displaced by excess production will be shifted to more productive employment if there are no barriers to trade. Experience, however, has led to grave doubts that this proposition always applies to agriculture; during periods of unemployment in industry, agriculture may continue to suffer from an excess of

1. See Calvin B. Hoover and B. U. Ratchford, "International Trade Policy," Chapter 17 in *The Economic Policies and Resources of the South*, Macmillan, New York, 1951, pp. 422–440.

2. Percy W. Bidwell in the Foreword to C. Addison Hickman, *Our Farm Program and Foreign Trade: A Conflict of National Policies*, Council on Foreign Relations, New York, 1949, p. vii.

workers. And even in periods of prosperity, agricultural surpluses are not uncommon.

To admit agricultural imports may only increase the disparity between farm and nonfarm incomes. As long as the income of most farm people was already relatively low, and farm workers could not find enough city jobs, there was little reason to believe that migration off the farm would be hastened by an increase in the disparity between farm and nonfarm incomes. The demand for agricultural workers has long been declining. To increase agricultural imports without shifting farm labor would redistribute income away from farmers to urban consumers. But the fundamental objective of trade is to raise the real income of both farm and urban people by shifting resources to more productive employment. If resources are not transferred and the effect is only to redistribute income, the case of agriculture deserves special consideration.

The Conflict in Policy

Agriculture has been a thorn in the side of American efforts to negotiate international agreements which would lay the framework for freer trade. In negotiating the Havana Charter for an International Trade Organization, for example, the United States delegates thought it necessary to demand (1) the use of quotas when domestic prices are maintained above world prices by restrictions on supply, and (2) the subsidy of agricultural exports. The ITO charter has never been ratified, but although duties on agricultural imports have been drastically reduced under the General Agreement on Tariffs and Trade and are now quite moderate, quotas and other restrictions have been imposed. Quotas and subsidies are so contrary to liberal objectives that severe criticism has been leveled at agriculture for these practices.[3]

There are grounds for criticism; nonetheless, it is easily possible to exaggerate the inconsistency between the apparent internationalism of our trade agreements policy and the nationalism of American agriculture. Those who stress the conflict have failed to emphasize that protection of established home industries has not been abandoned under trade agreement policies.[4] Under the "escape clause," no home industry is to be seriously injured, and it is only through the process of growth that resources may be shifted out of protected industries by reducing the tariff. The "liberalism" of our trade policy is narrowly circumscribed.

On the other hand, the new restrictionism in agriculture should not be confused with traditional protectionism. The *new* restrictionism does not

3. In addition to Hickman, *op. cit.*, see D. Gale Johnson, *Trade and Agriculture: A Study in Inconsistent Policies*, Wiley, New York, 1950.
4. See Chapters 5 and 19.

seek to increase America's self-sufficiency or to expand farm employment; its primary objective is to protect the income of people who would be employed in farming in any event. If this income is already low enough to encourage migration out of farming, the question is, "Do the restrictions on agricultural imports hamper a desirable decline of farm employment?"

In view of the dependence of American agriculture on exports, the charge is sometimes made that, in turning to restrictionism, the American farmer does not know his own best interest. While the United States buys over one quarter of the world's sugar exports and over one fifth if its wool exports, it supplies about half of the cotton exports and two fifths of the wheat and tobacco exports.

Although the United States seeks equality of treatment and elimination of restrictions against exports, it discriminates against agricultural imports by quotas and other quantitative restrictions. The reason for this is clear. As a remedy for the disastrously low prices of the 1930s, various government programs were inaugurated to raise farm prices. The inevitable result, when surpluses appeared, has been to divorce the domestic market from world prices. Under any program which attempts to raise farm income by raising prices, it is essential to provide for discrimination between domestic and foreign producers. Otherwise, the United States government would find itself attempting a task possibly beyond the powers of its resources—supporting world prices and indirectly subsidizing foreign producers. But this discrimination against agricultural imports should not be confused with traditional protectionism. Traditional protectionism results in the *misemployment* of resources. The purpose of the new restrictionism in agriculture is supposed to be protection against unfairly low incomes consequent to *underemployment*. Underemployment results from the failure of the market to shift resources rapidly enough to avoid surpluses. The fundamental objective of the farm program is not to keep resources employed in agriculture which can be more productively employed elsewhere, though in some cases that may be its effect.

With exceptions, like wool and sugar, the bulk of American farm products was not subject to protective duties until the collapse of prices following the first world war.[5] The misguided efforts to aid agriculture with a protective tariff in the 1920s ended in failure. Much of the attempt at tariff protection provided in the acts of 1921, 1922 and 1930 was based on the delusion that prices of crops of which the United States has an exportable surplus could be raised by tariffs.

These efforts to support farm prices by imposing duties on products

5. See Murray R. Benedict, *Farm Policies of the United States, 1790–1950*, Twentieth Century Fund, New York, 1953, Chapter 3.

produced in surplus at home were destined to fail. Thus, there is some basis for the charge that agriculture, as a whole, did not know its own interest in supporting higher tariffs as a general policy in the 1920s. A different problem is presented, however, by the demands for protective safeguards against an increase in agricultural imports under the price-raising programs inaugurated in the 1930s.

Some of the criticism directed at agriculture misses the mark when it states or implies that freer international trade offers a solution to the problem of low farm incomes. The fundamental cure is to prevent the production of surpluses by shifting any excess workers off America's farms. Unless this is accomplished, the potential gains from trade are limited. If trade policies restrict this migration, they are harmful and should be corrected. But the problem of internal maladjustment cannot be corrected by foreign trade. Agriculture does not seek to expand farm employment at the expense of industry, and trade agreement policy does not undertake to drive resources out of protected industries. The conflict in American foreign policy, therefore, is not so basic as may appear on the surface. As long as agriculture suffers from underemployment and the capacity to produce surpluses, the expansion of agricultural imports presents a special problem.

The continued contraction of farm employment is evidence that agriculture is subject to strong market pressures to adjust in the right direction, and can do so, even at advancing levels of farm income, when the economy as a whole is active. Indeed, probably no other industry can be found in which the reduction of employment has been so great as in agriculture and where competitive imports have been permitted in such large volume in the face of ample domestic resources and relatively low incomes. While there is certainly no reason for satisfaction with present restrictions on domestic prices and imports, the excess labor in agriculture created by the relatively high birth rate and the revolution in technology throws a heavy burden of adjustment on the farm community which must be taken into account in efforts to expand international trade. The basic issue is whether migration off the farm can be accelerated by increasing agricultural imports.

Source of Conflict

How fundamental is the quarrel between agriculture and trade?

The keystone of the present farm program is the support of farm prices above free market levels, and consequently above world prices. By direct government purchase, by nonrecourse loans and production controls, the government has raised prices of the principal farm crops.[6] In other agricultural commodities, control is exercised through marketing agreements

6. Johnson, *op. cit.*, provides a detailed account of the measures which conflict with liberal commercial policy. On commodity loans, see Jeffrey Shepherd, *Agricultural Price Control*, Iowa State College Press, Ames, 1945.

which restrict the supply in the several markets. Prices of individual crops are supported when they get substantially below the calculated parity price, that is, the relationship between the price, in some historical base period, of cotton, for example, and the average price of things that farmers buy.

The misuse of resources attributable to the farm program is partly a misallocation within agriculture, growing out of obsolete price relationships between parity prices for individual farm products. The parity price formula is based on individual price relationships in some historical base period and, for this reason, does not allow for (1) changes in consumer taste and (2) relative changes in cost among various farm products. Rigid parity prices would stimulate relative overproduction of some commodities and would not sufficiently encourage production of others.

The parity formula which has been established by law to provide criteria of fair prices to farmers has two aspects: (1) the over-all level of farm prices compared with nonfarm prices and (2) the individual price of farm commodities compared with each other. Even if we continue to use the old 1910–1914 relationship between farm and nonfarm prices as a test of fair prices to farmers as a whole, it is unmistakably clear that the parity price of wheat on this basis is too high compared with the parity price of beef cattle. This is because mechanization has greatly reduced the cost of producing wheat and other field crops while comparable economies have not been realized in producing animal products, fruits and vegetables. At the same time, demand for cereals has declined while demand for meats, fruits and vegetables has increased, owing to the rise of consumer incomes.

Modernization of the parity formula is urgently needed in the determination of parity prices for individual farm products even if the 1910–1914 base is retained to determine fair prices for farmers as a whole. The Agricultural Act of 1948 attempted to do this, to some extent, by relating the parity price of each commodity to the farm price during the preceding ten years. In cases of downward revision, the adjustment was to be no more than 5 per cent annually. Downward revision of parity prices for basic commodities was blocked completely, however, by the Agricultural Act of 1949 for the ensuing four years.[7]

Because of changes in demand and in relative costs since the base period, individual parity prices are not well suited to encourage migration out of surplus areas. But, on the other hand, farm incomes under the price support program are still not sufficiently attractive to prevent large-scale migration of hundreds of thousands of farm people to more productive nonfarm jobs. Individual parity prices are inappropriate, chiefly because of the relative surpluses and shortages that they would produce as between individual

7. For further details, see Benedict, *op. cit.*, pp. 474–483.

farm products. One redeeming feature is that the structure of parity price for individual commodities has not been rigidly imposed on agriculture.

Quotas and Subsidies

The price support program has led to the use of quotas, which are far more effective than tariffs in isolating the home market from the influence of world supplies. Unless domestic production is restricted, moreover, stocks may accumulate which cannot be disposed of in the home market without spoiling the price. This leads to the disposal of surpluses abroad.

Quotas are of two quite different types, tariff quotas and absolute quotas. Under tariff quotas, the lower duty provided by trade agreement concessions applies to a specified volume of imports, and the previous higher duty applies to any excess above the quota. Tariff quotas on agricultural products include rice, potatoes, shelled walnuts, dairy products and cattle.

Imports which materially interfere with domestic farm programs may be restricted under Section 22 of the Agricultural Adjustment Act as amended. If the imports in question are products on which the United States has given concession in trade agreements, such restrictions usually require investigation, public hearings and recommendations by the Tariff Commission. Imports of butter, milk products, cheese, oats, barley, rye, rye flour and peanuts have been restricted by quota under Section 22. Imports of filberts, almonds, flax seed, linseed oil and peanut oil in excess of specified quantities have been restricted by fees. These controls may be imposed, modified or withdrawn as conditions change in each marketing year. The United States has obtained a waiver of certain provisions of the GATT in order to accommodate import restrictions imposed under Section 22.

Wheat imports were placed under an annual quota of 800,000 bushels in 1941 and have remained at that level ever since. Of this amount, Canada is permitted to supply 795,000 bushels. The duty is now 21 cents a bushel. Four million pounds of wheat flour are admitted annually, 3,815,000 pounds from Canada, at a rate of duty of 52 cents per 100 pounds.

Cotton and cotton-waste quotas were fixed in 1939. Imports of long staple cotton are currently restricted by annual quotas of 46 million pounds. Long-staple cotton comes from Egypt and is not competitive with most American cotton. Owing to its high price its use is restricted to high-grade goods. Short-staple cotton is under a quota of 15 million pounds annually, allocated by country. There is a quota of 10 million pounds on harsh cotton, which is now imported from India and Pakistan and not grown in the United States. There is also a quota on cotton waste of 5 million pounds allocated by countries. Wheat and cotton quotas can be increased by the President.

Following the sharp increase in certain imports with the outbreak of war in Korea, the President was directed, under a broad grant of power, to control imports which unnecessarily burdened any domestic farm program.[8] As a result, cheese and a number of minor products were placed under quotas, and butter, rice, linseed oil and other minor products were embargoed in 1951.[9] In 1952, the stringency of this legislation was modified to permit the broad effect of such restrictions on international relations to be taken into account. Subsequently, quotas were increased on certain types of cheeses and removed on others.

The Department of Agriculture has power to license imports in support of almost any farm program.[10] Butter is the most important commodity that has been licensed.

The most flagrant inconsistency in our policies is between the subsidy of farm exports and our own antidumping law. The Tariff Act of 1922 provides special penalties on imports of foreign merchandise "sold in the United States or elsewhere at less than its fair value," when, as a result, any domestic industry "is being or is likely to be injured."

Export subsidies were born of the depression and are based on an unusually broad authorization of power, limited only by funds.[11] Some funds have been appropriated for this purpose and 50 per cent of import duties are available by law for export subsidies on agricultural products. These subventions are not tied to parity prices or to producer returns.

Significance of Restrictions

Special restriction on agricultural imports has embarrassed American leadership in international affairs and made the task of our negotiators more difficult. Quotas and embargoes such as those required on cheese by the Defense Production Act of 1950 are offensive to good judgment, handicap American leadership and provide only meagre benefits to farmers.

On the other hand, a number of the import quotas do not seriously distort rational channels of trade. The United States is a leading exporter of rice, wheat and cotton, the three most important crops subject to quotas. An important effect of the rice quota, for example, was to make world

8. Defense Production Act of 1950, as amended, Sec. 104.

9. Cf. U.S. Tariff Commission, *Operation of the Trade Agreements Program*, Fifth Report, "Restrictions under Defense Production Act of 1950," pp. 203–206, mimeographed.

10. Public Law 155, 81st Cong.

11. Authorization for subsidy was provided in the original Agricultural Adjustment Act of 1933, Sec. 12; later authorization is in Public Law 370, Sec. 32, 75th Cong. The Commodity Credit Corporation may, under some conditions, sell surplus stocks acquired through loans. The European Cooperation Act of 1948, Sec. 112, provides that farm products may be sold through the ECA at prices as low as 50 per cent below current market price.

supplies more directly available to other countries that are dependent on imports.

Some countries have obtained subsidized American exports of cotton, tobacco and dried fruits which, owing to balance-of-payments difficulties, they could not have acquired without increased American aid. This was particularly important when Germany, Austria and Japan were under military occupation. At the same time, if American aid had been used to buy Greek and Turkish tobacco and Italian dried fruits, it would have helped the dollar position of these countries, which were also receiving American aid. The Department of Agriculture recognizes the serious problem created by export subsidies and has called them a stopgap.

To say that the dumping of exports is inadmissible as a policy is correct, but does not go to the root of the matter. The real solution is not to stop subsidizing but to stop producing surpluses. And the important policy question is the extent to which subsidies have expanded production.[12]

The great increase in wool imports has been possible because of the growing prosperity in other branches of agriculture.[13] A similar adjustment would probably have taken place in sugar but for the quota restrictions. The potential increase in imports from removal of the sugar quotas is probably as great as for the removal of all other quotas added together.

Is Foreign Trade a Solution to the Farm Problem?

What effect would freer foreign trade have on American agriculture? This is a crucial question. The view has been expressed that

. . . freer trade would have little or no net direct effect on the number of job opportunities in agriculture. It is likely that the losses in job opportunities in sugar, wool, sheep, beef, butter, cheese, fats, and oil would about offset gains in cotton, tobacco, hogs, corn, fruits and wheat.[14]

This judgment is based on the assumption that increased agricultural imports will be offset by increased agricultural exports.[15]

12. For a recent evaluation of the farm program, see the papers and discussion at the Sixty-sixth Annual Meeting of the American Economic Association. M. R. Benedict, "The Impact of Government Programs on Farm Income," and D. Gale Johnson, "Competition in Agriculture: Fact or Fiction," *American Economic Review Supplement*, May 1954.

13. See pp. 84 ff.

14. Johnson, *Trade and Agriculture*, p. 52.

15. Aside from quota restrictions and export subsidies, it is estimated that total protected products account for about 15 per cent of labor requirements in farming while the export branches account for 30 per cent. The highly protected products, sugar and wool, account for only 2.4 per cent of the agricultural economy, measured by labor requirements. On the other hand, the farm products strongly dependent upon export markets account for 13.2 per cent of farm labor requirements. The mildly protected products, beef, dairy products and oil crops, account for 12.4 per cent of labor requirements, while the products mildly dependent on exports, corn, hogs, wheat, fruit and vegetables, account for 18.1 per cent of farm labor requirements. *Ibid.*, p. 53.

The view that total requirements for agricultural employment would not be reduced by freer trade is open to question. It may be that industrial rather than agricultural exports would be increased if we import more sugar and wool.[16] The nations from which we buy agricultural imports seem to want more of our industrial exports.

There remains a still more serious doubt about the assumption that increased imports will be balanced by increased exports. Although domestic employment in sugar beets is maintained by control of imports, it does not follow that agricultural exports have been correspondingly constricted. This is because of the large excess of American exports, both agricultural and industrial, that have been paid for by foreign aid, at the expense of the American taxpayer. It is highly desirable to reduce foreign aid by taking more imports. But the cessation of foreign aid, whether by increasing imports or by reducing exports, seems almost certain to reduce total demand for American farm products. This follows from the fact that American consumers will probably increase their consumption of farm products very little as the result of reduced foreign aid. Thus the view that increased agricultural imports will expand agricultural employment correspondingly in the export branches is a dubious one. The long-term trend has been a decline in the relative importance of agricultural exports.

If workers were shifted off the farm about as rapidly as they are displaced, this should be a welcome adjustment, for it would make possible an increase in nonfarm employment and in general living standards. But experience shows that the market has often failed to shift workers out of farming as rapidly as they are displaced, and it is for precisely this reason that the increase of agricultural imports presents an acute problem.

To eliminate the restrictions on agricultural imports is highly desirable. But to insist on this as a first step is to put the foreign trade cart before the domestic surplus horse. We have had farm surpluses because of the surplus of farm workers created by improvements in technology together with the frictions impeding labor mobility and the inelastic demand for farm products. An equally urgent step is to remove the excess of farm labor which perpetuates the production of surpluses. The home economy needs to be in reasonable balance in order to realize the full benefits of trade.

The farm problem is made up of two major parts. The first is associated with the shift of workers out of farming as productivity is raised by mechanization and improved methods. There is a backlog of underemployed farm workers in addition to those who are annually displaced and must migrate if the nation is to make the best use of its resources. The second is the

16. If it is assumed that the expansion of trade takes the triangular pattern and includes agricultural exports to Europe, it seems less likely that increased imports will be balanced by increased exports. Instead, foreign aid can be reduced.

instability of farm income, owing to the fact that farmers continue to work and produce in bad times as well as good. Farm income is more unstable than nonfarm income because neither the cost nor the selling price of farm products is subject to the private controls which characterize industrial costs and prices. Farm people continue to produce whether it is profitable or not.

More foreign trade is good, but it is not, as is sometimes implied, a solution for the farm problem. While more trade can raise real national income, including farm income under some circumstances, a disparity between farm and nonfarm income cannot be corrected by increasing agricultural imports. This is the nub of the issue. To increase agricultural imports which compete with farm labor when it is already underemployed as a whole and capable of producing surpluses may only shift farm income to nonfarm income.

It is sometimes assumed that more international trade, by expanding the export market for American mass production goods, can provide jobs for the surplus of farm workers. This is a mistaken view which confuses the problem of national growth with the growth of international trade. The workers displaced by an increase in imports may be absorbed by the corresponding expansion of export industries (with a net gain from the shift to more productive employment), but the surplus of workers who must be annually moved off the farm because of growth in population and increased productivity must be absorbed mainly by internal expansion of the domestic economy.

If price supports were removed, we might still have crop surpluses because we have a surplus of farm labor. Manifestly, the solution to this problem can only be found in the expansion of the home economy. International trade offers other benefits, but it can neither prevent nor cure unfavorable internal terms of trade for agriculture and the relative fall in farm incomes that result from the failure to shift labor to more productive nonfarm employment as rapidly as it is displaced on the farm.

This is one of the significant consequences of the changing structure of demand as people become richer; it is one of the far-reaching consequences of the advances in technology now going forward in agriculture.[17]

Resource Use

The fundamental issue is whether restrictions on agricultural imports hold resources on American farms which would be employed more productively elsewhere if these controls were removed. If import restrictions have made farming attractive enough to prevent migration to nonfarm employ-

17. T. W. Schultz, *Agriculture in an Unstable Economy*, McGraw-Hill, New York, 1945, p. 84.

ment, they should be removed immediately. But the evidence suggests that the rate of migration depends on the availability of nonfarm employment and that, broadly speaking, farm incomes have not been so high as to reduce nonfarm employment.

Migration off the farm has been highest in periods of prosperity and lowest in depression. The annual net migration of farm people to nonfarm areas was 675,000 in the years 1922–1929, but fell to less than 200,000 in the depression years 1930–1934. In the recovery 1934–1937 annual migration increased to 620,000, but fell to 450,000 in the depression of 1938–1939.

Although the war brought a much greater improvement in farm than in nonfarm income, the annual net migration off the farm was 1,400,000 in the years 1940–1944. Finally, in 1947, when relative farm prices reached a peak 15 per cent above parity, 600,000 people net moved off the farm.[18]

Farm population declined from 24 per cent of total population in both 1929 and 1935, to 18 per cent in 1947 and to 15 per cent in 1951.[19] Thus, the shift of population has continued despite the relative improvement in farm income and despite the fact that the natural growth of population is much greater in rural than in urban areas.[20]

The question of policy with respect to agricultural imports is primarily one of magnitudes rather than of principle. How rapidly can farm workers be shifted by market forces? If the expansion of nonfarm employment can be accelerated by increasing agricultural imports, the adjustment should not be too difficult. But if the effect of increased imports is only to lower farm incomes, the adjustment is a formidable one.

During the past twenty years it has been possible both to reduce agricultural employment and to expand agricultural output. Technological changes and other improvements in farm practices will make it possible for this trend to continue. The burden of adjustment created by increased imports, therefore, may be superimposed on the migration required by progressive improvements in farming. In order to accommodate these adjustments the forces of prosperity will need to be strong and sustained.

18. *Agricultural Statistics, 1950*, Table 632, p. 579; *Farm Population Estimates*, U.S. Department of Agriculture.

19. *Agricultural Statistics, 1952*, Table 653, p. 635.

20. Net reproduction rates in 1935–1940 were 1,616 for rural farm and 1,150 for rural nonfarm, compared with 726 for urban areas. Johnson, *Trade and Agriculture*, p. 45, note 1.

PART III

WHAT IMPORTS
MIGHT BE INCREASED?

Chapter 13

Agricultural Imports

THE DRAMATIC INCREASE of 40 per cent in domestic farm production from 1935–1939 to 1948 provided a 10 per cent increase in per capita food consumption for a rapidly growing population together with an 80 per cent increase in the quantity of exports and little change in imports. Consumption of food and fiber is generally still well below the productive capacity of American agriculture despite a net movement of 9 million people off the farm in the same period.[1]

Despite the impressive increase in consumption, the United States has become relatively less, rather than more, dependent on the rest of the world for agricultural products, reversing the trend from 1910–1914 to 1925–1929 when imports increased faster than domestic production whether measured by value or quantity. In the twenty years ending in 1948, total agricultural imports declined in quantity while agricultural production increased 36 per cent and real gross national product rose 86 per cent. In value terms the disparity was equally striking: agricultural imports increased only 36 per cent in current prices while cash receipts from farm marketings increased 178 per cent and gross national product increased 177 per cent.[2] Although import prices rose, *the increase in import values was roughly only about one fifth as great as the rise in cash receipts from farming.*

Over the next twenty years consumption of farm products as measured by quantity will be influenced far more by changes in population than by changes in national income. Consumption of food and fiber does not expand as rapidly as income. In the twenty years 1928–1948, total food consumption increased 25 per cent, compared with the 86 per cent increase in gross national product. The increase in food consumption reflects, of course, an increase in population of almost 18 per cent as well as a better diet. Per capita food consumption in the same period increased 9 per cent.

The capacity of American agriculture to support a higher standard of food consumption for a larger population has already been demonstrated. By far the most important increase in demand for foodstuffs as the popula-

1. *Agricultural Statistics, 1950*, U.S. Department of Agriculture, Table 632.

2. Cash receipts increased as fast as gross national product despite the much slower growth of farm production. This reflects an improvement in terms of trade for the farmer as a result of rising national income and world-wide improvements in the position of agriculture; governmental programs have been only a relatively minor factor.

tion grows and incomes rise will be the increased demand for meat and milk. Animal products account for the major part of the value of food production. According to the Department of Agriculture, the level of grain production reached in the peak year 1948 was probably adequate to support growing food and feed requirements a decade or more hence.

The Future of Imports

Before the inflationary stimulus of the Korean War, agricultural imports amounted to roughly $3 billion annually. These were divided about equally between "complementary" products such as coffee and rubber, which do not compete directly with domestic farm production, and "supplementary" products such as hides and wool, which, in some degree, do compete directly. The dividing line is not sharp: natural rubber is directly competitive with chemical rubber, which is not a farm product. In the broadest sense, of course, all goods compete indirectly for the consumer's dollar. Nonetheless, the classification of agricultural imports into competitive and noncompetitive groups is useful.

. Both competitive and noncompetitive agricultural imports have declined relative to the market value of domestic farm output since the 1920s. Agricultural imports equalled 21 per cent of the cash receipts from farm marketings in 1925, 15 per cent in 1935, 10 per cent in 1949 and 14 per cent in 1950. (See Table 33.) Some agricultural imports which complement home agriculture were displaced by the synthetic products of home industry and almost all of the competitive group lost ground to home production.

Both the quantity and price of agricultural imports are sensitive to inflationary developments and fear of shortages such as followed the outbreak of fighting in Korea. Increased private buying for inventory and official stockpiling of such items as rubber and palm oil were substantial factors after 1949. The rise in import values from $2.9 billion in 1949 to $4 billion in 1950 was due partly to volume and partly to price. The further increase to $5.1 billion in 1951 was virtually all due to price; there was almost no change in over-all volume. Half of the extraordinary increase in agricultural imports from 1949 to 1951 was accounted for by coffee and rubber.

Quite apart from the inflation of import prices, the rapid expansion of domestic production and the strain on domestic resources which followed the outbreak of war in Korea were highly favorable to imports. But the comparison between 1950 and 1951 provides a useful insight. The first impact of the Korean War was stronger in the United States than elsewhere and the volume of imports increased. But even the great expansionary pressures of 1951 including the stockpiling of some imports failed to produce a further increase in volume. The rise from 1948 to 1951 was about 7 per cent.

TABLE 33

RELATION OF AGRICULTURAL EXPORTS AND IMPORTS TO CASH RECEIPTS FROM
MARKETINGS, 1914–1950

(*Dollar Figures in Millions*)

| | | | Value of Agricultural Imports | | | Value of Agricultural Exports and Imports as Per Cent of Cash Receipts | | | |
| | | Value of Agricul-tural | | | | | Imports | | |
Calendar Year	Cash Receipts	Exports	Total	Supple-mentary	Comple-mentary	Ex-ports	Total	Supple-mentary	Comple-mentary
1914	$ 6,050	$ 997	$ 985	$ 598	$ 387	16.5	16.3	9.9	6.4
1915	6,403	1,608	1,088	636	452	25.1	17.0	9.9	7.1
1916	7,750	1,755	1,408	830	578	22.6	18.2	10.7	7.5
1917	10,746	1,981	1,818	1,066	752	18.4	16.9	9.9	7.0
1918	13,461	2,751	1,807	1,144	663	20.4	13.4	8.5	4.9
1919	14,602	4,093	2,608	1,565	1,043	28.0	17.9	10.7	7.1
1920	12,608	3,443	3,249	2,157	1,092	27.3	25.8	17.1	8.7
1921	8,150	2,114	1,319	735	584	25.9	16.2	9.0	7.2
1922	8,594	1,884	1,607	834	773	21.9	18.7	9.7	9.0
1923	9,563	1,820	2,028	1,094	934	19.0	21.2	11.4	9.8
1924	10,221	2,110	1,911	984	927	20.6	18.7	9.6	9.1
1925	10,995	2,136	2,340	1,001	1,339	19.4	21.3	9.1	12.2
1926	10,564	1,817	2,416	973	1,443	17.2	22.9	9.2	13.7
1927	10,756	1,885	2,221	996	1,225	17.5	20.6	9.3	11.4
1928	11,072	1,863	2,100	955	1,145	16.8	19.0	8.6	10.3
1929	11,296	1,693	2,218	1,017	1,201	15.0	19.6	9.0	10.6
1930	9,021	1,201	1,469	701	768	13.3	16.3	7.8	8.5
1931	6,371	821	1,008	447	561	12.9	15.8	7.0	8.8
1932	4,743	662	668	296	372	14.0	14.1	6.2	7.8
1933	5,314	694	732	366	366	13.1	13.8	6.9	6.9
1934	6,334	733	821	413	408	11.6	13.0	6.5	6.4
1935	7,086	747	1,072	589	483	10.5	15.1	8.3	6.8
1936	8,367	709	1,242	695	547	8.5	14.8	8.3	6.5
1937	8,850	797	1,579	868	711	9.0	17.8	9.8	8.0
1938	7,686	828	956	477	479	10.8	12.4	6.2	6.2
1939	7,877	655	1,118	526	592	8.3	14.2	6.7	7.5
1940	8,364	517	1,284	544	740	6.2	15.4	6.5	8.8
1941	11,181	669	1,668	786	882	6.0	14.9	7.0	7.9
1942	15,372	1,185	1,271	817	454	7.7	8.3	5.3	3.0
1943	19,434	2,095	1,513	1,059	454	10.8	7.8	5.4	2.3
1944	20,360	2,133	1,818	1,229	589	10.5	8.9	6.0	2.9
1945	21,520	2,294	1,709	1,041	668	10.7	7.9	4.8	3.1
1946	24,864	3,173	2,318	1,195	1,123	12.8	9.3	4.8	4.5
1947	30,014	3,957	2,760	1,406	1,354	13.2	9.2	4.7	4.5
1948	30,545	3,473	3,149	1,618	1,531	11.4	10.3	5.3	5.0
1949	27,518	3,576	2,897	1,443	1,454	13.0	10.5	5.2	5.3
1950	27,921	2,876	3,986	1,804	2,182	10.3	14.3	6.5	7.8

Source: Bureau of Agricultural Economics. Compiled from reports of the Bureau of the Census and BAE.

Clearly, war and near-war will produce spurts of additional imports.

The present survey, however, is concerned with long-term growth under more normal conditions and no weight has been given to the speculative increase in imports which followed the fighting in Korea.

The great agricultural resources of America are perhaps the most important single reason why our imports are relatively small compared with other highly industrialized nations. As a result of better methods of farming, total requirements for crop land have scarcely increased since 1919 and considerably less than half of our farm land is in crops.

Despite continued urbanization and intensification of industry, growth of agricultural imports has been retarded by the following developments from 1929 to 1950:

(1) production of crops per acre increased 27 per cent;
(2) production per animal unit increased 22 per cent;
(3) farm output per man-hour increased 82 per cent.

Barring a highly destructive war, productivity seems almost certain to increase in the future as in the past. This implies that domestic consumption will not keep pace with domestic capacity to produce, even if there is no increase in farm population.

Success in maintaining a healthy and vigorously expanding economy will encourage population growth, which appears to be affected by prosperity and depression. In the twenty years ending 1949, population increased from 123 million to 150 million.

The farm birth rate is much higher than the nonfarm rate. Consequently, the prospective increase in productivity of home agriculture can provide for food requirements and permit the continued migration of excess farm workers to nonfarm employment. *This does not bar the expansion of international trade, but it does suggest that no dramatic increase in agricultural imports relative to domestic production is probable.* Imports of rubber, wool, hard fiber and oils for soap may suffer further technological displacement. Only under conditions of sustained prosperity are agricultural imports likely to increase more rapidly than population. Modification of present commercial policy is probably required in order that imports may rise as rapidly as farm production. In any event, it appears that agricultural imports, which account for almost half of the total, will fall sharply relative to gross national product.

The individual items to be reviewed in this chapter account for almost 90 per cent of agricultural imports. The discussion assumes no fundamental change in commercial policy. Some policy problems were considered in Chapter 12 and will come up again in Chapter 19.

COMPETITIVE FARM PRODUCTS
Hides and Skins

The United States has long supplemented domestic production of hides and skins with a substantial volume of imports.

About 85 per cent of leather goes into footwear. Shoe production has expanded largely with the growth of population. The slight increase in per capita shoe production between 1929 and 1949 was in nonleather shoes. While per capita output declined somewhat in the worst depression years and increased somewhat during the war, annual production of leather shoes in more normal years has remained about two and a half pairs per capita for a generation. Owing largely to the 17 per cent growth in population, shoe production of all kinds increased 21 per cent between 1929 and 1949, while shoes with all-leather uppers increased 16 per cent. The income effect on leather shoe consumption has been small.

Leather substitutes have been used extensively for uppers and a major part of the soles are made of materials other than leather.

Substitutes have displaced leather to a far greater extent in the field of luggage and handbags. Twentieth-century automotive and air transport has made possible more extensive travel for more people, and technology has revolutionized not only the mode of transportation but also the traveler's luggage. Two thirds of the luggage produced in 1947 was designed for use by women. The mode requires lighter-weight luggage, a trend also emphasized by the higher cost of porter services. The most radical change in construction is a hand luggage series made entirely of aluminum. The newest material is a completely synthetic sheeting. Thus, traditional leather-covered luggage is another technological casualty. A major part of production in 1947 was from nonleather materials.[3]

Leather harness has been displaced along with the horse and the mule, while the new machine is more simply harnessed with a plastic belt.

What may seem surprising in the face of an absolute expansion of consumption is the drastic decline in imports of a product that can be regarded as marginal to domestic production. Imports of cattle and calf skins have fallen more than two thirds in relation to home production.

Cattle hides are a striking example of the danger of simple generalization with respect to the effect of economic growth on imports. The United States has long been a marginal importer of hides. Yet here we see a dramatic rise in income accompanied by an *absolute* decline in the volume of imports, which averaged 4.8 million in 1925–1929, 2.6 million in 1935–1939, 1.4 million in 1945–1949. (See Table 34.)

3. See "Luggage" in *Illinois Business Review*, May 1951.

TABLE 34

IMPORTS OF HIDES AS PER CENT OF DOMESTIC PRODUCTION, 1922–1949[a]

(*Number in Millions*)

Year	Cattle Hides		Calf and Kip Skins		Goat and Kid Skins		Sheep and Lamb Skins	
	Num-ber	As Per Cent of Domestic Production	Num-ber	As Per Cent of Domestic Production	Num-ber	As Per Cent of Domestic Production	Num-ber	As Per Cent of Domestic Production
1922	7.2	30	17.2	46	48.2	99	26.0	71
1923	6.7	26	7.6	41	49.8	105	31.4	78
1924	3.9	17	6.5	39	31.7	88	23.9	62
1925	3.8	17	4.9	35	47.5	112	25.2	76
1926	3.4	16	7.6	48	53.5	107	23.8	75
1927	5.1	24	7.0	41	49.0	91	22.5	63
1928	6.2	30	7.0	45	53.5	98	25.6	66
1929	5.5	29	8.8	57	60.1	108	25.8	66
1930	3.7	21	5.6	39	55.1	99	21.3	70
1931	1.9	12	5.3	43	48.9	100	16.3	50
1932	1.2	8	4.0	40	34.5	93	14.9	52
1933	2.8	16	6.3	48	50.8	115	21.9	65
1934	1.3	7	2.1	16	40.3	90	14.2	42
1935	2.7	12	3.0	21	48.8	101	18.6	48
1936	3.1	14	3.0	23	46.7	99	20.8	55
1937	2.6	12	2.7	22	51.8	111	22.6	66
1938	1.3	7	3.4	26	29.9	94	14.6	50
1939	3.2	15	3.9	28	39.0	97	28.7	73
1940	4.6	22	2.3	20	40.2	107	24.4	64
1941	8.7	31	3.6	28	49.5	109	42.1	81
1942	6.1	20	2.4	19	36.7	89	37.7	70
1943	4.5	18	2.4	22	35.4	95	34.5	58
1944	3.0	11	1.9	18	29.2	84	42.0	76
1945	0.9	3	0.9	8	24.4	101	38.6	74
1946	1.3	5	0.5	4	28.7	119	38.5	80
1947	1.3	4	0.6	5	37.5	101	21.4	59
1948	2.5	10	1.0	10	39.0	103	27.9	83
1949	0.9	4	1.0	10	36.2	104	25.1	87

Sources: Imports, *Foreign Commerce and Navigation*, compiled by U.S. Department of Commerce and Bureau of the Census; production, *Survey of Current Business*, compiled by Tanners' Council of America.

a. General imports, 1922–1933; imports for consumption, 1934–1949.

If the Hawley-Smoot tariff on hides had been high, there would doubtless have been a tendency to attribute the decline to the tariff. But in fact, the tariff was low: the 1930 tariff of 10 per cent on cattle hides was reduced to 5 per cent by trade agreement in 1941. The tariff has not been an important factor.

The striking decline in the imports of cattle, calf and kip skins since the 1920s can be attributed to four factors: (1) The demand for meat with rising income increased the marketings of cattle from 15.2 million head in

1930 to 23.1 million in 1949, and calves from 8.7 million to 12.4 million in the same period. Domestic production of hides was increased as a by-product. (2) Depletion of European herds during the war reduced the world supplies. (3) Nations in various parts of the world are encouraging the production of finished leather goods rather than the export of hides. Some countries are consuming more of their own supplies. Argentina's price policies in particular have reduced United States imports. (4) The use of leather substitutes in shoes has been significant. The major part of hand luggage is now made of nonleather materials.

Prospect for Hide Imports

Hides and skins of different animals cannot be substituted for one another except to a limited extent. Soles are made from cattle hides while uppers are most often made from skins of other animals. Different classes of skins are also used for dress and work shoes and for women's and men's shoes.

Specialization of use will require the United States to import goat and sheep skins unless substitute materials are developed. The decline of sheep raising in the United States means that imports of sheepskins will probably continue to increase in relation to domestic production. However, economic development in the rest of the world may well increase world shoe consumption and, by raising the world price of hides, encourage the development of substitutes in the United States market.

Imports of cattle and calf skins, which have been unusually low as a result of policies of the Argentine government, may increase modestly if hide prices are reduced. Maintenance of the unusually high prices encourages the use of leather substitutes. During the five years 1945–1949, imports were equal to 5.2 per cent of domestic production. If cattle hides are available at prices competitive with rubber and other substitutes, we shall probably import more than in the recent past, but it seems doubtful that imports of cattle hides will regain the relative position they held in the 1920s. (See Table 34.)

Sugar

Domestic production of sugar is more dependent on restriction of imports than any other crop. Still worse, the situation continues to deteriorate. Domestic production from beets is heavily dependent upon protection. The sugar duty was increased under the Hawley-Smoot Act of 1930 to 2.0 cents a pound on 96 degree raw sugar from Cuba and to 2.5 cents a pound on sugar of the same grade from other countries. This virtually excludes imports from countries other than Cuba. Imports from the Philippines and

TABLE 35

SUGAR PRODUCTION, IMPORTS AND PER CAPITA CONSUMPTION, 1909–1950

	(1)	(2)	(3)	(4)	(5)	(6)
Year	U.S. Mainland Production[a]	Shipments from Territories[b]	Columns 1+2	Imports	Column 4÷3	U.S. Per Capita Consumption (Refined)
		(1,000 Tons)			*(Per Cent)*	*(Pounds)*
1909	880	785	1,665	1,899	114	73.1
1910	901	818	1,719	2,076	121	74.8
1911	1,002	896	1,898	2,061	109	76.7
1912	904	922	1,826	2,155	118	75.2
1913	1,085	914	1,999	2,373	119	80.6
1914	1,019	927	1,946	2,692	138	80.3
1915	1,074	951	2,025	2,620	129	77.0
1916	1,189	1,035	2,224	2,765	124	76.2
1917	1,065	1,099	2,164	2,464	114	77.4
1918	1,099	907	2,006	2,576	128	74.1
1919	902	944	1,846	3,497	189	85.9
1920	1,345	964	2,309	3,873	168	84.9
1921	1,425	1,011	2,436	2,961	122	86.7
1922	1,024	929	1,953	4,851	258	103.6
1923	1,111	862	1,973	3,829	194	90.0
1924	1,256	1,070	2,326	4,172	179	98.8
1925	1,119	1,356	2,475	4,435	179	103.6
1926	1,008	1,307	2,315	4,529	196	103.8
1927	1,242	1,352	2,594	4,241	163	101.8
1928	1,271	1,554	2,825	3,912	138	103.1
1929	1,307	1,393	2,700	4,388	163	96.3
1930	1,508	1,681	3,189	3,894	122	109.0
1931	1,421	1,731	3,152	3,260	103	99.9
1932	1,717	1,922	3,639	2,873	79	94.1
1933	2,007	1,787	3,794	2,836	75	93.1
1934	1,508	1,802	3,310	3,200	97	93.5
1935	1,583	1,815	3,398	2,763	81	96.4
1936	1,807	1,868	3,675	2,999	82	97.2
1937	1,821	1,883	3,704	3,280	88	95.8
1938	2,207	1,810	4,017	3,073	76	95.0
1939	2,320	1,872	4,192	2,975	71	98.0
1940	2,104	1,855	3,959	3,006	76	95.2
1941	2,090	1,852	3,942	3,997	101	103.7
1942	2,151	1,607	3,758	1,928	51	86.4
1943	1,531	1,511	3,042	3,411	132	80.0
1944	1,512	1,548	3,060	3,928	128	89.1
1945	1,667	1,647	3,314	3,224	97	73.5
1946	1,900	1,504	3,404	2,687	79	74.4
1947	2,158	1,812	3,970	4,219	106	91.2
1948	1,917	1,734	3,651	3,320	91	95.7
1949	2,112	1,894	4,006	3,809	95	95.5
1950	2,460	2,081	4,541	3,859	85	96.3

(Notes opposite)

266

American territories are free of duty. In addition, imports are regulated by quota, which is the controlling factor under the Sugar Act of 1948.[4] This act limits and allocates imports in an arbitrary fashion. The international sugar agreement tends to rigidify world sugar trade.

Per capita consumption declined slightly from over 100 pounds in the late 1920s to 96 pounds in the late 1940s. Imports of 3.1 million tons annually in the 1940s compare with 3.7 million tons in the 1920s. Production on the mainland and supplies from the territories have increased since the 1920s, with the result that imports have declined drastically in relation to production. Imports amounted to 168 per cent of United States mainland production and shipments from territories in 1925–1929; 80 per cent in 1935–1939; and 94 per cent in 1945–1949. Mainland production and shipments from territories increased about one third from 1930 to 1950. (See Table 35.)

Without import restrictions, mainland production in the United States would probably decline from one third to one half. United States sugar production has been limited to 2.4 million tons. Supplies from the territories of Hawaii and Puerto Rico are not likely to increase appreciably over 2 million tons. With a 20 per cent increase in population, sugar imports, principally from Cuba, could increase by a million tons over the 3.8 million tons imported in 1949.

This assumes no further legislative increase in the domestic sugar quota— an unrealistic assumption in the light of recent experience.

Probably the most important change (in terms of value) that has been made under the Trade Agreements Program is the reduction of the duty on sugar. But this tariff reduction was coupled with quota restrictions of imports which favor domestic production. Although imports have increased, the increase has been less than it would have been if the duty were the only barrier. Since the price of sugar is maintained through restriction of supply by arbitrary quotas, the tariff reduction has served only to increase the price to Cuban producers. The result has been an improvement in terms of trade in favor of Cuba at the expense of the United States Treasury.

4. Public Law 388, 80th Cong., 1st sess., Chapter 519; Cf. William C. Pendleton, "American Sugar Policy—1948 Version," *Journal of Farm Economics*, May 1948, pp. 226–242. Public Law 140, 82d Cong. extended the Sugar Act in amended form.

Notes to Table 35

Sources: Foreign Commerce and Navigation, data from U.S. Department of Commerce, 1909–1934; Sugar Branch, PMA, U.S. Department of Agriculture, 1935–1950.

a. Cane and beet; raw value. U.S. Department of Agriculture, crop years, 1909–1934; calendar years, 1935–1950.

b. 1909–1934, U.S. Department of Commerce; 1935–1950, Sugar Branch, PMA, U.S. Department of Agriculture.

Wool

Wool, like sugar, is highly protected by the tariff but, unlike sugar, is not subject to import quotas. While sugar imports have fallen in relation to production, wool imports have increased sharply in relation to domestic production. In fact, the volume of wool imports has increased while the volume of domestic production has declined. Thus, the behavior of these two highly protected commodities is exactly the opposite. The rise of wool imports has already been explained in Chapter 4.

Consumption of wool per capita during the past generation has been unstable and is probably subject to further change. The decline in consumption of apparel wool from 2.7 pounds per capita in the early 1920s to 2.0 pounds in the late 1930s is usually attributed to improved heating in homes and transportation facilities. When the army was equipped during the war, consumption, of course, was greatly increased. Wool has not yet met the effective competition from artificial fibers that cotton and silk have suffered, but such competition is in the course of development now. It is also possible that wool, like leather, will be subject to increased world demand as a result of the economic development and higher incomes in the rest of the world. High wool prices would encourage use of the substitute fibers in the American market.

Domestic wool raising, despite tariff protection, has been a declining industry and the trend seems likely to continue unless halted by special legislation such as might be encouraged by a depression.

It is difficult to project future consumption: requirements would be sharply increased by the maintenance of a large army; on the other hand, wool may suffer seriously from competition by the new artificial fibers.

Imports have increased absolutely while domestic production has declined. This is almost unique among competitive imports. Imports were equal to only 37 per cent of domestic production in 1929, and 32 per cent in 1939, but climbed to 304 per cent in 1946. Although volatile, imports remained relatively high at 196 per cent of production in 1948 and 132 per cent in 1949. (See Table 36.)

The duty on wools finer than 44's, the class most competitive with domestic wool, was set at 31 cents per pound in 1922, raised to 34 cents in 1930 and reduced to 25.5 cents in 1948. The duty on the class not finer than 40's was reduced to 13 cents in 1941 and on that not finer than 44's, to 17 cents. The cost of producing our full requirements at home would, as in the case of sugar, be exorbitant and we shall continue to rely on large imports despite the duty.

Per capita wool consumption of 2 pounds annually would require substantial imports in the future. The continued substitution of imports for domestic production, together with the increase in consumption from

TABLE 36

PRODUCTION, IMPORTS AND PER CAPITA CONSUMPTION OF APPAREL WOOL,[a]
1918–1949

Calendar Year	Production (Shorn and Pulled)	Net Imports	Imports as Per Cent of Production	Per Capita Consumption
	(Million Lbs.)			(Pounds)
1918	130	227	175	3.55
1919	140	204	146	2.69
1920	129	127	98	2.48
1921	129	130	101	2.76
1922	119	116	98	2.84
1923	120	162	135	2.78
1924	124	76	61	2.19
1925	132	99	75	2.17
1926	141	104	74	2.17
1927	149	77	52	2.17
1928	161	47	29	1.93
1929	167	61	37	2.08
1930	182	46	25	1.62
1931	195	25	13	1.91
1932	185	9	5	1.50
1933	192	25	13	1.94
1934	188	21	11	1.32
1935	189	30	16	2.49
1936	185	76	41	2.33
1937	187	94	50	2.12
1938	187	20	11	1.68
1939	188	60	32	2.22
1940	190	118	62	2.33
1941	199	329	165	3.85
1942	200	457	229	4.22
1943	195	383	196	4.31
1944	184	342	186	4.15
1945	170	404	238	4.20
1946	153	465	304	4.29
1947	139	253	182	3.63
1948	125	245	196	3.29
1949	111	147	132	2.29

Source: Bureau of Agricultural Economics. Compiled from reports of the Bureau of the Census and the U.S. Department of Agriculture.

a. Scoured basis. These data have not been officially released owing to uncertainty about the conversion factor from a grease weight basis. However, they probably provide a more accurate comparison of imports with production than published series.

growth of population, would require a large increase in the volume of imports over the 1930s. But this seems highly uncertain. Unless there is drastic technological displacement, wool imports will, however, remain substantially higher than in the 1930s but may easily decline from the level of the 1940s. Expansion and contraction of the size of the armed forces will affect imports substantially.

The real threat from synthetics should serve to discourage efforts to protect domestic wool growing by raising the tariff again or by resorting to quotas. Only high level prosperity in agriculture as a whole, however, will permit continued displacement of domestic production by imports.

Fats and Oils

Imports of fats and oils have declined owing to changes in habits of consumption and technological advance. Despite higher incomes people eat less fats. Estimated per capita consumption in pounds in 1935–1939 and 1949 was as follows:[5]

	1935–1939	1949
Food	48	45
Soap	12	11
Drying	6	6
Miscellaneous	4	6
Total fats and oils	70	68

In the period 1935–1939, the United States was highly dependent on imported fats and oils, which amounted to 30 per cent of domestic production. By 1949, consumption had increased only about 10 per cent.

Total imports of fats and oils fell by almost one half in this period while domestic production increased about 60 per cent. Two factors were at work: on the production side, lard supplies[6] were drastically increased as a by-product of higher pork production while production of a relatively new domestic product, soybean oil, expanded ninefold. (See Table 37.) On the consumption side, technical research in the soap field has developed substitute detergents. Soap oils are by far the most important imports. These fell from 103 per cent of domestic production in the period 1935–1939 to 37 per cent in 1949.

The raw materials used to produce detergents are entirely different from those required in making soap. Although some synthetics are made from the hydrogenation of fats and acids, the great bulk are produced from petroleum products or coal-tar derivatives. Consumption of synthetics increased rapidly from one pound per capita in 1942 to 8 pounds per capita in 1950. This still represents less than one third of soap consumption and a further increase in the relative importance of detergents seems almost certain.[7]

5. Bureau of Agricultural Economics, Division of Statistical and Historical Research.
6. New breeds of lean, bacon-type hogs are beginning to displace the old lard-type.
7. See "The Billion Dollar Soap Industry," *Illinois Business Review*, January 1952.

TABLE 37

FATS AND OILS: PRODUCTION FROM DOMESTIC MATERIALS, 1935–1939 AND 1949

(*Millions of Pounds*)

Item	1935–1939	1949
Total	7,239	11,586
Food fats and oils	5,900	8,463
Butter	2,170	1,692
Lard	1,630	2,552
Other edible animal fats	219	166
Corn oil	128	224
Cottonseed oil	1,425	1,787
Olive oil, edible	4	5
Peanut oil	63	178
Soybean oil	261	1,859
Soap fats and oils	1,145	2,250
Inedible tallow and greases	879	2,126
Fish and marine mammal	266	124
Drying oils	178	763
Linseed oil	178	744
Tung oil	a	19
Other industrial oils, including cod and fish-liver oils	16	110

Source: Bureau of Agricultural Economics, Division of Statistical and Historical Research.

a. 3 million pounds in 1939.

Development of rubber-based paints has also displaced the use of drying oils. The principal uses of fats and oils are food, soap, drying and miscellaneous industrial uses. There is considerable but incomplete substitutability among the various uses.

While domestic agriculture is expected to produce a large surplus of lard, inedible tallow and certain oils, we shall need large imports of coconut oil and lesser amounts of palm oil and castor oil or the raw products.

Imports of olive oil and other food items fell drastically from 1935–1939 to 1949 as did linseed, tung and other drying oils. Imports of the soap oils declined about one third in this period, although some of these are stockpile items. (See Table 38.)

Under favorable economic conditions, domestic production of all fats and oils is expected to increase a further 10 per cent over the next twenty years, making a 75 per cent increase over 1935–1939. This will leave a large surplus of edible fats and inedible tallow above anticipated home consumption for which it may prove difficult to find export markets. At the same time, because of specialization of use, imports of linseed, tung and castor

TABLE 38

IMPORTS OF FATS, OILS AND OIL-BEARING MATERIALS, 1935–1939 AND 1949

(*Millions of Pounds*)

Item[a]	1935–1939	1949
Total	2,173	1,106
Food fats and oils	345	26
Olive oil	63	20
Others[b]	282	6
Soap fats and oils	1,184	821
Coconut oil and copra	632	655
Palm oil	321	82
Others[c]	231	84
Drying oils	480	78
Linseed oil and flaxseed	349	4
Tung oil and nuts	123	65
Oiticica	8	9
Other industrial oils	164	181
Castor oil and beans	60	141
Others[d]	104	40

Source: Division of Statistical and Historical Research, Bureau of Agricultural Economics.

a. Where oil-bearing materials are imported, the oil equivalent is given.

b. Mostly sesame seed and oil.

c. Mostly babassu kernels and oil, palm-kernel oil, palm-nut kernels, marine mammal oils, and inedible olive oil and foots.

d. Mostly fish-liver oils.

oil, which were low in 1949, can be expected to increase. Imports of drying oils, which were also extremely low in 1949, will rise above prewar levels if supplies are available. But, despite prospects for an increase in imports of olive oil from the low 1949 level, there seems to be little prospect that the food and soap groups will exceed half of the prewar ratio of imports to domestic production.

In sum, total imports are likely to rise in relation to domestic production. The ratio of imports to domestic production was only 9.5 per cent in 1949, compared with 30 per cent in 1935–1939. (See Table 39.) But there has been a revolution in the structure of world production in fats and oils and, under normal conditions, there is little prospect of a return to the prewar proportion.

By far the largest import items are in the soap category; here domestic production doubled between 1935–1939 and 1949 while per capita consumption declined.

TABLE 39

FATS AND OILS: IMPORTS AND PRODUCTION FROM DOMESTIC SOURCES, 1935–1939
AND 1949

(*Millions of Pounds*)

Item	Production 1935–1939	Production 1949	Imports 1935–1939	Imports 1949	Imports as Per Cent of Production 1935–1939	Imports as Per Cent of Production 1949
Total	7,239	11,586	2,173	1,106	30.0	9.5
Food fats and oils	5,900	8,463	345	26	5.8	0.3
Soap fats and oils	1,145	2,250	1,184	821	103.4	36.5
Drying oils	178	763	480	78	269.7	10.2
Other industrial oils	16	110	164	181	1025.0	164.5

Source: Bureau of Agricultural Economics, Division of Statistical and Historical Research.

Tariff movements do not account for the relative decline of imports. Some imports are not subject to protective duties and the trend has been downward. However, linseed oil and butter are restricted by quota, and free trade in fats and oils would substantially increase imports including also coconut oil and castor oil.

Cattle and Beef

Cattle imports in the period 1921–1949 ranged from less than one per cent of domestic production to a high of 5 per cent in 1939.

The ban on cattle imports from Mexico due to the outbreak of hoof and mouth disease in that nation reduced cattle imports sharply beginning in 1947. Total imports in 1949 were only 21,000 head, compared with 754,000 in 1939 and 493,000 in 1929. (See Table 40.) With continued progress in control of the disease, imports of feeder cattle from Mexico should be restored.[8]

The duty of 3 cents a pound in the Tariff Act of 1930 was decreased in 1936, 1939 and 1943, but tariff quotas were imposed. The importance of the duty was further decreased in postwar years by price rises.

Imports of fresh and canned beef show a tendency to rise, but have increased less rapidly than domestic production (dressed weight). Imports reached 199 million pounds and 149 million pounds in 1948 and 1949, respectively, compared with 115 million pounds in 1929. (See Table 40.) The duty was reduced from 6 cents to 3 cents a pound and the demand for beef increased with rising incomes. Nonetheless imports declined from 1.3 per cent of production in both 1926–1929 and 1936–1939 to 1.0 per cent in 1946–1949.

8. Since this paragraph was written, the ban has been lifted, but the immediate imports of Mexican cattle were small. The Mexican government prefers to export canned beef.

TABLE 40

IMPORTS OF SELECTED AGRICULTURAL COMMODITIES, 1919–1949

Calendar Year	Cattle, Dutiable[a]	Beef, Fresh and Canned[b]	Tobacco, Unmanufactured Leaf[c]	Cotton (478 Lb. Bales)[a]	Jute and Jute Butts[a]
	(1,000 Head)	(Million Lbs.)	(Million Lbs.)	(1,000 Bales)	(Long Tons)
1919	—	38.5	52.0	351	62,332
1920	—	50.2	59.7	628	96,039
1921	118[d]	32.4	60.9	291	62.416
1922	236	36.7	60.7	390	77,939
1923	137	23.6	63.2	392	83.982
1924	142	20.9	61.7	336	67,904
1925	173	20.1	64.9	328	64,551
1926	212	38.5	73.1	379	68,763
1927	436	69.0	79.0	430	92,415
1928	524	100.9	81.3	360	90,049
1929	493	115.4	82.1	467	87,819
1930	226	55.7	80.3	269	61,025
1931	85	19.6	69.8	128	64,622
1932	96	22.6	54.5	142	29,092
1933	75	43.5	51.5	156	51,287
1934	58	47.0	57.9	148	51,590
1935	364	84.8	63.3	105	65,537
1936	399	91.8	67.5	177	78,682
1937	495	92.8	71.7	247	118,609
1938	424	80.2	71.4	193	45,590
1939	754	88.2	82.4	148	35,849
1940	630	73.9	76.1	166	48,191
1941	732	142.6	75.7	329	104,393
1942	653	104.5	70.5	229	57,237
1943	630	107.9	72.1	143	77,839
1944	341	89.9	72.7	117	63,845
1945	489	58.4	76.0	254	30,908
1946	516	6.4	82.1	379	75,572
1947	54	30.4	90.4	349	42,095
1948	43	199.3	84.3	198	75,015
1949	21	148.9	87.9	148	61,696

Source: Bureau of Agricultural Economics. Compiled from Foreign Commerce and Navigation records of the Census.

a. General imports, 1919–1933; beginning 1934, imports for consumption.

b. Includes chilled or frozen and corned beef.

c. Imports for consumption.

d. Not available prior to May 28, 1921.

Cotton

The United States imports a small amount of long-staple cotton. The proportion of imports in recent years is below that of the 1920s but higher than in the 1930s. Imports amounted to 3.2 per cent of production in the

1920s, 1.3 per cent in the 1930s and 2.1 per cent in the 1940s. This compares quite different products, however.

Cotton imports are currently restricted by quota. A duty of 7 cents a pound was imposed on cotton imports in 1930 and reduced to 3.5 cents in 1942. Under Section 22 of the Agricultural Adjustment Act imports may be limited by quota to not less than 50 per cent of the level during a representative period, if imports threaten the effectiveness of domestic agricultural programs.

There are few uses for cotton that cannot be supplied by the rising production of longer-staple domestic upland. It must be assumed that expansion of cotton imports has a dim future.

Jute (Burlap)

The most important jute import is in the form of burlap. The rise in the value of jute imports through 1949 is entirely a result of the increase in price. With respect to quantity, the long-term trend of jute imports has been down, but this trend may have leveled off. In round numbers, imports of jute burlaps declined from 650 million pounds in 1929 and 1937 to 450 million pounds in 1949. Jute imports averaged roughly 90,000 tons in 1927–1929, 68,000 tons in 1937–1939 and 60,000 tons in 1947–1949. Cotton and paper are competitive and much depends on the relative price of cotton, jute and paper for bagging. If the price of jute were favorable, imports could rise somewhat. To some extent, however, jute is a technological casualty and is not likely to regain entirely the ground lost to paper.

Tobacco

While the trend has been slightly upward, tobacco imports have not risen as fast as cigarette production. The reason is that the proportion of imported leaf used in the blend has been gradually reduced since the 1920s. Imports declined from 10 per cent of domestic production in 1928, to 8 per cent in 1938, to 6 per cent in 1948. (See Table 41.) The ratio of imported cigarette leaf to cigarette production has probably declined somewhat more than is suggested by these figures, which include other types of tobacco.

Up to now, imports were indispensable to the blend, but the proportion was not invariable. In the future, the development of domestic production of aromatic types of tobacco for blending in cigarettes, which is now under way, may greatly reduce imports of Turkish-type tobacco.

The tariff was totally innocent of this decline in imports, which was caused by a change in taste and technology. The tariff remained unchanged after 1922 except for the product of Cuba. The rate against Cuban tobacco fell from the 1922 and 1930 rates of 28 cents a pound to 14 cents in 1942.

TABLE 41

IMPORTS OF UNMANUFACTURED TOBACCO AS PER CENT OF TOBACCO CONSUMED
IN MANUFACTURING, 1919–1948

Year	Per Cent	Year	Per Cent
1919	8	1934	7
1920	9	1935	8
1921	10	1936	8
1922	9	1937	8
1923	9	1938	8
1924	9	1939	9
1925	9	1940	8
1926	10	1941	8
1927	11	1942	6
1928	11	1943	6
1929	10	1944	6
1930	10	1945	6
1931	9	1946	6
1932	8	1947	7
1933	7	1948	6

Sources: "Tobacco Leaf Consumed in Manufacturing," *Historical Statistics of the United States, 1789–1945;* imports, U.S. Department of Agriculture.

Grains and Feeds

The United States is normally a heavy exporter of cereals. It is only in drought years that much grain is imported. In recent years, imports of grains, feeds and fodders have amounted to less than one per cent of the value of domestic marketings. Domestic production of food grains and feed in 1948 was almost double the 1935–1939 level. This striking increase in output has kept imports of grain, feeds and fodder to a minimum.

Despite high rates of consumption, the government acquired substantial grain stocks from the 1948 and 1949 crops. Under normal conditions a decade or more of growth may be required before domestic consumption catches up with the full current production potential of American farms.

Productive capacity will increase as further declines in the horse and mule population free additional land from pasture for cultivation and reduce feed requirements for horses and mules.

The most fundamental characteristic of food consumption is the shift from cereals to animal products as people grow richer. Consumption of meats and dairy products may increase 30 per cent in the next twenty years.

Domestic agriculture clearly has the capacity to produce future food grain requirements. The only question is the production of feed grains required for such an increase in consumption of meat and milk. Even here it appears more likely than not that, given normal improvements in farm practice, the feed grains needed to supply animal products for a growing and prosperous population can be met from domestic production. Export surpluses may be reduced and poor crop years may require imports. The problem in the immediate future, however, is likely to be surplus production with restrictions on imports.

The tariff on barley, oats and rye has been reduced from the high level of 20 cents, 16 cents and 15 cents a bushel in 1930 to 7½ cents, 4 cents and 5 cents under the General Agreement on Tariffs and Trade. Imports of wheat and oats are restricted by quota. The duty on feed has always been low. The Hawley-Smoot rate was 10 per cent ad valorem. It is now 2½ per cent on most feeds.

Dairy Products

Imports of dairy products declined absolutely in the twenty years 1929–1949 while domestic production increased 26 per cent. Exports greatly exceeded imports. The tariff on butter is 14 cents a pound and imports are rigidly limited by license. Butter imports of roughly half a million pounds in 1948 were less than one half the 1939 level.

Per capita consumption of butter has fallen more than one third. An important factor is competition from margarine. Moreover, the dietary trend is away from fats. Per capita consumption of all food fats and oils declined from 48 to 45 pounds between 1935–1939 and 1949.

Cheese imports fell from 55 million to 25 million pounds between 1939 and 1948. The decline was influenced by the scarcity of supplies in Europe and by high European prices, but it also reflects improvements in domestic production and changes in taste. Domestic blue cheese, for example, has probably displaced certain imports. While imports of cheese and other dairy products could easily increase from the low level of recent years, the total values are likely to remain a fraction of one per cent of domestic production. Imports of cheese are subject to an average duty of about 25 per cent,[9] and could rise appreciably if restrictions were eliminated.

Casein imports exceed domestic production by about 50 per cent and the trend is up.

NONCOMPETITIVE FARM PRODUCTS

Coffee

Coffee is the import par excellence that has behaved as some writers seem to think imports should behave: consumption has increased more rapidly than income. With a rise in per capita real income of less than one half, coffee consumption per capita increased more than one half in the twenty years 1929–1949. Actually this increase represents not only the effect of higher income but a change in taste and habit as well, for coffee

9. A quota on imported cheese was also established in 1951. This ill-advised action was taken in utter disregard of the relatively small volume of imports and the fact that our exports of cheese exceed our imports.

TABLE 42

IMPORTS OF COFFEE, CACAO, TEA AND BANANAS, 1919–1949

Year[a]	Imports				Imports Per Capita			
	Coffee	Cacao Beans	Tea	Bananas	Coffee	Cocoa	Tea	Bananas
	(Million Lbs.)				(Pounds)			
1919	1,338	391	108	1,850	11.7	3.5	.6	17.5
1920	1,297	344	98	1,966	11.6	2.9	.8	18.4
1921	1,341	305	72	2,168	11.9	2.7	.7	19.9
1922	1,246	345	86	2,255	11.7	3.0	.9	20.4
1923	1,410	414	97	2,198	12.6	3.5	.9	19.6
1924	1,421	378	105	2,369	12.1	3.3	.8	20.6
1925	1,284	382	93	2,774	10.5	3.1	.9	23.4
1926	1,493	426	99	2,812	12.3	3.6	.8	22.8
1927	1,433	425	97	3,050	12.1	3.3	.7	24.4
1928	1,457	379	90	3,215	11.9	2.9	.7	26.2
1929	1,482	508	93	3,257	12.1	3.9	.7	26.2
1930	1,599	373	86	3,141	12.4	3.0	.7	24.6
1931	1,742	416	87	2,793	12.9	3.4	.7	21.8
1932	1,501	480	90	2,473	12.4	3.2	.7	19.7
1933	1,586	474	95	1,981	12.7	3.4	.8	16.2
1934	1,524	442	88	2,384	12.3	3.5	.6	19.8
1935	1,755	606	84	2,751	13.3	4.8	.6	22.4
1936	1,739	632	84	2,915	13.7	5.0	.6	23.8
1937	1,697	619	92	3,329	13.2	4.0	.7	27.1
1938	1,987	453	86	2,962	14.8	3.5	.7	22.0
1939	2,014	664	90	2,856	14.8	4.7	.7	22.9
1940	2,055	729	100	2,617	15.4	4.9	.7	20.0
1941	2,255	693	102	2,583	15.8	4.8	.8	19.1
1942	1,715	239	94	1,361	13.5	3.8	.5	8.6
1943	2,200	574	52	1,236	12.9	2.9	.5	7.8
1944	2,608	682	91	1,584	15.7	3.6	.5	10.3
1945	2,718	621	90	2,048	16.3	4.0	.5	13.9
1946	2,738	595	87	2,695	19.9	4.2	.6	16.6
1947	2,501	598	90	3,008	17.3	4.1	.6	18.8
1948	2,774	558	78	2,961	18.2	3.8	.6	19.5
1949	2,924	629	89	2,771	18.6	4.1	.6	18.6

Source: Bureau of Agricultural Economics. Compiled from reports of the Census and U.S. Department of Agriculture.

a. Year ending June 30.

consumption increased in the low-income 1930s, as well as in the high-income 1940s. In fact, per capita consumption has increased each decade since 1919. As a result of the increase in per capita consumption and the growth of population, coffee imports jumped dramatically from 1.5 billion pounds in 1929 to almost 3.0 billion in 1949. (See Table 42.) The value of imports also increased owing to the sharp rise in price.

Coffee is distinctly atypical. It is America's largest import and there is no other product in its class. It seems unlikely that coffee will maintain the extraordinary rate of growth of the twenty years 1929–1949, but it probably will increase at least as rapidly as population. With lower prices, the increase could be somewhat greater.

There is no tariff on coffee and there is no prospect that one will be imposed.

Cocoa

Imports of cocoa, which were rising rapidly in the 1920s and 1930s, have failed to continue this trend. Dietetics discourage increased consumption. Moreover, most chocolate products now on the market contain much synthetic flavor. The result is that imports of cocoa have not kept pace with the consumption of chocolate products. Per capita consumption of cocoa increased from the 1920s to the 1930s, but was lower in recent years than in the late 1930s. (See Table 42.) Consumers seem to have accepted artificial flavor, and although per capita consumption is only about four pounds, imports do not seem likely to rise much more rapidly than population.

Tea

Unlike coffee and cocoa, per capita consumption of tea has declined since the early 1920s. In fact, total imports in recent years were lower than in the 1920s. (See Table 42.) Any significant expansion in tea drinking would probably be at the expense of coffee.

Bananas

Banana production has been impaired by plant disease and, as a result, imports, which enter duty-free, have not kept pace with the growth in population. Per capita consumption dropped sharply from 26 pounds in 1929 to 19 pounds in 1949, and total imports declined slightly in the same period. (See Table 42.) The future of imports depends on the success in fighting plant disease and on resolution of management problems in the producing countries. Production appears to be a limiting factor.

Hard Fibers

The cordage industry is affected by the level of shipbuilding activity, which, in turn, reflects war and peacetime requirements and special shipbuilding legislation. Except for war demand the trend of hard fiber imports has been down for a generation. Sisal and manila represent another though less dramatic instance of technological displacement in the following ways: gum tape has displaced packaging twine in the corner grocery, steel bands

TABLE 43

IMPORTS OF SISAL AND MANILA FIBER, SELECTED PERIODS,
1926–1949

(*Thousands of Long Tons*)

Period	Sisal and Henequen	Manila
1926–1929	127	60
1936–1939	122	39
1946–1949	118	53

Source: Bureau of Agricultural Economics.

have displaced many of the uses for heavy rope in industry, the combine has displaced grain binders in agriculture.

Although sisal imports have been supported by a new use in the growing popularity of sisal rugs, imports of sisal and henequen declined from 1926–1929 to 1936–1939 and again in the decade ending 1946–1949. (See Table 43.) The industry is continuing to suffer from newer technological developments. Both sisal and manila fiber enter duty-free.

Carpet Wool

Unlike apparel wool, carpet wool is not competitive with home production.

Carpets are luxuries, and sales are sensitive to income changes. Imports were lower in the years 1936–1939 than a decade earlier. The substantial increase since the war reflects both the high levels of income and a backlog of deferred demand. Imports of carpet wool in the period 1926–1949 were as follows (in millions of pounds):

1926–1929	109.5
1936–1939	92.5
1946–1949	164.8
1949	118.0

Although imports almost doubled from 1919 to 1929, the rise was only about 50 per cent over the two decades from 1926–1929 to 1946–1949. High prices are currently encouraging the substitution of artificial fiber and, to an even greater extent, cotton carpeting is displacing wool. Except for competition from substitute fibers, carpet wool imports might be expected to increase faster than population if high level incomes are maintained.

However, experience in other products indicates that artificial fibers for specific purposes[10] can be quite successful and cotton has already made substantial gains. Thus, the future of carpet wool is not promising.

10. The advantage of natural over synthetic products lies in their greater adaptability.

The duty on carpet wool is remitted so that, for all practical purposes, carpet wool is duty-free.[11]

Silk

From a leading import, silk has fallen as follows (in millions of pounds):

1926–1929	86.5
1936–1939	61.0
1946–1949	6.2
1949	2.8

Raw silk imports in 1946–1949 were about 7 per cent of the level in 1926–1929. Rayon had already made great inroads by the late 1930s when imports had fallen 30 per cent from a decade earlier. With the advent of nylon, synthetics virtually usurped the market while natural silk was knocked out during the war. While there may be some increase of imports from the extreme low in postwar years, the market for natural silk remains one of the outstanding technological casualties of the past twenty years.

There is no duty on raw silk.

Rubber

Rubber consumption increased from less than 300,000 tons in 1919 to more than 1,200,000 tons in 1949. With the rapid growth of the automotive industry, consumption reached 684,000 tons in 1929. Continued expansion of demand for tires, which accounts for two thirds of consumption, has been augmented by many other uses and from 1929 to 1949 consumption increased in the same general proportion as gross national product. Imports, however, are one of the most important technological casualties.

Consumption of natural rubber rose from 215,000 tons in 1919 to 592,000 in 1939, but was no higher in 1949 than in 1939. (See Table 44.) Reclaimed rubber declined from roughly one third to one fifth of consumption and is far below the potential supply.

The relatively low level of imports is, of course, due to domestic production of chemical rubber. The war-born synthetic industry, which developed one million tons of capacity, is here to stay. Small amounts of chemical rubber are also imported from Canada.

The rubber industry managed to achieve a ratio of only 15 per cent natural rubber to total production in 1945, but was unable to turn out a full line of rubber products at this ratio, which also involved some deterioration of quality. The minimum requirement for a full line of products has been estimated at 25 per cent. Synthetic is still not completely substitutable for

11. The 1930 duty of 24 cents a pound was reduced to 13 cents in the reciprocal trade agreement with Argentina in 1941.

TABLE 44

CONSUMPTION OF RUBBER, BY TYPE, 1919–1949

(*Long Tons*)

Year	Natural	Chemical	Total New Rubber[a]	Reclaimed	Total
1919	215,000	—	215,000	73,560	288,560
1920	206,000	—	206,000	75,300	281,300
1921	177,772	—	177,772	41,350	219,122
1922	301,499	—	301,499	54,480	355,979
1923	319,422	—	319,422	75,200	394,622
1924	328,769	—	328,769	78,500	407,269
1925	388,481	—	388,481	137,000	425,481
1926	366,158	—	366,158	164,500	530,658
1927	373,000	—	373,000	189,500	562,500
1928	437,000	—	437,000	223,000	660,000
1929	467,400	—	467,400	217,000	684,400
1930	376,000	—	376,000	153,500	529,500
1931	355,193	—	355,193	123,000	478,193
1932	336,738	—	336,738	77,600	414,238
1933	412,365	—	412,365	85,000	497,365
1934	462,480	—	462,480	100,855	563,335
1935	491,544	—	491,544	117,523	609,067
1936	575,000	—	575,000	141,500	716,500
1937	543,600	—	543,600	162,000	705,600
1938	437,031	—	437,031	120,800	557,831
1939	592,000	1,951[a]	593,951	170,000	763,951
1940	648,500	2,904	651,404	190,244	841,648
1941	775,000	6,259	781,259	251,231	1,032,490
1942	376,791	17,651	394,442	254,820	649,262
1943	317,634	170,891	488,525	291,082	779,607
1944	144,113	566,670	710,783	251,083	961,866
1945	105,429	693,580	799,009	241,036	1,040,085
1946	277,597	761,699	1,039,296	275,410	1,314,706
1947	562,661	559,666	1,122,327	288,395	1,410,722
1948	627,332	442,072	1,069,404	261,113	1,330,517
1949	574,522	414,381	988,903	222,679	1,211,582

Source: Bureau of Agricultural Economics. Compiled from records of the Office of Domestic Commerce, U.S. Department of Commerce.

a. Data on chemical rubber not available prior to 1939.

natural rubber. Truck and airplane tires, for example, require a relatively high proportion of natural. Chemical rubber, however, is being improved and the prejudice in favor of natural rubber seems to be waning.

Postwar legislation required a minimum production of 222,000 tons of chemical rubber. Imports of natural rubber were limited to this extent by the mixing proportions required by law. Production of natural rubber has not kept pace with world demand, however, and the domestic production of chemical rubber was more than double the minimum required by law.

The cost of synthetic has been well below the postwar price of natural rubber. Present acreage is past maximum-bearing age and is also much less productive than the new trees which can be planted. New plantings have not kept pace with the rise in consumption. Presumably this is due to unsettled political conditions and potential competition from additional synthetic capacity. It is not really known how much acreage can be expanded at costs competitive with synthetics. But it is certain that the present prices of natural rubber will have to come down and it is quite possible that competition for labor from other agricultural products will force costs up.

The price of synthetic, on the other hand, may rise as soon as government-owned plants are sold and price policy is controlled by private industry. Presumably this would tend to encourage expansion of domestic capacity.

Plastics will displace rubber for some uses, but consumption will probably continue its strong upward trend. It seems likely that demand in the United States will expand at about the same rate as gross national product and in the outside world will rise even faster.

Imports including stockpiling amounted to about one half of domestic consumption in 1948 and 1949. Taking into account the potential increase in world demand and the apparently favorable cost position of chemical rubber, it would be surprising if imports amount to much more than half of domestic consumption over the next twenty years.

Technological Change

Our attempt to evaluate the prospect for imports may turn out to be mistaken, particularly with respect to any single item. The main point is that it cannot be assumed that agricultural imports will rise as rapidly as domestic farm production, much less that they will rise as rapidly as national income.

The economic conditions which produce high prices are favorable to imports; but high prices will encourage substitution of synthetic products. On the other hand, the economic conditions which produce falling prices are unfavorable to imports because it means that we will have surpluses at home.

Agricultural imports have suffered severely from changes in technology and in the pattern of consumption. Natural silk and rubber are the outstanding casualties. There are also less dramatic instances which add up to a substantial total. Hides and skins have been displaced by synthetics in the making of shoes, luggage and other products. The most important imports of fats and oils are used in making soap, and soap is being displaced by detergents, which require less fat and oil. Hard fibers are being displaced by

TABLE 45

RATIO OF COMPETITIVE AND NONCOMPETITIVE AGRICULTURAL IMPORTS TO OUTPUT BY QUANTITY, 1910–1914 TO 1951

(*Index: 1924–1929=100*)

Calendar Year	Agricultural Imports	Noncompetitive Complementary Imports	Competitive Supplementary Imports
Average 1910–1914[a]	48	—	—
1915	63	—	—
1916	70	—	—
1917	76	—	—
1918	65	—	—
1919	84	—	—
1920	83	—	—
1921	75	—	—
1922	91	—	—
1923	90	—	—
1924	87	85[b]	89[b]
1925	97	96	99
1926	100	97	102
1927	103	103	102
1928	98	101	95
1929	116	119	113
1930	99	107	90
1931	93	111	71
1932	85	103	61
1933	90	102	74
1934	90	101	75
1935	112	117	103
1936	111	114	107
1937	106	105	107
1938	84	95	69
1939	91	102	78
1940	97	114	78
1941	114	120	107
1942	62	46	84
1943	64	41	93
1944	65	48	86
1945	61	53	72
1946	71	69	73
1947	72	78	65
1948	76	84	66
1949	71	78	62
1950	82	86	78
1951	81[c]	85 (est.)	77 (est.)

Sources: Imports, Office of Foreign Agricultural Relations, U.S. Department of Agriculture, unpublished calendar year data; production, *Historical Statistics of the United States, 1789–1945* and *Statistical Abstract of the United States.*

a. Average 1909–1910 to 1913–1914, calendar years thereafter.

b. Data not available before 1924.

c. Preliminary.

gum tape and other wrapping materials. Jute burlap is meeting severe competition from cotton and paper bags. Apparel wool may meet serious competition from new synthetic fibers which, along with cotton, are already being substituted for carpet wool.

These developments have seriously affected both competitive and noncompetitive imports. The increase in the quantity of agricultural imports was twice as great as the increase in domestic production between 1910–1914 and 1924–1929. Since that time, the ratio of imports to production has fallen by almost 20 per cent. (See Table 45.)

Tariffs and Quotas

In this connection it is difficult to judge the effect on imports of quantitative restrictions in support of domestic marketing programs. It would be a mistake, for example, to regard the imports which might come in at the present level of support prices as a measure of the imports which would come in with no price support program and no restrictions. Domestic prices of the restricted items would be lower without a support program and, hence, would attract fewer imports.

What can be said is that quantitative restrictions have offset, to an important extent, the effect of tariff reduction. On the other hand, the 50 per cent tariff reduction under trade agreement programs, and the further reduction resulting from rising prices and specific duties, have reached products not subject to quantitative restrictions. While quantitative restrictions are more effective than tariffs with respect to certain products, tariff reduction has been broader than the offsetting restrictions.[12]

12. On quota restrictions, see pp. 251 and 406 ff.

Chapter 14

Forest Products

SUPPORTED BY the growing demand for newsprint and high levels of building construction, the value of paper and wood imports reached well over one billion dollars in 1950 and is still growing.

Newsprint has become a leading import, rising from 4,845 million pounds in 1929 to 6,634 million in 1937 to 9,279 million in 1949. We now import about 75 per cent of our newsprint. The value of imports of "paper and manufactures," which is mainly newsprint, now exceeds half a billion dollars. Imports of wood pulp have risen to more than one third of a billion dollars and sawmill products now exceed a quarter of a billion. (See Figure 11.) Forest products account for roughly 10 per cent of total imports.

Lumber

The United States was a net exporter of lumber until the second world war. Imports have increased while the long-term trend of exports has been down since the cyclical peak in 1929. Thus, the United States has become a net importer of lumber and, by 1951, net imports amounted to nearly 5 per cent of domestic production. Gross imports increased from 4.4 per cent of production in 1924 to a peak of 8.7 per cent in 1950. (See Table 46.)

Lumber production at home has not kept pace with demand either in the prosperous 1920s or in the expansion since 1935. The rate of growth of all timber in the United States[1] in terms of cubic feet is approximately equal to the rate of depletion through cutting and natural losses. But the depletion of domestic forests is greater than the comparison of rates of cutting and of growth would indicate, for much of the drain is in saw timber, especially softwoods, whereas much of the growth is in low-grade trees and inferior hardwoods. The Department of Agriculture estimated that the cut plus natural losses of saw timber exceeded annual growth by 50 per cent in 1944.[2] The cut has since increased 18 per cent. Thus, there is little prospect of a large and sustained increase in domestic supply for some decades.

1. Growth figures tend to understate the productivity of forest lands. Virgin forest stands have a rate of growth of zero but occupy land where growth will occur once original forest is cut. Approximately 75 per cent of the volume of West Coast stands are virgin (35 per cent of the area). The West Coast supplies 45 per cent of total domestic lumber output. C. H. Stoltenberg drew this point to the author's attention.

2. *Long-Range Agricultural Policy*, Committee on Agriculture, House of Representatives, 80th Cong., 2d sess., 1948, p. 50.

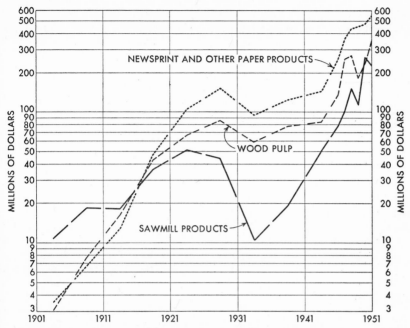

FIGURE 11. IMPORTS OF SAWMILL PRODUCTS, WOOD PULP, NEWSPRINT AND
OTHER PAPER PRODUCTS, 1901–1951

Source: Statistical Abstract of the United States, 1948, p. 919 and 1952, p. 853.

It is this excess of demand over domestic supply at current prices that
accounts for net imports. The rapid rate of cutting indicates that domestic
supplies will not increase rapidly in the near future, but the need for housing and other uses for lumber suggest that demand will continue to expand
if high levels of employment are maintained. We should anticipate accordingly a continuing rise in the price of lumber relative to other prices and a
pressure to increase imports of lumber relative to home production for the
next few decades.

Most imports come from Canada, where lumber resources relative to
depletion are in excess of those in the United States. The rate of growth in
Canada is not yet known,[3] but it is clear that Canadian resources will
permit a large increase in exports to the United States.

Improved Forestry Can Reduce Imports

Domestic lumber is at present in short supply and will be for some years.
Whether the United States will be permanently dependent upon supple-

3. Dominion Bureau of Statistics, *Canada Year Book, 1950,* p. 462.

TABLE 46

LUMBER: IMPORTS AND PRODUCTION, SELECTED YEARS, 1909–1951

Year	Production[a]	Imports[b]	Ratio (Per Cent) of Imports to Production
	(Millions of Board Feet)		
1909	44,510*	846	1.9
1914	40,500	925	2.3
1919	34,552*	1,149	3.3
1924	39,500	1,743	4.4
1929	38,745	1,543	4.0
1932	13,524	381	2.8
1935	22,943	138	0.6
1937	29,003	688	2.4
1939	28,754	718	2.5
1941	36,538	1,361	3.7
1942	36,332*	1,540	4.2
1943	34,289*	856	2.5
1944	32,938*	1,010	3.1
1945	28,122*	1,062	3.8
1946	36,382	1,238	3.4
1947	35,404	1,314	3.7
1948	36,828	1,867	5.2
1949	34,416	1,574	4.6
1950	39,384	3,432	8.7
1951	39,265	2,599	6.6

Sources: Data for years 1909–1946, *Long-Range Agricultural Policy: A Study of Selected Trends and Factors Relating to the Long-Range Prospect for American Agriculture*, for the Committee on Agriculture, House of Representatives, 80th Cong., 2d sess., 1948, p. 51; 1947–1950, U.S. Department of Commerce, *Business Statistics, 1951*; 1951, *Survey of Current Business*, February 1952.

a. Forest Service estimates through 1946 except when an asterisk (*) indicates census data.

b. *Foreign and Domestic Commerce and Navigation of the United States.* Fiscal years through 1918, calendar years thereafter.

mentary supplies of foreign lumber is conjectural. Much depends on whether or not higher prices lead to improved forestry in the United States.

By 1951 the wholesale price index for lumber had risen to more than 350, while all prices had risen to only 185 (1926 = 100). This relative rise in lumber prices may induce better forestry practices and increase the growth of domestic timber. It is estimated, for instance, that farm woodlands, which comprise some 30 per cent of all commercial forest land, contribute only one third to one half of their potential supply.[4]

Even a small increase in output would probably convert the United States into a lumber exporter once again, for gross imports were still less than 7 per cent of domestic production in 1951. Further rise in prices will

4. *Long-Range Agricultural Policy*, p. 49.

TABLE 47

PULPWOOD: IMPORTS AND PRODUCTION, SELECTED YEARS, 1924–1951

Year	Production[a]	Imports[b]	Imports as Per Cent of Production
	(Thousands of Cords)		
1924	4,739	5,539	116.9
1929	6,465	7,609	117.7
1932	4,919	5,596	113.8
1935	6,620	7,434	112.3
1937	9,392	9,454	100.7
1939	9,761	7,978	81.7
1941	14,250	7,425	52.1
1942	14,982	7,518	50.2
1943	13,617	6,936	50.9
1944	15,369	6,352	41.3
1945	15,295	7,956	52.0
1946	17,004	9,240	54.3
1947	18,542	7,998[c]	43.1
1948	20,026	8,501[c]	42.4
1949	17,619	7,698[c]	43.7
1950	20,712	8,495[c]	41.0
1951	25,123	9,685[c]	38.6

Sources: 1924–1939, American Paper and Pulp Association and American Pulpwood Association; 1941–1946, Bureau of the Census and Forest Service, as quoted in *Long-Range Agricultural Policy: A Study of Selected Trends and Factors Relating to the Long-Range Prospect for American Agriculture*, for the Committee on Agriculture, House of Representatives, 80th Cong., 2d sess., 1948, p. 51; 1947–1951, U.S. Department of Commerce, *Pulp, Paper and Board*, Industry Report, March 1952.

a. Derived from published statistics on domestic pulpwood consumed in the United States and on exports of pulpwood. Data for 1941–1946 based on domestic pulpwood received rather than consumed at United States mills.

b. Including equivalent pulpwood volume of wood pulp and paper.

c. Based on conversion ratios: 1 cord pulpwood = 1 ton paper; 1 ton wood pulp = .91 cord pulpwood. Conversion ratio used for earlier years unknown.

not only stimulate long-run production but will also increase the use of substitutes and stimulate discovery of new substitutes.

Pulpwood

In the twenty-seven years from 1924 to 1951, the consumption of pulpwood in the United States increased three and a half times. Domestic output increased more than five times while imports increased by only 75 per cent. The ratio of imports to domestic production fell from over 100 per cent to less than 40 per cent in this period. (See Table 47.)

Looking ahead, the upward trend in consumption of pulpwood will probably continue, and an increasing proportion of total supplies may come from domestic production with the continuation of the rapid development of the South as a producer of pulpwood. While total consumption has increased 4.8 times since 1919, consumption of southern pulpwood has quadrupled every ten years since 1919 and now accounts for over one half of total domestic supplies.

The Increase in the Relative Importance of Lumber Imports

Lumber imports are likely to increase, whereas imports of pulpwood seem likely to fall as a proportion of domestic production during the next few decades. In 1944 pulpwood accounted for 11 per cent of our timber cut;[5] six years later, this percentage had increased to approximately 14 per cent. Because of this relative increase in domestic pulpwood production, imports of pulpwood have increased much more slowly than those of lumber. The importance of lumber imports, measured in cubic feet, was half that of imports of pulpwood and pulpwood products in 1932 but was equal to it in 1949. The shift in relative importance of the two products in import volume is much greater if account is taken of the rapid fall in exports of lumber in contrast to the fairly stable level of pulpwood exports.

Future of Imports of Wood and Paper

Imports of newsprint have exhibited dynamic growth.

Given the preponderant importance of lumber in the consumption of all timber products it seems that imports of all timber products will rise as a proportion of timber consumption.

Forest products are a "growth" item in that imports of newsprint and timber products increased more rapidly in the past than did the gross national product. Further increases in imports of commodities in this group will have an appreciable effect in raising the general level of imports. The increase in the value of imports in the future will not be proportionate to the increase in volume, however, because of the relative shift from the valuable manufactured products, pulp and paper, to the less valuable product, lumber.

Should the national income fall below full employment levels there will be little pressure to increase timber imports, which are a marginal item.

Increased use of substitutes for wood is an important moderating influence on the growth of consumption and of imports. In the fifty years 1900–1950, per capita consumption of forest products declined by 50 per cent.

5. *Ibid.*, p. 51.

Chapter 15

Mineral Imports

DEPLETION OF OUR natural resources, it is sometimes assumed, will produce an increase in imports of raw materials that is more rapid than the rise in national income. We have concluded that this is most improbable for agricultural materials, our largest class of imports. (See Chapter 13.)

Minerals, which account for about 20 per cent of imports, comprise our next largest class of raw materials. Although the use of minerals has risen about twice as fast as that of other raw materials, the value of mineral imports failed to rise more rapidly than national income between 1929 and 1948, despite relative inflation of raw material prices.[1]

Although principal mineral imports rose sharply from $0.5 billion in 1929 to $1.4 billion in 1948, they failed to increase more rapidly than total domestic production of minerals. Imports amounted to 9.2 per cent of domestic production in 1929, but had fallen slightly to 8.8 per cent in 1948.[2]

The United States is relatively more deficient in metals than in other natural resources. Yet imports of metals failed to rise faster than domestic production from 1929 to 1948. Fuel imports declined from 4.4 per cent of domestic production in 1929 to 4.0 per cent in 1948. Other nonmetallic minerals increased sharply from 5.6 per cent of production in 1929 to 9.8 per cent in 1948. (See Table 48.) These ratios of gross imports to production overstate somewhat United States independence of foreign resources, com-

1. Imports for later years are more seriously distorted by demand for stockpiling and armaments production.

2. Domestic production figures used in calculating these percentages include only production from new ores while imports include scrap. Inclusion of secondary production from scrap would show a greater decline in the relative importance of imports owing to the growing importance of old scrap as a raw material for production.

Production is the Bureau of Mines "old series," which includes shipments from territories and possessions. See *Minerals Yearbook*, 1948, p. 17.

The import series used in this chapter does not include gold, silver, manufactured iron and steel, building materials, certain gem stones, chemicals, an insignificant volume of coal and other extremely minor items. Successive editions of the *Minerals Yearbook* differ greatly as to the items which are counted as mineral imports. In order to obtain comparable data from 1929 to 1948–1949, it was necessary to use Department of Commerce tabulations. The total of mineral imports included in Tables 48 and 50 is approximately the same for the overlapping year 1949 as the total figure shown for imports in Statistical Summary, Table 8, *Minerals Yearbook* (1951), although there are some differences in coverage. The series used here appears to include virtually all raw material mineral imports of economic consequence except fertilizer materials, which the Department of Commerce tabulated as chemicals rather than minerals and which declined from 1929 to 1948 and 1949.

TABLE 48
PRINCIPAL MINERAL IMPORTS[a] AND DOMESTIC PRODUCTION,[b]
1929, 1933, 1937 AND 1948
(*Dollar Figures in Millions*)

	1929	1933	1937	1948
Total minerals				
Domestic production	$5,888	$2,555	$5,413	$15,670
Imports	541	138	341	1,376
Imports as per cent of production	9.2	5.2	6.3	8.8
Fuels				
Domestic production	$3,191	$1,683	$3,201	$10,266
Imports	141	25	43	413
Imports as per cent of production	4.4	1.5	1.3	4.0
Metals				
Domestic production	$1,480	$417	$1,468	$3,510
Imports	315	91	227	748
Imports as per cent of production	21.3	21.8	15.5	21.3
Nonmetals				
Domestic production	$1,217	$455	$745	$1,894
Imports	68	15	56	185
Imports as per cent of production	5.6	3.3	7.6	9.8

Sources: Imports, Office of International Trade, U.S. Department of Commerce; production, *Minerals Yearbook*.

a. General imports in 1929, imports for consumption thereafter.

b. Production includes shipments from territories and possessions and represents output from new ores only. Imports include scrap. See note 2 in text.

pared with 1929, because of the decline in the quantity of American exports of those materials, like copper, which we export as well as import. The absolute rise in imports has been less than the net change in dependence on foreign supplies because the United States has shifted from a net exporter to a net importer of petroleum, copper, lead and zinc.[3] Stockpiling may be a factor explaining this shift.

Stockpiling

Both production and imports in recent years were inflated by purchases for stockpiling purposes under the Strategic and Critical Materials Stockpiling Act. (Public Law 520, 79th Cong., approved July 23, 1946.) This act provides for the acquisition and retention of stocks of strategic materials except fissionable materials, which are the responsibility of the Atomic

3. This fall in the volume of exports was insufficient to offset the effect of the rise in prices, however, and American mineral exports in 1949 were above those of 1929 by $18 million.

Energy Commission. About $242 million had been spent and $540 million obligated by the end of 1948. A year later $1,149 million had been spent and $416 million obligated. Deliveries of over $900 million in 1952 brought total inventory to some $4 billion. The effect is to increase the importance of imports whether domestic or foreign supplies are purchased directly for stockpiles. Without this act imports of minerals would have been substantially lower, particularly since 1949.

Technological Displacement and Scrap Materials

Why have imports of the resources in which the United States is most deficient failed to increase more rapidly? Expansion in production from new ores and in imports for normal use was not as great as might be expected for two reasons.

The first is the development of new techniques which save raw materials, as well as new materials which save imports. For instance, spectacular material-saving innovations have been introduced in making tin plate. As a result, the number of pounds of tin per ton of tin plate fell by almost one half, from 32 in 1935 to 17 in 1949. More important, metals have been economized by the substitution of plastics. This has been particularly significant for nonferrous metal, in which the United States is relatively deficient. (See Figure 12.) Still another type of displacement is the substitution of domestic aluminum for imported copper.

The second reason is the growing importance of scrap as a source of metals for re-use. Copper production from old scrap reached one half of primary production and lead reached 80 per cent in 1950. (See Figure 13.)

Stocks of metals in old equipment and in debris from the process of production become an increasingly important source of raw materials as a community becomes wealthier and its scrap heap grows in size. The amount of metal available for reclamation varies, of course, with the use to which it was put. Industrial diamonds and the zinc used in paint pigment, for example, disappear almost entirely whereas 90 per cent of the lead used in type metal is customarily recovered.

It is estimated roughly that about one fourth of the copper used in the past forty years has been produced from old scrap.[4] The recovery factor for lead was between 40 and 50 per cent from 1939 to 1947 and for zinc considerably less. Scrap iron and steel account for roughly one fourth of total use. Recovery between 1939 and 1947 was unusually low because of large exports and loss through destruction. The collection and sale of scrap is an important industry in industrially developed countries. In the United

4. Charles White Merrill, *The Accumulation and Conservation of Metals-in-Use*, United Nations Conference on the Conservation and Utilization of Resources, UNESCO, New York, 1951, Vol. II, Tables 1, 2 and 3.

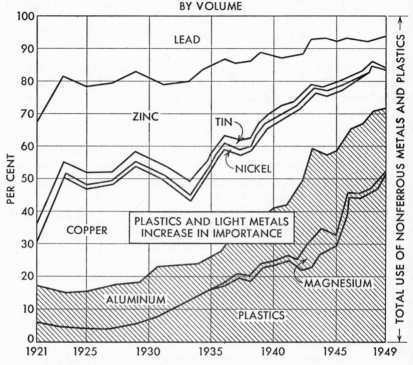

FIGURE 12. TECHNOLOGY BRINGS NEW MATERIALS TO THE FORE

Source: Resources for Freedom, The President's Materials Policy Commission, Vol. I, p. 11.

States 32,711,000 net tons of steel and iron scrap, 973,000 short tons of copper and 500,000 tons of lead were marketed in 1948, the total having a value of nearly $2 billion.

Economies in the use of metals and increasing use of scrap explain why both domestic production from new ores and imports have not expanded more rapidly. They do not necessarily explain, however, why imports of minerals have failed to increase as a proportion of domestic production. Such a development might have been expected to take place if the United States is indeed rapidly depleting its resources of minerals. The more important factor has been substitute materials.

Technical progress has not only produced man-made substitutes for natural resources and greater economy of use, but also new methods of extraction which have increased domestic supplies. As the United States exhausted its reserves of ores of the highest grade, new techniques of extraction were developed which lowered costs and allowed American

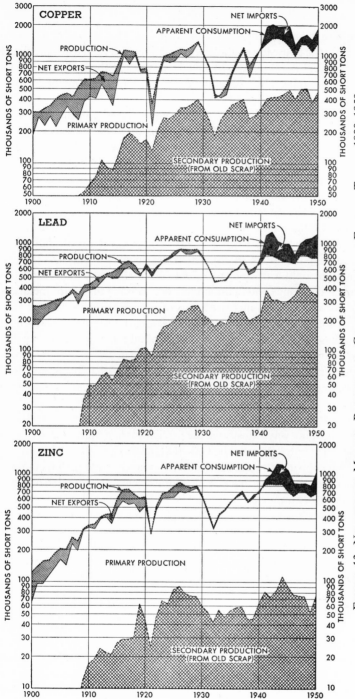

FIGURE 13. NONFERROUS METALS: PRODUCTION, CONSUMPTION AND FOREIGN TRADE, 1900–1950

Sources: Tables 51, 53 and 54.

producers to maintain their position vis-à-vis foreign producers though they were forced to use lower grade ores than they had been using previously.

Technological development in metals stands for three things: (1) new substitute materials, (2) economy of use, and (3) new methods of extraction.

In the minerals group imports there is great diversity in the behavior of individual items. The quantity of copper and tin imported was no greater in 1948 than in 1929. The index (1929 = 100) of the quantity of lead imports rose to 280, while that for zinc reached 1,824 in 1948. (See Table 49.) Rising prices brought the index of imported lead values to 790 in 1948 while that for zinc values reached 3,139 in the same year. (See Table 50.) The high index figures reflect the fact that imports were negligible in 1929. In the case of diamonds, on the other hand, the increase in the quantity index of imports to 1,460 in 1948 was largely offset by the fall of unit values, so that the index of import values increased only to 239. This represents not only a price change, but also a shift in composition from cut to uncut diamonds and diamond powder. Among the minor metals, the value of chrome imports increased much faster than manganese by value, but about the same by quantity. By and large, the largest rise was in the smaller items. This explains why the index of all mineral imports by value stood at only 255 in 1948.

The importance of this group and the diversity of influences affecting different minerals warrant an examination of the eight leading imports.

Copper

Copper in some ways illustrates the foreign trade pattern that we should expect for the United States. The United States has been the only industrial nation with copper resources more or less commensurate with its industry. Owing to the enormous increase in requirements, it shifted from a net exporter to a net importer with the advent of the second world war. This is precisely what one would expect, and the surprising thing is that the United States had not become increasingly dependent on imports at an earlier date.

Three developments explain why copper imports have not increased faster. One is the development of new techniques for treating ores, another is the increasing importance of old scrap metal as a source of supplies and the third is the decline in American exports.

By 1910 the main bodies of high-grade ore existing in the United States had been largely depleted and the main source of the metal was found in low-grade sulfide ores, the average copper content of which is, in some cases, even lower than one per cent. Exploitation of the reserves of sulfide ores was possible only with the development of techniques of mass mining,

TABLE 49

QUANTUM MINERAL IMPORTS, 1929, 1933, 1937, 1948 AND 1949

(Index: 1929=100)

	Unit	1929 Quantum	Index	1933 Quantum	Index	1937 Quantum	Index	1948 Quantum	Index	1949 Quantum	Index
Fuels											
Oil, crude and refined	1,000 bbl.	108,565	100	45,165	41.5	60,003	55.3	188,335	173.5	239,005	220.1
Metals and metallic ores											
Iron ore	1,000 long tons	3,139	100	861	27.4	2,442	77.8	6,109	194.6	7,402	235.8
Copper[a]	1,000 c.lb.	974,312	100	253,263	26.0	454,958	46.6	976,793	100.3	1,138,041	116.8
Lead[b]	1,000 c.lb.	238,294	100	67,815	28.5	32,599	13.7	666,080	279.5	830,375	348.5
Zinc	1,000 c.lb.	29,274	100	6,703	22.9	83,087	283.8	533,996	1,824.1	562,324	1,920.9
Bauxite	1,000 long tons	381	100	150	49.4	507	133.1	2,489	653.3	2,688	705.5
Tin, total	Long ton	87,255	100	63,741	73.1	88,266	101.2	87,438	100.2	99,046	113.5
Nickel	1,000 lb.	96,971	100	52,861	54.5	108,360	111.7	213,879	220.6	194,288	200.4
Manganese ore	1,000 c.lb.	724,450	100	316,864	43.7	1,040,595	143.6	1,405,553	194.0	1,347,293	186.0
Chrome or chromite	Long ton	317,630	100	116,511	36.7	247,056	77.8	607,788	191.4	476,420	150.0
Tungsten[c]	1,000 c.lb.	6,810	100	311	4.6	6,064	89.0	8,480	124.5	6,746	99.1
Cobalt ore and metal	1,000 lb.	1,241	100	838	67.5	1,660	133.8	7,834	631.3	7,526	606.4
Aluminum[d]	1,000 long tons	48,438	100	15,247	31.5	45,178	93.3	321,761	664.8	250,653	530.0
Nonmetals											
Mica	1,000 lb.	5,556	100	1,383	24.9	8,072	145.3	16,707	300.7	18,921	340.6
Asbestos[c]	Long ton	234,309	100	106,733	45.6	274,275	117.1	578,466	246.9	460,091	196.4
Diamonds	1,000 carat	818	100	471	57.6	2,501	305.7	11,947	1,460.5	7,350	898.5

Source: Unpublished tabulations by Office of International Trade, U.S. Department of Commerce, from census data.

a. Includes refined ingots, excludes manufactures.
b. Quantity figures include "lead manufactures, n.e.s."
c. Includes scrap and alloys.
d. Unmanufactured.

TABLE 50

VALUE OF MINERAL IMPORTS, 1929, 1933, 1937, 1948 AND 1949
(Dollar Figures in Millions; Index: 1929 = 100)

	1929 Value	1929 Index	1933 Value	1933 Index	1937 Value	1937 Index	1948 Value	1948 Index	1949 Value	1949 Index
Total	$540.6	100	$137.7	25	$341.4	63	$1,376.1	255	$1,466.4	271
Fuels	141.0	100	24.8	18	42.9	30	413.1	293	475.2	337
Oil, crude and refined	141.0	100	24.8	18	42.9	30	413.1	293	475.2	337
Metals and metallic ores	315.0	100	91.0	29	227.0	75	748.2	238	823.4	261
Iron ore	8.1	100	2.1	25	5.8	72	27.3	336	36.8	452
Copper[a]	153.7	100	14.8	10	52.6	34	203.0	132	219.1	143
Lead, total	13.5	100	2.6	20	1.5	11	106.4	790	121.8	905
Zinc and manufactures	1.3	100	.4	27	4.2	320	40.9	3,139	45.9	3,527
Bauxite	1.8	100	.9	51	3.6	206	15.8	902	16.4	932
Tin, total	91.9	100	51.3	56	104.4	114	176.2	192	212.3	231
Nickel	19.4	100	10.8	55	24.0	124	61.0	314	66.0	340
Manganese ore	8.5	100	3.0	36	10.7	127	23.3	276	26.8	317
Chrome or chromite	2.7	100	1.4	54	7.3	275	33.0	1,238	24.2	907
Tungsten ore and concentrates	2.5	100	.1	3	3.3	130	8.7	347	6.4	255
Cobalt ore and metal	1.8	100	.5	25	1.4	77	10.3	572	10.9	610
Aluminum and manufactures	9.9	100	3.2	32	8.2	84	42.2	426	36.8	362
Nonmetals	68.3	100	15.1	22	56.3	82	184.7	270	138.4	203
Mica	1.2	100	.3	23	1.7	138	12.9	1,062	17.2	1,418
Asbestos, unmanufactured	11.2	100	3.5	32	10.5	94	38.0	341	33.9	304
Diamonds	56.0	100	11.2	20	44.1	79	133.9	239	87.3	156
Miscellaneous[b]	16.3	100	6.9	43	15.2	94	30.2	186	29.4	181

Source: Unpublished tabulations by Office of International Trade, U.S. Department of Commerce, from census data.
a. Includes refined ingots, excludes manufactures.   b. Platinum-group metals, antimony, fluorspar, cryolite, mercury and graphite.
Note: Computations before rounding.

which involved a change from pit to open-face mining where large earth-moving machines could be used. Immense amounts of rock can be handled cheaply by this method, which is used with new mass methods of concentration through the flotation process.[5] These new mass mining techniques allowed the American producers to meet foreign competition and maintain their position in their own market.

The second factor depressing the level of copper imports is the growth in importance of secondary scrap copper as a raw material for new output. One quality of copper is its unusual durability and, as most of it is used in products which are not dissipated, it can be re-used more frequently than most metals. Data for the years 1910 to 1950 showing production from old scrap in relation to primary production are impressive. The proportion was about one eighth in 1910 and about one half in 1950. (See Table 51.) In 1936 Britain obtained about one third of her supply from reclaimed copper, according to the British Non-Ferrous Metals Federation.[6]

The last important factor depressing imports is the fact that American exports declined, thus causing a substitution of the domestic product for the imports which would otherwise have been required. From 1940 to 1950 imports were consistently above exports, an occurrence which had previously taken place only in the three depression years 1930–1932. In 1950 the United States imported almost 700,000 short tons of copper and exported about 200,000 tons. In 1925 imports had been about 325,000 tons and exports 525,000 tons. Thus, the United States shifted from a net exporter of about 200,000 tons in 1925 to a net importer of almost 500,000 in 1950. (See Table 51.) Furthermore, a shift in the composition of copper imports took place during this period. The proportion of imports of refined copper to unrefined copper was much greater in the later year. The value of imports, of course, increased by more than the increase in tonnage would indicate.

Under tariff item 1658, copper has free entry into the United States.[7] But imports have been subject to a discriminatory excise tax (Internal Revenue Code) since 1932. This tax was 4 cents a pound and was suspended during the war because the government was the sole importer. Under the General Agreement on Tariffs and Trade the rate was reduced to 2 cents. The tax was suspended from April 30, 1947 to June 30, 1950. The suspension was later extended from April 1, 1951 to February 15, 1953 as long as the price did not fall below 24 cents a pound.

5. Eric W. Zimmermann, *World Resources and Industries*, Harper, New York, 1951, p. 692.

6. Federal Trade Commission, *Report on the Copper Industry*, Washington, 1947, pp. 6 ff.; quoted by Zimmermann, *op. cit.*, pp. 696 ff.

7. A tariff imposed on copper in 1883 was repealed in 1884.

TABLE 51

U.S. COPPER PRODUCTION, CONSUMPTION AND TRADE, 1900–1950

(Thousands of Short Tons of Cu)

Year	Production Primary[a]	Production Secondary[b]	Net Exports[c]	Apparent Consumption	Price per Pound[d]
					(Cents)
1900	303	e	117[f]	186	16.54
1901	301	e	28[f]	273	16.40
1902	330	e	105[f]	225	11.96
1903	349	e	71[f]	278	13.62
1904	406	e	186	220	13.11
1905	444	e	163	281	15.98
1906	458	e	114	344	19.77
1907	424	e	129	295	20.86
1908	478	50[g]	222	256	13.39
1909	563	55[g]	181	383	13.11
1910	544	65	282	427	12.88
1911	557	76	226	407	12.55
1912	625	107	183	549	16.48
1913	618	92	260	450	15.52
1914	574	88	312	350	13.31
1915	744	121	186	679	17.47
1916	1,003	175	166	1,012	28.46
1917	948	195	292	851	29.19
1918	955	177	87	1,045	24.68
1919	606	153	44	715	18.90
1920	612	169	70	711	17.50
1921	233	132	140	225	12.65
1922	482	203	101	584	13.56
1923	739	271	77	933	14.61
1924	803	266	175	894	13.16
1925	839	291	198	932	14.16
1926	863	337	113	1,087	13.93
1927	825	339	180	984	13.05
1928	905	366	170	1,101	14.68
1929	998	404	13	1,389	18.23
1930	705	342	−32	1,079	13.11
1931	529	261	−13	803	8.24
1932	238	181	−31	450	5.67
1933	191	260	31	420	7.15
1934	237	311	100	448	8.53
1935	381	362	47	696	8.76
1936	615	383	74	924	9.58
1937	842	409	73	1,178	13.27
1938	558	267	174	651	10.10
1939	728	287	95	920	11.07

(Continued on following page)

TABLE 51 (*Continued*)

Year	Production Primary[a]	Production Secondary[b]	Net Exports[c]	Apparent Consumption	Price per Pound[d]
					(Cents)
1940	878	334	−56	1,268	11.40
1941	958	413	−568	1,939	11.87[h]
1942	1,080	427	−541	2,048	11.87[h]
1943	1,091	428	−414	1,933	11.87[h]
1944	973	457	−540	1,970	11.87[h]
1945	773	497	−712	1,982	11.87[h]
1946	609	407	−282	1,304	13.92[h]
1947	848	503	−208	1,559	21.15[h]
1948	835	506	−287	1,628	22.20
1949	753	383	−349	1,485	19.36
1950	907	475	−482	1,864	21.20

Source: U.S. Bureau of Mines, Office of Chief Economist.

a. Mine production, except for 1900–1905, when data are for smelter output (from domestic ores).

b. From old scrap only.

c. General imports include copper imported for immediate consumption plus material entering country under bond. Exports of domestic merchandise exclude "other manufactures of copper," for which figures for quantity are not available, 1926–1950; include copper sulfate 1913–1950; data not available prior to 1913.

d. Average prices of electrolytic copper in New York f.o.b. refinery, through August 1927. New York refinery equivalent thereafter.

e. Not available.

f. Imports of refined copper, plus estimated U.S. smelter production from imported pyrites, ores and matte (latter not available in foreign trade statistics).

g. Estimated.

h. Excludes government bonus payments to marginal producers.

Tin

Tin merits attention because it is one of the few natural resources for which the United States is wholly dependent on outside sources. Our consumption of primary tin was two fifths of the world's output in 1948. That year over one third of the tin consumed in the United States was used for tin plate. Because of extraordinary resistance to corrosion, acids, atmosphere and water, even a thin coating of tin provides a nontoxic protective covering on steel. "Through the ubiquitous tin can which is made of steel covered with a very thin coating, it (tin) has revolutionized the food habits and general living conditions of mankind."[8] The other main uses of tin are for making solder and for making brass and bronze.

The volume of tin imports has not increased very rapidly in the past because of the development of techniques for using tin more sparingly and

8. Zimmermann, *op. cit.*, p. 747.

because of substitutes. Tin requirements per ton of tin plate have been reduced by almost one half and a further reduction of similar proportions is in prospect.

The main technical development of the past few years has been the widespread introduction of the electrolytic process of making tin plate, which uses only about two fifths as much tin as does the older hot-dip method. The hot-dip method has also become more sparing of tin by about one eighth.

Between 1935 and 1949 the pounds of tin used per short ton of tin plate fell from 32 pounds to 17 pounds. (See Table 52.) This fall was primarily caused by the electrolytic process. After 1947, the tonnage of tin plate produced by the electrolytic process exceeded the hot-dipped tin plate. Thus far, the electrolytically plated tin can be used only for dry pack. If research now under way succeeds in adapting the technique to wet processed food, tin requirements will be still further reduced. A Tariff Commission study estimated that the electrolytic process saved 10 million pounds of tin in 1944.[9]

Except for tin plate, the principal use, the return on old scrap is quite high. Recovery amounts to 25–30 per cent on all uses.

The high price of tin relative to other metals has given an impetus to a search for tin substitutes, which has met with some success. Aluminum has been a competitor for many uses for which tin had formerly been used exclusively, such as foil and tubes. The possibility of further extensive displacement of tin by aluminum is a serious one. Cellophane also has displaced tin foil in some uses. The tin used in solder can be largely replaced by substitutes.

The status of the tin can itself is being challenged, although not yet seriously, by the development of frozen food in paper cartons.

Despite more economical methods of using tin and the development of substitutes, the volume of tin imports increased by 13 per cent between 1929 and 1949. A fraction of the tin imports are re-exported in the form of tin plate for, since 1941, the United States has become the world's principal source of tin plate. Annual exports of tin plate were approximately 600,000 tons from 1949 to 1952. This would involve less than 5,000 tons of tin content.

The value of tin imports has been altered in a way not reflected by the quantity of imports because of structural changes in trade necessitated by the war. Before the war tin ore both from Asia and Bolivia was smelted in England, Germany and the Low Countries. When the supplies from continental smelters were cut off during the war, the United States govern-

9. *Post-War Imports and Domestic Production of Major Commodities*, a Report (of the Tariff Commission) to the U.S. Senate, 78th Cong., 2d sess., p. 499.

TABLE 52

TIN CONTENT OF TIN PLATE PRODUCED IN THE UNITED STATES, 1935–1949

(Production in Thousands of Short Tons)

Year	Total Tin Plate (All Forms)		Tin Plate (Hot-Dipped)		Tin Plate (Electrolytic)		Waste (Waste, Strips, Cobbles, etc.)	
	Production	Pounds of Tin per Short Ton of Tin Plate	Production	Pounds of Tin per Short Ton	Production	Pounds of Tin per Short Ton	Production	Pounds of Tin per Short Ton
1935	1,927	31.7	1,927	31.7	—	—	—	—
1936	2,349	32.2	2,349	32.2	—	—	—	—
1937	2,820	31.2	2,724	31.2	—	—	95	30.5
1938	1,692	31.2	1,625	31.2	—	—	67	30.1
1939	2,645	31.0	2,546	31.1	—	—	98	30.0
1940	2,759	31.4	2,583	31.9	63	12.3	112	31.6
1941	3,388	29.7	3,189	30.1	88	11.6	112	30.9
1942	2,559	25.0	2,429	25.4	82	11.9	49	25.4
1943	2,077	23.4	1,685	25.8	328	12.2	65	19.2
1944	2,504	22.3	1,779	26.3	645	11.8	80	19.4
1945	2,656	21.9	1,709	27.2	860	11.9	87	18.4
1946	2,676	21.9	1,717	27.1	883	11.9	77	19.1
1947	3,731	18.6	1,872	26.5	1,735	10.3	125	15.1
1948	3,914	18.0	1,848	26.7	1,919	10.0	147	14.6
1949	3,864	17.2	1,648	26.7	2,031	9.7	185	14.4

Source: Bureau of Mines, July 1951, unpublished.

ment built the Longhorn smelter, the largest smelter in the world. This smelter handles concentrates chiefly from Bolivia, Indonesia and Thailand. The effect of smelting tin in this country is, of course, to reduce the dollar earnings from tin smelting in the rest of the world. Tin is duty-free.

Tin consumption will probably continue to rise very slowly. A decade or more may be required before imports rise above the 1950 level, which was unusually high owing to purchases for stockpiling.

Lead

The position of lead in the United States is similar to that of copper. The United States is the world's largest lead producer and yet has had an import surplus since 1940 equal to a third of its total consumption of lead.

The main uses of lead are for the manufacture of storage batteries, for cable coverings, for construction, for the anti-knock agent (tetraethyl lead) in gasoline and for pigments in paint. The past cheapness of lead has meant that few attempts have been made to find substitutes for it. Annual consumption has increased from 179,000 short tons in 1900 to 1,296,000 short tons in 1950. (See Table 53.) The very high price of lead which has prevailed since 1947 has stimulated attempts to use substitutes such as titanium in paints and cadmium in storage batteries. Plastics are also being substituted for lead in cable coverings and in paints.

The expansion in domestic production of primary lead was less than twofold in the first half of this century and did not keep pace with domestic demand. In 1900 the United States produced about 270,000 short tons of primary lead and exported about 82,000 tons. As domestic demand expanded, exports fell and imports rose until net imports reached 518,000 tons in 1950. (Figure 13.)

The third main source of lead, beside primary production and importation, is the recovery of secondary lead, which accounted in recent years for nearly one third of total supplies and from 1946 to 1948 exceeded the tonnage of primary production.

The importance of secondary lead arises from the possibility of reclaiming it after it has been used in its two primary uses, batteries and cables. With expected relatively rapid growth of these end uses, recovery of old scrap will continue to expand more rapidly than total consumption.

The inability of primary lead production to keep pace with the increase in demand in recent years indicates that this industry may have reached its fullest expansion, and that imports and secondary lead production will have to be relied upon to accommodate the further expansion of demand.

No reliable estimates exist of the amount of reserves of lead ore in the United States, for mining firms themselves are primarily concerned with calculations of ore reserves only for the period immediately ahead. Govern-

TABLE 53

U.S. LEAD PRODUCTION, CONSUMPTION AND TRADE, 1900–1950

(*Thousands of Short Tons of Pb*)

Year	Production Primary[a]	Secondary[b]	Net Exports[c]	Apparent Consumption	Price per Pound[d]
					(*Cents*)
1900	271	e	82	179	4.41
1901	269	e	89	180	4.36
1902	277	e	63	214	4.10
1903	290	e	54	236	4.26
1904	309	e	62	247	4.32
1905	319	e	24	295	4.70
1906	338	e	4	334	5.66
1907	365	23	29	359	5.35
1908	330	16	66	280	4.23
1909	385	37	62	360	4.30
1910	383	49	49	383	4.49
1911	427	48	85	390	4.46
1912	442	59	50	451	4.48
1913	483	64	32	515	4.40
1914	505	54	72	487	3.87
1915	542	69	116	495	4.67
1916	601	85	99	587	6.83
1917	629	82	84	627	8.71
1918	562	85	95	552	7.46
1919	430	107	31	514	5.81
1920	497	110	−68	675	8.08
1921	415	91	−51	557	4.55
1922	478	140	−23	641	5.71
1923	547	171	9	709	7.25
1924	596	180	21	755	8.08
1925	684	200	75	809	9.02
1926	684	244	20	908	8.42
1927	666	243	76	833	6.75
1928	633	272	73	832	6.31
1929	654	274	42	886	6.83
1930	558	225	20	763	5.52
1931	405	207	0	612	4.24
1932	293	175	11	457	3.18
1933	273	198	3	468	3.87
1934	287	183	−8	478	3.86
1935	331	238	−5	574	4.06
1936	373	231	8	596	4.71
1937	465	242	11	696	6.01
1938	370	198	36	532	4.74
1939	414	211	55	570	5.05

(*Continued on following page*)

TABLE 53 (*Continued*)

Year	Production Primary[a]	Production Secondary[b]	Net Exports[c]	Apparent Consumption	Price per Pound[d]
					(*Cents*)
1940	457	227	−95	779	5.18
1941	461	380	−415	1,256	5.79
1942	496	309	−524	1,329	6.48[f]
1943	453	311	−334	1,098	6.50[f]
1944	417	290	−319	1,026	6.50[f]
1945	391	310	−330	1,031	6.50[f]
1946	336	345	−136	817	8.11[f]
1947	384	445	−221	1,050	14.67[f]
1948	391	433	−332	1,156	18.04
1949	410	364	−414	1,188	15.36
1950	430	348	−518	1,296	13.30

Source: U.S. Bureau of Mines, Office of Chief Economist.

a. Mine production of recoverable lead. Production of refined lead from domestic ores and base bullion, 1900–1906.

b. From old scrap only. The figures for 1907–1938 are based on the assumption that 88 per cent of the total secondary lead recovered came from old scrap. Old scrap constitutes a net addition to lead supplies for the year.

c. Imports for consumption include miscellaneous products such as babbitt metal, type metal and antimonial lead. Exports are of domestic merchandise.

d. Average price of pig lead in New York.

e. Not available.

f. Excludes government bonus payments to marginal producers.

mental officials estimated reserves existing in January 1944 of 6,580,000 short tons of metallic lead. At the 1950 rate of extraction such a reserve would last for only fifteen years.[10]

The import duty on lead of ¾ cents per pound was suspended for specified periods.

Nickel

The United States has no domestic natural resources of nickel. Only a few tons of nickel are produced as a by-product of copper refining. But eight or nine thousand short tons of secondary nickel are reclaimed annually. This amounts to about 10 per cent of annual consumption.

The main use of nickel is as an alloy for steel. Nickel imparts to its alloys strength and lightness that are especially valuable in armor plate. It is also alloyed with other metals and is used in electroplating anodes and solutions. Consumption is especially high in time of war.

10. Joint Staffs of U.S. Geological Survey and Bureau of Mines, *The Mineral Position of the United States*, p. 257, quoted in Zimmermann, *op. cit.*, p. 740.

Imports of nickel into the United States declined for four years after 1943 but partly recovered in 1948 to 20 per cent above the previous years. The nickel content of imports in 1943, the peak year, was 245 million pounds as compared with 194 million pounds in 1948.[11] In 1929, 83 million pounds were imported. In all these years Canada, which produces about 80 per cent of the world output of nickel, was the chief supplier of nickel to the United States. During the period 1929 to 1948 the proportion of nickel oxide in total nickel imports increased markedly and that of ore and matte fell, their absolute volume remaining the same in 1948 as in 1929.[12]

The twofold expansion in the use of nickel in the period under examination is a little larger than the expansion in gross national product in physical terms. The increase was not as large as the expansion in the use of aluminum because the role of nickel is not so closely tied up with new industries such as aviation. Furthermore, new alloys have constantly been appearing which compete with nickel. On the other hand research, undertaken especially by the International Nickel Company of Canada, has constantly brought out new uses for the metal.

Nickel is duty-free.

Zinc

The United States is the world's leading producer of slab zinc. In 1949–1951 the output of United States smelters averaged about 40 per cent of the world output of zinc. However, not all this zinc is produced from domestic ores. In 1949–1951 approximately 30 per cent of the ore used was imported, chiefly from Mexico. Old scrap is a comparatively unimportant source of materials. It has rarely amounted to as much as 15 per cent of primary zinc production. Reclamation from old scrap is, of course, the relevant quantity when estimating yearly supplies. Secondary zinc made from new or currently produced scrap is not a net addition to supplies of that year.

Zinc is the mineral which is used to galvanize iron and steel to protect them from rusting, and the galvanizing industry is, in normal times, the main consumer of zinc. In 1948, approximately 370,000 tons of zinc were used in the United States galvanizing industry out of total consumption of 853,000 short tons. The manufacture of die castings is customarily the next largest zinc consumer, followed by brass products. In 1948 these two uses consumed 231,000 and 109,000 tons, respectively. In wartime the brass industry expands relatively to the others and becomes the major zinc consumer.[13]

11. *Minerals Yearbook, 1948*, p. 885.
12. *Ibid.*
13. *Ibid.*, p. 1296.

New uses which consume large quantities of zinc are not developing rapidly. Neither, on the other hand, is zinc being replaced by substitutes nor are technical developments making for more economical use of it. A moderate expansion in the consumption of zinc has taken place since 1929 but it has been much less than the nearly twofold expansion in the production of goods and services in general. The period of rapid expansion in the use of zinc was in the first quarter of the century.

As in the case of other base metals, the United States became an importing nation only in the late 1930s and markedly so only with the advent of the war. Before 1936 the United States had always had an export surplus. (See Table 54.) In recent years net imports supplied about one fourth of total domestic consumption. (See Figure 13.) In 1948 zinc ore and concentrates used in domestic smelting amounted to 264,000 short tons of zinc content. Eighty-three per cent of the 93,000 tons of slab zinc imports originated in Canada.[14]

The explanation for the increase in imports into the United States is to be found in the fact that American consumption is equal to nearly half of the total world smelter production of zinc. Despite the fact that the greatest ore fields in the world are located in the United States, domestic production of the raw materials including secondary zinc accounts for only two thirds of requirements. Further expansion of consumption will probably need to be supplied largely from foreign ores. Consumption is expected to rise less than half as fast as income, as it has since the 1920s.

The duty of $3/5$ cents per pound on ore and $7/10$ cents per pound on slab was suspended for specified periods.

Industrial Diamonds

As in the case of tin, the United States is dependent on foreign sources for its supply of diamonds.[15] Unlike tin, diamonds are as yet not being displaced by substitutes but, instead, the uses to which they can be put are increasing. Extensive experimentation in industrial laboratories in the United States and in the Diamond Research Laboratory at Johannesburg is increasing the number of possible applications and promoting more efficient recovery methods.

Imports of industrial diamonds increased greatly from about 50,000 carats in 1929 to 12 million carats in 1951. At the same time, however, the unit value dropped from $87 per carat to less than $4 per carat. This drastic decline in unit value is due mainly to the greater importance of diamond

14. *Ibid.*, p. 1306.
15. Small quantities of diamonds are received from Puerto Rico.
Since this chapter was written the General Electric Company has announced successful production of artificial diamonds. *Science News Letter*, February 26, 1955; *Time*, February 21, 1955.

TABLE 54

U.S. ZINC PRODUCTION, CONSUMPTION AND TRADE, 1900–1950

(*Thousands of Short Tons of Pb*)

Year	Production Primary[a]	Secondary[b]	Net Exports[c]	Apparent Consumption	Price per Pound[d]
					(Cents)
1900	124	e	58	66	4.24
1901	141	e	45	96	3.89
1902	157	e	61	96	4.64
1903	159	e	45	114	5.25
1904	187	e	51	136	4.97
1905	204	e	43	161	5.79
1906	200	e	58	142	6.10
1907	260	6	37	229	5.90
1908	235	6	44	197	4.62
1909	306	12	7	311	5.39
1910	328	17	18	327	5.42
1911	334	19	39	314	5.70
1912	385	24	16	393	6.93
1913	413	22	27	408	5.61
1914	416	21	86	351	5.11
1915	588	27	118	497	14.16
1916	703	29	160	572	13.57
1917	714	29	210	533	8.93
1918	636	30	117	549	8.04
1919	549	62	159	452	7.04
1920	588	45	124	509	7.77
1921	257	25	−8	290	4.67
1922	472	47	43	476	5.74
1923	611	67	72	606	6.66
1924	638	63	89	612	6.35
1925	711	85	175	621	7.66
1926	775	91	164	702	7.37
1927	719	79	111	687	6.25
1928	695	75	48	722	6.03
1929	724	74	36	762	6.49
1930	595	60	19	636	4.56
1931	410	53	8	455	3.64
1932	285	42	9	318	2.88
1933	384	55	4	435	4.03
1934	439	47	11	475	4.16
1935	518	54	4	568	4.33
1936	576	58	−6	640	4.90
1937	626	59	−35	720	6.52
1938	517	45	−5	567	4.61
1939	584	45	−47	676	5.12

(*Continued on following page*)

TABLE 54 (*Continued*)

Year	Production Primary[a]	Production Secondary[b]	Net Exports[c]	Apparent Consumption	Price per Pound[d]
					(*Cents*)
1940	665	64	41	688	6.34
1941	749	81	−88	918	7.48
1942	768	73	−176	1,017	8.25[f]
1943	744	84	−464	1,292	8.25[f]
1944	719	113	−452	1,284	8.25[f]
1945	614	91	−414	1,119	8.25[f]
1946	575	77	−272	854	8.73[f]
1947	638	75	−133	846	10.50[f]
1948	630	74	−149	853	13.58
1949	593	52	−162	807	12.15
1950	618	75	−382	1,075	13.87

Source: U.S. Bureau of Mines, Office of Chief Economist.

a. Mine production of recoverable zinc. Smelter production from domestic ores, 1900–1906.

b. Old scrap only. 1907–1938, old scrap calculated at 25 per cent of total secondary.

c. Imports for consumption include pigments; exclude manufactures of zinc, for which weight not available. Exports of domestic merchandise. Includes slab zinc made from foreign ore.

d. Annual average, Prime Western slab zinc, East St. Louis.

e. Not available.

f. Excludes government bonus payments of marginal producers.

powder, which is a low-priced product. Prices were cut at the beginning of the war but had substantially regained their prewar levels by 1946. Sales of industrial diamonds to the United States reached their peak during 1944 as might have been expected. A brief fall in imports of industrial diamonds occurred in 1946 and 1947, followed by importation in 1948 of 11 million carats valued at $33 million. The very large sales of diamonds beginning in 1948 were made to American industries, which purchased a normal amount, and also to the American government, which purchased large quantities of diamond powder in London for its stockpile.

Iron Ore

Although imports of iron ore have been small, they are increasing rapidly. Owing to depletion of high-grade ore reserves in the Mesabi Range, the prospects are that imports will continue to rise at a rapid rate. While domestic reserves of low-grade ores, mainly taconite, are extensive, it will probably prove more economical to exploit the immense ore bodies currently under development in the Quebec-Labrador area of Canada, in Venezuela and in Nigeria.

Iron ore is duty-free.

American industry continues to show a gargantuan appetite for iron and steel despite competition from the light metals and plastics. Potential expansion of iron ore imports appears to be greater than for other leading metals.

Aluminum

During the peak war years consumption of aluminum exceeded one million tons annually, most of which was produced at home. After a drastic cut-back at the end of the war, production is again rising and may be expected to exceed copper in less than a decade.

The growing importance of aluminum is well known. It has substituted for many uses of nonferrous metals and will doubtless continue to do so. Moreover, it is expected to displace steel and wood on an increasing scale. The principal uses are in durable goods, construction and transport.

Aluminum has the strength of steel with about one third the weight. It is almost as good as copper as a conductor of electricity and heat and has high resistance to corrosion. Production can be expanded almost without limit, requiring only abundant electric power although imports of bauxite are needed to keep costs low.

The use of aluminum is expected to rise much faster than that of other major metals and probably will increase several times as fast as income. It would be economical to import more aluminum from Canada. The limiting factor should be military security.

The duty is 1½ cents per pound on ingots and 3 cents per pound on plates, sheets and bars.

Dependence on Mineral Imports

The United States is fully self-sufficient in coal, sulfur, molybdenum, magnesium, phosphate and potash. By contrast, we are almost entirely dependent on imports of tin, nickel, manganese, chromite, asbestos and mica. These minerals are not competitive with domestic production.

The United States produced 10–25 per cent of requirements of cobalt and the platinum group, which includes antimony, mercury, fluorspar, cryolite and graphite.

Many minerals are on the strategic and critical materials list, which has been greatly expanded. The Munitions Board is stockpiling a score of minerals including minor items.

Some minor metals, like manganese, play a strategic role in industrial processes. While these imports are of critical importance because the United States is almost entirely dependent on outside sources, the dollar values are not large. Imports of manganese, chrome, cobalt and tungsten amounted to only $75 million in 1949 so that even a large percentage increase will not affect total imports substantially.

The Tariff

Duties on minerals are not highly restrictive at the present time and should be *gradually* eliminated. The military security argument for protection neglects the fact that better means are available for obtaining marginal supplies. We should, indeed, look to our security but direct subsidies to high-cost producers are cheaper than protective tariffs, which subsidize all producers. Moreover, in the case of natural resources which face depletion it is doubly important that we know more precisely what we are doing than is possible when subsidies in the form of general tariffs are used.

Most dutiable minerals bear specific duties, which have been greatly reduced by the rise in prices. In addition, most dutiable items have been cut 50 per cent by trade agreements. Duties on copper, lead, steel scrap and aluminum scrap have been suspended for various periods during and since the war.

Tin, nickel, iron and antimony ore, cobalt and industrial diamonds are duty-free. The ad valorem rate at prices in recent years on leading mineral imports ranges from about 5 to 15 per cent. On semifabricated forms the duty usually runs appreciably higher. Where foreign supplies are regulated by monopoly as in the case of mercury, retention of duties may be justified.

The order of magnitude of the increase in imports which might result from elimination of duties is believed to be about 10 per cent.

The Future of Imports

The advent of war in Korea inflated the demand for mineral imports. Production of armaments chews up metals somewhat faster than a civilian boom although the more important effect may have been private inventory buying and public stockpiling. The present evaluation is concerned with the long-term outlook and not with the build-up period of the defense program started by the Korean War. Both imports and production have been stimulated by stockpiling and by defense spending.

Mineral imports including stockpiling amounted to $1.4 billion and $1.5 billion in 1948 and 1949, respectively. As a result of accelerated stockpiling, increased demand and higher prices, the value of mineral imports averaged $1.8 billion in 1950–1951. Imports rose 28 per cent from 1949 to 1951 compared with an increase of 27 per cent in domestic production (new series). Further growth of domestic consumption will support the trend toward smaller exports of metals. A 60 per cent peacetime expansion in gross national product might double or triple mineral imports from 1948–

1949 levels. Petroleum would account for the major part of such an increase and for this reason the next chapter is devoted to it. The future of copper imports depends upon the adequacy and quality of domestic ores compared with foreign ones. Already the American reserves are of a lower grade than those of major producing areas abroad such as the Belgian Congo. However, technological developments have so far made it feasible to exploit increasingly low-grade ore in the United States. Increased use of scrap will also moderate the rate of growth of imports.

American consumption of copper in 1940 was 36 per cent of world consumption and its production was 33 per cent of world production although United States reserves of ore which it is thought feasible to use under present conditions were only 26 per cent of total reserves. This means that the United States is using up its reserves more rapidly than the rest of the world and will be pushed to using lower-grade ores sooner, thus increasing its costs of production relative to costs of foreign producers.

The rise in relative cost may be retarded, as in the past, by new discoveries and by technical progress of a type more suited to American than foreign conditions, thus enabling American copper producers to maintain their position in the domestic market. But such innovations cannot be counted on. Although new discoveries in the past have about kept pace with the growth of production, exhaustion of good ores in the United States and its effect on foreign trade are already evident in the decline of American exports. More rapid exhaustion of reserves in the United States than abroad combined with their generally lower grade indicates that we can expect the present high level of imports to continue and increase.

Tin is a prime example of an import which has been adversely affected by technological progress, for it has suffered both from the development of substitutes and from more economical ways of using it.

Lead, too, has been affected by the development of substitutes, but these are of more recent origin and the displacement has not been as great. There are two further factors moderating the expansion of lead imports in the future. The first is that old scrap is of more importance for this metal than for others and is likely to increase in importance as the price of lead rises. The second is that lead is not closely associated with the most rapidly expanding parts of our economy; rather its uses are in industries which are established and unlikely to expand as rapidly as the average.

The development of highly delicate and refined industrial processes and the increasing use of very hard materials indicate that the demand for industrial diamonds will continue to increase rapidly.

Zinc, like lead, is not closely associated with new industries. On the other hand metal substitutes have failed to appear. This, together with the unimportance of old scrap and especially with the exhaustion of lower cost reserves in the United States, indicates that further increases in consumption will have to be satisfied by imports.

Iron ore imports in 1948 amounted to only 6 million tons. Barring technological displacement, requirements are expected to rise in proportion to the growth of gross national product. A 60 per cent increase in gross national product would increase iron ore requirements to 165 million tons, about half of which would represent import requirements owing to exhaustion of rich domestic ores. Provided foreign reserves are developed, imports might reach $400 million compared to $27 million in 1948.

Aluminum is vital in the new and rapidly expanding industries of aircraft production and electricity and is also being substituted for some uses of other metals, such as copper and steel.

Increasing use of aluminum should bring about increased imports from Canada as it did during the war. It will also increase imports of the raw material, bauxite, which amounted to $16 million in 1948 and which could easily rise about twice as fast as income.

In sum, the increase in mineral imports of petroleum, iron ore, ferroalloys and nonferrous metals that can be anticipated with a 60 per cent peacetime expansion of gross national output amounts to $1.5 to $2.5 billion, which represents a two to threefold increase over 1948 levels. Petroleum accounts for a major part of the estimated total increase. If the petroleum projection should prove wrong owing to the discovery of wholly unanticipated domestic fields or subsidy of synthetic fuel as a national policy, mineral imports might rise no faster than income. And if steel should be displaced by Fiberglas and aluminum in the next generation as nonferrous metals have been displaced by plastics in the past generation, imports might rise by less than income. In addition to the factors already mentioned which have held down the expansion of imports, American designers may well reduce requirements by "engineering out" of the scarce metals. Thus, the future of mineral imports is highly dependent on what happens in the field of technology.

Iron ore and petroleum are the two mineral imports with the greatest potential for future expansion. In both instances, the potential rise is definitely circumscribed by low-grade domestic resources which it would be feasible to exploit at prices somewhat above current levels. Although the rich deposits of the Mesabi Range are nearing exhaustion, virtually unlimited taconite ores limit the increase in the price of foreign iron ores and, with advancing technology, could become competitive. On the side of consumption, the growth of iron and steel may suffer from substitution of Fiberglas, which has already been used by the automobile industry to produce sports models.[16]

16. Judging by the extremely high ratio of price to earning for shares of Owens-Corning Fiberglas Company, investors are betting heavily on the future of Fiberglas.

Potential imports of petroleum, too, are circumscribed by the real possibility of technological change which will utilize domestic instead of foreign resources. In fact, if the government were to provide capital at low interest rates, shale oil could be produced currently at competitive prices according to some authorities.

Attempts to project the future of imports have little predictive value. They may serve, however, as a wholesome antidote to popular misconceptions.

President's Materials Policy Commission

A draft of the present chapter was completed before the *Report of the President's Materials Policy Commission* (the Paley Report) was available and has been permitted to stand, substantially unchanged, as an independent effort at appraisal. The present chapter mentioned that mineral imports might increase two or three times as fast as income; the Report to the President, which is far more detailed and authoritative, projected an increase of 250 per cent in minerals imports with a 100 per cent rise in income. There is, however, a decided difference in tone in that the present chapter has emphasized more than does the Report that technological change might easily result in a much more moderate rise in imports.

The projections of the Paley Report must, of course, be interpreted in the light of the assumptions that were made in deriving them. "Changes in technology which appear highly likely have been projected as taking place within the next twenty-five years; *others, whose 'wrinkles' have yet to be ironed out, have not been allowed for at all.*"[17] While this is a prudent assumption for any single commodity, *it would be surprising if it should prove correct for all materials.*

A chart in the Commission's Report shows the relative growth of plastics and light metals at the expense of copper, lead and zinc. Taking the total use of plastics and nonferrous metals as 100 per cent, plastics jumped from 5 per cent of total use in 1925 to over 50 per cent in 1949. The older nonferrous metals, on the other hand, fell from more than 80 per cent of total use in 1925 to less than 30 per cent in 1949, while the light metals, aluminum and magnesium, rose from roughly 10 to 20 per cent of total use. (See Figure 12.)

The focus of the Paley Report differs from that of the present study. The Commission was concerned with the adequacy of material resources in the free world for future expansion of living standards and for *national* security. Consequently, a dualism pervades the Report, which emphasizes expansion of both domestic production and imports.

The detailed analysis of the Paley Report brings out a relationship that

17. *Resources for Freedom: The Outlook for Key Commodities*, Vol. II, June 1952, p. 118. (Italics supplied.)

is easily overlooked, namely, that consumption of all minerals is now expected to rise less rapidly than income. Thus, with a 100 per cent rise in income from a 1950 base, projected consumption of copper, lead and zinc rises only 40–50 per cent while tin rises only slightly. Aluminum, on the other hand, rises almost 300 per cent. The Report's projection of imports is a residual derived by subtracting estimated domestic production from projected consumption. On this basis, imports of copper, lead and zinc would need to rise by 60 to 125 per cent from the 1950 level.

Implication of Technology for Foreign Trade

No attempt has been made to consider the effect on the pattern of metal consumption of current developments in supersonic speed which require resistance to very high temperatures.

Technological change may lead to an increase in imports as with uranium and cobalt, as well as to displacement as with copper, tin, lead and zinc. Is the implication of technological advance neutral in this respect for a country with the vast capital resources and varied natural resources of the United States?

The evidence seems to be that in the past generation it has not been neutral. Displacement of imported materials appears to have exceeded the new imports resulting from technological advance.[18] The importance of capital costs in making synthetics and the substitution of chemical materials for natural resources afford some basis for supposing that an advanced capital-rich nation which is richly endowed with natural resources may show a very general tendency to reduce the relative importance of its gross imports of raw materials.

At the same time, the shift from a net exporter to a net importer of materials emphasizes the growing absolute dependence of the United States on imported materials. Despite relative displacement by plastics, imports of nonferrous metals have shown rapid growth.

18. Cf. technological displacement of agricultural imports, Chapter 13.

Chapter 16

Petroleum Imports

PETROLEUM IMPORTS have a greater potential for future increase than imports of other commodities and for this reason are singled out for special attention. They had already increased more than sixfold from 1939 to 1952. Under favorable circumstances, petroleum imports could increase by as much as one billion dollars within a decade. No other import with a potential of this magnitude is visible.

Petroleum imports will be strongly affected by three of the most important factors, in addition to commercial policy, which affect the future of imports in general. These are (1) the rate of growth of the home economy, (2) depletion of the nation's natural resources, and (3) technological developments. Unlike the metals, energy resources cannot be reclaimed and used again.

The United States is the largest consumer of oil in the world and consumption is expected to double in the next twenty-five years. The potential growth of petroleum imports is indicated by the fact that this nation consumes more of the world's output than it possesses resources. Demand has outstripped production since 1948 and America has again become a net importer. (See Figure 14.) Gross imports in 1952 amounted to about 14 per cent of domestic production. Nonetheless, as with other natural resources, technological developments may reduce the apparent need for greatly increased imports. The industry estimates that it would become feasible to produce crude oil from domestic shales with present techniques at somewhat higher prices. Some experts hold that shale oil could be produced currently at competitive prices.[1] Reduction of the cost of hydrogenation and synthesis of coal could provide still another domestic source of supply.

Prospective Shortage

American production may continue to rise for many years, but at rising costs. Foreign production is expected to rise faster than domestic.

Rapid increase in the demand for petroleum products, continual fluctuations in the discovery of oil fields and technical changes in methods of processing crude oil have combined to create an unstable industry and widely changing expectations as to future supplies. The vital importance of

1. It depends on the rate of amortization on the huge capital investment required.

317

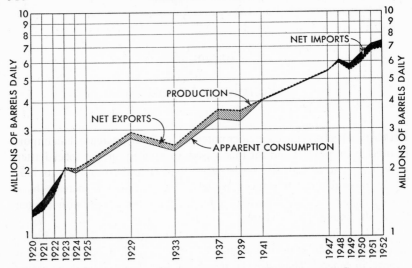

FIGURE 14. CRUDE PETROLEUM AND PRODUCTS[a]: PRODUCTION,[b] CONSUMPTION
AND FOREIGN TRADE, SELECTED YEARS, 1920–1952

Source: Appendix 5.
a. Mainly imports of residual oil.   b. Crude oil and natural gas liquids.

petroleum to the economy and to military power has given great importance
to the vigorous controversy about public policy affecting conservation and
imports. The importance of import policy is enhanced by the fact that the
value of oil imports can rise rapidly, and unless interfered with, oil may
become of dominating importance in American imports.

Imports are rising because for seventy years domestic reserves have been
depleted more rapidly than foreign reserves. Agreements within the domestic industry and between industry and government regulating output and
maintaining inefficient producers in operation also contribute to higher
domestic costs and attract imports.

Consumption of oil is growing rapidly in the United States. The automobile and the airplane use increasing amounts; railroads have shifted to
diesel engines. There has also been considerable conversion from coal for
space heating and power. An increase in imports of over a billion dollars
a year is easily possible within two decades. If consumption were to dupli-
cate the expansion of the 1930s with no further growth in domestic production, imports would increase to more than 500 million barrels within one
decade.[2]

2. At the Oklahoma-Kansas price in 1950 of $2.57 per barrel, this is more than a billion
dollar import. Cf. testimony before the Senate Special Committee Investigating Petroleum Resources, June 27, 1945, cited by Leonard M. Fanning, *American Oil Operations
Abroad*, McGraw-Hill, New York, 1947, p. 133.

Petroleum is extractable from a wide variety of sources including crude petroleum in subterranean pools, shale, coal and methane gas. These sources provide an abundance of liquid fuels in the United States for many decades—but at a wide range of costs. In the present state of technical knowledge, the cost differences favor the exploitation of crude petroleum as the unique source of the liquid fuel.[3] Shrinkage of low-cost sources of fuels and lubricants relative to the growing demand is the meaning of the prospective "oil shortage." Imports and competing sources of fuel tend to place a ceiling on the future rise in prices. Production of crude oil both in the Middle East and in Venezuela has increased in relative importance.

Foreign Sources

Early in its industrial history the United States acquired a gargantuan appetite for oil and the production to satisfy it. During the ten years immediately following the Civil War, American petroleum met the requirements of domestic consumption and upwards of 80 per cent of foreign requirements as well.[4] By the end of World War I, the United States had faced the heavy consumption of mechanized warfare and oil-powered navies. A petroleum shortage, it was then believed, had arrived in the United States.

The United States Geological Survey pointed out that the United States was consuming twice as much oil as the rest of the world combined, although it owned no more than one seventh of the world's reserves. The Bureau of Mines believed that domestic production would decline in a period of two to five years after the war with the result that domestic oil fields would be unable to meet home demands under existing methods of utilization and manufacture. This fear of shortage was combined with fear of a petroleum monopoly in the hands of a British-French-Dutch combination.

These projections were badly mistaken. Vast new fields were discovered at home. Moreover, the over-all situation was conducive to the expansion of the American petroleum industry abroad.[5]

The federal government paved the way for a broad expansion of American participation in foreign petroleum production by providing strong

3. A small amount of gasoline is produced currently by the process of synthesizing methane from natural gas and oxygen, but processes for the liquification of shale and coal have not yet put the solids into competition with crude petroleum. There is, however, a difference of opinion as to the economy of production from shale.

4. Fanning, *op. cit.*, p. 225. In 1865 U.S. exports were 73.6 per cent of "indicated total foreign domestic demand," but were above 80 per cent in each of the following nine years. Part of Fanning's data consist of private information and estimates.

5. *Ibid.*, pp. 3–4. This account relies heavily on Fanning, who made full use of the Report of the Group on American Petroleum Interests in Foreign Countries submitted to the Senate Special Committee Investigating Petroleum Resources under the chairmanship of Senator Joseph C. O'Mahoney.

TABLE 55

INVESTMENTS OF AMERICAN OIL COMPANIES IN FOREIGN COUNTRIES BY MAJOR
ACTIVITIES, 1935–1941

(*Millions*)

Activity	1935	1937	1939	1941
Total gross amounts	$2,062	$2,398	$2,499	$2,329
Exploration and production	517	703	876	940
Refining	301	312	365	356
Transportation	112	103	145	145
Marketing	743	728	791	588
All others	390	510	322	301

Source: Leonard M. Fanning, *American Oil Operations Abroad*, McGraw-Hill, New York, 1947, p. 193.
Note: Computations before rounding.

diplomatic support.[6] Prior to the outbreak of World War I, American interests had been operating in only two foreign countries—Mexico and Rumania.[7] In the period following the war, American geologists and technicians participated in the development of many of the most productive foreign fields and were active in nearly all areas outside the Soviet Union.[8]

Foreign Investment

New private foreign investment by oil companies today doubtless serves the national interest, particularly in the Middle East, which is directly exposed to any Soviet expansion. It is estimated that 95 per cent of American imports of crude and 70 per cent of imports of refined oil are due to the investments of private American companies.[9]

During the twenty-year period 1919–1939, the investments of American oil companies in foreign countries increased from roughly $400 million to $2,500 million. Investment initially was directed largely to the expansion of marketing facilities, but in later years a large share was devoted to exploration and development of production. Even during the period of relatively slow industrial growth in the late 1930s, gross assets employed by American oil companies in foreign areas increased by one fourth, or about $500 mil-

6. There had been some support for the creation of a quasi-governmental corporation for this purpose, but the idea was dropped. This bit of history was repeated during World War II when it was proposed that the United States buy the companies that held the rights to develop the oil of Saudi Arabia and Bahrein. Both this and the substitute proposal that the federal government finance the construction of pipeline in Saudi Arabia were abandoned in favor of diplomatic cooperation, which produced the Anglo-American Oil Agreement of 1945. For an account of this episode in petroleum diplomacy, see Herbert Feis, *Seen from E.A.*, Knopf, New York, 1947, Episode Number Two.

7. The term "interest" refers to both American corporations and locally organized subsidiaries of such corporations whether or not there are material minority interests.

8. They assisted in the development of Soviet production but as hired technicians rather than entrepreneurs.

9. *Survey of Current Business*, December 1953.

TABLE 56

PRODUCTION OF PETROLEUM BY AREAS, SELECTED YEARS, 1933–1949

(*Millions of Barrels*)

Year	Africa	Asia, Middle and Far East	Europe (including U.S.S.R.)	North America	South America	World
1933	2	115	215	941	169	1,442
1939	5	207	275	1,315	284	2,086
1945	9	215	198	1,766	406	2,595
1946	9	271	208	1,791	467	2,747
1947	9	338	236	1,920	519	3,022
1948	14	480	270	2,087	575	3,425
1949	16	587	287	1,922	567	3,389

Source: *Causes of Unemployment in Coal and Other Specified Industries*, S. Rept. No. 2042, 81st Cong., 2d sess., 1950, p. 85 (Neely Hearings).

lion. Investment in exploration and production increased even more rapidly—from roughly one fourth in 1935 to approximately 40 per cent of the total in 1941. (See Table 55.)

Investment by American oil companies accounts for the bulk of private foreign investment since the second world war. The general effect of heavy investment, whether American or foreign, in oil concessions abroad has been to increase the relative importance of foreign production, although as yet the shift has not been substantial. North American production, of which all but a small fraction is accounted for by the United States, still amounted to well over half of total output in 1949. (See Table 56.)

The *potential* contribution of foreign production to world supply, however, is much greater, particularly from the Near and Middle East. Nearly 64 per cent of the cumulative world production through 1944 came from the United States, against less than 4 per cent from the Near and Middle East. But the United States at the beginning of 1945 had only 32 per cent of the world's estimated reserves, against more than 41 per cent in the Near and Middle East.[10] These figures suggest a large increase in imports if we follow prudent policies in regard to prices and conservation.

The long-run productive efficiency of Middle Eastern petroleum industries, barring disruptive political disturbances, has probably been enhanced by limited drilling as contrasted with competitive drilling in American fields. At the beginning of 1947 there were only 193 producing oil wells in the Middle East, but the average daily yield was nearly 4,000 barrels compared with only 11 barrels a day from about 424,000 producing wells in the United States.[11] (See Table 57.)

10. Hearings of the Special Committee of the Senate Investigating Petroleum Resources, cited by Feis, *op. cit.*, p. 102.

11. *Petroleum for National Defense*, Hearings, House, Special Subcommittee on Petroleum, 80th Cong., 2d sess., 1948, p. 113. Hereafter referred to as *Short Hearings*.

TABLE 57
PRODUCING OIL WELLS AS OF JANUARY 1, 1947, BY MAJOR AREAS

Area	Number of Wells	Number of Barrels Daily per Well
Total, world[a]	447,293	15.6
United States	424,286	11.1
Other North American	3,037	51.3
Venezuela	4,975	218.4
Other South American	10,503	21.2
Europe	3,473	5.9
Africa	229	104.9
Middle East	193	3,930.9
Far East	597	12.0

Source: *Petroleum for National Defense*, Hearings, House, Special Subcommittee on Petroleum, 80th Cong., 2d sess., 1948, p. 113.

a. Does not include U.S.S.R. and some other countries such as Japan, Germany and Italy.

The contrast between number of wells and production by areas is, indeed, striking. It suggests that foreign production costs will not constitute a barrier to imports when shortages develop.

Overproduction and Scarcity

Overproduction rather than scarcity has most often been the problem in the past.[12] As early as 1872 new discoveries in Pennsylvania undermined prices and ruined producers. A movement soon developed, according to one historian, "to organize a shutdown of producers . . . Over-production, with agitation for organized curtailment, was a recurrent feature of Pennsylvania history, as of the history of most other oil regions."[13] The disease was chronic throughout most of the period between 1923 and World War II. Fear of shortage and of foreign monopoly, which led to the aggressive petroleum diplomacy of the early 1920s, had given way in a few years to general concern about surpluses. Output increased nearly 50 per cent in the short period between 1922 and 1925, and by 1929 production had reached one billion barrels a year, nearly double the output of 1922.

Many companies which had participated in the search for foreign oil withdrew in favor of home operations, and the industry began to experiment with methods of controlling production. Restrictive practices, which had been tried on a voluntary basis periodically since the flush period of Pennsylvania production, were publicly sanctioned by the state conserva-

12. The term "overproduction" describes a situation in which production is so great that falling prices fail to relieve the pressure of supply on existing storage facilities and above-ground waste removes an inordinate part of the surplus.

13. John Ise, *The United States Oil Policy*, Yale University Press, New Haven, 1926, p. 13.

TABLE 58

U.S. PRODUCTION, EXPORTS AND IMPORTS OF CRUDE PETROLEUM, SELECTED YEARS,
1910–1950

(*Millions of Barrels of 42 U.S. Gal.*)

Year	Domestic Production	Exports	Imports	Net[a] Exports or Imports (—)	Imports as Per Cent of Domestic Production
1910	210	6	1	6	0.3
1914	266	3	17	−14	6
1919	378	6	53	−47	14
1920	443	9	106	−97	24
1921	472	10	125	−116	27
1922	558	11	127	−117	23
1923	732	18	82	−65	11
1924	714	18	78	−60	11
1925	764	13	62	−49	8
1929	1,007	26	79	−53	8
1933	906	37	32	5	4
1937	1,279	67	28	40	2
1939	1,265	72	33	39	3
1941	1,402	33	51	−17	4
1947	1,856	46	99	−53	5
1948	2,016	40	129	−89	6
1949	1,840	33	158	−125	9
1950	1,972	35	173	−138	9

Sources: U.S. Geological Survey and Bureau of Mines (as quoted in Leonard M. Fanning, *American Oil Operations Abroad*, McGraw-Hill, New York, 1947, pp. 226–227) and *Survey of Current Business*.

a. Does not include petroleum products (mainly residual oil).

tion laws of the 1930s, the Interstate Oil Compact and the Connally "Hot Oil" Act.

Scarcity was not again a problem until after the beginning of World War II, when the demands of mechanized warfare and the interruption of trade put an extraordinary drain upon domestic resources and again shifted the United States from a net exporter to a net importer. Even after the end of the war, the continued scarcity of drilling and production equipment hampered the expansion of output, while higher levels of income resulted in heavier demands. The situation appeared so critical that strong sentiment developed in favor of limiting exports and encouraging imports. The nation's position in the event of further warfare was viewed in the light of imminent shortages. Chairman Short opened the 1948 hearings before the House Armed Services Committee with the statement: ". . . it requires no insight or extensive study to realize that this nation is becoming so dependent on petroleum that even in peacetime vital demands of the economy are outstripping the productive capacity of the oil industry."[14]

14. *Short Hearings*, 1948, p. 1.

TABLE 59

RATIO OF KNOWN DOMESTIC RESERVES TO DOMESTIC DEMAND,[a] 1919–1947

Year	Ratio	Year	Ratio
1919	16.6	1934	13.0
1920	14.7	1935	12.4
1921	15.7	1936	11.3
1922	14.7	1937	11.2
1923	11.7	1938	13.6
1924	11.1	1939	14.1
1925	10.3	1940	13.9
1926	10.9	1941	12.8
1927	11.0	1942	13.5
1928	12.2	1943	13.2
1929	11.7	1944	12.0
1930	14.2	1945	11.5
1931	15.1	1946	11.6
1932	15.6	1947[b]	11.1
1933	14.2		

Source: Bureau of Mines, quoted in *Petroleum for National Defense,* Hearings, House, Special Subcommittee on Petroleum, 80th Cong., 2d sess., 1948, p. 101.

a. Known reserves at beginning of year divided by domestic demand during year.
b. Estimated.

Apparent consumption of oil in the United States increased by one quarter between 1945 and 1948. Production increased by only one fifth. This shifted America from a net exporter to a net importer.

Consumption and domestic production of crude oil fell by approximately 10 per cent in the slight recession from 1948 to 1949. While some recovery took place in 1950, domestic production failed to regain 1948 levels. Imports, however, continued to rise, despite the fall in production. Between 1947 and 1950, imports of crude oil almost doubled and net imports nearly tripled. Although net imports in 1950 were less than 10 per cent of domestic production, compared with nearly one fourth during the scarcity period after the first world war, they were still increasing. (See Table 58.)[15]

The widespread concern which had been expressed before 1948 of a threatened oil shortage was immediately transformed into fear of surplus at prevailing prices, leading to agitation by interested groups for curtailment of the still increasing oil imports. Nothing more was heard of an oil famine until the difficulties of the Anglo-Iranian Oil Company in 1951 threatened to restore Europe's dependence on American petroleum. This threat did not materialize, however.

It is impossible to draw inferences from the history of American production which will allay the shortage controversy. In the past, discovery of new

15. No adjustment has been made in these statistics for imports bonded for exports after refining. While the amounts in the 1920s were large, this type of trade has decreased with the expansion of refinery capacity abroad.

TABLE 60

NUMBER OF MAJOR DISCOVERED FIELDS IN THE UNITED STATES BY YEAR OF
DISCOVERY, 1938–1945

Year	Number of Major Fields Discovered[a]	Per Cent of All New Fields
1938	39	17.48
1939	21	12.65
1940	32	13.97
1941	19	7.01
1942	14	5.46
1943	16	5.73
1944	13	5.30
1945	5	2.34

Source: Petroleum for National Defense, Hearings, House, Special Subcommittee on Petroleum, 80th Cong., 2d sess., 1948, p. 105.

a. A "major field" is one having reserves of ten million barrels or more.

reserves which could be exploited with known techniques has about kept pace with the increase in consumption. The increase in reserves has been possible only with the development of deep drilling and other expensive techniques. Known reserves were about eleven times the annual demand in peak production years of the late 1920s and in the late 1940s. (See Table 59.) This figure had not changed significantly by 1951.

The declining rate of discovery of major fields would seem to foreshadow the future need for imports. While 39 major fields were discovered in 1938, only 5 were discovered in 1945. This is the meaning of the argument that the "big fish" are strained out first. Major discoveries declined consistently in relation to all discoveries in the period 1938–1945. (See Table 60.)

The importance of exploration to future costs lies in the fact that the rate of discovery must keep pace with the rate of consumption if future shortages are to be avoided. Proven reserves cannot last long even at the current rate of consumption, and consumption is expanding. Output per well and per field declines as more oil is extracted and recovery costs mount. Secondary recovery must eventually be used to extract oil.[16] While new discoveries will continue, it seems most improbable that production can be increased as rapidly as consumption at costs which are competitive with imports.

The cost of expanding crude oil production in the Middle East and Venezuela is well below that in the United States. It is difficult to forecast the pattern of trade in petroleum which will develop, even if it is not disrupted by tariffs and quotas. In 1922 nearly all imports came from Mexico. In 1949 Venezuela supplied 60 per cent of total imports and much of the rest came from the Middle East.

16. Secondary recovery is a method of using water to force oil into pockets from which it can be pumped.

Shifts in the volume and source of imports cannot be attributed entirely to differences in cost. Company policy and local and international politics also influence the pattern.

Despite the difficulty of calculating costs and the presence of other factors in the determination of trade, the tendency is doubtless toward an increasing volume of imports.

Other Factors Affecting Imports

"The international oil industry usually has sought new customers and markets, in the confident belief that all the oil that could be sold would be found. But the quantities demanded have increased remarkably rapidly."[17]

In spite of increasing demand, discovery has moved in jumps—jumps which were sometimes in advance of demand. There must have been times when the producing companies sought new customers on the theory that what has been found must be sold. The development of the Middle Eastern resources, which promised to free Europe from dependence upon American petroleum, gave the participating American companies an additional selling job. With contractual commitments to other customers, the disposition of remaining production in the American market must have been based on calculations to maximize profits.

The integration of the importing firms complicates their calculations of cost and profit. They are concerned not only with the price of imported petroleum but also with the influence of imports on domestic prices, and with the relationship between the price of crude and the price of finished products. The large companies find it advisable to maintain stable prices for the end-products which are sold to the public. They wish to have adequate profit margins for refining, processing and distributing, and this aspect of their operations offsets their interest in high prices for crude oil.

The organization of the petroleum industry is flexible enough to adapt the pattern of sales to such calculations of relative advantage. The importers of petroleum products, with one principal exception, are American firms, and the foreign and domestic operations of these companies are integrated vertically. They control both foreign and domestic oil wells, ocean and inland transportation, refineries, bulk stations and other facilities for marketing end-products. Imports of crude petroleum for the purpose of supplementing domestic production are, therefore, readily available to refineries in the necessary quantities. Since the same companies operate both ends, there is no marketing problem in the usual sense, though the refining activity of the importing companies is partially dependent upon the crude oil produced by "independents."

17. Herbert Feis, "The Effect of the World Distribution of Petroleum on the Power and Policy of Nations" in W. E. Pratt and Dorothy Good (Eds.), *World Geography of Petroleum*, Princeton University Press, Princeton, 1950, p. 393.

In 1945 twenty-one major integrated companies held 82 per cent of the total refining capacity, but produced less than 62 per cent of the crude oil.[18] Partly estimated data relating to the operations of twenty-three of the largest refiners in the 1930s indicated a tendency on the part of refiners to enlarge their ownership of crude petroleum resources. This group produced a little less than 55 per cent of its refinery requirements in 1934 and a little less than 59 per cent in 1937.[19] Expanding ownership of foreign petroleum resources reduces dependence upon "outside" petroleum. Thus importing firms can use imports as a lever to affect the domestic price of crude oil.

The domestic producer interest of those firms which are mainly concerned with foreign operations is dominated by their commitment to exploit foreign concessions. When the large companies were criticized for importing crude oil in excessive amounts, one of them replied: "With domestic crude in good supply, the company's imports of crude oil are being kept to a minimum consistent with the maintenance of its foreign sources of oil . . ."[20] Operations should be technically efficient, but they must also be consistent with staying in business in the political circumstances.

Impact of Technology on Foreign Trade

Petroleum illustrates the varied ways in which technology may affect the pattern of our foreign trade.

The drilling of much deeper wells has brought in vast new fields at home as well as abroad, and has postponed the shortage which seemed imminent when the United States became a net importer in the early 1920s. New fields were discovered and the number of barrels of new domestic reserves per foot drilled has been maintained during the past fifteen years while new reserves per well completed have increased.

Measured by the value of output in constant prices, the efficiency of refining has also increased modestly. The value of refined output per barrel of crude increased from $3.50 in 1929 to $3.90 in 1947. This change, which reduced supplies of residual oil, and the advent of the diesel engine, which increased the demand, have helped to create a niche in the American market for imports.

18. Eugene V. Rostow, *National Policy for the Oil Industry*, Yale University Press, New Haven, 1948, pp. 10–11. The data are from *The Independent Petroleum Company*, Hearings, Senate Special Committee Investigating Petroleum Resources, 79th Cong., 2d sess., 1948.

19. *Petroleum Industry Hearings* before the Temporary National Economic Committee, as published by the American Petroleum Institute, 1942, p. 228. Hereafter cited as *Petroleum Hearings, A.P.I.*

20. *Causes of Unemployment in Coal and Other Specified Industries*, S. Rept. No. 2042, 81st Cong., 2d sess., 1950, p. 456. (Neely Hearings.) This statement was intended to be descriptive of the attitude of Standard Oil (New Jersey).

Residual fuel oil, sometimes called "heavy" oil, is used for power by industry, railroads, trucks and buses. Imports increased tenfold from 1925–1929 to a daily rate of 350,000 barrels in 1952. Domestic supplies of this fuel oil, which must be distinguished from the lighter distillates and home heating oil, have declined relatively because of the increasing efficiency of the refining process. Residual oil is a low-priced by-product. As refining has obtained increasing percentages of high-value products, the domestic output of residual oil has declined.

Foreign refining activity, on the other hand, has risen without an increase in the consumption of residual oil commensurate with that of gasoline and distillates. The effect of this imbalance was to create large supplies of residual oil which could best be sold in the expanding American market. Moreover, transportation costs were held at a relatively low level through the increased use of larger tankers. Thus, easy supply together with a growing price disparity between coal and oil hastened the long-term trend toward a relative increase in oil consumption. The great increase in residual oil imports after 1946 was also partly the result of uncertainties of coal supply and the rising cost of coal. Many industries either converted or added supplementary equipment to burn oil as conditions warranted.

Imports and Import Taxes

Whether import tax [21] reduction played any substantial part in this increase in imports is questionable. The "independents" tried, from time to time, to blame reciprocal trade agreements for the ills that beset them. The import tax on crude and fuel oil was reduced from 21 cents to 10½ cents a barrel in the Venezuela agreement of 1939. A spokesman for the Independent Petroleum Association pointed out that 25 per cent of the companies engaged exclusively in the production of oil went out of business in the period from 1938 to 1942.[22] Considering that production increased during those years, the causal connection between reduction of the import tax and difficulties of domestic producers is easily exaggerated. The trade agreement concession applied only to a quota of no more than 5 per cent of the petroleum processed in American refineries during the preceding calendar year.

These reduced rates were incorporated in the Mexican agreement of 1943 without the quota provision. But by the time this agreement had been set aside by the two governments in 1950, the Oklahoma price had increased from $1.19 to $2.57 a barrel and the tax had become correspondingly less significant.

21. The term "import tax" is used instead of duty because petroleum in the Tariff Act is on the free list. The import tax rates are found in the Internal Revenue Code.

22. Statement of Russel B. Brown in *Extension of the Reciprocal Trade Agreements Act*, 1945, Senate Hearings, pp. 47 and 51.

The ad valorem equivalent of the 21 cent per barrel tax, which was the rate applicable to all foreign oil after termination of the Mexican agreement (except that eligible for admission under the quota arrangement with Venezuela), was cut back roughly to the Mexican agreement rate by the rise of prices. The evidence suggests that factors other than the tax were mainly responsible for the behavior of imports in this period. Not the least of these factors was the belief in the importing section of the petroleum industry that domestic supplies of crude were not sufficient to satisfy the requirements of the trade.

New Venezuelan Agreement

When the Congress debated extension of the Trade Agreements Act in 1951, it was assured by the administration that no new major negotiations were contemplated for the next three years. This did not preclude a new agreement with Venezuela in 1952, supplementing the bilateral agreement of 1939.

Without opening new fields, Venezuelan production has risen to about 14 per cent of world production and now accounts for about 90 per cent of all Venezuelan exports to the United States. The 1952 Venezuelan agreement is notable because it involved the first experience with the peril point amendment requiring the Tariff Commission to determine *in advance* the limits beyond which tariff reduction would endanger home industry. A majority of the Commission was unable to agree on the "peril points" and concessions were granted beyond the limits found by all Commissioners.

The quota restriction limiting the 1939 concession to 5 per cent of domestic refinery output was eliminated. President Truman reported to the Congress that experience had shown that the reduced tax of 10½ cents a barrel was not likely to hamper development programs at home. Thus far, the trend of tariff restriction has been down. The 10½ cent tax on imported crude and fuel oil does not hamper imports significantly, although the much higher taxes on gasoline and lubricating oil protect domestic refineries.

Protectionists, however, appear to have mustered increased strength, as is indicated by debates in the Congress on the proposed Simpson Amendment (1953) and later proposals to limit imports by quota. Once quotas are introduced, the danger is that they will gradually be made more restrictive as has been the experience with sugar.

Domestic Restrictions on Production and Imports

Prorationing is a system of public regulation of petroleum production which grew out of private efforts to restrict output in order to control prices. According to one definition: "Proration of oil production is the rationing of allowable production to individual units—wells, groups of wells, or geographic areas—whose collective capacity to produce exceeds the total allowable."[23] Contemporary defense of the system is based upon the "conservation" argument, but it is not clear that conservation, as administered under the proration laws, has been anything more than a happy by-product of commercial restrictionism.

Some producing companies experimented with voluntary agreements to restrict production in the late 1920s and by 1932 domestic restriction was supported by limitations on imports. Under the 21 cents per barrel excise tax imposed by the revenue act of that year, and a subsequent voluntary restrictive agreement between the principal importing companies and the Secretary of the Interior, the companies agreed to limit imports to the average of the last six months of 1932. These restrictions were incorporated into the N.I.R.A. Petroleum Code and the companies continued to abide by them after termination of the codes in 1935.[24]

During this period domestic restriction was organized and made compulsory under state laws. The governments of several states empowered regulatory bodies to prorate production among fields and among the common owners of each field on the basis of an equitable division of allowable production in order to prevent waste.

In 1935, six states—Texas, Oklahoma, Kansas, New Mexico, Colorado and Illinois—entered into a compact obligating each participating state to enact and enforce conservation laws and to cooperate through an Interstate Oil Compact Commission. The Compact was approved by Congress and supported by the Connally Act, which prohibited the interstate movement of petroleum produced in violation of state laws. While some important producing states were not members of the compact, these states frequently sent observers to the Commission's sessions.

Proration and Price

Total production prorationed among the various producers and fields approximates estimated "market demand" adjusted for desirable changes in the stocks of crude oil. The Bureau of Mines prepares advisory estimates of demand (we are not told at what price), which are subdivided into state allocations. These are checked by the state regulatory authorities against nominations of the buyers. Estimates of future imports are subtracted, thus

23. *Petroleum Hearings*, *A.P.I.*, p. 296, statement by E. DeGolyer.

24. This account of restriction and operation of the proration system is based largely on the testimony of Joseph E. Pogue before the Temporary National Economic Committee. Since Mr. Pogue, then Vice President of the Chase National Bank, appeared as a witness for the American Petroleum Institute his statement is assumed to represent the thinking of the industry on those aspects of proration covered in the statement. The statement, dated September 25, 1939, is contained in the official T.N.E.C. Hearings, pp. 7435–7457. The page references cited below are to *Petroleum Hearings*, *A.P.I.*

providing a guide for the determination of production allowables for the ensuing period. A slump in domestic demand, as reflected in buyer nominations, is followed by a cutback in production. It is difficult to test the effect on prices of such regulation.[25] An industry admission that prices in the 1930s were higher than they would have been without prorationing is doubtless correct, but the long-run effect could be greater stability.

Spokesmen for the petroleum industry generally deny that prorationing has continued to be a price-fixing device. Under the Interstate Oil Compact, measures for limiting production for the purpose of fixing prices, creating or perpetuating monopoly, or promoting regimentation are specifically prohibited. However, insofar as prorationing is effective in decreasing domestic supply it raises the price of petroleum by increasing its scarcity and consequently attracts imports. Furthermore, the variable costs of oil extraction are raised by prorationing, which may keep production below the optimum output and which may keep high-cost producers in the business. If domestic supplies last longer as a result, presumably future imports will be lower than without "conservation."

Prorationing has provided the integrated companies with an additional incentive to import. Except for the effect of imports, the system of restriction strengthens the hands of the independents by guaranteeing to them some administratively determined share of the total output which they might not retain if market forces were permitted to eliminate high-cost production. To the extent that those shares are at the expense of the domestic production of the importing companies, the importers are able to compensate for the loss by drawing on foreign output.[26]

Proration and Conservation

Proration programs are supported on the ground that they promote conservation of American petroleum resources, which are in danger of depletion to the detriment of economic and military power. The "conservation" argument is somewhat peculiar. Existing wells must be exploited, it is argued, in order to provide profits to discover new ones, for profits promote exploration and technological advance. Moreover, it is argued that maximum physical production of oil conserves natural resources, and that the abandonment of "stripper" wells and other marginal producers is contrary to this goal. The goal of maximum physical production neglects to mention the waste of resources in extraction of high-cost oil.

Conservation of domestic petroleum resources at the cost of wasting resources in the process of extraction is justifiable only if it is the best way to maintain reserves against the possible needs for war. Under peaceful condi-

25. *Ibid.*, p. 234.
26. *Ibid.*, pp. 52–53.

tions the economic well-being of the United States would be advanced by the use of cheap petroleum, part of which was imported, rather than by artificially priced petroleum as a result of restrictions on production.

If it is desirable to restrict the rate of use of domestic petroleum resources for military reasons, prorationing is a dubious way of achieving this goal. Conservation is not promoted by keeping up the price of petroleum in order to encourage discovery, for the encouragement to discovery exists only because the extraction and sale of oil is profitable. Extraction is the very thing that true conservation should seek to diminish.

If it is desirable for purposes of national security to discover new fields at a more rapid rate than is provided by the incentive of free market prices, subsidies for exploration, not profits for exploitation, would promote the same end with the use of less resources. Allocating part of the market to marginal producers in order to obtain maximum physical output is unworthy of support since the output of anything, even oil, cannot be unrelated to cost. Maximum production is only possible at exorbitant costs.

The most important factor making for rapid exploitation of oil fields is the existence of competitive drilling, a practice which reduces total supply of oil recoverable at reasonable cost. Production in most fields is undertaken by a number of competitive groups operating under the traditional rule of capture. Each has a stake in rapid extraction lest other wells get more than their share. Present programs do nothing to alter these conditions.[27]

The "independent" section of the petroleum industry, which generally has no interest in foreign production, has never been sympathetic to the idea of "hoarding" domestic reserves. This idea was widely discussed before 1930 because of the possibility of scarcity, and some domestic petroleum producers sensed a plot to promote the use of imported oil at the expense of domestic oil. To meet the threat the "independents" organized the Independent Petroleum Association of America, which did much to obtain adoption of the import tax on oil in 1932.[28] Should a depression reduce the consumption of petroleum, the same interest will undoubtedly press for quota restrictions and higher import duties. In fact the signs point in this direction in any event.

Parts of the industry oppose large imports on the ground that incentives for exploration and development are undermined as a result. Imports lower prices, and the argument is that the discovery of new reserves will be impaired if profits are impaired. But producers already receive favorable treatment under our tax laws, and precisely for this reason.

27. Joe E. Bain, "Rostow's Proposals for Petroleum Policy," *Journal of Political Economy*, February 1949, pp. 55–60.
28. *Petroleum Hearings, A.P.I.*, p. 64.

In computing their tax liability producers are permitted to deduct 27½ per cent of gross income for depletion so long as the deduction does not exceed 50 per cent of net income. This means that the tax-free recovery over the life of the property may exceed the investment.

Prospects

Petroleum imports may be expected to grow markedly unless new restrictions are imposed.

First, home industry has no monopoly either of the most advanced technology or of the best-known reserves. The cost of foreign oil need not rise as rapidly as the cost of domestic oil because good domestic resources are now less abundant and the domestic practice of competitive drilling is more expensive.

The second reason for believing that imports should rise substantially is that the automotive industry as well as millions of consumers have a serious interest in keeping the price of gasoline down. It should be possible to arouse the entire electorate against import quotas which will raise the price of gasoline and fuel oil. The great danger is that, once introduced, quotas might be gradually made more restrictive without arousing public opposition.

Recent attempts to restrict imports of petroleum are likely to appear again from time to time. An industry with the growth potential of petroleum should rarely be protected from foreign competition except as a temporary expedient. The problems of adjustment created by petroleum imports are quite minor compared with those of agriculture and relatively stagnant manufacturing industries.

Demands for protection against imports derive much of their strength from instability of the domestic market. To regulate imports for this reason would only throw the burden of unstable domestic demand on foreign producers.

As for problems of the coal industry, it is quite clear that displacement of coal by substitute fuels is largely independent of the rise of petroleum imports.[29]

Should petroleum imports increase, the world's net dollar earnings would increase by less than the value of additional imports, for most imports are made by American firms which employ American equipment and services in foreign production. Additional dollar earnings require additional dollar costs. The foreign exchange position of the producing countries would improve to the extent of royalty payments and the earnings of their residents in the petroleum industry.

29. See pp. 171–172.

Europe's position will be directly improved insofar as European firms export to the United States, and indirectly improved when non-European producing countries buy in Europe with dollars (or draw down fewer dollars from their convertible bank accounts in Europe). Thus, should petroleum imports increase by $1 billion in the next decade, petroleum will probably have done more by far than any other item of merchandise trade to improve the dollar position of the rest of the world.

The importance of opposing new restrictions on petroleum imports must be emphasized. The potential growth of petroleum imports may be, perhaps, as large as the total increase in imports which would result from drastic reduction of all protective tariffs.

Moreover, serious restrictions on imports would discourage foreign investment, which is vital to the producing countries and to American foreign policy.

Chapter 17

"Luxury" Imports

A MAJOR PART of American imports have been considered in the immediately preceding chapters. Relatively few of these items have increased faster than national income. The question naturally arises, "What are the imports which consumers might be expected to buy in increasing quantities as they become more affluent?" No scientific pretensions are attached to the term "luxury"; it is only a label for those imports which a rich people might be expected to buy relatively more of, as their incomes rise. The reader may find that the individual items shed more light on the import problem than the totals. But it does seem worth while to consider, in connection with the relative failure of other classes of imports, how those items have fared which some writers believe should increase more rapidly than national income. This view was expressed recently in particular connection with the need for increasing imports from Europe.

It would be difficult to imagine that public taste for luxury and semi-luxury goods which figure so largely in these imports had materially declined. So far as concerns the dependence of these markets on income, the proportion should have increased markedly since per capita national income in real terms has recently exceeded even the prosperity level of the latter 'twenties, and imports from Western Europe are highly income elastic.[1]

The author further argues that American tariffs must be responsible for the relative failure of luxury imports.

The Nonfood Group

We may begin with diamonds and jewelry. By the standards of past ages, people with today's middle class incomes would buy jewels. But today, Americans buy machine-stamped costume jewelry, which is a distinctly American product. The rise of costume jewelry is an expression of the adaptation of taste in a mass society to mass methods of production.

Demand for diamonds for industrial uses has increased tremendously, but imports of both jewelry and diamonds (except industrial) have failed to increase since 1929 as rapidly as consumer expenditures. The index of consumer expenditures (1929 = 100) reached 226 in 1948, 229 in 1949, and 246 in 1950. The index of diamond imports was 194 in 1948, 134 in 1949 and

1. Howard S. Ellis, *The Economics of Freedom*, Council on Foreign Relations, Harper, New York, 1950, p. 83.

199 in 1950. Jewelry imports in 1950 had not yet reached the 1929 level and stood one half below that level in 1948 and 1949. The complete destruction of the prewar jewelry center of Pforzheim, Germany, by the United States Air Force may have been a contributing factor in some slight degree. But machine-stamped, domestic jewelry probably provides better values.

The outstanding characteristic of the luxury and semiluxury imports[2] other than foods is the sharp disparities in rates of growth. Imports of beads, perfumery, tulip bulbs, silk and flax products declined absolutely from 1929 to 1950. China, porcelain and artificial flowers reached about the same levels in 1950 as in 1929. Toys and sporting goods increased slightly. Photographic goods and musical instruments increased, but less than the increase in consumer expenditures. The largest increase was in sewing machines, automobiles and motorcycles. It seems doubtful whether these items should be included in the luxury category. To some extent, they are mass-produced, as distinct from the handmade products where Europe's skills and lower labor costs are supposed to bring a competitive advantage. The only other nonfood imports which increased more rapidly than consumer expenditures were watches, smokers' articles and fancy handkerchiefs. (See Table 61.)

Altogether, luxury and semiluxury imports in the nonfood group declined by one third from 1929 to 1950. If silk is excluded, the increase is less than one half. This means that this group of imports, which were selected because they naturally might be expected to increase more rapidly than incomes, actually fell drastically relative to the rise in consumer expenditures. In fact, the nonfood group even fell by about two thirds as a share of total imports. (See Table 62.) Some of these imports have increased substantially since 1950, the cut-off date for the special tabulations in this chapter.

The Food Group

Luxury and semiluxury foods fared better than the nonfood group. Imports of coffee, cocoa, lobster and fish in oil increased more rapidly than consumer expenditures from 1929 to 1950. But fruits, nuts, tea, cheese and olive oil failed to rise as rapidly as expenditures. The index (1929 = 100) of lobster imports reached 770 in 1950 while that for cheese was only 108.

Repeal of prohibition marks a nonrecurring increase in imports during this period. It is extremely doubtful if coffee should be included in the group. The index of luxury foods excluding coffee and the liquor group (including hops) reached 220 in 1948, 178 in 1949 and 229 in 1950. Including

2. The individual items in Tables 61 and 63 include all luxury and semiluxury products from a breakdown of imports into about 275 classes. Omissions are entirely due to the fact that not all "luxury" products were shown separately in this tabulation, which was prepared by the International Economic Analysis Division, Office of International Trade, U.S. Department of Commerce.

TABLE 61

IMPORTS OF "LUXURY" PRODUCTS OTHER THAN FOODS, 1929, 1933, 1937 AND 1948–1950[a]

	1929 Value (Millions)	1929 Index	1933 Index	1937 Index	1948 Index	1949 Index	1950 Index
					(Index: 1929=100)		
Total	$809	100	27	43	69	54	68
Total excluding silk	343	100	32	67	152	118	146
Silk and manufactures	466	100	23	25	9	7	12
Furs, undressed	108	100	31	73	147	95	93
Tobacco, unmanufactured	54	100	46	59	144	136	142
Diamonds (except industrial)	52	100	19	72	194	134	199
Flax and manufactures	48	100	46	73	68	68	91
Clocks, watches and parts	17	100	12	64	355	300	339
China, porcelain table and kitchen articles	9	100	25	46	78	86	100
Toys and sporting goods	7	100	32	57	67	76	109
Photographic goods	7	100	37	111	109	99	141
Beads	6	100	13	13	52	47	47
Tulip bulbs[b]	6	100	9	26	65	68	69
Jewelry and parts	5	100	5	9	50	48	83
Musical instruments	5	100	36	102	219	216	216
Cigarette paper	4	100	90	103	0.1	0.1	2
Perfume materials	3	100	30	57	53	57	77
Automobiles, parts and motorcycles[c]	3	100	13	48	831	417	833
Artificial flowers	3	100	19	59	29	66	100
Linen: embroidered or lace handkerchiefs	2	100	50	164	274	357	326
Perfumery and toilet waters	2	100	37	33	33	83	84
Smokers' articles	1	100	33	56	72	139	329
Cotton: embroidered or lace handkerchiefs	1	100	4	2	351	347	400
Firecrackers	1	100	33	104	274	223	145
Sewing machines and parts	0.5	100	48	56	332	1899	2612

Source: Office of International Trade, U.S. Department of Commerce, from census data. *Note:* Computations before rounding.

a. General imports in 1929, for consumption thereafter.   b. Includes lily and narcissus bulbs.   c. Includes certain other "vehicles."

337

TABLE 62

IMPORTANCE OF LUXURY IMPORTS IN TOTAL IMPORTS AND CONSUMER EXPENDITURES, 1929, 1933, 1937 AND 1948–1950

	1929	1933	1937	1948	1949	1950
Total imports	$4,399	$1,433	$3,010	$7,092	$6,598	$8,735
			Value (*Millions*)			
Total luxury imports[a]	1,322	447	745	1,805	1,695	2,289
Luxury food imports	513	228	398	1,245	1,258	1,736
Luxury nonfood imports	809	219	347	560	437	553
Luxury imports excluding silk	876	338	627	1,765	1,663	2,235
Luxury imports excluding coffee	1,020	323	594	1,107	899	1,198
Luxury imports excluding coffee and silk	574	214	476	1,067	867	1,144
			Index (*1929 = 100*)			
Luxury imports	100	33.8	56.4	136.5	128.2	173.1
Luxury imports excluding silk	100	38.6	71.6	201.5	189.8	255.1
Luxury imports excluding coffee	100	31.7	58.2	108.5	88.1	117.5
Luxury imports excluding coffee and silk	100	37.3	82.9	185.9	151.0	199.3
			Per Cent of Total Imports			
Luxury imports	30.1	31.2	24.8	25.5	25.7	26.2
Luxury imports excluding silk	19.9	23.6	20.8	24.9	25.2	25.6
Luxury imports excluding coffee	23.2	22.5	19.7	15.6	13.6	13.7
Luxury imports excluding coffee and silk	13.0	14.9	15.8	15.0	13.1	13.1
Luxury foods	11.7	15.9	13.2	17.6	19.1	19.9
Luxury nonfoods	18.4	15.3	11.5	7.9	6.6	6.3
			Per Cent of Consumer Expenditures			
Luxury imports	1.7	.97	1.1	1.0	.95	1.2
Luxury imports excluding silk	1.1	.73	.94	1.0	.93	1.2
Luxury imports excluding coffee	1.3	.70	.89	.63	.50	.6
Luxury imports excluding coffee and silk	.73	.47	.71	.60	.48	.6

Source: Office of International Trade, U.S. Department of Commerce, from census data.
a. See Tables 61 and 63 for the specific items.

TABLE 63

IMPORTS OF SPECIFIED "LUXURY" FOODS, 1929, 1933, 1937 AND 1948–1950

	1929 Value	1929 Index	1933 Index	1937 Index	1948 Index	1949 Index	1950 Index
	(Millions)			(Index: 1929=100)			
Total	$513	100	44	78	243	245	338
Total, excluding coffee and liquor group	210	100	45	83	220	178	229
Coffee	302	100	41	50	231	263	361
Fruits and preparations	59	100	49	81	173	168	192
Cocoa and cacao beans	49	100	38	106	391	252	338
Nuts and preparations	28	100	31	71	212	171	199
Tea	26	100	53	83	175	176	209
Cheese	22	100	49	58	57	76	108
Olive oil	16	100	38	55	95	47	118
Fish in oil	7	100	93	130	288	250	455
Lobsters, not canned	2	100	78	149	594	669	770
Liquor, still wines and hops	1	100	a	a	a	a	a

Source: Office of International Trade, U.S. Department of Commerce, from census data.

a. Because of the repeal of prohibition, the index is not significant.

Note: Computations before rounding.

339

coffee and the liquor group, the corresponding figures were 243, 245 and 338, respectively. (See Table 63.)

Food and Nonfoods

That luxury and semiluxury goods account for a substantial fraction of total imports is quite clear. But contrary to the expectations of some writers, they declined from 30 per cent of total imports in 1929 to 26 per cent in 1948, 1949 and 1950—a period in which consumer expenditures rose almost 150 per cent and total imports fell relative to national income. Excluding coffee, the decline of the luxury groups was from 23 per cent in 1929 to 14 per cent of total imports in 1950.

It is indeed surprising to find that in 1950 American consumers devoted only 0.6 per cent of their total expenditures to luxury imports (excluding coffee), compared with 1.3 per cent in 1929—a relative decline of more than one half. The major part of this fall was due to the displacement of silk. But excluding both silk and coffee—two giants which moved in opposite directions—the change in relative importance was still down from 0.7 per cent of expenditures in 1929 to 0.6 in 1950. (See Table 62.)

The relative decline in the importance of luxury and semiluxury imports cannot be blamed on tariffs because (1) a large fraction of those items are duty-free or bear low duties and (2) duties on others have been substantially reduced as a result of inflation and tariff concession.[3] Some of these imports may rise substantially as Europe's economic position improves and as American marketing is emphasized. But this class of imports seems to be the victim of basic changes in the pattern of consumption.

The behavior of these imports raises the broad question of whether or not "luxuries" to the American consumer are likely, in the main, to be mass-made products.

Most Luxury Items Have Lost Rank among Other Imports

Eight of the twenty-five leading imports, as classified and ranked by order of importance in *Foreign Commerce and Navigation of the United States*, fell in the luxury and semiluxury category. These are coffee, cocoa, furs, fruits, precious and semiprecious stones, beverages, tobacco and manufactures of flax. Only two of the eight items, coffee and cocoa, increased in rank during the twenty years 1929 to 1949.[4] It is a conspicuous fact that neither of the items that has risen in rank comes from Europe and neither is a manufactured product.

Each of the remaining six luxury items failed to hold its rank among the twenty-five leading imports.

3. Nonetheless, duties on many of these items are still highly restrictive. See Chapters 19 and 20.

4. The most recent year for which these data were available.

1. Furs fell from 7th place in the 1920s to 8th place in the 1930s to 14th place in 1949. Since the tariff on skins is not high, this appears to represent changes in taste and style as well as increased home production.

2. Precious and semiprecious stones, which ranked 14th in the years 1926–1930, declined one place to the 15th position in 1949. This item is especially sensitive to depression and ranks much lower in depression years.

3. Fruit and fruit preparations fell in rank from 16th place in the late 1920s to 20th place in 1949. This decline may be associated with production problems in bananas rather than with demand.

4. Beverages, which ranked among the 25 leading imports only since the repeal of prohibition, fell from 8th place in 1936–1940 to 18th place in 1949.

5. Tobacco rose from 17th place in the 1920s to 14th place in the 1930s, but fell to 21st place in 1949. In the face of the enormous increase in tobacco consumption this represents a reduction in the proportion of imported tobacco used in blending.

6. Flax and hemp no longer place among the 25 leading imports. Linen is going out of mode.

It seems clear that some further explanation is required of the failure of luxury imports.

Imports and the Way of Life

The essence of economic development is enough efficiency to permit a surplus of labor that can be shifted out of the production of food. The shift from agriculture to manufacturing to the services is the normal pattern of growth. One aspect of the structural changes in the growth process which has been neglected is the rise in the cost of services implicit in rising incomes. Average wages are higher in manufacturing than in agriculture and become higher in the services than in manufacturing.[5]

Thus, while the expansion of income provides a growing surplus of "luxuries" over subsistence, the rising labor cost in the service field appears to play a significant role in the type of "luxuries" consumed. The entire mode of living appears to be decisively affected by the rising cost of services that is implicit in the growth of wealth.

It is a familiar fact that the middle class and well-to-do in the United States enjoy less in the way of personal service than comparable economic groups in poorer societies. Getting rich has its paradox; for in a mass society, the richer we become, the fewer servants we can afford. In the United States, our standard of living has risen so high that most of us can

5. Colin Clark, *The Conditions of Economic Progress*, 2d edition, Macmillan, London, 1951, pp. 440–451. According to Clark the principle might fairly be called Petty's Law. On scanty evidence, Sir William Petty wrote in 1691: "There is more to be gained by *Manufacture*, than *Husbandry*; and by *Merchandise* than *Manufacture*."

no longer afford servants. The reason, of course, is that the growth of capital has increased the value of labor.

This leads to the whole question of mass and class. To what extent is our mode of living conditioned by the dramatic rise in labor cost that is inherent in the process of economic development by which the mass society becomes rich? And, of course, only the mass society can become rich in terms of total national output.

There is a way of life that goes with cheap labor; the mode must necessarily change as labor becomes more valuable. It may be that the newly well-to-do do not have the same habits of sumptuous living as those who combine wealth with "background" and leisure.

To live on the grand scale requires a degree of personal service quite beyond the citizens of the richest nation. Some of the goods affected by the mode of life are fine china and glassware, elaborate silver service, linen, jewelry, heavy leather luggage and "valuable" goods in general. The decline of entertaining at home on a sumptuous scale has affected the demand for quality dinner sets and elaborate glassware, which characterize upper classes in the rest of the world. Synthetic table mats and paper napkins displace fine linen, the high cost of laundry discourages popular use of linen clothing, and the linen handkerchief gives way to Kleenex—except as birthday gifts.

No one has better epitomized the mass versus class standards of consumption than Mrs. Roosevelt in writing of her meeting with Britain's Royal Family during the war.

. . . Both the king and I had rather bad colds, which necessitated a good deal of attention to our noses. As we drove away from Windsor Castle my aunt said to me in shocked tones: "Darling, I never was so humiliated in my life. Your using those nasty little tissues and wadding them up in your hand while the king used such lovely sheer linen handkerchiefs! What could they have thought!"[6]

Moderately well-to-do Europeans buy custom-tailored shirts while richer Americans buy standardized, factory-made, short-tail shirts. The buyer's time is valuable and few Americans would spend the time and cost for fittings. Moreover, the standardized sizes are better than anything but the best tailoring. Double cuffs and cuff links are a disappearing symbol of largesse, and even where worn, the European chain cuff link that virtually requires valet service does not compete with the simply designed, gold-filled, domestic product which retails for $1.50 to $2.50. As incomes in Europe rise it seems more likely that American mass production methods will displace Europe's custom tailoring in their own market than that the European mode will replace the factory system in the American market.

6. *This I Remember*, Harper, New York, 1949, p. 276.

Taking shirts as a symbol, it must be so—otherwise Europe can never be rich.

Labor is more efficient on the assembly line and, therefore, cheaper than labor in the repair shop, a truth which contributes to the practice of frequent turn-ins of automobiles and other durable goods. Most upper-income-class Americans prefer two cars to the lifetime model of Rolls-Royce quality.

In general the relatively high cost of maintenance, repair and storage in a high-income society discourages ownership of the most valuable types of consumption goods. Building costs place a premium on storage space. It becomes cheaper and more convenient to use the less valuable types of goods, throw them away and acquire new ones more often. These are not absolutes, of course, but tendencies fostered by the rising value of labor.

Considering the enormous increase in wealth, the decline in the popularity of furs seems difficult to explain. By the standards of an earlier generation almost everyone today could afford furs which, if properly cared for, last almost a lifetime. The experts will attribute the disappearing fur to changes in style. The high cost of services may well be of fundamental importance. It is a commonplace that furs are no longer worn to keep warm, but if they could be used only as the mark of distinction, they would be more popular. Is it the cost of frequent re-tailoring imposed by changes in styles in addition to storage and repair charges that discourages ownership? The trite but significant expression, "It's not the initial cost, it's the upkeep," expresses the economics of owning goods with high service costs.

The relevance of "service costs" to the import question is that the luxuries of life in a high-income society tend to become the mass-produced goods rather than the more valuable handmade products or the more durable quality products requiring high-cost maintenance and storage. The economist correctly points out that we should import those commodities the production of which requires a relatively high proportion of labor, and export those requiring a high proportion of capital costs. But, on the import side, this fundamental proposition of economics neglects the "service costs" that cannot be imported. For while it is true that rising incomes make a class market of a mass market, it is truer that high "service costs" make a mass market of a class market.

Rising labor costs have also produced more efficient retailing, which depersonalizes the sales relationship with the customer. Highly differentiated products require more "selling" than standard items and must bear higher selling costs. *The rise in incomes in a mass society has as a necessary corollary the even greater rise in "service costs" which causes us to take our luxuries in the mass-produced forms.*

Chapter 18

Tourism, Shipping and Other Services

IN 1951 the United States paid $3 billion for foreign services and received $2.8 billion from other countries for services (excluding income on investments). This compares with commodity imports of $10.8 billion and commodity exports of $14.9 billion in the same year. Thus, services amounted to about 28 per cent of commodity imports and 19 per cent of commodity exports.

International trade in the form of services has increased much faster in the past generation than has trade in commodities. United States exports of services increased from about 10 per cent of the export of goods in the 1920s to 15 per cent in the 1930s and to 19 per cent in 1951.

Services imported by the United States increased from 22 per cent of commodity imports in the 1920s to almost 30 per cent in the 1930s and remained near this level after World War II.

The relative importance of services to commodity imports (28 per cent) and to commodity exports (19 per cent) is distorted by four factors: (1) economic and military aid, which creates a large surplus of commodity exports over imports; (2) the net export of shipping services as a result of the indirect subsidy of the American fleet in connection with foreign aid; (3) the large "import" of services for American military personnel stationed overseas; (4) the foreign governmental restrictions on foreign travel in the United States. Restoration of more normal conditions will bring the proportion of services to imports and to exports closer together.

Tourism is an important source of dollar earnings for other countries. But the increase in travel expenditures by foreigners in the United States during recent years has been slightly larger than the increase in tourist expenditures by Americans, so that on balance the net earnings of other countries in 1952 declined slightly to about $400 million. The world's net earnings from travel have been less than net payments to the United States for shipping in most years since the end of World War II.

Expenditures by American military agencies and their personnel add roughly one billion dollars to the earnings of other countries for services.

Receipts from American private services to other countries (film rentals, management fees, etc.) are increasing and amount to roughly $400 million net.

Net payments of only $200 million on all services in 1951 were the end result of America's (1) net payments on tourism, (2) net receipts on shipping, (3) net payment on governmental expenditures for other services, and (4) net receipts on private expenditures for other services.

POSTWAR TOURISM

Expenditures by American tourists abroad are one of the largest sources of dollar earnings to other countries. These are listed in the international account as payments for services and count as United States imports in the balance of payments. A new peak was reached in 1952 when Americans abroad spent $1 billion including travel on foreign ships and planes.[1] Foreigners spent about $600 million on travel in the United States—a receipt to the United States which counts as an export in the balance of payments. On balance we paid other countries $400 million for travel and other things which tourists buy.

Receipts from travel by foreigners increased more rapidly from 1950 to 1952 than from 1946 to 1950. The annual increase averaged $76 million from 1950 to 1952, compared with $62 million before 1950.

The average annual increase in payments for expenditures of American tourists abroad during the postwar years averaged $86 million; but the rate of increase has declined. The rise from 1950 to 1952 was only 14 per cent. In the same period, the rate of increase in receipts from travel in the United States was about twice as great. On balance, net payments declined slightly in 1952.

The $1 billion spent abroad by Americans in 1952 compares with tourist expenditures of roughly $650 million in 1929, and is less than might have been expected considering the rise in American national income. The number of Americans traveling in Europe in 1952 was still less than in the prewar peak year 1929–1930.[2] One important reason for this is the decline in America's foreign-born population. A second factor is lack of transportation. Cabin-class space on ships has been a bottleneck. Introduction of tourist-class air travel increased the available transportation to Europe and helps to account for the rise in expenditures in 1952.

Europe and the Mediterranean accounted for about one third of total United States tourist expenditures in 1952, compared with 45 per cent in 1929. In 1952 tourist expenditures were substantially larger in Canada than in Europe and the Mediterranean. Mexico, the West Indies and Central America combined earned about as many tourist dollars as did Europe and the Mediterranean.

1. This is substantially less than the value of the largest commodity import; coffee imports in 1951 were $1.36 billion.
2. "One Billion Travel Dollars Go Abroad," *Survey of Current Business*, June 1953, pp. 9–11.

About one half of the American tourists in Europe in 1952 were foreign-born Americans. This represents a large decline both absolutely and relatively from 1929. The decline in foreign-born American tourists will continue. Only 7 per cent of America's present population is foreign-born. The limitation of immigration since World War I will soon reduce the number of foreign-born to insignificant proportions.

The secular downward trend in European travel by foreign-born Americans has not been fully offset by the rising number of native-born American travelers. However, native-born American tourists spend about 70 per cent more per trip than do foreign-born travelers, most of whom visit friends and relatives. The average expenditure of native-born American tourists in Europe and the Mediterranean was $935 in 1952; the corresponding expenditure of foreign-born Americans was $548. These trends will tend to cure the transport bottleneck without reducing total expenditures.

More than 75 per cent of American tourists in Europe come from nine states which have less than half of our total population but nearly 70 per cent of the foreign-born population. New York State alone accounts for one third of the American tourists in Europe.

American travel in Europe has declined sharply from the prewar ratio of tourist expenditures to income. The decline of foreign-born population and the shipping bottleneck do not sufficiently account for the sharp break from the prewar pattern of tourist expenditures.

One study of American tourist trade in Europe for the prewar years 1923–1938 indicates that the important factor determining tourist expenditures was national income.[3] The income most relevant is the disposable income in the three or four years before the trip to Europe is made. Evidently the rate of exchange on foreign currencies and the level of foreign prices had little to do with the decision to travel.

A projection of prewar experience into the postwar period indicates that a disposable income of $200 billion in the United States would be accompanied by tourist expenditure in Europe alone of approximately $1 billion, including payments to European companies for transportation. Actually, tourist expenditures in Europe amounted to only one third of that amount in 1952, when disposable income reached $235 billion.

Travel to Europe by foreign-born Americans to visit relatives will continue to decline as they decline in number. Increased proportions of native-born American tourists as well as any absolute increase in the number of tourists will probably require expansion of tourist accommodations.

3. Kathleen M. Longmore, "American Tourist Expenditure and the European Balance of Payments," *Bulletin of the Oxford University Institute of Statistics*, March 1950, pp. 65–73.

Can Tourism Be Expanded?[4]

Whatever the difficulties which limit exports of Europe's goods to the United States, there is one type of "trade" which avoids almost all the barriers and obstacles which most imports have to meet, namely, the services and goods sold to American tourists while abroad. Of course no tariffs or other trade restrictions apply to payments for food, lodging, transportation and other services rendered to American tourists. Furthermore, most of the difficulties in connection with the scheduling of production, sales promotion and actual sales of European consumer goods in the United States market do not exist when the American tourist goes directly to the merchandise in Europe. Also, the exemption from tariff of goods amounting to $500 per person usually eliminates the effect of our protective tariff on the purchases of the average tourist.

Tourism played an important role in the balance of payments of the E.R.P. countries with the United States. Total dollar earnings of these countries from this source were estimated to have been $345 million in 1950. Expenditures of United States travelers alone amounted to $230 million and fares paid to E.R.P. carriers for transatlantic travel added $115 million more. The figure of $230 million amounted to slightly more than 18 per cent of the value of the merchandise exports of E.R.P. countries to the United States. It exceeded the combined export value of several of the most important commodities from Europe to the United States. Yet to one who visits these countries as a tourist, keeping an eye out always for ways in which the volume of tourism could be expanded, the potentialities for increasing expenditures are immense.

New Tourists Need Different Accommodations

The character of American tourism to Europe has greatly altered between 1929 and the present time. The typical American-born tourist of today is not relatively wealthy, not even as wealthy as the American tourist of 1929. This shift in the income level of the average American-born tourist is one source of some of the current limitations on satisfactory facilities for tourists. Also, the decline of foreign-born tourists who return to visit relatives means that relatively more tourist accommodations are required.

Paris may serve as an example for many European cities. The large hotels of Paris were built to serve, not primarily the tourist of today, but the pre-World War I upper classes of Great Britain, the United States, Germany and Russia. The latter part of the nineteenth century and the first decade

4. This section by Calvin B. Hoover reflects observations made in Europe in the summer of 1950. Cf. Chapter 11.

and a half of the twentieth were the heyday of luxury travel. Two wars in the twentieth century, accompanied by the economic and social upheavals of our day, have meant the decline, if not the disappearance, of those travelers *de luxe* who characterized the period before World War I.

A new type of hotel accommodations, more appropriate for the new tourist drawn largely from a different economic class, is now in demand. The decline in travel *de luxe* has been less pronounced in the United States than in Europe, yet it profoundly affects the possibilities for the expansion of American tourism in Europe.

The new type of tourist presents a problem, but a great opportunity as well. There has been an immense expansion in the number of potential American tourists to Europe simply through the widespread extension of vacations with pay throughout the United States. It is true that most paid vacations are not of a length sufficient to make possible a European vacation which includes a sea voyage. Air passage is still too expensive for many. Yet the current development of the tourist or coach type of air transport makes it possible for literally hundreds of thousands of people to take a vacation in Europe at least once or twice in a lifetime. Furthermore, air travel makes possible the out-of-season trip to Europe by short-term vacationers, which would immensely facilitate the solution of the "peak load" problem in hotel and other tourist accommodations.

Much needs to be done, and much can be done, to tap a market for tourism which could easily double within a very few years the number of Americans now going to Europe. There needs to be an increase in the tourist type of steamship accommodation,[5] for which the demand far exceeds the supply. Still further development of the coach type of air transport and further use of the low-price off-season rate are needed. Fortunately this particular development is currently being planned on a substantial scale.

Another requirement is the expansion of hotel accommodations in Europe, particularly of the type which fits the middle-income purse. A beginning has already been made in the construction of a few hotels having small, comfortable rooms with individual shower baths but with a minimum of plush and gilt.[6] There is a real opportunity for the development of the European *pension* into something a bit more like the "tourist home" or even the "motel" in the United States. Apart from the provision of things like shower baths and a little catering to American tastes in food, it would be most helpful to list *pensions*, together with their prices, at the railway stations and other points to which tourists first come when they arrive in a city.

5. The New Maasdam is an example of such a ship.

6. One hotel of this type has recently been opened in Copenhagen and another in Gothenburg.

Improvement of information furnished to tourists would immensely facilitate tourism. On the simplest level, much could be done by placing explanatory signs in railway stations, at ferries, frontier points and the like. These signs should be in three or.four of the principal languages. A sign in almost any language, is, however, much better than none. It often turns out that the native is sometimes almost as bewildered as the foreigner.

For example, even a native needs explanatory signs when he comes to a ferry crossing an arm of the sea between Sweden and Denmark, with the necessity of changing from train to ship, going through two complete systems of customs, money control and passport inspection, and perhaps a bus to be caught to make connections with the next train. The absence of either signs or guides at such points is likely to discourage tourist travel in areas where great opportunities for expansion otherwise exist.

In addition to signs, travelers' aids or guides in the principal railroad stations would greatly lessen the dependence of tourists on conducted tours or on travel bureaus. Exceedingly useful though conducted tours and travel bureaus are, reduction of the need for their services would materially lower costs and thus perhaps make scores of thousands actual instead of potential tourists.

There is a great need for information for tourists as to the relative occupancy of the various tourist areas at particular times. Much could be done to space out the pressure for accommodations among the various areas by some planning and coordination of promotional advertising by the various European countries and the various tourist resort areas. Tourist advertising, like other advertising, is carried on for competitive reasons, but much would be gained by some cooperation. Often at the moment when hotels are most crowded in Paris, for example, hotels will be almost empty in the Alpine resorts, because "the season" has only begun, even though "the season" is not sharply determined by reasons of climate.

Just when American tourists are flooding into England in June, many vacancies exist in the hotels of the French and particularly the Italian Riviera. Most American tourists who go to England do not visit Italy at all. Those who do are likely to go to Italy when the weather is warmer and when Italians themselves are vacationing at the sea coast and taking up the accommodations there. The custom of going to England first is traditional and is caused partly by the fact that steamship accommodations are available to England but only to a limited extent to Italy. With the further development of air transport this can be partially overcome.

In any event, much could be done to encourage cooperation between steamship lines so that, for example, a tourist who can spend most of the summer in Europe could come to Italy on an Italian ship in June, move up through France and England and later sail for home on a British, French,

Dutch or Scandinavian ship. There are endless variants which could be worked out which would require the cooperation of guided tours, travel bureaus, steamship lines and the governments of the various countries through their organizations for the promotion of tourism.

This means that, just as in the case of intra-European trade in commodities, a central organization to further the common interests of all European countries is needed. Such an organization has indeed been set up, but much still needs to be done. Additional funds spent on the promotion of tourism are likely to afford greater returns per dollar spent than those to encourage the export of commodities. Much can be done, moreover, simply by combining specific advice and information with general promotional efforts in advertising. The additional cost would be almost negligible.

Tourist Purchases

There is probably no phase of tourism which presents so great an immediate opportunity as increasing the amount of consumer goods sold to American tourists while they are abroad. The American tourist fails to use even half of his tariff exemption of $500 per person. It is true that many of the typical "bargains" formerly available to American tourists no longer exist. For example, it used to be possible to purchase men's suits and topcoats in England, either ready-made or custom-made, at a lower price than in the United States. Even after devaluation of the pound, this is no longer true. Other similar comparisons in various countries of Europe might be cited. The demand for commodities by the European domestic market is so strong that prices are forced up while the dollar exchange rate remains pegged. Indeed, in many cases quantities in the market are not sufficient to serve all comers.

This combination of high prices and inadequate quantities of goods reflects a combination of inflationary pressures and failure to allow exchange values of European currencies to fall to the point where their actual purchasing power in comparison with the dollar would be truly reflected. The remedy for this situation would evoke far-reaching problems of national and international economic policy which cannot be developed here.

Quite apart from fundamental changes in foreign exchange parities and apart from special measures like those which have already been taken, such as remission of the purchase tax in Britain and the special exchange rate for tourist purchases in France, there are many things which could be done to facilitate a greatly expanded purchase of goods in Europe by American tourists.

Even though the average present-day American tourist is not wealthy, he still is more likely to buy goods of high grade and quality than anything else. This is because European manufacturers cannot, in most cases, hope to produce articles of mass consumption more cheaply than those in the United States. If an American tourist is to be induced to buy appreciable amounts of goods, either he must be able to find what he wants more cheaply than in the United States or he must be able to buy something which he cannot obtain in the United States.

This means that the tourist will purchase at least limited amounts of high-quality linens, woolens, *de luxe* silks and rayons, leather goods, silver, china, wines and liquors, food specialties and the like, to the extent that these are available, reasonably priced and transportable, *if he knows where they can be most advantageously obtained.* In short, the American tourist is still willing to purchase the type of goods which several European governments are unwilling to allow their own nationals to use scarce foreign exchange to purchase in other countries.

Handicaps to the sale of this type of commodity could be measurably overcome. First, an immense improvement in the sale of goods to tourists would result from making more and better information available with respect to *where* goods can be bought. This cannot be done at all adequately simply by individual advertising. Some sort of cooperative advertising which would, for example, point out the merits of leather goods to be found in Florence, Italy, accompanied by advertisements of individual shops, could be combined with general tourist promotional literature dealing with Italy.

Beginnings have been made in this sort of thing. Small booklets listing shops where particular goods can be bought, together with lists of restaurants, theatres and special tourist attractions, are now placed in the coaches of boat trains coming to Paris from the Channel coast. A very limited attempt has been made to get out a small booklet for a similar purpose in Rome. Yet what has been done falls short of what needs to be done or could be done.

This problem of finding where goods can be bought is illustrated by this writer's effort to find where Sèvres china could be purchased in Paris. There was no listing of Sèvres in the telephone directory. Neither the telephone switchboard operator nor the portier at the Crillon could say where the sales office of this government manufactory was located. The portier finally suggested that one might find out by actually going to Sèvres, in the suburbs of Paris. A trip to Sèvres found only the museum of ceramics open (indeed, the portion of the museum representing Sèvres china was closed while undergoing repairs). Persistent inquiry at the museum yielded the alleged address of the business offices in Paris of the Sèvres manufactory. Upon return to Paris this address turned out to be wrong. Further inquiry seemed useless as it dawned on the writer that even if the offices could be found they would be closed, since it was Saturday. Indeed, since it was also the month of August the offices were probably not open during the entire month.[7]

During August many of the shops and business offices are completely closed for vacation. This custom of closing up shop for a month during the height of the tourist season reflects another failure to exploit effectively all possibilities for increasing dollar earnings from tourist purchases.[8]

One result of this situation is that the producers of quality products complain that there is no future in the manufacture of their type of commodity while simultaneously the commodity can be found only with difficulty on the retail market. Even if one admits that the problem of producing and marketing high-quality goods requiring skilled workmanship presents great difficulties, improvement in the promotional methods so as to develop and service a strong and continuous demand among American tourists would surely help the situation considerably.

One practical limitation on the sale of goods to tourists is the problem of getting goods to the United States after purchase. The tourist may and often does "lug" his purchases with him from London through Paris and Rome and perhaps back to London. This process is obviously not conducive to extensive purchases of articles of large bulk or high specific gravity.

It would be helpful if more shops would offer, for an appropriate charge, to wrap the goods and ship them to the United States for the purchaser. It would be useful if the services of travel agencies in wrapping and shipping aggregates of purchases to the tourist's home address could be more widely developed and popularized. Finally, there might well be a further development of what already has begun in at least one European port of embarkation—the setting up of branch shops selling the kinds of goods which tourists want and delivering them suitably wrapped aboard ship.

These are "homely" suggestions, but it is largely on overcoming the inconvenience aspect of tourist shopping that expansion of purchases by tourists depends.

Shipping

The merchant marine of the United States emerged from World War II as the largest fleet in the world. Yet it costs about $200,000 more to operate a 7,500-ton freighter for one year under the American flag than under the British or Norwegian flags. An American fleet is considered essential for the national defense. The question arises then, as it has before, how much support the merchant fleet should be given by the government.

7. A comparable experience, with the actual incidents differing but with essentially the same frustrating conclusion, had resulted when an economist friend had attempted to locate this same elusive Sèvres sales agency during a previous year.

8. The opera and many of the theatres close during this same period.

Economic considerations alone would dictate the use of foreign fleets for American commerce. Capital costs, wages, subsistence and maintenance costs are higher for American than for foreign ships. If competition determined who got the business, foreign fleets would earn American dollars by carrying American goods. Yet the opposite has prevailed in postwar years despite the fact that the United States has been trying to sell the idea of free competition to the rest of the world. On balance, other nations have had to pay dollars for services rendered by the American merchant fleet because of direct and indirect subsidies to United States shipping.

Shipping represents a substantial item in the balance of payments and a significant part of America's export surplus. In 1949 the United States sold foreign countries more than $1 billion of shipping services including port charges. On balance other countries paid United States ship operators about $500 million for shipping services in contrast to the prewar years, when they earned dollars from us.

Shipping is a clear case where, on economic grounds alone, the United States would hire foreign services—a form of importing—that would enable the rest of the world to earn dollars and would be advantageous to American exporters and consumers because it would be cheaper than shipping under the American flag. The American merchant marine is essential, however, in the event of war and therefore we have been unwilling to permit competition to work. This is an admissible policy as long as the nation subsidizes only as much shipping as is essential for strategic purposes. The criticism is that by indirect subsidy the United States has gone beyond this. As a result the other countries are denied the opportunity to earn dollars in the most important single industry where otherwise they would be able to do so.

As the fleets of other nations have been rebuilt since 1946, the proportion of American foreign trade carried in American ships has declined, but is still far above prewar levels. In 1951 net foreign exchange payments to the United States for shipping still amounted to more than $500 million. This is due in large part to the discrimination enforced by law against hauling American goods in foreign ships. This is not a rational method of supporting a fleet for national defense. The proportion of foreign trade carried by the American merchant fleet will automatically decline as foreign aid is reduced and as our imports rise.

Governmental Policy

In 1789 the Congress passed an act limiting registration of ships under the American flag to those built in the United States and belonging to United States citizens. Moderately favorable rates of duty and discriminatory taxes were used to protect American ships. In 1817 the Congress passed another navigation act, the lasting provision of which was the reservation of coastal trade to American ships. Largely because of basic economic advantages, the American merchant marine flourished until the Civil War and the era of steam. Then it entered a long decline.

During the first world war a Shipping Board with wide authority engaged in a shipbuilding and ship-purchasing program. However, less than one sixth of the tonnage built under its authority was delivered before the Armistice.

The Merchant Marine Act of 1920 was an attempt to maintain a peace-time merchant marine which could be relied upon for national security in time of war. The purpose was to subsidize the American shipping industry in such a way as to offset its comparative disadvantage. A revolving con-struction fund of $12.5 million was set up. But private firms were unwilling to construct merchant vessels in the United States because of the high costs.

The Merchant Marine Act of 1928 doubled the revolving fund and also provided direct subsidies to offset the higher operating costs of the Ameri-can fleet. Mail contracts came into prominent use. Despite this further aid, American shipping stood at only 4.5 million gross tons in 1935.

The Merchant Marine Act of 1936 was a much more aggressive measure than the earlier efforts to rehabilitate American shipping. It set up a United States Maritime Commission with responsibility for (1) increasing the com-merce handled by United States ships and (2) providing additional vessels for use in the event of war. The purpose was to create a merchant marine capable of carrying all coastal waterborne cargo as well as a substantial portion of American foreign commerce. Subsidies and generous terms of payment were provided. Shipbuilding increased under this act, and in 1939 twenty-eight ships were built in the United States. In addition to construc-tion subsidies, the Maritime Commission was permitted to aid private firms in covering operating expenses.

During the second world war an unprecedented level of shipbuilding was carried out under the direction of and for the Maritime Commission.

The United States emerged from the war with a fleet of 61 million net registered tons entered in foreign trade, as compared with the prewar total world fleet of 69 million tons. Because of war losses of the foreign merchant marine, the United States had about 65 per cent of the total merchant tonnage of the world in 1945–1946. With the rebuilding of foreign fleets, this had declined to 41 per cent in 1951, still far above the prewar figure of 26 per cent.[9]

Because of the cheaper cost of operation under foreign flags, as of Jan-uary 1950, 362 American-owned vessels were under foreign registry—about 100 more than before the war.

9. *Statistical Abstract of the United States, 1952*, Table 663, p. 546.

The American fleet today is maintained both by subsidies on shipbuilding and by indirect subvention in the form of discrimination in favor of hauling American cargo in American vessels.

Discrimination against Foreign Shipping

In 1949–1950, some 250 ships were directly subsidized to the extent of approximately $60 million a year. It was assumed that about 100 additional ships would be able to operate without direct subsidy. The objective was that a substantial proportion of American commerce on essential trade routes should be carried by American flag ships. But instead of 100 additional ships, some 300 vessels, practically all of which are privately owned, were able to operate without direct subsidies. Thus, it was not necessary to subsidize the entire American fleet directly.

Apparently the main reason that shipping under the American flag can be profitable without subsidy, despite the fact that foreign vessels are much cheaper to operate, lies in the preferential treatment given American vessels in carrying government-financed cargo.

The combined result of discrimination and direct subsidy was to create an American fleet substantially larger than was necessary in peacetime to carry out the objective of hauling a substantial part of our commerce on its essential trade routes in American ships.[10]

Several laws provide cargo preference for the American fleet. At least 50 per cent of the shipments financed by the ECA and military aid programs have had to be carried by American ships. The precedent goes back almost half a century when the Congress required the Army and Navy to move all their cargo in American vessels. Similar legislation was enacted in the 1930s covering cargoes financed by government loans.[11]

This indirect aid to the shipping industry is more important than the direct subsidies. Indicative of the care which officials in the executive branch of the government bestow on the shipping interests was the transport of cotton to occupied areas as though a 100 per cent preference for American vessels were required, although Public Law 820, 80th Congress, carries no preferential requirement in shipments to occupied areas. In the same spirit, other cargoes for occupied areas were first considered as coming under the 100 per cent preference rule; they were later placed under the 50 per cent preference required by the act which established the ECA, governing shipments not to occupied areas but to Marshall Plan countries.

No matter what size fleet is regarded as necessary for security reasons, the device of cargo preference is an undesirable method of achieving it.[12]

10. This information comes from "competent authority" that prefers not to be quoted.
11. Public Res. 17, 73d Cong., 1934.
12. *Report to the President on Foreign Economic Policies*, 1950, p. 89.

A sound general rule is that subsidies should be open and direct, since concealed subsidies are not subject to the same scrutiny. By indirect aid in the form of cargo preference the cost of the shipping subsidy has been shifted to the budgets of ECA, Mutual Security and other government agencies. The American merchant marine at times has been kept more than one half larger than is called for by the recommendation of responsible authorities. The whole point about cargo preference is that it has been used *indirectly* to increase total aid to the American merchant marine.

Future Policy

The United States will doubtless wish to retain a merchant fleet under the American flag and to insure a nucleus shipbuilding industry capable of expansion. Some American shipping is essential for security. The question is how much.[13] In making this decision the costs should be weighed. A large merchant fleet is a drain on American resources. Together with our allies, we can have more security for the same cost by producing planes, for example, in America and allowing our allies to produce and operate more of the shipping. To the extent that we decide to produce our own ships and operate our own fleet, it means that we must accept less of something else, because American shipping is wasteful of resources.

The reason the United States is unable to compete in shipbuilding is because ships are substantially made to order. This process involves much labor relative to other costs and does not lend itself to the mass production techniques in which the United States has an advantage. Other nations can operate ships more cheaply because their labor costs, which amount to 20 per cent or more of the cost of operation, are no more than one half as great as American labor costs. The perquisites that must be maintained for the crew also cost other countries less than they cost the United States. By subsidies, by exclusion of foreign ships from coastal trade and by discrimination in foreign commerce, United States citizens use their own resources uneconomically and deny their allies the opportunity to earn dollars. This loss of dollar receipts is especially serious today when other nations are trying to earn enough dollars to support themselves.

When a ship is operated under the American flag, the United States is exporting or selling services. European allies must pay the United States for shipping services instead of selling shipping services. The effect of discrimination on the dollar shortage of allies is thus twofold. By eliminating cargo preference, the United States would both reduce exports and increase imports of services. The effect on the balance of payments would, therefore, be twice as great as the charge that is involved. Consequently, the discrimi-

13. Cf. Calvin B. Hoover, *International Trade and Domestic Employment*, McGraw-Hill, New York, 1945, pp. 110–120.

natory treatment which supports one 7,500-ton vessel in the American fleet may increase the dollar shortage by about $500,000 annually.

The elimination of cargo preference would produce savings to the United States in two ways. First, the real cost of shipping would be lower. Second, foreign aid could be reduced. The taxpayers' bill for economic and military aid could be reduced by perhaps $150 million annually by elimination of the cargo preference rule. Here is one way that the taxpayers' burden can be reduced.

In addition to the fleet of ships that are operating at a given time, the United States has also a large stock of ships in "mothballs" which can be drawn upon in times of emergency. Moreover, the American stockpile is not necessarily the only consideration. European allies in the North Atlantic Treaty Organization are the world's principal maritime nations, with a distinct advantage both in shipbuilding and in shipping. The United Kingdom is currently building 40 per cent of the world's new ships. In the event of war, their tonnage is available as allied tonnage. In addition, American-owned vessels now sailing under foreign flags remain under American control in event of war.

The Canadian government, which faced the same problem with respect to shipping, has resolved the issue by reducing the size of its fleet. It has decided against maintaining a large merchant fleet because of the high cost of construction and operation and the need to encourage imports of shipping services from the United Kingdom and other countries. Canada proposes to maintain a small merchant fleet of a few vessels and a modest building program in a few yards and to rely upon the cheaper shipping services of her partners in the North Atlantic community to supply the shipping she needs. The ships owned by the Canadian government and by private individuals above the minimum required were transferred to the British flag in order to take advantage of the lower cost of operations for ships registered in that country.

SERVICES AND THE DOLLAR GAP

Tourism is an important source of net dollar earnings to foreign countries and one that can be increased without precipitating the difficult problem of injury to American industry. The extent to which this could narrow the dollar gap is contingent on what happens to foreign travel in the United States and other expenditures for services, which are increasing. Many foreign governments control the dollar expenditures of their citizens for travel, especially travel for recreation. The balance earned by Europe on tourism would be reduced if controls on travel expenditures in the United States were eliminated, as is eventually desirable. It is not clear that payments by Americans for tourism and other private services will rise faster than receipts, except insofar as foreign governments restrict dollar expenditures of their citizens.

The large balance paid the United States for shipping services can be reduced by eliminating the cargo preference which laws now impose in favor of hauling government-financed goods in American ships. This balance will decline in any event as (1) foreign economic and military aid is curtailed and (2) American imports rise. In fact, the increase of private trade whether of imports or exports will reduce the share of foreign trade that is carried by the American fleet.

Some indication of the magnitude of shipping receipts to the United States on account of government-financed cargo in 1951 is provided by the following figures: (1) Net receipts on ocean transportation of this cargo in 1951 totaled $577 million. (2) Net "cash" payments for ocean transportation by foreign governments were $390 million. (3) The difference of $187 million represents United States government payments under various foreign aid programs to the American fleet for shipping services.[14]

As a result of America's expanded role in world affairs, the expenditures by State Department and other government employees will remain far above prewar levels. But the world's total dollar earning from services will suffer a large decline if United States military establishments overseas are reduced or withdrawn.

The magnitude of such a decline could greatly exceed the potential increase in dollar earnings from the growth of tourism, for example.

On the other side of the balance of payments, the receipts from sale of American services (other than tourists or shipping) to foreign countries are increasing. In addition to travel expenditures, foreign countries purchased roughly $700 million of "other services" from the United States. These include film rentals estimated at $129 million in 1951, private sale of service to foreign governments and international organizations of $114 million, and management fees and contractors' receipts of $190 million. The net receipts to the United States for "other private services" purchased by foreign countries was about $450 million in 1951.

14. *Survey of Current Business*, May 1952, p. 19.

PART IV

WHO WOULD BE HURT?

Chapter 19

Injury and the Escape Clause

THE FUTURE OF America's foreign trade, insofar as it is affected by tariffs, depends on the policy that is adopted with respect to the injury of home industry. It is sometimes asserted that additional imports amounting to no more than 1 or 2 per cent of national production can do no harm. "America has nothing to fear from imports." As a generalization about the economy as a whole this may be true. But, under present policies, official investigations have found that imports can seriously injure individual industries— for example, imports of about $1.5 million have distressed the women's fur felt hat industry. The fact that imports representing an infinitesimal fraction of 1 per cent of national production do not injure total American industry does not meet the issue raised by the "escape clause" of tariff legislation.

Almost equally misleading is the view that additional imports can be absorbed without serious dislocations *because* far greater internal dislocations are already absorbed by the dynamic American economy. The oversight in this approach lies in failure to recognize that *the measure of the adjustment problem is the sum of the dislocations from both internal expansion and foreign trade*. A major part of the adjustment has little or nothing to do with trade barriers but is inherent in dynamic growth. The foreign trade adjustment is quite small and, by itself, would not usually create serious problems. However, the evidence suggests that the impact of additional imports will be concentrated chiefly on those sectors of the home economy which already suffer from internal dislocations. This should be taken into account in deciding where and when to add another straw to the camel's back.

American sensitivity to imports is indicated by official investigations of injury at a time when (1) total imports have declined relative to domestic production since the 1920s and (2) the economy as a whole is strong and prosperous. The present chapter is concerned chiefly with investigations by the Tariff Commission. The next chapter deals with the exposed import-competing industries which are subject to potential injury.

To show that the claims of injury made by interested parties are exaggerated and sometimes fatuous does not prove that the problem is not a serious one. Injury is a neglected subject. The literature advocating expansion of trade is enormous, but the question of injury has been left almost

361

entirely to those in the protectionist camp who rarely rise above the viewpoint of immediately interested parties.

The escape clause makes no provision for consideration of the national interest beyond allowing the President some discretion. It provided that

. . . if, as a result of unforeseen developments and of the concession granted by the United States on any article in the trade agreement, such article is being imported in such increased quantities and under such conditions as to cause, or threaten, serious injury to domestic producers of like or similar articles, the United States shall be free to withdraw the concession, in whole or in part, or to modify it, to the extent and for such times as may be necessary to prevent such injury.[1]

The peril point amendment carries the idea one step further and attempts to prevent injury rather than relieve it. The Tariff Commission determines *before* concessions are granted whether or not proposed concessions represent a threat to home industry. The President must justify his action to the Congress if he goes beyond this peril point.

An important part of our policy since 1951 is that tariff relief under the escape clause is to remain effective only so long as necessary to avoid injury to the domestic industry concerned. Under Executive Order 10401, October 14, 1952, the Tariff Commission has reviewed developments with respect to those items on which concessions have been modified.

The Hat Case

Those who believe that imports can be substantially increased under present trade agreement policies should consider the hat case. Increased imports of only about $1.5 million in 1949 caused the President, on unanimous recommendation of the Tariff Commission, to suspend American tariff concessions on hats under the General Agreement on Tariffs and Trade. Thus, duties on specified items were raised by 25–40 per cent. The

---

1. Executive Order 9832, February 25, 1947. Similar language in bilateral trade agreements and the General Agreement gives the same privilege to the other contracting party. Cf. superseding Executive Orders 10004, October 5, 1948 and 10082, October 5, 1949. On the origin of the escape clause, see *Congressional Record*, June 14, 1948, p. 8032.

Later policy is governed by the language of the Trade Agreements Extension Act of 1951. No tariff reduction or binding of tariff rates or other concessions "shall be permitted to continue in effect when the product on which the concession has been granted is, as a result, in whole or in part, of the duty or other customs treatment reflecting such concession, being imported into the United States in such increased quantities, either actual or relative, as to cause or threaten serious injury to the domestic industry producing like or directly competitive products." Sec. 6(a).

It is the President who acts both to make tariff concessions and to withdraw them. The Congress has been somewhat concerned when the President has failed to carry out recommendations of the Tariff Commission that would restore higher duties. The act of 1951 requires the President to report his reasons for so doing to the Congress. The act also requires the Tariff Commission to investigate possible injury promptly at the request of any interested party, either House of the Congress, the Senate Finance Committee, the House Ways and Means Committee, the President, or the Tariff Commission itself.

question whether injury follows tariff concessions depends on how much or how little of the home economy is considered. It was not the national economy which was injured, or the clothing industry, or the hat industry, or producers of women's hats, but "producers of women's fur felt hats valued at $9 to $24 per dozen." Eleven firms were considered in the Tariff Commission's survey.

The hat case illustrates four important aspects of the incidence of increased imports: (1) Home industries likely to suffer from imports are usually in trouble already from other causes. More often than not, imports are only the coup de grâce. As a general rule, it is not the rapidly growing industries but the declining or relatively stagnant industries which are most seriously affected by tariff reduction. (2) The impact of additional imports is often highly concentrated on small firms in geographical areas which are already suffering from internal dislocations. (3) The industries which would be displaced by imports are not typically the highly mechanized mass production industries, but those with a relatively high proportion of labor cost to total costs. (4) It is not the large firms in the monopolistic industries but the highly competitive home industries which are most exposed to serious injury by potential competition from imports.

The hat industry was suffering from a change in consumer habits, and the women's fur felt hat industry in particular from a change in style. The hatless mode has reduced consumption. In addition, styles changed in favor of fur felt hats with napped or pile finishes, a finish that required relatively more handwork. Consumption of women's fur felt hats declined from more than a million dozen in 1937 to about half that volume after the war. In the same period, imports increased from less than 5 per cent of domestic production in 1937 to 21 per cent in 1949, and further to 30 per cent in 1950 (January–June). Although still quite small in absolute volume, the increase in imports was about 125 per cent.

Imports did not increase following the tariff concession in 1938 to Czechoslovakia or following the concession to Britain in 1939. Concessions were again made in the General Agreement (effective January 1, 1948). In 1948 imports were still below the 1937 level. The increase appears to have been associated with later changes in style favoring a napped or pile finish. But for the change in style, imports might not have increased in such volume as to injure domestic producers.

Some producers specialize, but most produce both men's and women's hat bodies. For the industry as a whole, women's hats are much less important than men's. Although men's hats account for two thirds or more of the output of the industry as a whole, women's hats account for 90 per cent of the output of about 20 firms. Thus, the finding of injury from imports was for a product of specialization by the domestic industry under the narrow definition of "industry" used by the Tariff Commission. Presumably the hat industry as a whole was not injured.

Domestic producers have held the low end of the price range while imports have supplied the higher-priced items. That is, imports do not seriously compete below $9 per dozen or above $24 per dozen hat bodies. But between $9 and $24 per dozen the competition is direct, and in 1949 and the first half of 1950, imports increased "under such conditions as to cause serious injury to the domestic industry producing like or directly competitive products, and as to threaten continuance of such injury."[2]

Italy and Czechoslovakia supplied over 90 per cent of the imports by quantity.

Not all home industries share equally in general prosperity. Additional imports of $1.5 million could have been absorbed without injury if domestic producers of women's fur felt hats had been prosperous and expanding instead of suffering from a 50 per cent fall in consumption between 1937 and 1947.

The domestic fur felt hat industry making both men's and women's hat bodies is highly concentrated in a few cities on the eastern seaboard. Principal centers are Danbury and Norwalk, Connecticut; Reading and Philadelphia, Pennsylvania; and Amesbury, Massachusetts. Danbury, Norwalk, and Amesbury are highly dependent on the manufacture of felt hats. It is estimated that about 85 per cent of the factory wages in Danbury, and 50 per cent of those in Norwalk, are ordinarily paid by the hat industry.[3]

The wording of the escape clause was changed in the Trade Agreements Extension Act of 1951. The earlier phrasing was: "if as a result of unforeseen developments and the concession granted . . ." Since it is unthinkable that under trade agreement policies tariff concessions would be granted to produce foreseeable injury, the escape clause is a safeguard against "unforeseen" changes in styles, relative costs, conditions in the industry and, possibly, general economic conditions. This shows the fragile character of increased foreign trade under trade agreements. Imports may not increase for ten years after concessions are granted and the injury may arise more from the condition of the domestic industry than from the absolute volume of imports.

There are strong reasons for believing that most of America's import-competing industries will be unable to keep pace with increasing productivity in the more dynamic domestic industries. If the forces of prosperity are strong enough and wages are raised equally among the various industries by competition for labor, the import-competing industries which lag

2. *Women's Fur Felt Hats and Hat Bodies*, U.S. Tariff Commission, Report to the President, September 1950, p. 2, mimeographed.
3. *Ibid.*, p. 25.

behind in advancing productivity will find that foreign producers have gained advantage as a result of the relatively more rapid increase of productivity in the more dynamic home industries. In other words, American import industries with small improvements in productivity will have to pay high wages in order to compete for labor with other industries that have had a large rise in productivity. In the long run, the chief hope for a substantial increase in competitive imports lies in this development. But those who look to this development to increase substantially our foreign trade have reckoned without the escape clause.

Spring Clothespins

The duty on clothespins was twice reduced by trade agreements: first, from 20 to 15 cents per gross and, then, to 10 cents. Because of these concessions and the rise in prices, the ad valorem equivalent fell from 139 per cent in 1931 to 24 per cent in 1949.

The duty was prohibitive before the war and imports were negligible. Because of the backlog of consumer demand, consumption immediately after the war was four or five times as great as prewar. This provided a greatly expanded market for both imports and domestic production, the lion's share going to imports. In 1945 and 1946 imports were three times as great as domestic production. Thereafter, however, imports fell sharply to one third or less of domestic production.

The Tariff Commission (Gregg dissenting) found that imports had greatly increased but were not "entering under such conditions" as to injure domestic industry. "Even since the middle of 1948, when the backlog of demand was filled and when stocks were increasing and prices were declining, domestic producers have actually increased their sales substantially at the same time that imports have been falling off."[4]

This would seem to be a clear case where imports served as a stabilizing influence in the domestic market. The expansion of domestic output to fill the accumulated backlog of demand was less because of a great increase in imports in 1945 and 1946. But imports fell drastically after 1946 while domestic production held up well.

Clothespins indicates what small industries must be considered in connection with injury from imports. More important, clothespins shows the conditions under which imports may be increased without running afoul of the escape clause. The Tariff Commission found no injury although the increase in imports represented a larger percentage of total consumption than in the case of hats.[5] Injury depends not only on (1) the absolute volume of imports and, (2) the increase of imports relative to domestic production,

4. *Spring Clothespins*, U.S. Tariff Commission, Report No. 168, 1950, p. 3.
5. *Ibid.*, p. 1.

but also (3) on "conditions" under which imports take place. The ratio of imports to domestic production had increased from 33 per cent in 1947 to 41 per cent in August 1949. The market for clothespins had expanded and could absorb the additional imports; the market for hats could not.

The clothespin decision was not unanimous, and the following considerations led Commissioner Gregg to dissent from the majority decision of no injury: (1) Domestic producers lost sales to imports in the recession of 1949. (2) Inventories accumulated and prices fell. (3) The evidence showed foreign costs to be substantially below domestic costs.[6]

The basis for a more liberal interpretation is found in the argument as to legislative intent in the "additional comments" of Commissioner Edminister. Noting that the Congress had adopted the policy of expanding trade by gradually reducing tariff barriers, he held that it was not intended to construe the delegation of power to negotiate agreements so as to "foredoom it to sterility."

. . . it must be presumed to have been foreseen that reductions in United States duties in trade agreements would result in offers for the importation of many foreign articles into the United States market at prices lower than those at which they would have been offered in the absence of duty reductions on them; and further that, in many cases, this would result in substantial increases in the actual quantities imported of products directly competitive with articles produced in the United States. In short, it must have been foreseen that the duty reductions made in trade agreements would operate to limit to some extent the domestic production of certain articles, whether by actually reducing production or making expansion of it less profitable than it would otherwise be.[7]

It is clear enough that imported clothespins are a substitute for the domestic products, although domestic clothespins sold at higher prices than imports because of the superior quality of wood and metal used in manufacture. Goods of inferior quality may be highly competitive with those of better quality, particularly when the difference is a question of durability.

One cannot escape the impression that the most significant difference between the hat and clothespin cases was that the domestic hat industry had been declining for a number of years while the market for clothespins was in a robust condition after the production "holiday" imposed during the war years.

Hatters' Fur

Hatters' fur was the second escape clause proceeding in which imports had increased in such quantities as to seriously injure home industry and

6. *Ibid.*, pp. 6–16.

7. *Ibid.*, p. 4. Presumably this view was not shared by all the Commissioners who concurred in the decision.

to require the suspension of tariff concessions (effective February 8, 1952).[8] The total value of imports of hatters' fur was $382,000 in 1950 and $618,000 in January–August 1951.

The most important point brought out in this case is that, under the escape clause, domestic industry can be seriously injured by extremely small quantities of imports both absolutely and relatively. This is because of the condition of the industry owing to other factors. Imports amounted to only 5–6 per cent of domestic consumption in 1950–1951.

The reason that such small quantities of imports were injurious is that hatters' fur is a declining industry. Imports were the last straw. The long-run trend of consumption has been down (1) because men and women do not wear hats as much as formerly; (2) and, to a lesser extent, because of the displacement of fur felt by other materials for making hats. Consumption of hatters' fur declined from 7.9 million pounds before the war to 5.9 million pounds in 1947, to 5.4 million pounds in 1950.

The 1930 duty was 35 per cent ad valorem. This had been reduced to 27½ per cent in the 1935 bilateral agreement with Belgium, and further reduced to 15 per cent in the General Agreement. Imports of hatters' fur before the war were negligible. Imports supplied roughly 1 per cent of domestic consumption in 1948, 3 per cent in 1949, 5 per cent in 1950 and 6 per cent in the first part of 1951. Imports in recent years consist largely of low-grade furs and account for 15 to 20 per cent of domestic consumption of the lower grades. Domestic production of the closely comparable grade accounts for 30 per cent of total production of hatters' fur.

Belgium was the principal source of imports, supplying more than two thirds of the total.

"Practically all of the raw skins used by the domestic fur cutters are imported and come from the same sources"[9] as those which supply hatters' fur. The only question is whether the furs are imported in raw or processed form. The tariff protects domestic fur cutters from foreign competition.

The 35 per cent duty provided in the act of 1930 was restored on imports valued at $1.36 or less per pound, the concession rate of 15 per cent was continued on imports valued at $3.17 per pound, and a specific duty of 47½ cents per pound was established on imports valued between $1.36 and $3.17 per pound.

Motorcycles

The principal issue in this case was whether imported motorcycles are "like or directly competitive" with domestic production.

8. *Hatters' Fur*, U.S. Tariff Commission, Report No. 178, 1953.
9. *Ibid.*, p. 3.

The 10 per cent duty on motorcycles under the act of 1930 was bound against increase in the trade agreement with the United Kingdom effective January 1939.

Before the war imports amounted to only 3 per cent of domestic production. Domestic production in 1947 and 1948 was two and three times as great as in 1937. The increase in imports was still greater, amounting to 45 per cent of production in 1947. Domestic production reached a peak of 48,600 motorcycles in 1948 but declined to 17,500 in 1951 while imports increased relatively from 24 per cent of domestic production in 1948 to 52 per cent in 1951. This is the essence of the case for injury. That case was supported by the dissenting views of Commissioners Brossard and Gregg. Among other things, they also pointed out that the profits (before taxes) of Harley-Davidson (the only important domestic producer) "which averaged about 9 per cent during the 3 years 1946–1948 (and were appreciably higher during the 3 years 1937–1939), had declined to between 4.5 and 5.6 per cent of sales during the 3 year period 1949–1951."

The majority of the Commission found that the domestic industry was not injured by imports on the ground that imports are a much lighter motorcycle for sports use and do not compete directly with the heavier type of domestic motorcycle used by police.

The increase in the use of motorcycles for sport is due in part to the development of demand for lightweight and middleweight motorcycles, almost all the domestic consumption of which was supplied before 1948 by imports. Acquaintance with machines of these types was acquired during World War II by Americans who were serving in United States mili forces abroad and by other Americans during the years immediately after the war, when domestic motorcycles were not available in sufficient numbers to supply the demand. A further factor was the large increase and wider dispersion of sales agencies, resulting in broader contacts with the buying public.

In the 1949–1951 period there would have been considerably larger sales of domestic motorcycles had it not been for the marked decline in sales of the Indian Motorcycle Co., whose difficulties have been due mainly, if not wholly, to causes other than the competition of imports.[10]

Blue-Mold Cheese

Should the escape clause protect domestic producers whose output was greatly expanded during the war when imports were cut off? This issue was clearly presented in the case of blue-mold cheese, but was not brought to a clear decision owing to the fact that imports were restricted by quota under the Defense Production Act before the Tariff Commission's investigation of injury was completed.

10. *Motorcycles and Parts*, U.S. Tariff Commission, Report No. 180, 1953, pp. 3–5.

Blue-mold cheese is made by substantially the same process as Roque-fort, but is made from cow's milk instead of sheep's milk. Blue-mold is a "new" domestic cheese. Commercial production began in the 1930s and expanded rapidly during the war. Peak production of over 12 million pounds was reached in 1946 when imports were negligible.

Before the war, annual imports, chiefly from Denmark, Italy and France, were about 3.5 million pounds. The case for injury is shown by the following figures (in millions of pounds):

	Production	Imports
1939	Very small	3.3
1949	8.1	1.3
1950	7.7	3.5
1951	5.2	5.0

The 1930 duty was 7 cents a pound but not less than 35 per cent ad valorem. In 1936 this was reduced to 5 cents a pound but not less than 25 per cent ad valorem by trade agreement with France. This concession was continued under the General Agreement. The duty was reduced again in May 1950 to 3 cents a pound but not less than 15 per cent ad valorem.

Because of the quota controls, a majority of the Tariff Commission found that no action was necessary under the escape clause, but added that "if the import restrictions under section 104 should be terminated, a situation might develop which would require prompt action. . . ."[11]

Commissioner Gregg vigorously dissented from the majority view of the Commission. Even though domestic production was established while imports were cut off during the war, Gregg held that the evidence of injury was obvious. Domestic production had declined by more than one half (from 1946) as imports increased. Moreover, the absolute volume of imports exceeded prewar levels.

The acrimonious exchange in this report between Commissioner Gregg and some other members of the Commission, though ostensibly over the question of procedure, seems to indicate radically different views within the Commission as to what constitutes "serious injury."

Garlic

The investigation of injury to domestic producers of garlic presented the issue of truck gardeners who could avoid injury by substituting one crop for another. Garlic is a convenient crop to use in rotation and accounts for only a small part of the total gardening product of the great bulk of domestic garlic producers. In the case of a few specialized producers, however, garlic was the principal crop.

11. *Blue-mould Cheese*, U.S. Tariff Commission, Report No. 179, 1953, p. 4.

Before 1943, garlic imports ranged from about one fifth to one half of domestic production. The absolute increase in imports was more than threefold, from 5 million pounds in 1935–1939 to 16.7 million pounds in 1951. Domestic production increased slightly from 11 million pounds in 1940 to 12.9 million pounds in 1950. In the four years 1948–1951, imports were as great or greater than domestic production. Apart from the effect of imports on price, the displacement of domestic production by imports was relative rather than absolute.

A majority of the Commission (Brossard, Durand, Gregg and McGill) found that the domestic garlic industry was injured by imports (July 1952). Essentially the basis for this finding was the *relative* increase in imports and the fact that prices for 1949–1951 had declined more than one third from the 1944–1948 level. The majority held that evidence before the Commission indicated that the price "must be at least 12 cents a pound to be remunerative."[12] Actual prices in the three years 1949–1951 were 8.5 to 10 cents a pound.

The decision was four to two. Commissioners Ryder and Edminister dissented from the majority recommendation on the following grounds: (1) Garlic production is only a very small part of the *business* of most producers. (2) "Closely related to the preceding point is the fact that the labor, the land, and most of the equipment used in the production of garlic can be and has been used in the production of other crops. This fact limits the extent of any injury which garlic growers can experience as a result of a deterioration in the market for garlic."[13]

The key fact in the garlic case would seem to be that domestic producers continued to expand production absolutely when alternative crops for which there were profitable markets could have been substituted within their own business.

The duty on garlic had been reduced by tariff concessions from 1.5 cents to 0.75 cents a pound; as a result of higher prices, the ad valorem equivalent of the 1930 specific duty (1.5 cents) was reduced from 40 to 22 per cent. Thus, the combined effect of both factors reduced the equivalent ad valorem rate from 40 to 11 per cent—a reduction of almost three fourths.

Restoration of the full 1930 duty of 1.5 cents a pound, according to the majority of the Tariff Commission, "would be inadequate to remedy the serious injury to the domestic industry concerned." The Commission, therefore, recommended quantitative controls as "the only adequate remedy for such injury that can be applied by the President"[14] and proposed quotas for individual countries as follows (in millions of pounds):

12. *Garlic*, U.S. Tariff Commission, Report No. 177, 1953, p. 5.
13. *Ibid.*, p. 5.
14. *Ibid.*, pp. 2–3.

Mexico	6.3
Italy	4.8
Chile	.9
Argentina	.4
All others	.4

Thus, one important point that emerges from the garlic case is that tariff reduction with the escape clause may lead to more rigid restrictions on imports than if the duty had been left unaltered.

Garlic and the National Interest

The President rejected the majority recommendation of the Tariff Commission. In addition to citing some facts from the dissenting view of Commissioners Ryder and Edminister, President Truman expanded on the importance of trade in his identical letters of July 21, 1952 to the Chairmen of the Senate Finance Committee and the House Ways and Means Committee.[15]

If the standards employed by the majority were to be applied generally to American imports, I am confident that our trade agreements program would soon be impaired beyond all possible remedy, and gains from the negotiated tariffs completely nullified.

The Trade Agreements Act provides no guarantee to American producers against increased competition from imports. All that the escape clause provides for is protection against "serious injury." There is no evidence in this case that these increased imports are causing serious injury to American producers of garlic and that resort to an escape clause action would be justified.

On the contrary, there are many reasons for welcoming the increase in imports of Italian garlic. The United States has a stake in the strength and prosperity of Italy. We have recognized that fact in the aid we have given to Italy under the European Recovery Program and under the Mutual Security Act.

Italy has done a good job with that aid. Her production has increased. The strength of her Communist Party has declined. But Italy still needs to find ways of earning more dollars, and she is trying earnestly, and with some success, to earn them. Every obstacle the United States puts in her way in these efforts is a step harmful to our mutual security and costly in the end to the consumer and American taxpayer.

Yet lately our laws have forced us to put a good many obstacles of this sort in Italy's way. We recently raised our tariff on hats and hatters' furs, which the Italians sold us in considerable quantity. We recently put a large import fee on foreign almonds, most of which come from Italy. Our cheese amendment to the Defense Production Act, which restricts imports of foreign cheeses, has been hurting Italy more than any other single country, and Italy sees more trouble ahead in some of the escape clause applications which the Tariff Commission is now studying. All this seems to run contrary to a sensible policy toward Italian imports.

15. *Ibid.*, pp. 27–28.

As pointed out earlier, the Tariff Commission proceedings on garlic imports have taken place pursuant to the escape clause provisions of Section 7 of the Trade Agreements Extension Act of 1951. While the idea of an escape clause in the trade agreements program is not new, it was not written into the law until the Trade Agreements Extension Act of 1951 was enacted. When I signed that Act, I was disturbed by the protectionist overtones of this provision and a number of other provisions which it contained. I said this at the time I signed the Act.

Those misgivings now seem to have been justified. It is my understanding that the Tariff Commission has been flooded with escape clause applications— applications on blue-mold cheese, motorcycles, glaced cherries, clothespins, and a host of other products. Each one of these, of course, will be for determination on its merits—with the principles and objectives of the Trade Agreements Act as the fundamental guide. . . . Escape clauses, peril points, and the like, must be realistically administered in the light of this general objective, despite protectionist pressures that may be brought to bear against the Commission.

This is all the more important in view of the international crisis we face today. Normal economic life, in the form of the exchange of goods, is an essential requirement of friendly international relations. If we are restrictive in our trade with other countries, they must find other areas with which to trade. Cooperation in the economic field is fundamental to other forms of cooperation.

Just as important is the fact that a way must be found for these countries to carry their share of defense costs without continued reliance on our aid. It is to their own benefit—and to the benefit of the American taxpayer—that we find ways and continue to improve them, as quickly as possible, to the end that substantial foreign imports may become a substitute for direct foreign aid. In the total economy of the United States and, it seems to me, in the economy of the several domestic producers, garlic plays a minor part; to restrict imports of garlic under the circumstances portrayed in this report would violate the spirit as well as the intent of our trade agreements program.

Very sincerely yours,

HARRY S. TRUMAN

These remarks of the President are somewhat in the nature of obiter dicta. They are not material to the question of whether imports have seriously injured domestic producers of garlic. The President was here raising questions of the *national interest*. Such considerations are important and should play a role in American commercial policy. But they are not material to the question of injury to a specific industry, and the evidence seems fairly clear that the Congress has failed to sanction a policy which would injure home industry in the national interest.

The escape clause makes no provision for consideration of any interest except that of the "domestic producers of like or similar articles."[16] On the other hand, it can be argued that the President was given the power to reject the Tariff Commission's recommendations precisely in order to take

16. Legislative history of the Trade Agreements Act of 1955 may imply that the President's discretion involves consideration of national interest. For further comment on the same issue, see watches, p. 445.

broader considerations into account, and that, otherwise, no such discretion would be needed. Moreover, it might be said that the President has an obligation to overturn the Commission's recommendation where the national interest is at stake.

This view has far-reaching implications, indeed. If account were taken (1) of the injury to exporters from withdrawing tariff concessions and (2) of the need to make American commercial policy serve the dictates of our foreign policy, the escape clause would become harmless, and also relatively useless. But this would mean that the President's action *accepted* injury and called for the sacrifice of a specific industry in order to serve the national interest. In no case has the President so acted and it seems doubtful if his discretion goes this far. Such a policy would raise the question of equity and possible compensation for injury sustained in the national interest.

Groundfish Fillets

Increased imports of groundfish fillets are an indirect consequence of technological advance. In earlier chapters it was shown that technological change has taken a heavy toll of American imports.[17] The question naturally arises whether technological advance may not increase some imports while displacing others. In the present study we have searched for such instances and here is an example.[18]

Groundfish fillets are fresh or frozen strips of flesh cut from the sides chiefly of cod, haddock and rosefish (ocean perch). The domestic catch of groundfish, which also includes pollack, hake and cusk, is taken almost entirely by the New England fishing fleet. The market for groundfish was greatly widened by new methods of freezing in the filleted form. In addition, the product has become more popular in the new form.

The same revolutionary change in methods of marketing which stimulated consumption in areas distant from landing ports has also enabled imports of groundfish fillet to compete in the domestic market. The advent of freezing and filleting has extended the geographical market and improved the competitive position of Canada and Newfoundland, which are close to abundant fishing grounds.

Foreign production plants for filleting are expanding. Canada has three large plants under construction and others are reported to be planned. Iceland has expanded production facilities in recent years and Norway is building filleting plants.

The broad outlines of the competitive problem are quite clear. Imports have expanded ninefold since before the war. But the same improvements

17. See, for example, agricultural and mineral imports, Chapters 13 and 15.
18. Other examples are uranium and cobalt.

TABLE 64

IMPORTS OF GROUNDFISH FILLET AS PER CENT OF CONSUMPTION, 1939–1951

Year	Per Cent	Year	Per Cent
1939	13	1946	36
1940	14	1947	31
1941	10	1948	34
1942	19	1949	27
1943	26	1950	37
1944	29	1951	41
1945	40		

Source: U.S. Tariff Commission.

in marketing which have increased imports have also expanded the market. Consumption of groundfish fillets increased from 110 million pounds in 1939 to 236 million pounds in 1951. Moreover, the Tariff Commission found no evidence of a decline in the rate of growth.

Domestic production increased from 100 million pounds in 1939 to 149 million pounds in 1951. The issue presented by the investigation of injury is the question of relative shares of the market. By the absolute test, domestic production expanded by almost 50 per cent. By the relative test, the domestic industry lost ground to imports, which claimed an increasing share of a growing market. (See Table 64.) A majority of the Commission—Ryder, Edminister and McGill—held that the domestic industry was not injured. "An important indication of whether there has been improvement or deterioration in the condition of an industry, obviously, is whether production has been rising or declining. By this test it is clear that . . . domestic production . . . has gone up, not down."[19] Commissioners Brossard and Gregg dissented.

Spring Clothespins Again

After finding no injury to domestic producers of spring clothespins in its decision of December 1949, the Tariff Commission was again requested to investigate imports in later years.

In 1950 domestic production of spring clothespins reached a record level of three times prewar production, despite a large increase in imports. In 1951 imports increased while domestic production declined. In the first five months of 1952, imports declined abruptly relative to domestic production. Thus, there seems to be no established trend since 1946. (See Table 65.)

The Commission also considered wages, employment and profits. The number of workers employed in December 1951 was 578. Wages averaged

19. *Groundfish Fillet,* U.S. Tariff Commission, Report No. 182, 1953, p. 8. For later investigations see Appendix 7.

TABLE 65
SPRING CLOTHESPINS: PRODUCTION AND IMPORTS BY SPECIFIED YEARS,
1924–1952
(*Thousands of Gross*)

Year	Production	Imports	Imports as Per Cent of Production[a]
1924	843	101	12
1929	824	66	8
1931	835	11	1
1937	1,152	17	1
1939	1,335	7	0.5
1945	300	984	328
1946	1,135	3,168	279
1947	2,748	876	32
1948	3,237	1,065	33
1949	3,102	734	24
1950	3,670	985	27
1951	3,085	1,252[b]	41
1952 (Jan.–May)	1,248	399[b]	32

Source: U.S. Tariff Commission.
a. Percentages calculated before rounding.
b. Preliminary.

$1 per hour compared with $1.59 in all manufacturing industries. The increase in wages between 1946 and 1951 was 40 per cent in clothespins compared with 47 per cent in all manufacturing industries.

A majority of the Commission held that the

extremely wide contrast in the profit experience of the several concerns . . . tends to support the conclusion that the spring clothespin industry, *as an industry*, is not being seriously injured by imports. Some of the concerns have consistently made high, or at least substantial, profits. Those who have done less well on their clothespin operations either have consistently made fairly good earnings on their overall operations—and usually a profit on their spring clothespin operations as well—or, where the latter was not the case, have been so situated as regards their overall operations as to raise considerable doubt concerning the significance of their profit and loss figures on spring clothespins.[20]

This was only one of several factors taken into account. Consideration of the over-all profit position of an industry is clearly of great importance in establishing the criteria of injury. If over-all profits rather than the profitability of the specific products were accepted as a general principle, it would permit imports to displace domestic production of a specific product in a multiproduct industry.

A majority of the Commission again found that imports were not injuring the spring-clothespin industry. Commissioners Brossard and Gregg again dissented. They held that the competitive position of the industry

20. *Spring Clothespins (1952),* U.S. Tariff Commission, Report No. 181, 1953, p. 8.

has further deteriorated, and that domestic producers of spring clothespins are now in serious difficulty as a result of import competition.

Imports have continued to increase, both absolutely and relative to domestic production, and laid-down prices of clothespins in the principal markets of the United States have continued to favor the imported article. Employment in the domestic clothespin industry has declined; shipments of domestic manufacturers have fallen; and domestic manufacturers of clothespins (in the aggregate) suffered a loss in 1950 and realized a profit of only 2.9 per cent (before taxes) in 1951 *on that part of their business relating to clothespins.*[21]

Silk Scarves

The 1930 duty of 65 per cent on screen-printed silk scarves was reduced by 50 per cent under GATT. The Tariff Commission unanimously found that domestic producers were seriously injured and recommended withdrawal of the concession. President Eisenhower remanded the case to the Commission on grounds that international conditions demand our most earnest cooperation under trade agreements, and that action under the escape clause should be taken with great care and only after the facts are "clearly established and well authenticated." In short he told the Commission to go slow in recommending higher duties to him.

Clearly, it is beyond the Commission's competence to evaluate the effect of its recommendations on international relations. Although the issue in this case is rather complex and the facts are incomplete, it does appear that domestic producers of screen-printed silk scarves were injured as a result of the increase in imports. It does not follow, however, that "the industry" was injured, provided that industry is defined to include producers of all screen-printed products. The Commission made a supplementary report but failed to answer this question.[22]

Dried Figs

Dried figs is the third instance of serious injury under the escape clause. As a result of imports in the amount of one million dollars in 1951, duties were increased August 30, 1952.

Nearly all of the domestic crop is grown in California, where acreage reached a peak in 1930 and declined steadily for the next twenty years. But production increased almost consistently from 1930 to 1947 because of better control of pests and disease and because of higher yields from older trees.

As production increased, imports declined in importance from 30 per cent of production in 1931–1932 to 11 per cent in 1937–1938. The volume of imports which seriously injured home industry was relatively smaller

21. *Ibid.*, p. 9. (Italics supplied.) In 1954 the Commission divided 3–3.
22. *Screen-Printed Silk Scarves*, 1954 (processed).

than in any year prior to 1932. Imports amounted to 23 per cent of production in 1950, 15 per cent in 1951 and 10 per cent in 1952.

The essence of the case for injury appears to rest on the effect of imports on prices. Increased imports were held responsible for the weakness of packers' prices and the abnormal carryover of the 1950 crop. This carryover and the prospect of continued high-level imports led to a 30 per cent decline in the price that packers offered for the 1951 crop.[23]

Other Escape Clause Investigations

Candied cherries presented an issue somewhat similar to the garlic case. Candied cherries are produced in part by the same process and with the same equipment and labor that are used to produce other candied fruits or maraschino cherries. The "industry" affected by imports is, therefore, the candied fruit industry. Since candied cherries are a minor part of the business defined in this way, producers of candied cherries could not show that their gross sales or profits were seriously reduced as a result of higher imports in 1951.

A second factor was that increased imports in 1951 were due to the short crop and consequent high prices of sulphurated cherries, from which candied cherries are made. A third factor was that beginning in 1952 substantial imports of candied cherries were rejected by the Food and Drug Administration and foreign producers faced difficulties in conducting their operations so as to meet the standards of the Food and Drug Administration.

Consequently, the Tariff Commission found, with Brossard and Gregg dissenting, that imports had not caused and were not threatening serious injury to the domestic industry.

In the case of pregnant mare's urine, the Tariff Commission decided unanimously that domestic producers were not injured by imports. Natural hormones produced from pregnant mare's urine sold at about 6 cents per pill. Synthetic processes for hormone production subsequently resulted in drastically lower prices for the synthetic product. There is an argument whether synthetic and natural hormones are fully competitive. The decision of the Tariff Commission, however, did not settle the interesting question whether the escape procedure can be invoked when the injury is due primarily to competition from another industry which produces a substitute product if the substitution is imperfect. The Commission rejected the appeal on the ground that the producers were engaged in the business of buying and selling horses and that production of pregnant mare's urine was not their primary "business."

23. *Figs, Dried*, U.S. Tariff Commission, Report No. 188, 1953.

The Tariff Commission found that domestic producers of briar pipes had been injured by increased imports. Imports of briar pipes had increased absolutely and domestic production had declined absolutely. The market was disturbed by the Army's release of surplus PX stocks. The President rejected this decision on the ground that the imported pipes were noncompeting. The imported pipes which had increased in volume were novelty items selling for 10–20 cents.

A majority of the Tariff Commission, Commissioners Brossard and Gregg dissenting, found that notwithstanding the recent substantial increase in imports of wood screws of iron or steel, such imports were not causing or threatening injury to the domestic industry. In this case, no hearings were held, since in the opinion of the majority no evidence of injury was apparent in the premises. After a third investigation the Commission divided evenly, 3–3, and the President declined to invoke the escape clause.

Other escape clause investigations include chalk, woodwind musical instruments, canned bonita and tuna fish, and household china. Among the earlier applicants were producers of candied chestnuts, hops, reeds, narcissus bulbs and berets.

Summary of Escape Clause Actions, 1948–1952

During the four years ended June 30, 1952, 38 applications were made to the Tariff Commission for investigation under the escape clause. Under Executive Order the Commission could dismiss a petition for insufficient evidence after preliminary investigation. The act of 1951 requires an investigation and report. Sixteen of 20 applications in the earlier period were dismissed on the ground that the evidence did not justify formal hearing on investigation. Action was deferred in one case and the application was later withdrawn.

Twenty-two applications presented sufficient evidence to warrant investigation, or investigation was required by law. (1) Injury was found and concessions modified in three cases. (2) No injury was found by the President in nineteen cases; in four of these the Tariff Commission had recommended modification of concessions. (See Table 66.)

The problem of injury became increasingly serious in 1951–1952. The thirty-eight applications for restriction of imports provide a valuable clue as to the incidence of injury. (See Appendix 6.) (1) Only five applicants could be called producers of durable goods and these were all relatively small industries—motorcycles, bicycles, watches, musical instruments and screws. (2) Five applicants were producers of minerals—petroleum, aluminum and lead. All of these applications were filed at the time of the slight recession in 1949 and early 1950. (3) Almost three fourths of the ap-

TABLE 66

DISPOSITION OF APPLICATIONS FOR INVESTIGATION UNDER ESCAPE CLAUSE,
1949–1952

Year	Number of Applications	Dismissed without Investigation	Investigated	
			No Injury	Injury
Total	38[a]	16	19	3
1949	9	8	1	0
1950	11	8	1[b]	2
1951	3	0[c]	3	0
1952	15	0[c]	14[d]	1

Source: Appendix 6.

a. Two applications regarding aluminum and two regarding lead are duplicates. Three others are repeat cases: berets, clothespins and wood screws. Thus, the total represents 33 different "industries."

b. Action deferred in glove case and application withdrawn in 1951.

c. Investigation required by act of 1951.

d. The President rejected recommendations of the Tariff Commission which had found serious injury to producers of garlic, watches, pipes and silk scarves.

plicants and all the cases of injury were producers of agricultural products or nondurable goods. (4) No large-scale industries or firms were among the applicants except for minerals.

The industries claiming injury were so small (except minerals) that, even if they were all injured, the volume of increased imports would not go far toward solving the problems of international trade.

A review of escape clause investigations fully vindicates the administration's claim that American industry has not been seriously injured as a result of tariff concessions. But the other side of the coin is that the Trade Agreements Program has failed, thus far, substantially to increase imports. In relation to the vastness of the undertaking, the increase in imports has been meagre indeed. Never before were such large-scale negotiations sustained over such a long period. Reduction of the tariff mountain has produced a mouse. (For later investigations see Appendix 7.)

After eighteen years of experience under trade agreements, only three cases of injury have required the suspension of tariff concessions—fur felt hats, hatters' fur and dried figs. It should quickly be added that injury has been avoided by quantitative restrictions on a number of agricultural products. The Tariff Commission found injury in four other cases—watches, garlic, scarves and smoking pipes. But the President, correctly, rejected these recommendations, though not always for the right reasons.

As will be shown presently, there are a number of instances in addition to escape clause actions where increased imports can be attributed to tariff reductions. The magnitudes, however, are small.

War and postwar dislocations have, of course, seriously interfered with normal trade. We are now reaching a period when past tariff reductions can be expected to become increasingly effective. But should other countries build new plants to supply American imports so long as the escape clause hangs over any expansion of trade which may injure any branch of American industry, however insignificant? Owing to the escape clause, foreign producers and import wholesalers who might expand facilities and develop American markets face great uncertainty in risking the capital outlays that are usually necessary to develop an American market. In some respects, temporary tariff reduction is worse than no reduction at all—namely, when producers and importers are lured into making capital investments and then their market is destroyed by governmental action.

To proceed slowly and cautiously was prudent. To preserve the program, it was necessary to avoid serious injury. But this does not prove a program so preserved is worth saving. The energies of liberal forces have been exhausted in promoting a Janus-faced program which promised substantial benefits of trade without the injury which might be caused by increased imports to any interested group of producers.

In support of the program it is claimed that a healthy industry will not protest against imports even if they are increasing and, hence, that escape clause actions are no guide to increased imports. Automobiles are a good example. But automobiles also illustrate the truly formidable competition that imports face in such cases. The auto industry is not apprehensive because it is confident that the effect of imports on the domestic market will be negligible. It would doubtless be a different story if the price of automobiles was seriously affected by foreign competition. Moreover, aluminum illustrates a healthy, growing industry which has asked for escape clause protection. The electrical industry is certainly healthy, yet some members actively seek to maintain the extra protection afforded by our "Buy American" laws. Members of the chemical industry, despite prodigious expansion and profits, remain very active in protectionist ranks.

More important is the claim that trade agreements have prevented the raising of duties on "new competitive situations," that is, where changes in comparative costs have resulted in more serious competition from foreign producers. This issue still hangs in the balance. All duties reduced or bound are subject to escape clause action and the other duties are vulnerable to far more restrictive action under the flexible tariff provision of the act of 1930.[24] This provides for adjustment of protective duties to equalize costs between domestic and foreign producers and was expressly designed to afford additional protection to meet new competitive situations. Flexible tariffs remain available for the protection of those goods not subject to trade agreement

24. Section 336, Title III. See pp. 114–115 and pp. 184–185.

concessions. If duties have not been increased on "new competitive situations," the most probable reason is that such imports do not threaten serious injury.

Other Actions to Avoid Injury

In a handful of cases, chiefly under the so-called third-country clause, steps have been taken to avoid injury to home industry.

Tariff concessions on handkerchiefs were made to Switzerland in the 1936 agreement. Injury to domestic producers was threatened in 1940 by large imports of certain kinds of handkerchiefs from third countries which benefited by the reduction. The concession was withdrawn under the third-country clause permitting such action.

Duties were reduced on live silver or black foxes and furs in the 1939 trade agreement with Canada. When European markets were closed after the outbreak of war in 1939, Canadian exports were diverted to the United States in increased quantities. Domestic silver fox farmers complained and the administration immediately negotiated a separate agreement with Canada limiting annual imports. This quota was continued until the end of the war.

Imports of potatoes from Canada increased considerably in late 1948. By agreement with Canada, further imports of table stock potatoes were eliminated and seed potatoes were restricted to seed outlets only. This arrangement was terminated in June 1949. Imports of oats were similarly restricted in 1953.

Tariff concessions on linen fire hose were made in the 1939 trade agreement with Canada. Domestic producers were threatened with imports from other countries in 1947. As a result, the concession was withdrawn and the preagreement rate re-established.

Previous tariff concessions were withdrawn at Torquay by negotiation on three items: (1) women's and children's leather gloves seamed in part by hand; (2) stencil silk valued at more than $5.50 per pound; and (3) onion powder. The reason for the withdrawal was that a custom's court decision had classified gloves seamed in part by hand and onion powder in a lower tariff category than had been intended. The stencil silk withdrawal grew out of an escape clause application. Because of the reduction in duty to 25 per cent on certain dyed silk fabrics, it was alleged that imports for industrial purposes, which had traditionally been imported in undyed condition at rates of 55–60 per cent, were being imported in excessive quantities in dyed condition in order to take advantage of the lower rate.

The act of 1951 prohibited imports of certain furs from the Soviet Union and Red China and withdrew all trade agreement concessions from Communist-dominated countries.

Criteria of Injury

Neither the original act nor Executive Orders provide any criteria of injury. In this important matter the Tariff Commission has made policy. Moreover, the decisions clearly reveal sharp and more or less consistent disagreement within the Commission.

When the act was extended in 1951, the Congress called for consideration of the following information, though not to the exclusion of other factors:

a downward trend of production, employment, prices, profits, or wages in the domestic industry concerned, or a decline in sales, an increase in imports, either actual or relative to domestic production, a higher or growing inventory, or a decline in the proportion of the domestic market supplied by domestic producers.[25]

The inadequacy of these criteria is evident from the fact that on full investigation only a few of the Tariff Commission's decisions were unanimous as of June 30, 1952.[26] The Commissioners holding protectionist views were more prone to find evidence of serious injury than those with a more liberal outlook on trade.

While most of the industries subject to escape clause investigations are small and in this sense unimportant, the problems discovered and the principles which emerge are far-reaching in their implications. Four principal issues have emerged in the Tariff Commission's consideration of injury: (1) relative versus absolute displacement of domestic production of imports; (2) displacement of a single product of the multiproduct home industry; (3) the question whether or not the import is directly competitive; and (4) the definition of "industry."

(1) The most important principle is that additional imports may be absorbed by an expanding market. Although a minority of the Commission have dissented, the relative increase of imports at the expense of the potential growth of home industry does *not* constitute serious injury. This doctrine, which is entirely sound, opens the way for genuinely freer trade in expanding markets as long as domestic production is not absolutely curtailed. There are two possibilities: (a) Imports may create their own market, that is, the domestic market may be expanded as a result of the lower prices or sales efforts on imports. In this case, the total market would be larger than if imports were kept out. (b) Expansion of the market may not flow directly from imports, but imports may, nonetheless, take the growth share away from domestic producers. If this doctrine were made to stick, it would

25. Section 7(b).

26. Although we cannot expect unanimity in difficult decisions, it is a source of concern that split decisions should tend to follow party lines. President Truman acted on three unanimous decisions of the Commission and rejected one. For later decisions see Appendix 7.

mean that some home industries are condemned to stagnation but not to extinction as the result of increased competition from imports. The principle has, also, a negative implication that is more highly restrictive than its liberal side. It means that tariffs or quantitative controls will be raised to avoid the absolute displacement of any home industry by increased imports.

For reasons which will be discussed more fully later, if this principle offered the only opportunity for increased imports, it would probably result in the disintegration of America's foreign trade. This is not a matter of logic, but of history. The evidence suggests that, as a general rule, imports do not have a competitive advantage in America's rapidly growing markets. On the contrary, most of the goods which can be produced relatively more cheaply abroad are agricultural products, nondurable goods and specialities for which the market is rather inelastic.

(2) The severity of the first criterion, which would limit increased imports to the growing market, is mitigated by the second, which would permit the absolute displacement of domestic production *in case the product is produced by a healthy multiproduct industry*. If it is held that that test of injury is the over-all position of the industry, then the multiproduct industry may be required to absorb "injury" on one or more individual products.[27] Since almost all of America's largest industries produce scores of products, the principle that injury depends on the total market of any industry creates opportunities for the expansion of imports without abandoning the doctrine of no injury. This criterion, like the first, has a negative or restrictive (as well as a liberal) implication, for it means that freer trade will be restricted as necessary to maintain healthy conditions in the over-all operations of any home industry. Industrial integration and the large-scale corporation provide a structure of home industry that is more favorable to imports, under this doctrine, than specialization and small-scale business. As will be shown presently, there are many niches in Big Business where imports could compete successfully if tariffs were drastically cut, but as a general rule the incidence of potential imports lies elsewhere. Consequently, the principle of absorption of "little injuries" by Big Business, while liberalizing in principle, offers only limited opportunities for the expansion of imports.

(3) The third principle which emerges concerns the meaning of "like or directly competitive" products. The way has been opened for increased imports by a fine distinction between imports which are like or unlike domestically produced goods: (a) Light motorcycles for recreation are sufficiently

27. This recalls the principle of cost absorption employed by the Office of Price Administration during the war. It appears, however, that the possibility of requiring domestic producers to absorb injury on a portion or subdivision of their business will be blocked by amendments to the act of 1955.

unlike heavy motorcycles for police and business use that they are not directly competitive. (b) The garlic case opened up the question of different geographical markets within the United States and whether imports were competitive in all areas. (c) For perishable products, a similar issue exists with respect to seasonal supplies. Tomato imports, for example, seriously compete in one season but not in another. (d) Another possibility is that imports may not compete fully with domestic supplies for all uses. (e) There was even some suggestion in the first spring clothespin case that imports of slightly cheaper metal and wood than domestic clothespins were not fully competitive. These distinctions offer the possibility for such increased imports as can be absorbed through interstices in the structure of American production.

(4) The fourth principle concerns the breadth or narrowness of the industry or business that is injured by imports. The Tariff Commission has considered extremely narrow segments of an industry for purposes of determining injury. To some extent this offsets the liberalizing effect of the second and third principle outlined above. Industrial classification for tariff purposes is extremely narrow—too narrow. If hats rather than women's fur felt hats were treated as an industry, there would probably have been no injury.

Possibly a fifth consideration should be mentioned. There is some evidence that a majority of the Tariff Commission consider the increase of imports relative to domestic production on a prewar base. This means that domestic producers who expanded at the expense of imports during the war, and who now lose this share of the market, are not likely to be regarded as injured by such increased imports.[28] The evidence on this point, however, is not entirely clear.

The liberal elements in the first three of these criteria have no status except in case histories. While they are drawn from the cases the Commission has disposed of, they are not well established. Under less favorable economic conditions or a new President,[29] the liberalizing factors could all be thrown overboard. In fact, a majority of the Tariff Commission did not require the absorption of injury in the garlic, watch and silk scarf cases. (1) The rule requiring absolute instead of relative injury seems to have a fair chance of survival although Commissioners Gregg and Brossard rather consistently rejected it. (2) The rule of absorption of "little injuries" by the healthy multiproduct industry rests, thus far, on very slim support. Only Chairman Ryder, backed by the President, supported this criterion in the garlic case. (3) The interpretation which draws a fine line permitting im-

28. See chinaware, for example, p. 394 and Table 67.
29. Harry Truman was President during the period covered. President Eisenhower's actions indicate support of these criteria except in the watch case.

ports that are not "like or directly competitive" was rejected by two commissioners in the motorcycle case. (4) The Tariff Commission accepts the highly restrictive definition of industry, and there is apparently no chance of a more liberal criterion on this score.

Absorption of Imports via Domestic Growth

Apparently, the only real possibility of substantially expanding competitive imports lies in long-term growth. The evidence thus far, however, suggests that under the escape clause, an import-competing home industry will not be permitted to wither on the vine as a result of increased imports. The escape clause cases in which tariff concessions have been maintained are industries where home production has continued to expand, though less rapidly than imports.

The most important investigation involving this principle concerned watches and, for this reason, Chapter 22 is devoted to the watch industry. The Tariff Commission was split three-three on existing injury, but since one commissioner found a threat of serious injury, the Commission recommended four to two that duties be raised. President Truman emphatically rejected the recommendation, which President Eisenhower later accepted. The decisive principle of how far America will permit imports to increase at the expense of domestic growth still hangs in the balance.

The intent of the Congress was to permit though not to require a finding of serious injury when imports increased relative to domestic output. The act expressly provides that consideration of injury must include "an increase in imports, either actual or relative to domestic production, . . . or a decline in the proportion of the domestic market supplied by domestic producers."[30]

The escape clause is invoked when increased imports, either actual or relative, are *in part* a result of trade agreement concessions. That is to say, the offending imports do not need to be *wholly* a result of concessions.[31]

The constructive results, limited as they are, have been realized under extremely favorable economic conditions prevailing during the postwar boom. A depression, a recession, or even less inflationary expansion would leave most import-competing industries more vulnerable to injury from imports. Both the intent of the Congress and investigations of the Tariff Commission indicate that serious injury depends on the condition of home industry as well as on the absolute or relative volume of imports. Consequently, it cannot be assumed that trade agreement concessions will be maintained under less favorable economic conditions. In the future, injury

30. Section 7(b), Act of 1951.
31. Section 6(a), Act of 1951.

may be found under the escape clause because home industry is in a less healthy condition.

Other countries are apprehensive concerning the escape clause threat to their exports. Italy and Britain have expressed concern, a Belgian concession was withdrawn after the United States withdrew its concession on hatters' fur, Turkey increased several duties on United States exports and Greece requested new concessions to offset the increase of duties on its export of figs to the United States. The fur felt hat action precipitated a working party investigation by members of GATT.

One reason why tariff concessions have been rather ineffective may be the uncertainty that attends the escape clause principle. This means that the policy and attitude of the American government toward foreign trade may often be as important as the actual reduction of duties. And on this matter, the split between the Executive Branch and the Congress is expressed in the two faces of the Trade Agreements Program. The administration calls for freer trade while the Congress seeks to avoid the consequences. Only the President's emphatic rejection of some of the Tariff Commission's recommendations has prevented a more restrictive interpretation of the escape clause.

The escape clause can easily become a retreat to protectionism without amending the Trade Agreements Act. All that is needed is for a majority of the Tariff Commission, supported by the President, to find evidence of the *threat* of serious injury.

Everything considered, the Tariff Commission is to be congratulated on its majority decisions. Given the doctrine of permitting no injury, a beginning has been made toward making the escape clause as sensible a policy as is practicable in view of the attitude of the Congress. This is not to say that the escape clause is a desirable policy. What is lacking in the doctrine of no injury to home industry is any consideration of (1) the injury to other industries, to consumers and to taxpayers, (2) the obligation to create an orderly basis for international trade, and (3) the foreign-policy implications of commercial policy. In other words, the escape clause places the interest of a single industry, narrowly defined, above the national interest. This is the most important issue in American commercial policy today.

Later Investigations under Escape Clause

The results of later investigations under the escape clause can be summarized as of January 7, 1955. (See Appendix 7.)

President Eisenhower raised tariffs on (1) watch movements and (2) alsike clover seed. He declined the Tariff Commission's recommendations to invoke the escape clause on (1) scissors and shears, (2) groundfish fillets and (3) lead and zinc.[32] In eight additional investigations the Commission found no serious injury and in three additional cases the vote was evenly divided.

In all, Presidents Truman and Eisenhower had invoked the escape clause five times as of January 7, 1955, and declined the majority recommendation of the Tariff Commission seven times.

Crippling Amendments of 1955

Legislation extending the Trade Agreements Act for another three years passed the Senate only after crippling amendments had been added by the Finance Committee.[33]

1. The most serious of these provides, under the escape clause, that domestic producers are eligible for tariff relief on that portion or subdivision of their business (producing competitive products in commercial quantities) that is seriously injured or threatened by imports.

2. Escape clause action may be invoked if imports "contribute substantially" to the threat of serious injury.

3. The President is authorized to restrict imports which threaten to impair the national security.

Our policy is already unduly restrictive in that tariff relief is available to small segments of an industry. These amendments are a further step in the wrong direction and represent a miscarriage of the principle of relief from *serious injury*. It is difficult to see how a firm whose total business is affected only to a slight degree can be seriously injured as a result.

A constructive approach would require both the firm and the industry to adjust to tariff concessions, where possible, by changing the composition of its output or shifting to other fields. This is the best means of escape from foreign competition. Such an adjustment is uncomfortable but it offers real benefits. The problem is most serious for those home industries which are already declining or relatively stagnant. This is one of the problems considered in the next chapter.

32. See p. 392 on lead and zinc. See Table 66 on earlier investigations.

33. These amendments, which leave a measure of discretion to the President, are preferable to commodity amendments, which otherwise threatened the program with higher tariffs and quotas at the hands of the Congress. The Senate vote of 75–13 reflects approval of the compromise.

Chapter 20

Injury and Potential Imports

TIME IS OF THE ESSENCE in making adjustments to imports. On the supply side, in some cases imports can be increased immediately by diverting supplies from the home market and from third markets to the American market. In other cases foreign production will need to be expanded.

On the demand side, imports of some products can be increased merely by the growth of the American market. But for reasons which will be indicated later in this chapter, the great bulk of America's potential imports will displace domestic production.[1] Increased imports of food, textiles and shoes depend more on the contraction of domestic production than on the expansion of consumption. The major issue, therefore, is the shift of domestic production out of the industries exposed to competitive imports. For this reason, the potential expansion of imports over a period of ten to twenty years is much greater than in the short run, *provided that internal growth is sustained enough and rapid enough to draw resources out of the exposed industries.* If alternative employment is not available in the durable-goods and service industries, agriculture and the nondurable-goods industries meet foreign competition with lower prices. Thus, the magnitude of the increase in imports from tariff reduction depends on time and on sustained prosperity at home. In order to absorb such increased imports, the economy must not only expand, but the rate of growth in the progressive sectors must accelerate.

One factor to bear in mind in judging the effect of tariff reduction is that the transport and marketing costs on most manufactured imports are probably roughly equal to the foreign price. A 20 per cent decrease in duty will usually reduce the retail price by only 10 per cent. But because imports may displace domestic production as well as expand the total market, the

1. The findings in this chapter are a result of the following procedure: (1) Trade associations and labor organizations were queried as to whether foreign competition, actual or potential, was regarded as a serious threat to their industries. (2) Statistical summaries and commodity analyses prepared by the staff of the Tariff Commission were reviewed to locate those industries most exposed to foreign competition. (3) Personal interviews were conducted at plants in New England, New York, Pennsylvania, Ohio and West Virginia. (4) Officials of the Department of Agriculture were consulted concerning the imports that are regarded as most troublesome to agriculture. (5) Hearings on commodities proposed for trade agreement concessions were reviewed, as were the data prepared by the Tariff Commission.

potential increase of imports of any one product is far greater than is indicated by the potential expansion of its consumption.

The seriousness of injury from competitive imports is not indicated by the ratio of imports to production alone. In an expanding market, imports may rise from virtually nothing to 10 per cent of domestic production without serious injury. But in a contracting market, the rise of imports from 1 per cent to 10 per cent of production may seriously injure the competing industry. If the market is inelastic with respect to price and if domestic resources are not shifted, tariff reduction may increase foreign competition and force domestic prices and incomes down without a substantial increase in imports. For this reason, neither the actual increase in imports nor the unemployment which may result is an adequate measure of the adjustment problem. Prices of agricultural and textile products may have to fall so much in order to absorb a relatively small increase in supply that domestic producers will be injured by an absolute increase in imports which seems small when expressed as a per cent of domestic production. Injury depends both on (1) the growth of the market and (2) the alternative opportunities which are available for employment.

Unless otherwise stated, the current imports shown in the following pages are for 1951. The figures have been rounded to rough approximations. In most cases specific duties have been expressed ad valorem.[2]

Metal Products and Machinery

The American iron and steel industry is not likely to be damaged by lower trade barriers. This is not only because the volume of additional imports would be small relative to domestic production but also because the impact of freer trade could be absorbed mainly by a shift in the composition of output. This illustrates how large integrated firms producing a variety of products may avoid injury from imports that would seriously affect small specialized companies. The relative volume of imports and exports suggests, in fact, that the gains to large steel firms from a greater

2. Most of the figures cited are from reports prepared by the staff of the U.S. Tariff Commission. See *Summaries of Tariff Information*, 16 volumes (processed); *Trade Agreement Digest* (processed). These voluminous reports, issued at various dates, have been supplemented by digests on specific commodities obtained directly from the Tariff Commission. These reports contain information on sources of imports, tariffs, production and the structure of industry. Cf. an earlier study, *Postwar Imports and Domestic Production of Major Commodities*, Sen. Doc. 38, 79th Cong., 1st sess.

For a most useful handbook comparing imports and domestic production by tariff categories, see Howard S. Piquet, *Aid, Trade and the Tariff*, Thomas Y. Crowell, New York, 1953. Piquet's over-all estimates of the effect of temporary tariff suspension are useful but suffer from the method of partial equilibrium analysis. It may be, however, that the range of his estimates of imports is sufficient to allow for this difficulty.

A draft of the present chapter was circulated privately before Piquet's book was available. Although both studies rely heavily on Tariff Commission sources, the present analysis of the problem of injury differs very substantially from that of Piquet.

volume of exports might well exceed the losses resulting from a larger volume of imports.

For about two decades after the Civil War, the United States imported large quantities of rails from Britain. But beginning in the 1890s exports greatly exceeded imports. They were eight times greater during 1926–1930 and twenty times greater during 1936–1940. They were almost ten times greater than the 11,000 tons of imports recorded for 1951.

The United States usually exports vastly greater quantities of plates and sheets than are imported. They were nineteen times greater during 1926–1930 and 88 times greater during 1936–1940. The steel shortage associated with the Korean War reduced exports and increased imports many fold so that exports were only 1.6 times greater than imports in 1951–1952.

Exports of wire rods were about double the volume of imports during 1926–1930 and eight times greater during 1936–1940. They were nine times greater in 1949, but imports jumped from less than 6,000 tons in 1949 to 122,000 in 1951 while exports dropped from 53,000 tons to 4,000.

Imports of rails, wire rods, and plates and sheets totaled 233,000 tons in 1952, which is a negligible amount in relation to the volume of domestic production.

Structural iron and steel is our most important import of steel mill products. Exports normally exceed imports. They were roughly twice as great during 1926–1930 and about five times as great during 1936–1940. In 1949 exports were four times greater than imports of 115,000 tons. Owing to the shortage associated with the Korean War, imports rose fourfold in the next two years and exceeded the volume of exports. In 1952, imports amounted to about 6 per cent of production. The duty is 7½ per cent on fabricated shapes and quite nominal on unfabricated steel.

In 1952 total exports of steel mill products, including semimanufactures and advanced manufactures, totaled $932 million compared with imports of $237 million.

The duty of 60 cents per ton on pig iron is nominal and, despite transport costs, imports reached almost $50 million in 1951. Other forms of ferroalloys are imported in substantially greater value. The total amounts to 1–2 per cent of domestic production.

American merchants have been scouring the world for possible imports of iron and steel scrap. The duty of 37 cents per ton was suspended until June 30, 1953.[3] Imports of $13 million compare with domestic production of nearly $3,000 million.

Imports of metal household products are negligible. The duty runs as high as 40 per cent. Before the volume of imports could amount to much,

3. Public Law 66, 82d Cong.

it would be necessary to standardize specifications and provide for adequate repair services.

Apparently a niche has been discovered in the structure of American machinery production where imports can undersell domestic producers. The number of cases that have arisen under the Buy American rule indicates that heavy electrical generating equipment is sufficiently a custommade rather than a mass production product so that imports may be able to establish a substantial market if they are not discriminated against. Only a very few domestic producers can make the huge equipment for power plants, and it appears that potential imports of this item may exceed the effect of tariff reduction on all other machinery items added together.

Although imports of machinery and vehicles have increased rapidly, it is unlikely that domestic industry would be seriously damaged by lower trade barriers. This is because of a growing market and a strong competitive position. Machinery exports of $4.7 billion are almost twenty times greater than imports. This suggests that the machinery industries would be much more likely to suffer if foreign trade were restricted.

Imports of automobiles of about $25 million were less than 10 per cent of exports and negligible in relation to domestic production of $7 billion. Elimination of the 10 per cent duty is highly desirable. It seems most improbable that the resulting increase in imports would appreciably affect America's automobile industry. But if it should, it is virtually certain that domestic companies would turn out competitive small cars and continue to hold the domestic market.

Motorcycles and bicycles are another niche where imports have a chance. The American market for light- and medium-weight sports motorcycles has already greatly expanded, and elimination of the 10 per cent duty (15 per cent on parts) would help but not greatly expand the $3.5 million market.

Bicycle imports, which amounted to only about one per cent of domestic production before the war, have increased sharply since 1949. Duties have been reduced from 30 per cent to an average of 11 per cent (the range is from 7½ per cent to $2.50 per bicycle). Imports have reached about 10 per cent of production and are five times larger than exports. The domestic market has nearly doubled in quantity consumed since 1937 but is off sharply from the peak years 1947–1948. The first escape clause investigation found that imports had not seriously injured the domestic industry. A second investigation recommended higher duties to the President.

An application for tariff relief by producers of cotton-carding machinery was declined after investigation by the Tariff Commission.

Imports of sewing machines amount to $15 million and the duty is 10 per cent. Imports equal about 10 per cent of domestic production and could be expanded. The Singer Sewing Machine Company controls the companies in a number of foreign countries. Japan is now a leading exporter.

In view of the high labor content of machine tools, America's competitive position is notable. Imports increased greatly to a peak of $50 million in 1952. This compares with exports of $122 million and production of $1,126 million.

Lead and Zinc

Domestic producers of lead and zinc have suffered from sharp fluctuations in market demand since the second world war. From this position the industry was threatened with continued high-level imports and in 1954 the Tariff Commission recommended an increase in duties. President Eisenhower rejected this recommendation and chose the alternative method of aiding domestic producers by increasing purchases of lead and zinc for the stockpile program. Purchases of 200,000 tons of lead and 300,000 tons of zinc were indicated for fiscal 1955.[4]

Chemicals

Total exports of chemical products reached almost $1,000 million in 1951 compared with imports of $300 million. Although imports of industrial chemicals have increased greatly, they are still substantially below exports.

Duties collected on chemicals, oils and paints averaged 38 per cent in 1934 compared with 12 per cent on imports in 1952.

Imports of $60 million, equal to almost one third of domestic production, make ethyl alcohol one of the largest chemical imports. Even so, the duty of 7½ cents per gallon is probably highly restrictive.

Chlorine is protected by a duty of 12½ per cent; imports are negligible.

Calcium carbide is protected by a duty of 15 per cent and imports of $2 million amount to about 2 per cent of domestic production.

The basic chemicals which are used in large volume by industry are sulfuric acid, soda ash and caustic soda. Imports of each of these are negligible. The duty of one fourth of a cent per pound on soda ash and caustic soda is probably mildly restrictive. Specific duties on many chemical products have been reduced by rising prices, but imports still amount to only a fraction of one per cent of domestic production.

Duties on coal-tar products receive special treatment in the Tariff Act. They are based on "American selling price" rather than "foreign value," which is the usual standard. As a result, the effective rate may be several times the stated duty of 25 per cent and up. American imports of dyestuffs declined from roughly 1,500 metric tons in 1937 to 400 metric tons in 1948, while exports increased from 8,000 to 21,000 in the same period.

4. *Foreign Commerce Weekly*, Washington, August 16, 1954.

It is easy to understand why the chemical industry would not wish to become highly dependent on foreign sources of basic and intermediate chemicals. Indeed, the national interest probably dictates that domestic capacity be maintained to meet the bulk of our requirements. But this is not the issue.

There is plenty of room to increase imports and still produce the great bulk of requirements at home. Is it necessary to produce virtually all of such products at home? An enlightened view of the national interest might allow imports of the basic chemicals as large as 10 to 15 per cent of consumption. On the assumption that the margin of profit is relatively low on these products, the industry itself might find it more profitable to concentrate production on the newer products where profit margins are higher. If put to the test, home industry might, because of integrated production, meet foreign competition to the extent of holding imports to less than 10 per cent of consumption. Freer trade would produce no flood of chemical imports and, if profits of the chemical companies were shaded a trifle, no real damage to the national interest would result.

Optical Goods

Optical glass is a high-duty item. The necessary high quality cannot be maintained with mass production techniques. Because optical glass must be produced in small batches, American producers are at a competitive disadvantage. For reasons of security, however, it would not be prudent to liquidate completely this home industry. Even if it were feasible to cut the duty enough to share the market equally between domestic production and imports, the volume of imports would still be negligible, that is, about a quarter of a million dollars.

The market for manufactured optical goods is an entirely different story. The duty on high-grade field glasses has already been reduced by 50 per cent. Yet present duties on optical instruments still range from 18 to 50 per cent. Imports of $6 million amount to more than 10 per cent of domestic production. If it would not injure national security to give half this market to imports, they could be increased $20–25 million by tariff reduction.

The duty on cameras with valuable lenses is highly restrictive. Yet exports of photographic goods greatly exceed imports and the President of Bell and Howell makes a brilliant case for lower tariffs.[5]

Scientific and laboratory instruments of many kinds bear a duty of 50 per cent. Imports in 1953 were over $500,000.

5. See House Hearings on H.R. 1 (1955), pp. 623 ff. On optical goods and glassware, see *Federal Register*, June 25, 1954, p. 3882.

Pottery and China

Pottery is one of the larger potential manufactured imports. The market has shown slow and irregular growth. Domestic production of earthenware increased less than 7 per cent (by quantity) in twenty years from 1929 to 1949, while imports declined from 17 to 5 per cent of production.

Production of chinaware increased about 10 per cent in the twenty years from 1929 to 1949, while imports fell from 111 to 31 per cent of production. (See Table 67.)

Interruption of international trade in chinaware during the war created an opportunity for domestic producers of earthenware and semivitreous china to enter the production of new lines of higher quality china.[6] It is reported that before the war only one domestic manufacturer produced as a sole product china dinnerware highly competitive with imports. Subsequently, other domestic producers converted old capacity and added new plant for the production of vitrified china. The old pattern of specialization whereby the domestic industry produced chiefly hotel and household dinnerware in low- and medium-price brackets gave way to greater diversification.

The market for chinaware was taken over by domestic producers during the war and imports have been displaced, both absolutely and relatively, despite tariff reduction on parts of quality china. While imports have greatly increased since the war, they had still not regained their prewar share of the market in 1951. Here we see an illustration of the very limited effect of trade agreements. Competition from imports is limited chiefly to quality chinaware for household use, partly because of the much higher protection on cheaper wares. The tariff structure is a complex one and present duties amount to about 30 per cent on quality china and 65 per cent on cheaper wares. The average realized duty of 55 per cent in 1951 compares with 80 per cent in 1939.

Imports of those items on which duties were reduced increased almost threefold from 1937 to 1951 and trade agreement china increased from roughly 5 per cent to 20 per cent of total imports of chinaware. Nonetheless, imports of quality china have declined absolutely from prewar years while production has increased many times. Trade agreement concessions have not prevented expansion of new investment. The number of workers employed has increased and output per man-hour has substantially increased, owing to improvements in equipment.

The foreign sources are Japan, Britain, Germany, Italy and France, in that order.

6. Domestic production of handmade glass also expanded during the war with similar postwar troubles. Cf. Chapter 21.

TABLE 67

IMPORTS AND DOMESTIC PRODUCTION OF EARTHENWARE, STONEWARE AND
CHINAWARE, SELECTED YEARS, 1929–1949

(*Thousands of Dozen Pieces*)

	Earthenware and Stoneware			Chinaware		
Year	Imports	Production	Imports as Per Cent of Production	Imports	Production	Imports as Per Cent of Production
1929	5,525	33,000	17	9,137	8,200	111
1932	2,375	16,600	14	4,490	3,700	121
1935	4,870	22,200	22	5,183	5,600	93
1937	4,992	24,500	20	6,185	6,900	90
1938	2,463	24,200	10	3,510	5,600	63
1939	2,879	27,000	11	3,584	6,300	57
1943	803	33,000	2	129	10,500	1
1946	1,061	37,000	3	203	11,600	2
1947	1,237	42,285	3	654	12,324	5
1948	1,645	45,700	4	2,087	11,380	18
1949	1,877	39,200	5	2,790	9,020	31

Source: U.S. Tariff Commission.

If duties were cut drastically imports would probably take over half the market. An escape clause investigation found that imports had not seriously injured this industry.

Woolen Products

Woolens and worsteds is one of the most important industries exposed to potential competition from imports. As of this writing the industry has not applied for an escape clause investigation, or for the higher duties specifically provided for by the General Agreement. But imports increased sharply relative to domestic production in 1950–1951 and if this rise were to continue, woolens and worsteds could become the most important American manufacturing industry to be seriously affected by imports. Correspondence released by the Economic Cooperation Administration in reply to inquiries from a New Jersey senator indicated that, even before the sharp rise of 1950–1951, an American producer[7] of fine quality woolens was disturbed by ECA's policy of encouraging imports.

Potential imports of woolens and worsteds deserve attention for two reasons. (1) A 50 per cent further cut in duty would probably produce a large increase in imports. (2) This is an industry where Britain can supply additional quantities with a minimum readjustment in her own economy. Britain was the source of about 70 per cent of imports in 1951; Italy supplied about 12 per cent.

7. The Forstmann Company.

TABLE 68

WOOLENS AND WORSTEDS: PRODUCTION, EXPORTS AND IMPORTS, SPECIFIED YEARS, 1929–1951

Year	Production[a]	Domestic Exports	Imports for Consumption	Ratio to Production[b]	
				Exports	Imports
		(1,000 Pounds)		*(Per Cent)*	
1929	269,591	469	10,766	0.2	4.0
1931	193,605	201	9,852	0.1	5.1
1937	314,288	216	5,604	0.1	1.8
1939	308,947	310	6,626	0.1	2.1
1943	439,836	30,721	2,497	7.0	0.6
1946	493,719	24,861	2,154	5.0	0.4
1947	413,122	17,298	2,490	4.2	0.6
1948	407,201	5,391	4,703	1.3	1.2
1949	333,876	3,077	4,278	0.9	1.3
1951	c	c	c	c	4.0

Source: U.S. Tariff Commission.

a. Does not include wool blankets, pile fabrics, upholstery cloths and woven wool felts.

b. Calculated before rounding.

c. Not available in pounds: production (est.), 465,000,000 square yards; imports, 18,700,000 square yards. (Howard Piquet, *Aid, Trade and the Tariff*, Thomas Y. Crowell, New York, 1953.)

The high duties of 50–60 per cent (plus a specific duty to compensate for the duty on raw wool) in the Hawley-Smoot tariff were reduced, first by the British trade agreement of 1939 and again by the General Agreement. The duty protecting wool manufacturers is now 25 per cent.

The United States is the world's largest producer of woolens and worsteds. Production is highly concentrated geographically in New England, Pennsylvania and New Jersey. Although several producers are large concerns, most firms are small. Representatives of the industry assert that the effect of lower tariffs has been reflected in the profit margins and financial position of domestic companies rather than in a substantial increase in imports.

Output was greatly stimulated by military demand during the war, as were exports. Imports were equal to 4 per cent of production in 1929 and to 2.1 per cent in 1939. Imports recovered only slowly after the war, as the domestic industry had greatly improved its production of fine quality woolens. By 1949, imports were equal to only 1.3 per cent of domestic production, but had increased to about 4 per cent by 1951. (See Table 68.) Although this is only a small share of the market, it is double the 1939 share and equal to the 1929 share.

The prospect for a substantial rise in imports is not promising. If imports continue to increase, duties will probably be increased as specifically provided for by the General Agreement. The United States reserved the right to increase the ad valorem rate on woolens and worsteds to 45 per cent on imports of any fabrics which exceed 5 per cent of domestic production in the three immediately preceding calendar years.

Imports of wool yarn, which have reached almost $4 million, are an example of the effect of tariff reduction under trade agreements. The duty was cut twice, first in the British bilateral agreement of 1939, and again at Geneva. Imports have risen in each instance, but are still almost negligible in relation to domestic production, and the duty is still high. Domestic production exceeds half a billion pounds. Yarn is produced, chiefly, in integrated mills and raises the same problem as imports of fabrics. Additional imports of yarn and woolen cloth would be offset, in part, by lower imports of wool.

Imports of woolen gloves supply one third of the domestic consumption although domestic producers are protected by a duty of some 40 per cent. Knit gloves constitutes apparently a relatively stagnant industry. A request for an escape clause investigation was deferred by the Tariff Commission and later withdrawn. Later investigations found no injury.

Cotton Cloth

Domestic production of cotton cloth in 1951 was 10.3 billion square yards, compared with 8.3 billion in 1939 and 7.7 billion in 1929. Imports in 1951 amounted to 0.4 per cent of production compared with 1.4 per cent in 1939 and 0.7 per cent in 1929. (See Table 69.)

Exports in 1939 were 3 times larger than imports; in 1949, they were 43 times larger (by quantity). Imports increased twofold from 1949 to 1951, while production and exports rose only moderately. By value, exports in 1951 were roughly 14 times greater than imports.

Britain supplied roughly one third of imports in 1951, India one fifth and Switzerland one seventh.

America's principal export markets in recent years were the Philippines, Cuba, Canada, and Central and Latin America.

Duties on fine cotton cloth were reduced (1) about one sixth by trade agreement with Britain in 1939 and (2) about one third or less below the original rates of 1930 by the General Agreement. Duties on coarse cloth were not reduced. The present range is from 7½ per cent on coarse cloth to 47½ per cent on fine cloth.

Duties collected on imports of cotton manufactures averaged 22 per cent in 1952, a reduction of 41 per cent from 1930 rates.

TABLE 69
COTTON CLOTH: PRODUCTION, EXPORTS AND IMPORTS, SPECIFIED YEARS, 1929–1951

Year	Production	Domestic Exports	Imports for Consumption	Ratio to Production[a] Exports	Imports
	(Million Square Yards)			(Per Cent)	
1929	7,670	558.1	55.9	7.3	0.7
1931	6,493	365.7	33.9	5.6	0.5
1937	8,727	230.5	147.3	2.6	1.7
1938	b	315.5	58.3	b	b
1939	8,266	359.3	111.8	4.3	1.4
1943	10,500	521.4	19.7	5.0	0.2
1946	9,100	759.6	43.8	8.3	0.5
1947	10,140	1,438.2	15.9	14.7	0.2
1948	10,000	915.6	31.8	9.1	0.3
1949	8,500	867.8	19.7	10.2	0.2
1951	10,300	b	45.8	b	0.4

Source: U.S. Tariff Commission.
a. Calculated before rounding.
b. Not available.

Despite the fact that imports are a fraction of one per cent of domestic production, the fine goods sector of cotton textiles has been a chronic plaintiff in the tariff debate. In the finest grades imports amount to a considerable part of domestic production.

Experience has shown that where fine quality imports of a somewhat unique character located a profitable niche in the market, domestic producers have moved in.[8]

On general principles, it has usually been assumed that the cotton textile industry would be seriously affected by freer trade. The volume of exports suggests that the American industry may be able to give a better account of itself in a free market than has usually been supposed. Some well-informed students believe that the industry could hold its own with foreign competitors except the Japanese.

Matthew J. Cuffe, President of the Textile Export Association, told the American Cotton Manufacturers Institute that "There are no mills in the world which can produce denim, percales, chambrays, vat-dyed twills and drills, corduroys, sheets, towels and other items at prices equal to ours when quality factors are taken into consideration."[9]

The industry's position is stated by the American Cotton Manufacturers Institute:

8. J. Bachman and M. R. Gainsbrugh, *Economics of the Cotton Textile Industry*, National Industrial Conference Board, New York, 1946, p. 35.
9. *Trade Talk* from the Committee for a National Trade Policy, February 18, 1955.

The industry (textile) does not advocate and never has advocated the doctrine of exclusion. In those instances of luxury items, embracing novelties, unique specialties, unusual designs, handicraft products, etc., existing tariff rates are no bar to importation, or consumption. Those customers who wish such items are not deterred by current tariff duties.

But additional imports of cotton goods of the type which would respond to lower duties are quite another matter. If their entrance should be permitted in sufficient volume to narrow perceptibly the "dollar gap" which is the purpose intended, they would have to invade our full range of standard constructions displacing in proportion American production and employment, while at the same same time undermining the American wage and price structure.[10]

The shift of the American industry from New England to the southern states indicates that New England mills would probably be seriously affected by increased imports.

Because of the development of synthetic yarn, new fabrics and the relocation of plants, the textile industry is in the throes of dynamic changes. At the same time, cottons and woolens suffer from both unstable markets and relative stagnation. Consumption of apparel wool showed little change from the end of the first world war to the beginning of the second, although population increased substantially. Woolen and worsted (Bradford) spindles in place declined about 2.3 million between 1923 and the end of the second world war. In the same period, cotton spindles in place declined about 14 million.[11]

The expansion of foreign capacity to supply the American market must take account of the risk of rapid technological obsolescence, which these countries can ill afford. Possibly we are on the verge of technological improvements establishing continuous production processes in textiles, which would largely wipe out differentials in labor cost due to higher American wages.

Other Textile Products

Linen manufacturers were highly protected. New fabrics and the high cost of laundry on linen clothing have reduced the market for linen clothing. Towels, handkerchiefs and fire hose are among the other linen articles which are restricted by the tariff. Imports of towels amount to about $1 million, or one fourth of domestic consumption. The 40 per cent duty is highly restrictive. Imports of handkerchiefs amount to over $2 million, or one fourth of consumption. The duty is 25 per cent on hemmed and 10 per cent on unhemmed handkerchiefs. Imports of hemmed could be much increased by cutting the duty to 10 per cent.

10. Statement of the American Cotton Manufacturers Institute, Inc., and others, before the Committee for Reciprocity Information, May 17, 1950, pp. 11–12.

11. *Cotton Cloth*, War Changes in Industry Series, U.S. Tariff Commission, Report No. 27, p. 34; *Woolens and Worsteds*, Report No. 29, pp. 52–55.

It was demonstrated that tariff concessions would increase imports of linen fire hose. This is an item that our dragnet would have missed but for the action withdrawing the concession under the third-country clause. If the duty of 25–30 per cent were suspended, imports, which are now negligible, might rise to $1 million. At present the yarn is imported.

Lace is a highly protected industry and must be protected if it is to exist because labor costs represent a high fraction of total costs. Duties range from 35 to 75 per cent. Imports of about $9 million account for about 25 per cent of domestic consumption. The imported types of lace are not generally produced domestically.

The silk scarf sector of domestic industry has virtually disappeared. Imports have seriously injured screen-printing firms because conversion was unattractive economically even if it had been feasible technically. The dress and nappery divisions already suffer from overcapacity. Thus the problem of injury to one division of industry depends on conditions in related sectors. Apparently American screen-printers could meet foreign competition if they could obtain their materials at competitive prices. The hand-rolling division in Puerto Rico needed protection against the Japanese. Without such protection, screen-printers in the United States are unable to compete against imports from Japan.[12]

Rayon has affected cotton and wool and has seriously displaced silk fabrics. The making of broadsilks is a declining industry. The alternative for producers with high-speed automatic machinery is rayon, which has been profitable. Production of broadsilk declined from 140 million yards in 1937 to 27 million in 1950, while imports increased from 28 million to 42 million. This means that imports increased from 20 per cent of production in 1937 to 156 per cent in 1950. The value of imports is roughly $15 million. The duty ranges from 25 to 65 per cent and is highest on the cheaper fabrics, which are produced domestically.

Producers of rayon fabric are protected by a 30–35 per cent duty. Imports are negligible. Demand in foreign producing countries is growing rapidly and it is only in the long run that imports could be substantially increased. America is the world's largest exporter of synthetic fabrics. Manufactured exports of all kinds reached a peak of $226 million in 1951 compared with imports of $52 million.

Imports of rayon staple fiber reached 90 million pounds in 1950, or about 25 per cent of domestic production. The duty is 15 per cent. Further important expansion of imports would probably require the expansion of foreign chemical supplies. The older textile industries have lost ground to rayon. Thus, imports of cotton and woolen fabrics would seriously injure some sectors of domestic industry, while imports of rayon staple reached

12. See p. 376 regarding tariff relief.

25 per cent of domestic production. At this level the industry was apprehensive and imports were discouraged by a dumping charge. Integration in
the industry may be a means of escaping more serious injury from both
domestic and foreign competition.

Partly as a result of changes in price and composition, average duties on
all synthetic textiles have been reduced from 72 per cent on 1934 imports
to 18 per cent on 1952 imports.

Imports of rayon yarn are negligible relative to domestic production. The
duty is 25–30 per cent. Increased imports would require time for foreign
capacity to expand.

Leather Goods

Leather goods constitutes one of the home industries most exposed to
potential competition from imports. The glove industry numbers over 200
factories and is centered in Fulton County, New York. The business in
Gloversville dates back to the colonial period. Duties on women's and children's gloves were reduced 10 per cent at Geneva. Some specific rates on
men's gloves were reduced at Geneva and others bound. Rising prices have
also reduced the effect of specific duties. Nonetheless, duties are still highly
protective, ranging from 25 to 75 per cent.

Production of leather gloves is a declining industry. Production of
women's and children's gloves fell from 726,000 dozen pairs in 1939 to
468,000 dozen pairs in 1948; at the same time, imports fell from 37 to 8 per
cent of production. Domestic production of men's gloves declined from
964,000 dozen pairs in 1937 to 761,000 dozen pairs in 1948, while imports
increased from 0.2 per cent to 0.4 per cent of production. (See Table 70.)

Imports of all leather gloves in 1951 amounted to $3 million, or about
6 per cent of production. Tariff reduction would increase imports several
fold and, because of the stagnant market, would seriously injure home
industry.

Domestic production of women's handbags was greatly expanded during
the war and has been subject to readjustment as a result of both market
conditions and supplies of raw materials. Plastics are used less than during
the war and production of leather handbags is well above prewar levels.
The industry is competitive both at home and abroad and the duty of 20
per cent is highly protective. Imports in 1951 of $3 million amounted to
about 5 per cent of domestic production. Imports could be expanded
several fold if duties were cut.

The domestic shoe industry is growing slowly with the growth of population. Production of 360 million pairs in 1939 compared with 372 million
pairs in 1949. Imports were very small before the war and are now negligible
in relation to domestic production. (See Table 71.) Duties have been

TABLE 70

LEATHER GLOVES[a]: PRODUCTION AND IMPORTS, SELECTED YEARS, 1937–1949

	Women's and Children's				Men's		
Year	Production	Imports	Ratio of Imports to Production	Year	Production	Imports	Ratio of Imports to Production
	(1,000 Dozen Pairs)		(Per Cent)		(1,000 Dozen Pairs)		(Per Cent)
1937	716	522	72.9	1937	964	2	0.2
1939	726	265	36.5	1938	583	1	0.2
1943	758	7	.9	1939	814	2	0.2
1945	812	79	9.7	1943	790	2	0.3
1946	920	146	15.9	1945	730	18	2.5
1947	653	49	7.5	1946	975	8	0.8
1948	468	38	8.1	1947	866	3	0.3
1949	b	40	b	1948	761	3	0.4
				1949	b	2	b

Source: U.S. Tariff Commission.
a. Except horsehide or cowhide.
b. Not available.

402

TABLE 71

LEATHER FOOTWEAR: PRODUCTION, EXPORTS AND IMPORTS, SPECIFIED YEARS, 1937–1949

Year	Production	Exports	Imports	Ratio of Imports to Production
		(1,000 Pairs)		(Per Cent)
1937	336,000	1,431	3,749	1.1
1938	324,000	1,759	3,412	1.0
1939	360,000	2,492	2,081	0.6
1946	396,000	11,066	1,335	0.3
1947	408,000	5,487	697	0.2
1948	384,000	5,609	531	0.1
1949	372,000	4,396	581	0.2

Source: U.S. Tariff Commission.

reduced but still reach as high as 35 per cent. Imports of only $11 million in 1951 could be greatly increased if protection were eliminated. Britain is the largest supplier at present since imports from Czechoslovakia are cut off by economic sanctions directed against the Czechoslovakian government.

Leather imports of $25 million amount to only 1 or 2 per cent of production and could be much increased if the duty of 10 to 15 per cent were cut. Imports of cattle hides and calfskins reached $50 million in 1951 or more than 10 per cent of domestic production. The duty of 5 per cent is only very slightly restrictive.

The leather goods industries would be seriously injured if the protective duties were drastically cut. The potential increase in imports of each item cannot be added together, however. More imports of shoes, gloves and handbags would mean smaller imports of hides and leather.

Floorcovering

Imports of linoleum are negligible. Protected by a duty of 15 and 25 per cent, domestic production probably amounts to $75 million. Over a long period, Great Britain has demonstrated superior competitive ability in world markets. New products are appearing in this field, however, and it remains to be seen whether the British linoleum industry, which before the war was larger than the American, will hold its dominant position. American exports were almost $1.5 million in 1951. Judged by prewar competitive ability, Britain would be able to take an appreciable share of the American market if duties were cut and Britain would introduce the more colorful patterns favored here. These inlaid patterns are protected by the higher duty of 25 per cent.

Quality rug imports of $10 million are protected by a 25 per cent duty. Imports account for less than 5 per cent of home production and could be increased at lower duties. These rugs come from Europe, chiefly Belgium. Other wool floor coverings are protected by duties as high as 40 per cent. Imports in this category of $3 million could be greatly increased, particularly from Japan.

Clay floor and wall tile are protected by duties ranging from 25 to 40 per cent. Imports of less than $2 million are about equal to exports and amounted to less than 5 per cent of domestic production in 1951. Production of tile was not much greater in 1949 than in 1926 because of competitive inroads of substitute materials for floor coverings, such as plastic, asphalt, rubber and cork.

Because of the weight, transport costs are an important consideration and may explain why domestic industry is able to export to certain markets. This is a fairly well-standardized product and imports to areas that can be served by ocean transport would be greatly increased if duties were cut. The industry is keenly aware of the potential competition from imports[13] and has published its views in a brochure under the title *The Threat to the American Tile Industry*.

Toys

Toys including dolls comprise one of the items usually cited as an example of the highly restrictive effect of American tariffs. Various investigations of the market indicate that this is justified with respect to simple,[14] low-priced toys and, at the other extreme, those toys which are substantially handmade. But the fact that American exports are nearly double imports supports, as do market investigations, the view that American producers can compete in the bulk of the toy market because of mass production techniques and modern designs. A drastic cut in duties, which range from 25 to 90 per cent, would increase imports of certain types very substantially, but it seems doubtful if imports would exceed 10 per cent of domestic production unless foreign producers revolutionized their whole conception of both design and production technique.

Paper Products

Abandoned paper mill towns are reported to have been a familiar sight after newsprint was placed on the free list forty years ago. Today, newsprint is a prime example of how a large increase in imports can be absorbed

13. See testimony before the Committee for Reciprocity Information, Panel E, May 31, 1950, p. 116.

14. One survey found that buyers regard American-made dolls as more durable. See *The Market for United Kingdom Consumer Goods in the United States*, Time, Inc., 1948; *What American Stores Are Buying in British Markets*, American Chamber of Commerce, London, 1950.

without serious damage to home industry. The explanation, of course, lies in the growth of consumption. Imports rose from a monthly average of 197,000 tons in 1935 to 414,000 in 1951. Production increased somewhat less rapidly, from 257,000 tons to 460,000. Nor did foreign competition spoil the market. Prices rose from $40 per ton to $111.

Imports of all paper products rose from an average of $217 million in 1936–1940 to $958 million in 1951, chiefly as a result of increased imports of newsprint and higher prices for wood pulp. Domestic companies that do not own forest resources claim to have suffered from the shift of Canadian exports from wood pulp to end-products. Other complaints concern the shift in grade of Canadian exports as a result of changes in duty on certain paper products. Although profits margins are said to have been squeezed by Canadian competition, the industry is in a healthy condition. The publishing industry has been a powerful influence resisting attempts to place a tariff on newsprint.

The paper industry illustrates why the growth of consumption will often have a more important influence on foreign trade than the further reduction of trade barriers. The accommodation of the paper industry to larger imports stands in striking contrast to the adjustment that would be required in order to accommodate a similar increase in competitive agricultural imports.

Imports of various forms of paper products (other than newsprint) total about $25 million and in each category amount to less than one per cent of domestic production. Reduction of the duties, which range from 10 to 20 per cent on various classes of paper products, would doubtless increase imports, but the total would still be small.

Selected Items

Imports of certain musical instruments are highly competitive with domestic production. The skills required to produce woodwinds require careful training and long experience. An escape clause investigation denied that the industry was seriously injured by tariff concessions. Imports of band instruments supplied 10–20 per cent of the domestic market before the second world war. Domestic production is concentrated in Elkhart, Indiana, where four concerns account for about 70 per cent of total production.

Imports of cheap jewelry are subject to duties of 67 per cent after trade agreement concessions. In 1945 the Tariff Commission estimated that imports would probably increase fivefold if duties were cut 50 per cent. Imports have amounted to 2 per cent of production both before and after the second world war.

Cutlery is among the high-duty imports. The tariff ranges from 53 per cent to 107 per cent on folding knives, scissors, shears and razors even though some rates have already been cut by 50 per cent.[15] Imports of roughly $700,000 are less than 5 per cent of production. America is able to compete in third markets in this field, as is indicated by the excess of exports over imports. In part the explanation may be that imports and exports are of a different quality and not fully competitive.

Scores of articles are still subject to a protective tariff of 50 per cent or higher. The description of such items, however, is exceedingly narrow in most cases. For example, the duty of 69 per cent on paints or colors for students and artists refers only to tubes, jars, cakes, etc. not exceeding 1½ pounds each and valued at less than 20 cents per dozen pieces. The duty on Vermouth in containers of one gallon or less has been reduced to 10 per cent and imports have increased substantially. But in containers of more than one gallon the 1930 rate was 122 per cent and the present rate is 57 per cent. *The tariff is excessively discriminating with respect to quantity, size, value, and decoration or adornment of articles with handmade work.*

The duty is at present 50 per cent or higher on articles of clothing and furnishings containing lace, embroidery or other ornamentation; bamboo baskets, porch and window blinds; pistols; fishing rods; thermos bottles; dried mushrooms and dried eggs; neutral spirits for beverages; brandy in containers of more than one gallon; jute cordage and twine of two or more yarns not treated; chloroform and ether; coal-tar photographic chemicals; sodium nitrate; certain types of locks; zippers valued at less than 4 cents each. The complete list is extensive but the high-duty categories are often very narrow.

Perhaps the most needed reform is to simplify the almost unbelievable complexity of tariff classes. The Congress has asked the Tariff Commission to consider this problem but without changing the duties, which is an essential part of the task. One complicating factor, in addition to questions of protection, is that many tariff rates serve as a special excise tax on luxury articles.

Agricultural Imports

Sugar is the most highly protected industry in America. The demand for sugar is inelastic. Per capita consumption has been declining. Elimination of quotas, duties and excise taxes would probably increase imports by $250 million, which would displace half the domestic industry. There is probably no other import for which the potential is so large within an adjustment period of five to ten years.[16]

15. For a complete list of articles bearing a duty of 50 per cent or higher, see *Federal Register*, June 25, 1954, pp. 3881–3899. An escape clause investigation of scissors and shears found serious injury.

16. It is always possible, however, that recent improvements in mechanization will improve the competitive position of domestic beet growers.

Butter is one of the two or three largest potential imports, at least over the short run. At present imports are virtually excluded by quota. The duty is 14 cents a pound.

The butter problem is serious and complex. Per capita consumption has declined by half since before the second world war. In part, this is because the price is artificially high and consumers have substituted margarine, and in part, it has arisen from the decline in per capita consumption of all fats and oils. Domestic producers are in trouble, therefore, because of a serious loss of market. The situation is further complicated by the fact that the price of fluid milk is partly determined by the butterfat content, which means that it is closely related to the price of butter. Moreover, per capita consumption of fluid milk and other dairy products has continued to expand. The acute import problem is a by-product of (1) the sharp divergence in the trend of demand for butterfat and for other milk products and (2) the historical practice of determining the price farmers receive for milk by the butterfat content. In supporting the farm price of dairy products, the government has acquired large stocks of butter.

It seems fairly clear that the dairy farmers who supply butterfat are faced with the necessity for contraction. Dietetics and the mode of the slim figure have changed eating habits. It is chimerical to call for the removal of the tariff and quota on butter until domestic production is adjusted and the government stops acquiring surpluses.

The domestic price of butter has been held far above world prices, and if the quota and tariff were removed, imports would rise to perhaps 10 per cent of domestic production, which exceeded $800 million in 1951. Butter illustrates the fact that home industry may be injured by imports equal to less than 10 per cent of domestic production. Quotas were imposed when imports of all dairy products were negligible if expressed as a percentage of domestic production.

Specialty types of cheeses are also restricted by import quotas. The potential increase in imports and the potential injury to home industry are much less serious in this case. Restrictions on imports serve chiefly to protect domestic processors of specialty cheeses. Farmers receive no more for milk sold to these processors than for other similar uses.

Wool imports in 1951 amounted to 200 per cent of domestic production. As far as we have noted, no other import has increased as much at the expense of domestic production. The duty ranges from 8 cents to 37 cents per pound. Some specialists believe that wool imports would be substantially increased by elimination of the duty. Some doubts may be expressed on this score except for the long run. (1) Sheep are raised for mutton as well as wool, and meat prices are favorable. (2) To an important extent sheep are a side line which on many farms graze pasture and woodlands too poor for any other use. (3) The displacement of sheep by cattle may have gone too far because of the long cycle of rising cattle prices when heifers were withheld from the market to expand cattle herds.

A number of the oils are moderately restricted by tariffs. The most important restriction in this field is the prohibition on imports of linseed oil. In 1947, before the quantitative restriction, over one million pounds were imported. The duty of 4½ cents per pound was raised to 50 per cent in 1953.[17] Linseed oil was in short supply during the war and immediate postwar years and, as a result, domestic acreage of flaxseed was greatly expanded to more than double the 2.1 million acres harvested in 1939. With more plentiful supplies, the domestic acreage declined from 5.3 million acres in 1949 to 4.1 million acres in 1951. Domestic consumption in recent years exceeded 500 million pounds.

The present structure of duties as between oil and seeds favors the importation of flaxseeds. These are restricted, however, by the Argentine government's regulation of exports. Elimination of quantitative restrictions and tariff barriers would result in imports of linseed oil of perhaps $25 million.

Peanuts and peanut oil were restricted by quotas and tariffs in 1953. Edible almond and filbert nuts were restricted by special duties and quantity controls beginning in 1952.[18]

The duty on coconut oil is 18 per cent while the raw material, coconut meat, is duty-free; this situation of course restricts imports of the oil.

The 10 per cent duty on edible olive oil is only slightly restrictive and imports of $13 million supply most of domestic consumption.

Imports of castor oil amounting to $18 million supply about two thirds of consumption. This is an example of an import which apparently has been increased as a result of the 50 per cent cut in duty at Geneva. Castor oil also exemplifies a shift in imports from the raw material, castor beans, to the manufactured product as a result of structural changes begun during the war. At present prices, the duty amounts to about 7 per cent. Judging from experience since Geneva, imports would respond to a further 50 per cent cut in the duty.

Palm oil is not produced in the United States, but domestic producers of competing fats and oils for making soap are mildly protected by a processing tax of 3 cents per pound.

17. *Specified Manufactured Dairy Products, Flaxseed and Linseed Oil, Peanuts and Peanut Oil, Tung Nuts and Tung Oil*, U.S. Tariff Commission, 1953, processed. The governments of Argentina and Paraguay agreed to restrict their exports of tung nuts and oil to the United States during the marketing year 1955.

18. *Edible Tree Nuts*, U.S. Tariff Commission, Report No. 183, 1953. In addition to restrictions under Section 22 of the Agricultural Adjustment Act, imports of certain dairy products, oils and nuts are licensed under Section 104 of the Defense Production Act of 1950. This system restricted imports of dairy products but licenses on some items were issued freely.

The various fats and oils compete to some extent with one another but the substitution is imperfect. Thus, the United States has a surplus of some fats and oils and a shortage of others. The apparent potential increase in imports of individual items should not be added together because one may be substituted for another and the more pressed oil is imported, the less the raw material will be imported.

Imports of wines totaled about $17 million. The duty is 15 per cent on table wines but rises to 30 per cent on heavy wines. Producers of certain types of wines would probably be injured by substantial cuts in duties.

Duties on wines, hard liquor and other beverages have been reduced from 81 per cent to 23 per cent (based on 1952 imports).

Imports of cigar tobacco total $26 million and are equal to 20–25 per cent of domestic production. The duty discriminates in favor of Cuba. The duty on Cuban cigar filler is 15 per cent, on imports from other countries about 50 per cent. The duty on wrappers is about 20 per cent. Over the long run, the effect of tariff reduction would probably be substantial and the injury to domestic producers would be serious. Duties on all tobacco products have been reduced from 89 per cent on 1934 imports to 20 per cent on 1952 imports.

The embargo on live cattle on account of hoof and mouth disease has encouraged the export of canned beef to the United States. In fact, when the sanitary embargo was lifted for a time, the Mexican government restricted exports of live animals in order to export the more valuable canned product. The duty on live cattle and dressed beef is only 5 or 6 per cent, but on canned beef the duty is 20 per cent.

Imports of live cattle, chiefly from Canada, are regulated by quota and amount to less than $100 million. Imports of canned beef, chiefly from Argentina, are about half as great. The dollar value of the potential increase in imports from tariff reduction and suspension of quotas is substantial.

One of the larger imports on which duties have not been reduced under trade agreements is green olives. Imports amount to about $20 million, a major part of which are olives stuffed by hand. The tariff is 30 cents per gallon on the bulk of imports. Domestic production is chiefly ripe olives. Green olives are among the numerous dutiable imports which could be increased appreciably by tariff reduction only if total consumption could be increased. In this particular instance, to increase imports would also require the planting of new trees abroad as the United States takes virtually all of Spain's crop.

Fish

Imports of sardines and other canned fish amount to $13 million and are severely restricted by duties which range from 15 to 45 per cent.

TABLE 72
CANNED TUNA: PRODUCTION AND IMPORTS, SPECIFIED YEARS, 1933–1951

Year	Production	Imports	Ratio of Imports to Production[a]
	(Million Pounds)		(Per Cent)
1933	33	14	44.2
1935	55	8	15.0
1937	70	11	15.7
1938	60	7	11.9
1939	82	10	12.3
1943	54	0.5	0.9
1946	90	5	5.2
1947	109	6	5.7
1948	132	8	6.3
1949	138	4	3.2
1950	173	36	21.0
1951	160	4	2.3

Source: U.S. Tariff Commission.
a. Calculated before rounding.

Canned tuna is a $100 million home industry, highly protected by a duty of 45 per cent on tuna in oil. The industry expanded rapidly from 33 million pounds in 1933 to 160 million pounds in 1951, while imports fell precipitately from 44 per cent of production in 1933 to 2 per cent in 1951. The unusual increase in imports to 21 per cent of production in 1950 followed the announcement that duties would be raised from 22½ per cent to 45 per cent, effective January 1, 1951. (See Table 72.) Japan is the principal source of imports.

Tuna is an example of a home industry that has expanded rapidly and at the expense of imports, and now feels the effect of foreign competition. The duty on tuna in oil was increased under the flexible tariff[19] from 30 to 45 per cent in 1934. The trade agreement with Mexico reduced the rate by one half, to 22½ per cent, in 1943.[20] The duty was restored to 45 per cent with termination of the Mexican trade agreement. Imports of canned tuna in oil are directly competitive with home production and probably could be increased many times if the tariff were drastically cut.

Imports of tuna canned in brine and bonito were negligible until recent years when duties were reduced by 50 per cent. Tuna in brine is not as tender as tuna in oil and the original 25 per cent duty was cut to 12½ per cent by trade agreement with Iceland. The 44 per cent duty on bonito in oil was cut to 22 per cent by exclusive concession to Cuba in GATT, and

19. Section 336, Act of 1930.
20. But the United States reserved the right to withdraw the concession on termination of the unlimited national wartime emergency.

the general rate was reduced to the Cuban rate at Torquay. These lower duties have apparently created a market. Imports increased sharply to 9 million pounds of tuna in brine and 10 million pounds of bonito. As a result, imports of all canned tuna and bonito reached 16 per cent of domestic production in 1951, which is slightly above the prewar ratio. After an escape clause investigation, the Tariff Commission found, with two members dissenting, that the tuna fish industry had not been seriously injured.

The Whole and the Parts

The total possible expansion of imports would be substantially less than appears from the sum of the individual items considered separately. There are two reasons why the apparent potential market for individual items cannot be added together. (1) Raw material imports compete with imports of finished goods produced from the same materials. (2) Domestic resources in agriculture may be shifted out of wool, cattle or dairying into other agricultural products, but it is much more difficult to shift them out of agriculture altogether. Thus, the increase of one agricultural import makes the increase of the second more difficult. Both factors are important because of the particular structure of American imports.

If we import more woolen cloth and clothing, we shall import less raw wool. Increased imports of leather goods will reduce imports of hides and leather. Still other examples are hides, canned beef and live cattle. Wool carpets illustrate the competition between the free list and dutiable imports. Carpet wool is duty-free while wool carpets are highly protected. If the duty were cut, imports of carpet would rise but imports of wool would be reduced. Similarly for fabricated nonferrous metals and a long list of other products.

A number of the most highly restricted agricultural products compete rather directly for domestic resources. Imports of wool and canned beef have been stimulated by the embargo on cattle imports and the quantitative restrictions of imports of butter, cheese and oil. Increased imports of sugar, butter, cheese and linseed oil would shift land into pasture for beef cattle and sheep. Or if more soybeans are raised, competition with imported fats and oils may be increased. The potential increase in agricultural products taken severally is much greater than the total. Since sugar, wool, butter, and other fats and oils are among the largest imports or potential imports, and each competes with cattle or with each other for resources, the effect of freer trade in all agricultural products would be quite different from freer trade in one or two, with restrictions maintained on others.

In cases where joint demand exists, increased imports of one product will necessarily increase imports of another. Motorcycles and motorcycle parts are such an example. But these cases appear to be relatively unimportant.

Will increased agricultural imports increase agricultural exports and thus absorb the displaced resources within agriculture? This is possible but not probable, first, because American tobacco and cotton can supply the export market without drawing additional resources into these areas, second, because the reduction of foreign aid is likely to leave excess resources and the capacity to produce surpluses in most of the export branches of agriculture. The conclusion is that partial equilibrium analysis doubtless gives an exaggerated impression of the potential market for imports.

One further comment about magnitudes. Total imports in 1951 were $10.8 billion; of these, $6 billion were duty-free and $4.8 billion were dutiable. Roughly $1.8 billion of the dutiable imports probably could not be substantially affected by tariff reduction because (1) they are not produced at home, or (2) they are specialty items which already account for virtually the entire market, or (3) the volume is dictated almost entirely by industrial requirements. The expansion of these items by tariff reduction depends entirely on the elasticity of consumption. Potential imports the consumption of which would be greatly increased by lower prices are the exception rather than the rule. In general, high price elasticities depend on displacement of domestic supply. A number of the minor minerals are dutiable but not produced in significant quantities at home. Such imports depend almost entirely on the level of industrial production. Others, like molybdenum, bear a high duty although the United States has 90 per cent or more of the world's known reserves. Stuffed olives are dutiable, but imports already account for virtually the entire market. Imports of synthetic rubber are not likely to be substantially increased by tariff reduction.[21]

Excluding such items, the base level of imports against which the effect of tariff reduction should be measured is roughly about $3 billion of 1951 imports. And the elasticities that would induce a $1 billion increase in imports if tariffs were reduced and quantitative restrictions were eliminated are not quite so low as they appear in relation to total dutiable imports of $4.8 billion. Moreover, as was already noted, individual price elasticities are not a reliable guide to the over-all effect of reducing trade barriers because individual imports may increase at the expense of competing imports as well as at the expense of domestic production.

Who Will Be Injured?

Who will be injured by a policy of freer trade? The evidence seems reasonably clear. With few exceptions, the durable-goods and newer industries will not be injured. (1) The exposed branches of agriculture will be injured. (2) Many of the older nondurable-goods industries will be injured. Possibly as much as half of the total potential increase in imports are agri-

21. Information in this paragraph largely from Piquet, *op. cit.*, p. 42.

cultural products, whereas agriculture accounts for less than 8 per cent of national income. In a number of the older nondurable-goods industries, such as pottery, chinaware and handblown glass, imports could displace half of domestic production.

The question whether imports will injure home industry depends chiefly on how rapidly the market will expand. For those dynamic industries which enjoy a growing market, imports may increase relative to domestic production without creating serious problems. But in the more stagnant industries where the market is rather inelastic, the increase of imports will liquidate home industry and require the shift of resources, including the relocation of industry and the migration of workers.

Increased imports of chemicals, automobiles, steel, machinery, electrical equipment, rubber, paper, instruments and other products in this category will not, as a rule, seriously injure the competing home industries for three reasons. (1) The increase in imports will be relatively small. The argument that America has nothing to fear from imports is valid in these fields, where we generally have a comparative advantage in the cost of production. (2) The market is expanding rapidly enough so that additional imports will not displace established industries, destroy capital values and require the migration of workers. (3) These industries are dominated by giant corporations producing scores of products. Therefore, even if imports should seriously compete with a single product, neither the industry as a whole nor the individual company as a whole would be seriously injured.

The position of agriculture and many older nondurable-goods industries is more or the less the opposite. (1) To the extent that other countries have a cost advantage and can compete seriously in the American market, their advantage lies largely in agriculture and the nondurables. Some parts of these industries employ comparatively simple techniques and use less industrial equipment per worker. (2) The market for foods, textiles, shoes, hats, floorcovering and earthenware expands more slowly than the market for automobiles, electrical appliances and chemicals. The market for some nondurables is declining absolutely; for others the rate of growth is dependent chiefly on the growth of population. (3) Many more producers are competing in agriculture, textiles and shoes than in automobiles, steel and chemicals. Competition is on a basis of price. Because the domestic market is more competitive and is expanding more slowly, profits and wages in these industries are relatively low. The incidence of potential competition from imports is concentrated in the competitive rather than in the monopolistic home industries.

Unless the forces of expansion are strong, lower tariffs may lower prices and incomes without shifting domestic resources to more productive employment. Competition for labor in the dynamic industries must be strong and sustained in order to raise wages enough in the relatively stagnant industries to permit imports to displace domestic production.

In the nineteenth century, the tariff was associated with trusts and monopoly. Today, the opposite is more nearly true. It is no longer the monopolistic industries with relatively inflexible prices or the industries dominated by giant corporations which most need tariff protection in order to survive.

The concentration of potential imports in the relatively stagnant, low-wage industries helps to explain (1) why America imports so little, (2) why the response to lower tariffs has been so small, and (3) why the resistance and threatened dislocations from additional imports may seem disproportionate to their volume.

Imports of goods competitive with American products in which labor cost is decisive have been relatively low because the more stagnant home industries have customarily suffered from excess resources and underemployment. Witness, that even during the acute shortage of labor during the war, when millions of workers were drawn into the armed forces and shifted to the war industries, agriculture and most of the relatively stagnant industries were able to expand production significantly.

Any large increase in competitive imports in stagnant industries will require actual liquidation and the shift of workers and other resources to the more dynamic industries. The adjustment to imports is more difficult than if trade could be expanded by increased imports in the dynamic home industries, which would not require the actual shift of resources. This adjustment is all the more formidable because rapid technological advance and other changes are already displacing workers in many of these same industries, so that the import displacement is superimposed on other dislocations.

Geographical Incidence

The incidence of potential injury from increased imports of manufactures is concentrated in New England manufacturing where the older nondurable-goods industries were originally located. A major part of many and a substantial part of most industries which are subject to serious potential competition from imports are located in New England:

Woolens and worsteds	Jewelry (low-priced)
Hats	Cutlery
Shoes	Musical instruments
Leather handbags	Fish
Cotton textiles	Cigar tobacco
Lace	Clothespins

Another group of exposed industries is concentrated in southeastern Ohio and the adjacent West Virginia border. These are pottery, chinaware and handblown glass. Some plants producing clay floor tile, another exposed industry, are also located in this area.

The Ultimate Problem

Granted that some industries will be injured, how serious is the over-all problem of adjustment to freer trade? Additional opportunities for jobs must be created to absorb the workers who will be displaced. By lowering wages and profits in those industries where earnings are already relatively low, the dislocation may also take the form of underemployment. By lowering prices, increased foreign competition will redistribute income away from the import-competing industries. And as a result of lower American prices and wages, the actual volume of increased imports may be rather small. Thus, neither the actual increase in imports nor the unemployment which results is an adequate measure of the effect of foreign competition.

Time will be needed to make the adjustment, but time is not the only requirement. In agriculture and most of the older nondurable-goods industries, taken as a whole, the rate of growth of consumption probably cannot be accelerated by the expansion of international trade. This is the nub of the problem, for it means that those parts of the economy which are already growing most rapidly—durable goods, newer industries and services—must accelerate in order to compensate for unemployment and underemployment in the relatively stagnant industries exposed to increased competition from imports.

The adjustment to $1 billion of additional competitive imports cannot be fairly compared to the cancellation of $1 billion of war orders, for example. Because of the incidence of imports, the foreign trade adjustment is far more difficult.

The export branches of agriculture and industry, which are benefited by foreign aid, will suffer a smaller contraction from abandonment of foreign aid if the rest of the world is able to increase its dollar earnings by selling more goods in the American market. But, in a sense, this only makes the import adjustment more difficult because it means that the export branches, which are already expanded, may not absorb any workers who may be displaced by increased imports. By increasing imports, the adjustment to reduced foreign aid is transferred from the export trades to the import trades, provided that the reduction of foreign aid does not result in comparable reduction of taxes to consumers, and that they in turn do not use their increased purchasing power to buy the imports. Only expansion of the level of living at home will avoid unemployment and underemployment in agriculture and the import industries. By itself, this adjustment would be easily manageable. But the magnitudes of total adjustment are seriously misconceived by isolating the foreign trade adjustment from all the other dislocations that are inherent in a dynamic and progressive economy.

The American level of living will need to expand rapidly enough to take care of three things: (1) the expansion of output from continued mechanization and from new improvements in technology and methods, (2) the consumption at home of the goods formerly shipped abroad as foreign aid, and (3) the gains from the expansion of mutually beneficial trade.[22] The first is much the largest and the third is much the smallest of the three. But the fact that the third is a minor part of the total adjustment does not mean, as is often stated, that it will be easy. To get the benefits of increased trade, the economy must expand rapidly enough to absorb all the workers who are displaced for whatever reason, insofar as standard working hours are not reduced.

This is not an argument for maintaining protection. It does suggest that the adjustment problem is a serious one which should not be brushed off because the foreign trade adjustment by itself is relatively minor.

The significance of potential injury from freer trade lies primarily in the factors which determine the rate of growth for the economy as a whole.

22. It will require possibly only 75 per cent as much labor to produce the exports required to pay for additional imports as is now required to produce the goods at home. Thus 25 per cent of the labor now engaged in producing potential imports will be freed; this represents the gains from trade.

Chapter 21

Injury from Domestic and Foreign Competition: Handmade Glass

THE CLAIMS MADE for freer trade are often ambiguous. On the one hand, it is said that American industry has nothing to fear from imports. On the other, it is claimed that tariff reduction offers great benefits. In point of fact, benefits and "injury" are two sides of the same process. If there is to be an increase in international trade relative to home production, certain home industries must suffer. This will free resources. "Freeing" of labor resources can also be called unemployment. This represents virtual injury. But under the proper conditions, the unemployment will be temporary, and if the displaced workers and other resources are shifted to more productive employment, the expanding home industries will gain to the net benefit of the entire community; and the displaced workers will have a better opportunity. The "injury" will become a benefit.

The productivity of American industry has increased more rapidly than that of most other nations. As a result our industry is less dependent on tariff protection than it used to be. But the dictum that all home industry has nothing to fear from imports goes too far. Although our most dynamic industries have less and less to fear from import competition, certain industries, usually small ones, remain highly dependent on tariff protection.

Handmade Glass Dependent on Protection

The glass industry is a case in point. Domestic production of glass was valued at over a billion dollars in 1949. However, it is not the billion-dollar industry which is acutely apprehensive over imports, but that part of it which produces handmade glass. Sales of handmade glass in 1949 were estimated at about $32 million, or roughly 3 per cent of sales for the entire glass industry. Technologically, handmade glass is a separate industry although it must compete with machine-made wares.

The handmade glass industry presents a clear picture of the issue arising from increasing imports into the United States.[1] The benefits accrue to consumers and to the export industries; the burdens are borne by the owners and workers of small industries like this one. The fact that the benefits ex-

1. The views of management and workers expressed in this chapter were obtained by personal interview. One company was later forced to close.

417

ceed the burdens may be beneficial to the nation but is of no help to the handmade glass industry. And even the benefits would be so widely diffused that scarcely anyone would notice the difference, while the injury would be highly concentrated among a few producers and a small number of workers in certain communities. In the spring of 1950, handmade glassware, as far as could be judged by personal inquiries, was one of the industries most aggrieved by the Trade Agreements Program.

Handmade glass is produced by essentially the same process that has been used for centuries. The industry is located chiefly in West Virginia, Ohio and Pennsylvania. The location was originally dictated by the presence of natural gas for fuel. Technology has improved the quality of the product: the modern firm uses iron molds instead of wooden molds and provides wind to cool the molds (and, in summer, the workers), which makes it possible to work somewhat faster. Labor cost, however, remains, as always, the principal cost. For this reason, foreign costs are a fraction of those prevailing in the United States since foreign wage rates are far lower than American wages and, apparently, the difference in productivity in this branch of industry is small.

Handmade glass is a prime example of a high-labor-cost product that can be produced more cheaply by those countries having less capital per worker than does the United States. The productivity and hence the standard of living of the world, including the United States, could be raised (if full employment were maintained) by liquidation of the United States industry and the shift of labor now engaged in domestic handmade glass to the mass production export industries which use more capital per worker.

In most of the mass production industries, because of technique and the high capital-labor ratio, American unit costs are lower than foreign costs despite the much higher American wage rate. Consumers both at home and abroad could buy both handmade glass and mass-produced commodities more cheaply by trading our exports for their glass. The same amount of work in each country will produce more glassware and more machines if we specialize and trade. Average wages are higher here because labor is generally more productive, having a large amount of capital with which to work. This is why our expensive labor should be used only in highly capitalized industries while foreign countries should employ their less highly paid labor to make such things as handmade glass, which do not require so much of their relatively scarce and expensive capital.

Early in 1950, foreign prices of handmade table, stem and ornamental glassware were often one half or less of the American manufacturers' price. The countries with the lowest prices at this time were Czechoslovakia and Poland, which now controls the Silesian (formerly German) glass industry. Sweden also makes some inexpensive wares as well as higher-priced quality products. The American industry complained also that Holland had obtained glassware under a trade agreement with eastern Europe and resold the product in the American market. Japan, with financial assistance from the United States government, was also getting into a position to undersell the higher-cost American wares.

It is necessary to look at the specific industry to be liquidated in order to appreciate the difficulties in the way of adjustment to the potentially higher productivity and higher standard of living attainable by greater international specialization.

The problem arises from the fact that the benefits of specialization and trade are widely dispersed among millions of consumers while the costs of the adjustment, which are serious in a free market economy, are concentrated on the owners and workers in a few specific plants. One geographic area in the United States will gain at another's expense. The adjustment may involve the displacement of one community and the geographical shift of workers and capital to American export industries. In a market economy, the social overhead costs of the adjustment are borne by a few individuals.

The domestic industry to be displaced by imports naturally feels that it should not be put out of business by foreign competition in the interest of expansion in the export industries. Those in peril see their congressmen. The skilled workers who are articulate feel an injustice in a policy that would require them to abandon their skills and move from the community where they have lived and own their homes to start over again in the larger cities where most of the mass production industries are located. The average wage of skilled workers is high, their experience is usually limited to a single industry, and their emotional roots and property ties are in a single community.

Their position is not essentially different from that of workers in an obsolescent industry threatened by technological change—e.g., carriage makers after the advent of the automobile. But it seems different because it involves a dispute over change in an existing law.

Adjustment to Both Domestic and Foreign Competition

The position of the handmade glassware industry is weakened, not only by the competition of foreign handmade glassware but also, in some lines such as tumblers and the cheaper grades of stemware, by the development of the quite efficient domestic machine-made ware. American machine-made lines are able to compete in foreign markets and, in 1947, exports of machine-made tumblers and stemware alone were greater than total imports of all handmade table and ornamental glassware. Exports of machine-made table and kitchen glassware were three to five times larger than imports of handmade ware in postwar years.

The vigorous growth of the machine-made glassware industry has taken most of the market and made the handmade glass industry especially sensitive to increases in imports. Domestic competition has made foreign competition more onerous. This important part of the adjustment problem is usually neglected by those who are concerned with foreign trade. It is not merely the displacement from imports, but *the total competition, both domestic and foreign*, which is the measure of the industry's adjustment problem. A relatively small increase in imports may tax the capacity for adjustment if it is strained already by the shift of resources dictated by domestic competition.

The major adjustment problem will be present even without imports. In the period 1935–1950, machine-made wares increased from roughly 50 per cent to 70 per cent of the market in which both compete. Machine-made production rose more than fourfold while handmade production doubled in value.

Glass as a whole is a rapidly growing industry. Output of $400 million in 1939 rose about 150 per cent to over $1,000 million in 1949. Handmade glass received a special stimulus during the war years when most imports were cut off. Domestic production rose 83 per cent by value in the period 1939–1949.

The competition which the handmade industry faces from domestic machine-made wares is far more important than the competition from imports, and is reported to be increasingly severe. With rising wage rates, we should expect this to be the case. Nonetheless, a small handmade glass industry has been able to survive domestic competition. The industry believes that free competition from imports would represent the coup de grâce. Evidence on production costs supports this view.

Tariff Concessions Already Made

Concessions have been made on handmade glassware at Geneva and Annecy.[2] The important reduction was at Geneva when the duty on table, kitchen and art glassware (except engraved ornamental glassware valued at not less than eight dollars each, and bubble glass) was reduced to fifty cents each but not less than 30 per cent nor more than 50 per cent ad valorem, effective January and April 1948. (See Table 73.)

For imports valued under one dollar each, an important category in total imports, the duty was thus reduced from 60 per cent under the Act of 1930 to 50 per cent ad valorem. The duty on engraved ornamental glassware was reduced from 30 per cent to 15 per cent at Annecy, effective April 30, 1950.

In the 19th century protection became almost synonymous with monopoly. But today the American industries that would be most seriously

2. See Chapter 6 for a summary of these multilateral negotiations.

TABLE 73

GLASSWARE BLOWN OR DECORATED (EXCEPT PRESSED UNPOLISHED): CHANGES IN
UNITED STATES RATES OF DUTY

Item	Tariff Rate in:		
	Act of 1930	1945	1950
Table and kitchen articles and utensils, and all articles of every description not specifically provided for (except Christmas tree ornaments), composed wholly or in chief value of glass, blown or partly blown in the mold or otherwise, or colored, cut, engraved, etched, frosted, gilded, ground (except such grinding as is necessary for fitting stoppers or for purposes other than ornamentation), painted, printed in any manner, sand-blasted, silvered, stained, or decorated or ornamented in any manner, whether filled or unfilled, or whether their contents be dutiable or free:			
Articles primarily designed for ornamental purposes, decorated chiefly by engraving and valued at not less than $8 each	60%	30%[a]	15%[b]
Other, commercially known as bubble glass and produced otherwise than by automatic machine (except articles cut or engraved and valued at not less than $1 each)	60%	30%[c]	30%[d]
Other, blown or partly blown in the mold or otherwise, if cut or engraved, and valued at not less than $1 each	60%	45%[e]	50¢ each; min. 30%
All other	60%	60%[f]	max. 50%[g]

a. Trade agreement with Sweden, effective August 1935.

b. Annecy (effective April 30, 1950).

c. Trade agreement with Mexico, effective January 1943; rate previously reduced to 50 per cent in trade agreement with Czechoslovakia, effective April 1938 to April 1939.

d. Bound, Geneva, 1948.

e. Trade agreement with the United Kingdom, effective January 1939; rate previously reduced to 50 per cent in trade agreement with Czechoslovakia, effective April 1938 to April 1939.

f. In the trade agreement with Czechoslovakia, effective April 1938 to April 1939, rate was reduced to 50 per cent.

g. Geneva, 1948.

affected by foreign competition are not, as a rule, the more monopolistic industries. On the contrary, they are industries which, for one reason and another, are already facing severe competition within the national economy. Nor are the home industries which most need protection the large-scale industries; they are generally small firms and are often located in the less densely industrialized areas. The home industries which would benefit most from free trade tend to be the mass production industries, while those which

TABLE 74
GLASS AND GLASSWARE: IMPORTS AS PER CENT OF PRODUCTION, 1939 AND
1946–1949

	1939	1946	1947	1948	1949
Total	1.3	0.5	0.6	0.6	0.7
Flat glass	0.9	a	0.2	0.4	0.4
Glass containers:					
Machine and handmade	0.2	a	a	a	a
Pressed and blown glassware:					
Machine-made	b	b	b	b	b
Handmade	7.0	6.1	8.5	6.1	7.6
Illuminating ware	1.5	1.3	1.5	2.8	1.9
Technical, scientific, industrial					
and other	7.4	0.8	0.7	1.3	2.8
All other	2.5	b	b	0.1	0.1

Source: Compiled by the U.S. Tariff Commission from U.S. Department of Commerce data.
a. Less than 0.1 per cent.
b. Not available.

would suffer most are small firms, using essentially the same technology that has been employed for generations.

Imports of Glass

The insignificance of glass imports relative to the entire home industry is indicated by the fact that all imports were equal to only 0.7 per cent of production in 1949. Moreover, this represents a decline of almost one half from 1939, when imports were equal to 1.3 per cent of production. Although imports of illuminating ware increased slightly in relative importance, they still amounted to only 1.9 per cent of production in 1949. In the category of technical and scientific wares, imports fell from 7.4 per cent of production in 1939 to 2.8 per cent in 1949. (See Table 74.) However, imports of handmade glass relative to domestic production were more important than these figures for the entire industry would indicate. Imports which appear insignificant for an entire industry are, at the same time, a serious threat to part of the industry.

Imports of handmade table, kitchen and art glassware amounted to 10 per cent of domestic production in 1935, 15.4 per cent in 1937 and 8.7 per cent in 1939. During the war years, trade was cut off and the home industry emerged from the war with production of $35.5 million in 1946, compared with $17.5 million in 1939. Before the tariff concessions at Geneva, imports amounted to 6.9 per cent of production in 1946 and 8.7 per cent in 1947. The Geneva concessions became effective in January and May 1948, but home production increased in that year while imports remained about the

TABLE 75
HANDMADE TABLE, KITCHEN AND ART GLASSWARE: UNITED STATES PRODUCTION
AND IMPORTS, SPECIFIED YEARS, 1925–1951

Year	Domestic Production[a]	Imports[b]	Ratio of Imports to Production
	(Thousands)		(Per Cent)
1925–1929	c	$3,315	c
1935	$16,000	1,595	10.0
1937	19,000	2,926	15.4
1939	17,500	1,528	8.7
1946	35,500	2,458[d]	6.9
1947[e]	37,500	3,307[d]	8.7
1948[e]	41,000	2,322	5.7
1949[e]	32,000	2,866[f]	9.0
1951[e]	31,500	4,468	14.6

Sources: U.S. Tariff Commission and U.S. State Department.
a. Estimated.
b. Products imported under tariff paragraph 218(f), except Christmas tree ornaments. Possibly includes very small amounts of machine-made ware.
c. Not available.
d. Includes glass jewelry, estimated at $450,000 in 1946, and $750,000 in 1947, which in other years shown above was dutiable as jewelry under paragraph 1527.
e. Preliminary.
f. Includes imports valued at $350,040 from Canada, which consisted largely of glass television tubes.

same, so that the ratio of imports to production fell to 5.7 per cent. Contrary to the usual cyclical pattern, imports increased in 1949 in the face of a sharp fall in home production, with the result that the import ratio reached 9 per cent. (See Table 75.)

Imports did not regain their prewar position relative to home production until 1951. But in the meantime machine-made wares had gained a much larger share of the market. The principal problem would appear to be that of the home industry's adjustment to postwar competition—both foreign and domestic. Yet the industry was fearful of imports and the apprehension was probably justified. Wage costs in the United States for this industry may have increased more than in competing countries in the decade 1939–1949, so that higher rather than lower duties may have been needed in order to maintain prewar protection.

Industry Views

The industry emphasizes that it is not opposed to competition and does not seek a tariff wall high enough to eliminate foreign competition. What it wants is "fair" competition, by which the industry's spokesmen mean a tariff that is adequate to compensate for differences in the wage cost. Competition in design and marketing is regarded as fair, and is acceptable.

The most-favored-nation principle and, indeed, the principle of uniform tariff rates to all nations is objectionable to those in the handmade glass industry, whose view on this point is shared by a number of comparable small industries.[3] The multilateral policy of one duty for all is regarded as altruistic because it does not take account of the different wage costs among the various nations. The conclusion is drawn that because wage costs differ from country to country a fair tariff would be one which, by meting out different rates, would equalize the effect of different wage costs. The low-wage cost in Czechoslovakia, Silesia and Japan is held to be not only unfair to American labor but also to other friendly countries like Britain and Sweden. "Ultimately, the countries—our good friends—who are trying to raise labor rates, eventually are squeezed out of the market . . . by tariff reductions we actually are helping only the low wage countries."[4]

Two further points are made against tariff reductions that would permit more imports of glassware. First is the national defense argument. Workers in the home factories, it is said, are needed because of their skill in making scientific and laboratory ware and because, with only a little additional training, they can make radar and radio tubes, running lights and lenses, instrument parts and hospital equipment. The skill of experienced glassblowers is required for production of the glassware required by the armed forces. During the war years, the industry produced to the limits imposed by skilled labor and equipment, and output for military use is reported to have averaged about $7 million annually. This, it should be noted, was 25–30 per cent of production.

The second point is that there is a value in craft industry for its own sake, that the American economy is already lopsided, that not every person wants to be a machine worker. "A country," it is said, "without the uplifting influence of the hand arts is like a community without a church."

However, the hard core of the industry's case against tariff reductions is the low-wage argument. The industry feels that the onus of tariffs belongs on the low-wage sweatshop nations who "oppress their own nationals with Negro wages and depressed social conditions."

Potential Japanese Competition

Conflict of interest also emerges in connection with foreign policy objectives. In order to enable the Japanese economy to support itself and pay for food imports from the United States, the Department of the Army, as the agency responsible for the occupation, was concerned with the rehabilita-

3. Including pottery, fur felt and wool hats, and cutlery.

4. The industry's argument is illustrated in the following example. The scale of wages in Britain is about $4.00 per day, compared with $1.00 in Japan. The duty is 50 per cent ad valorem. Thus one day of Britain's labor must sell for $6.00 and one day of Japan's for $1.50. The customary distribution markup is 100 per cent. Thus a day's labor in Japanese glassware is sold to the consumer for $3.00 compared with $12.00 for the British.

tion of export industries. Japanese businessmen were encouraged to visit the United States, learn our methods and acquire modern equipment. The United States handmade glass industry was reluctant to cooperate in assisting the Japanese to learn the American way. The industry objected to public financial aid to develop Japanese competition to destroy American industry (though if this were done by private loans, it would, in this respect, not be regarded differently) and made the rounds in Washington voicing their objections.

Attempts to Obtain Governmental Support

In the spring of 1950, when the concern about unemployment created in the slight recession of 1949–1950 was still in evidence, representatives of the industry attempted to see the President. They were able to present their case to an Assistant to the President, John R. Steelman. Labor representatives in the group assert that Mr. Steelman advised them to seek employment in some other industry. One particular worker happened to be a 54-year-old, highly skilled worker who had been in the industry since he was 18, owned his own home and regarded such a suggestion as outrageous. Skilled workers, in an industry like glass which requires specialized skills, have organized and achieved a good wage and a high degree of immobility. Wartime experience indicates that skilled workers did not migrate as did the unskilled.

Following the interview, Mr. Steelman wrote the following letter, the effect of which was only to embitter the industry. The letter was reproduced and distributed as an indictment of the administration's policy. The escape clause was held up by Mr. Steelman as the proper means of relief, although he took a dim view of the future of handmade glass in the United States. The recommendation that the area find a new industry was the equivalent of waving a red flag. If anyone must move to a new industry, in the view of glass workers, it should be the Japanese and the Czechs.

> The Little White House
> Key West, Florida
> March 24, 1950

Dear Congressman:

. . . I am rather surprised to learn that no application has been filed with the Tariff Commission for an investigation under the "escape clause" provision of the Trade Agreements Act. Such investigations are for the purpose of determining "whether as a result of unforeseen developments and of a concession granted on any article by the United States in a trade agreement . . . such article is being imported in such increased quantities and under such conditions as to cause or threaten serious injury to the domestic industry producing like or directly competitive articles." From a cursory examination of the Department of Commerce estimates of domestic production and imports of handmade glassware, I suspect that it may be difficult to show that competition between foreign and domestic glassware has been much affected by tariff concessions in trade agreements. Nevertheless, I believe that this approach should be explored with the Tariff Commission and the industry.

The problem of competition from imports of glassware from Japan is a difficult one. You realize, of course, that the United States is anxious to assist in the development of sound Japanese foreign trade as an essential part of the rehabilitation of the Japanese economy. However, I understand that the problem of the effect of imports of Japanese glassware on the glassware industry in this country has been raised with officials of the Department of the Army who are in touch with glassware manufacturers and are investigating the situation. . . .

As I indicated to you . . . I cannot be very hopeful of the prospects for United States production of handmade glass to return to high levels achieved directly after the war. The problem of attracting new industries to replace declining ones is extremely difficult and your district is faced with an unusually critical problem. I am convinced, however, that there is more hope in the direction of attracting new industries than in attempting to support the handmade glass industry except at a reduced level.

Since the President asked me to direct activities to alleviate unemployment in particular areas last summer, I have become increasingly convinced that coordinated community planning by local groups is essential to any real solution of unemployment problems. Such local action is particularly important in areas faced with declining employment in a number of industries. I suggest that you may want to consider this approach in your district.

Sincerely,
(Signed) John R. Steelman

Honorable Harley O. Staggers
U.S. House of Representatives
Washington 25, D. C.

This is President Truman's Answer to Us through His Assistant John R. Steelman.

The above was the only comment that the industry felt was needed. The letter was circulated in the confidence that it spoke for itself.

The labor representatives, after three trips to Washington, wrote:

Nothing has been accomplished—so it leaves us with one thought—and that is —they are passing the buck—and have no interest whatsoever in the handmade glass industry in this country. They leave us with a very bitter thought—that the men and women who have helped to build this country are now being sold down the river in order to rehabilitate foreign countries at the expense of many hand craft workers of this nation. Candidly speaking, no agency has given us much hope of our industry being helped.

Dollar Gap

The dollar gap, in the view of President Orme of the Cambridge Glass Company, is an artificial creation of American policy which operates to the benefit of the large companies in the export business.

It seems unfair that we should give up our total domestic market and turn it over to these foreign countries with the result being bankruptcy, and our thousands of workers thrown into idleness. . . . American dollars have created the dollar gap by financing all exports to these countries. Having created a big export business with our dollars—now certain industries, particularly the handmade glass industry, is asked to give up its domestic market to help balance the gap we created . . . had not the millions of dollars been poured into these countries to create the dollar gap it would not have been necessary to increase the imports into this country from them to try to close it. Since our handmade glass industry has not contributed to the creating of the dollar gap by exporting to these countries—why should it be saddled with the responsibility of closing it by sacrificing its entire domestic market?

Mr. Orme also referred to "the interference of our government authorities encouraging the American public to purchase these imports to the point where many of our citizens believe they are unpatriotic if they do not buy them in preference to merchandise produced by American workmen who created the buying power of the nation."[5] Reference was made to the International Fair in Chicago in 1950, and glass company officials pointed to a picture of public officials on the brochure who were "promoting the sale of foreign goods against the domestic." It was felt that "Paul Hoffman's running around this country telling people to buy in Europe" was favorable to the big automobile industry at the expense of the little handmade glass industry.

Boycott of Imports

Labor union officials did not take the prospect of increased imports lying down but aggressively carried the issues to the retailers. The President of the American Flint Glass Workers' Union, Harry H. Cook, distributed a letter[6] to all department stores in the United States and to all labor unions affiliated with the A. F. of L. "Steps are being taken by our Union," wrote Mr. Cook "to directly meet with the more than eight million members of the A. F. of L. with which our union is affiliated. We are going to tell our fellow workers of the A. F. of L. in the confident belief that they will sympathize and cooperate with us in our endeavor to boycott the merchants who are promoting the sale of cheaply produced European handmade glassware and reward those who have remained loyal to American products . . . Nor shall our efforts end there. We shall seek, and I am confident we will secure, the same sympathetic understanding of other large American unions." The threat of unemployment was added to the argument: "Your

5. Based on personal interview at the plant and statement made by W. L. Orme before the Committee for Reciprocity Information, Washington, June 7, 1950.
6. Letter dated May 16, 1950, signed by Harry H. Cook, International President, American Flint Glass Workers' Union of North America (A.F. of L.).

business, if not directly, then indirectly, cannot help but be adversely affected by the growing unemployment in our contract glass plants, for the economic chain cannot be stronger than its weakest link . . ."

The action of longshoremen helped the industry. In the wake of the outbreak of fighting in Korea, longshoremen threatened not to unload, and in some cases refused to unload, goods from the Soviet and satellite countries. It was reported that one of the ships not unloaded carried a cargo of $25,000 worth of foreign glassware.[7] The instance receiving the most publicity was Soviet crab meat that had been shipped here directly by Britain, which has long been a customary channel for distribution of this product with the United States. Relief from satellite competition in the latter half of 1950 apparently resulted from informal discrimination against satellite products by American buyers.

Talk of boycott in the trade, together with the action of longshoremen, apparently was effective in stopping further large-scale purchases of glassware from behind the Iron Curtain. A further factor doubtless was the uncertainty of supplies in the future. At least one large department store attempted at this time to make a deal whereby some of the leading department stores were to buy all their handmade glass from certain United States companies and, in return, the companies were to sell to no one else. The companies interviewed refused, in the belief that their "bread and butter" sales lay in the large number of small retail outlets.

Do Retailers Benefit from Lower Import Prices?

The markup on handmade glass is about 100 per cent over factory cost, the retailer absorbing transportation and packaging charges. By reason of the lower cost of foreign-produced glassware, the retailer is able to enjoy a larger markup and, at the same time, advertise modest cuts in the retail price.[8] It is this experience which is back of the view expressed by many industries, including glass, that consumers do not receive the benefits of the lower manufacturers' price of imports.[9] While this may be true with respect to the earlier batches of imports, it probably would not continue over the long run if importing were organized as a regular source of supply.

Dumping

Among the countries which seem to offer the strongest threat to the weakest American industries are the satellite nations of eastern Europe and the defeated enemy nation, Japan. With their planned economies and com-

7. This was later reported to be a shakedown racket. The embargo was lifted on suitable payment to the union.

8. Transportation, breakage and other losses are higher on imports and the distributor's margin needs to be higher than on domestic goods.

9. This is standard doctrine in the American Tariff League.

pletely controlled foreign trade, these nations are able to sell imports without regard to the costs of the individual firm. At one American plant the writer's attention was called to an official magazine *Czechoslovakia Glass Review*, stating that Czechoslovakia would not be undersold. This is quite different from a firm in a market economy announcing that it will not be undersold. The general problem of trading with a country with nationalized industries that can export without regard to cost is, however, not limited to the glass industry, and the United States has legislative safeguards to prevent dumping.

The United States Anti-Dumping Act of 1921 provides special duties if it is found that the imported wares are priced below costs of production. Pending an investigation of dumping in early 1951, the Treasury Department placed a long list of handmade glassware imports from Czechoslovakia under bond equal to 150 per cent of the assessed value of the merchandise. The order issued by the Bureau of Customs states:

> The settlement of customs duties on the glassware in question from Czechoslovakia is being suspended and such glassware will be released to importers only if they post special bonds to protect the revenue pending a determination of whether any special dumping duties are assessable on such glassware under the Anti-Dumping Act of 1921.[10]

"AMERICAN DOLLARS FOR CZECH INSULTS" was the title of an editorial in the *Philadelphia Inquirer* (June 4, 1950) accompanied by a feature story "UNITED STATES NEGLECTS THE ECONOMIC FRONT IN THE COLD WAR AGAINST CZECHS." "Operating under the Iron Curtain wage scales, Czechoslovakia is now beginning to land some items—such as bone china, glass and shoes—into the American market under tariff concessions." "It is one thing," said the editor, "to accept some goods made in friendly countries of Western Europe which we are trying to help through the Marshall Plan, even if these imports do create problems in our own industries. But it is a very much different matter, and entirely indefensible, when we permit and even encourage competing imports from behind the Iron Curtain."

The conclusion of the feature story was "although it may put American workers on the relief rolls, our State Department has no intention of getting mad enough to end this good thing for Czechoslovakia or any other Russian satellite." The time, it will be remembered, was June 1950 when the State Department was under fire from some quarters for allegedly harboring Communists.

The West Virginia Glass Workers Protective League has printed a number of brochures linking Communism with the destruction of American industry by imports from the East market.

10. *National Glass Budget*, 66th Year, No. 30, Pittsburgh, January 27, 1951.

Glass making is America's oldest industry, having its beginning in the early settlement in Jamestown, Virginia.

In the development of glass America has far outdistanced all other countries. Art, scientific and commercial glassware has here reached peaks of perfection equalled nowhere else in the world.

Glass is one of the pillars of our economic and cultural structure. Without glass and our own glass industry in this position of leadership, not only will our everyday existence be disrupted but our National Security would be seriously jeopardized.

The destruction of the American glass industry by communism is well under way.

Enormous and increasing amounts of glassware made in communist Czechoslovakia are now being sold in America, causing widespread unemployment among our workers, huge financial loss to the industry, while building up the war machine with which Russia hopes to destroy us.

GIVE AMERICANISM A CHANCE

Buy American made Products, from merchants who sell American Merchandise only.[11]

Escape Clause

When asked why the industry had not taken advantage of the "escape clause" the reply was: "If a gun is pointed at a man, there is no injury until the trigger is pulled—then it is too late." The industry's view of the way the escape clause works is "you are out of business before you have a case." Whether justified or not, it was clear that, as a result of the conference with State Department and White House representatives, the industry had no confidence whatever in relief measures. "If there would be the slightest possibility that the State Department or the President would recognize the injury, what relief would be granted? I can only feel that the answer would be NONE." This comment was circulated in the trade by a spokesman after visiting Washington.

While the escape clause has so circumscribed the Trade Agreement Program as to seriously impair its effectiveness, the glass industry believes that it fails to protect them. It was described with extreme cynicism as "a useless device that had been adopted in the first place for the express purpose of forestalling inclusion in the Trade Agreements Act of some more effective device for the protection of domestic industry."

The industry had not sought at this time (December 1950), and probably could not have obtained, revocation of concessions under the escape clause. While the rate of profits has sometimes been reduced by foreign competition, the level of profits generally remained "pretty fair" until the spring of 1950. The evidence, as distinct from the fear, of injury to date consists

11. A second brochure states that to spend billions fighting communism, while adopting policies which permit glass imports to create unemployment in the United States, is "un-American, indefensible, and downright dumb."

largely in reduction of operations to a three-day week in the first half of 1950 as a result, it was believed, of imports from eastern Europe. In the earlier postwar years foreign production had not been sufficiently restored. This illustrates the widely held view among critics of the Trade Agreements Program that the real danger in concessions already made lies in the future.

The historian who looked only at the statistical record might well conclude that there has seldom been so much fuss about so little. Imports in 1949 were less than $3 million and were no larger than those in peak prewar years while home production had expanded substantially. Despite their improved position compared to prewar, domestic producers felt pained at having to meet postwar foreign competition with reduced tariff protection. During the postwar boom and before the complete recovery of foreign industries, the domestic industry had been in an especially favored position. The restoration of foreign production and the general contraction of the market forced a curtailment of domestic production in 1949 when the foreign share of the market rose to about the 1939 level. The reduction in the proportion of the market supplied by domestic producers from the overextension of the immediate postwar period was undoubtedly unpleasant, but it was to be anticipated. The violent complaints of ruination were anticipatory.

Following summer vacation in 1950, many companies did not have sufficient orders to warrant returning production to a normal work week. They took a chance and began producing for inventory. Post-Korean expansion in the American market and the grabbing for inventory together with discrimination against imports from satellite nations restored the domestic market in the last half of 1950. As its own representatives interpret developments, the handmade glass industry was granted a reprieve by events. They remained, however, embittered and fearful of the Trade Agreements Program. In 1951 imports increased substantially.

Tariff reduction probably contributed to the rise of imports from $2.3 million in 1948 to $4.5 million in 1951. But domestic production of handmade glass fell by $9.5 million in this period, from $41 to $31.5 million. Domestic competition from machine-made ware was apparently the more serious factor.

If duties were cut drastically, imports might well take more or less half of the market for handmade glass. This would represent a 300 per cent increase, but would still be a very small market with only a limited future.

The industry received some relief from foreign competition when all trade agreement concessions were suspended (effective June 30, 1952) on imports from Communist-dominated countries. This affected imports from Czechoslovakia, Poland and the Soviet zone of Germany. The industry has since applied for relief under the escape clause, which was denied.

Chapter 22

Imports without Injury: Watches

AN ARTICLE in *Fortune* magazine in 1949 told this story:

One day early last February (1949) Mr. Truman was seated at his desk, thinking about whatever successful candidates think about, when there was ushered into his office a delegation headed by Governor Paul Dever, newly elected, of Massachusetts; said delegation including the harassed Mayor of Waltham, Massachusetts (John F. Devane), the Mayor of Elgin, Illinois (Walter E. Miller), the Mayor of Lancaster, Pennsylvania, where Hamilton watches are made (Dale E. Cary), together with Representatives Donahue of Massachusetts and Dague of Pennsylvania. The proposition that these gentlemen laid before the President seemed simple enough. The ancient Waltham Watch Co., which pays a fifth of the wages in Waltham, Massachusetts, was on the rocks; implicated was Switzerland, that great competitor (population 4,500,000) of the U. S.; a cure was to throttle the Swiss watch industry so that the American watch industry could survive.[1]

On December 28, 1948, the century-old Waltham Watch Company petitioned the federal district court in Boston for reorganization. Two and a half years later, only 350 workers out of the original force of 2,300 were at work at the Waltham plant, mainly on non-watch work; about 1,200 had found work in other plants, and 650 (excluding women who had withdrawn from the labor force) were still unemployed.

Waltham's financial embarrassment was seized by interested parties as the occasion for an effort to curb imports, and Waltham became perhaps the first instance of bankruptcy attributed to tariff concessions under the Trade Agreements Program.

But Waltham Company has a history.[2] Up to about 1880, the company had been able to increase productivity and lower costs, outcompete the Swiss, expand exports to the United Kingdom and pay good dividends. In 1883, approximately 2,000 employees were producing 1,200 watches per day, compared with an output of 50 watches per day for 200 employees in 1859. The improvement in output per man was attributed largely to the development of automatic machinery and to simplification of design. Also, the expanding market led to economies of scale. By 1876 three fourths of

---

1. *Fortune*, April 1949, p. 84.

2. This discussion of Waltham's history is based mainly on C. W. Moore, *Timing a Century* (History of the Waltham Watch Company), Harvard University Press, Cambridge, 1945. Reliable observers have the impression that the copies of this book were bought up by interested parties to avoid its further dissemination.

the parts employed in British watch production had disappeared from American models.[3] Such improvements made possible the substitution of workers with relatively less skill.

During the period 1864 to 1872, watch imports from Switzerland more than doubled, but the Waltham Company achieved a similar increase in sales. After 1872 imports of Swiss movements declined and Waltham sales exceeded total imports. Even after the Swiss had adopted American methods and regained some ground, Waltham sales in 1884 were more than 75 per cent greater than total Swiss imports.[4]

The subsequent history of the Waltham Company is a story of successive bankruptcies and reorganizations. While the number of man-days required to produce a watch was reduced from 4 in 1859 to 1.5 in 1905, little improvement occurred thereafter.

Moore notes that visitors at Waltham (presumably in the 1940s) were shown equipment that had been in operation for fifty years.[5] The advances in production and selling techniques apparently were made by Waltham's competitors. Advertising was regarded as a waste of money. But whatever the specific causes, the company was in difficulty, periodically, for nearly fifty years. In 1949 inventories were disposed of at half-price, and the cry to stop imports went into full swing.

"The Waltham Mess" has been characterized by *Fortune* magazine[6] in plain language. The collapse of Waltham, it said, was caused by bad management rather than Swiss competition. Red ink was a familiar color on the Waltham ledger long before there were trade agreements. Founded in 1850, Waltham went bankrupt for the first time seven years later and has since been reorganized five times. In the twenty years of more or less profitable operations, little was spent on research, design, new machinery or advertising.

Reports from many quarters indicate that Waltham as a watchmaker was permitted to wither on the vine. It is reported that dividends to stockholders were parsimonious while the net worth of the company was built up, apparently with a view to selling the company rather than improving its watch-making facilities. The war doubled Waltham's sales, and its management, whose operation of the New Haven Railroad has also occasioned a good deal of critical comment, sold out of the Waltham concern.

Waltham appears to be a clear case of an effort to subvert international trade in order to protect inefficiency and poor business management. The moral, according to *Fortune* magazine, is that we should not "justify bad

3. *Ibid.*, pp. 59–60.
4. *Ibid.*, p. 67.
5. *Ibid.*, p. 232.
6. April 1949.

management, condone bad banking and give false life to a company that has demonstrated its inability to compete."[7] At the same time, it should be recognized that imports may give the coup de grâce to the inefficient company that is already in trouble.

The failure of Waltham was treated as an omen of disaster by the two remaining domestic manufacturers of quality[8] jeweled watches. Imports of Swiss movements had increased rapidly following elimination of the restrictions in the Swiss agreement in 1947.[9] Also, the market had softened in 1949 and large inventories produced occasional price-cutting. Early in 1950, Elgin National and Hamilton were reported as employing 2,000 fewer people than in February 1949.[10]

As a result, the administration was charged with violating the promise to avoid injury to home industry, and Waltham became a *cause célèbre* in the issue of imports versus home production. Under pressure, the administration obtained the consent of the Swiss government in October 1950 to include the escape clause in the Swiss trade agreement. Four months later, some observers wondered if the involvement of the Reconstruction Finance Corporation in the future of Waltham affected the government's attitude toward imports.[11] No evidence was found to support this view.

As is frequently the case with protected industries, watches raises the serious question of national defense. The making of fuses, timing devices and other high precision work requires a degree of skill that cannot be quickly provided except by keeping a small but indispensable reservoir of skilled workers.[12] But, clearly, national security does not dictate the protection of every individual company, however inefficient. To the contrary, our national power is weakened by preservation of inefficient companies. *If industries are to be protected in the interest of national security, it is doubly*

7. *Loc. cit.*

8. Jeweled watches of quality are distinguished from watches containing clock-type movements. The distinction is based primarily on the type of escapement, a mechanism which governs wheel speed. Jeweled watches of quality contain jeweled escapements, and clock-type watches contain pin-lever escapements. The adjective "quality" is further justified on the ground that some watches with pin-lever escapements may also be jeweled, largely for merchandising reasons.

9. See p. 437.

10. Statement of J. B. Shennon, President of the Elgin National Watch Company, before the Committee for Reciprocity Information, June 14, 1950.

11. A broader question of great importance is whether or not the extension of the role of the government, including government ownership as in Britain, will operate to reduce or to increase economic nationalism in a democracy.

12. In comparison with the policy of France and even the United States, the British assumed a more generous attitude towards the rehabilitation of German industry immediately following World War II. One of the few industries, however, that they wished to suppress as a means of encouraging the industry in Britain was the watch industry. Caught at the beginning of the war without a watch industry, Britain was handicapped as a result.

important that the individual companies should be well-managed. Patently, it is the industry as a whole and not the individual company which is vital.

Home Production versus Imports

The salient facts with respect to the jeweled watch market are these: the total market has about doubled since 1926–1929, but sales of domestic watches have increased only about 55 per cent while the increase in imports has been about two and a half times as great.

In the late 1920s, imports were increasing at the expense of domestic sales, but beginning in 1929 imports fell sharply from 66 per cent of the total market to 40 per cent in 1933. In 1935, before the Swiss trade agreement, imports amounted to 48 per cent of the market; by 1939 the figure was 60 per cent. During the war years, domestic watch makers were engaged in war production and imports reached 80 to 90 per cent of total sales. In 1950, imports accounted for 75 per cent of the market. (See Table 76.)

The important domestic producers are Elgin and Hamilton. Benrus and Longines-Wittnauer import and assemble Swiss movements. Bulova and Gruen engage in both operations. The American market for quality jeweled watches increased between four and five times from 1935 to 1950.[13] Sales of domestic watches more than doubled in this period. The domestic industry stands aggrieved but not liquidated by competitive imports. It has been "injured" only in the relative sense that it now has a smaller share of a much larger market. Moreover, the expansion of the market itself may be largely due to the lower price and aggressive advertising of the importers.

Many fewer jeweled watches would have been sold if the domestic market had been more severely restricted to the watches offered by domestic producers. Moreover, home industry has retained the cream of the market. The great bulk of the increase in domestic production has been in watches with seventeen or more jewels. This would appear to be the easiest possible adjustment to serious foreign competition. The same workers at the same benches in the same plants now produce a much larger quantity of more expensive watches than before the increase of imports.

Thus far we have not considered the effect of foreign competition on domestic producers of cheap watches with pin-lever movements. Both production and consumption of this type of watch have declined since 1936–1940. Increased production of pin-lever wrist watches has been more than offset by the declining popularity of pocket watches. That decline, however, cannot be attributed to imports of pin-lever watches, which were quite small. It is difficult to evaluate the effect of imports of jeweled movements on the domestic market for pin-lever wrist watches. They are only slightly

13. Except for a few clocks, imported watches and movements are virtually all of Swiss origin.

TABLE 76
JEWELED WATCH SALES OF DOMESTIC MANUFACTURERS AND IMPORTS OF JEWELED WATCHES AND MOVEMENTS (EXCLUDING 0–1 JEWEL), 1926–1950

Year	Domestic Manufacturers' Sales[a]	Imports (Excluding 0–1 Jewel)[b]	Total Watch Supply	Per Cent of Total Domestic Sales	Imports
		(Thousands of Units)			
1926	1,864	2,600	4,464	41.8	58.2
1927	1,834	3,000	4,834	37.9	62.1
1928	1,679	2,600	4,279	39.2	60.8
1929	1,739	3,400	5,139	33.8	66.2
1930	1,175	2,300	3,475	33.8	66.2
1931	976	815	1,791	54.5	45.5
1932	534	422	956	55.9	44.1
1933	647	433	1,080	59.9	40.1
1934	957	842	1,799	53.2	46.8
1935	1,246	1,138	2,384	52.3	47.7
1936	1,815	2,133	3,948	46.0	54.0
1937	2,089	2,957	5,046	41.4	58.6
1938	1,257	2,135	3,392	37.1	62.9
1939	1,768	2,700	4,468	39.6	60.4
1940	2,171	3,265	5,436	40.0	60.0
1941	2,601	4,044	6,645	39.3	60.7
1942	1,816	5,108	6,924	26.2	73.8
1943	1,570	7,609	9,179	17.1	82.9
1944	1,502	6,757	8,258	18.2	81.8
1945	987	8,708	9,696	10.2	89.8
1946	1,696	9,039	10,735	15.8	84.2
1947	2,340	7,357	9,697	24.1	75.9
1948	2,922	7,830	10,752	27.2	72.8
1949	2,631	6,840	9,471	27.8	72.2
1950	2,625	8,075	10,700	24.5	75.5

Source: U.S. Tariff Commission, *Investigation No. 4 under Part III of Executive Order 10082 Covering Watches, Watch Movements, Watch Cases, and All Other Articles Classified under Paragraph 367, Tariff Act of 1930, as Amended*, Brief in Behalf of American Watch Association, Inc. (This is the importers' brief.)

a. For further details of domestic manufacturers' sales and sources of data see Table F, p. 35, Brief in Behalf of American Watch Association, Inc. Totals for 1935–1950 exclude combined export sales of Elgin, Hamilton and Waltham.

b. Import data (excluding 0–1 jewel) were compiled from U.S. Foreign Commerce and Navigation reports, Census FT-110, and U.S. Tariff Commission reports.

competitive. In any event, the displacement of cheap pocket watches has been more than offset, in value, by expanding sales of other items. Total annual sales of domestic producers of pin-lever watches rose from $25 million in 1936–1940 to $58 million in 1946–1950. In the same period, watches declined from 36 per cent of total sales to 31 per cent. This sector of the industry has adjusted to substantial changes in the market by shifting the composition of its output.

Why Imports Have Increased

Watches constitutes a rare instance of a manufactured product competitive imports of which have increased faster than national income and illustrates the market conditions which make this possible. These conditions suggest why, in most cases, it is extraordinarily difficult for manufactured imports to expand more rapidly than home production.

In the first place, the total market has expanded relative to income. Second, imports have been sold aggressively. The cost of imports is below domestic costs and they can bear a large advertising budget. Third, expansion of the market has been supported by a decline in durability, by a rise in repair costs, and by style factors. Even so, imports of Swiss watches amounted to less than $40 million in 1949.

Not only has the total market expanded, but jeweled watches have become more favored over cheap clock-type watches. Greater variety and new designs have encouraged ownership of more than one watch. Watches have become jewelry and, for an important range of imports, relatively cheaper.

The domestic watch industry lost some of its market to imports while serving the needs of the nation during the war. At a time when the market would have absorbed an enormous increase in output, the industry was engaged in producing specialized timing pieces and other military equipment. This is an important point in the industry's claim of injury from imports.

Historically, the home industry has been plagued with overcapacity—a problem that seems to antedate the depression. Capacity production was never sustained. Production of movements in 1928 was less than 1.8 million and in 1941 less than 2.7 million. Capacity was estimated at 3.7 million movements in 1929.[14]

The Postwar Market

After the wartime suspension of production, domestically made watches were not again available until 1946, by which time importers dominated the market so completely that domestic producers feared they would be faced with great difficulty in re-entering it. They feared also that the large sales of Swiss watches had absorbed the pent-up demand which would have facilitated the transition to a peacetime basis.[15] Domestic manufacturers prevailed upon the American government to reach an informal agreement with the Swiss to limit exports to the United States. The Swiss undertook to limit direct shipments during 1946 and the first quarter of 1947 to the annual rate of 1945.

14. *Postwar Watch Markets*, Domestic Commerce Series No. 21, 1950, p. 25.
15. *1945 Extension of the Reciprocal Trade Agreements Act*, Hearings, Senate Finance Committee, pp. 222–226.

Marketing difficulties appeared soon after the termination of the restrictive agreement. Though shortages of certain nationally known makes continued throughout 1947, unknown makes were in easy supply. The supply of watches increased because of contract commitments between importers and suppliers which could not be cancelled, and competition was intensified. In later years shortages of well-known brands had disappeared.

"In the resulting scramble some of the weaker companies were compelled to sell portions of their inventories at well below customary markups; this has been an unsettling market factor throughout most of 1949. . . ."[16]

The recent irregularity of the business is shown by the experience of one company. In 1950 it could have produced 500,000 more watches than were either sold or produced. In early 1951 it had a considerable number of unfilled orders.[17]

Increasing Importance of Expensive Models

The high level of personal income following the war has been accompanied by a marked rise in the median quality of watches sold. This rise has affected both imported watches and domestic watches but the latter more strongly.

In the prewar period Swiss imports had the range between the cheap clock-type watches and the jeweled watches of quality to themselves. Domestic producers contend that this specialization was not voluntary, that they were first driven out of the seven-jewel fields, which had been a mainstay in earlier years, and later pushed out of the fifteen-jewel field by Swiss competition.

Since the war, competition has been concentrated among watches with high jewel counts because of the tendency of both imports and domestic producers to increase the number of jewels. In 1931, 8 per cent of all the watch movements made by one domestic company contained sixteen or seventeen jewels. In 1941 the proportion was 45 per cent.[18] Today no jeweled watches with fewer than seventeen jewels are produced domestically.

The tendency toward more jewels is also apparent in the trend of imports. During the war, the proportion of imported sixteen- and seventeen-jewel models increased. By 1946, about 65 per cent of total imports were of this type.

16. *Postwar Watch Markets*, p. 7.

17. U.S. Tariff Commission, *Hearings on Watches and Parts*, May 15, 1951, p. 110, Statement by James B. Shennon, President of the Elgin Watch Company. The unfilled orders were not very consoling, Mr. Shennon continued: "Our salesmen a few months ago were riding high . . . Now they are struggling hard to sell watches, and they are very apprehensive about the fall." *Ibid.*, p. 111.

18. U.S. Tariff Commission, *Watches*, War Changes in Industry Series, Report No. 20, 1947, p. 10.

Swiss Competition

Swiss-made watches sell in the domestic market at about all levels of quality and price. Nationally advertised, expensive Swiss watches compete with the American quality jeweled watches. The Swiss industry also dominates the market in the retail price brackets from $6 to $30 where domestic manufacturers are inactive. In the lower range these imports compete with clock-type watches, but they are also substitutes for the higher-priced domestic models. The domestic industry is unable to compete in the low jewel-count field because importers can provide watches with more jewels at the same price.

The competitive strength of seventeen-jewel Swiss watches, the most popular model, is based not only on cost, but also on the imaginative promotion and sales techniques employed by importers.

The three domestic firms in the quality watch industry are the survivors of a much larger number of firms in the nineteenth century. They have usually "suggested" retail prices to distributors. Their methods of distribution have been traditional and slow in evolution. Believing that service ought to be available at the point of purchase, these firms distributed through wholesalers who in turn sold to jewelry stores.

The importers, however, developed other types of outlets such as department, drug and tobacco stores and have lowered distribution costs. They also pioneered direct selling to retailers as well as selling on credit. In part, the great expansion of the market is attributable to such innovations. One representative of the domestic industry considered the diversion of business from jewelry stores to be a form of injury resulting from import competition.[19]

Sales have also been stimulated by new developments in watch making, most of which are of Swiss origin. Though the domestic industry has made notable advances in engineering, such as the development of a new long-lived mainspring, the changes which have attracted most consumers were initiated by the Swiss. The wrist watch is probably the most spectacular development, but other changes include water-resistant, shock-resistant and self-winding features. Domestic companies have manufactured only few water-resistant watches and, until the middle of 1950, they did not manufacture self-winding or shock-resistant watches.[20]

New marketing techniques, new designs and new features have aided the aggressive and successful sales effort of the importers. There is no doubt, however, that the source of their competitive strength lies in the lower cost at which the Swiss can produce watches.

19. U.S. Tariff Commission, *Hearings on Watches and Parts*, May 15, 1951; testimony of J. B. Shennon, President of Elgin National Watch Company.
20. *Postwar Watch Markets*, p. 33.

The Swiss have developed a degree of internal specialization which is more typical of America than of Europe.[21] While some manufacturers produce most of their own parts, a few specialize in the production of jewels only, and still others specialize in the production of incomplete movements called "chassis." Standardization of parts makes for interchangeability within quality, size and style categories. Such interchangeability and an abundance of spare parts have facilitated the servicing of watches which is necessary to a continuous market.[22] In watches, the Swiss have outstandardized America.

The two leading American manufacturers, by contrast, are nearly self-contained. While they continue dependent on imported jewels, virtually all other parts are made and assembled into completed watches by the individual firms. To a considerable extent, domestic firms also produce their own tools as requirements have never been large enough to justify development of a separate machine tool industry. The Swiss, on the other hand, have not only developed a tooling industry, they also export its products—sometimes on onerous terms—to foreign manufacturers.

The competitive strength of the Swiss industry is indicated by its continued domination of the market for jewel bearings. Manufacture of these minute parts, which are essential to the accuracy and long life of a watch, was undertaken by the domestic industry during the war, but was discontinued because the Swiss can supply them at one fourth to one third of the domestic cost of production.[23]

Domestic watch manufacturers argue that expansion of the home industry would make possible the reduction of costs. Thus, tariff protection is said to be necessary in order for the home industry to achieve the economies of large-scale production. Importing companies, on the other hand, charge that the remaining domestic companies have made it more difficult to start new, integrated companies in the United States.

They have followed the practice of producing under one roof all of the component parts of the watches they manufacture, although this is a far more expensive method of operation than other methods which could be made available. It is their established practice not to sell machinery or parts of watch movements to other domestic watch manufacturers or assemblers.[24]

21. In the period 1936–1940 the United States market absorbed nearly 52 per cent of Swiss exports of watch movements, but less than 1.5 per cent of the exports of cased watches. *Watches*, p. 143.

22. *Postwar Watch Markets*, p. 18.

23. *Ibid.*, p. 40.

24. U.S. Tariff Commission, *Investigation No. 4 Under Part III of Executive Order 10082 Covering Watches, Watch Movements, Watch Cases, and All Other Articles and Parts of Articles Classified Under Paragraph 367, Tariff Act of 1930, as Amended*, Brief in Behalf of American Watch Association, Inc., p. 19. (This brief became available after the present study was largely completed.)

The Tariff and Imports

The tariff on watch movements was increased by the act of 1930. Since these duties were specific, the rate was further increased relative to prices by deflation in the following years. The trade agreement with Switzerland reduced duties in 1936 and the ad valorem equivalent rate has been further reduced by price inflation since that date. As a result, average duties on imports in the following periods were:

Year	Per Cent	Year	Per Cent
1926–1930	53	1941–1945	41
1931–1935	83	1945–1950	36
1936–1940	64	1951	36

Duties averaged 81 per cent in 1935, the year before the Swiss agreement. The effect of inflation on specific duties relative to price is shown by the fact that the calculated rate on 1950 imports at 1930 duties is 59 per cent. This was reduced to 37 per cent as a result of concessions made to Switzerland. The rise in prices since the Swiss agreement has reduced the ad valorem rate by the same absolute amount that specific duties were reduced in the agreement.

Before reviewing the question of protection, it is well to recall that imports consist very largely of watch movements. Their average unit value was $4.75 during 1950–1951. The point is that tariffs represent an extremely small part of the retail price of watches even though they may seem fairly high when expressed as a percentage of import values.

By trade agreement the tariff was reduced by 28 to 42 per cent. Rates before and after concessions were:

	Act of 1930	Trade Agreement
Watch movements, etc., having more than 1, but not more than 17 jewels:		
Over 1.5 inches wide	$1.25	$0.90
Over 1.2 but not over 1.5 inches wide	1.40	.90
Over 1 but not over 1.2 inches wide	1.55	.90
Over 0.9 but not over 1 inch wide	1.75	1.20
Over 0.8 but not over 0.9 inch wide	2.00	1.35
Over 0.6 but not over 0.8 inch wide	2.25	1.35
0.6 inch or less	2.50[a]	1.80[b]

a. Plus 15 cents for each jewel in excess of 7 jewels.

b. Plus 9 cents for each jewel in excess of 7 jewels. Par. 367, Tariff Act of 1930, and Swiss trade agreement of 1936. Self-winding watches also bear a duty of one dollar. More than 17 jewels bear a duty of $10.75.

Specific duties remained substantially unchanged from 1936 to 1954. These reductions were on movements containing more than one but not more than seventeen jewels. Watches with less than seven do not compete seriously with quality domestic watches and the duty on watches with more than seventeen jewels remained at the high rate of $10.75. Duties were reduced moderately on cases, adjustments, certain parts and the larger sizes of movements having no jewels or only one jewel.

Domestic manufacturers claim (1) that they have been injured by tariff concessions and (2) that the lower duties are not passed on to the consumer in lower prices. In proposing higher duties a representative of Elgin's management said: "We believe ample room exists for all of such increase to be absorbed by the Swiss importer and the Swiss cartel."[25] The argument was that tariff reduction has produced higher profits instead of lower prices and that the gains have gone into a fund for promoting sales of imported watches.[26]

Importers were placed in the position of having to show that higher duties would restrict their sales. Since the duty usually amounts to only $1.50 more or less, they argued that the duty is pyramided by the use of percentage markups so that a 50 cent increase in duty would amount to about $1.50 in the retail price and a total duty of $1.50 would amount to about $4.50. While domestic producers were not anxious to stress the pyramiding effect of percentage markups, apparently it seemed the best position to support their charge of injury from tariff reduction.

It is difficult to evaluate the effect of tariff reduction.

From the testimony of domestic watch makers themselves, it is difficult to show that imports were increased *as a result* of tariff concessions since they argue that the benefits were not passed on to consumers in lower prices. It can be argued that tariff reduction helped indirectly to foster advertising. But apart from this issue, the percentage reduction of 28 to 42 per cent in duty may easily be misleading. It amounts to only 35 cents to 70 cents (plus 6 cents for each jewel in excess of seven) on watch movements which sell to consumers completely assembled in the price range of $25 to $60. The distribution markup greatly overshadows factory cost and the tariff is less important than excise taxes except as it is cumulated by the percentage markup of distributors.

The relative unimportance of the tariff on watches of seventeen jewels and less is indicated by a Tariff Commission study of 1939 data. In 1939, a seventeen-jewel movement cost about $3.00 f.o.b. Switzerland. Total cost including case and duty was $8.00 to the American importer. After markups of 50 and 112 per cent by assembler and retailer, respectively, the price

25. *Hearings on Watches and Parts*, May 15, 1951, p. 25.
26. *Ibid.*, p. 137.

to the consumer was $25.50.[27] As prices have advanced substantially since 1939 while the specific duty remains the same, the tariff became even less important than in 1939.

Wages of American companies are reported to be 144 per cent higher than those paid by Swiss watch makers. Although wages represent a large part of the factory cost of a movement, they account for less than one eighth of the American retail price. The remaining costs consist of tariff and assembly costs plus wholesale and retail markups which approximately triple the factory price.

How important was tariff reduction to the increase of watch imports? *It seems likely that the policy of the American government with respect to imports may have been more important than the actual changes in duty.* Entrepreneurs could not be expected to risk the costs entailed in developing a market for imported goods if it were national policy to destroy their business when their efforts proved successful. But the actual dollars and cents cost of the tariff is such a small part of the final price to the consumer that the duty itself would seem to be a minor factor. Much depends on whether or not the practice of percentage markups in distribution is regarded as unalterable. The importance of this point extends to many other products.

Injury

The principal casualties in the American watch industry occurred well before the trade agreement with Switzerland in 1936. Twelve companies disappeared between 1914 and 1929.[28] There has been no net contraction in number of firms since duties were reduced. While the Waltham Company[29] has declined, Bulova, a major importer, has developed a domestic manufacturing business about equal to Waltham's. Sales of domestic manufacturers' jeweled watches have increased, and aggregate profits of the two leading domestic producers, Hamilton and Elgin, are above pre-trade-agreement levels including allowance for changes in price level.[30]

The fact that American watch makers have turned to importing as well as manufacturing does not indicate an immediate decline of home industry. It may reflect the fact that importing has been *relatively* more profitable than manufacturing.

27. *Watches*, p. 105. The average unit value of imported watch movements in 1951 was $4.68.

28. U.S. Tariff Commission, *Investigation No. 4*, p. 16.

29. Witnesses appearing in behalf of Waltham have stated that the company has the equipment to produce a million movements a year.

30. The profit *margin* on sales, however, is down from the 1935–1939 level. See the brief of the watch importers, U.S. Tariff Commission, *Investigation No. 4*, Tables K and L, pp. 67–68.

Nonetheless, the domestic industry claims injury on the grounds that expanding imports have stifled "the natural growth of American industry." "The fact that imports from Switzerland have absorbed substantially all benefits of our dynamic domestic economy alone constitutes the gravest sort of injury."[31]

The crucial fact is that while sales of domestic watch makers have increased, the increase in imports has been several times as great.[32] Despite the increase in their own sales, the domestic industry insists that a smaller share of a larger market "constitutes one class of injurious competition."

The necessity to adjust the pattern of domestic production to meet competitive imports is also regarded as injurious. In seven-jewel watches, American consumers preferred the cheaper Swiss watch to the more expensive American watch. As a result, the domestic producer was forced to switch to more expensive watches with more jewels.[33] This, it is charged, represents a definite injury to the Elgin National Watch Company. "We felt that it is uneconomic and an evidence of injury for Elgin not to make a full line of watches."[34]

A Key Policy Decision

The policy decision regarding watch imports is of cardinal importance. The first question is whether imports which create their own market by expanding total American consumption can injure the domestic industry which is directly competitive. A second question concerns the role of the tariff.

The weight of evidence is that the growth of the watch market has been due to the lower prices, new styles and aggressive selling of imported watches and that tariff reduction by itself was of minor importance. An extenuating circumstance is that imports gained ground during the war when domestic producers were engaged in war work.

The tariff itself is a very small part of the consumer price. If, in fact, the consumer demand were so elastic that a reduction in price of one or two dollars per watch would greatly expand sales, we are justified in believing that profits would be increased by cutting the distribution margin by this amount and profiting from the larger volume of sales. At the same time, it is obvious that tariff reduction does enable importers to shade prices slightly or to spend more in advertising.

When additional imports can be absorbed by expanding the domestic market, there is little or no direct dislocation of home industry. Watches,

31. *Hearings on Watches and Parts*, May 15, 1951, p. 16.
32. Imports of nineteen and twenty-one jeweled units have remained negligible in importance. *Ibid.*, p. 46.
33. *Ibid.*, p. 104.
34. *Ibid.*, p. 122.

therefore, represent the easiest type of adjustment to increased imports. The case for imports is even stronger when it is the importers who take the lead in expanding the market by innovation and by aggressive selling. If the doctrine of injury is interpreted to mean that the protected home industry is entitled to a constant share of a growing market, the prospect for increasing competitive imports is dim indeed.

Findings of the Tariff Commission

Three members of the Commission found that the domestic watch industry was suffering injury from imports and three found no such injury. However, Commissioner Edminister found a *threat* of injury. As a result, the vote was four to two in favor of raising duties by 50 per cent but in no case higher than the 1930 rates.

In addition to the share-of-the-market argument, the three Commissioners' statement of the case for injury rested on the shift of domestic production from seven-jewel watches to watches with seventeen or more jewels. This meant that the shift of domestic production to a more remunerative segment of a growing market was regarded as evidence of injury.

Although cheap pin-lever watches are not imported, the fact that the total market for such watches has not expanded was also included in the considerations supporting the finding of injury. On this point, the Commissioners who found no injury showed that producers of pin-lever watches had more than offset any loss of market with production of other things so that total sales and employment had been maintained.

President Truman emphatically rejected the majority recommendation that duties be increased. The President's decision was the correct one. In addition to a cogent statement of the evidence, the President declared:

The impact which the tariff increase now proposed would have on Swiss-American relations would be extremely serious. United States imports from Switzerland in 1951 totalled only $131 million of which over 50 per cent were watches. Thus, tariff action on watches would strike at Switzerland's most important export to us, affecting adversely an industry tailored in large part to the United States market and employing one out of every ten industrial workers in the country. In addition, the industry is concentrated in a part of Switzerland where there is relatively little other industry and the possibilities for transfer of employment small.

During 1951, Swiss imports from the United States totalled over $216 million and were comprised of a long and varied list of commodities such as wheat, cotton, tobacco, automobiles, machinery, office appliances and pharmaceuticals. United States exports to Switzerland are therefore almost double our imports from Switzerland and the Swiss market is one of the very few that remains free of restrictions against dollar imports. If, in these circumstances, we should erect new barriers against the importation of Swiss watches, we would at the same time be erecting barriers against our own export markets. More than that, we would be striking a heavy blow at our whole effort to increase international trade and permit friendly nations to earn their own dollars and pay their own way in the world.[35]

These considerations are clearly of the highest importance. But, as in the garlic case, they seem to be obiter dicta.

The injury of American export industries is material to the national interest but not to the possible injury of the watch industry. *Injury to both domestic and foreign exporters is implicit in the policy of protecting home industry against serious injury from imports.* The broad objectives of international trade and American leadership indicate that the United States should accept injury to home industry under some conditions. If such a policy were accepted by the Congress, the escape clause would be emasculated and the prospect of expanding foreign trade under trade agreements would be improved.

Duties on Watches Increased in 1954

The Tariff Commission reported its investigation of injury under the escape clause in the summer of 1952. Two years later President Eisenhower ordered that trade agreement rates be increased by up to 50 per cent. The Office of Defense Mobilization, said the President, had found from an interdepartmental report that preservation of the unique skills of the watch industry is "essential to the national security." Apparently this advice was accepted without adequate review.[36]

According to *Time* Magazine, more than two months before Eisenhower made his decision, Department of Defense officials had studied the watch industry and reported: "No special nor preferential treatment is necessary. . . . It is apparent that manufacturers outside the jeweled watch industry . . . are capable of producing the mechanical time fuses and rear fitting safety devices" needed for mobilization.[37]

If other nations were to act precipitately on issues of this sort, the abuse of the national security argument for tariff protection could impair rather than strengthen the defenses of the free world.

35. *Watches, Watch Movements, Watch Parts, and Watch Cases*, U.S. Tariff Commission, Report No. 176, Second Series, pp. 79–80.

36. The Symington Amendment (1954) prevented tariff reduction if the President found that "such reduction would threaten domestic production needed for projected national defense requirements."

The government also brought an antitrust suit against importers owning Swiss companies, although such ownership is necessarily subject to Swiss law on cartels. The Treasury moved to reclassify and raise the duty from $3.75 to $10.75 on watches with seventeen jewels that could be converted to a higher jewel count.

37. *Time*, April 4, 1955, p. 92.

PART V

THE SUMMING UP

Chapter 23

The Future of Imports

WHAT IS THE FUTURE of America's import deficit?

Earlier chapters have shown that the most important factor affecting the level of imports is the sustained growth of the domestic economy at high levels of production and employment. An American depression, on the other hand, by reducing the demands of consumers and business for imports, would probably precipitate an acute crisis in other nations, and even a recession could have serious consequences.

The prospect that domestic growth will increase imports enough to relieve the chronic disorder in world trade that is loosely described as the dollar shortage depends, mainly, on whether or not there is a shift in world demand toward dollar goods. Domestic growth will undoubtedly increase the absolute level of American imports. On the other hand, growth of the outside world, together with changes in the technique of production, tastes and the distribution of income, may well result in an even greater increase in demand for dollar goods and services. Such a change seems to have taken place since the 1920s. The growth of leading American imports has been seriously retarded by technological displacement and, on the other hand, the potential market for American exports is greater than ever before. The world has acquired a strong taste for American goods and because of innovation, higher productivity and lower unit costs, leading American industries are in a strong competitive position with respect to both the home market and export markets.

What is needed, for many reasons, is an increase in international specialization and trade as well as the normal expansion of trade that is derived from growth of national income. This requires an increase in the ratio of imports to national output. Relative expansion of imports from Europe, which declined in quantity from 1925–1929 to 1950, is especially important. Although our tariffs have been greatly reduced, they bear more heavily on imports from Europe and Japan than elsewhere. In 1950, average rates on all dutiable imports were 13 per cent compared with 19 per cent on dutiable imports from Europe and 28 per cent on dutiable imports from Japan. Also, a much smaller part of imports from Europe than elsewhere are duty-free.

A notable increase in both imports and exports of goods and services has taken place since 1948. In part, this is a result of rapid expansion of produc-

449

tion both at home and abroad and disappearance of the absolute shortages which plagued the outside world in the immediate postwar years. In part, the rise of American imports is also due to our stockpiling program and to extraordinary expenditures by our government in connection with its military establishments overseas.

Institutional factors and structural changes which have operated to reduce the relative importance of American imports since the 1920s were discussed in earlier chapters. We return now to the questions posed in Chapter 1. Why does America import so much less than she exports and what problems would be created in eliminating this troublesome import deficit? Beyond this, why is it so difficult to raise living standards by raising the level of both imports and exports through increased specialization?

On the American side, although tariffs have been drastically reduced, imports are still restricted by tariffs, quotas, customs regulations and Buy American legislation. On the foreign side, they are restricted by artificial exchange rates, high costs of production and the failure of other nations to live within their means.

The slogan "trade not aid" seems to imply that America's trade barriers are the main problem. This implication should not be taken too seriously. Only when foreign nations suffer unemployment in their export industries will it be easy for them to offer more exports to the American market. If full employment prevails, foreign nations can substitute trade for aid only by giving up goods which are presently consumed at home or exported to third countries in exchange for imports.

While the competitive position of other nations is much improved, they will still need to reduce their real wages in order to sell much more in the American market. This may be a difficult task. If they let wages rise faster than productivity, the disorder in world trade will persist, because their goods will be priced too high to sell in the American market. Restoration of balance in the balance of payments may involve unemployment in Britain and Europe that will be difficult to cope with. For one thing, it is much easier to shift resources by inflating moderately than by deflating. Also, some countries do not have enough capital to employ all their workers at the customary wage. Other nations must also keep pace with the continued rise in American productivity or adjust their exchange rates.

A major part of the problem of avoiding a dollar shortage lies in the hands of other nations. This is no excuse, however, for not getting our own house in order.

The assumption that the United States could replace the need for foreign aid solely by reducing trade barriers and thus importing more goods is open to serious question. It implies, in its crudest form, that commodity imports are now obstructed mainly by import duties, and that if tariffs and quotas were sufficiently reduced, Americans would buy enough more foreign goods to avoid a "dollar gap." Desirable though lower tariffs and trade barriers are on other grounds, there are reasons to doubt that reduction of trade barriers alone would solve the problem.

The Dimensions of the Problem

The total import deficit of the United States, including both goods and services, was approximately $5 billion in recent years. While imports have increased greatly since 1948, the increase in exports has been only somewhat less great and, consequently, the gap was reduced only from $6.7 billion to $4.7 billion in a five-year period ending in 1953. Military aid has increased as economic aid was reduced.

The gap between imports and exports, however, represents a somewhat arbitrary measure of the existing dollar shortage. This is because the volume of American exports is arbitrarily restricted by the controls which other governments have placed on the spending of dollars. If these restrictions had been even more severe, American exports might have been arbitrarily held down to the level of our imports. On the other hand, if the restrictions had been removed altogether, the demand for American exports would unquestionably have been much greater. There is no way of knowing precisely the dimensions of the suppressed demand. But under prevailing conditions, the dollar gap might be greatly increased if other countries could find some means to finance such a deficit. The actual export surplus of $5 billion in recent years was determined largely by the amount of foreign aid made available. Thus, to measure the need for aid by the realized excess of exports over imports would involve circular reasoning.

The relation of military aid and world tensions to the future dollar shortage presents some difficult problems of interpretation. It is well recognized that a substantial part of our exports is financed by military aid, and this is sometimes regarded as independent of the dollar shortage. But it is often overlooked that the dollar shortage has been substantially reduced by the increase in American imports that is due to our own military expenditures abroad. The dollar earnings of foreign countries from our government's expenditures abroad for military goods and services amounted to $2.5 billion in 1953. Thus, both sides of the balance of payments are currently enlarged as a result of world tensions.[1]

Moreover, the distinction between economic and military aid is a tenuous one with respect to the dollar shortage. Both forms of aid represent a net addition to the resources available to foreign countries. Some military grants are made to purchase raw materials and equipment for production of military end-items; others provide revenue to meet military expenditures.

1. *Economic Report of the President*, January 1954, p. 219.

In either case, military aid enables the receiving nation to direct more of its own resources to production of civilian goods. The distinction between economic and military aid becomes clear-cut only when it is assumed that the other country would sacrifice its national security rather than its living standards if the United States failed to furnish military aid.

Foreign Investment as a Means of Buying Time

Private investments abroad constitute a possible means of financing a part of the import deficit, aside from any governmental aid. However, the character of investment and pattern of postwar trade would have to be substantially altered. And even if this were possible, foreign investments would only postpone the problem of increasing imports.[2]

Foreign investment is a means of exporting without importing, *but only so long as investments are continuously increased*. Because each new investment is expected to yield gains which represent a return flow of imports, investment postpones the import problem rather than solving it. Once begun, the investment process must inevitably lead to increased imports, or to the reinvestment abroad of the ever-growing profits and amortization on ever-growing investments.

Foreign investment is a way of buying time, but it increases the dimensions of the future import problem. The world needs to buy time and it is highly desirable that foreign investment should increase. Under favorable conditions investment in underdeveloped countries might expand for a long time. It is often said that we have an obligation to reduce tariffs because America is a creditor nation. This is a fallacy if it implies that free trade would turn our export surplus into an import surplus or that a creditor nation ought to have an import surplus. In the absence of political barriers, we would normally expect a continued outflow of capital from the United States so long as we remain richer than the rest of the world and have more capital to invest. Individuals may liquidate their investments, but creditors as a class do not usually seek repayment of principal either from foreign or domestic investments. A creditor nation has no occasion to import more than it exports so long as the rate of growth of its foreign investment exceeds the yield. The political risks are so great, however, that there is no basis for anticipating the type of investment that will create free dollar exchange in sufficient volume to cure the dollar shortage.

It is often assumed, to be sure, that the dollar shortage can and should be reduced by expansion of private investment abroad rather than by expansion of American imports. This view overlooks the fact that foreign investment today is largely direct investment which involves the shipment

2. Similarly, domestic investment only postpones the problem of raising consumption relative to personal incomes, but no one seems to worry about this. Cf. p. 14.

of American exports of machinery and equipment. Only that part of direct foreign investment which is spent for local labor and materials becomes available to relieve the dollar shortage. The portfolio type of investment which created free dollar exchange for the use of foreign borrowers has been insignificant since 1930.

With reference to both portfolio and direct investment abroad, there are greatly exaggerated ideas current of the extent to which the capital movement involved can serve an important or lasting function in providing dollar exchange to meet the requirements of foreign countries for imports of dollar goods and services. . . .

The investment abroad of American capital in the years ahead will undoubtedly make a significant contribution to the development of the resources of foreign countries and the industrialization of their economies. All things considered, however, the prospective amount of such investment cannot be expected to play more than a minor role in the balance of payments of the United States. It would be folly to rely upon it either in theory or in practice, as a substitute for increased purchases by the United States of goods and services from foreign countries as a means of maintaining or raising the level of exports.[3]

A Complex Picture

Elimination of an export surplus does not depend on increase of commodity imports alone. Services form an appreciable part of foreign trade. Import of services can be increased in several ways, for example, by a rise of American travel abroad—a type of import which is not restricted by any duty, and one the enlargement of which would not injure any specific American industry. If the United States should revise its policy of subsidizing shipping, another important means of increasing service imports would appear, since foreign ships could certainly carry more American trade if allowed to compete on even terms.

On the other hand, American imports of miscellaneous service items have already reached extraordinary proportions. In 1952 and 1953 they exceeded the combined dollar expenditures on foreign travel and transportation. Expenditures for services by American military personnel and establishments overseas have made an important contribution to reduction of the dollar shortage. Eventually, we hope to be able to *reduce* this import item. If this should become possible, it may prove quite difficult to find a substitute and the dollar problem will become more acute.

It should not be assumed that every dollar derived from a higher level of American imports will be used to finance the dollar deficit. Some part of the additional dollar earnings will almost certainly be used to purchase additional dollar goods. We should anticipate, therefore, that the dollar exchange available to the outside world will need to rise by an amount much

3. August Maffry, "Direct Versus Portfolio Investment in the Balance of Payments," *American Economic Review*, Papers and Proceedings, May 1954, pp. 618 and 625.

greater than the dollar shortage. Many of our imports which can be increased by reduction of trade barriers will come from outside Europe and, after allowing for three-cornered trade, at least part of the proceeds will be spent for additional American exports. Even those nations receiving foreign aid may find it necessary to import more dollar goods in order to expand their exports by a larger amount. Moreover, it is highly desirable to raise the level of American imports enough to permit other nations to eliminate the discrimination against our exports which they have imposed as a result of the dollar shortage.

Finally, American imports have been enlarged by the stockpiling of strategic and critical materials, and some allowance must be made for a decline in demand for imports, once this program is complete. Deliveries to the stockpile totaled $900 million in 1952, which raised the total in inventory to some $4 billion. An additional $1.8 billion was under contract with an eventual objective of $7.5 billion at 1952 prices.[4]

Considering these imponderable elements, we may conclude that in order to avoid a chronic dollar shortage the United States may need to raise the level of its imports by several billion dollars. Even this would not solve all the dollar problems of countries which genuinely need aid. But such an increase would make it possible, insofar as our own policies are a barrier to trade, for other countries generally to pay for the American exports that are essential to their well-being and security.

This study does not consider further the possibility of increased foreign investment. Tourism and shipping subsidies have been discussed in preceding chapters. The following remarks apply only to the increase of commodity imports, which is the hard core of the problem.

Nature of Required Adjustments

Unless the other balance-of-payments factors are changed, cutting American foreign aid would be felt in reduction of American exports. This would injure export industries in the United States, including important branches of agriculture, and would adversely influence either the present or the future levels of living abroad—the present level insofar as imports from America are used for consumption, and the future level insofar as they are required for replacing or enlarging facilities for production.

If the United States were to replace foreign aid by an increase of imports, other adjustments, not necessarily easy or comfortable, would be required both abroad and at home. Foreign nations must avoid inflation and adjust the exchange value of their currencies in order to compete successfully in American markets. In some products they may also have to reduce their

4. For a discussion of the stockpiling program, see *Survey of United States International Finance, 1952*, Princeton University Press, 1953, pp. 214–221.

real costs—a process which might be achieved in the course of time without loss to living standards by a sufficient increase in productivity, but one which is frequently obstructed by customs and prejudices as well as by lack of capital. Manufacturing and selling methods would have to be adjusted to the requirements of the American market. General deflation of costs is not regarded as a practicable policy. Some reduction of real wages with the end of foreign aid is the most that can be expected.

If imports are to be encouraged by a more liberal tariff policy, some American industries may be injured, either by absolute decline or by a restricted opportunity to grow. Most duties have already been drastically reduced; further liberalization should include modification of the "escape clause" and of import quotas, which now protect the industries subject to the most injury. A reduction of the duty on woolens and worsteds could probably enlarge imports from Britain. Elimination of the escape clause could encourage imports of such commodities as fur felt hats, hatters' fur and dried figs, domestic producers of which are safeguarded because the Tariff Commission has decided that lower duties would injure them. The mere existence of the policy protecting every industry against serious injury may, in some cases, discourage foreign exporters from risking the efforts that would be required to expand their American market.

Higher Imports versus Lower Exports

Which adjustment will be more onerous, the rise of imports or the fall of exports? Most writers who favor expansion of trade state or imply that the adjustment to increased imports would be easier to accommodate than the adjustment to lower exports. This appears extremely doubtful.

Except for agriculture, the export industries helped by foreign aid are chiefly growing industries. Broadly speaking, the loss of foreign markets by the manufacturing industries can be offset by the expansion of domestic consumption and investment in the same broad sectors of the economy. Moreover, in many if not most instances, the export industries are large-scale industries producing many products so that the adjustment will consist chiefly of a change in the composition of output within the industry and within the firm. It seems probable that no important migration of people will be required. On the other hand, the adjustment needed to accommodate increased imports will require contraction of the relatively stagnant industries which already suffer from a tendency toward chronic overproduction. In the main, they are small businesses. Some of the displaced employees will have to move from the location where these small industries are concentrated. This is a more onerous adjustment.

In agriculture, it is a toss-up between higher imports and lower exports. Either way, more people will need to move off the farm with the end of foreign aid. If exports are reduced, wheat, cotton and tobacco could suffer. If imports are increased, sugar, dairy, oils, wool and cattle may be displaced.

The belief that increase of imports represents the more difficult adjustment rests on the presumption that: (1) the export branches of industry are, broadly speaking, the sectors of the economy which supply the kind of goods that will be demanded by rising living standards at home; (2) total consumption of the kind of goods produced by the import industries will expand but little as a result of the end of foreign aid; (3) the large-scale multiproduct export industries with some degree of monopolistic prices can more easily adjust to minor dislocations than the more highly competitive import industries. (The expression "import industries" refers to import-competing industries and not to importers.)

Expansion of Imports Is the Better Device

Though expansion of imports may be more difficult to achieve and temporarily more painful, it would lead ultimately to greater benefits.

Balance at low levels of trade can be restored merely by cutting off foreign aid. What would happen in this event? American exports must fall. Other countries would probably maintain and increase their restrictions and discriminations against our exports. At the same time they would turn to expanding their trade in nondollar markets. This resolution of the problem would move even farther away from free multilateral trade. It means that Europe would import food and raw materials at higher prices than the same goods could be obtained in the American market, but would also sell exports at higher prices than could be obtained here. We should have two worlds of trade, the dollar market and nondollar market, with different levels of prices and costs in each. This has been the situation, but our objective is to prevent it from becoming permanent.

Since the war, other countries have needed, chiefly, a net addition to their resources. Because foreign production has increased substantially, these countries are now better able to sacrifice their production for export. With the end of aid, they will need a larger dollar market for exports. But as their exports to America rise, there will be strong and irresistible pressures to increase their imports too, though not necessarily in the same proportion. This means that trade can move toward a balance with less difficulty for the rest of the world if the world's imports from America rise by some fraction of its rising exports to America. If American imports were to rise more rapidly than exports, it would assist other countries to eliminate exchange controls and other measures that discriminate against dollar goods. This offers the best pattern of adjustment, for it combines the end of foreign aid with expansion, rather than contraction, of mutually beneficial trade.

Perils of Readjustment

On the American side, the standard of living, including investment, must rise as foreign aid is reduced, and imports and exports are brought into balance. The only alternative is unemployment, or high expenditures for national security.

Whether the end of foreign aid will tend to deflate the American economy and create unemployment or will raise living standards depends on conditions at the time. In any case, this is an issue we must face. The threat of unemployment at home is not a valid reason for maintaining foreign aid. If necessary, spending for public works is preferable to foreign aid merely to provide domestic employment. If foreign aid is ended, taxes can be reduced and taxpayers can spend correspondingly more on the goods of their choice. If savings are increased, particularly by reduction of business taxes, investment must rise or unemployment will result. With the end of foreign aid, it will be easier to balance the budget, and this of itself will be either counterinflationary or deflationary. Moreover, there will have to be some readjustment in the structure of domestic production and employment because our own people will not buy the agricultural products which now make up part of our export surplus.

In sum, the end of foreign aid will require: (1) some check to the rise of foreign living standards including investment, and the rise of American living standards including investment, (2) a shift of resources and readjustment of the structure of production and employment both at home and abroad. Finally, if world trade is to be balanced without extensive governmental controls, other countries must avoid inflation and America must avoid deflation. The balancing of world trade could intensify unemployment problems both at home and abroad, though for different reasons. Other countries would have to pursue a policy of disinflation. They may run into trouble if they have to cut imports of raw materials and foodstuffs and they may face strikes if the standard of living is reduced.

At home it is a question of getting the standard of living up and raising investment, which has already been maintained at very high levels for about as long as the market economy usually expands without a depression. The long-term problem of balancing trade by increasing imports is to shift resources out of the import industries. In agriculture and other cases this will require an absolute reduction in employment; in other industries retardation of their growth may be sufficient.

Tariff Reduction Less Important Than Economic Growth

In the future, tariffs may become the main barrier to the substitution of mutually beneficial trade for foreign aid, but they have not been in the past. The excess of American exports over imports is not chiefly a result of tariffs and cannot be cured solely by commercial policy. On the other hand, it is urgent that we avoid raising tariffs and quotas on an *ad hoc* basis as individual imports threaten to increase.

The level of imports is determined basically by (1) relative prices and (2) the level of national income. Of these, national income is the more influential (within the range of changes that have occurred in historical experience).

Tariffs affect imports through prices. Changes in technology and productivity also affect imports through costs and prices. However, the price system works imperfectly owing to a host of institutional factors, which are particularly important for nonstandardized manufactured products.

National income affects imports in two ways: (1) the growth of industry requires more raw materials like tin and nickel, and with rising incomes consumers naturally buy more imported consumer goods; (2) imports not only rise and fall owing to changes in total demand for specific products, but domestic producers can satisfy a smaller proportion of the demand when domestic resources are fully employed than when unemployment prevails. When wool growers were asked why they are raising fewer sheep, they replied, "Too busy on other things, had to cut down on something." This is one of the keys to enlarging imports.

Impact of Technology on Imports

A new and vital development is the revolution in technology, which has taken a heavy toll of America's raw material imports, although it might have been expected that a rapidly growing industrial nation would need to import relatively more primary products.[5]

Manufactured imports have declined in relative importance for more than a century. Although the trend continues, the rate of change in the past generation was less than in the previous generation. From the Civil War to the 1930s, the growth of total imports was sustained consistently by the relatively rapid rise of crude material imports and, at times, by agricultural imports.[6] In recent decades, however, imports of both crude industrial materials and agricultural products have declined relative to expansion of domestic production. This signifies that capital equipment and technique have been substituted for natural resources including land.

The displacement of imports by the rise of the chemical industry has probably exceeded the increase in imports resulting from tariff reduction of about 75 per cent.

5. Changes between 1939 and 1950 in production and consumption of important primary products in the United States and the free world are given in *The Midyear Economic Report of the President*, July 1951, by the Council of Economic Advisors, pp. 74 and 242.

6. This statement refers to quantities. The relative decline in the value of crude material imports began after the first world war.

Chemical rubber has displaced natural rubber, chemical fiber has displaced natural silk, plastics have displaced metals and leather, detergents have displaced soap (fats and oils), paper has displaced jute burlap, and synthetic fertilizer has displaced natural nitrate. Medicine uses more synthetic drugs. Wool is in danger of becoming another technological casualty. We feed, clothe, doctor, travel and scrub by using more capital and relatively less natural resources.

These developments are a major factor explaining the decline in the relative importance of imports since the 1920s. But they are not a complete explanation. Advancing technology may increase as well as displace imports. Development of the automobile industry originally produced a great expansion of rubber imports. Exploitation of atomic energy in the present decade has produced a new import, uranium. An improved process of quick freezing has increased imports of fish. It is quite clear, however, that in the past twenty years the direct increase in imports due to technological advance has not been commensurate with the displacement. To some extent this is because research and innovation were consciously directed toward the goal of reducing our dependence on resources overseas. The war spurred the development of synthetic rubber. The indirect increase in imports from technological change is discussed later in the present chapter.

The United States is relatively more deficient in many minerals than in other resources and has shifted from a net exporter to a net importer of all minerals except coal and molybdenum. Our absolute dependence on imports has increased; nonetheless, owing to technological advance and changes in the composition of production, the prospect is that mineral imports, with the exception of petroleum and iron ore, will not rise as fast as gross national product in the next twenty years. The prospective rapid growth of imports of petroleum and iron ore may be retarded by innovations which will exploit domestic shale oil and taconite ore. Substitution of aluminum for steel might result in larger imports of metals. But the importance of such possibilities to foreign trade will probably continue to be overshadowed by the substitution of plastics and other synthetic products for natural raw materials.

Foreign Supplies

Sustained growth of the American economy will require a great increase in world supplies of raw materials and foodstuffs which are not produced in America or which can be produced in greater quantities only at rising costs. Some students foresee an exceptionally favorable American market for foreign supplies with relatively high prices for raw materials and foodstuffs.

Looking forward after the first world war, primary producers also anticipated expanding markets but paid dearly for their optimism as prices tumbled even before the great depression. Judging from unit values, the terms of trade on all imports and exports in 1953 were somewhat more favorable to foreign suppliers than in the earlier period 1923–1925. Those who now foresee even more favorable price relationships are more likely to be proved correct if foreign producers do not gear their production plans to such optimistic projections. The disastrous experience of the 1930s and recent barriers to foreign investment have probably retarded expansion of primary production abroad and contributed to the present high prices of coffee and certain raw materials. Some time is required to open new mines and expand acreage of tree crops like coffee and rubber. Moreover, everyone is probably aware that the present American demand for imports is influenced by stockpiling and by high-level military expenditures which may require larger imports of materials than normal civilian consumption. Experience suggests that primary production is eventually expanded to meet sustained demand and that prices move in longer or shorter cycles depending on the time that is required to bring in new production. High prices not only stimulate world production of raw materials, they also spur development and use of substitute materials.

Largely as a result of technological displacement, the quantity of our total commodity imports barely increased at all from 1928–1929 to 1948–1949. Innovation, however, proceeds by fits and starts rather than at an even pace. In the recent period 1948–1953 the quantity of imports rose 29 per cent while gross national product in constant prices rose 26 per cent. As indicated in earlier chapters, imports normally increase faster than national income during short periods of rapid growth.

Tariffs and the Effects of Rising Productivity

Tariff protection today is less vital to American industry than it was in the nineteenth century; therefore there is less chance of increasing imports by reducing it. This is the kernel of truth in the dictum that America has nothing to fear from imports. It is now the rest of the world which fears American competition. The old argument that high-wage American labor cannot compete with cheap foreign labor is nonsense, as is demonstrated by the fact that American exports compete with and undersell the products of cheap foreign labor all over the world. The United States is an exporter not only of manufactured goods in competition with Europe and Japan, but also of agricultural products, including rice, which we sell in competition with the lowest subsistence labor of Asia.

This is possible because of American mechanization and technique. *Our wages are high because productivity is high.* However, America's superior competitive ability arising from higher productivity is only one side of the coin. *The other side of the same coin is that other countries enjoy a competitive advantage in those industries which do not lend themselves to mechanization and mass production techniques.* Italy's advantage in making fur felt hats is not derived merely from the fact that Italian wages are low, but from the fact that hat making is not highly mechanized. If competitive advantage were merely a question of wage levels, Italy could undersell the United States in virtually everything. Patently this is not the case.

The conclusion is that wage levels are substantially determined by productivity; regardless of the difference in wages between nations, each can always undersell the other in some things.[7] This is the foundation of international trade. The necessary corollary is that someone will be hurt when trade barriers are eliminated. Thus, while America is less dependent on tariffs than in the nineteenth century, the fact remains that some industries rely on protection and will be injured if imports are increased. These exposed areas are certain branches of agriculture and nondurable goods. American industries which use much labor and little machinery have something to fear from imports, provided that their wages must be competitive with wages in the more progressive industries.

This proposition is important in connection with technological advance. By reason of the mass market at home and the unsurpassed wealth available for research, innovation and development, American industry is able to turn out new products and improve some of the old at a rate which offers formidable competition to the rest of the world. In the economy of mass production and in our matchless capacity for innovation and modernization, we possess a double advantage. *But the consequence of our own technological advance is to confer a competitive advantage on other countries in those home industries which are not susceptible to mechanization and therefore are unable to keep pace with rising productivity in the more progressive home industries. If rising productivity in the dynamic industries raises costs in all industries through domestic competition for resources, the less progressive import-competing industries will face higher costs which are not matched by higher productivity.* This explains why technological advance, under favorable conditions, will indirectly increase some imports while directly displacing others.[8] The necessary condition is (1) mobility of labor at home, (2) sustained prosperity and sufficient competition that wages in hats, shoes and textiles will be raised equally with the rise of wages in chemicals, automobiles and other dynamic industries where labor is more productive because it works with more capital equipment.

7. The important requirement is that prices be proportional to marginal opportunity costs.

8. Under certain conditions, development of capital-intensive industries would raise marginal opportunity costs in labor-intensive industries and, as a result, additional labor-intensive imports would tend to be substituted for home production.

The revolutionary speed with which American industry has forged ahead, both in new methods and greater mechanization,* is the principal reason why our tariffs could be reduced so drastically without substantially increasing imports. At the same time, it must be assumed that competition from imports will become increasingly severe as wage costs are increased in some branches of agriculture and the relatively stagnant home industries. These processes of adjustment depend on competition for labor and other resources between home industries.

Rising American wages, dictated by advancing productivity in the dynamic industries, will leave the relatively stagnant home industries less able to compete against imports.

Those American producers who are apprehensive because they have been exposed to foreign competition by tariff reduction have a point. Their fears cannot be brushed off merely by showing that they have not been injured yet. Perhaps we have not yet seen the full effect of the tariff reduction that has already taken place because other countries initially failed to control inflation and because of the implication of rising productivity on relative costs at home. It is inconsistent to argue that (1) tariff reduction is important and (2) no one will be hurt. The degree to which resources are shifted is the best measure of the ultimate gains to all of removing protection, because the benefits are derived from the shift of resources out of the injured industries into more productive employment.

Inelastic Markets and Competitive Imports

One of the most important considerations is that America's comparative advantage is preponderantly in the more rapidly growing industries. Therefore, the possibility of directly expanding imports competitive with them by expanding consumption is rather limited. Duties should be eliminated on such items as automobiles, machinery, electrical equipment, chemicals and petroleum; but we should not anticipate a large increase in imports as a result.

Almost half of total imports are agricultural products. If to this we add lumber, manufactured foods, textiles, apparel, pottery, chinaware, glassware and leather goods, *it is evident that the bulk of imports consists of products of agriculture and the older nondurable-goods industries.*[9] More-

9. The expression "older nondurable-goods" is used to exclude products of the relatively dynamic newer nondurable-goods industries—petroleum, chemicals, rubber and certain paper products. Employment in each of the older nondurable-goods industries declined relative to all manufacturing employment during the period of rapid expansion from 1939 to 1947. In textiles, the most important import-competing industry, employment increased 6 per cent. In machinery, the most important export industry, employment increased 153 per cent. The increase of employment in ten durable- and newer nondurable-goods industries was three times greater than in ten older nondurable-goods industries. *Regional Trends in the United States Economy,* U.S. Department of Commerce, 1951, Appendix Table 30.

over, the potential increase in imports from elimination of tariffs and quotas consists of an even higher proportion of such products.[10] According to Howard Piquet's estimates, which are based on individual commodity analysis by experts of the Tariff Commission, roughly 85 per cent of the increase in imports from suspension of tariffs and quotas would consist of products of agriculture and older nondurable goods.[11] The total market for most of these products is relatively inelastic and any substantial expansion of imports depends on contraction of domestic employment.

If this situation were reversed so that the great bulk of our potential imports could be absorbed directly by expansion of consumption, the problem of adjusting to lower trade barriers would be much less difficult. Tariffs can be eliminated on those products which compete with rapidly growing domestic industries. But owing to America's comparative advantage in this area, the instances where this will produce a substantial increase in imports are the exception and not the rule.

Even an across-the-board cut in trade barriers would produce no flood of imports. The problem is a serious one only because the great bulk of potential imports impinge on areas of the domestic economy which already suffer from the dislocations of internal growth.

ADJUSTMENT TO FREE TRADE

The following discussion concerns the adjustment to free trade, which means that it does not deal directly with noncompetitive imports or those imports, like petroleum, which may be required in greatly increased quantities to supplement domestic production. The thesis is developed that American imports will rise not only in response to growth of national income, but also that the increase of imports from the price effect of lower tariffs will be greater if internal expansion is rapid enough and balanced enough to draw resources from relatively stagnant import-competing industries and thus avoid the relative deflation and underemployment that have afflicted these industries in the past.

The Dynamic Setting

America's import problem is a corollary of the dynamics of internal growth. Nowhere is the nature of the problem illustrated so well as in agriculture. Chronic surpluses at home are a barrier to expansion of imports from abroad. Farm workers who are displaced by the tractor must be shifted off the farm and reabsorbed by the expansion of industry before

10. See Chapters 19 and 20.

11. *Aid, Trade and the Tariff*, Thomas Y. Crowell, New York, 1953, Tables 4 and 7, pp. 37 and 63. The individual imports covered by Piquet's analysis account for 80 per cent of dutiable imports in 1951.

imports which will displace additional farm workers can be substantially increased. And since farm labor can be shifted to nearby textile mills and pottery plants, surplus farm labor is also a barrier to expanding imports of textiles and pottery.

The import adjustment competes with internal adjustments for the market's limited capacity to transfer resources in time. These internal adjustments include: (1) migration of about 300,000 people out of agriculture annually owing to the relatively high farm birth rate,[12] (2) technological displacement and related structural changes in production and employment, (3) the shift of industry to the South, particularly at the expense of New England.

If the import displacement were the only adjustment, it would be comparatively simple to shift 300,000 people out of agriculture annually, permitting an important increase in agricultural imports. As it is, a far greater number—about 10 million people net—migrated out of agriculture in the period 1940–1948 while the reduced farm labor force increased production enough (1) to raise domestic consumption and exports and (2) to reduce the relative importance of imports.

We have more good and fairly good land per capita than the rest of the world (except Russia). Greater use of the tractor and equipment that goes with it have reduced labor requirements. A family-size farm can now use economically more capital equipment than the average investment per worker in manufacturing, although many farms, particularly in the South, are not yet mechanized. The rest of the world cannot afford this degree of mechanization.

Displacement of the horse and mule is freeing thousands of acres of hay and pasture land annually for the production of food for human consumption. New developments in mechanized harvesting of high-protein hay are among the important technological improvements that affect the cost of animal products. These factors will continue to prevent any dramatic rise in agricultural imports. But since changes in productivity are unequal among various farm products, technological advance dictates the increase of certain imports as well as the displacement of others, provided resources are mobile and the domestic economy is kept in balance. The best use of resources requires an increase in certain agricultural imports. In the case of sugar, this adjustment should not be too difficult. But a general policy of free and rational trade in farm products will be difficult to achieve owing to farm surpluses and to disparities in income both within agriculture and between farm and factory.

12. Such migration is needed in order to avoid a relative decline in per capita farm income owing to the higher farm birth rate. D. Gale Johnson, *Trade and Agriculture*, Wiley, 1950, p. 48.

Some branches of agriculture could be injuriously affected by lower quotas and tariffs, and others might benefit from increased exports. But in principle we have an import problem for the same reason that we have a farm problem, namely, the excess of workers in agriculture. How can we expect to increase the relative importance of such imports as long as domestic resources remain underemployed and capable of producing surpluses?

The answer is that internal consumption and investment must expand more rapidly in order to absorb both the excess workers displaced by the revolution in technology and the additional workers who would be displaced by increased imports. This means that the barriers to acceleration of the rate of internal growth are also barriers to foreign trade because segments of most import-competing industries seem to suffer chronically from relative deflation.

Textiles, apparel, leather, china, glass, food and kindred products are all among the relatively low-wage home industries. One reason competitive imports have failed to increase as rapidly as domestic production is that most of the durable goods and new products demanded by the rising American standard of living can be produced more cheaply at home.[13] But this is only a provisional answer. A double play is required to increase the importance of competitive imports relative to production; workers must be shifted from agriculture and nondurable manufactures into the growing industries in order to make a place for imports of food, textiles and other nondurables with relatively inelastic markets.[14]

Unbalanced Growth Retards Foreign Trade

The magnitude of the adjustment required to increase competitive imports relative to home production is deceptive because of potential internal growth.

Relatively high prices and incomes in the growth industries, while necessary to attract resources, hamper the expansion of exports from the growth industries. At the same time, relatively low wages and prices in the stagnant industries, while necessary to contract employment, hamper the expansion of imports which must compete against these industries.[15]

Relatively low wages in the import industries are explained by inelastic markets and the relative excess of labor which make it possible to increase production faster than consumption. High wages in the export industries

13. On the marketing problems, see Chapter 10.

14. Because of the potential growth of consumption, imports of petroleum are the most notable exception. Even here, domestic coal mining may be adversely affected. See p. 171.

15. The fact that we do have foreign trade shows that marginal costs in the import-competing industries are high relative to the price of imports. The argument is simply that equalization of factor returns between import and export industries would tend to expand foreign trade.

are explained by the growing market and rising productivity in these industries. In addition, the import industries are highly competitive while most of the export industries have fewer producing units. Low wages in the import industries afford the same safeguard against imports as a protective tariff. Therefore, elimination of the relatively low wages in the import industries is as essential to the expansion of international trade as elimination of tariffs. However, the restrictive effect of the disparity in American wages may be mitigated by a similar disparity in foreign wages.[16]

America's peculiar disability with respect to foreign trade is that, as a general rule, its capital-intensive exports are handicapped by the relatively high prices necessary to attract domestic resources while its imports must compete against the low-wage home industries.[17] It is difficult to absorb additional competitive imports, because any failure to realize internal potential growth will first result in relative deflation of the import-competing industries and affect the growth of imports. The adjustment required to accommodate most competitive imports tends to come last, because any failure to realize maximum internal growth means that underemployed resources are not drawn out of the home industries against which imports must compete. The internal disparities between the low-wage import industries and the high-wage export industries appear to increase in periods of depression and stagnation and to decline in sustained periods of prosperity.

The average annual wage per worker in the nation's six low-wage manufacturing industries increased 142 per cent from 1939 to 1947. The increase was 99 per cent in seven high-wage industries and 115 per cent in seven medium-wage industries during the same period.[18]

America's largest reservoir of underemployed labor is located in the thirteen southern states which extend from the Potomac to the Rio Grande. Some notion of the importance of this factor is indicated by the relative growth of income in the South during periods of rapid expansion. Income payments rose 245 per cent from 1929 to 1950 compared with 149 per cent in the remaining 35 states. All of this relative gain occurred in two brief

16. Little is known about comparative international wage structures, but in the broadest terms, the wage structure of industrial countries is probably similar since the pattern of growth is similar. Otherwise, we should not have as much international trade as we do. But the differentials are not likely to be identical and, indeed, the structure of income and employment must differ if free market forces are to shift resources out of the import-competing industries in America and into these same industries in other countries.

17. America's export surplus supported by foreign aid and investment has tended to obscure the fact that American exports of consumers' durable goods are rather lower than would be expected. Charles Kindleberger calls attention to this fact. *The Dollar Shortage*, Technology Press of Massachusetts Institute of Technology and Wiley, New York, 1950, p. 13.

18. *Regional Trends in the United States Economy*, U.S. Department of Commerce, 1951, Table 28.

periods, 1932–1934 and 1941–1944, when demand for labor was rising rapidly. After the war, the South sustained small relative losses of income.[19]

Given sufficient total demand, what limits the rate of growth of the American economy—an absolute shortage of resources or the problems of transferring underemployed resources into the growing industries? One authority on agriculture writes that "Most of America's agriculture for most of the time has employed altogether too much labor . . ." The evidence suggests that "more than half of the labor force devoted to farming has an output (value productivity) less than half the standard output of comparable human resources in the American economy taken as a whole."[20] Despite the rapid growth of production, labor is not equally scarce and, therefore, not equally productive as between farm and factory, between textiles and automobiles, and between North and South.[21]

In a perfect market, labor would be shifted out of the more depressed regions of agriculture and into the growth industries by lower farm prices. Through competition for resources, lower farm incomes would increase urban labor supply and reduce wages and prices in petroleum, chemicals and durable-goods industries, and this in turn would accelerate expansion of production and employment in these industries. This is the point at which the market adjustment breaks down to some extent, and it may be critical to the import adjustment. Increased competition from agricultural imports may lower farm prices, but wages and prices in durable goods will not usually fall as a result. If the obstacles to labor mobility prevent the nation from deriving full advantage from its own technical progress, may they not also prevent full advantage from greater freedom in international trade?

Nondurable Goods and New England

The excess of agricultural labor, which is concentrated in the South, is drawing industry to that area. This competition has been felt particularly by New England industry. New England textiles have already been displaced by competition from southern mills.[22] In other words, New England is already subject to the same dislocation that would result from increased imports. But industry has been shifted to the southern states instead of to Britain or Japan. *The dislocation and adjustment that would be required to*

19. B. U. Ratchford, "Patterns of Economic Development," *Southern Economic Journal*, January 1954, pp. 218–219.

20. Theodore W. Schultz, *Production and Welfare of Agriculture*, Macmillan, New York, 1949, pp. 36 and 61.

21. For a discussion of the North-South wage differential and its significance for trade, see Calvin B. Hoover and B. U. Ratchford, *Economic Resources and Policies of the South*, Macmillan, New York, 1951, pp. 393–412.

22. See Seymour E. Harris, *The Economics of New England*, Harvard University Press, Cambridge, 1952, Chapters 2 and 7.

expand foreign trade is taking place in domestic trade, and we have so little of the one because we have so much of the other. This is evidence of the dynamic quality of the American economy, but the adjustment to imports is more and not less onerous because it is superimposed on similar adjustments dictated by internal growth.

The importance of these internal adjustments is indicated by the following changes in the structure of southern industry from 1930 to 1950: (1) Agricultural employment declined 40 per cent. (2) Expansion of manufacturing absorbed less than half of the workers who left agriculture. (3) Although the South has displaced most of New England's cotton textiles, the relative importance of textiles in southern manufacturing declined.[23]

The shift of cotton textiles from New England to the South affords an excellent example of the role played by internal wage differences in foreign trade.[24] If southern wages had been fully competitive with New England wages, imports would have had a better chance of displacing domestic industry. On the other hand, if southern wage costs can be reduced as tariffs are reduced, New England production may be displaced, but imports will face tough competition from the South. More than any other one thing, the North-South wage differential probably represents the failure of industry to expand rapidly enough to absorb the excess labor in southern agriculture.[25] *The persistence of the differential demonstrates that low farm incomes do not create enough factory jobs.*

The situation with respect to wage and income disparities was substantially improved at the end of the second world war, but has since deteriorated. In cotton textiles, the differential wage rate between southern and New England mills has tended to shrink from about one half near the beginning of the century to about one fifth in 1952. An appreciable wage

23. Ratchford, *op. cit.*

24. Decentralization of the domestic shoe industry also appears to have resulted from the movement into low-wage rural areas where shoes were not previously produced. George P. Shultz, *Pressures on Wage Decisions*, Technology Press of Massachusetts Institute of Technology and Wiley, New York, 1951, Chapter 2.

Employment in the leather industry increased 6.5 per cent from 1939 to 1947, but New England suffered a decline of 8 per cent.

25. With reference to relative changes in farm wages during the war, one study found that "Not only were customary wage differentials within the region preserved, but the South as a whole undisputedly remained the region of lowest farm wages in the country at the end of the war. . . .

"The degree to which such wage differentials have enabled southern operators to meet their production problem by reliance on low cost labor is conspicuously brought out by B.A.E. findings that although farmers in the Cotton Belt used nearly a third of the total hired labor employed on American farms in 1945, they paid only about a fifth of the country's annual cash farm wage bill." James H. Street, "The 'Labor Vacuum' and Cotton Mechanization," *Journal of Farm Economics*, August 1953. The reference to the findings by the Bureau of Agricultural Economics is to *Wages by Type of Farm and Type of Farm Work, United States and Major Type-of-Farming Regions, 1945*, Washington, July 1947, p. 32.

increase for northern workers in 1951 was not matched in the South.[26] The problem seems likely to be a persistent one, although we may anticipate smaller differentials than have prevailed most of the time in the past.[27]

Southern wage rates are lower and the work load is higher than in New England. The southern textile worker operates more looms. Taxes and fuel costs are also lower. Furthermore, only about 10 per cent of southern mills are organized. Consequently, it is conceivable that wages might be cut, if necessary to meet increased foreign competition.

Southern textile mills do not hire Negro workers although they are employed by cigarette factories in the same towns. Potential competition from Negro workers is probably one factor which holds down southern wages even in mills which do not hire them.

Each new tractor displaces farm workers who are available for factory employment. Cotton acreage is down nearly one half and yield per acre has nearly doubled since 1929. The advent of the mechanical cotton picker not only displaces farm workers, it is slowly shifting cotton production from the Carolinas to the more favorable terrain of Texas, Arizona and California. Thus, the reservoir of surplus labor available to mills in the old cotton belt is further augmented.

The adjustment facing the older nondurable-goods industries is similar to that facing agriculture. Soft spots have appeared in textiles, hats and hosiery despite rapid expansion in the economy as a whole. New England textile towns suffer substantial unemployment even in periods of prosperity. In an effort to meet southern competition, wages were cut slightly in a period when wages generally were rising. The textile industry suffered recessions in both 1949 and 1951–1952. Wages of knitters were reduced in North Carolina in 1952 allegedly because more women were going without stockings.

The question again is whether tariff reduction in the stagnant industries where wages are already relatively low will accelerate the rate of growth in competing industries and thus provide new jobs. Instead of raising real incomes by shifting resources to more productive employment, the threat of increased imports may only deflate wages generally in the low-wage in-

26. *Report of the New England Textile Industry by Committee Appointed by Conference of New England Governors*, Seymour E. Harris, chairman, 1952, p. 100. The Committee recommends "(1) that the Government reduce tariffs for the most part only on growing industries; and (2) that no trade concessions be made on textiles in the immediate future."

27. The historical perspective provided by one study is that "On the whole, the southern wage level for all jobs covered was no closer to that of the Northeast in 1945–1946 than it had been in 1907 and 1919. The considerable improvement in the position of the South relative to the Northeast which took place between 1931–1932 and 1945–1946 merely reduced the differential to that prevailing during the two early periods." Joseph W. Bloch, "Regional Wage Differentials, 1907–1946," *Monthly Labor Review*, April 1948, p. 374.

dustries. Consumers would be able to buy food, clothing, pottery and leather goods a few cents cheaper at the expense of workers whose wages were already relatively low. National income would be redistributed rather than increased to the maximum.

When the foreign trade adjustment is placed in a dynamic setting, three separate aspects of the same problem emerge: (1) The spread between incomes in the stagnant and growth industries that is appropriate to the shift of resources hampers international trade during the adjustment period because imports must compete against relatively low wages while the export industries must pay relatively high wages. (2) Agriculture and the older nondurable-goods industries are more competitive than the growth industries. The acceleration of growth is hampered by relatively inflexible prices and wages in the durable-goods industries. Does anyone suppose that lower prices and wages in agriculture and low-wage industries will accelerate expansion of steel, aluminum, machinery and automobiles by reducing wage costs through the labor market? (3) The growth adjustment breaks down in depression and a backlog of excess labor builds up in agriculture. Foreign trade suffers not only from the fall of demand, but also from the failure of internal growth to draw resources out of the import-competing industries. Thus, the business cycle is intimately related to the growth adjustment. The hypothesis was advanced in Chapter 3 that deflation in the import-competing industries is relatively greater than in the rest of the economy. *Imports are marginal to internal growth in the sense that the failure to expand internally may produce an absolute decline in imports.* Even the leveling off of internal expansion would leave excess resources in the import-competing industries.

Inflation and Imports

The unique character of America's import problem seems to be indicated by the relatively low level of imports despite acute shortages since the second world war which have resulted in general inflation. Although tariffs were greatly reduced, buyers have purchased fewer imports relative to domestic consumption than in earlier decades when domestic supplies were more abundant. This is a remarkable phenomenon, for nothing is so favorable to imports as a round of domestic inflation.

Why have buyers failed to reach out for additional imports rather than pay higher prices as inflation spread at home? One critical factor was the relatively greater inflation abroad, at least until 1949. But this was offset to some extent by special measures to stimulate dollar exports and by widespread devaluation of foreign currencies in 1949. Following the Korean War American imports did rise faster than domestic production. But a substantial part of the acceleration was due to special factors and something more is needed to explain the relatively low level of imports in the midst of domestic shortages.

It might be supposed that once full employment were reached imports would rise precipitately, as long as aggregate demand exceeded aggregate supply. America's failure to import as an alternative to inflation is evidence that, as a rule, the kinds of additional goods which are widely demanded to raise living standards either cannot be bought from foreign producers or can be produced more cheaply at home. It seems to be evidence of the formidable adjustment that is required in order to expand domestic consumption enough to increase the relative importance of imports by substituting imports for domestic production. Prices in agriculture and textiles turned soft before those in the more dynamic industries. Even an inflationary rate of expansion failed to eliminate underemployment and relative deflation in the leading import industries.

Under a full head of prosperity steam, the growth industries erupt in inflation before the excess resources are completely drawn out of agriculture and the relatively stagnant industries, particularly in the South. Here is the root of the difficulty. *The expansion of demand is directed chiefly at the growth industries and, in part, escapes in inflation before reaching the stagnant import industries which are relatively deflated.* If Europe enjoyed a comparative advantage in the production of automobiles, refrigerators, air conditioning and other durable consumer goods, some of which Europe scarcely makes at all, our imports of these products could be expanded rapidly. But the actual adjustment requires that resources be drawn out of the import industries before prices and wages are raised in the export industries. If we are to import much additional sugar, butter, cheese, textiles, hats, china and floor coverings, domestic production and employment in the durable goods and services must expand more rapidly than they have. Otherwise, the labor which would be displaced by additional imports will not be absorbed. The bottleneck problems of wartime production are familiar. Similar problems are posed by any rapid expansion to new peaks of production, for higher levels of consumption require a new pattern of production and employment.

The ultimate indication of America's peculiar disability to enlarge imports is underemployment in the import industries in the midst of over-all inflation. If price and wage increases in durable goods could have been held back longer, with a corresponding increase in demand for their products, and production had been expanded more rapidly by drawing additional labor out of agriculture and the import industries, with a consequent rise in the prices of their products, then we could have experienced a corresponding increase in imports. Thus the barriers to expansion of foreign trade are as deep and broad as the barriers to acceleration of the rate of domestic growth. Living standards must be increased, but the problem of growth without inflation is more than a question of sufficient total demand.[28] On the supply side, the rate of growth is limited not only by the over-all scarcity of resources, but also by investment bottlenecks, housing shortages, noncompetitive prices and wages, subsistence farming and other rigidities which hamper the shift of resources. *Underemployment and potential internal growth are so great and the market so imperfect that imports moderate inflation only to a minor extent.* Nonetheless, once unemployment is mopped up, removal of trade barriers may further moderate the impulse toward inflation.

The long delay in expanding basic steel capacity probably contributed to disparities within the American economy. We appear to have produced about as much durable goods in the immediate postwar years as steel capacity would permit. Because of investment bottlenecks, wage demands by organized labor, and price increases to compensate for them in the more dynamic industries, expansion of consumer demand was partly dissipated in inflation before resources were shifted from the relatively stagnant import industries to the growth industries.

Because of the cost structure and relative price rigidity of most industries producing durable goods, they usually yield exceptionally high profits at capacity levels of production. This leads to demands for higher wages by organized labor. Management has acceded to wage demands in the growing industries before wages in the rest of the economy reached fully competitive levels. This retarded the elimination of relatively low wages in the import industries, which is a prerequisite to maximum foreign trade. These adjustments are complex and are characterized by many crosscurrents and circular effects. The rapid rise of agricultural prices since 1939 substantially increased living costs and reinforced the demand for higher wages in industry.

For a time, administered pricing in industry was a stabilizing influence: prices of chemicals and automobiles were sometimes held below free market prices. It was scarcely possible to hold prices and wages down in the dynamic industries long enough for prices and wages in the low-wage industries to be brought into line. But higher prices and profits in the growing industries do not necessarily accelerate the rate of expansion. Eventually, concern as to the duration of prosperity is a more important consideration to those who might expand than higher profits. Time is necessary to expand the new industries and new products. These considerations are

28. Cf. Walter S. Salant, "The Domestic Effects of Capital Export Under the Point Four Program," *American Economic Review*, Papers and Proceedings, May 1950, pp. 509–510.

relevant to foreign trade because they emphasize that relatively low wages in the import industries do not automatically disappear with full employment.

To some extent we still suffered at the close of the war from the disparities accumulated during a decade of unemployment in the 1930s. A tremendous backlog of deferred demand was released at the end of the war, and consumers tried to raise living standards faster than the structure of employment and production could be reorganized to fit the new pattern of consumption.

Judged by historical standards, the postwar expansion of output is a very creditable performance. The market was called on to make the adjustments of two decades in one. Another decade or two of sustained prosperity might go a long way toward equalizing incomes between industries, eliminating underemployment and creating conditions favorable to the relative expansion of imports. At the same time, two decades of sustained prosperity without a major depression would be without historical precedent, at least since the Civil War.

Exports

The prospect of tolerable adjustment to freer trade is improved from the export side of the picture. The chief requirement is sufficient expansion of employment in the growth industries which produce exports rather than further deflation of stagnant industries which compete with imports. Even in prosperity the disparities associated with internal growth are usually great enough to encourage the shift of resources. In fact, relative decline of agricultural employment has been consistently greater in decades of strong expansion than in decades of relative stagnation.

Potential expansion of our export industries, however, is influenced by the fact that they are already expanded by the export surplus financed by foreign aid and by direct subsidy of exports of farm surpluses. Moreover, we have been exporting a large volume of labor-intensive exports, in part presumably because of underemployment and relatively low returns to factors of production in agriculture and labor-intensive manufacturing industries.

The fact that exports of cotton textiles were 5.5 times greater than imports in 1952 would suggest that freer trade might expand exports of certain items at the same time that imports of other textiles displaced domestic production. Presumably, low-cost southern mills would be the chief beneficiary while New England would suffer more acutely from foreign competition. The immediate background is that exports of cotton textiles were distended by foreign aid and postwar shortages and have dropped about 50 per cent from 1947–1948 to 1953.

In addition to the obvious effect of changes in productivity, labor-intensive exports are also influenced by relative wage rates compared with other home industries. Changes in these disparities may be as important as changes in tariffs. The increase of wage rates in cotton manufacturing was more than 50 per cent greater than in all manufacturing from 1939 to 1946. In southern manufacturing, which is predominantly labor-intensive, the increase of annual wages was about 25 per cent greater than for the nation as a whole.

More recently, however, farm income has declined and wage increases in steel and automobiles have not been matched by textiles. Aggressive bargaining by labor unions in mass production industries and relative declines in agriculture and textiles have probably increased disparities between labor-intensive and capital-intensive sectors of the economy since 1947. Although such developments support continued exports of labor-intensive products, the long-run trend of agricultural exports has been down. By value, they declined in relative importance from 47 per cent of total exports in 1921–1925 to 23 per cent in 1952 and, except for wheat, the quantity of agricultural exports declined absolutely.

The more successful we are in expanding at a rate that will eliminate underemployment and equalize factor costs,[29] the more rational and beneficial our foreign trade may become. Such developments imply relatively higher factor costs in labor-intensive industries than have prevailed in the past. This would encourage both labor-intensive imports and capital-intensive exports and also would imply reduction in the importance of our labor-intensive exports. Relatively higher wage costs in low-wage industries might well retard expansion of labor-intensive exports of cotton, cottonseed oil, cotton textiles and tobacco.

On the other hand, the effect of mechanization and other improvements is to retard the rise of labor costs by making production less labor-intensive.

In the case of machinery and automobiles, which accounted for one third of total exports in 1952, lower trade barriers will encourage expansion of exports and cushion the effect of reduced foreign aid. Broadly speaking, expansion of capital-intensive exports will benefit the more dynamic branches of manufacturing, which are already expanding rapidly.

In sum, expansion of exports will assist the transfer of resources that is required to produce maximum benefits from foreign trade. But the export side of the picture points to the same problem that we face with imports. Increased specialization and exchange of capital-intensive exports for labor-intensive imports are marginal to internal growth because they require more of the same basic adjustment that is dictated by internal growth.

29. Equal wages do not include inequalities due to quality of labor, differences in skill, attractiveness of the job, etc.

Redistribution of Income

It may be recalled that foreign trade is a substitute for foreign investment and immigration. The United States can export capital, or employ the capital at home and export the products of its capital-intensive industries. Although foreign workers are barred from the United States by immigration laws, much the same result can be obtained by importing the products of labor-intensive industries.[30]

Less hampered foreign trade can raise over-all productivity, but the effect on land, labor and capital will not be the same. At the present stage of America's economic development we have relatively less labor and relatively more capital than the rest of the world.

If we import more sugar, the Colorado land now in sugar beets may be shifted to pasture, since the technique of grass farming has been greatly improved in recent years. This will reduce farm labor requirements and quite possibly the return per acre of land. Free imports of wool will give us access to the extensive land area of Australia, as free imports of cattle will give us the use of Canadian and Mexican land.

In sum, freer trade will encourage expansion of capital-intensive industries, discourage labor-intensive forms of employment, lower the return on land most suitable for raising imported products, and raise the return on land most suitable for export products. The net effect on land may be unfavorable relative to capital because trade may encourage, chiefly, the more capital-intensive exports of manufactures.

Expansion of foreign trade can serve as substitute for both the immigration of labor from foreign countries into the United States and the expansion of American investment abroad and, if carried far enough, will tend to produce similar results. Under free trade, land and labor will become relatively more plentiful because we shall import the goods which require much land and labor, to wit, wool and sugar, respectively; capital, on the other hand, will become less plentiful because we shall export the goods that require much capital, to wit, durable goods. The *relative* return to labor will go down and the *relative* return to capital will go up.

Income will be redistributed between geographical areas for the same reason.

As a practical matter, the implied redistribution of income may not be too significant, for two reasons: (1) The potential expansion of foreign trade relative to potential internal growth is so small that the change in income because of foreign trade may be slight. (2) If the income which is

30. Under certain theoretical conditions, prices and marginal returns to factors of production between two nations can be equalized by international trade. In the real world, the imperfect market does not attain this objective even within the home economy.

redistributed unfavorably to labor is a higher real national income, labor's real income would not necessarily be less.[31]

The practical effect of increased imports on the distribution of income may be significant for a quite different reason, namely, the possible danger that the adjustment process might accentuate the tendency of other internal dislocations to depress incomes of farmers and small business over a long period of time. The same may be said of New England as a region and of small areas in southeastern Ohio and adjacent West Virginia which produce pottery, china and handblown glass. The people involved are concerned with the total effect of all dislocations rather than the foreign trade adjustment alone.

In the exposed import industries where demand is inelastic and incomes are already relatively low, a small increase in imports may further depress prices and incomes substantially if the expansion elsewhere is not rapid enough to take up the slack in agriculture and nondurables. Competition from imports cannot be viewed as an isolated adjustment.

The effect of free trade on distribution of income makes it impossible to generalize about benefits to the nation as a whole unless compensation is provided to those who are injured.

The actual unemployment that would be created by freer trade is relatively small, not only because the volume of additional imports would be small, but also because additional foreign competition may result in relative deflation of the import-competing industries rather than actual expansion of imports. Unemployment is not an appropriate measure of the magnitude of the dislocation. Farmers, for example, do not become unemployed; as long as they remain on the farm, they continue to work and produce. Additional foreign competition will reduce the market value of their produce, and their income will fall. To a lesser extent, the same may be true of other highly competitive import-competing industries. Unless resources are transferred, the effect of lower tariffs on products with inelastic consumer demand may severely reduce prices and incomes of domestic producers even though the actual increase in imports is relatively small. In sum, the dislocation may take the form of *underemployment* with relative overproduction and low incomes in the import-competing industries.

The Question of Injury

Thus far we have had largely the form of tariff reduction without the substance of increased imports which displace home industry. In some

31. Stolper and Samuelson have shown that under certain theoretical conditions, the real return and the relative return to a particular factor of production are likely to move in the same direction as a result of tariff changes. "Protection and Real Wages," *Readings in the Theory of International Trade*, Blakiston, Philadelphia, 1949. But this, of course, takes no account of the effect of innovation on productivity.

cases the trade agreements themselves provide specifically for restoration of higher duties as imports rise. Under the farm price support programs, the government is acquiring larger stocks of commodities as farm prices drop. Continued restriction of agricultural imports seems probable under present policy. Some of the future increase of imports which gets by the escape clause may be killed by recourse to the flexible tariff, which can still be used to raise duties on imports not covered by trade agreements.

Liberal forces in America today are trapped by hostages that were given to the future in the pledge to avoid serious injury from tariff cuts. As the issue has been drawn since 1949 at least, it has been a struggle to renew the Trade Agreements Act and the most that liberal forces could win was to maintain present policies. Merely to hold the present policy line represents an orderly retreat instead of a rout. Under present policies imports may be increasingly restricted. The most urgent policy issue is to avoid raising trade barriers as specific imports rise.

Those who favor freer trade have given too little attention to the problem of adjustment. It is no use to sugar-coat the import pill. Absolute or relative injury to some is an essential and inevitable result of the shift from a protected market to a free market.

The shift to free trade is comparable to technological progress. The new structure of production and employment is more productive, but the older must be displaced. We pride ourselves on technological improvement but resist the same potential gain in the form of more foreign trade. Additional imports would displace domestic employment but would create exports which cost less to produce.[32] Improved technology comes to the same end: some workers are displaced and more productive jobs are created as a result. There is no difference in principle between increasing productivity with more technique and increasing productivity with more trade.

But this does not quite dispose of the real issue, which is one of relative magnitudes and not one of principles. To add one uncomfortable adjustment to the other makes the total adjustment more difficult. The proper goal is not to avoid all injury but to avoid displacement of resources which are not reabsorbed with reasonable dispatch. If the adjustment takes place in a reasonable length of time, the injury from imports is bearable. As a practical matter, the conditions are all-important. This brings us to the criteria of injury.

An attempt was made in Chapter 19 to explore how far we can go under the escape clause policy. (1) We can tolerate imports in the growth industries so long as domestic production is not absolutely displaced. (2) Big business can absorb imports without injury in the multiproduct industries

32. Of if foreign aid is reduced, new jobs can be created by tax reduction and higher private spending.

and firms. (3) We can accept imports through the interstices in the structure of production which do not compete directly with "like products" of home industry.

These criteria must be regarded as the outside limit of tariff concessions under present laws and the present state of public opinion. They rest on very slim precedent. They are not accepted by a minority of the Tariff Commission and the Congress has not given them statutory sanction. Certainly, present prospects for expanding trade would be somewhat improved if these principles were sanctioned. But even if well established, these criteria of injury do not get us far. The policy of making small segments of an industry eligible for tariff relief leaves little scope for requiring the industry to adjust to foreign competition by shifting the composition of its output. This restrictive amendment was enacted in 1955.

In the garlic case, President Truman rejected the majority recommendation of the Tariff Commission essentially on the ground that alternative opportunities were available to domestic producers within their own business. Similar considerations led President Eisenhower to deny tariff relief to domestic producers of silk scarves.[33]

In these cases, no one was forced to change his job or his business to avoid serious injury. The alternative opportunity for profitable production and employment was available within the same business. At least, this was the argument. This doctrine seriously limits the possibility of increasing competitive imports because of the concentration of potential imports in certain branches of agriculture and industries of small firms.

By a change in policy this principle might be extended to take account of alternative opportunities in other industries and geographical areas. This would permit injury to an *industry* as long as the *people and resources* had alternative opportunities for employment.

More than half of domestic wool production has been displaced by imports without injury because cattle raising, dairying and other types of farming offered profitable alternatives. Thus, wool imports have reduced the price of beef. Cattle raisers were not injured as long as the growing demand for beef sustained profitable prices. On the other hand, wool imports have contributed to a surplus of butter because of government support of prices and decline in consumption. Butter differs from beef in that consumption of butter and whole milk has dropped 19 per cent since the end of the war as a result of higher prices and reducing diets.[34]

33. Both the industry and labor union involved have challenged the finding of facts in the case of silk scarves.

34. This figure comes from a dairy association which will spend $6–$10 million in the next year touting milk as the "ideal food" for a reducing diet. A survey by the association reports that about one third of the population is on a diet. *Time* Magazine, August 10, 1953, p. 81.

With the relative fall of farm prices since 1947 and the absolute fall since early 1950, conditions are much less favorable for the expansion of agricultural imports. Cattle herds were built up over a period of years while wool imports were rising, and in 1952–1953 cattle prices dropped about one third. The government has acquired burdensome stocks of butter in supporting dairy prices and it seems clear that the structure of dairy prices should have been overhauled while prices were rising.

The adjustment to rising wool imports was tolerated as long as alternative opportunities were profitable. Politically, support prices for wool made it difficult to argue that wool growers were seriously injured. Adjustment to increased imports of wool is the most outstanding achievement since the change in our tariff policy in 1934. This notable success required great courage by the Truman administration when intense pressure to restrict wool imports developed at the time of the GATT negotiations in Geneva. Heavy losses have been incurred, however, during a decade of price supports. The necessary adjustment may be aggravated in the future by the rise of synthetic substitutes for wool and a decline in consumption of natural wool similar to that in butter.

Because of imperfections of the market and the magnitude of the total adjustment, we cannot, as a general rule, count on automatic price adjustments, as a result of tariff reduction, to absorb the displaced resources in more productive employment. In this respect, one of the standard arguments for freer trade needs qualification.

Free trade at home, it is said, has made the American economy dynamic and progressive and, therefore, free foreign trade will make it that much more dynamic and productive. This argument misses the mark in that foreign producers can give us little competition in the industries where we need it most and can give us serious competition in the industries where we need it least. More competition is needed in the industries with administered prices and rapid improvements in technique. Because of innovations, these industries enjoy high profits and pay high wages. But the serious increase in competition from tariff reduction will be highly concentrated in those home industries which are already highly competitive in price, and thus will tend to exacerbate the disparity between the more and the less competitive home industries.

According to Piquet's estimates, for example, increased imports of cotton and cigar tobacco under free trade may be as great as or greater than the increased imports of steel.[35] He also estimates that increased imports of all farm products may be twenty-two to thirty times greater than increased imports of all chemicals, machinery and vehicles. It may be doubted if more competition in cotton and tobacco will accelerate the rate of internal

35. *Aid, Trade and the Tariff*, pp. 63, 152–153, 203.

growth; where competition is needed is in those industries with inflexible prices which must absorb the displaced resources.

The Long Run

It is commonly assumed that these difficult problems of adjustment are automatically solved by the "long run."

Time is indispensable to making the adjustments that are required to raise the level of foreign trade: (1) because the bulk of imports that can be increased by changes in policy will displace home industry and require the shift of resources, and (2) because the adjustment is superimposed on much larger internal adjustments in the same area and in the same direction. Time is needed for preparatory adjustments in the domestic farm program. However, time alone will not necessarily take care of the adjustment.

Owing to existing disparities between the relatively stagnant import-competing industries and the more dynamic growth industries, it cannot be assumed that the transfer of resources will automatically accelerate if the disparities are further increased. Where farm incomes are already low enough to encourage migration and nonfarm employment does not expand *because* farm income falls, additional foreign competition may only exacerbate the problem of underemployment and chronic surpluses.[36] Similarly, where relative deflation of the older nondurable-goods industries is already sufficient to redirect investment and employment, there may be some question as to whether further deflation of this area will accelerate the growth of durable goods and services. If, for any reason, the economy expands at less than the maximum rate of potential growth, the maladjustment will only compound in the long run. On the other hand, in those import-competing industries where lower prices and income will accelerate the transfer of resources, the long-term effect of lower trade barriers will be salutary.

The American economy has demonstrated enormous capacity to adjust, but it is unrealistic to assume that no limit is imposed on the rate of growth by the problem of shifting resources.

The adjustment to free trade and a durable international order will require not only a long time, but also favorable over-all economic conditions. An expansionary fiscal policy is probably a minimum requirement. If the over-all climate is even mildly deflationary, the foreign trade adjustment will suffer.

36. The popular view would seem to be that a fall in farm income usually retards the expansion of nonfarm employment. Conceivably, the disparities could become great enough to have this effect through changes in the propensity to consume. Further investigation of this problem is needed.

Protection and Revenue

A major part of our imports are duty-free and not even the Tariff League wishes to exclude noncompetitive imports. Domestic production has been supplemented with large imports of wool, sugar, fruits and nuts, fish, nonferrous metals, petroleum, newsprint, wood pulp and sawmill products. The economy has been spared the cost of extreme protection. The real disagreement concerns probably one billion dollars more or less of competitive imports, which within a few years would displace, absolutely or relatively, competing home industries.[37] These are not the vital, key materials for want of which the economy will suffer acutely. They are chiefly products that are now produced at home, though at higher costs than they could be obtained in exchange for exports. The net gain from one billion dollars of additional trade is only a fraction of one billion dollars because the cost of exports must be subtracted from the cost of producing the imports at home. And from this must be subtracted the loss of revenue, which, at present duties, will be substantial relative to the gain (except for those imports now restricted by quota).

At one extreme, reduction of highly protective duties may increase revenue by increasing imports. At the other, further tariff reduction may fail to produce positive economic benefits if loss of revenue is taken into account. Our earlier statements of the case for trade have taken scant account of revenue aspects of the problem. Under present world conditions, it would seem to be a poor policy for the rich United States to tax its trade with the rest of the world in order to collect revenue.

Average duties of 40 per cent on imports in 1929 produced revenue of $585 million. Average duties of 12.7 per cent in 1952 produced revenue of $570 million. Dutiable imports rose 208 per cent, by value, during this period, or less than the 233 per cent rise in gross national product. In a number of important instances, like sugar, tariffs were cut but imports have been restricted by quota. This means that foreign producers gained enormously because the United States lost revenue and the potential benefits were not passed on to consumers via lower prices.

The purpose of our policy of reciprocal tariff reduction was to expand American exports. But since exports have been controlled largely by the dollar shortage, reciprocal tariff reduction may have served chiefly to avoid less favorable terms of trade.

Foreign Policy—and Domestic Equity

We are concerned not only with the balance of trade and economic development but with the national interest in the most profound sense.

37. Displacement includes not only liquidation but also serious loss of income.

Institutions which protect the dignity and worth of the individual are challenged by the threat of Soviet expansion, and the values of western civilization are at stake. The requirements of American foreign policy dictate expansion of our foreign trade. The economic benefits of freer trade are widely regarded as less important to us than the responsibility of American leadership at a time of great disorder in world affairs.

American aid is welcome, but foreign nations grow restive under continued dependence on appropriations by the Congress. Free nations would like to be able to support themselves and defend themselves. It becomes increasingly clear that continued aid is no substitute for leadership and that gifts win neither love nor loyalty.

The idea that the richest and strongest nation should discriminate against and restrict trade with weaker countries is offensive—the more so since we are disposed to preach the virtues of competition and the free market to poorer countries for whom the adjustments will be more onerous than for ourselves. Moreover, we are in the vulnerable position of trying to restrict Europe's trade with Russia and Japan's trade with China, while failing ourselves to trade enough with our Allies to enable them to pay their own way.

The costs of the economic adjustment to freer trade seem small, indeed, in relation to the objective of national security in a friendly world of free nations. When we attempt to go beneath these generalities, however, disquieting questions appear. If imports are raised to serve the dictates of foreign policy, why should a few citizens in the exposed industries bear the entire cost of adjustment? Why, for example, should the handblown glass industry pay for the cold war? A case for financial assistance to those who are seriously injured by imports can be made on economic grounds alone: the injury results from a basic change in America's historic policy of protectionism.[38] The case is even stronger if the overriding objective is national security. In matters as important as this, we need not limit our efforts to conventional methods.

38. The difficulty, however, of distinguishing between injury from foreign competition and injury from domestic competition should not be underestimated. Potential injury from imports may be serious only because it is the last straw. The Tariff Commission already faces this problem in its escape clause investigations.

Chapter 24

Conclusions

THE PEOPLES of the world are demanding higher living standards in more strident tones than ever before. Their hopes and aspirations can be gratified only by sustained growth of production, based on higher productivity throughout the world from year to year.

To achieve this end, the rest of the world needs to trade with the United States. Trade is a source of strength because it is one way of raising productivity. It would be cheaper for all to exchange imports for exports than to maintain protected home industries. But the United States imports so little that it has been virtually impossible for other nations to pay for the goods they would like to buy here.

Creditor Nation

Ever since the United States became a creditor nation, it has been said that we have an obligation to reduce trade barriers. Desirable as this is for other reasons, the creditor nation argument is misleading. The United States is so much richer than other countries that growth of foreign investment could exceed the yield for a long time, if economic considerations were paramount.

Private foreign investment, however, no longer plays the role that it played in the nineteenth century. Other nations fear American domination. A new nationalism has arisen that associates foreign control of investments with colonial exploitation. At the same time, the drive of native peoples for development and industrialization is stronger than ever. And success or failure of their hopes and plans will affect the security of the United States, because growth and stability are safeguards against Communist subversion.

Limited foreign investments make it even more important to avoid restriction on foreign trade, because trade is a substitute for investment. If we do not invest our capital in development of foreign lands, at least we can make it possible for other peoples to obtain the products of industrial progress through mutually beneficial trade. (See Chapter 1.)

The Dilemma

After a long history of high tariffs, the United States has moved slowly in the opposite direction. Since 1934 the average tariff collected on dutiable imports has been reduced by almost 75 per cent. So far, this drastic cut has been largely ineffective. (See Chapters 5 and 6.) Under favorable conditions, lower tariffs may become more effective in raising the future level of trade than they have been in the past.

The marked shift of sentiment toward freer trade does not signal a popular demand for imports so much as it reflects the growing strength of our export industries and the acute need to strengthen the free world against the threat of Soviet expansion. The consensus now seems to be that more trade would be a "good thing," but we are not prepared to accept the consequences. (See Chapter 7.)

The key to the dilemma is that we are embarked on a program of tariff reduction without accepting the principle that the gains from trade outweigh the damage to home industry. This Janus-faced attitude has compromised our Trade Agreements Program from the beginning. On one side, it seeks to expand mutually beneficial trade; on the other, it promises that no branch of home industry, however small, will be seriously damaged as a result. (See Chapter 19.)

President Eisenhower's special message to Congress spoke boldly: "The Nation's enlightened self-interest and sense of responsibility as a leader . . . require a foreign economic program that will stimulate economic growth in the free world through . . . free enterprise and competitive markets." In contrast to the vigor of his message, the President asked for very little and received even less. The Congress (in 1955) authorized further tariff reduction. But if even a segment of home industry is seriously injured or threatened, protection may be increased. Thus, the President is authorized to move forward and backward at the same time.

The Cheap-Labor Fallacy

The argument that the United States cannot compete against cheap foreign labor is disproved, in part, by the plain fact that our high-wage industries do compete in foreign markets, and very successfully too. In addition, domestic production has displaced imports in the home market in the face of lower tariffs.

This was possible because of high productivity, which means high wages and low unit costs. Our great mass production industries no longer need protection. Indeed, they would profit under free trade. Industries like the automobile industry, which use little labor in relation to their capital equipment, have nothing to fear. Certain competitive imports of chemicals or machinery may substantially affect domestic production of these specific items, but such industries would not be seriously injured. Growing industries can absorb additional imports by expansion of consumption. Large firms producing a wide range of products can absorb the impact of increased foreign competition by expanding output of some lines at the same time that growth of others is retarded. The adjustment can usually take place within the industry and firm, and will sometimes produce a net gain. Steel, machinery, electrical equipment, instruments, chemicals, petroleum, rubber, and parts of the paper industry probably fall in this category. (See Chapter 20.)

Some imports, like watches, may expand chiefly by creating their own market. Domestic sales have increased, although imports have increased even faster. (See Chapter 22.)

Domestic producers of bicycles and motorcycles may face a more serious problem, partly because they have concentrated on designs that do not satisfy the taste of domestic consumers.

Proponents of free trade go too far when they imply that all branches of home industry can become strong enough to withstand foreign competition. Such arguments claim too much for they imply that all competitive imports could be eliminated if each home industry were able to lower its costs sufficiently. This is the same fallacy found in the argument about cheap foreign labor.

Some industries will always progress less rapidly than others, however great the rise in productivity. And these will be vulnerable to foreign competition even though their real costs are below their foreign competitors'. In textiles, for example, American industry uses labor more productively than Britain or Japan. But our textile industry must compete with the even higher productivity of our automobile industry. In other words, foreign trade in textiles depends not only on comparative costs in textiles, but also on comparative costs in automobiles. It is profitable to import goods that we can produce 25 per cent more cheaply than other countries so long as we pay for them with exports that we produce 50 per cent more cheaply than other countries.

Who Would Be Injured?

Although free trade would produce no flood of imports, the impact would be concentrated on certain branches of agriculture and the older nondurable-goods industries. These sectors are vulnerable because they are technically less advanced and less mechanized than the durable-goods and newer nondurable-goods industries, like chemicals and petroleum refining. They are also vulnerable because their markets are relatively inelastic and the prospect of absorbing imports by expanding consumption is rather limited. In contrast to large-scale mass production, our leading import-competing industries are made up of farmers and small businesses.

It is impossible to predict with certainty who would be injured by free trade, but it is certain that some would suffer.

Imports of sugar, handblown glass, earthenware and chinaware might displace as much as half of domestic production. It appears that producers of butter, wool, certain tree crops, oil crops and fish would be substantially affected. The vulnerable manufacturing industries appear to include woolens and worsteds, leather goods, floor coverings, lace, certain segments of cotton textiles, hats, cutlery, jewelry, musical instruments and more than a score of quite minor products.

No one proposes to establish free trade suddenly, and if foreign competition were the only adjustment, the problem of getting out of these industries gradually should not prove too difficult. The problem is an acute one, chiefly because employment is already declining, absolutely or relatively, in our leading import-competing industries as a result of technological displacement and inelastic markets.

Freer trade is like introducing a new machine or a new technique. It makes possible higher productivity and living standards, but it imposes one uncomfortable adjustment on top of another. Imports are only the last straw.

Workers displaced by the revolution in technology must be shifted off farms and away from stagnant industries before imports, which would displace additional workers, can be substantially increased. And unless this adjustment is accelerated by more rapid expansion of the growing industries, the chief effect of free trade would be to redistribute income away from declining industries where wages and incomes are already relatively low.

The excess of farm labor is concentrated in southern states where manufacturing is also predominantly labor-intensive. Southern competition has displaced New England textiles, and competition for farm labor has decentralized the leather industry.

Precisely the same adjustment that might have increased foreign trade is taking place in domestic trade, and we have so little of the one because we have so much of the other. (See Chapter 23.)

It is the combined displacement of domestic *and* foreign competition which measures the adjustment that is required. The handblown glass industry is vulnerable to foreign competition because it is a labor-intensive industry in a capital-intensive nation. It has already been substantially displaced by vigorous expansion of domestic machine-made glassware. The capital-intensive branch of domestic industry is able to compete against cheap foreign labor. Its exports exceed imports of handblown glassware. (See Chapter 21.)

Long-Term Growth

Tariff changes do not appear to have been the controlling factor determining the over-all importance of imports. (See Chapter 4.)

In the earlier period of our history, the attempt to restrict imports of manufactured goods was probably frustrated, to some degree, by the favorable effect of tariffs on the terms of trade. This means that the price of raw material exports compared with manufactured imports remained favorable to domestic production of raw materials.

As manufacturing developed, some imports rose in response to expanding national income at the same time that other categories were restricted. In any event, the growth of imports since the Civil War, though interrupted by depression and war, appears to have kept pace with domestic production of commodities, except for a displacement near the end of the nineteenth century, and again in the 1930s. (See Chapter 2.)

Every major depression has produced a greater fluctuation in imports than in output. Imports are sensitive not only to the rise and fall of national income, but also to the relative deflation of our import-competing industries that apparently takes place in depression. (See Chapter 3.)

Invisible Tariff

Imports are restricted not only by tariffs but also by antiquated, cumbersome and ambiguous customs regulations. These involve costly delays and needless expenses. Classification and valuation formulas are needlessly complex and the results are sometimes inequitable. Whatever tariffs may be imposed, nothing can be said in favor of restrictions that create uncertainty and burden foreign trade with unnecessary expense. (See Chapter 9.)

Laws requiring government agencies to buy American-made goods are contrary to the national interest and should be repealed. In the meantime, the degree of discrimination can be reduced by executive order.

Institutional Handicaps

Manufactured imports face a host of institutional handicaps. These include technical specifications, inventory controls, distribution facilities, delivery dates, advertising costs, and problems of adapting foreign production to the American market. Substantial differences in comparative costs between domestic and foreign manufacturers have resulted in a small volume of trade because of problems of distribution. (See Chapter 10.)

European producers are appalled at the risk and expense of expanding their American market. They are apprehensive that if a large market were developed, American producers with greater resources would recover it with mass production methods. These problems are sometimes exaggerated in the minds of European exporters. They are deterred from finding out if they can compete by the risk that American tariffs will be raised if they are successful. (See Chapter 11.[1])

Agriculture

Agricultural products account for almost half of total imports. These have suffered technological displacement. (See Chapter 13.)

Although tariffs have been reduced, a number of important imports are restricted by quota. This means that foreign producers gain from higher prices because the United States Treasury loses revenue and the potential benefits are not passed on to consumers in lower prices.

Displacement of domestic production by imports of wool offers an enlightening illustration of the adjustment process. On the western ranges, sheep gave way to cattle; farther east, wheat, soybeans and dairying claimed more of the farmer's labor. Displacement of domestic wool by imports expanded production of cattle and soybeans, which, in turn, displaced imported hides, vegetable oils and dairy products. Woolens and beefsteak are cheaper as a result, but the problem of surplus butter, wheat and vegetable oil has been aggravated. (See pp. 84–87 and 478–479.)

The excess of farm labor created by the revolution in technology throws a heavy burden of adjustment on the farm community. No other branches of American industry with declining employment and ample resources have permitted so large a volume of competitive imports.

Whatever is done to raise farm income, it should not interfere with the shift of workers to nonfarm employment or with better use of resources within agriculture. (See Chapter 12.)

Minerals

Minerals account for about 20 per cent of total imports, chiefly because the United States is more deficient in metals than in other natural resources.

Although consumption of minerals has increased faster than consumption of other raw materials, expansion has been moderated by new techniques which save materials and by new materials which displace imports. (See Chapter 15.)

Projections of growth of national income foretell a great increase in demand for raw material imports. But such projections make inadequate allowance for the effect of technological advance on which the validity of the income projections depends. At the same time, the shift of the United States from a net importer to a net exporter of materials emphasizes our growing dependence on foreign sources of supply.

Petroleum appears to be the import with greatest potential growth and, consequently, it is important to avoid a policy of restriction. (See Chapter 16.)

1. By Calvin B. Hoover.

Luxuries

Luxury and semiluxury products account for a substantial part of American imports, and some writers have supposed that these would rise faster than national income. Apparently this did not happen, at least from 1929 to 1950.

The present study suggests that sumptuous living on the grand scale has been affected by the rise of labor costs. Getting rich has its paradox; for in a mass society, the richer we become as a nation, the fewer servants we can afford. Rising incomes result in an even greater rise of "service costs."

Mass production and high service costs do not encourage sumptuous living. This has affected demand for luxuries, such as fine linens, chinaware, glassware, elaborate silver service and jewels. (See Chapter 17.)

Tourism

American tourist expenditures are one of the largest sources of dollar earnings to other countries. Considering the rise of our national income, luxury expenditures for the grand tour of foreign countries have increased less than might be expected. Calvin B. Hoover makes some "homely" suggestions for expanding tourism.

American payments for tourism exceed receipts, but receipts from the sale of other private services exceed payments to other countries. In considering the implication of tourism for the dollar shortage, it should be remembered that foreign demand for American services may rise as fast as or faster than American payments. (See Chapter 18.)

Shipping

It costs much more to operate a merchant vessel under the American flag than under foreign flags. Yet more vessels fly the American flag than any other.

If competition determined who got the business, foreign fleets would earn dollars carrying American goods. The "American Flag Rule," however, requires that government-financed cargo be hauled in American vessels.

A fleet is essential for national defense, and direct subsidy is justified in order to operate the number of vessels needed for this purpose. We have gone beyond this point, however, as a result of indirect subsidy provided by the rule of cargo preference. A fleet that is subsidized beyond the recommendations of competent authorities drains American resources and denies European countries the opportunity to earn dollars in the most important single industry where otherwise they would be able to do so.

Cargo preference is incompatible with the objectives of American foreign policy. (See Chapter 18.)

Policy Criteria

Adjustments to free trade pose serious problems because, although gains exceed losses, the distribution of benefits is inequitable. Some industries and communities may suffer hardship while others benefit as a result.

The fact that dynamic internal growth also imposes inequitable adjustment does not necessarily justify a change of national policy that would add one dislocation on top of another. This is especially relevant to tariff questions because support of foreign policy seems to carry more weight than potential economic gain in shaping American attitudes toward foreign trade.

The problem is best viewed as a struggle for labor and other productive resources between competing home industries.

1. Tariff protection for domestic industries that show pronounced growth can be eliminated. Growing industries have no legitimate claim to protection in order to attract workers and expand employment at the expense of competing American industries that would otherwise be able to employ these resources to produce goods and services of greater value.

2. The same principle can be applied to the *output* of industries producing a variety of products. So long as a growing industry can adjust to foreign competition by shifts in composition of output, it has no valid claim to protection on a minor segment of its business.

3. Protected industries that are relatively stagnant or declining may be kept under pressure to contract through normal attrition of labor force and depletion of fixed investment. But such industries may fairly claim that the rate of total adjustment, rather than the dislocation from foreign trade, is the relevant consideration. A change of national policy should avoid creating greater disparities in income than are needed to redirect resources into more productive employment. Periods of adjustment may extend over a generation in manufacturing industries and even longer in agriculture. A minimum requirement is an expanding national economy that bumps the full employment ceiling fairly hard and fairly often.

4. Specific programs to alleviate hardship and facilitate adjustment may be justified in the case of declining industries and communities.

5. Tariff reduction is not likely to be fully effective in stimulating trade so long as the escape clause promises to restore protection if imports threaten serious injury. Temporary tariff reduction is a dubious expedient. It is more important to avoid raising some tariffs than to reduce others.

COMMITTEE REPORT

Chapter 25

Import Policy for Security and Progress*

I. WHY AMERICAN IMPORT POLICY IS IMPORTANT

IF STRICTLY ECONOMIC factors were the only considerations affecting a country's external economic relations, the making of foreign economic policy would be a comparatively simple matter. In such circumstances, the objective of policy would no doubt be to achieve and maintain the kind of foreign trade and investment most helpful to the development and economical use of the country's resources. But, in the conditions of the mid-twentieth century, no nation can in practice determine its import and export policies completely, or even mainly, on the basis of purely economic considerations. Generally speaking, the policies governing the foreign trade and payments of most countries tend to reflect two types of concerns: (1) that of the national community as a whole to ensure the national capacity for self-defense and for economic self-support and continued growth; and (2) those of politically powerful special interest groups for maintaining or increasing their own shares of domestic or foreign markets or of the national income. In most countries these two types of considerations are both influential, and actions in one category will often necessitate counter or supporting measures in the other category.

A. The International Position and Responsibilities of the United States

The foreign economic policy of the United States has naturally expressed those concerns, and their relative influence on policy has tended to reflect the changes in the international position of our country. Before World War I, the United States was not generally regarded by the rest of the world as a leading nation politically, militarily or economically. Distant from the main centers of world power and absorbed in our own national development, Americans did not have—and did not need to have—a responsible foreign policy. Instead, the United States tacitly relied—as did most other Western nations—upon Britain's political influence, economic power and naval might to ensure the peaceful and efficient working of the nineteenth

---

* This chapter is a policy statement prepared by the Committee on International Policy of the National Planning Association based on the data and analysis presented in this study. The names of NPA International Committee members signing the policy statement will be found at the end. The Committee wishes to acknowledge the assistance of Theodore Geiger, NPA's Chief of International Studies, in the writing of this statement.

century world polity and economy. In such circumstances, American import and export policies could be—and were—formulated almost exclusively in terms of domestic economic needs and interests, as these were then understood and as conflicts among them were reconciled through domestic political processes.

In the years after 1914, a profound change occurred in the international political, military and economic position of the United States relative to that of other countries. For a variety of reasons, the United States became the wealthiest, strongest and economically most influential nation—a change which reflected both its own progress and the decline of other world powers. During the interwar period, however, neither the United States nor other countries explicitly recognized the implications of this change for American policies or for those of other nations. In the main, the foreign political and economic policies of the United States continued to reflect domestic political and economic trends and needs. The start of the Reciprocal Trade Agreements Program in 1934 marked the beginning of a broader conception of the purposes and strategy of American foreign economic policy, but it too was publicly justified largely in terms of the increased American exports—and hence domestic employment—it was supposed directly to stimulate.

It was only after the outbreak of World War II that a fuller understanding of the consequences of our new position in the world began rapidly to impress itself upon the consciousness of official policy makers and of the public generally. During the war, a major reorientation of the whole of American foreign policy—political, military, economic, psychological—occurred, which the events of the postwar period have confirmed and strengthened. Today, the disparity between the economic and military strength of the United States and the persistent weakness of many other non-Soviet countries would make our leadership responsibilities within the free world unmistakable even in the absence of the Soviet threat. The menace of Communist imperialism greatly increases the difficulty and the urgency of these responsibilities.

The special position which the United States now occupies in the non-Soviet world may be seen in a comparison of economic capabilities. Our total production of goods and services is almost double that of the four leading industrial nations of Western Europe combined—the United Kingdom, France, West Germany and Italy. Our average output per man-hour is at least twice that of any other country (except Canada). Owing to the continental size of our economy, to the abundance and variety of our natural resources, and to the balanced and dynamic character of our economic development, the economic stability and growth of the United States have not in recent years been strongly affected by economic conditions and trends abroad. In contrast, the economic health of many other free countries, particularly those with industrial economies, has been sensitive to changes in the level of demand in the American economy because of the extent of their dependence upon American markets and sources of supply. Thus, the American economy exerts a major influence upon economic conditions and trends in other parts of the world while itself enjoying comparative immunity to adverse economic changes in its external environment.

The disparities between our economic capabilities and those of the other non-Soviet countries, and the nonreciprocal character of our economic relations with the rest of the free world, would not be matters for special concern were it not for two factors already noted—the persistent economic, political and military weaknesses of many of the other free countries and the ceaseless efforts of Soviet Communism to exploit these difficulties for its own imperialist purposes. These weaknesses express in varying degrees and different forms the inability of many free countries to achieve rates of economic growth sufficient to meet their minimum economic requirements for self-support, self-defense, internal social cohesion and political stability. In the absence of constructive measures by which such poor economic health could be overcome, these countries are driven to counteract their economic weaknesses negatively, by reducing their dependence on foreign trade and by insulating their national economies against the adverse effects of external economic changes. Such efforts are among the main reasons for the trade and payments restrictions which today form so important a part of the foreign economic practices of many nations. In turn, other countries may be compelled to adopt similar restrictions in order to protect their own domestic or foreign markets from the discriminatory policies of their trading partners. The result of this self-reinforcing tendency toward trade and payments restrictions has been a serious impairment of the efficiency and calculability of the international economy, which, in consequence, can no longer provide the competitive stimuli and the expanding market opportunities needed by many national economies if they are to maintain adequate rates of economic growth, i.e., good economic health. Thus, national economic weaknesses have led to international economic inefficiency, which in turn has fostered national economic weaknesses in a complex vicious circle.

Owing to the serious political, psychological and military consequences, the countries suffering from poor economic health are vulnerable to internal Communist subversion or external Soviet aggression. This dangerous situation is of vital concern to the United States. It is one of the generally recognized facts of life in the mid-twentieth century that the survival and progress of other free societies—of our allies and friends abroad—are necessary conditions for the continued freedom and progress of the United States. Since, among the non-Soviet countries, the United States possesses to the greatest degree the requisite resources, influence and freedom of action, we have been compelled to assume the responsibilities of leadership in the inescapable task of preserving and advancing the cause of human freedom.

The effective discharge of these leadership responsibilities has meant that the United States has had to have a dynamic and worldwide foreign policy for the first time in its history. This new foreign policy has had to cover a much wider range of actions than anything we have attempted before—political, military, economic and psychological. In particular, the economic aspect or dimension of American foreign policy has assumed greatly increased importance in a world whose problems tend to express themselves in economic forms or to have serious economic consequences. At the same time, economic means have proved to be among the most effective of those available for working toward the general goal of American foreign policy—a free, peaceful and increasingly prosperous world. As we have seen, the nations among whom the United States exercises leadership are heavily dependent upon the American economy, which, in the aggregate, has been their single most important source of primary products, manufactured goods, capital funds and technological innovations. Hence, by easing or impeding their access to the American economy, the United States can advance or retard the economic improvement of many other non-Soviet countries.

American foreign economic policy is an intrinsic aspect of foreign policy, and its proximate objectives and means can only be adequately understood and validly determined in the light of the general goals and strategy of American foreign policy as a whole. Viewed in this context, the interest of the United States requires our foreign economic policy to work toward decisive improvements in the effectiveness of the international economy and in the economic health of its component national economies. These proximate objectives can be achieved in two ways: (1) by conducting our own foreign economic relations and our domestic economic policies in a manner that minimizes their adverse effects on the international economy and maximizes their contribution to its more effective functioning; and (2) by inducing and helping other non-Soviet countries to undertake necessary changes in their own policies and actions, individually and collectively.

B. How American Import Policy Could Serve the Purposes of Foreign Policy

The import policy of the United States is particularly relevant to the first method, for it is one of the factors determining the nature, extent and calculability of the access other countries have to the American economy.

Its relative importance compared with other factors is, however, a matter of dispute. Opinions differ as to the extent to which changes in American import policy would improve the functioning of the international economy and as to how drastic these changes would have to be before their external effects would be worthwhile.

A point of view which assigns maximum importance to American import policy is perhaps best exemplified by the more extreme proponents of the recent "trade not aid" campaign. Their argument appears to be based on the implicit premises (1) that the "dollar shortage" is the major problem of the international economy, and (2) that it results mainly from the failure of the United States to buy enough goods and services from the rest of the non-Soviet world to enable the latter to purchase all of the American products it needs or desires. The abolition or drastic reduction of American tariffs, quotas and other restrictions on the import of foreign goods and services would, on this view, automatically increase the dollar earnings of the rest of the non-Soviet world to a level at which the difficulties of the international economy would soon disappear. Hence, this school of thought tends to regard changes in American import policy as the panacea for the free world's economic problems.[1]

The opposite view is characteristic of the so-called "neutralist" opinion in Western Europe and of the isolationists and protectionists at home. For quite different reasons, both groups believe that the best way to improve the functioning of the international economy would be for the rest of the non-Soviet world to reduce its trade with the United States to the absolute minimum and concentrate instead upon expanding nondollar markets and sources of supply. The American supporters of this view would argue that the import restrictions of the United States contributed in no significant way to the difficulties of the international economy and should, indeed, be increased to encourage other countries to become more independent of the American market as well as to protect the "welfare" of the United States.

The trouble with the opposing views is that each ignores too many im-

1. A much less extreme variant of this view, especially fashionable among economists in the classical tradition, finds the causes of international trade and payments problems primarily in the inflated costs, prices and incomes of other countries and only secondarily in American import barriers. The remedy considered appropriate, though rarely seriously proposed as a practical objective of American policy, is currency devaluation and deliberate deflation of costs and prices by other countries severe enough to reduce their import demand and to stimulate their export sales to the point where a balance could be maintained without quota and currency restrictions. This prescription is not seriously pressed because a deflation severe enough to accomplish its objective would in all likelihood provoke fatal political crises in some countries, would in any event be unacceptable on moral grounds, and would not necessarily even be the most efficient way to make European and Japanese exports more competitive in the world market. Though on this view American import barriers would not be considered major causes of international economic difficulties, neoclassical economic doctrine would also argue for a general reduction of American trade barriers in accordance with the principles of comparative advantage and international specialization.

portant factors. The first overlooks the fact that the dollar shortage is only one aspect or symptom of the economic ill health of many non-Soviet countries, and that the nature of the American economy is a more important obstacle to increased imports into the United States than tariffs, quotas and other deliberate restrictions. The second not only ignores the extent to which the United States is the indispensable residual source of supply of many important raw materials and manufactured goods for the rest of the free world. It is also dangerously indifferent to the importance of growing and mutually beneficial economic relations in maintaining the political and military solidarity of the free countries in the face of the Soviet threat.

A more adequate approach to settling the controversial issues of American foreign economic policy, particularly those of American import policy, would, we believe, have to be based upon a much better understanding (1) of the nature of the difficulties of the contemporary international economy and of their relation to political, social and military factors; and (2) of the way in which the structural characteristics of the American economy affect its demand for imports and help to determine the possible kinds of foreign economic policies which the United States could reasonably be expected to follow. These two lines of empirical investigation are in fact complementary, for the first is directed outward toward analysis of the capabilities and limitations of the contemporary international economy as a whole, while the second is focused inward upon evaluation of the corresponding aspects of the domestic American economy.

The National Planning Association's Committee on International Policy has been fortunate in being able to participate in two fundamental studies along these lines. It has joined with the Woodrow Wilson Foundation in sponsoring a study group of nine businessmen, economists and political scientists who have explored from new perspectives the nature of contemporary international economic problems and their consequences for American foreign economic policy.[2] Earlier, the Committee agreed to examine the implications for American policy of the factual data and economic analysis presented in the import study, and to make recommendations for appropriate changes in American import policies. The International Committee has been impressed by the fact that these two independent investigations, starting in different directions and analyzing opposite aspects of fundamental international economic relationships, have arrived at mutually supporting conclusions.

Before presenting the Committee's analysis of the policy implications of the Twentieth Century Fund's study of American imports, it may be helpful

2. See *The Political Economy of American Foreign Policy: Its Concepts, Strategy and Limits*, Report of a Study Group sponsored by the Woodrow Wilson Foundation and the National Planning Association, Henry Holt and Company, New York, 1955.

to clarify the basis on which the Committee approached its task. In the making of policy recommendations, the interpretation of the relevant factual data influences the choice of economic goals and of the means effective for achieving them. In turn, preconceived evaluations of the relative importance of the political, social and individual interests affected by the choice of economic goals and means inevitably color the interpretation of past events and the estimation of possible future developments. Thus, the making of policy always involves conscious or unconscious judgments of value. The foregoing pages have attempted to make clear the Committee's judgments of the relative importance of the various purposes which the foreign economic policy of the United States should serve. These may be briefly summarized here:

1. As a leader of the non-Soviet world, the United States must, in its own interest and in that of humanity, have a foreign policy which actively and continuously seeks to maintain and extend the freedom and progress of mankind.

2. Foreign economic policy is an inseparable part of foreign policy and constitutes one of the most important means for carrying out this world leadership responsibility of the United States.

3. Foreign economic policy can most effectively and legitimately serve the purposes of American foreign policy by seeking, within the limits set by domestic economic capabilities and political possibilities, to improve the functioning of the international economy and the economic health of other free countries. One of the ways by which these results can be achieved is an appropriate import policy.

II. MAIN CONCLUSIONS DERIVED FROM THE IMPORT STUDY

A study as detailed and comprehensive as that produced for the Twentieth Century Fund by Dr. Don D. Humphrey will directly or indirectly yield several different kinds of conclusions. First, there are conclusions about the facts—what imports were actually made, when, in what quantities, and in what circumstances. Then, there are the conclusions which seek to account for these factual and statistical data, to explain why American import patterns and trends have had the character they did, and how these explanations are derived from, or may necessitate modifications in, the generally accepted body of economic theory. Finally, there are conclusions about the significance of these factual and analytical interpretations for the achievement of human purposes—individual, group, national and international. The latter may be called "policy conclusions" and are the ones with which this statement is mainly concerned. But policy conclusions cannot be

TABLE 77

UNITED STATES GROSS NATIONAL PRODUCT AND IMPORTS, 1929, 1939 AND 1952

	1929	1939	1952
Billions of Current Dollars			
Gross national product	$103.8	$91.3	$348.0
Imports, total	4.4	2.3	10.7
Imports of finished manufactures	1.0	.4	2.1
Index Based on Current Dollars (1929 = 100)			
Gross national product	100	88	335
Imports, total	100	52	244
Imports of finished manufactures	100	44	211
Index of Quantity (1929 = 100)			
Gross national product	100	106	200
Imports, total	100	82	133
Imports of finished manufactures	100	70	118

considered in isolation from the other two types of conclusions. Accordingly, this section will summarize the main conclusions of fact and interpretation stated or implied in the study which have important implications for the import policy of the United States.

A. Historical Trends in American Imports

While the quantity of American imports has increased over the past quarter century, it has grown less rapidly than the gross national product of the United States. In other words, the quantity of imports has declined as a proportion of the gross national product. (See Table 77 for a comparison of these rates of growth.)

In the main, this lag of imports behind gross national product reflects certain characteristic trends in the American economy—increasing industrialization, growing efficiency, and gradual substitution of domestically produced synthetic materials for imported natural ones.[3] Increasing industrialization means that imports will consist more and more of raw and semiprocessed materials; growing efficiency means greater economy in the use of raw and semiprocessed materials in terms both of quantity and of price. As the gross national product rises, the consumption of raw materials rises less than proportionately. Hence, imports, which consist increasingly of raw materials, will also grow less than proportionately.

The historical data presented in the study reveal these trends most clearly. Throughout the nineteenth century, the bulk of American imports consisted of finished manufactures. About the turn of the century, imports

3. The import study also shows that part of the relative decline of imports has been due to the growing importance of services in the gross national product.

TABLE 78
MERCHANDISE IMPORTS BY ECONOMIC CLASS, SELECTED YEARS, 1821–1952

Year or Yearly Average	Total	Crude Materials	Semi-manu-factures	Finished Manu-factures	Manu-factured Foodstuffs	Crude Foodstuffs
Millions of Current Dollars						
1821	$ 55	$ 3	$ 4	$ 31	$ 11	$ 6
1850	174	13	26	95	21	18
1871–1880	535	92	70	177	111	86
1901–1910	1,158	395	201	287	139	137
1929	4,399	1,559	885	994	424	539
1952	10,745	2,935	2,567	2,093	1,081	2,068
Percentage Distribution						
1821	100	4.7	7.5	56.9	19.8	11.2
1850	100	7.2	15.1	54.9	12.4	10.4
1871–1880	100	17.2	13.0	33.0	20.7	16.0
1901–1910	100	34.1	17.3	24.8	12.0	11.8
1929	100	35.4	20.1	22.6	9.6	12.2
1952	100	27.3	23.9	19.5	10.1	19.2

Sources: *Historical Statistics of the United States, 1789–1945*, and *Statistical Abstract of the United States, 1953*.

Note: Components may not add to totals because of rounding.

of crude and semiprocessed materials surpassed finished manufactures and have continued to increase their lead ever since, rising very rapidly during the first quarter of the twentieth century and more slowly during the second quarter. In recent years, semiprocessed industrial materials appear to be the most rapidly growing category of imports. Crude material imports have not increased as fast, owing in part to the displacement of formerly imported raw materials by domestically produced synthetics (rubber, natural fibers and fertilizers, etc.) and in part to the encouragement of higher cost domestic production during and since World War II for reasons of national security. (See Table 78.)

These general shifts in the composition of imports have been accompanied by an acceleration of the tendency for the imports of a smaller and smaller number of commodities to account for a larger and larger proportion of total imports. Over the past twenty-five years, the aggregate increase in the value of the imports of eight commodities has been about equal to the total increase in imports.[4] These eight commodities are (in order of their rates of increase in recent years): coffee, nonferrous metals, newsprint and woodpulp, petroleum and products, manufactured wool, machinery and vehicles, watches and clocks, and industrial diamonds. In

4. This does not mean that only these eight commodities have increased. It means that the declines in the imports of certain commodities were sufficient to offset the growth in the imports of all other commodities except the eight noted above.

TABLE 79

CYCLICAL CHANGES IN UNITED STATES PRODUCTION OF FINISHED COMMODITIES
AND IN MERCHANDISE IMPORTS, 1920–1938

(*Per Cent*)

Period	Domestic Production[a]	Merchandise Imports
	Constant Prices	
1920–1921	−6	−15
1921–1929	+57	+77
1929–1933	−30	−34
1933–1937	+44	+50
1937–1938	−12	−29
	Current Prices	
1920–1921	−32	−53
1921–1929	+49	+77
1929–1933	−52	−67
1933–1937	+74	+108
1937–1938	b	b

Source: Based on Table 11. The output series in Table 11 is based on Simon Kuznets' estimates of finished commodity output at producers' prices as published in *Commodity Flow and Capital Formation*, Vol. I, National Bureau of Economic Research, New York, 1938. Kuznets' estimates, which run through 1933, were extended to 1939 on the basis of estimates by William H. Shaw and unofficial data from the Commerce Department. Data for later years are not given because of the lack of conceptually comparable output data.

a. Finished commodity output at producers' prices.

b. Not available.

consequence of this trend toward concentration, the twelve commodities imported in the largest amounts (by value) accounted for 64 per cent of total American imports in 1952 compared with only 43 per cent in 1929. (See Table 5, p. 35.)

Finally, the historical series presented in the study confirm the generally held impression that, in periods of declining economic activity, the value and volume of American imports have fallen more than domestic production. In periods of economic expansion, the prices of imports tend to rise more rapidly than do domestic prices. (See Table 79.)

B. Factors Determining the Composition and Level of Imports

The foregoing changes in the composition, volume and value of American imports are the resultants of two sets of factors—those operating within the American economy to determine the pattern and level of demand for imports, and those operating in the international economy to determine the willingness and ability of foreign producers to meet this demand.

1. The Nature of the American Economy

Of all these factors, internal and external, the one which has had by far the most massive influence is the nature of the American economy itself. As already noted, the American economy is of continental size, has a favorable ratio of population to natural resources, and has enjoyed a balanced economic growth. Indeed, it is simultaneously the largest producer of industrial and of primary commodities in the non-Soviet world and, except possibly for Canada, has the highest rate of growth of productivity.

These structural characteristics are in part the results of the entrepreneurial vigor of American producers and of the freedom of enterprise implicit in the values and institutions of American society. In turn, the continental size and balance of the American economy has helped to preserve its freedom and vigor. Most sectors of American industry (and to a lesser extent parts of American agriculture) find the competitive stimuli and the expanding market opportunities necessary to maintain a satisfactory rate of productivity growth within the American economy itself—the largest, wealthiest and most competitive domestic market in the world. In consequence, growing mass production for rising mass consumption is the distinctive feature of contemporary American economic life.

Today, no other industrial country enjoys the beneficial effects on its entrepreneurial vigor and rate of productivity growth of a domestic market remotely approaching that of the United States in size, balance, dynamism or competitive intensity.[5] As a result, in those sectors of the American economy characterized by mass production for mass consumption—by a very wide margin the largest and most rapidly growing portion of our gross national product—imported commodities are generally not competitive with domestically produced goods either in price or in the equally important nonprice aspects of competition (product design, styling and merchandizing, sales effort, delivery, servicing, terms of payment, etc.).[6] The bulk of American imports—over 70 per cent—consists of tropical agricultural products and of raw and semiprocessed industrial materials not available in the United States or not produced here in sufficient volume. Such commodities are, however, only a small fraction—2 to 3 per cent—of the total goods and services of all kinds consumed by Americans. Beyond these

5. Except for Canada, whose domestic market is in many respects an extension of the American, the domestic markets of the other industrial countries are too small and rigidified, and the international economy is too incalculable and unexpansive, to provide them with the competitive stimuli and the increased market opportunities which are among the conditions necessary for maintaining adequate rates of growth of productivity. This is one of the major reasons for the economic difficulties of Western Europe and Japan.

6. There are exceptions, of course, which will be noted below, but these are small relative both to total imports and to total American demand for such products.

small necessary imports, the overwhelming portion of the vast quantities of goods bought and sold in the American market are bound to be the products of domestic factories, mines and fields.

In sum, the American economy is in the paradoxical position of being, on the one hand, the world's largest importing nation in terms of the absolute value of the goods and services it buys abroad and, on the other hand, only a very minor importer relative to the total value of the goods and services it consumes. By its nature, the American economy in the aggregate is only very marginally dependent upon foreign trade. In recent years, exports have averaged a mere 4 to 5 per cent of gross national product and imports somewhat less. Thus, the pattern and level of American imports are mainly determined by the structural characteristics of the American economy—its size, balance, growth and competitive ability—and the influence of legislatively or administratively imposed barriers against imports is, by comparison, insignificant. Indeed, depending upon their magnitude and duration, the cyclical fluctuations in national employment and income, to which any dynamic free enterprise economy is susceptible, may have a greater effect upon imports than existing tariff and quota restrictions.

2. The Tariff

Within the relatively narrow limits on potential imports set by these structural characteristics of the American economy, the tariff has probably had the greatest effect on the actual pattern and level of trade. From 1865 to 1934, the general trend of tariff rates was upward, except for brief reversals during the administrations of Grover Cleveland and Woodrow Wilson. In the twenty years since the initiation of the Reciprocal Trade Agreements Program, the general trend has been toward lower and lower rates. (See Table 19, p. 74.)

Attempts to assess the effects of specific tariff acts on the level of imports are difficult owing to the fact that the tariff is only one of the many factors involved. After examining the available evidence for the period 1865–1934 in considerable detail, the import study concludes:

Short-term changes in the value of imports appear to correlate more closely with prosperity and depression than with changes in the tariff. With the possible exception of the Dingley tariff, the changes in duties which began in 1872 did not decisively reduce the over-all importance of imports in relation to domestic output. In this respect, the McKinley tariff of 1890 seemed to have had no important effect. Similarly, there is little evidence of a decisive change in the relative importance of total imports due to changes in the tariff during the first three decades of the twentieth century. *Tariff levels were not the controlling factor in determining the over-all importance of imports.*

For the period since 1934, when the Reciprocal Trade Agreements Program was started, the evidence is even more difficult to evaluate and its interpretation is highly controversial. The qualified conclusions reached in the study cannot be accurately summarized and hence will be repeated here in full:

First, all experience shows that American imports increase more rapidly than home production in periods of rapid expansion. Yet the quantity of imports rose less than 4 per cent in the twenty years 1929–1949, a period in which real gross national product increased by two thirds. In part as a result of the war in Korea, the quantity of imports increased 20 per cent from 1949 to 1951 while real gross national product increased 16 per cent. The increase in imports after 1946 includes substantial inventories for the stockpiling of strategic materials.

Second, efforts to check the specific items which might be expected to increase most as a result of tariff reductions have turned up relatively few instances where imports have increased faster than domestic production. More important, domestic producers themselves are alert to competition from imports. Requests for relief under the escape clause provide a good indication of the relative unimportance of the industries where imports have increased faster than domestic production as a result of tariff concessions. Escape clause proceedings show only three "industries" which had been seriously injured as of June 30, 1952: (1) women's fur felt hats, (2) hatters' fur, and (3) dried figs. Imports of filberts and almonds were also found injurious to domestic marketing programs. Up to January 1955, the escape clause was also invoked on alsike clover seed and watch movements.

The President has declined to invoke the escape clause, as recommended by the Tariff Commission, on garlic, tobacco pipes, scissors and shears, groundfish fillets, lead and zinc, handblown glassware, spring clothespins, screen-printed silk scarves and screws.

Imports of certain agricultural products on which tariffs were reduced are restricted by quota; otherwise, some of these imports would have increased substantially, in part as a result of tariff concession, but also as a result of growth of population and incomes.

Compared with prosperous prewar years, the quantity of imports has fallen drastically in relation to national product. It may be, of course, that without tariff concessions the relative decline would have been still greater. But the overwhelming weight of evidence is that the increase in America's trade as a result of tariff reduction has been in no way commensurate with the magnitude of the undertaking.

Nonetheless, the comprehensive reduction of duties (1) by about 50 per cent as a result of tariff concessions, and (2) by a like amount as a result of rising prices, may produce more substantial results in the future, particularly if a high rate of internal growth is maintained and business fluctuations are moderated. *In time, it is probable that the dynamic changes in relative costs will produce an increase in imports if the present level of duties is held and if unemployment can be avoided.* This may not be possible, however, under the escape clause.

In sum, though reductions in tariff rates have been substantial, the increase in imports of the commodities on which rates have been reduced has been quite small. In the main, the effect of rate reduction to date has been to eliminate the *excess* protection in the tariff structure—excess protection either originally embodied in the Hawley-Smoot Tariff Act of 1930, or generated subsequently by changes in general price levels and in the relative costs and prices of competitive foreign and domestic goods. Therefore, reduction of the rates not yet cut under the Trade Agreements Program and further reduction of rates already cut are the only ways by which tariff liberalization is likely to increase imports significantly.

3. The Non-Tariff Obstacles to Imports

In addition to tariffs, there have been other types of legislative and administrative obstacles to imports. These include import quotas and subsidies for domestic production;[7] customs regulations and practices; discriminatory excise taxes; "Buy American" legislation; food, drug, sanitary, and plant and animal health regulations; state and local building and other codes; copyright and patent laws; and private restrictive arrangements and discriminatory actions. Import quotas and customs regulations and practices are by far the most important. As in the case of the tariff, it is difficult to evaluate their effects on imports. Though the impact of these non-tariff restrictions may never be accurately measured, their importance cannot be doubted.

4. Factors Influencing the Ability and Willingness of Foreign Producers to Export to the United States

The structural characteristics of the American economy, and deliberately imposed trade barriers, operate either to restrict American demand for imports or to reduce the ability and willingness of foreign producers to export to the American market, or, usually, in both ways.

The superior competitive ability of most branches of American industry in the domestic market (and in many foreign markets as well) reflects, as we have seen, the disparities between the rates of productivity growth and the entrepreneurial motivations of the American economy and those of other industrial economies. For European producers to become more competitive with American producers over significantly wider areas of the American market requires an acceleration of their rates of productivity growth and an intensification of their entrepreneurial vigor. But increased competitive stimuli and expanding market opportunities, which are among the necessary preconditions for such changes, are not likely to be found either in the existing small and rigidified domestic markets of the European countries or in the present relatively unexpansive international market, with its high degree of incalculability and restrictiveness. Thus, the effects of the structural characteristics of the American economy on the American demand for

---

7. For example, import quotas on agricultural products and subsidies for shipbuilding and operation, etc. A subsidy to a domestic producer which enables him to reduce his selling price has an effect similar to that of a protective tariff rate.

imports parallel and reinforce the effects of the structural characteristics of European and other economies on the ability of their producers to export to the American market.[8]

The competitive ability and entrepreneurial vigor of many foreign producers tend to be further impaired by the effects of tariff and other deliberate trade barriers in the United States. Even where goods are not absolutely excluded by tariff rates or import quotas, customs regulations and procedures may effectively discourage foreign exporters from making the effort and incurring the risks of attempting to enter the American market or of expanding their share of it. In many cases, it is not so much the restrictive effect of existing trade barriers as the fear that barriers would be raised in the future which deters foreign businessmen from investing the substantial amounts of energy and capital necessary to develop an American market for their products and to expand their own production accordingly. For experience has taught them that if they successfully introduce a new product into the United States, or substantially expand their share of the American market for an old product, changes in the tariff or in other forms of import restrictions may soon make continuation of their new export business impossible. Hence, foreign producers and exporters are unlikely to risk the investment required for increasing their exports to the United States unless they have greater confidence in the stability of American import policy.

C. Factors Affecting Future Import Growth

In the past, the major factor operating to increase American imports has been the growth of the American economy. There can be little doubt that, over the long term, depletion of natural resources, increase in population, or continued rise in living standards would singly or in combination generate substantial increases in crude and semiprocessed materials imports even without any change in American import policies. The President's Materials Policy Commission (Paley Commission) has estimated that, by 1975, the population of the United States might grow by 27 per cent, the gross national product might be doubled, and industrial raw materials imports might increase from $860 million in 1950 to $3 billion in 1975, or by 250 per cent. Increased population or rising living standards or both could also be expected to result in corresponding increases in nonindustrial raw materials imports, e.g., coffee, cocoa, other tropical foodstuffs, etc. Thus, the best prospects for steady, substantial and virtually

---

8. Ignoring these fundamental structural factors is largely responsible for the fallacy in the argument that the major problems of the international economy could be overcome by practicable American actions designed to balance the external economic relations of the United States at a high and rising level of trade.

automatic increases in imports are raw and semiprocessed industrial materials and tropical agricultural products.

However, continuation of the trend toward increased concentration of imports among a few commodities would seem to qualify to some extent the prospect for a steady, automatic growth of raw materials imports. Technological advance may at any time eliminate or drastically reduce the demand for one of the few remaining categories of major imports, as it did in the case of silk, rubber, natural fertilizers and tin. Indeed, the import study shows that, despite the depletion of American mineral resources, gross imports of minerals increased no more rapidly than the gross national product or than domestic production of minerals during the period 1929–1949. Technological innovation and substitution played a large part in this result. Changes in popular taste for consumer goods could indirectly have similar inhibiting effects on raw materials imports.

With respect to future imports of manufactured goods, there seems no reason to believe that they will ever again constitute the largest category of imports, or that their proportion of total imports will grow appreciably, or even that it will cease to decline. Several considerations combine to support this conclusion.

The *first* relates to the newer and most rapidly growing branches of industry. The sectors of the American market in which per capita domestic demand is increasing most rapidly are, with certain exceptions, the sectors in which tariff protection and other import restrictions do not exist or are of minor importance. These are the dynamic sectors of the American economy, characterized by mass production methods, rapid technological advance, enormous sales efforts, etc. Today (and increasingly in the future) the products of these industries make up the largest proportion of American consumption of manufactures, not only producers' goods but virtually all of the newer forms of consumer goods (e.g., electrical, mechanical and electronic consumer durables, synthetics, plastics, etc.). These are precisely the fields in which the manufacturers of other industrial countries have the most difficulty in competing with American producers, not only in the American market but in many foreign markets where demand for such products is also rising more rapidly than for the older types of manufactures. Moreover, as we have seen, the American competitive advantage is not limited to price; indeed, other factors may more than offset occasionally higher American prices. These other factors include: more varied and modern designs, more aggressive sales efforts, shorter delivery dates, ability to supply larger quantities, more favorable credit terms, prompter and more satisfactory servicing of products and provision of replacement parts, greater "prestige" value of American products, etc. These competitive disparities between American goods and those of other industrial nations are the results of the differences in the structural characteristics and the entrepreneurial attitudes of the countries involved. No practicable changes in American import policies could by themselves overcome the competitive disadvantages of European and Japanese goods in most of these newer lines of production, for which both American and world demand is growing most rapidly, and which already supply the overwhelming proportion of the manufactured products sold in the American market.

There are, of course, notable exceptions to this generalization about American competitive superiority in the newer industrial fields. Among mass-produced products in which foreign manufacturers can compete with American may be mentioned bicycles, small automobiles, baby carriages, small sewing machines, and several other commodities described in the import study. In addition, there are a number of other producers' goods not mass-produced in which the Europeans appear to enjoy a comparative advantage, for example, some of the organic chemicals which cannot be manufactured by the continuous production method but must be produced in small, carefully controlled batches. Another type of producers' goods in which European manufacturers seem to enjoy a major competitive advantage is heavy electrical generating equipment. These products, too, are not mass-produced nor are most of their components mass-produced; they are specialty items, tailor-made for particular installations, and their labor component is large. However, in the aggregate, all of these exceptions are too small to qualify significantly the conclusion that American manufacturers enjoy competitive advantages in the general field of mass-produced capital and consumer goods.

The *second* set of considerations relates to the older branches of industry and of world trade. In general, these are the sectors in which the producers of the other industrial countries enjoy a comparative advantage over those of the United States. Two types of goods may be distinguished in this category. The first, and smallest, consists of manufactures (and specialty foodstuffs and beverages) whose sale in the United States is relatively easy because of the absence of domestically produced goods of similar kind or quality; because of long-standing consumer preferences unaffected by price competition, e.g., "snob appeal"; and because of other nonprice considerations. In the main, these are luxury products which, by their nature, can never enjoy a mass market. Hence, the total volume of such goods sold in the United States is, and will always be, very small relative both to total American imports and to the dollar needs of the exporting countries.

The largest and most important type of goods in the category of older industrial products consists of imported manufactures (and specialty foodstuffs and beverages) which, in the absence of tariff protection, would tend to have comparative advantages over domestic goods and which in any event do compete directly with them. Most of these are consumer goods, such as textiles, leather products, ceramics and glass products, cutlery, optical goods, watches and clocks, etc. With certain exceptions, these are the products for which per capita domestic demand has been growing least rapidly and in some cases has actually been declining. Technological advance has been relatively slow in some of these industries, many of which tend to be labor-intensive rather than capital-intensive. Consumers' preferences have been changing.

It would, however, be a mistake to conclude that competitive disadvantage is without exception characteristic of all the American industries producing commodities of this type. In some industries the generalization is uniformly true—the handblown glass industry is perhaps the classic case. But in others, it is true in varying degrees of many, not necessarily all, of the particular branches of the industry and of individual producers within each branch. For example, the American textile industry is in the aggregate probably the most advanced in the world in terms of technological innovation, product design, managerial competence and labor efficiency. Important and rapidly growing sectors of it find no difficulty in competing with foreign products not only in the home market but even abroad, e.g., synthetic fibers; new mixtures, weaves and designs immediately reflecting rapidly changing consumers' preferences; many types of industrial textiles, etc. Even in the American woolen and worsted industries, major technological changes have been occurring in the last few years. In general, it is precisely those branches of the textile industry and those individual producers within these branches that have lagged furthest behind the industry as a whole or their domestic competitors that have also been most strongly affected by foreign competition.

Even when these qualifications have been taken into account, it is nonetheless true that, in the aggregate, these less expansive—and in some cases, stagnant—sectors of the American market make up a much smaller and relatively declining component of total American consumption than do the more expansive or buoyant sectors, and that they tend, to a greater or lesser degree, to have a competitive disadvantage as compared with certain foreign producers. Thus, it is not an accident that these are precisely the sectors of the American market in which tariff and other import barriers are most formidable.

In the light of the foregoing analysis, it is clear that a dilemma exists with respect to the problem of increasing American imports of manufactured goods. On the one hand, in the largest and most rapidly growing sectors of the American market, tariff and other protective restrictions are relatively unimportant, but foreign goods are generally not competitive with domestically produced goods. On the other hand, in the smallest sector of the

American market—where foreign manufactures tend to have, and are likely to continue to have, comparative advantages—demand is growing more slowly, if at all, and import barriers are a formidable obstacle. Any policy designed substantially to increase imports of manufactured goods must find some way of resolving this dilemma.

III. THE IMPLICATIONS FOR POLICY OF THESE CONCLUSIONS

The main conclusions of the study, summarized in the preceding section, have important implications for the foreign economic policy of the United States with respect both to the objectives of policy and to the means appropriate for achieving them.

We have stated in Section I the reasons for our conviction that the general purposes of American foreign economic policy are to work toward a more effectively functioning international economy and a decisive improvement in the economic health of many of its national economies. These objectives cannot be accomplished automatically by relying upon the long-term growth of the American economy to balance the external economic accounts of the United States at a high enough level of trade. Moreover, we have outlined our reasons for rejecting the view either that the external trade and payments of the United States are likely to be balanced at so high a level in the foreseeable future, or that this objective, if it could be achieved, would indeed overcome the economic difficulties of the rest of the non-Soviet world, particularly of the other industrial nations.[9]

But, while high, rising and better-balanced American external trade and payments are not the panacea for the free world's economic problems, they are nevertheless among the necessary and desirable preconditions for the achievement of economic health by many non-Soviet countries and for the more effective functioning of the international economy as a whole. Thus, the question is not whether we should strive to balance the trade and payments of the United States at a high and rising level, but to what extent, and by what means, is it possible to make significant progress toward this objective in the foreseeable future.

The maintenance of steady growth and reasonable stability in the American economy as a whole is an indispensable means for achieving the objectives of American foreign policy. As we have already noted, American economic growth would make a greater quantitative contribution to the

9. For the so-called "dollar shortage" is merely a symptom or result of certain structural inconsistencies and functional maladjustments in the international economy. It often helps to perpetuate these difficulties, but a reduction or even temporary disappearance of the dollar shortage does not mean that basic problems have been overcome or have vanished of their own accord. We cannot here even begin to describe the broad outlines of these more fundamental problems, which are not solely economic but are also political, social and moral in their causes and consequences. Exploration of them forms the subject of a separate NPA study. (See footnote 2 on page 498.)

expansion of foreign trade than any conceivable changes in American policies. Conversely, in its absence, attempts to liberalize American import policy would be more and more futile. We must also stress our view that one of the essential conditions for an effective American foreign policy is the prevention of depressions in the American economy.

Policies which more directly seek increased and better-balanced American participation in the international economy must perforce be actively concerned with the development of American imports. As the preceding section has made clear, the greatest obstacle to increased imports into the United States is the disparity between the structural characteristics of the American economy and those of the countries which have the most need to expand their trade with us. These "structural" discrepancies set narrow limits upon the possible increases in imports that might result from the reduction of other kinds of obstacles which changes in policies could immediately and directly accomplish.

Though the quantitative increases in imports achievable by policy changes are small compared with total domestic production of goods and services, they are nevertheless worthwhile when measured against the dollar earnings and needs of many of the countries which could be expected to expand their markets in the United States if deliberate trade barriers were permanently reduced. Moreover, the significance for American foreign policy of a reduction of tariff and other import restrictions cannot be evaluated solely, or even mainly, in quantitative economic terms. Indeed, the qualitative political and psychological effects of a lowering of American import barriers are in themselves of sufficient importance to justify a substantial effort toward this objective. The reasons may be summarized as follows:

1. A reduction of American trade barriers would be one of the most effective means for counteracting the Soviet economic offensive against the free world and for cementing more strongly the unity of the free countries. Recent shifts in Soviet economic policies, particularly the apparent willingness to purchase larger quantities of manufactured goods from the other industrial countries of the free world, underscore the importance of making access to the American market easier and more calculable for our allies and friends abroad. Even if no concrete trade benefits for the latter result from current Soviet tactics, it is nevertheless most undesirable to provide plausible grounds for Soviet propaganda which seeks to create the impression that the Russian economy is a prospectively better trading partner for the non-Soviet world than is the American economy.

2. Apart from the Soviet economic offensive, there are other strong political and psychological reasons why a reduction of American import

barriers would be desirable. Rightly or wrongly, our major allies in Europe and many of our best friends among the independent underdeveloped countries have convinced themselves that liberalization of American import policy is today the major test of American economic leadership in the free world. Moreover, a permanent reduction of import barriers may help to encourage European and other producers to undertake the investments required to expand their exports and to improve their competitive positions not only in the American market but throughout the international economy.

3. Finally, reduction of import barriers would benefit the American economy itself—domestic producers as well as consumers. If we wish convincingly to expound to the rest of the world the view that one of the evils of continued foreign discrimination against American goods is that it fosters high-cost, stagnant economies abroad, we must be willing to apply the same logic to the relatively less expansive sectors of our own domestic economy.

Enabling the other industrial countries to expand their exports to the United States means, as we have seen, removal or reduction of precisely those barriers which restrict the importation of the manufactured goods in which foreign producers tend to have a comparative advantage over domestic producers. Thus, changes in American import policy likely to increase imports would be bound to affect some domestic producers adversely. Many of these domestic producers are concentrated in a small number of industries. Often these industries, or the segments of them most likely to be hurt by increased imports, are in turn concentrated in certain local communities and regions where their contribution to local employment and income is out of proportion to their contribution to American national income as a whole. Hence, the reduction of protective barriers will involve a concentration of damage, small in the aggregate, but severe for affected businessmen, farmers and workers, and for the communities in which they happen to be important—sometimes the only—producers and consumers.

Many of these industries and communities have already been suffering from the competition of lower-cost domestic producers in other parts of the country, and from other competitive uses of consumers' incomes. Since their capacity for self-adjustment to such domestic changes in competitive conditions and in consumers' preferences has been so small, increased foreign competition would further complicate the adjustment problems they already face. If economically and socially undesirable results are not to occur, it will be necessary to help these depressed industries and communities undertake the required adjustments.

Facilitating the adjustment of affected industries and communities to increased foreign competition is necessary and desirable not only on humanitarian grounds; if the reduction of import barriers is to be substantial enough to be worthwhile, facilitating these adjustments will be necessary for political reasons as well. The domestic interest groups involved—business, farm and labor—are well organized and strong, and wield considerable political influence, particularly compared with consumers generally, importers, and other direct beneficiaries of lower-cost or increased imports. Hence, it is unrealistic to expect that any significant reductions can be made in import barriers unless alternative means can be found for meeting the legitimate needs of these groups.

IV. The Requirements of a Program of Action

It is clear that if a substantial reduction of import restrictions is to be achieved, two types of actions will be needed. These are (1) measures for easing or forestalling the adverse effects of such reductions on American employers, employees and local communities; and (2) effective changes in existing legislation, executive powers and administrative procedures relating to the tariff and other forms of restrictive devices.

A. Facilitating the Adjustment to Increased Imports

Two methods have generally been suggested by which domestic producers could be helped to adjust to the effects of reductions in import barriers. The first is by direct payments to producers (both employers and employees), either as continuing subsidies to enable firms to remain in business, or as compensation for losses incurred by firms in liquidating their businesses and by workers in obtaining new employment. The second method is by "depressed industries and communities programs" which would involve federal support of local and state initiative in helping certain industries and communities to adjust to adverse changes in their economic environment arising from any cause, or set of causes, and of such magnitude as to be beyond their own capacity for self-adjustment without undesirable economic or social consequences.

Widespread use of the method of direct federal subsidy or compensation is definitely undesirable for a variety of reasons. Subsidies ostensibly given for the purpose of enabling an industry to continue operations for a transitional period while it adjusts to increased competition tend instead to be used indefinitely to offset the higher production costs of relatively uneconomic methods, thereby forestalling precisely those changes which the subsidy is supposed to facilitate. If the payments are intended to compensate for actual or prospective damage, major practical difficulties will be encountered in trying either to relate the loss of profits or assets to any single cause, or to measure its quantitative effects. For these reasons, as well as for the undesirable political consequences of subsidy programs, it would be well to limit direct subsidies to those industries which have to be maintained for national security purposes. Even in this case, however, the use of long-term purchase contracts would be preferable. Where such contracts cannot be used and a continuing direct subsidy is the only remaining means available, federal subsidies could perhaps be held to a minimum if they were made an integral part of the Defense Department's portion of the national budget and not an unrelated civilian item.

With this exception, the main reliance for facilitating adjustments to increased imports should be placed on programs for transforming depressed industries and communities which originate at the industry, local or state level and are effectively supplemented by the federal government in various ways. The importance of local initiative and control should not be underestimated either for political reasons or as a practical matter. Unless the people directly affected are willing and able to assume some of the responsibility for making necessary changes, there is little that can be done for them from the outside except indefinite subsidization, which only perpetuates their plight.

It is also clear that, in many cases, local and state resources will be insufficient for the task of economic transformation or relocation. Several federal agencies already have responsibilities and powers which are relevant to the problems involved in readjustment programs. But local programs are now receiving very little active assistance from the federal government. In some cases, this is due to lack of funds; in others, it results from inadequate interest and ingenuity on the part of the federal agencies concerned. Even without a broadening of existing federal functions, much more could be done to assist local programs than is now being undertaken by federal agencies.

In addition to the provision of adequate unemployment benefits, there are various appropriate ways in which the federal government could assist local readjustment programs. Federal aid to local and state readjustment agencies could be provided in the form of grants for the retraining of labor; for meeting workers' costs of moving to new locations where employment is available; for research into the possibilities of diversifying the industries of individual communities and regions, and improving technology and managerial skills, etc. Federal loan funds might be made available to state and local development authorities for such purposes as the building of new plants, and the modernization of old ones, for sale or rental to private companies; the construction of needed transportation, power and other public utilities, etc. Finally, low-interest federal loan funds and accelerated amortization certificates might be given directly to business firms willing to undertake costly readaptations which would have a reasonable chance of making their operations profitable in the changed competitive situation.

The effectiveness of federal support for such programs will depend directly upon the principles governing the use of federal funds. Federal benefits available to private persons, state government organizations and local communities should generally be for the purpose of paying part of the cost of readjustment, and not as compensation for injury. Where benefits are granted, they should normally be contingent upon evidence that the readjustment is actually being made. Finally, the federal government should always require the presentation of a plan or program developed on local initiative, for without adequate local interest in self-help, federal efforts are unlikely to accomplish positive improvements, though they would certainly help to ameliorate distress.

The development of long-term readjustment programs by depressed industries and communities, and adequate federal assistance in carrying them out, will foster not only the growth and stability of the American economy but the foreign policy of the United States as well. In cases where the difficulties of a depressed industry or community result wholly or in part from changes in import policies, a vigorous readjustment program could provide the increment of energy and resources needed to make an affected domestic industry more efficient or to enable affected businessmen and workers to shift to other activities or locations. General recognition that the private groups and the local, state and federal agencies concerned were willing and able to cooperate in the formulation and execution of such programs would help to mitigate the objections of many businessmen, workers and farmers to significant reductions in American import barriers.

B. Reducing American Import Barriers

A worthwhile and practicable program for reducing American import barriers must strike a balance between two opposing requirements. To be worthwhile, the reductions must be substantial enough actually to increase imports; to be practicable, they must not be so drastic as to create insuperable political obstacles. Harmonizing these requirements is not always an easy task. The political difficulties may be eased if it is clear from the beginning that import barriers will be reduced only gradually; that, for many commodities, differential degrees of protection will still remain which will reflect as far as possible the relative competitive positions of American and foreign products; and that effective readjustment efforts will be vigorously supported for those industries and communities adversely affected by tariff cuts. At the same time, it must also be emphasized that every economy has marginal industries and every industry has marginal producers; that the marginal industries and producers have no inherent right to protection against competition, domestic or foreign; and that a valid case for continued or increased protection of them can be made only if important national or humanitarian interests are involved which cannot be satisfied by more desirable means. Finally, it must be recognized that the reduction of import barriers will necessitate internal economic adjustments which would obviously be easier to make in conditions of full employment than when significant portions of the labor force and of the nation's productive capacity are unemployed.

The determination of the specific reductions to be made, and their timing, requires a careful and dispassionate weighing of the national and private interests involved. If the objectivity and flexibility needed for this purpose are to be ensured, the primary responsibility for decision and action should remain where it has been for the past twenty years—with the President, acting under authorization of the Congress and in accordance with general policies specified by it.

None of the official and semiofficial studies of import policies in recent years has involved a thorough examination of the existing structure of import restrictions for the purpose of evaluating the need for, and effectiveness of, its individual items in terms of the valid national and private interests concerned. The existing tariff rates and classifications are the results of a quarter of a century of piecemeal reductions from an original pattern which intervening economic changes have in any event long since rendered obsolete. Before major decisions about further tariff reductions are made, a thorough reappraisal of the existing tariff structure, and an analysis of possible and desirable reductions, should be undertaken by a responsible government body on the basis of principles which provide adequate guidance through the various conflicting considerations of national policy—foreign and domestic, economic and defense—involved in lowering of import barriers.

Accordingly, we suggest that the President formally appoint a top-level interdepartmental committee which should make a detailed and comprehensive study along the foregoing lines and should recommend specific reductions in import barriers to the President. Both the President and the interdepartmental committee should be guided by general principles—some of which are suggested below—which might be formulated and approved by the Congress. The committee should be composed of representatives from all executive departments concerned with foreign policy and domestic economic affairs, including the Department of Labor, and should be authorized to call upon the Tariff Commission and other government agencies for the necessary factual studies.

The effectiveness of the committee's work will depend not only upon the competence and good judgment of its members but also upon the principles which guide its decisions. The major objective of the committee should be to determine the maximum specific reductions in import barriers consistent with national security and the maintenance of vigor and stability in the American economy. But, in examining individual industries and products, the committee should not only assess their importance to the national defense and the national economy; it must also keep in mind the extent to which competitive imports can help to stimulate improvements by domestic industries in productive efficiency, in the variety and design of their products, and in their prices and sales practices.

In recommending reductions in tariff rates and liberalization of other import restrictions, the committee should give urgent attention to those branches of existing industries, and to the specific products, in which there have been, or are likely to be, long-term declines in demand, capacity or employment, or in which there is evidence that producers are already being adversely affected by increased imports. Special consideration for transitional periods would be appropriate in those cases where alternative employment opportunities are not readily available either locally or in other convenient places. However, except where national security must be the major consideration, even temporary maintenance of existing restrictions should not generally be favored if they would encourage the production of goods or the rendering of services which are not now provided by domestic producers in significant volume and which are being, or could be, provided by imports.

If Presidential action pursuant to the committee's recommendations is actually to result in increased imports, the Congress will have to broaden the President's authority to reduce import barriers, particularly tariff rates. As explained in Section II, B-2, a substantial expansion of imports through changes in the tariff can be achieved only by a further lowering of rates already reduced and by a lowering of rates not yet reduced. The reason is that the reductions hitherto made under the Reciprocal Trade Agreements Program have, with certain exceptions, merely eliminated the excess protection embodied in the Tariff Act of 1930 or generated by economic changes over the past twenty-five years. Hence, if imports are to be increased through tariff liberalization, the President will have to be empowered to make further substantial cuts in tariff rates already reduced. In addition, the "peril point amendment" will have to be abolished, and the "escape clause" at least modified along the lines indicated below, to enable the President effectively to use his existing authority to cut those rates not yet reduced under the Reciprocal Trade Agreements Program.

There is both a feasible maximum and a worthwhile minimum to possible changes in the legislation governing import restrictions. These limits can be illustrated by the respective recommendations of two recent official bodies—the February 1953 Report of the Public Advisory Board for Mutual Security (the Bell Committee), and the January 1954 Report of the Commission on Foreign Economic Policy (the Randall Commission).

The Bell Committee's recommendations represent the maximum reductions likely to be politically feasible in the foreseeable future. These include:

(1) The adoption of the concept of the national interest as the guiding principle of import policy in place of the necessity of avoiding injury to particular domestic industries or groups—a change which the Bell Committee believed would necessitate abolition of the escape clause and the peril point amendment.

(2) The preparation of a new simplified tariff providing for general reduction of duties and eliminating present uncertainties in the classification of goods by consolidating the many hundreds of present tariff rates into seven basic schedules—a Free List; four groupings of commodities bearing duties of 10, 20, 30, and 40 per cent ad valorem; a Specific List for basic agricultural and mineral raw materials; and an Extraordinary List where commodities might be placed whose importation, for security or other reasons, should be limited by quotas or other restrictions, or by exceptionally high rates.

(3) The President should be authorized without limit of time to enter into reciprocal trade agreements and to reduce tariffs, within the limits specified in (2) above, unilaterally or in return for reductions in tariffs or trade restrictions by other countries.

(4) Other recommended reductions include simplification of customs procedures; revision of agricultural import quotas; easing of mandatory shipping restrictions; and liberalization of government procurement policies (i.e., "Buy American" restrictions).

In contrast, the recommendations of the Randall Commission probably represent the minimum that could be considered politically worthwhile. The Commission proposed:

(1) The existing escape clause and peril point amendment should be retained but modified to permit the President to disregard the findings of the Tariff Commission on injury to domestic producers whenever he deems it in the national interest.

(2) Instead of a comprehensive revision and reduction of the tariff, piecemeal studies of commodity definitions and rate schedules should be authorized by the Congress, and the President given authority to promulgate individual modifications and simplifications provided they do not materially alter the total duties collected on any existing group of rates.

(3) The Reciprocal Trade Agreements Act should be renewed for three

years and the President authorized to reduce existing rates by not more than 5 per cent each year in return for reciprocal trade concessions.

(4) In addition, the President should be authorized to reduce rates, with or without reciprocal concessions, on commodities not now imported or being imported in negligible volume, provided the reductions do not exceed 50 per cent of the 1945 rates and are spread over a period of three years.

(5) Other recommendations include some simplification of customs procedures, some Presidential flexibility under the "Buy American" Act, repeal of the mandatory shipping restrictions, etc.

For reasons already indicated, the NPA International Committee believes that increases in imports are likely to be quantitatively significant only if reductions in import barriers are of the magnitude advocated by the Bell Committee. Hence, those who believe that better integration of the American economy into the international economy is one of the necessary conditions for the security and progress of the United States and of other free countries should not cease to work for a liberalization of American import policy at least as substantial as, though not necessarily identical with, that recommended in the Bell Report. However, until such a policy can be achieved, we cannot afford to undertake less than the minimal measures recommended by the Randall Commission. While the Randall Commission's proposals would probably not increase imports very appreciably, they would nevertheless maintain at least a sense of movement toward desirable goals. In the absence of such momentum, not only our allies and friends abroad but the American people as well are likely to suffer a serious weakening of their faith in the capacity of American leadership to grapple effectively with the critical problems of world economic order in the mid-twentieth century.

* * *

The task of reducing import barriers is, at bottom, one of reconciling national and private interests, the foreign policy of the United States and the economic self-interest of domestic groups. In some cases, conflicts can be disregarded, both morally and politically, because satisfying the demands of certain private interests may actually be harmful to the national interest. In other cases, conflicts can be avoided because acceptable alternative means can be found for meeting the legitimate needs of domestic groups or of our allies and friends abroad. Nevertheless, an important area of actual or potential conflict still remains which cannot be ignored and for which alternative means of satisfaction are not available. In such circumstances, a choice must be made, a choice which cannot be based solely, or even predominantly, on purely economic considerations. Moral, political and defense interests must be taken into account if the choice is to be wise.

When due weight is given to all of the values involved, we believe that the national interest, in its broadest conception, must be regarded as paramount in the special conditions of the mid-twentieth century.

NPA International Committee Members Signing the Statement

Frank Altschul, *Chairman*	Kenneth Holland	Lithgow Osborne
Louis Brownlow, *Vice Chairman*	Isador Lubin	Clarence E. Pickett
Stanley Andrews	T. G. MacGowan	Victor G. Reuther
*Solomon Barkin	John C. McClintock	Morris S. Rosenthal
Richard M. Bissell, Jr.	Helen Hill Miller	Wayne Chatfield Taylor
John F. Chapman	Philip E. Mosely	Robert West
Carter Goodrich	George Nebolsine	Walter H. Wheeler, Jr.
Luther H. Gulick	Paul Nitze	David J. Winton
	Charlton Ogburn	

* See statement following.

Supplementary Statement

The statement of the NPA International Committee uses the general need for American policies which promote the economic health of the free countries of the world to justify a specific program for the maximum liberalization of American import policies. It is the latter aspect of the Committee's statement, particularly the last section (IV-B), to which these dissenting remarks are addressed. My disagreement relates to the timing of an import liberalization program, to its importance for the foreign policy of the United States, and to the criteria of national interest on which it should be based.

At no time in the postwar era could the subject of American import policy be publicly debated under less favorable circumstances than now. With unemployment and economic uncertainty prevailing in the United States, people generally are not disposed to consider further dislocations in the domestic economy from outside causes. Present difficulties make it abundantly clear that our resources and thoughts must first be directed toward the restoration of our own economic health. The achievement of this goal will benefit not only our people but other countries as well. The maintenance of a less than full employment economy in the United States will be injurious to us and will sharply curtail our capacity for absorbing imports. A liberal import policy is no substitute for a full employment economy even for the purpose of promoting a high level of imports.

This is hardly the time for the promotion of an import liberalization program. The research study of American imports, on which the Committee's statement is based, makes clear that "trade is good—not because it will create additional jobs, but because it will make some jobs productive." Today, we are not primarily concerned with increased productivity or more buying power for the consumer's dollar, welcome as they might be, but with creating more jobs and preventing further contraction in employment. Hence, a program for positive action in the field of import policy must be shelved until such time as government and industry have restored and guaranteed full employment. Only in such periods are resources and initiative available to create the new employment and industries necessary to absorb displaced people, stranded enterprise and idle capital. Personal and business adjustments necessitated by the contracting of an industry will then be most easily made.

However, even if the American economy were now enjoying full employment, I would not by any means be convinced that the benefits which could be derived from a more liberal American import policy would be worth the effort of getting such a policy adopted or the damage it would do to certain domestic producers. As the first three sections of the Committee's statement make abundantly clear, the American economy has by its nature a very limited capacity to absorb the kinds of imports which Western Europe and Japan can ship to us. Moreover, the economic problems of these countries, including their dollar shortage, are not caused by American import barriers, nor could they be cured by the lowering or removal of such barriers. As the Committee's statement intimates, the poor economic health of Western Europe and Japan is the result of long-term changes both within their own economies and in the world economy as a whole. Among the most important and dramatic of these changes are the increasingly competitive character of international trade in manufactures and the superior competitive ability of a large, dynamic economy like that of the United States; the stifling of enterprise and initiative within the small, cartelized economies of Western Europe and the addiction of European business groups to the short-sighted policy of low wages, restricted markets and excessive profits; the so-called "revolution of rising expectations" on the part of the working people in Western Europe who are now seeking to obtain a fairer share of the benefits which democracy and industrialization can provide; and the new political freedom or increasing economic independence of the vast raw-material-producing areas in Asia, Latin America, Africa and Oceania which were formerly subordinate to the European (and Japanese) imperial powers. The effects of these basic economic, social and political trends have been aggravated over the past half century by two world wars and the intervening great depression, and are aggravated still further today by the cold war and the subversive tactics of the communists. The dollar shortage is only a symptom of these profound changes in the twentieth century world. In these circumstances, the extent to which liberalization of American import policy could contribute to alleviating the causes of Western Europe's and Japan's poor economic health is small indeed—so small, in fact, that it would hardly be worth the political difficulties and the economic distress it would create within the United States.

On balance, foreign aid is a more effective means of offsetting our excess of exports over imports than either a reduction of exports or an increase of imports. It contributes to a higher level of activity and employment within the American economy, which export reduction would not, and which import liberalization is supposed in theory to do but which it does not necessarily do in practice. Also, foreign aid is an effective tool of foreign policy, for it enables the United States directly and consciously to influence the economic policies and practices of other countries in directions more conducive to the restoration of their economic health and the welfare of the free world.

In this connection, it is important to recognize the speciousness of the "trade, not aid" slogan. It was first pronounced by Europeans anxious to gain greater entrance into the American market. In the United States it has been enthusiastically—and ironically—adopted by two groups diametrically opposed to each other: by isolationist politicians who want neither trade nor aid, and by doctrinaire economists and government officials who still imagine that the nineteenth century British free trade theory is a relevant basis for policy making in the mid-twentieth century. The Committee's statement properly recognizes, as does the research study, that in today's world even the most liberal changes in import policy would not result in an increase in imports of anything like the magnitude of the dollar shortage. Though the dollar shortage might temporarily disappear when the free world is enjoying unusually favorable economic and political conditions, even the complete removal of American trade barriers would not be sufficient to abolish it permanently. As already noted, the dollar gap is the result not of American import policies but of long-term changes in the European economies and of the structure of the American economy. The ratio of American imports to domestic production has been declining in terms of value though it has been maintained in terms of physical volume. American imports have been concentrated in crude agricultural materials and semimanufactured goods. Our continental economy naturally has a high degree of self-sufficiency. While our pattern of economic growth "enlarges demands for foreign goods," there is no assurance that "imports into the United States will grow." Even the most liberal trade program would, therefore, yield disappointing results in terms of the value of imports. Hence, it is important that the slogan "trade, not aid" be played down. It encourages foreign countries to believe that this prescription is the solution for their problems—which it cannot be, as the Committee statement itself points out.

A more liberal American trade policy is at best only a minor tool in developing a new balance in international economic relations. Indeed, the Committee itself regards a more liberal import policy only as a precondition for the accomplishment of the broader objective and the Committee refers to other studies being currently conducted for the other necessary measures. In the public debate on import policy, the more extreme advocates of trade liberalization should follow the Committee's example and define the need for a liberal American trade policy within the context of a more comprehensive program for achieving a better international economy. Such a grand design must be created if international economic stability is to be realized. Unfortunately, few of the devotees of trade liberalization, here or abroad, have paid much attention to the other, much more important, parts of the program.

Finally, I would like to comment on the criteria of national interest involved in a reduction of import barriers. The proponents of liberal trade policies have identified themselves as representing the national interest. However, they overlook the fact that the private beneficiaries of such policies may often be promoting them with enthusiasm, finances and claims far exceeding the possible public gain. More significantly, the argument has been presented in terms of general foreign policy and over-all domestic injury. This argument does not, however, adequately take into account either the smallness of the benefit to general foreign policy or whether it is in the public interest to destroy or contract specific industries or sectors thereof through sweeping tariff reductions. At the same time, the protectionists have argued in terms of specific private interest, and their contentions about the relationship of these industries to the general national interest have not been adequately supported. The disputants have not really come to grips with the issues of national interest involved in protecting or not protecting specific industries and products.

For this reason, I agree with the Committee's recommendation for a "reappraisal of the existing tariff structure, and an analysis of possible and desirable reductions." Until a thorough study has been made, there appears no justification for taking any action to liberalize imports. However, by endorsing the Bell and Randall reports, the Committee is by implication sanctioning actions which may be injurious to the public interest, for neither report envisages the kind of detailed appraisal of the existing tariff structure which the Committee itself proposes as a precondition for tariff reduction. Moreover, both reports have evaded the specific challenge of the affected industries. In any event, action should be postponed until a stable level of full employment is realized. I join in the Committee's emphasis on the importance of high or full employment and economic activity as a prerequisite to the maintenance of a maximum volume of imports.

The immediate need is to develop a list of criteria of public interest by which to determine the specific industries to be maintained, contracted or destroyed. What degree of protection should be afforded specific industries in the national interest? In accordance with what orderly procedure should the existing levels of protection be lifted to enable domestic industries, workers and communities to adjust thereto?

I believe that the following considerations of national interest are binding upon the American people, and that, where applicable, they justify the maintenance and protection of industries, or necessary proportions thereof:

(1) Industries producing goods or employing persons with skills required for national defense or for maintaining the balance and dynamism of the American economy.

(2) Industries which are measurably more efficient and productive than foreign competitors and are undersold in the United States primarily because of wage differentials, and which provide technological and managerial leadership and design leadership to their competitors in other countries.

(3) Industries which for any reason, domestic or foreign, are undergoing serious upheavals resulting in plant closings, geographical migration, large-scale employee displacement, marked increase in machine efficiency; and industries in which large capital investments are currently being made for modernization.

(4) Industries located in economically depressed or contracting areas and in single-industry communities.

(5) Industries in which producing units and capital resources are small, and the work force is of advanced age.

(6) Industries which are declining not only in the United States but also in the countries which have traditionally exported their products.

Careful enumeration of the criteria of national interest will provide a basis for determining the specific industries to be protected in whole or in part through tariff rates. For those which are not so protected and which will be subjected to an increasing amount of foreign competition—except as they may be able through innovation and ingenuity to offset the advantage of lower-priced imports—a precise schedule of reductions should be fixed beforehand, to be suspended if national employment should decline from full employment levels for any significant period. For people and communities who are personally injured, I believe that the depressed industries and communities program endorsed by the Committee should be supplemented by provision for an earlier retirement age under old-age and survivors insurance.

The adoption of the course of action proposed by the undersigned might make such protective devices as the escape clause, the peril point amendment and the "Buy American" Act unnecessary. None is really satisfactory to the diverse groups affected. The protectionists find them inadequate since they have been administered, particularly by the present administration, with uncompromisingly liberal trade tests which have rendered them useless and deceptive. The system of tariff rates developed by the procedures herein advocated must, of course, be protected against currency manipulation, subsidies, assistance to exporters, dumping and similar devices fostered by state trading schemes and other practices of foreign countries.

SOLOMON BARKIN

APPENDICES

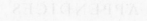

APPENDIX 1

(*Index*[b]: *1919=100*)

Calendar Year	Current Prices[c]	Constant Prices[c]
1869	147	150
1879	136	143
1889	138	147
1890	151	161
1891	142	150
1892	145	155
1893	129	139
1894	128	142
1895	140	146
1896	124	129
1897	125	134
1898	99	108
1899	109	112
1900	104	107
1901	101	103
1902	106	105
1903	104	101
1904	107	106
1905	113	114
1906	111	110
1907	112	110
1908	99	101
1909	114	111
1910	113	108
1911	109	112
1912	117	118
1913	111	110
1914	115	116
1915	111	115
1916	113	109
1917	105	95
1918	88	85
1919	100	100
1920	124	110
1921	86	99
1922	99	113
1923	105	104
1924	103	102
1925	110	104
1926	110	103
1927	108	107
1928	100	104
1929	103	112

(*Continued on following page*)

APPENDIX 1 (*Continued*)

Calendar Year	Current Prices[c]	Constant Prices[c]
1930	87	106
1931	77	104
1932	67	97
1933	70	105
1935	70	107
1937	84	110
1939	66	91

Sources: Output, 1869–1919, William H. Shaw, *Value of Commodity Output since 1869*, National Bureau of Economic Research, New York, 1947, pp. 62, 63, 76, 77; 1919–1933, Simon Kuznets, *Commodity Flow and Capital Formation*, National Bureau of Economic Research, New York, 1938, Vol. I, pp. 138, 159; 1933–1939, U.S. Department of Commerce (unpublished). Imports, 1869–1915, *Monthly Summary of Commerce and Finance*, December 1911, p. 1051; December 1915, p. 59; 1916–1939, *Foreign Trade of the United States, 1936–1949*, International Trade Series No. 7, U.S. Department of Commerce, 1951.

a. Output excludes construction materials. General imports through 1933; imports for consumption thereafter.

b. The output series of Shaw, Kuznets and the Department of Commerce (unpublished) have been tied together for overlapping years.

c. The output series of the National Bureau in constant prices represent "output destined for consumption," that is, production adjusted for the net foreign trade balance. The output series in current prices are not so adjusted. Imports deflated by wholesale prices before 1919; quantity index thereafter.

APPENDIX 2

QUANTUM IMPORTS AS PER CENT OF INDUSTRIAL PRODUCTION, 1919–1950

Year	Quantum Imports	Industrial Production[a]	Imports as Per Cent of Industrial Production
	(*Index: 1919=100*)		
1919	100	100	100
1920	108	104	104
1921	92	81	114
1922	118	101	117
1923	123	122	100
1924	120	114	105
1925	130	125	104
1926	138	133	104
1927	141	132	107
1928	142	138	103
1929	163	153	107
1930	138	126	109
1931	121	104	116
1932	97	81	121
1933	107	96	112
1934	106	104	101
1935	130	121	107
1936	144	143	100
1937	161	157	102
1938	115	124	93
1939	132	151	87
1940	139	174	80
1941	165	225	73
1942	123	276	44
1943	137	332	41
1944	148	326	45
1945	151	282	53
1946	159	236	67
1947	152	260	59
1948	173	267	65
1949	169	244	69
1950[b]	206	278	74

Sources: Imports, *Foreign Trade of the United States, 1936–1949,* International Trade Series No. 7, U.S. Department of Commerce, 1951, Table 13; industrial production, *Federal Reserve Bulletin,* May 1951, p. 549.

a. Production of manufactures and minerals.

b. Preliminary.

APPENDIX 3

INDEXES OF RATIO OF VALUE OF AGRICULTURAL IMPORTS TO CASH RECEIPTS FROM
DOMESTIC MARKETINGS AND RATIO OF QUANTUM AGRICULTURAL IMPORTS TO
AGRICULTURAL PRODUCTION, 1910–1914 TO 1950

(*Average 1909–1910 to 1913–1914 = 100*)

Year	Ratio of Value of Agricultural Imports to Cash Receipts from Farm Marketings	Ratio of Quantum Agricultural Imports to Agricultural Production[a]
1910–1914 average[b]	100	100
1915	115	133
1916	124	148
1917	115	160
1918	109	136
1919	121	176
1920	85	174
1921	110	158
1922	127	192
1923	144	188
1924	127	183
1925	145	204
1926	155	210
1927	140	216
1928	129	206
1929	134	244
1930	111	208
1931	108	196
1932	95	178
1933	94	188
1934	88	190
1935	103	235
1936	101	232
1937	122	222
1938	85	176
1939	97	191
1940	104	204
1941	102	240
1942	56	131
1943	53	134
1944	61	137
1945	54	129
1946	63	149
1947	63	152
1948	70	160
1949	70	149
1950	97	—

Sources: Production, *Historical Statistics of the United States, 1789–1945*, Series E 72 and E 88, and *Agricultural Statistics, 1950;* imports, Office of Foreign Agricultural Relations, U.S. Department of Agriculture, unpublished calendar year data.

a. Production for sale and home consumption.

b. Average 1909–1910 to 1913–1914, calendar years thereafter.

APPENDIX 4

IMPORTS OF SELECTED CRUDE MATERIALS, 1850–1950[a]

(*Millions*)

Year	Hides and Skins	Furs[b] and Manufactures	Rubber, Crude	Tobacco, Un-manufactured	Silk, Raw
1850	$ 5	$ 1	—	$ 0.3	$ 0.4
1860	11	2	$ 1	1	1
1865	5	2	1	1	1
1870	14	2	3	3	3
1871–1875	17	4	5	5	5
1876–1880	18	5	6	4	8
1881–1885	25	7	13	6	13
1886–1890	24	7	14	11	19
1891–1895	25	10	18	13	22
1896–1900	39	9	25	11	31
1901–1905	56	15	35	17	45
1906–1910	83	21	61	25	66
1911–1915	103	19	83	32	80
1915–1920[c]	202	48	192	51	214
1921–1925	93	81	193	65	348
1926	97	120	506	61	393
1927	113	138	340	75	390
1928	151	122	245	55	368
1929	137	126	241	54	427
1930	92	69	141	41	263
1931	50	56	74	37	191
1932	22	28	33	23	114
1933	45	37	46	25	103
1934	35	41	102	25	72
1935	46	53	119	26	96
1936	55	82	159	30	102
1937	71	86	248	32	107
1938	30	46	130	36	89
1939	47	55	178	37	121
1940	50	80	318	37	125
1941	83	109	418	38	62
1942	78	69	118	37	0.1
1943	66	91	33	42	d
1944	61	126	76	60	d
1945	50	144	99	75	1
1946	77	238	233	86	101
1947	86	126	317	91	16
1948	108	165	309	78	15
1949	73	109	240	73	7
1950[e]	119	109	458	76	21

Source: Statistical Abstract of the United States, 1948 and 1953.

a. General imports through 1932, imports for consumption thereafter.

b. Largely undressed furs.

c. Average for period July 1, 1915, to December 31, 1920.

d. Not published.

e. Reflects speculative buying of hides and stockpiling of rubber.

APPENDIX 5

U.S. PRODUCTION, EXPORTS AND IMPORTS OF CRUDE PETROLEUM AND PRODUCTS,
SELECTED YEARS, 1920–1952

(*Thousands of Barrels Daily*)

Year	Domestic Production[a]	Apparent Consumption	Exports	Imports[b]	Net Exports or Imports (—)
1920	1,240	1,319	218	297	−79
1921	1,327	1,484	196	353	−157
1922	1,565	1,734	204	373	−169
1923	2,066	2,059	280	273	7
1924	2,018	1,956	320	258	62
1925	2,170	2,072	312	214	98
1929	2,910	2,761	447	298	149
1933	2,577	2,409	292	124	168
1937	3,647	3,331	473	157	316
1939	3,614	3,258	518	149	369
1941	4,073	4,041	298	266	32
1947	5,451	5,438	450	437	13
1948	5,922	6,069	367	514	−147
1949	5,477	5,795	327	645	−318
1950	5,906	6,451	305	850	−545
1951	6,720	7,142	422	844	−422
1952	6,868	7,384	436	952	−516

Source: U.S. Bureau of Mines.

a. Crude oil and natural gas liquids.

b. Mainly imports of residual oil.

APPENDIX 6

APPLICATIONS FOR INVESTIGATIONS UNDER ESCAPE CLAUSE PROVISIONS OF TRADE AGREEMENTS, AS OF JUNE 30, 1952

Commodity	Name and Address of Applicant	Date Received	Status
1. Marrons (candied chestnuts)	G. B. Raffeto, Inc., New York, N. Y.	April 20, 1948	Dismissed after preliminary inquiry.
2. Whiskies and spirits	U.S. Distillers Tariff Committee, Washington, D. C., on behalf of 28 distilling companies	Sept. 7, 1948	Dismissed after preliminary inquiry.
3. Spring clothespins	DeMerritt Co., Waterbury, Vt. (6 other producers)	Nov. 10, 1948	No modification in concession recommended.
4. Knitted berets, wholly of wool	American Basque Berets, Inc., New York, N. Y.	Feb. 11, 1949	Dismissed after preliminary inquiry.
5. Crude petroleum and petroleum products	Independent Petroleum Association of America, Washington, D. C.	Feb. 15, 1949	Dismissed after preliminary inquiry.
6. Hops	United States Hop Growers Association, San Francisco, Calif.	Mar. 28, 1949	Dismissed after preliminary inquiry.
7. Reeds, wrought or manufactured from rattan or reeds, cane, etc.	American Rattan & Reed Manufacturing Co., Brooklyn, N. Y.	May 20, 1949	Dismissed after preliminary inquiry.
8. Narcissus bulbs	Northwest Bulb Growers Association, Sumner, Washington	June 9, 1949	Dismissed after preliminary inquiry.
9. Sponges, n.s.p.f.[a]	Sponge Industry Welfare Committee, Chamber of Commerce, Board of City Commissioners, and Greek Community, all of Tarpon Springs, Florida	June 14, 1949	Dismissed after preliminary inquiry.

APPENDIX 6 (*Continued*)

Commodity	Name and Address of Applicant	Date Received	Status
10. Knit gloves and knit mittens, finished or unfinished, wholly or in chief value of wool Gloves and mittens, embroidered in any manner, wholly or in chief value of wool Gloves and mittens, knit or crocheted, finished or unfinished, wholly or in chief value of cotton	Association of Knitted Glove and Mitten Manufacturers, Gloversville, N. Y.	Aug. 5, 1949	Action deferred to study further developments November 22, 1949. Application withdrawn July 1951.
11. Knitted berets, wholly of wool (second application)	American Basque Berets, Inc., New York, N. Y.	Nov. 23, 1949	Dismissed after preliminary inquiry.
12. Woven fabrics in the piece, wholly of silk, bleached, printed, dyed or colored, and valued at more than $5.50 per pound	Textile Section of the Manufacturers Division of the Greater Paterson Chamber of Commerce, Paterson, N. J.	Jan. 5, 1950	Dismissed after preliminary inquiry.
13. Women's fur felt hats and hat bodies	Hat Institute, Inc. and United Hatters, Cap & Millinery Workers International Union, New York, N. Y.	Jan. 24, 1950	Certain concessions withdrawn by presidential proclamation of Oct. 30, 1950.
14. Stencil silk, dyed or colored	Albert Godde Bedin, Inc., New York, N. Y.	Jan. 30, 1950	Dismissed after preliminary inquiry.
15. Beef and veal, fresh, chilled or frozen	Western States Meat Packers Association, San Francisco, Calif., and Washington, D. C.	Mar. 16, 1950	Dismissed after preliminary inquiry.

Product	Applicant	Date	Disposition
16. Aluminum and alloys, in crude form (except scrap) Aluminum in coils, plates, bars, rods, etc.	Reynolds Metals Co., Louisville, Ky.	Mar. 24, 1950	Dismissed after preliminary inquiry.
17. Aluminum and alloys, in crude form (except scrap) Aluminum in coils, plates, bars, rods, etc.	Kaiser Aluminum & Chemical Corp., Washington, D. C.	April 7, 1950	Dismissed after preliminary inquiry.
18. Lead-bearing materials, lead and lead scrap	Emergency Lead Committee, New York, N. Y.	May 11, 1950	Dismissed after preliminary inquiry.
19. Lead-bearing materials, lead and lead scrap	New Mexico Miners and Prospectors Association on behalf of Lead Producers of New Mexico, Albuquerque, N. Mex.	May 16, 1950	Dismissed after preliminary inquiry.
20. Hatters' furs, or furs not on the skin, prepared for hatters' use, including fur skins carroted	Hatters' Fur Cutters Association of the U.S.A., New York, N. Y.	June 22, 1950	Concession modified by presidential proclamation of January 5, 1952.
21. Jeweled watches and watch movements containing 7 but not more than 17 jewels, and parts therefor	Elgin National Watch Co., Elgin, Ill. Hamilton Watch Co., Lancaster, Pa.	Feb. 13, 1951	Modification in concession recommended to President. Recommendation rejected by President, Aug. 14, 1952.[b]
22. Motorcycles and parts	Harley-Davidson Motor Co., Milwaukee, Wis.	May 21, 1951	No modification recommended.
23. Blue-mold cheese	National Cheese Institute, Inc., Chicago, Ill.	June 11, 1951	No modification recommended.

APPENDIX 6 (*Continued*)

Commodity	Name and Address of Applicant	Date Received	Status
24. Screws, commonly called wood screws, of iron or steel	United States Wood Screw Service Bureau, New York, N. Y.	Aug. 15, 1951	No modification recommended.
25. Spring clothespins (second application)	Clothespin Manufacturers of America, Washington, D. C.	Aug. 22, 1951	No modification recommended.
26. Fresh or frozen groundfish fillets	Massachusetts Fisheries Association, Inc., Boston, Mass., and others	Sept. 10, 1951	No modification recommended.
27. Garlic	Robert S. Stapleton, Gilroy, Calif.	Oct. 8, 1951	Restriction by quota recommended. Rejected by President.
28. Bicycles and parts	Bicycle Manufacturers Association of America, New York, N. Y. Cycle Parts and Accessories Manufacturers Association, New York, N. Y.	Oct. 11, 1951	No modification recommended.
29. Cherries, candied, crystallized or glace	Maraschino Cherry and Glace Fruit Association, New York, N. Y.	Oct. 26, 1951	No modification recommended.
30. Bonito, canned in oil; and tuna and bonito, canned, not in oil	California Fish Canners Association, Inc., Terminal Island, Calif.; and others[e]	Nov. 28, 1951	No modification recommended.
31. Tobacco pipes and tobacco pipe bowls of wood and root	American Smoking Pipe Manufacturers Association, New York, N. Y.	Dec. 29, 1951	Modification of concessions recommended. Rejected by President.
32. Specified household china tableware, kitchenware, and table and kitchen utensils	Vitrified China Association, Inc., Washington, D. C. National Brotherhood of Operative Potters, East Liverpool, Ohio	Feb. 11, 1952	No modification recommended.

33. Dried figs	California Fig Institute, Fresno, Calif.	Mar. 17, 1952	Concessions modified by President.
34. Screws, commonly called wood screws, of iron or steel (second application)	United States Wood Screw Service Bureau, New York, N. Y.	April 1, 1952	No modification recommended.
35. Pregnant mare's urine	National P.M.U. Producers Association, Farmer City, Ill.	April 8, 1952	No modification recommended.
36. Chalk or whiting or Paris white dry, ground or bolted	Southwark Manufacturing Co., Camden, N. J.	April 10, 1952	No modification recommended.
37. Screen-printed silk scarves	Association of Textile Screen Makers, Printers and Processors, Inc., New York, N. Y.	April 14, 1952	Modification of concessions recommended. Rejected by President.
38. Woodwind musical instruments and parts	Penzel, Mueller and Co., Inc., New York, N. Y.	April 29, 1952	No modification recommended.

Source: U.S. Tariff Commission.

a. Not specifically provided for. Apparently this case arose because of a mistake in customs classification.

b. Duties were increased in 1954 on the ground that preservation of skills in this industry is essential to national defense.

c. Applications were received from the Columbia River Salmon and Tuna Packers Association, Astoria, Oregon, on December 12, 1951; the Pacific Coast Fish Producers Institute, Westport, Wash., on December 19, 1951; the American Tunaboat Association and Lower California Fishermen's Association, San Diego, Calif., on December 20, 1951; and the International Association of Machinists, Lodge 389, San Diego, Calif., on January 4, 1952.

537

APPENDIX 7

STATUS OF ADDITIONAL ESCAPE CLAUSE INVESTIGATIONS[a] AS OF JANUARY 7, 1955

Tariff Commission Decided against Action under Escape Clause

1. Cotton-carding machinery (unanimous), July 29, 1953.
2. Metal watch bracelets and parts (unanimous), August 20, 1953.
3. Rosaries (unanimous), August 21, 1953.
4. Mustard seeds (unanimous), December 10, 1953.
5. Ground chicory (unanimous), September 7, 1954.
6. Coconuts (unanimous), October 25, 1954.
7. Wool gloves and mittens (5–1), December 28, 1954.
8. Glue of animal origin and inedible gelatin (unanimous), January 7, 1955.

Tariff Commission Recommended Escape Clause Action

9. Scissors and shears (4–2), March 12, 1954.[b]
10. Groundfish fillets (3–2), 2d investigation, May 7, 1954.[b]
11. Watches, movements and parts (4–2), 2d investigation, May 21, 1954.[c]
12. Lead and zinc (unanimous), May 21, 1954.[b]
13. Alsike clover seed (unanimous), May 21, 1954.[c]

Vote of Tariff Commission Evenly Divided (3–3)

14. Handmade blown glassware, September 22, 1953.[b]
15. Spring clothespins, 3d investigation, October 6, 1954.[b]
16. Wood screws made of iron or steel, 3d investigation, October 27, 1954.[b]

Pending Investigation

17. Bicycles, 2d investigation.
18. Hardwood plywood.
19. Red-fescue seed.

Application Dismissed at Applicant's Request

20. Hard fiber cords and twines, January 14, 1953.
21. Fluorspar, acid grade, November 23, 1953.

Investigation Terminated without Formal Findings

22. Straight pins (unanimous), June 22, 1954.
23. Safety pins (unanimous), June 22, 1954.

Source: Trade Agreements Extension, Hearings, House Ways and Means Committee, 84th Cong., 1st sess., pp. 390–391.

  a. Vote of Tariff Commission is shown in parentheses.

  b. The President declined to invoke the escape clause.

  c. The President invoked the escape clause.

INDEX

INDEX